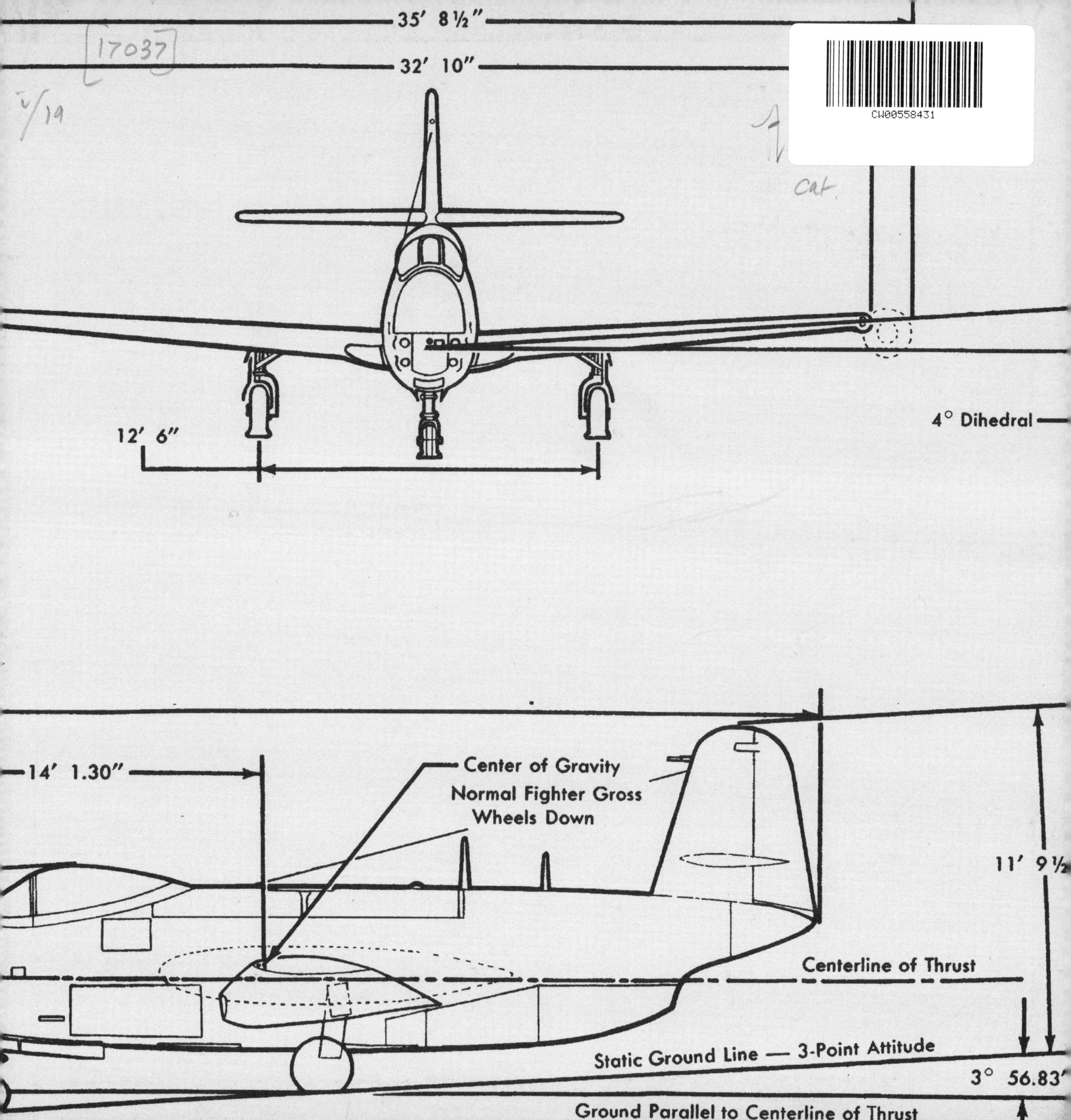
35′ 8½″
32′ 10″
4° Dihedral
12′ 6″
14′ 1.30″
Center of Gravity
Normal Fighter Gross
Wheels Down
11′ 9½
Centerline of Thrust
Static Ground Line — 3-Point Attitude
3° 56.83′
Ground Parallel to Centerline of Thrust

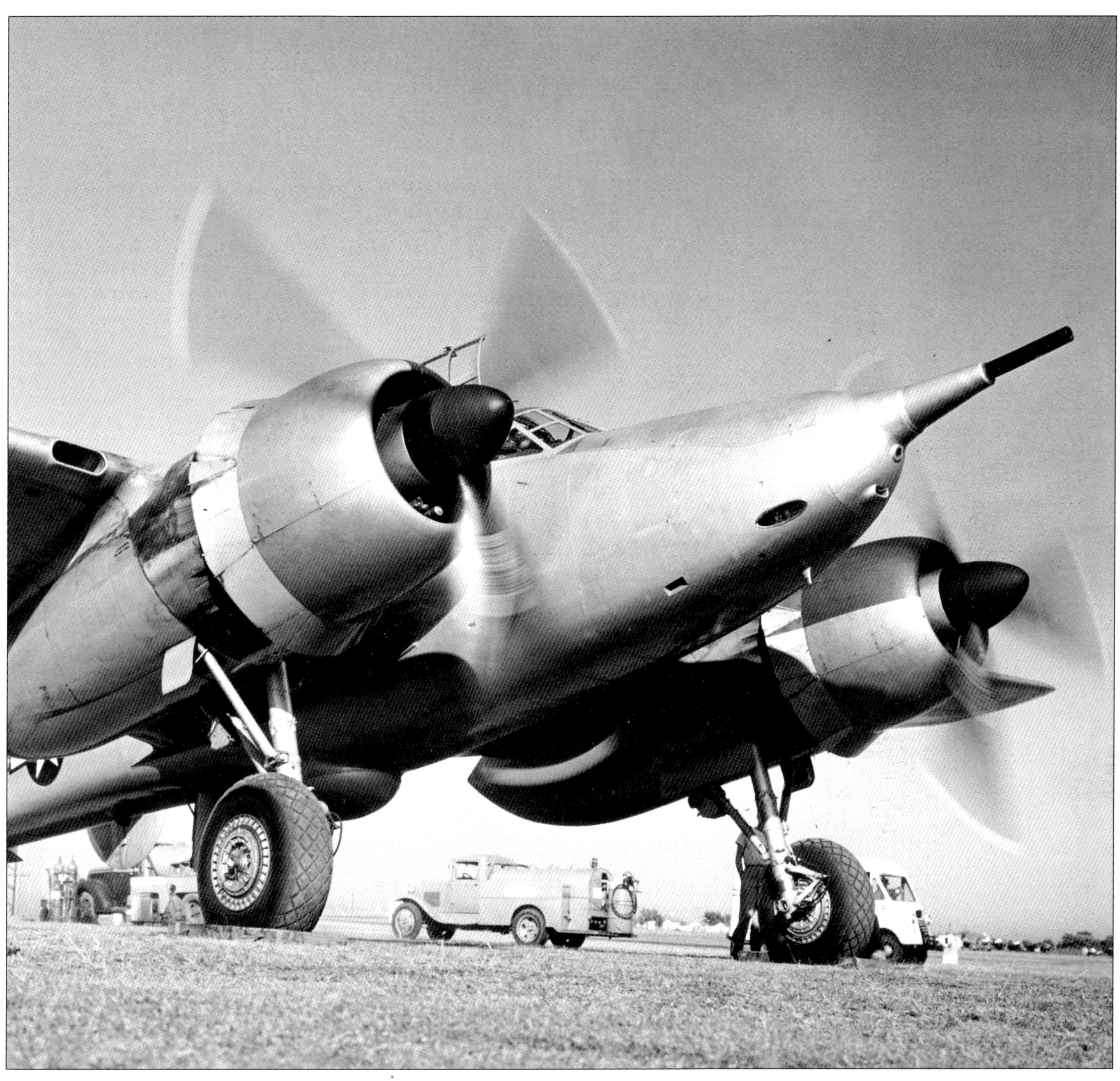

specialtypress
PUBLISHERS AND WHOLESALERS

Edited by Nicholas A. Veronico
ISBN-13 978-1-58007-109-3
Item Number SP109

39966 Grand Avenue
North Branch, MN 55056 USA
(651) 277-1400 or (800) 895-4585
www.specialtypress.com

Printed in China

Library of Congress Cataloging-in-Publication Data

Norton, Bill, 1959-
US experimental & prototype aircraft projects : fighters, 1939-1945 / by Bill Norton.
p. cm.
Includes bibliographical references and index.
ISBN 978-1-58007-109-3
1. Research aircraft--United States--History--20th century. 2. Fighter planes--United States--Design and construction--History--20th century. 3. World War, 1939-1945--Aerial operations, American. I. Title. II. Title: Fighters, 1939-1945.
UG1242.F5N66 2008
623.74'64097309044--dc22
2008015662

On the Front Cover: ***The U.S. Army Air Force's first jet fighter, the Bell XP-59A Airacomet, was limited by security measures and rushed. While it proved disappointing, much was learned from the effort. This example is seen in flight over California's Mojave Desert.*** (National Museum of the United States Air Force)

On the Front Dust Jacket Flap (Top photo): ***The Allison V-1710 (here on the XP-51F) was the only American inline, liquid-cooled engine in series production throughout World War II. All others never progressed beyond the experimental stage. Production of the UK's Rolls-Royce Merlin engine under contract by Packard provided the only other alternative.*** (San Diego Aerospace Museum)

On the Front Dust Jacket Flap (Bottom photo): ***The rapid adaptation of the British turbojet to an American-designed airframe, all in a very short time, yielded the Army's Bell P-59. Although a remarkable achievement, it is understandable that this new type of fighter did not measure up as a fieldable weapon.*** (Air Force Flight Test Center)

On the Back Dust Jacket Flap: ***The growing capabilities of combat aircraft prompted the Navy to explore combined-mission airframes that would define postwar attack aviation. One expression of this was the Curtiss XBT2C-1 with cannons and bomb bay, the first example shown here. It flew at the close of the war and so had no future.*** (Naval Aviation Archives)

On the Front/Back Endsheets: ***The third naval jet fighter project initiated in the last year of the war was the Vought XF6U-1 with the J34. Note the intent from the first to install wing tip tanks, but many other changes would intrude before the aircraft entered fleet service.*** (Vought Aircraft Heritage Foundation)

On the Frontis: ***A fine example of American late-war aeronautical achievement is the XA-38 with 75-mm cannon in the nose. From Beech Aircraft, a firm with little combat aircraft experience, it was a very reputable weapon that may have been produced and deployed if circumstances had been different.*** (Jay Miller Collection)

On the Title Page: ***Consolidated-Vultee's XP-81, ship 2, reveals the NACA inlet trough ahead of the left shoulder-mounted inlet for the rear J33 turbojet. This hybrid also had one of the new XT31 turboprop engines in the nose. The T31 was too immature and the overall aircraft performance too lackluster to justify production.*** (Tony Landis Collection)

On the Back Cover:
Top: ***The long and frustrating P-60 program culminated in this one YP-60E. It was flown twice and then ferried to Wright field where it is seen in this photo. There it received little attention and never flew again.*** (National Museum of the United States Air Force)

Middle: ***The XFR-1 Fireball's mixing of jet and reciprocating propulsion is evident here with the propeller in front and jet exhaust in back. The second XFR-1, Bureau number 48233, cruises over Southern California on an early test mission in 1944. Other than being a bit thick in the middle, it appears a conventional late-war fighter.*** (San Diego Aerospace Museum)

Bottom: ***The Curtiss XF15C-1 began in the last months of 1943 to provide the Navy a powerful composite aircraft, mixing turbine and reciprocating engines as a step beyond the Fireball. It became enormous in size for a single-seat, carrier-based aircraft.*** (Naval Aviation Archives)

U.S. EXPERIMENTAL & PROTOTYPE AIRCRAFT PROJECTS

FIGHTERS 1939-1945

Bill Norton

Table of Contents

ACKNOWLEDGMENTS

The author would like to thank, in alphabetical order, Dick Atkins and the Vought Aircraft Heritage Foundation, Gerald Balzer, Kase Decker, Hayden Hamilton and Paul Minert of the American Aviation Historical Society, Larry Feliu and the people of the Northrop Grumman History Center, Dennis Jenkins, Lloyd Jones, Tony Landis, Norman Malayney, Jay Miller and the people of the Jay Miller Collection, Alan Renga and the folks at the San Diego Aerospace Museum, Brett Stolle and the National Museum of the United States Air Force, Warren Thompson, Curtiss Utz and the staff of the Naval Aviation Archives, Ray Wagner, Dr. Jim Young and the people of the Air Force Flight Test Center History Office, and the United States National Archives.

INTRODUCTION

There is, of course, no distinct demarcation between various groups and types of aircraft that are customarily referred to loosely as "fighters." Even aircraft intended only for air-to-air fighting may eventually have been adapted for air-to-ground missions as the beginning of what became Air Force fighter-bombers and Navy attack aviation. The Army's World War II attack aircraft were generally on the scale of what would conventionally be regarded as fighters. Likewise, Navy aircraft operating off carriers during the war, even those designated for bomber and scout missions, were "fighter-esque" in generally having a single engine and pilot and being equipped with forward firing guns. One can be assured the pilots of all these aircraft referred to themselves as fighter pilots! Consequently, the author has used his own judgment in selecting the aircraft subjects to include in this volume. This will certainly not be met with universal satisfaction.

The contents seek to address projects that were intended to yield new combat aircraft or improvements to existing fighters. Fighters or fighter-like aircraft employed for purely research and experimental purposes have been left to a future work. This distribution helps ensure a focused, yet even examination of the subject to a suitable depth for enjoyable reading. Focusing almost exclusively on official programs, and especially those that entered development, provides more than sufficient interesting material of adequate depth to fill these pages. Attempting to cover all design concepts and proposals would greatly reduce the coverage of those programs that advanced beyond preliminary stages, yet fail to cover the entire subject completely because of the paucity of source material. The Bibliography at the back of the book provides a guide to research material for the reader seeking the larger picture.

Although the United States of America entered World War II only in the last month of 1941, with the conflict more than two years old, this book covers the period from September 1939 and the declaration of war in Europe to August 1945 and the cessation of hostilities with Japan. American aircraft were operated by foreign combatants from the first days of the conflict. Americans were also engaged in the hostilities before the U.S. declaration of war, although mostly in an unofficial capacity as volunteers. There were official U.S. military aviation operations in the early war years, such as convoy protection in the Atlantic, albeit as a neutral force. Even before the outbreak of open warfare, the American military expansion had begun and the aviation industry was growing to support rearmament. These manufacturers were soon the principal external suppliers of combat aircraft to friendly countries at war or preparing to meet any eventuality. Aviation programs slowed little after the defeat of Germany, as Japan remained a determined foe of uncertain capabilities that was expected to require prodigious quantities of equipment to completely defeat. Hence, the time period examined is entirely appropriate.

In setting the stage for the review of these aircraft," all of the production fighter types and models will be discussed superficially, as these formed a basis for comparison in pursuing advanced development. Consequently, nearly all American "fighters" will be presented to some extent, inclusive of Army, Navy, Marine Corps, and foreign operators. Aircraft "characteristics" are presented for the most common standard fighters and the projects that actually flew during the war to allow a measure of comparison in size, performance, and capabilities for assessment of the advances presented by each model. Americanized English units are used exclusively, consistent with the U.S. practice at the time.

The fighter projects are set in the context of the overall evolution of American military aviation, the aircraft industry, and technological maturation during the war. In this way, this volume provides illumination of little-known or minimally documented aircraft that significantly advanced the science and technology of aeronautics, propulsion, aircraft systems, avionics, and ordnance, even without going into full-rate production and deployment. The introduction of advanced technology, such as jet engines and electronics (radar, compensating bombsights, navigation aids, etc.) is a key theme throughout. How all this work contributed to actual fielded weapons systems is a particular point, with discussions of failures, course changes, and close-run competitions. The interaction with allies, knowledge of enemy systems or reaction to their introduction, and the effect of mobilizing the nation's industries for total war is also touched on. The effects of emergency measures, haste, budgets, resources, evolving doctrine and strategy, the general course of the war, Allied achievement of air superiority, and leadership biases are considered.

The reader will find few references to actual combat experiences and associated personalities between these covers. Instead, the war stories are those of staffs, engineering teams, and test pilots struggling against short schedules and tight resource constraints to develop new aircraft for an ongoing war while pushing the bounds of technology. These epic and sometimes life-threatening endeavors were as vital to the war effort as actual combat operations.

Most projects addressed within this volume were the subject of thousands of hours of labor by dedicated pilots, mechanics, engineers, and managers, even if the efforts were not taken to their ultimate conclusion. Although some projects are dealt with in a comparatively brief manner, this is in no way meant to diminish the efforts of those assigned to the development. Indeed, some readers may judge the author's treatment of such efforts to be rude or unnecessarily satirical, if not dismissively brief. Such is not the intent. Level of detail is based on importance of the project to the overall course of fighter development, how far the program progressed, and the extent of available information. As made clear through the author's own professional experience, projects are cancelled for fiscal, political, or strategic reasons entirely apart from their technical merit or engineering excellence. The manner of treatment within the text is not meant to reflect negatively on the efforts of those assigned to a project or the manufacturers.

A personal motivation for the author in undertaking this project is a sense of frustration that a comprehensive examination of American aviation projects of the war period has been lacking. However, the efforts of other nations are documented, if only as used books. Particularly German "secret projects" and advanced aircraft designs have been detailed to a point of excess. Many recent books have lavishly reviewed "projects" or designs that were fantastic to the point of infeasibility, too far ahead of the state of the art in materials, structures, propulsion, stability, and control technology to be realized in a wartime environment. Yet, these publications show detailed drawings and computer-generated art for many concepts that never advanced beyond the stage of a notional sketch. The author's research makes it clear that American designers sketched similar innovative designs, but the industry and military wisely restricted themselves to efforts that had high potential for yielding a militarily useful weapons system in a reasonable time and within available technological means. While the results may have been less wondrous than the German efforts, they were generally more numerous, more successful, proceeded farther along in development, and some carried on beyond the war. The perception of some that Germany was far advanced of the Allies in aviation technology, and the American contribution to victory was essentially mammoth materiel supply of modest-quality weapons developed and operated by personnel of average capabilities is far from true. This book may help to dispel this notion.

Lastly, the text presupposes the reader has a fundamental understanding of airplanes, how they fly, how piston and jet engines work, and the basic course of the Second World War.

The author welcomes feedback and additional research material, particularly images. Readers may contact Bill Norton at williamnorton@earthlink.net.

Glossary

Adverse Yaw – the tendency of the aircraft to yaw away from the direction of a roll, reducing turn rate and increasing drag. It is normally countered by applying rudder to bring the sideslip to zero (coordinate the turn).

Afterburning – also known as augmentation, reheat, and secondary combustion, this is the injection of fuel into the hot exhaust of the turbine, forward of the nozzle, to produce additional thrust from a turbojet engine.

Air-cooled Engine – a piston engine employing the passing air to cool the cylinders and other components. This requires a properly formed cowling and baffling encircling the engine, and usually cowl flaps to regulate the flow of air while reducing cooling drag.

Airfoil – a wing cross-section shape determining lift characteristics.

Angle-of-Attack – angle between the wing mean chord line and the incident airflow.

Arrestment – means of capturing and decelerating an airplane landing on an aircraft carrier deck. This usually consists of a series of parallel cables stretched across the deck, one of which is engaged by a tailhook hanging below the aft fuselage of the landing aircraft. The cable is played out and decelerated by an energy absorption system below deck.

Axial-flow Jet Engine – a turbine engine through which air flows along the longitudinal axis without being radically redirected as through a centrifugal compressor.

Barrier – with respect to an aircraft carrier, refers to cables strung above the deck beyond the arrestment cables. An aircraft missing the cables would engage the barrier and be abruptly halted, although usually with damage.

Block – a group of aircraft in a production-model series with like physical attributes.

Bombsight – an optical device for estimating the impact point of bombs dropped from an aircraft at considerable altitude.

Boundary Layer – the thin layer of air adjacent to a surface in an air stream in which the flow goes from zero velocity at the surface to freestream velocity. A thick or turbulent layer would possess greater skin friction drag than a thin or laminar boundary layer.

Catapult – a means of launching an airplane off an aircraft carrier deck, usually by a bridle between the aircraft and a shuttle in a slot along the deck. The shuttle is propelled by a hydraulic or pneumatic piston below deck to accelerate the aircraft to takeoff velocity.

Center of Gravity – (cg) is the point at which the aircraft would balance if suspended from that point, i.e., the center of gravitational attraction acting on the mass of the aircraft. A cg too far forward or too far aft could render the airplane uncontrollable.

Centrifugal-flow Jet Engine – a turbine engine through which air flows through a centrifugal compressor, redirecting the air radially outward to pass through combustors on the outer periphery of the powerplant.

Chord – the width of a wing or the line between the leading and trailing edges, usually referred to as chord length, or a mean chord for a tapered wing.

Compressibility Effects – refers to the effects on aircraft performance and control resulting from air compressing into shock waves as the aircraft approaches the speed of sound at the operating altitude.

Contra-rotating Propeller – also known as a dual-rotation propeller or contraprop, this employs two propellers, in tandem, turning in opposite directions on coaxial power shafts.

Control Reversal – a phenomenon of control sense reversing, such as displacing the control column to the right to produce a left rolling acceleration instead of the normal right roll. Reversal is normally the result of structural deformation under airloads (wing twist in the example of roll reversal) or the action of compressibility shocks on control surfaces.

Counter-rotating Propeller – propellers on opposite sides of the aircraft (as in a twin-engine aircraft) that rotate in opposite directions to eliminate torque effects.

Critical Mach Number – the flight velocity at which compressibility shocks first begin to appear on the aircraft.

Dive Brakes – flaps or other deployed surfaces intended to slow the aircraft and prevent exceeding the Critical Mach Number.

Dive Flaps – flaps allowing recovery from a dive for which pullout is rendered ineffectual by compressibility effects.

Drag – the resistance of the air to passage of an aircraft. It is made up of "induced drag" from the creation of lift and "profile drag" created by moving the aircraft through an air mass. Profile drag includes skin friction drag, the overall frontal area offered to the incident air, cooling drag from air passing through a cowling and engine baffling, and other elements.

Dual-rotation Propeller – (see Contra-rotating Propeller)

Flaps – an articulated portion of a wing trailing edge that enhances lift at the expense of drag, and is usually employed on approach to allow a reduced landing speed. The split flap is a lower portion of the trailing edge that rotates down. The Fowler flap slides aft and down, usually creating a slot between the wing mainplane and flap surfaces.

Flutter – an unstable oscillation of a portion of the aircraft or control surface that can grow to catastrophic levels. The instability is induced by unsteady air loads interacting with elastic deformation of the structure or control surface rotation at like frequencies (resonance).

Gunsight – a mechanism for aligning guns and cannon with a target. This is usually in front of the pilot or gunner allowing visual sighting through an optical device.

Hardpoint – a strengthened structural portion within the bottom surface of a wing or fuselage with fittings for carriage of weapons or fuel tanks.

Inline Engine – a reciprocating engine in which the pistons are arranged in one or more longitudinal lines parallel to the center power shaft. An upright or inverted V-arrangement is typical.

Intercooler – one or more heat exchangers cooling air passing to a supercharger to increase density.

Laminar Flow – boundary layer of air adjacent to a surface in an air stream with an even pressure distribution as opposed to turbulent, and possessing less skin-friction drag. A laminar flow wing is one with an airfoil designed to maintain laminar flow for more of the chord length than typical airfoils.

Lend-Lease – U.S. government policy by which weapons and other materiel assistance was purchased by the United States and provided as a form of loan to nations fighting or arming to fight the Axis powers.

Liquid-cooled Engine – a piston engine employing recirculated liquid to cool the cylinders and other components. The coolant fluid is cooled via one or more radiators open to the passing air.

Load Factor – a measure of acceleration in the vertical axis of an aircraft defined as units of gravitational pull on the surface of the Earth (1 g). This is a primary criterion for structural design to ensure the airframe can withstand maneuvering airloads and inertia, plus a factor of safety.

Mach Number – the speed of sound at the aircraft's operating altitude.

Pressurization – a system that pumps compressed air into a sealed cockpit to maintain safe pressure as the aircraft climbs into the rarefied air at high altitude.

Propeller Cuff – fitting near the base of a propeller blade that expands the width (chord) to improve thrust or alter the flow off that portion of the blade for improved passage of cooling air into an engine cowling immediately aft.

Propwash – the flow of air off a propeller passing back over the aircraft directly aft (assuming a tractor propeller). The propwash can create asymmetrical moments on the aircraft but also ensures control effectiveness at low aircraft velocities for those surfaces within the wash.

Radial Engine – a reciprocating engine in which the pistons are arranged radially about the center power shaft. One or two rows of radially grouped cylinders are typical.

Slats – a segment of a wing leading edge that slides forward to increase wing camber (inflexion) to add lift. This usually creates a slot between the surface and the wing mainplane through which air is accelerated to energize flow downstream and delay stall.

Slot – A narrow spanwise opening between the lower and upper surface of a wing allowing high-pressure air below to accelerate up and over the top of the wing to energize the flow and delay stall.

Specifications – An agreement between a manufacturer and the customer as to the characteristics of an aircraft yet to be designed and built.

Spin – An out-of-control condition produced by the stall of one wing coupled with a high aircraft yaw angle. The result is a descending flight path, with the aircraft rotating about the vertical axis.

Stall – The turbulation and separation of air on a wing or other surface due to high angle of attack and adverse pressure gradients within the boundary layer that causes a large loss of lift.

Supercharger – a spinning compressor impeller, usually driven off the engine accessory gearcase, through which the fuel-air mixture from the carburetor is ported before passing into the intake manifold. This "boost" helps maintain intake pressure nearer sea level, even with the lower air density at altitude, for sustained high engine power output.

Torque – the moment (lateral displacement tendency) created by a propeller, especially at high power on takeoff and low speed on landing. This is a combination of mechanical effects from turning the heavy prop as well as the asymmetrical airflow effects on the aircraft elements aft of the propeller.

Turbojet – a gas turbine (jet) engine for which the motive output is an accelerated mass of air for thrust.

Turboprop – a gas turbine (jet) engine for which the principal motive output is shaft torque to a propeller.

Turbosupercharger – a turbine spun by engine exhaust gases that, in turn, spins a compressor to "charge" air taken in via a ram air duct. This air is then passed to the carburetor or supercharger.

Water Injection – the introduction of a metered flow of water (usually a water-alcohol mixture) into the cylinder of a piston engine or combustion chamber of a jet engine to reduce temperatures, allowing more fuel to be burned in the combustor for greater power or thrust output. For the piston engine, the leaner fuel-air mixture permits higher intake manifold pressures.

Acronym List

AAB	Army Air Base
ADF	Automatic Direction Finding
AEW	Airborne Early Warning
AI	air intercept
approx.	approximately
APU	auxiliary power unit
AR	Aircraft Rocket
ASB	air-to-surface Type B
ASV	air-to-surface vessel
ASW	anti-submarine warfare
BAC	Brewster Aeronautical Corporation
BuAer	Bureau of Aeronautics
Buno.	Bureau Number
cal.	caliber
Caltech	California Institute of Technology
carquals	carrier qualifications
CBI	China-Burma-India theater
cg	center of gravity
CV	aircraft carrier (earliest U.S. Navy models)
CVB	aircraft carrier, battle
CVE	aircraft carrier, escort
CVL	aircraft carrier, light
DLI	deck-launched interceptor
DF	direction finding
eng.	engines
ext.	external
fpm	feet per minute
fps	feet per second
ft	foot, feet
g	acceleration due to gravity
gal	gallon, gallons (U.S. units)
GCI	Ground Control Intercept
GE	General Electric
GM	General Motors Corporation
GW	gross weight
HF	high frequency
hp	horsepower
HVAR	High Velocity Aircraft Rockets
IFF	Identification Friend or Foe
int.	internal
JATO	Jet-Assisted Take-Off
JPU	jet power unit
lbf	pounds force (thrust)
lbs	pounds
LSO	Landing Signals Officer
M	million
MAD	magnetic airborne detector
max.	maximum
mi	statute miles
Mil	Military Power
min.	minimum
Mk	Mark
mm	millimeter
mod	modification
mph	miles per hour
NAA	North American Aviation
NACA	National Advisory Committee for Aeronautics
NAMU	Naval Air Modification Unit
NAS	Naval Air Station
NATC	Naval Air Test Center
p	page
pp	pages
prop	propeller
qual	qualification
RAAF	Royal Australian Air Force
RAF	Royal Air Force
recip	reciprocating engine
recon	reconnaissance
RFP	Request for Proposal
RN	Royal Navy
rpg	rounds per gun
RO	radar operator
shp	shaft horsepower
spec(s)	specification(s)
TBO	time-between-overhauls
torp	torpedo
UK	United Kingdom
USAAC	United States Army Air Corps
USAAF	United States Army Air Forces
USMC	United States Marine Corps
USN	United States Navy
USSR	Union of Soviet Socialist Republics
VBT	bomber-torpedo, carrier-based
VDB	Vengeance Dive Bomber
VF	Fighter, carrier-based
VHF	very high frequency
VJ-Day	Victory over Japan day
VTOL	vertical take-off and landing

Chapter 1

Wind tunnels operated by the military, NACA, and educational institutions were vital resources supplementing those owned by private industry. Langley's full-scale tunnel, accommodating the actual aircraft, was an invaluable aid to designers. The Bell YP-59A Airacomet is seen in the tunnel during efforts to understand its poor handling qualities. (Jay Miller Collection)

BACKGROUND TO GROWTH

In the 1920s and first half of the 1930s, the United States of America's military aviation forces were professional and motivated, but ill-equipped. Only one-quarter to one-third of its airplanes were frontline aircraft. As war approached, the American military was in approximately fifth place among the world's nations.[1]

Pent-up Capability

The American aviation-manufacturing sector had become virtually a cottage industry by the latter half of the 1930s. This neglect was due to extremely constricted military and commercial budgets during the Great Depression, competing military priorities in which aviation was still seen as needing to prove itself, and an isolationist tendency with lawmakers who saw no need for a large military with a preponderance of "offensive" weapons. These factors set the Unites States a step behind Germany in aeronautical science, as the Nazis ensured generous funding and support for advanced design tools and experimentation years before the Americans went into high gear. Yet, from raw materials to skills and national will, the United States had tremendous latent capabilities.

Assisting development efforts, American military services had laboratories for technological research and testing. The government had established the National Advisory Committee for Aeronautics (NACA) in 1927 that, with its labs and test centers, provided research and development tools too costly for the private sector. There was no lack of vision, talent, and means ready to expand aircraft capabilities with new types pushing the bounds of technology.

By law, aircraft procurement was performed on a competitive basis to ensure equal treatment and as an incentive for innovation and excellence in design. This was typically initiated by a statement of need from a combat organization that was translated into a Request for Proposal (RFP) released to industry by a development agency of the service. Resulting proposed designs were submitted as drawings and substantiating figures. These were evaluated against equitable measures and detailed specifications for the aircraft created in cooperation between the service and the winning manufacturer. Contracts usually followed for one or two experimental articles, with a mockup and other progress subject to review and potential redirection by the military. A dozen or so service test examples might be purchased for field evaluation. Adjustments to the design were introduced and tested as required.

The mockup stage of a development project was crucial and permitted a perspective difficult to obtain from drawings alone. This mockup of the Curtiss XP-46, photographed on 4 August 1939, was above average in being nearly complete and mobile, although control surfaces are not indicated. (San Diego Aerospace Museum)

The National Advisory Committee for Aeronautics (NACA) was a U.S. government-funded research establishment. An example of its contribution is this Army A-17A at Langley on 3 April 1940, heavily modified with a fully enclosed cowling around the air-cooled radial and alternate air paths added in the wing roots. (San Diego Aerospace Museum)

Even during the war, the U.S. military aircraft procurement processes usually included ordering one or two prototypes of any new aircraft for testing prior to a production contract. Vought's prototype of the Corsair, the XF4U-1, differed significantly from the first production models, validating the value of prototyping. (Military Aircraft Photographs)

The threat of total war arose again in 1939 with hostilities in Europe and tensions with Japan over its war on the Asian continent. As with so many other nations, America began rearming. Large aircraft orders placed by foreign nations in the run-up to war and after were a contributor. The concurrent production of aircraft meeting foreign – as well as American – orders facilitated rapid expansion of the aeronautical industry and workforce skills prior to the United States' entry into the conflict in December 1941. Designers were introduced to actual combat requirements as their customers found themselves at war with well-equipped adversaries. With passing of the

Wind-tunnel models, such as this Vultee XP-54 flutter model, were a vital means of collecting aerodynamic, stability, and control data on aircraft designs. The specialized model-making skills and national wind tunnels operated by NACA and the War Department were of tremendous value in the fast-moving wartime projects. (San Diego Aerospace Museum)

Lend-Lease Act of 11 March 1941, America was essentially buying everything provided to foreign nations. The Joint Aircraft Committee sought to standardize configurations as much as practical between American and foreign (namely British) models, facilitating higher production rates.

When war opened in Europe during September 1939, President Franklin D. Roosevelt declared a "limited national emergency" and the military began moving to a war footing. The mobilization of the nation generated a remarkable increase in industrial capacity. Within the first two years, this capacity roughly doubled.

Airpower was given priority in expenditures both before and after the declaration of war. These acts of the President and Congress overcame any remaining institutional inertia, placing the air arms on equal footing with the other combat branches. However, the services had just begun reequipping with world-class warplanes when plunged into combat. Other advanced designs were still in development and test, bearing fruit only later. Consequently, the first year of combat was tough, with marginal equipment and lack of combat experience. With the urgency of war, aircraft were placed into production before testing had been completed or even begun. Some of these designs still needed maturing to meet the unique circumstances of the conflict and as enemy systems evolved.

Building a war-winning aerial force, providing for training, and replacing combat losses required an enormous number of fighter aircraft like these F6F-5s awaiting delivery in Bethpage. Grumman contributed admirably, with F6F production alone exceeding 500 per month, with more than 12,000 delivered by November 1945. (Northrop Grumman History Center)

The United States facilitated a tremendous expansion of its industrial capacity in order to meet the demands of total war and defeat the Axis powers. Aircraft production especially outpaced all other nations combined. Notable among the producers was Grumman, manufacturing thousands of exceptional naval airplanes like these F6F-5s. (Northrop Grumman History Center)

The engineering, manufacturing, and testing behind U.S. combat aircraft was both prodigious and excellent. An example is this drop test of an F6F-5 at Grumman, released to simulate an extreme landing. In the background is an airframe likely subject to static loads testing to demonstrate structural safety margins. (Northrop Grumman History Center)

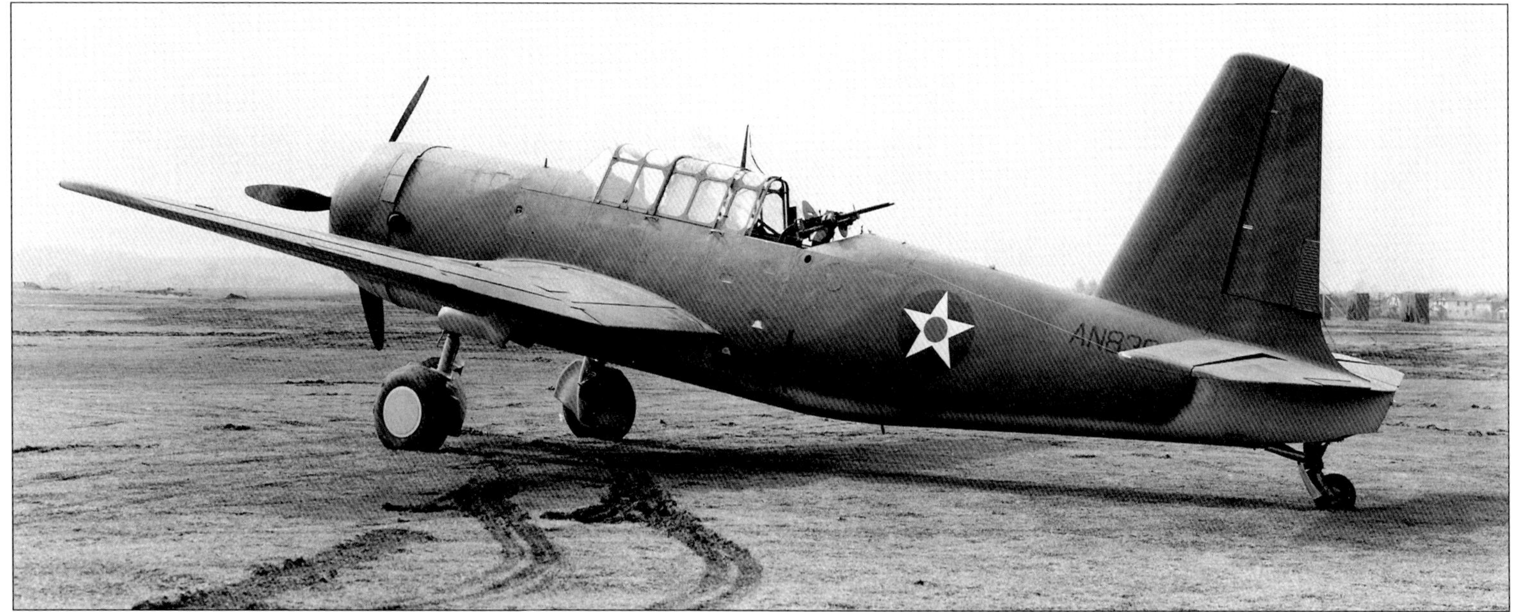

This Vultee A-31, one of the requisitioned RAF Vengeance dive-bombers, is equipped with a pair of .30-cal. machine guns in a flexible mount for the rear gunner. Even two of the weapons were proving too light in firepower but nearly too heavy for manual manipulation. (National Archives)

The eventual force of technically excellent warplanes in superior numbers matched with well-trained personnel had the most telling effect beginning in about mid-1944, when the Allies achieved air superiority. This was a major contributor to ultimate victory.

March of Progress

Prewar aircraft developments set the stage for a tremendous leap in military aircraft reliability, performance, and mission capability. Numerous technologies contributed to this dramatic acceleration in the evolution of military airpower during the war years.

Weapon Moves

The ubiquitous, air-cooled .30 caliber (cal.) and .50-cal. aircraft machine guns (weighing about 30 and 64 pounds, respectively) were steadily improved. The prewar standard of one each of these weapons in the engine cowling was shown to be inadequate by early combat. The .30 cal. soon became ineffective against enemy aircraft metal structure and armor. Even the .50 cal. was falling short near the end of the war. More and heavier guns meant a fuselage mount became impractical. Wing mounting also eliminated the need for an interrupter gear to avoid rounds striking the propeller. However, this then mandated converging streams of fire that required a suitable gunsight, prompting further developments in this equipment.

This early P-40 was too lightly armed with only the pair of .50-cal. machine guns in the nose. Initial efforts to address the deficiency saw two to four .30 machine guns in the wings, although the .30 was rapidly losing its effectiveness. Later models would have four .50s in the wings. (National Museum of the United States Air Force)

The .50 cal. was seldom suitable in a flexible, hand-operated mounting on a fighter, contributing to the demise of this feature. Instead, turrets were the design option of choice for a time. These could be heavy, "draggy," and complex, generally requiring power systems and possibly a stabilized periscopic sight for the gunner.

The need for firepower heavier than the machine gun compelled adoption of cannon with explosive shells. Initially, the U.S. Army favored the Madsen 37mm cannon, weighing about 200 pounds and firing a 1.25-pound explosive shell up to 12,000 feet. However,

The heavier armament required for fighters to successfully engage enemy aircraft with armor and other protective features is typified by this P-38F Lightning from June 1942. The weapons concentrated in the nose consisted of six .50-cal. machine guns with 500 rpg and a centerline 20mm cannon with 150 rounds. (National Museum of the United States Air Force)

manufacturing issues with the 37mm and fewer rounds made the 20mm, at about 115 pounds and with a higher rate of fire, the desired weapon. The French Hispano-Suiza 20mm cannon was produced in the United States by Bendix, becoming available for U.S. mounting in late 1941.

The telescopic gunsight, with its limited field of view, was finally replaced with the reflector sight in December 1941 on all fighters. Common initially were units that projected a lighted ring through a collimating lens to eliminate parallax, some with a fixed reticule pipper in the center. A British reflector sight was eventually adapted

The speed of newer fighters and the need for heavier armament led to the introduction of turrets, although few fighters featuring turrets reached production. One such prototype was the Douglas XSB2D-1 Destroyer with two remote-controlled turrets, in dorsal and ventral position, each with a .50-cal. machine gun. (San Diego Aerospace Museum)

The singular Curtiss XP-36F (H-75L Hawk), s/n 38-172, carries a trial installation of a 23mm Madsen cannon in this photograph dated 5 November 1938. The Army Air Corps was then performing tests of airborne cannons, mostly foreign products, seeking a suitable weapon for domestic production. (National Museum of the United States Air Force)

This XF4F-3 is equipped with the Navy's standard telescopic sight in a photograph dated 21 June 1940. The narrow field of view and inability to provide adjustment for converging fire from wing guns made the sight too limiting for World War II combat. (American Aviation Historical Society)

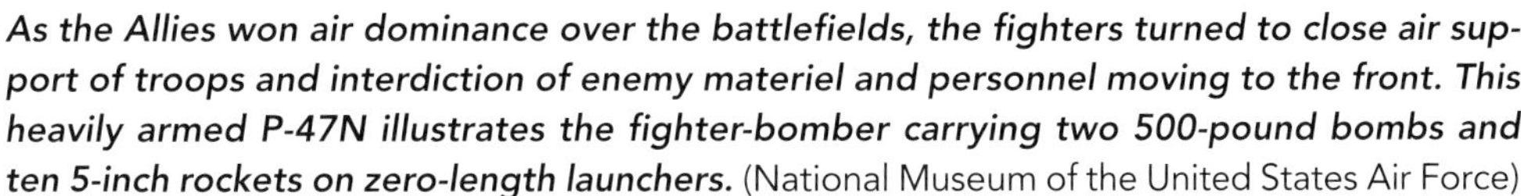

As the Allies won air dominance over the battlefields, the fighters turned to close air support of troops and interdiction of enemy materiel and personnel moving to the front. This heavily armed P-47N illustrates the fighter-bomber carrying two 500-pound bombs and ten 5-inch rockets on zero-length launchers. (National Museum of the United States Air Force)

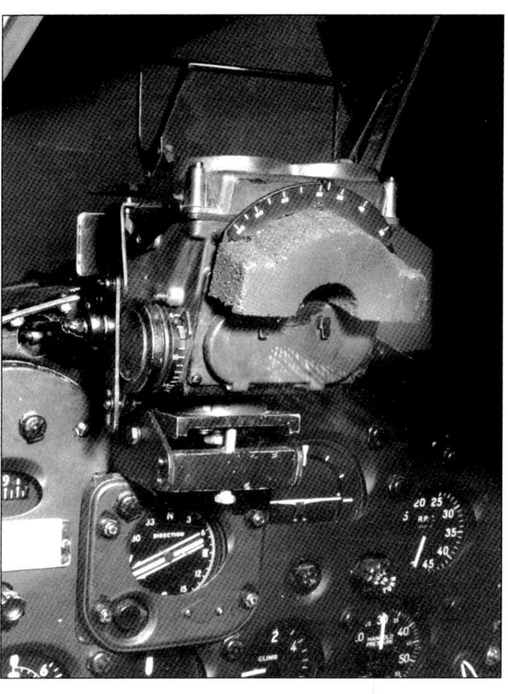

A Mk 21/23 gyro-stabilized computing sight is shown installed in an F6F-5 in this photo dated 23 May 1944. This compensated for aircraft movement while maintaining the lead for a deflection shot at the target. The larger field of view was a welcome change from earlier reflector sights. (Northrop Grumman Historical Center)

The basic reflector sight replaced the telescopic sight in this F4F-3 that also features a thick armored windscreen. An aiming reticle is projected onto the combiner glass, with a means to adjust for converging wing gunfire. Note the simple ring sight remaining on the glareshield as a backup. (Northrop Grumman Historical Center)

and standardized while more advanced indigenous products were developed. The U.S.-manufactured variant of the Ferranti unit with fixed or gyro optical sight compensated for relative movement between the attacker and target. The pilot dialed in the target's wingspan and approximate range. A gyro-stabilized lead-computing sight was also developed and fielded by the Army, but on only a very limited basis by the Navy. This required both altitude and airspeed settings, making the sight less desirable than the illuminated sight ring. A fire-control system for flexibly mounted guns combined the sight and compensation functions in a servo mount.

The Norden bombsight was initially included in Navy bombers. However, this was found to be of little value when performing horizontal bombing against maneuvering vessels. Land targets and stationary vessels were better attacked with dive-bombing or glide-bombing techniques.

As fighters became fighter-bombers in the late war years, they carried a larger assortment of air-to-surface weapons. The selection of iron bombs changed little, but rockets were a new addition. As with other weapons, the example was already set for the United States by the warring nations in Europe. The California Institute of Technology (Caltech) developed the American rockets. The first was the 4.5-inch diameter, 3-foot long Bazooka rocket fired from a 10-foot-long triple-tube launcher. This apparatus was cumbersome, heavy, and inaccurate. More suitable was the 3.5-inch Caltech aircraft rocket at 34 pounds with a solid steel warhead, initially fired off 6-foot rails. The

A new weapon for American fighters was the rocket. This was developed following the British example and evolved through several iterations during the war. Among the first was the 4.5-inch rockets fired from the M10 triple-tube assemblies like that carried by this P-51D. (National Museum of the United States Air Force)

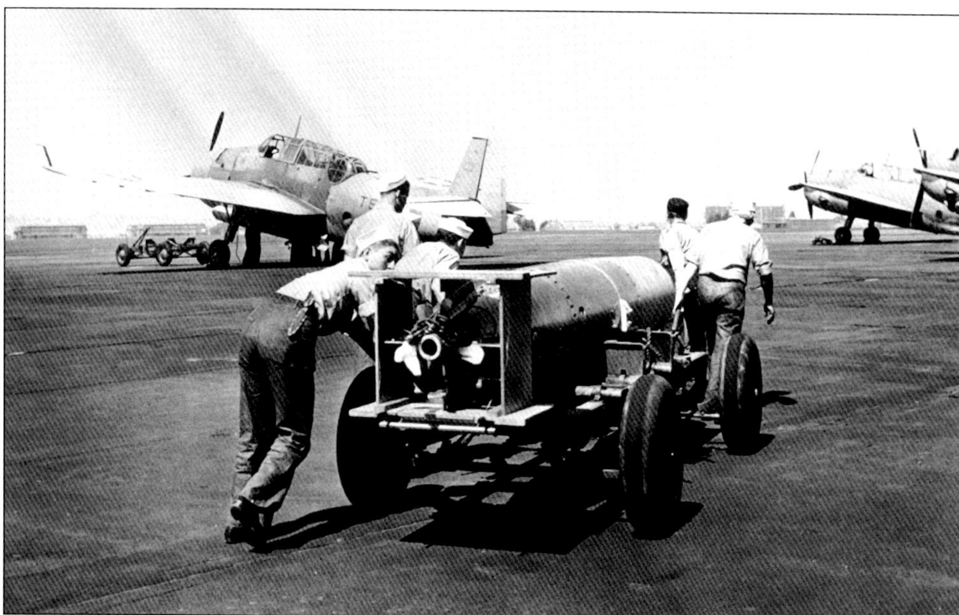

The Navy's standard Mk 13 torpedo weighed around 2,000 pounds and was more than 15 feet long. Here a TBF-1 receives the fish for its bomb bay. The weapon had numerous problems early on that required some time to remedy, making for many ineffectual attacks with many aircraft and aircrew lost. (Northrop Grumman History Center)

first 3.5-inch projectile was air-launched in August 1943, and used in combat for the first time on 11 January 1944. A 5-inch anti-aircraft shell was adapted to the 3.5-inch aircraft rocket, entering service by the end of 1944. These weighed 80 pounds and velocity decreased to 710 fps. They were also initially fired off rails, but these were particularly draggy. It was soon found that the rockets could be launched from standoff stub posts alone, and this method was adopted in spring 1944. Recovering the velocity decrement meant substituting a 5-inch motor for the High Velocity Aircraft Rockets (HVAR), or "Holy Moses," fired off the zero-length stubs. The projectile weighed 140 pounds, was 6 feet long, and possessed 1,375 fps velocity.

The Navy went to war with the Mk 13 aircraft torpedo that dated from 1935. This was a large weapon at 13.4 feet long and 22 inches in diameter, and it weighed 1,935 pounds with a 401-pound TNT warhead. The launch conditions were initially a very restrictive 100-foot altitude, 120 mph straight and level, and no more than 1,000 feet from the target. These exposed the aircraft to enemy fire and gave very poor results – including failure to run properly, home, or detonate. The Mk 13 was slow by international standards and the warhead comparatively light. Corrective actions began immediately; changes included options to add a pickle barrel drag ring on the nose and sometimes a wooden ring tail frame surrounding the fins. These ensured proper water entry and running for a much broader delivery profile, such as increasing the deployment height to 300 feet. The Mk 13 Mod 1 version increased the overall weight to 2,216 pounds with a 600-pound warhead, and the length was increased to 22.5 feet. Delivery profile was expanded in later models, to as much as 800 feet altitude and 300 mph. By fall 1944, the revised torpedoes were proving nearly 100-percent effective and were possibly the best in service with any nation.

Systems Complexity

Aerodynamics was not neglected, with NACA doing invaluable research into airfoils

High-lift devices became common on designs late in the war as aircraft height increased yet low approach and landing speed remained important. The slotted Fowler flaps on this Martin XBTM-1 are a fine example of this design option. In this case, the flaps are equipped with integral dive brakes. (San Diego Aerospace Museum)

Extending range via ever-larger external fuel tanks became an important element of evolving fighter designs. Experiments on this XP-47N during October 1944 employed modified P-38 ferry tanks of 330-gal capacity made of plywood, probably intended only for ferry. (National Museum of the United States Air Force)

and high-lift devices. The laminar flow airfoil derived from these efforts reduced drag by one-third to one-half for improved speed performance.* The airfoil had to be used in conjunction with very smooth construction that included flush riveting and very tight fit tolerances. There was concern that finish deterioration in service would render all this moot. However, laminar flow surfaces remained one aspect of performance gains by American combat aircraft.

Split flaps were common in the 1930s, but the new and more-efficient Fowler flaps were soon being adopted. These were more complex, shifting aft as well as down and forming one or more slots between the wing and flap. Likewise, leading-edge slats and slots began to appear. Such devices permitted the ever-heavier and faster fighters to continue landing at acceptable speeds.

The press for more speed and growing reliability of systems overcame any reluctance to adopt fully retractable landing gear. Although retractable gear became common, the tricycle undercarriage was only gaining popularity near the end of the war. However, these only rarely had nose-wheel steering. This meant the use of wheel

** Laminar flow refers to a boundary layer of air adjacent to the surface with even pressure distribution compared with a turbulent layer that contributes substantial drag. A laminar flow wing features an airfoil (cross section) that maintains laminar characteristics for more of the chord length (wing width) for lower overall drag. NACA had devised several such airfoils that were exploited by a number of American aircraft projects for improved performance. The United States was the leader in the field of airfoil characterization and design.*

brakes for directional control on the initial portion of a takeoff roll until aero surfaces became effective, lengthening the takeoff distance. The Navy had more fundamental concerns regarding tricycle-gear compatibility with carrier-deck launch and arrestment systems.

Lessons were also learned regarding self-sealing fuel tanks and armor for crew and vital systems. These were only just being adapted when America was plunged into war. The weight of added armor became a necessary evil. The self-sealing feature reduced internal tank volume. For the P-38, this equated to 410 gallons going to 300, and 160 to 147 gallons for the F4F. External tanks were innovative for the U.S. Army when World War II began having shunned external tanks because of hazard and drag. These drop tanks were quickly found to be essential given ferry and combat requirements. They had long been in use by the Navy.

Adapting warplanes to operating conditions required innovation and quick reaction. Examples were winterizing gear for Aleutians operations or sand filters for North Africa. Blown or bubble canopies were derived from new Plexiglas technology that permitted curved plastic transparencies. This was first seen on the Royal Air Force (RAF) Typhoon and understood by all to possess superior all-around vision, although there was a drag penalty. Pilots, however, wished to ensure adequate armor protection even with the bubble. Shore-based naval fighters commonly received pneumatic tail-wheel tires to replace the solid rubber units employed aboard ship.

War brought some earlier practices to a halt in the interest of weight saving or expediency. The practice of collecting spent shell casings in a fairing bin under the aircraft to prevent them from striking other aircraft was abandoned in wartime. By mid-1943, it was recognized that Army frontline aircraft would seldom last more than 500 flight hours in frontline service. Hence, camouflage was dispensed with on fighters to save weight and production time. The pre-war Navy had considerable standardized gear to which a new aircraft had to conform. Among these was a requirement for inflating flotation bags in each wing and a life raft stored in a compartment the pilot could readily access after ditching. These were quickly sacrificed in the interest of weight savings and reduced production demands.

Avionics came of age in the form of more practical aircraft radios, airborne radar, navigation aids, and electronic warfare equipment, with the United States at the forefront of this technology. However, this also contributed to fighter weight growth. The vacuum tube technology of the period was bulky and heavy, and additional capabilities came with more weight. At the beginning of the war, the common Air Corps transceiver, with one high-frequency (HF) transmitter channel and low-frequency receiver, weighed 40.3 pounds and required 1.3 cubic feet of volume. In 1942, the common radio was 93.5 pounds in 1.9 cubic feet, although bringing with it four very-high-frequency (VHF) transmit/receive channels. By 1944, the Identification Friend or Foe (IFF) radar transponder set was common, at 44.0 pounds. Some fighters were also fitted with a tail warning radar set (AN/APS-13 with antennae protruding from the tail) at 20.2 pounds, and VHF Homing Adapter at 17.5 pounds (direction finding or DF loop). The addition of radar further increased weight. All these units included antennae, shock-mount racks, cabling/connectors, and control heads, introducing cockpit complexity, pilot workload, and maintenance chores.[2]

Engine Challenges

America ranked with Britain and Germany as world leaders in superior aero engines and propellers. The Army championed the liquid-cooled inline engine (designated with an "I" prefix or a "V" for V-configuration), along with considerable private investment by the engine manufacturers, because of the promise of reduced frontal area and overall drag of the installation compared with the air-cooled radials ("R" prefix). Racers and foreign military types were

Such examples as the German Me 109, with liquid-cooled inline engines, and the desire for drag reduction, was motivation for the Army Air Corps to pursue the design option with vigor that has since met with criticism. This captured Me 109F was photographed on 22 May 1943 at Wright Field. (National Museum of the United States Air Force)

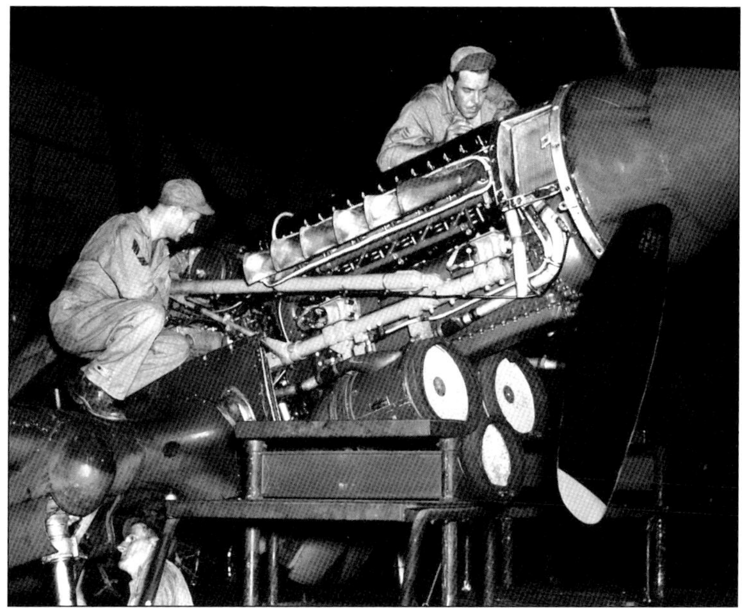

The Allison V-1710 (here on a P-40) was the only American inline, liquid-cooled engine in series production throughout World War II. All others never progressed beyond the experimental stage. Production of the UK's Rolls-Royce Merlin engine under contract by Packard provided the only alternative. (National Archives)

The single-row R-1820 Cyclone hung in the port nacelles of the Grumman XF5F-1 Skyrocket and delivered 1,200 hp via the 3-blade Curtiss Electric propeller. The 1939 installation is fairly simple by comparison to the engine mount, oil cooler, supercharger, and cowling to come. The propeller employed electrical pitch change versus hydraulics. (Northrop Grumman History Center)

showing the potential of the liquid-cooled engines. However, the coolant system could be heavy and complex, and the radiator(s) required careful design to avoid negating any drag savings. Although five firms had liquid-cooled engine projects in advanced stages during the war, only the Allison V-1710 reached quantity production. American production of the British Merlin inline was fortuitous, the P-51 benefiting most. However, as the Mustang moved to the ground-attack mission, its vulnerable cooling system became an Achilles heel.

When first introduced, the inlines produced less power per weight of engine than radials, yet promised imminent advances. The U.S. Army Air Corps (USAAC) dictated inlines for most of its new designs in 1939 and 1940 as it held the most promise for performance gains. However, radial development continued as well, as demonstrated when the Navy's F4U-1 exceed 400 mph with its R-2800. The Army reconsidered, and the P-47 received a radial. Radial-engine U.S. aircraft outperformed inlines in most cases.

The Navy had invested considerable sums over many years to assist in developing reliable air-cooled engines. The attraction for them was eliminating the need to carry coolant and other spares aboard ship. The compromise was the requirement for careful radial engine cowl design and cowl flaps for suitable cooling airflow.

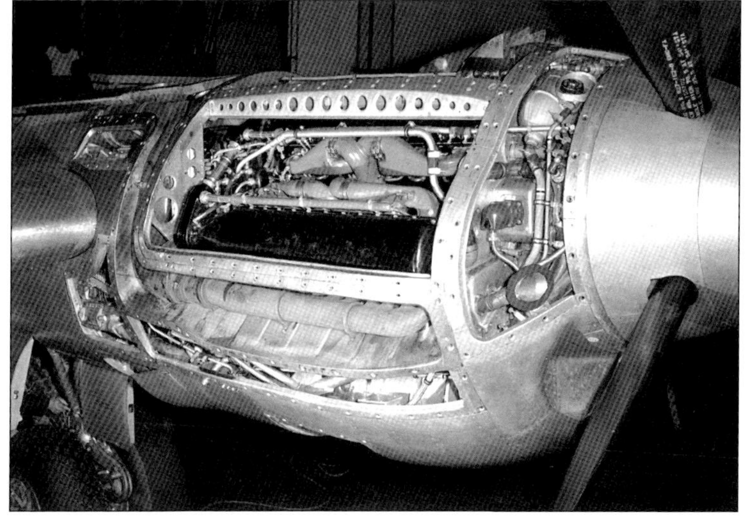

An example of the monster engines developed for the tremendous power required of the larger and fast fighters is this Allison V-3420 in the Lockheed XP-58 (shot 12 September 1944). The enormous 24-cylinder, liquid-cooled powerplant delivered 3,000 hp at 28,000 ft altitude with turbosupercharger. It never entered series production. (Air Force Flight Test Center)

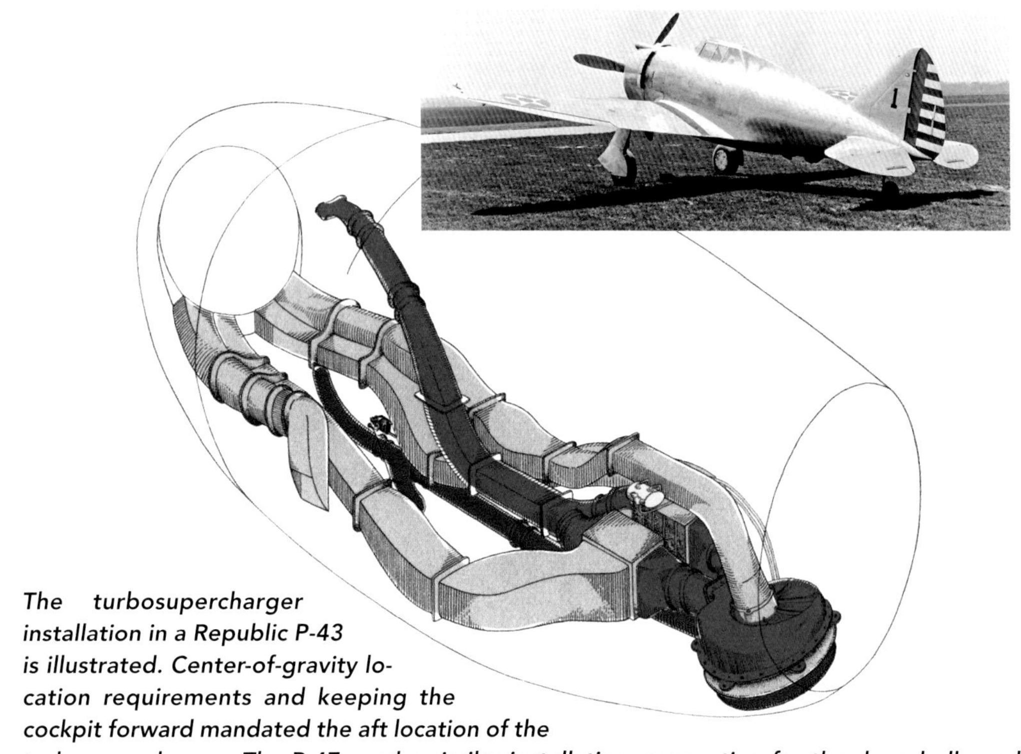

The turbosupercharger installation in a Republic P-43 is illustrated. Center-of-gravity location requirements and keeping the cockpit forward mandated the aft location of the turbosupercharger. The P-47 used a similar installation, accounting for the deep belly and some frustrating maintenance chores. (USAF and National Museum of the United States Air Force)

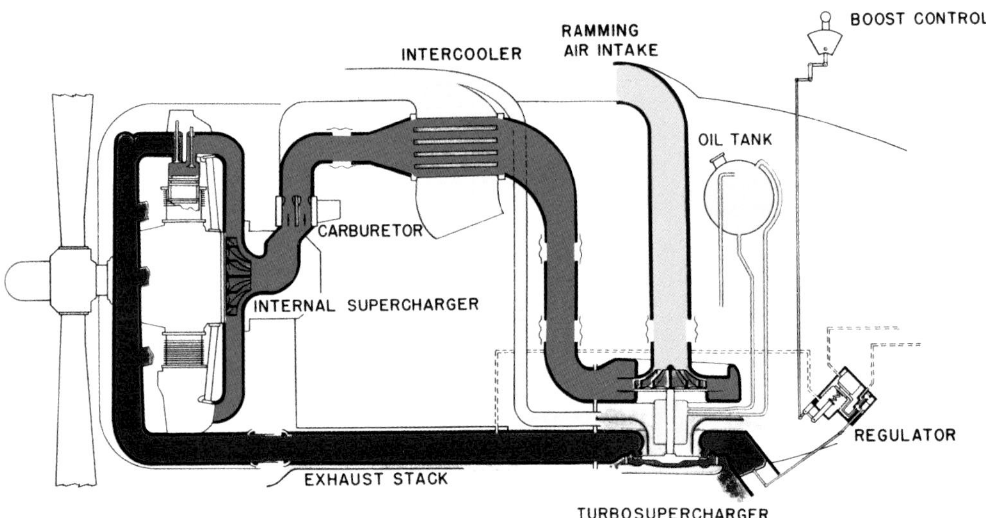

This training diagram shows notionally the components of a turbosupercharger used to improve altitude performance of an aero engine. Variations include the basic supercharger alone and perhaps multiple stages of compressors and intercoolers, two speeds of booster selectable, and automatic adjustments, adding further complication. (USAF)

Propeller cuffs were introduced to production aircraft in 1940 as another measure to improve flow into the cowling for enhanced engine cooling.

The never-ending demand for greater speed to propel the growing weight of fighters demanded ever-greater horsepower. By mid-war, 1,600 hp was considered the minimum for a frontline fighter. Water injection permitted bursts of extra power (referred to as Combat Power or War Emergency [WE] Power by some manufacturers, although WE could refer to other means of briefly increasing power). The fluid (actually a water-methanol mix) provided a leaner fuel-air mix but was also used to keep heat down, slowing the combustion to avoid detonation while permitting higher manifold pressures. The weight of the water tank and lines was the tradeoff. The Allies also adopted 100-octane fuel by 1942 and 100/130 in mid-1944 that allowed higher manifold pressures if care was taken to avoid knocking or uneven combustion within the cylinders. This was an advantage over the Axis, who continued to use 87-octane fuel.

Through the 1930s, the United States eschewed high-altitude performance for its fighters. Such would only be required for bomber intercept, and the prevailing notion was that the "bomber would always get through." However, as "bomber-destroyers" came into vogue and the general advantage of altitude over adversaries was appreciated, doctrine changed. The need to retain performance of normally aspirated piston engines as the aircraft climbed into thinner air was given extensive attention with considerable aircraft design impact.

The solution for altitude performance was the supercharger (boost) to maintain intake manifold pressures nearer sea level even with the lower air density at altitude. The fuel-air mixture from the carburetor is ported through a spinning compressor impeller, usually driven off the engine accessory gearcase, and the flow then ducted to the intake manifold. Complexity in attaining this added power (Military Power or Mil for some manufacturers) grew with two stages of compression in series, two speeds via gearing, and one or more intercoolers (using passing air for convective cooling) to reduce the temperature of the compressed induction air.

Initially, the turbosupercharger used the exhaust gases to spin a turbine that in turn spun a compressor to charge air taken in via a ram air duct. This air was then passed to the carburetor or supercharger. First introduced on a U.S. Army fighter in 1932, the turbosupercharger could throw blades due to cyclical heating-induced metal fatigue or even explode and generate fires. By World War II, continued effort had made the units reliable, easier to control, and much more effective than a supercharger alone. This required steady metallurgical research and compressor-design advancement. They exceeded anything existing abroad. Elements in the U.S. government resisted export of turbosuperchargers until spring 1941. The units were then still produced in comparatively low numbers and considered sensitive military technology.

A serious bottleneck in expanding aircraft production, both for domestic and foreign sales, was the limited aero engine design and manufacturing capability. Although there were numerous aircraft manufacturers, there were only three principal high-power military powerplant producers: Allison, Pratt & Whitney, and Curtiss Wright. The development of engines historically took longer than aircraft, making the parallel development of an engine for a specific new aircraft a very chancy proposition. This made the potential of producing British designs very attractive in meeting urgent wartime needs and offering more model choices for new airframes. Propeller development and production was similarly constrained, with only Curtiss, Hamilton Standard, and Aeroproducts as the principal producers of propellers suitable for fighters.

Speed Limit

The increasing maximum airspeed of each new-generation fighter was creating problems for airframe designers. In dives, the fastest aircraft began experiencing compressibility effects. As speed approaches the velocity of sound (approximately 700 mph at 22,000 feet), the air adjacent to the vehicle begins to compress into shock waves with a manifold increase in drag. The speed at which this occurs varies based on an aircraft's external shape and is called the critical Mach number. Mach number is the ratio of the velocity of the vehicle to the speed of sound at the specific flight condition. The air behind the shock wave is at lower velocity, reducing lift on the wing and tail, thereby decreasing control-surface effectiveness. The combined effect could mean the steepening of a dive, known as tuck-under. In this condition, stick forces grow dramatically or some controls become ineffective, and the airflow is also turbulent, causing heavy buffeting. Large and unexpected trim changes are experienced and are especially startling because they tend to exacerbate the dive angle. Many pilots came away shaken, and some did not come away.

Some aircraft would eventually be fitted with "dive flaps" that shifted the center of pressure of the air forces acting on the aircraft while also delaying shock formation. This gave a nose-up pitching moment to aid in recovery from the "graveyard" dive and restored some of the lost lift in the "shock stall." Others received "dive brakes" that were deployed to prevent exceeding critical Mach.

Demands for increasing speed were pushing the limits of propeller design. High flight speed combines with propeller speed to give tip velocities approaching the speed of sound – where flow breaks down and propeller efficiency drops off sharply. A measure to combat this was the introduction of "paddle-blade" propellers that moved the greatest thrust-producing portion of the blade toward the hub where velocity is lower. Advanced designs were being investigated, including swept scimitar-shaped blades to permit increased airspeed prior to the onset of sonic tip velocities. Such were tested on the P-61.

The propeller-tip velocity limit and the drag rise of straight wings suggested the practical speed of prop-driven conventional designs was approximately 550 mph. It is unlikely any such World War II fighter exceeded Mach 0.85—in one piece from a screaming dive—or Mach 0.70 in level flight. One worthy approach suggested by pre-war literature was to sweep wings and tail surfaces backwards, delaying the onset of shocks. Machmeters were introduced with new fighters, especially the later jets, so pilots could readily recognize when they approached critical Mach.

Jets Emerge

It was already evident to most involved in aircraft development that piston powerplants and propellers were reaching their practical limits. Late-war fighter engines had about 2,400 to 3,000 hp and 18 or more cylinders. With approximately one hp per pound, weight plus size and cooling demands of the engines were becoming critical. The next logical step, to 4,000 hp, would require 36 or more cylinders. Such growth appeared prohibitive. Design complexity and manufacturing requirements were already extremely demanding, with years spent developing a new engine and thousands of man-hours to build each unit. Operating tolerances were becoming daunting, and maintenance complexity challenged military suitability. Pilot controls and instruments were increasingly complex, with throttle, mixture, boost, water injection, cowl flaps, radiator shutters, propeller condition, carburetor air heat, starter, etc. Although the United States was a world leader in propeller design, the ability to convert high engine-output to thrust with efficient airscrews was also approaching its peak. This led to such complex and heavy solutions as contra-rotating (dual-rotation) propellers.

By the mid-1930s, many theorists and engineers were looking at the possibilities of gas turbines (jet) engines to replace reciprocating powerplants and propellers to achieve higher airspeeds.* The turbojet engine was theoretically more efficient in generating thrust from powerplant weight, this actually increasing with speed, although fuel economy would suffer. Jet engines appeared simpler, did not demand the ground clearance of the propeller, promised less vibration, and would eliminate the powerful yawing moments that can be produced by using propellers, generally summarized as "torque."† The fundamental challenges would be the extreme temperatures and rotating speeds of components that would demand specialized materials for blades and casings, and marked increases in achievable compression ratios and turbine efficiencies, while keeping fuel economy within tolerable limits. Design studies and research work along these lines were underway in other countries during the prewar years.

Captured aircraft were evaluated, sometimes including flight test, to determine capabilities. American engineers were offered the opportunity to examine the aircraft for useful insights, examples being these captured Japanese aircraft including a B6N2 Tenzan "Jill" (foreground) and N1K1 Kyofu "Rex" floatplane fighter. (Jay Miller Collection)

Engineers in American military laboratories, at NACA, and some aero manufacturers had discussed gas turbine aero engines in technical publications and performed some preliminary experiments. The United States' lead in turbosuperchargers was a natural jumping-off point for such research. However, focus in the country remained on advanced reciprocating engine/propeller combinations.

Hard Lessons

The United States adapted many lessons, most "written in blood," from the British and other combatants in the early war years. Their own experience and the unique circumstances of the Pacific Theater served as further guidance. Captured enemy aircraft were examined in detail, and flown if possible, to document capabilities and derive insights for application to domestic development. Test and engineering organizations in all services and combatant countries undertook this work. The results were recorded and shared within the services and industry, and with allies. Manufacturers examined and flew the aircraft.

The services held conferences with designers from the aviation manufacturers to share such intelligence, explain the changing needs of the air war, and introduce new technology or research data. Company "Tech Reps" and pilots were sent to training bases and combat theaters to learn firsthand about the issues arising from use and maintenance of their products, and to provide demonstrations of how to get the most from the weapons systems. Little research and development was undertaken during the war unless it held promise of short-term and direct impact on production warplanes.[3]

Shifting Plans

Aircraft development projects were initiated in response to combat requirements, enemy measures, and advances in engines, aerodynamics, weapons, and electronics. Developing and fielding

** At that time, reaction propulsion systems were referred to colloquially as jets in that they all produced a high-velocity jet of compressed and heated air (or other gas from rocket combustion). Hence, both jet engines and rocket motors, in addition to aircraft employing either, might be called jets.*

† The propwash aft of the propeller produces unequal forces across the aircraft that produce yaw. This generally requires use of rudder or rudder trim to compensate. Just the spinning mass of the propeller generates torque that will tend to roll the aircraft in the opposite direction. Further, a spinning propeller inclined to the incident airflow will produce asymmetrical loading or thrust across the disk. This is because the blades on one side are experiencing the flow at a greater angle of attack than the other side and so generate greater thrust. The yaw resulting from all these contributors, most evident at high power during takeoff, is referred to as P-factor. For the fighters with conventional landing gear and large propellers that produced enormous thrust that predominated in World War II, these torque effects required careful pilot attention. In some fighters, the yaw developed suddenly or rudder was inadequate if not fed in early. In such cases, the unwary pilot paid for his inattention with a ground loop that could damage or destroy the airplane.

a new aircraft typically required two to three years of iterative design and testing, and this could be accelerated only so much at heightened risk of disappointing results. Engine development was even longer. Adopting new technologies like advanced engines, cockpit pressurization, advanced systems, new weapons, and more electronic-intensive elements, all worked against rapid development. This paced some aircraft programs or caused others to perish. Carefully managed materials, engineering manpower, and test facilities were limiting factors that stretched out work.

All the complex work might still yield a warplane that represented only a marginal improvement or fell short of goals despite the best efforts of all involved. Many designs dropped by the wayside in competition, or as advances and combat made them obsolete or no longer required. Early war fighters were rushed to production and then incrementally improved while later prototypes tended to be drawn out as those in production were sustained to ensure adequate combat resources.

The most expedient measure was to improve existing warplanes while new designs marched toward combat introduction. Hence, marginally useful aircraft were produced in the thousands until late in the war. Some models and sub-variants had a dizzying variety of engines with supercharger or water-injection combinations, propeller changes, weapons-loading capabilities, fuel capacities, plus self-sealing cells and expanding armor protection, all in response to parts availability and the evolving requirements of combat.

As a means of promoting advances where practical and ensuring at least one successful design, more projects were begun than could be taken to production. It was also indicative of the continuing challenge of producing truly competitive fighters, the rapidly evolving state of technology, and the general sense of ill preparedness that followed Pearl Harbor and the gains of the Axis powers. In a few cases, American products lagged combat needs and U.S. forces adopted British aircraft, as the United Kingdom was frequently a step ahead owing to having been at war more than two years longer.

Army Struggles

The USAAC became the Army Air Forces (USAAF) on 20 June 1941. Gen. Henry H. "Hap" Arnold was the branch's chief of staff, then commanding General USAAF, throughout the war. When he took the post in 1938, the USAAC had 20,000 personnel and 300 combat aircraft – an unimpressive force by the standard of world powers. By 1945, the USAAF was the most powerful aerial force in the world, with 2.5 million personnel and 8,000 aircraft, most of the latter state-of-the-art. Arnold's strong leadership was a major element in this effective growth. In addition, emergency laws enacted in 1940 included granting military leadership temporary privileges to negotiate contracts for materiel without regard to acquisition laws ensuring competition and restrained profits.[4] Gen. Arnold used these powers to notable effect, becoming the ultimate decision authority on aircraft development and production.

Within the Army, there was a continuing evolution of aviation doctrine. However, the majority of Army commanders considered aircraft as a support element for the ground campaign. In the late 1930s, fighters were required only to sustain air dominance, ensuring prosecution of ground attack, and to conduct aerial observation missions. Specialized attack aircraft were employed for direct support of ground troops. To ensure fighters ("Pursuit" aircraft) were not diverted to ground support missions, policy prohibited their carrying external ordnance. Doctrine did not foresee a need to fight enemy aircraft more than 200 miles from friendly troops, so external drop tanks were unnecessary. Bomber escort was not expected to be a major mission element since the prevailing notion was that bombers had sufficient guns for self-defense.

Flight testing was an essential element of developing new aircraft. This image shows the first Vultee XP-54 prototype fighter on the dry lakebed at Muroc AAB, California, surrounded by engineers and technicians in preparation for another test flight in early 1943 on the vast and flat lakebed. (San Diego Aerospace Museum)

Flight testing of experimental and modified aircraft was a hazardous business. This is exemplified by the wreckage of the Curtiss XP-55, following a 15 November 1943 unrecoverable inverted spin. Such hazards bred the specialized test pilot and flight-test engineer, and development of airborne data collection, transmission, and recording equipment. (San Diego Aerospace Museum)

The rise of militarist regimes overseas prompted the beginning of Air Corps expansion and more attention to defense of territories abroad. After the Munich crisis in western Europe, and considering Japanese aggression in Asia in which airpower was very important, it became clear the USAAC would need to grow considerably if America was to be poised to meet any threat. The Air Corps Expansion Act was signed on 26 April 1939 with the goal of increasing the front-line force from 2,320 to 5,500 aircraft. On 16 May 1940, President Roosevelt announced a plan to build 50,000 warplanes. The ramp-up of production was agonizingly slow. A year after the war had begun, September 1940, American fighter production amounted to just 117 aircraft, consisting almost entirely of P-40s. Only the XP-38 was clearly in a new class, but it was suffering serious development problems.

By 1940, Army fighters had come to incorporate the now-familiar features of single-seat, single-engine, cantilevered monoplanes. As always, fighter technology moved faster than all other types, guaranteeing at least two generations of aircraft during the war. Unfortunately, the war came with Army airfields dominated by inferior types like the P-39, P-40, and P-43. It was more than a year before new designs began to be delivered in quantity, and another year before they matured and entered combat in telling numbers. In the interim, Army pilots were at a decided disadvantage against Japanese and German airman flying superior airplanes and backed by years of combat experience.

The center of Army aircraft development activities was the Materiel Division organizations at Wright Field, Dayton, Ohio, soon an element of Materiel Command. Between September 1939 and December 1940, more than two dozen fighter projects were begun that explored many design options. Choices were made that concentrated effort on a few successful types that could equip forces quickly. Other projects were begun to exploit new technologies or meet combat requirements, often via advanced models of existing designs. Yet, requirements evolved and rendered some projects irrelevant. Consequently, many programs were cancelled without production decisions.

Navy Steam

Carrier aviation was still relatively new to the U.S. Navy as war loomed. The service's first carrier, *Langley* (CV-1) was commissioned in 1922. The heart of the carrier fleet was the *Lexington* (CV-2) and *Saratoga* (CV-3). These were the largest and fastest warships in the world at the time launched; *Saratoga* carried more than 80 warplanes. Purpose-built carriers of differing capabilities were introduced beginning in the mid-1930s. These included *Ranger* (CV-4), *Yorktown* (CV-5) and *Enterprise* (CV-6), each carrying between 81 and 86 aircraft, more than foreign counterparts.

As with all elements of the U.S. military, the improvement and expansion of carriers and Naval aviation moved at a slow pace in the interwar years. Apart from isolationist and economic impediments, there were also international disarmament agreements limiting the number and size of carriers, plus resistance from traditionalists within the service. With the motivation of rearmament, the 17 May 1938 Naval Expansion Act permitted naval aircraft to reach 3,000 while new carriers were ordered. *Wasp* (CV-7) went to sea in 1940, and *Hornet* (CV-8) joined the fleet just as the United States entered the war. Radar was introduced to the vessels in 1940.

The carriers' flush-deck catapults were generally used when the deck was full of aircraft and too little distance remained for normal running takeoffs. It was only toward the end of the war that

Elevators aboard carriers transported aircraft from hangar deck to the flight deck. These were constantly evolving with new vessels, especially in terms of location. Their dimensions were constraints on aircraft size, requiring such design measures as the folding wing on this Grumman F6F-3. (Naval Aviation Archives)

catapulting became more common with the general increase in aircraft weight.* During aircraft recovery, launches were generally not possible until the postwar advent of the angled deck. Consequently, some vessels had a hangar-deck catapult to permit defensive fighters to be maintained overhead. During aircraft recovery aboard ship, the pilot approached at just the right descent angle to snatch an arrestment cable with the tailhook and be brought to a stop by deceleration devices (typically hydraulic) below deck.

The opening of war in Europe and the fall of France galvanized America into action, and an enormous naval expansion began. The 14 June 1940 Naval Expansion Act allowed for 4,500 frontline aircraft. Actual aircraft on strength was 1,741 at the time. After the fall of France, the Two-Ocean Navy Act was signed on 19 July 1940, authorizing 15,000 naval aircraft. Also funded was the necessary expansion of shore installations and training. Of course, the planes were not sitting on shelves. By December 1941 there were only about 5,250 aircraft and 5,900 pilots in both the Navy and Marine Corps, but perhaps only 2,500 combat types, of which about 350 were fighters.

The Bureau of Aeronautics (BuAer) supervised acquisition and development of Naval and Marine aircraft. Its selection of aircraft types and their roles were continuing to evolve as experience was gained through annual fleet exercises and as capabilities increased with each generation of warplane. In 1941, Navy "flattops" were filled with aircraft focused in four mission areas; fighters (VF, "V" for airplane or heavier-than-air craft), the scout-bombers (VSB, dive-bombers) that were displacing scout-observation, and torpedo-bombers (VTB).

The U.S. Navy's pre-war carrier force and aviation assets were a sound basis upon which to grow a war-winning fleet. However, it was a near-run thing, and the Navy just strong enough, and new ships and aircraft arriving just in time, to hold the Japanese and begin to press them. Four of the carriers would be sunk in early fighting. There remained many senior commanders with little experience employing carriers and aviation.

The construction of aircraft carriers became one of the most outstanding examples of American industrial prowess aiding the fight. At an extraordinary average rate of 18.5 months to build a carrier, and dozens on order, the United States vastly expanded its aviation-capable fleet in just a few years. During the war, 17 Essex-class carriers (designated CV) were delivered. These 27,000-ton vessels were maneuverable and fast, capable of speeds in excess of 30 knots, while carrying more than 80 aircraft. Nine Independence-class light carriers (CVL) were built as a rapid means of increasing carrier assets. These displaced 11,000 tons, could touch 33 knots, and carried about 45 aircraft. Also delivered were 114 escort carriers (CVE) in six classes, with 38 provided to the UK under lend-lease. By July 1943, these CVEs were being turned out at a rate of one per week! As the name implies, they were intended to provide air cover for shipping convoys, fighting off enemy submarines and aircraft. These "baby flattops" were slow, matching their convoy charges, and usually had a composite squadron of around 15 to 32 aircraft. They were soon found useful in offensive operations such as supporting amphibious

** The catapult consisted of a shuttle moving in a groove within the deck, driven below deck by a piston powered via hydraulics or compressed gas. Pulled by the shuttle was a steel cable bridle with eyelets at the ends that fit around hooks in the bottom of the aircraft. On launch, the bridle fell away. Near the aft end of the aircraft was attached a holdback link with shear pin to restrain the aircraft until shuttle force had built to the required level.*

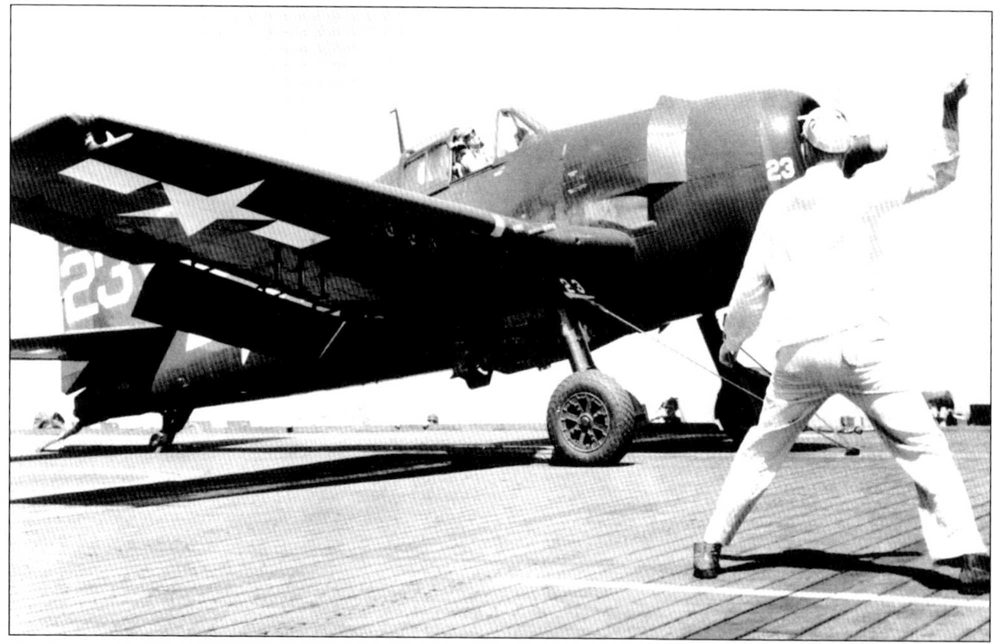

This F6F-5 of VF-74 Squadron is about to be shot off the USS* Kasaan Bay *(CVE-69), supporting the invasion of southern France on 15 August 1944. The photo shows well the bridle between the aircraft and the catapult shuttle, and the holdback link at the rear of the fighter. (Northrop Grumman History Center)

An SB2C-1 decelerates after snatching an arrestment cable aboard USS* Charger *(CVE-30) on 14 May 1943. The aircraft is brought to a stop by deceleration devices below deck. To the right can be seen barrier cables raised above the deck to stop the aircraft, should it pass that far. (Naval Aviation Archives)

landings. The big Midway class battle carrier (CVB) was intended for the large aircraft coming down the development "pipeline" while also improving survivability with an armored deck and better damage-control design. These vessels displaced 45,000 tons, were nearly 1,000 feet long, yet could exceed 33 knots and accommodate upwards of 130 aircraft. The CVB did not reach the fleet before the end of hostilities.

It was autumn 1943 before the first of the new Essex-class, light, and escort carriers became available for action. The U.S. Navy soon had a carrier fleet exceeding that of all the world's navies combined. This permitted the adoption of new tactics and multi-carrier task forces. They were a tremendous contribution to Allied victory, but not without cost. One light carrier and six American escort carriers were lost in action.

When America went to war, its Navy and Marines had only around 350 fighters, consisting of the second-rate F2A and the worthy F4F. Half the fighter units were in training.[5] Its principal attack aircraft were 100 torpedo bombers and 709 scout bombers. The "slow but deadly" SBD dive-bomber was limited, and TBD was clearly obsolete. The Marine Corps had a much smaller force of similar aircraft, although some were even more dated. In development to fill the decks to come were the F4U and F6F fighters, the TBF torpedo bomber, and SB2C dive bomber. The first of these new types would not enter service in meaningful numbers until 1943.

For the first six months or so of the war in the Pacific, the Japanese "Zero" fighter was a grave threat to U.S. aircraft due to its excellent aerodynamic design, greater numbers, and war-tested pilots with excellent training. However, once the United States began to adopt improved tactics, even the aircraft with which the war began would meet the Zero on relatively equal terms. America's introduction of new types forced open the quality gap further while Japanese pilot skills degraded with more hastily trained aircrew replacing losses.

The carrier shipboard environment was a difficult one for aircraft operations. Salt spray, limited resources, and confined conditions were just some of the challenges. This flight deck is crowded with Avenger torpedo-bombers and F6F-3 Hellcat fighters running up engines with wings folded, prior to launch. (Naval Aviation Archives)

The heavier armament, armor, and self-sealing tanks that came at the expense of slowing initial introduction of new models or types, and the general ruggedness of American aircraft, proved a decided advantage. Japanese aircraft were generally lighter, breaking up, catching fire, or exploding with much greater ease than American aircraft.

The kamikaze tactic first emerged at the end of October 1944. The suicide pilots made flattops their priority targets. Responding to the threat, fighter strength in the U.S. Navy shipboard air groups was increased at the expense of bombers. One means of boosting carrier fighter strength was introducing Marine units to carriers beginning in April 1945. Air groups entirely made up of Marine squadrons were eventually embarked on escort carriers. Operating under radar guidance was also a telling advantage for American naval fighters.

By the end of June 1945, the U.S. Navy carrier aviation force had grown to include 4,937 torpedo bombers and 5,101 scout bombers. These aircraft were instrumental in changing the character of naval warfare by sinking the majority of the Japanese warships destroyed by the U.S. Navy and enormous numbers of support vessels. A similar number of fighters had nearly swept Japanese aircraft from the skies. This permitted Navy and Marine aviation to contribute measurably to ground combat with bombing and close-air-support.

The United States more than made up for its carrier losses. This allowed the Navy to operate task forces of several carriers and support vessels during major operations, as suggested by this 31 January 1944 image. The formation is of jeep carriers (CVE), two TBF-1Cs aboard the one on the foreground. (Naval Aviation Archives)

Chapter 2

The Grumman F4F-3 was just entering fleet service in significant numbers when war was visited upon the United States. The Wildcat squadrons initially suffered grave losses against the more numerous Japanese. However, in the hands of a competent pilot, it gave as good as it got. (Naval Aviation Archives)

NAVY FIGHTER BAZAAR

Like other branches of the armed forces, the Navy began World War II ill-equipped to meet the challenges offered by the opposition. Nonetheless, the Americans felt they were more than a match for Japan in the Pacific region and Asian mainland. This delusion was quickly and violently dispelled. However, persistence, rugged airplanes, and courageous teamwork held the situation from becoming desperate while newer aircraft were acquired and more air and ground crews trained.

Core Competency

The F2A was the mainstay carrier and Marine Corps fighter, although represented in what would soon be comparatively small numbers. It was clearly a dated design by the standards of the day. Even some Grumman F3F biplanes remained in service until just before America's entry into the war. The F4F was just entering service while the F6F and F4U were nearing production. Hard work at home and the exigencies of war allowed new single-seat fighters to be introduced just as they were required to meet the Axis forces in battle.

Unfit for Duty (F2A, XF2A-4)

The Navy bought 162 Brewster F2As in three models by December 1941, the design dating from 1936. Hundreds more went abroad as B-239s and B-339s in foreign sales or lend-lease, where they were known as Buffalos. The final U.S. Navy order was primarily to keep the Brewster Aeronautical Corporation (BAC) workforce in Long Island, New York, occupied while other projects were in development. With the rapid advances in fighter design during the late 1930s, the once-hot Buffalo was emphatically second-rate by 1941. However, it was at hand at a time when every fighter that could be built was needed somewhere.

In 1938, the F2A-1 (Model 239) was the first American monoplane naval fighter, adopted as the U.S. Navy struggled to realize increased performance over biplanes that were reaching the apogee of their potential. The aircraft possessed then-advanced features like an enclosed cockpit, hydraulically retracted undercarriage, all-metal construction with flush riveting, and remarkable range for the period, at around 1,000 miles. It provided a marked increase in capability that permitted more offensive tactics by carrier fighters. The final variant, the F2A-3 (Model 439), packed four .50-cal. machine guns, with a rack for a 116-pound bomb under each wing. Incorporating lessons from the war overseas, armor, additional fuel, and self-sealing tanks were installed. Consequently, the weight leapt nearly 50 percent over the F2A-1. However, a change to the 1,200-hp, nine-cylinder Wright R-1820-40 Cyclone held performance almost unchanged.

Brewster F2A-3 characteristics:			
span	35.0 ft	weight empty	4,732 lbs
length	26.3 ft	gross	6,321 lbs
height (top of tail)	12.1 ft	maximum	7,159 lbs
wing area	209 ft²	speed, max. (16,500 ft)	321 mph
fuel capacity (int. + ext.)	110-240+0 gal	cruise	161 mph
service ceiling	33,200 ft	range, normal	965 mi
average climb rate	2,290 fpm	ferry	1,680 mi

An attempt to breathe new vigor into the design came during 1941 with a two-stage, two-speed supercharged engine added to an F2A-3 along with cockpit pressurization. The further increase in weight was not balanced by an increase in performance, and the XF2A-4 did not advance beyond prototype.

A Marine unit took the F2A into combat during the June 1942 Battle of Midway but was decimated by superior A6M Zero fighters flown by superbly trained and war-honed Japanese pilots. This marked the end of the F2A's front-line American service. The dumpy little fighter became symbolic of the marginal state of the armed forces' readiness. Apart from Finland's successes against Soviet opposition, foreign operators found the Buffalo equally lame. A handful of Aussie Buffalos, exported B-339Ds (F2A-2 with a commercial engine), and B-439s, made their way to USAAF pilots for in-theater training.

The Mitsubishi A6M3 Type O fighter was an outstanding performer, being the first naval aircraft to better its land-based counterparts. It was a rude surprise for the Americans when first encountered. This Model 31 Zero-Zen Hamp was acquired in Australia for evaluation by U.S. forces. (National Museum of the United States Air Force)

Brewster's F2A Buffalo left its mark as the Navy's first monoplane. However, by the time the United States entered the fray, the F2A was practically worthless on the frontlines. This F2A-3 was photographed on 2 August 1942 with NAS Miami below, by this point consigned to Training Command. (San Diego Aerospace Museum)

Some Grumman F3F biplanes still served in the fleet as the U.S. Navy and the nation was plunged into war. Powered by the 950-hp Wright R-1820-22 radial, this F3F-3 reached 264 mph at 15,200 feet, possessed one .30-cal. machine gun with 500 rounds and a .50 with 200 rounds. (San Diego Aerospace Museum)

Hard Worker (F4F, FM)

During 1941, the Grumman Aircraft Engineering Corporation F4F-3 Wildcats, with non-folding wings, were just beginning to fill Navy and Marine squadrons, and many more were on the way. These were powered by the 1,200-hp Pratt & Whitney two-row, 14-cylinder R-1830-76 Twin Wasp with two-stage/two-speed supercharger and carried four .50-cal. wing machine guns with 430 rpg. The 285 F4F-3s were supplemented by 90 F3F-3As powered by R-1830-90 engines to ensure against issues with the R-1830-76 holding up production. The F4F-4 featured the -90 engine, but added another pair of .50 cal. guns with just 240 rpg, had external tanks, and manually folded wings. Notably, 1,164 of this model were delivered during 1942, compared with just 248 F4F-3 and -3As with the fleet and Corps at the end of 1941.

Grumman F4F-3 characteristics:

span	38.0 ft	weight empty	5,342 lbs
length	28.8 ft	gross	7,002 lbs
height (level attitude)	11.8 ft	maximum	8,152 lbs
wing area	260 ft²	speed, max. (21,000 ft)	329 mph
fuel capacity (int. + ext.)	147-160+0 gal	cruise	147 mph
service ceiling	37,500 ft	range, normal	845 mi
best climb rate	2,265 fpm	maximum	1,690 mi

The Wildcat underwent a typical series of upgrades to remain relevant in the changing air war. Thousands were built by autoworkers, here represented by scores of FM-2s awaiting delivery at Linden, New Jersey. (Naval Aviation Archives)

Eastern FM-2 characteristics:			
span	38.0 ft	weight empty	5,448 lbs
length	28.9 ft	gross	7,487 lbs
height (level attitude)	12.9 ft	maximum	8,271 lbs
wing area	260 ft²	speed, max. (28,800 ft)	332 mph
fuel capacity (int. + ext.)	126+116 gal	cruise	164 mph
service ceiling	34,700 ft	range, normal	900 mi
best climb rate	3,650 fpm	maximum	1,310 mi

Once the United States entered the conflict, its automobile industry was under-employed, owing to gasoline rationing and materials diversions to war production. Consequently, five General Motors Corporation (GM) plants in mid-Atlantic states were converted for aircraft production as the Eastern Aircraft Division with Wildcat final assembly in Linden, New Jersey. These started with what were essentially F4F-4s, but carrying four machine guns, built as FM-1s. GM's performance was phenomenal as it retrained and retooled for aircraft production. Beginning in January 1942, it had its first Wildcat in the air by September. GM eventually produced 893 FM-1s, even after Grumman ceased producing Wildcats in 1943.

Seeking a fighter best suited for the small escort carriers, the U.S. Navy had Grumman design and build two lightweight XF4F-8 prototypes during the later half of 1942. This model employed the nine-cylinder R-1820-56 of 1,300 hp with a single-stage/two-speed supercharger, sacrificing high-altitude performance as unnecessary for the convoy protection role. It returned to the two pair of .50s with 430 rpg, and two 250-pound bombs or six 5-inch rockets could be carried under the wings. It also had a larger horizontal tail, fin, and rudder, and substituted slotted flaps for the earlier split design. The XF4F-8s, 500 pounds lighter than the F4F-4, served as patterns for the FM-2. This became the definitive Wildcat, with 4,437 manufactured between September 1943 and May 1945, some with water-injected engines.

The Vought F4U-1 and FG-1 Corsair were the highest-performing deployed naval fighters of the war and superior to most Army fighters. However, problems bringing them aboard carriers limited their contribution until the start of 1945. Still, they proved to be standout performers in both air-to-air and air-to-ground combat. (Naval Aviation Archives)

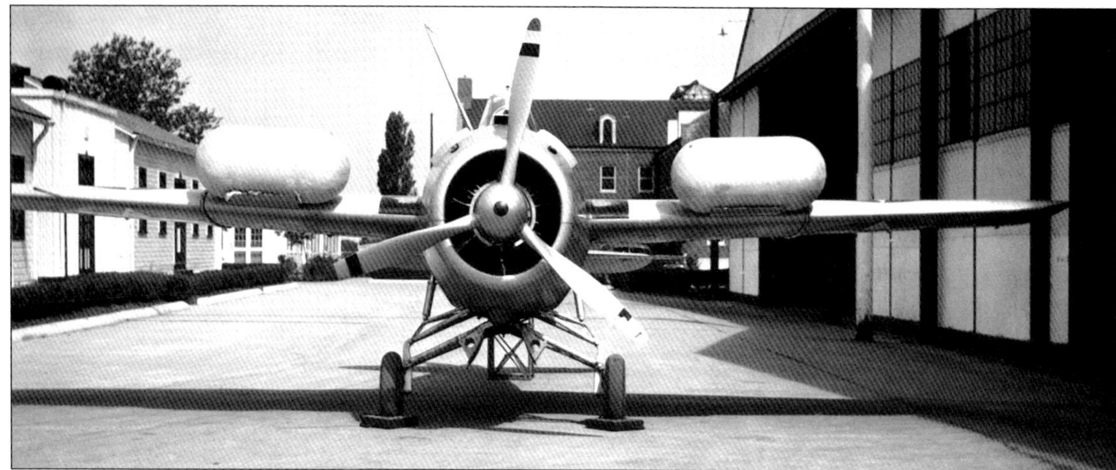

Navy design requirements prior to the war included flotation bags stored in the wings and activated in the event of ditching, demonstrated here by an XF4F-2. The bags were deleted, after a number of uncommanded deployments in flight, to reduce weight in the interest of wartime performance and production expediency. (American Aviation Historical Society)

Grumman and Eastern eventually produced 7,905 Wildcats through May 1945. Exported to Royal Navy's (RN) Fleet Air Arm were about 1,100 as Martlets and Wildcats, including aircraft originally destined for France and Greece.

Although becoming dated by 1943, and initially suffering under the weight of superior Japanese forces, the rotund little Wildcat came out on top in most engagements, owing to well-trained pilots exploiting the aircraft's advantages and the enemy's disadvantages. The supposedly obsolete fighter (still with hand-cranked undercarriage) claimed 1,327 enemy aircraft destroyed by Navy and Marine pilots. The Wildcat was substantially eclipsed by newer fighters during the latter half of 1943, but it remained predominant on escort carriers owing to its small size, and served reputably throughout the conflict – the only Navy fighter to do so. It was rugged and had few vices.

Late Bloomer (F4U, FG, F3A)

The Vought Corsair (Model V-166) stemmed from a 1938 competition to employ the Pratt & Whitney R-2800-8 Double Wasp, 18-cylinder twin-row powerplant developed by the Navy, with a two-stage/two-speed supercharger.* Converting the 2,000 hp to thrust required an enormous three-blade, 13.3-ft diameter, Hamilton Standard propeller, the largest fitted to a fighter to that time which gave a nose-high stance. Consequently, the designers introduced an inverted gull wing to ensure modest gear-strut length. Flush riveting and spot welding helped maintain a clean exterior surface. Like some other fighters of this period, the Navy initially had Vought design 10 shallow bays into the wings for twenty 5.2-pound anti-aircraft bombs. These were to be dropped on bomber formations, with aiming through a window in the belly. This feature was wisely deleted for production.

The striking design took flight for the first time in May 1940. It was the first U.S. fighter to exceed 400 mph in level flight and, at 9,000 pounds, the heaviest Naval fighter. It was hot, and the Navy was eager to get it to the fleet, placing an initial order for more than 500 aircraft. However, development was slowed by the need to address lessons of the war overseas. This included adding heavier armament, self-sealing tanks, and armor. A fuel tank was added aft of the firewall, requiring the cockpit to be relocated 3 feet farther aft, and a centerline hardpoint took a 175-gallon external tank. For ease of maintenance and producibility, the two .30 cal. machine guns under the cowl with 500 rpg were deleted and another pair of .50s added in each wing. The six guns had 400 rpg for the inboard and center pair and 375 rpg for the outboard weapons. The hydraulic gun charger would be praised as relieving the pilot of an onerous task in the heat of battle. With all these changes, it was June 1941 before the first production contract was let and a year later before the F4U-1 flew. The Navy began accepting these aircraft in October 1942.

Goodyear Aircraft Corporation and Brewster had been selected at the end of 1941 to supplement Vought's Stratford, Connecticut, production line. Goodyear's first examples flew in spring 1943 as the FG-1, manufactured in a newly built Akron, Ohio, plant while Brewster's F3A-1 was built in Johnsville, Pennsylvania. Goodyear would go on to roll out more than 4,000 Corsairs while Brewster imploded, owing to multiple problems after delivering 735 examples through July 1944. More than 8,500 F4U-1s and FG-1s were produced.

* *Chance Vought and Sikorsky had combined as the Vought-Sikorsky Aircraft Division of United Aircraft Corp. in April 1939. They separated in January 1943. The name Vought will be used throughout in referring to all these entities.*

The Marines took the F4U-1 into combat from land bases while the Navy undertook carrier qualifications (carquals). The carquals did not go well. The unusual aft position of the cockpit degraded forward visibility during an approach, there was a strong yaw on touchdown, the port wing stalled first such that the left wheel hit first, and the stiff landing gear could cause the fighter to bounce and miss the cables and sometimes the barrier. These characteristics required a higher approach speed for safety, but this was not enough for consistent engagements. Design changes included raising the cockpit, installing a new canopy with a blown, taller hood to permit the seat to be raised a few inches for improved sightline (also assisting deflection shooting), replacing the oleo valve to reduce the bounce on landing, lengthening the tail-wheel strut, and placing a stall strip on the starboard leading edge. Aircraft reflecting these changes were referred to as A models.

Vought F4U-1 characteristics:			
span	41.0 ft	weight empty	8,982 lbs
length	33.3 ft	gross	12,039 lbs
height (taxi attitude)	15.1 ft	maximum	14,000 lbs
wing area	314 ft²	speed, max. (19,900 ft)	417 mph
fuel capacity (int. + ext.)	361+175 gal	cruise	182 mph
service ceiling	36,900 ft	range, normal	1,015 mi
best climb rate	2,890 fpm	ferry	2,220 mi

The F4U-1 was eventually found acceptable for shipboard operations – although it remained among the most difficult planes to bring onboard. All this delayed carrier introduction until mid-1944. The production lines had rolled on, aircraft being modified after delivery to combat-ready configurations. With renewed urgency owing to the kamikaze threat, combat operations from U.S. Navy carriers in theater finally began on 3 January 1945.

Upgrades to the Corsair began immediately. Water injection was introduced with the R-2800-8W (indicated by the W), giving boosts to 2,130 hp at 12,400 feet. Aircraft bound for shore basing, principally with the Marines, dispensed with the hydraulic wing fold mechanism. An overhead rearview periscope was replaced with a mirror. The F4U-1B denoted Corsairs provided to Britain with cockpit and wing modifications. The 200 F4U-1C was fitted with four 20mm cannons, with 120 rpg, in place of the wing machine guns. This innovation, with so many fewer rounds, was not met with much enthusiasm. Reflecting the increasing emphasis on ground attack, the F4U-1D deleted unprotected wing tanks. It retained the machine guns but received 2,000-pound capacity hardpoints under each inboard wing section for drop tanks or ordnance in place of the centerline station – although combat units had already introduced these as improvised field modifications. Late F4U-1Ds and FG-1Ds were also fitted with eight outboard wing zero-length rocket stub mounts.

The F4U-4 was ordered in September 1944 and introduced to combat the following April. These featured the R-2800-18W delivering 2,100 hp at takeoff and 2,380 hp in Combat Power. It was characterized by a chin intake under the cowling and a four-blade Hamilton Standard propeller. The reliable .50s in the wings were retained with 400 rpg, as well as the 1,000-pound capacity hardpoints and eight 5-inch rocket launchers. The 297 F4U-4Bs were delivered with four 20mm cannon (984 rounds) in place of the machine guns, but these did not reach the field before the armistice. Vought delivered 1,912 F4U-4s during the war.

The expanded stores capacity of the F4U-1D and -4 were put to use in the growing ground attack role. The aircraft proved a formidable dive-bomber, able to descend at an 85-degree angle

With the ground war taking center stage in the island-hoping campaign of the Pacific, the Corsair began to be optimized for the role. The comparatively small number of F4U-1Cs featured four M-3 20mm cannons. The installation is seen in this 15 May 1944 image of Buno. 82277. (Jay Miller Collection)

Vought F4U-4 characteristics:			
span	41.0 ft	weight empty	9,205 lbs
length	33.7 ft	gross	12,420 lbs
height (taxi attitude)	15.1 ft	maximum	14,670 lbs
wing area	314 ft^2	speed, max. (26,200 ft)	446 mph
fuel capacity (int. + ext.)	234+300 gal	cruise	215 mph
service ceiling	41,500 ft	range, normal	1,005 mi
best climb rate	3,870 fpm	ferry	1,560 mi

without dive brakes. The Corsair was favored for these tasks, hitting targets within 10 feet of friendly troops. Although designed as a fighter, the F4U could carry the same 2,000 pounds of stores as the SB2C but at greater airspeeds (albeit shorter range) and remained a fighter when free of the stores.

The U.S. Marine Corps introduced napalm bombs during the battle for Okinawa in April 1945. Naval crews had earlier created the gasoline bomb as a field lash-up. The drop tanks were filled with gelled gasoline and an igniter was added. Army P-38s employed 165-gallon drop tanks fitted with fins for a more predictable and stabilized ballistic path. Napalm proved effective against bunkers and caves where the flaming liquid flowed into openings.

The AN/ASG-10 Bomb Director for "toss bomb" delivery was fitted to 48 of the F4U-4s. The technique involved acquiring the target, diving down for speed, then pulling up to release the bomb with an upward trajectory. The weapon would continue up, arc over, and drop on the target with a ballistic trajectory. The gyro-stabilized director indicated when the pilot should begin the pull-up and would then automatically release the bomb to hit the target given the gunsight's settings.

The Corsair's under-wing rockets were augmented with a much larger weapon. The Tiny Tim rocket was developed for anti-shipping use, allowing an attack without the long and slow, predictable run-in required for torpedo or bombing strikes. Caltech proposed the weapon in March 1944, and it was immediately approved with the highest priority. The 11.75-inch diameter allowed oil-well steel tubing to be used for the motor casing, also matching the diameter of a 500-pound bomb chosen as the warhead. The weight goal of 1,000 pounds matched the bomb racks on most fighter bombers. The first example was fired in late April 1944 at Inyokern, California. Air launch was problematic given the tremendous motor blast, as demonstrated with a damaged wing on an SB2C test aircraft. Instead, the weapon was released and a lanyard played out to ignite the motor when more than 4 feet from the airplane. The final rocket weighed 1,290 pounds, was 10.25 feet long, and reached 810 fps velocity above the launch aircraft's speed. It was fielded in time to be used in the final battles against Japan in 1945. It was fired against buried or hardened bunkers, with the F4U the most frequently used delivery platform.

Corsair deliveries during the war saw 1,236 serving in Navy units and 8,874 with Marines by August 1945, plus 1,972 provided to Britain's Fleet

These Marines are attaching a tank to the centerline of an F4U that will soon be filled with gelled gasoline. Napalm was first used in action on Okinawa where it was effective against underground positions. The Army also adopted the weapon. (Vought Aircraft Heritage Foundation)

Air Arm and 424 to New Zealand. The F4U was rapidly established as one of the outstanding fighters of the war, and certainly the premier carrier-based fighter. Even land-based initially, it was a tremendous asset, helping to deplete Japan's air capability and win American air dominance. Its late introduction to the carrier reduced its initial contribution, but this was made up for during the very tough landings during 1945 when it became a tremendous close air support asset. Orders for thousands were cancelled at the end of the war, including 2,900 FG-4s terminated on VJ-Day (Victory over Japan) with none delivered. However, production continued with new models through 1952, longer than any other World War II piston fighter and the last such in U.S. production.

Staunchness (F6F, FV-1)

In the fast-changing world of fighters, the Wildcat was clearly falling behind by 1941. Following a December 1940 VF competition, the Navy turned to its reliable supplier for the F4F replacement and for an airplane clearly derived from the earlier design. It was also meant as a backup in the event the F4U's development floundered.

A 30 June 1941 contract to Grumman for two F6F Hellcat

The F4U-4 was optimized for air-to-ground work with hardpoints under each inboard wing segment. This F4U-4 is captured on film at Stratford in 1944, carrying an 11.75-inch Tiny Tim rocket on each wing station. Designed as an anti-shipping weapon during 1944, it found use as a bunker-buster. (Jay Miller Collection)

The Hellcat was developed as insurance against the Corsair stumbling along its path to fleet service. It proved a wise decision, with the Grumman fighter leaving a noted legacy. This F6F-3 from VF-4 was photographed near NAS Alameda, in Northern California, during May 1943. (Jay Miller Collection)

This pair of F6F-5s shows off the 150-gal drop tank and rocket stub mounts during summer 1943. The large Grumman fighter was vital in the U.S. Navy winning air superiority in the Pacific and cutting the legs out from under the Japanese defense strategy. (Northrop Grumman History Center)

prototypes was coincident with the initial F4U production contract. The company moved promptly, urgency added by United States' entry into the war and revelation of the A6M Zero. The XF6F-1 (Model G-50) was powered by a Wright XR-2600-10 Cyclone-14, twin-row radial capable of 1,700 hp and, to reduce wing loading, had the largest wing of any single-seat Navy fighter to date. As with the Hellcat's contemporaries, a move to production was slowed by what the Navy felt to be essential changes reflecting combat lessons from abroad and the early experience in the Pacific. These were the usual armor, additional armament, and self-sealing tanks.

Grumman still came through expeditiously, flying the production-representative XF6F-3 in July 1942 with the 2,000 hp R-2800-10 fitted with a two-speed/two-stage supercharger and a three-blade prop. The first production F6F-3 followed in October and 10 more rolled out by year's end. Fleet deliveries began in the new year and they were committed to battle beginning in August 1943, reaching carrier decks in half the time it would take the F4U. A new plant was built at Bethpage, New York, to turn out the fighter, and 1943 alone saw 2,545 Hellcats delivered. This extraordinarily fast pace of development and production ramp-up was a credit to the highly experienced Grumman team.

Following the example of the F4U, the Hellcat was a heavy aircraft and heavily armed with six .50-cal. machine guns with 400 rpg.

Grumman F6F-5 characteristics:

span	41.8 ft	weight empty	9,238 lbs
length	33.6 ft	gross	12,740 lbs
height (over tail, level)	13.1 ft	maximum	15,413 lbs
wing area	334 ft²	speed, max. (23,400 ft)	380 mph
fuel capacity (int. + ext.)	250+450 gal	cruise	168 mph
service ceiling	37,200 ft	range, normal	1,090 mi
best climb rate	2,980 fpm	maximum	1,590 mi

The usual upgrades were introduced almost immediately. A 150-gallon centerline external tank began appearing in August 1943. January of the following year saw the R-2800-10W hung on new Hellcats. Production of this F6F-3 model numbered 4,156 units.

The F6F-5 emerged in early summer 1944, and was also fitted with the water-injected R-2800-10W for spurts of 2,200 hp. A proposed bubble canopy and cut-down turtledeck to improve rearward vision was rejected in the interest of maintaining a high production rate. Doing its share in helping the ground-pounders, the new model also featured hardpoints for a pair of 1,000-pound bombs or Tiny Tim rockets under the inboard wing segment, and three rocket stub mounts under each outboard wing. Increased armor protection was added, and some received quad 20mm cannons in place of the machine guns, in addition to other improvements. Grumman delivered 6,436 F6F-5 fighters.

The Hellcat rapidly displaced the F4F as the frontline carrier-based fighter and, because of the Corsair's troubles being cleared for routine carrier ops, remained so for the rest of the conflict. It especially filled the big decks of the new Essex-class carriers as they were launched. A total of 12,275 F6Fs were built through November 1945, exceeding 500 per month, with more than 1,000 supplied to Britain. Planned production of the F6F-1 by Canadian Vickers, as the FV-1, fell through.

Although not a standout in any particular measure of fighter potency, the Hellcat was well-rounded and got the job done with little fuss. It accounted for more than half the total Navy and Marine Corps kills during the war, while also performing meritorious service in ground attack.

Variants and Deviants

Wildcat Litters (XF4F-5, XF4F-6, XF2M-1, G-33)

An effort to extend the F4F-3's range was addressed with a non-jettisonable 42-gallon conformal external tank attached under each wing just outboard of the guns. Several F4F-3s and -3As were modified to carry these tanks. However, the tanks appear to only have been used as a jettisonable centerline unit following field improvisations in Hawaii.[1]

An early effort to imbue more range into the Wildcat was Grumman's modification of this F4F-3 with two conformal under-wing tanks. Of 42-gallon capacity and non-jettisonable, these do not appear to have been employed in service. However, some appeared as jettisonable centerline tanks on a few field-modified aircraft. (Northrop Grumman History Center)

The prototype Model G-36A for the Aéronautique Navale is shown in a mix of French national and U.S. civil markings at Bethpage, probably in May 1940. The atypical 7.5mm Darne machine guns in the upper fuselage are evident. Less evident is the Wright R-1820 Cyclone engine under the cowl. (San Diego Aerospace Museum)

There was a series of engine shuffles during F4F production, partially to improve performance and partially in response to powerplant availability. The French had ordered their Wildcats with R-1820 engines. Fearing a shortage of the new XR-1830-76 in the F4F-3, and because the two-stage/two-speed supercharger was still giving overheating trouble, the Navy decided to have a look at this combination. Two F4F-3s, Bureau Numbers (Bunos.) 1846 and 1847, were assembled in June 1940, fitted with single-stage, two-speed supercharged R-1820-40s as XF4F-5s. These were evaluated at the Navy's principal flight test facility at NAS Anacostia, Maryland, beginning in July 1940. Except above 15,000 feet, the performance was little improved over the -3 and the matter was dropped.

During winter 1942-43, the XF4F-5s were re-engined. Buno. 1847 received an XR-1820-48 with two-stage supercharger and jet exhaust, and oil cooler under the cowling vice the wings.* Buno. 1846 was fitted with a turbosupercharged R-1820-54. These aircraft were then subjected to comparative flight testing during February 1943. As one would expect, the aircraft with turbo did better at high altitude (340 mph at 26,400 feet) and the one without did better at low altitude. Reports were filed and the Navy moved on.

This Grumman XF4F-5, dated 8 February 1943, (Buno. 1846) has the single-row R-1820-54 engine fitted with a turbosupercharger. By February 1943, even Wildcats with such performance boost were being eclipsed by much superior fighters, so nothing more came of the work. (American Aviation Historical Society)

The Navy made moves to introduce improved altitude performance to the Wildcat with single- and two-stage engines or with turbo supercharger. One of these tests was the XF4F-6 with single-stage, supercharged R-1830 photographed on 22 October 1940. All were shelved as newer fighters worked high while the F4F stayed low. (Northrop Grumman History Center)

* *Jet exhaust refers to an engine exhaust designed to derive thrust from the expelled gases. A Rolls-Royce design was called the ejector exhaust.*

A look at the XF4U-3 reveals a nightmare complexity in an image dated 31 October 1944. The Double Wasp is backed up with the carburetor ducting leading eventually to the turbosupercharger seen just behind the circular intake below. Proximity to the wing root inlets for intercoolers and oil coolers is evident. (Jay Miller Collection)

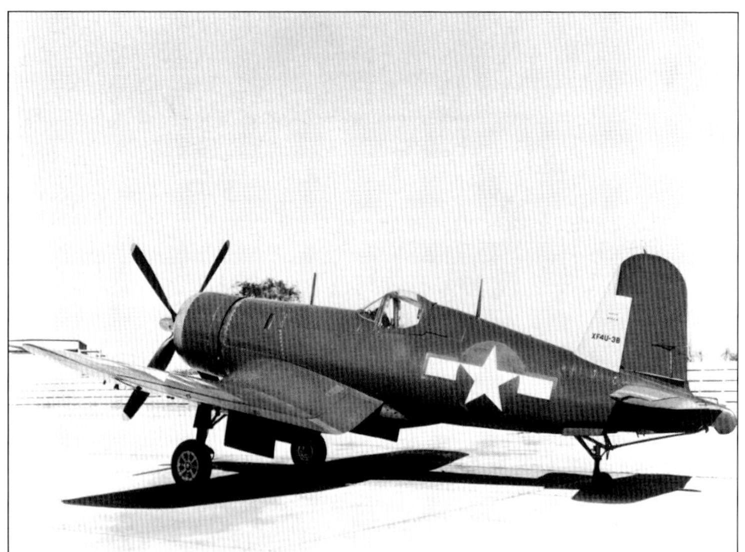

The XF4U-3B (49664) had a powerplant installation like the XF4U-3 (redesignated the XF4U-3A) except substituting the R-2800-14W engine with water injection and retaining the four-blade prop. The aircraft is otherwise a standard F4U-1 fighter. Location is most likely Vought's Stratford, Connecticut, plant. (Jay Miller Collection)

Seeking improved high-altitude performance, experimental XF4U-3 models were ordered using the XR-2800-16 engines with turbosupercharger. This required a scoop under the nose to feed the turbosupercharger and a four-blade propeller. Aircraft 17516 was one of three such aircraft flying in 1944. (Jay Miller Collection)

The Navy directed Grumman to build an airframe (Buno. 7031) with the single-stage 1,200-hp R-1830-90 for the same reasons the XF4F-5 was built. This flew on 11 October 1940 as the XF4F-6 and passed to Anacostia two weeks later. Again, nothing more came of it.

Eastern Aircraft was asked to investigate squeezing more speed from the Wildcat by general clean up and with the addition of the more powerful turbosupercharged R-1820-70W. Design work on three XF2M-1s (Bunos. 82855/7) was begun in October 1942 with assistance from Grumman. The project was cancelled in spring 1943 as unnecessary and potentially slowing production. Grumman

Goodyear F2G-2 characteristics:

span	41.0 ft	weight empty	10,249 lbs
length	33.8 ft	gross	13,346 lbs
height (taxi attitude)	16.1 ft	maximum	15,422 lbs
wing area	314 ft²	speed, max. (16,400 ft)	431 mph
fuel capacity (int. + ext.)	309+300 gal	cruise	190 mph
service ceiling	38,800 ft	range, normal	1,190 mi
best climb rate	4,400 fpm	maximum	1,955 mi

The F4U-1WM was a -1 Corsair modified to take the four-row R-4360 engine and four-blade propeller, strictly for powerplant testing purposes. Lacking supercharger intercoolers, the root intakes were reduced to accommodate just the oil coolers while a separate duct was added atop the nose. (Jay Miller Collection)

undertook a similar exercise on its own initiative, looking at the feasibility of incorporating a twin-row radial as the G-33. While eventually set aside as unpromising, the work found use in development of the F6F.

Corsair Rarities (F4U-1WM, XF4U-3, FG-3, F2G-1, F2G-2)

On 14 June 1941, the U.S. Navy tasked Vought with exploring possibilities of a high-altitude interceptor variant of the F4U, a contract following in March 1942. This came to focus on integrating the XR-2800-16 engine fitted with a Birmann 1009A turbosupercharger. A four-blade propellor swung in front of a scoop added below the cowling to aspirate the turbosupercharger. The scoop displaced the catapult bridle hooks, ensuring it would be a shore-based U.S. Marine Corps asset. The Navy intended to convert 100 F4U-1s to the new F4U-3 standard.

Vought was contracted for three XF4U-3s as modifications to F4U-1s (02157, 17516, 49664) and there were plans for Goodyear to assemble 27 as the FG-3. Bill Horan flew the first example (17516) on 26 March 1944. It could sustain 2,000 hp up to 30,000 feet for 412 mph with a 300-pound weight penalty. Because of powerplant availability problems, 49664 was given an R-2800-14W (water tanks in the outer wing panels) and designated XF4U-3B. Aircraft 17516 subsequently became the XF4U-3A. Taking flight initially on 20 September 1944, the installation in 49664 providing 2,800 hp with water and 2,100 hp continuous. Buno. 02157 crashed before contributing much and was not replaced. The remaining two test aircraft were passed to the Navy during the first half of 1945. In the meantime, Goodyear modified 13 FG-1s as FG-3s during 1944 before the program was halted. The performance increase was not sufficiently greater than the new F4U-4 model, and essentially nonexistent below 23,000 feet, to warrant continuing. The FG-3s joined the Vought aircraft at the Naval Air Modification Unit (NAMU) in Johnsville (previously the Brewster plant) in summer 1945 where they were used for high-altitude research.

An F4U-1 (02460) was modified by Pratt & Whitney with a longer cowling to serve as a flying testbed for its enormous 28-cylinder, 4-row, 3,000-hp XR-4360 X-Wasp (Wasp Major). This was first run while installed on 23 May 1943 and then flown on 12 September as the F4U-1WM (WM for Wasp Major). Pratt & Whitney employed Buno. 02460 for testing at its Hartford, Connecticut, plant from 31 May 1944 through August, with A. Lewis McClain flying.

Goodyear took the F4U-1WM design a step farther to the XF2G-1 "Super Corsair" by eliminating the turtledeck behind the cockpit and installing a bubble canopy. A sub-rudder, barely visible, displaced on takeoff to counteract the healthy torque of the giant 3,000-hp engine, and to aid in landings. (Vought Aircraft Historical Foundation)

As projects for enhancing effectiveness of the Corsair proliferated in the last year of the war, Vought required testbeds for the modifications. The two XF4U-4s were turned to this purpose as F4U-4Xs, 49763 shown. As they took on different characteristics, they were differentiated with additional suffixes, 49763 becoming the F4U-4XA. (Jay Miller Collection)

The carrier-capable F2G-2 added the taller tail with a sub-rudder that automatically moved to counter low-speed torque effects, and was to have eight .50-cal. machine guns. One of only five F2G-2s, Buno. 88462 was photographed at NAS Pearl Harbor soon after the war and appears to have only six guns. (Joe Genne via Rob Mears)

Two F4U-1As were modified with the features of the eventual F4U-4 model; these soon differentiated with an A and B suffix. The F4U-4XA (49763) is shown at Stratford with a broad-chord, square-tipped Hamilton Standard propeller, and spinner. This project dates from late in the war and was shelved. (Jay Miller Collection)

The second F4U-4 prototype, F4U-4XB (50301), was photographed at Vought's Stratford, Connecticut, plant on 31 March 1945. These twin airplanes became perennial testbeds for other work. Here it carries two non-jettisonable wingtip fuel tanks. (Jay Miller Collection)

In a photograph from summer 1945, an XF4U-4 is shown with a six-blade Aeroproducts contra-rotating propeller, the blades instrumented for a vibration survey. The advantages of such a propeller on an otherwise standard F4U-4 is unclear. (Jay Miller Collection)

The Navy saw advantages in the F4U-1WM configuration, and Goodyear was proposing the similar F2G variant. Achieving the highest practical speed on the deck would permit the fighter to intercept enemy attackers short of their target vessels. Seven Goodyear FG-1s were ordered on 7 February 1944 to be modified as XF2G-1s (13471/2, 14691/5) with R-4360-4s, but progress was slowed by delays in engine deliveries. Donald Armstrong finally flew the first XF2G-1 (13471) on 26 August 1944. The third (14692) was passed to the Navy on 27 November. Integrating the engine without the supercharger meant smaller wing-root cooling openings for only the oil coolers. Goodyear went farther by introducing a shallow sub-rudder at the base of the extended fin. This surface deflected 12.5 degrees when the aircraft was configured for approach to automatically counteract propeller torque effects at low speeds. Internal fuel was increased to 308 gallons. They also installed a bubble canopy and eliminated the turtledeck behind for improved rearward visibility, in addition to internal cockpit improvements. The first two XF2G-1s retained the original canopy.

The XF2G-1 "Super Corsair" achieved 399 mph on the deck and 431 mph at 16,400 feet, or a 30- to 40-mph improvement. Incorporation of water injection to get a surge to 3,650 hp for 450 mph at 16,500 feet was discussed. A further increase in internal fuel capacity was also intended. A 22 March 1944 contract funded production of 418 F2G-1 shore-based (manual wing fold) aircraft and 62 F2G-2 carrier-based planes with the vertical stabilizer lengthened one foot to accommodate the sub-rudder. Each had four .50-cal. machine guns with 1,200 rounds.

By 1945, the F2G type was seen as a potential answer to the kamikaze threat. However, by May the impending end of the war plus advent of the F8F and jets suggested the Super Corsairs would not be required. The order was reduced to 408 examples and then terminated at end of hostilities. Only 10 production examples, 5 F2G-1 (Bunos. 88454/8) and 5 F2G-2s (88459/63), were completed.

Other Corsair oddballs were also birthed, assisted by the two XF4U-4s (converted F4U-1As) that became testbeds as F4U-4XA (50301) and F4U-4XB (49763). Fixed-tip tanks were tried on 50301. A Hamilton Standard propeller with spinner was tested on the 49763, and an Aeroproducts six-blade contra-rotating prop evaluated on Buno. 02460. All of these projects came in the final months of the war and found no postwar application.

Hellcat Vigor (XF6F-2, F6F-3F, XF6F-4, XF6F-6, G-69)

The original development contract for the F6F called for two XF6F-1 prototypes, the first (Buno. 02981) with an R-2600-10 and the second (Buno. 02982) with the turbosupercharged version of the engine. However, the turbosupercharger option was set aside and the second plane became the prototype XF6F-3, chosen as more easily rushed to production. Confusing matters, the Bureau Numbers were swapped between the two airframes. All the

Grumman tested turbosupercharged engines for the Hellcat on the XF6F-2. The test aircraft has tufts on the exterior surface to visualize local airflow, earning it the name "Fuzzy Wuzzy" on the left side of the cowling. Not seen is the four-blade propeller, while the atypical spinner is evident. (Jay Miller Collection)

The fastest Hellcats were the two XF6F-6, 70913 seen in this photograph. It is distinguished here by the four-blade propeller turned by a Pratt & Whitney R-2800 with turbosupercharger delivering a maximum 2,380 hp. Testing during summer 1944 demonstrated 417 mph top speed at 21,900 feet. (San Diego Aerospace Museum)

powerplant integration work may have prompted a Hellcat to be designated for such testing, apparently leading to a -3 airframe devoted to the work as F6F-3F.

The redesignated Buno. 02981 was rebuilt after an accident and given an R-2800-27 with two-speed supercharger to become the XF6F-4. This flew on 3 October 1942, and four 20mm cannons were fitted in April 1943, each with 200 rounds. It was subsequently revised to match the -3 standard and sent on to the customer. However, the service requested studies in July 1943 of an F6F-4 suitable for escort-carrier duty. Like the XF4F-8, this Hellcat was to be lightened by reducing armament to two .50-cal. guns, removing some fuel tanks, and further reducing wing loading by increasing area and span. Although the proposed design would have been faster than the Wildcats populating escort-carrier decks, fewer would have been accommodated. There seemed little to recommend interrupting Hellcat production to insert the F6F-4, and it faded away.

The dormant XF6F-2 (G-18) was finally created from the last -3 (Buno. 66244) and flown in January 1944 with an R-2600-15 and four-blade propeller with spinner, promising 2,000 hp at 25,000 feet. The engine was later changed to the R-2800-21, first operating as such on 7 January 1944 with Carl Alber at the controls. The F6F-2 was characterized by a deeper cowling incorporating ducting to the Birmann turbosupercharger in the lower quarter, with the unit exhausting out the back of the cowl. In both incarnations, the type displayed expected performance improvement, but the turbosupercharger suffered from reliability issues and the Pacific Theater had too little need for a high-altitude fighter to interrupt production.

Two XF6F-6s were assembled from F6F-5s (Bunos. 70188 and 70913) with the 2,100-hp R-2800-18W and four-blade propeller, the first flying on 6 July 1944. Combat Power delivered 2,380 hp at sea level and 2,080 hp at 23,300 feet, while the two-speed/two-stage supercharger held 1,700 hp at 25,000 feet in Mil. Although the aircraft raced out to 417 mph at 21,900 feet, there did not appear to be enough of the engines to meet F4U-4 demands and the planned start of F6F-6 production in September 1944. Grumman also considered adopting a laminar flow wing for the aircraft, but it did not appear that the performance improvement justified it. Subsequently, the F6F-6 matter was shelved.

Grumman examined other engine replacements for the Hellcat. Integrating a 3,000-hp R-4360 was considered in August 1943 as the G-59 (single-stage/variable speed supercharger) and G-60 (two-stage supercharger), but this would have required too many major changes to the airframe for too little performance benefit. The G-69 would have had the R-2800-22 at 2,100 hp for a purpose-built fighter-bomber variant, but this found no traction either.

Last But Not Least

Two new model Grumman aircraft entered production during the war years. These advanced designs were among the finest propeller-driven fighters developed in the United States during that period, albeit too late to enter the fray.

Feline Twins (F7F)

Grumman's G-51 twin-engine fighter design was submitted in March 1941 for Navy evaluation, leveraging off earlier work on the experimental XF5F-1, XP-50, and the concurrent Army XP-65 program (all which see). The Navy ordered the Grumman twin on 30 June as two XF7F-1s, aimed at the Midway-class carriers. The proposed powerplant was the 1,800-hp R-2600-14.

Grumman F7F-1 Tigercat characteristics:

span	51.5 ft	weight empty	15,906 lbs
length	45.4 ft	gross	21,523 lbs
height	15.2 ft	maximum	25,852 lbs
wing area	455 ft²	speed, max. (20,000 ft)	422 mph
fuel capacity (int. + ext.)	426+300 gal	cruise	182 mph
service ceiling	40,000 ft	range, normal	1,115 mi
best climb rate	4,600 fpm	maximum	1,740 mi

After years of tinkering with the concept, a carrier-based twin, and one with tricycle landing gear, was finally brought forth in the form of the F7F-1. The Tigercat appeared in time to reach the combat zone – on literally the last day of the war. (San Diego Aerospace Museum)

With the distinct late-war trend to fighter-bombers, Tigercat production shifted to a variant with greater attack capability. The F7F-3 featured under-wing hardpoints and rocket launchers outboard, and greater centerline store capacity. The Navy remained leery about putting the twin on a carrier, and the Marine Corps needed the aircraft more. (Naval Aviation Archives)

The XF7F-1 mockup inspection occurred in September 1942. Thereafter, things progressed slowly as the F6F was the necessary focus of attention. It was summer 1943 before the Navy made the final powerplant selection, choosing the narrower 2,000-hp R-2800-27 with single-stage supercharger for the first prototype because of immediate availability, and the preferred 2,100-hp R-2800-22 for the second airplane. These turned three-blade Hamilton Standard propellers. The F7F also incorporated radar, the antenna in the nose, as standard equipment on all examples. There were four .50-cal. machine guns in the nose with 300 rpg and four 20mm cannons in the wings with 200 rpg. As expected at this point in the war, armor and self-sealing tanks were standard, and hardpoints under the inboard wing sections and centerline could facilitate a variety of external stores. It would be the Navy's first production tricycle-gear fighter and twin bound for a carrier, possessing the heaviest armament of any of its aircraft, and with a top speed faster than any fleet fighter.

The Tigercat finally came to fruition with the first XF7F-1 flying on 3 November 1943. It was written off following an accident in May 1944, but testing continued with its sibling. This went well, although some directional-stability inadequacies made it necessary to add a dorsal fin extension. Spins were found to have some unfortunate characteristics and so were forbidden. The first aircraft from the 1943 production order for 650 examples were fitted with a pair of 2,100-hp, water-injected R-2800-22W engines. The spinners were soon dropped, and a three-piece windscreen replaced the molded section installed on the prototypes. A 150- or 300-gallon centerline tank could be carried. A few issues remained, including problems with directional stability, harmony of control forces, and machine-gun jamming and cannon-blast damage to the wing.

Still hesitant to bring such a fighter aboard carriers, the first lot of 34 F7F-1s (Bunos. 80259, 80260, 80262/80293) went to the Marines beginning in April 1944, with the last delivered in October. The radar suggested night fighting would be enhanced with a radar operator, so a second seat was added in the 65 subsequent F7F-2N models (see Chapter 10). These had an 80-gallon tank installed in the rear cockpit and the canopy replaced with a translucent panel, and .50-cal. machine guns—normally removed with the radar in place—were reinstalled, to become F7F-2s. Shallow strakes installed

Grumman F7F-3 Tigercat characteristics:

span	51.5 ft	weight empty	16,270 lbs
length	45.4 ft	gross	21,720 lbs
height	16.6 ft	maximum	25,075 lbs
wing area	455 ft²	speed, max. (22,200 ft)	435 mph
fuel capacity (int. + ext.)	455+300 gal	cruise	180 mph
service ceiling	40,700 ft	range, normal	1,200 mi
best climb rate	4,530 fpm	maximum	1,830 mi

Evaluation of a captured Focke-Wulf Fw 190 was a factor leading to the F8F-1 Bearcat, bucking the trend in fighter design toward heavier aircraft. The Fw 190 was commonly flown at under 10,000 pounds gross weight, achieved more than 400 mph, and generally matched the Spitfire. (Jay Miller Collection)

under the aft fuselage addressed lingering stability issues and four rocket-launch stubs were added under each wing.

Production shifted to the F7F-3, with first flight and deliveries in March 1945, possessing a vertical tail/rudder further revised to finally resolve stability concerns, the height raised 1.4 feet. The wing was also strengthened to permit maneuvering at higher gross weights. An engine change to the 2,100-hp R-2800-34W and 33 gallons more fuel gave a marginal increase in performance. The -3s also had the rocket launchers changed to the single-posts that could also accommodate racks for 250-pound bombs, pylons added to pre-existing hardpoints under the inboard wing sections for 1,000-pound weapons or 150 gallon tanks, and the centerline station was upgraded to a 2,000-pound capacity, making it possible to carry a Mk 13 torpedo. At this point in the war, the aircraft's heavy armament made it an ideal choice for the Marine Corps' ground-attack role.

Approximately 250 Tigercats were on hand before the ceasefire, but only a handful of Marine F7F-1s arrived in theater just as the curtain fell. Production was greatly curtailed thereafter. Despite successfully completing carquals in November 1944, albeit with difficulty, no Tigercats went to sea during the war, and seldom thereafter.

Worthy But Too Late (F8F-1, F3M-1)

Grumman was cognizant of the trend to heavy fighters and sensitive to the fact that its Hellcat was primarily limited to the big carriers. With more powerful engines struggling to reach production and yet greater performance required to meet advanced designs sure to be introduced by the enemy, an effort to change the power-to-weight ratio while continuing with current powerplants was desired. Consequently, in summer 1943, the company began an internally funded study, designated G-58, to develop the smallest airframe that would fit around the powerful R-2800 engine. This somewhat followed the example of the German Fw-190 that company officials had examined and flown in the UK during the spring. Grumman submitted the design in autumn as an unsolicited proposal, and BuAer responded enthusiastically. The Navy believed that the G-58 could be the first deck-launched interceptor (DLI), sent off at radar warning of a hostile bogie and fast enough for intercept at safe range from the carrier.[2] Such a high-performance fighter could compensate if the jet projects being initiated failed to measure up. Two XF8F-1s (Bunos. 90460/1) were ordered in November 1943.

Grumman did not disappoint. It agreed to an extraordinarily short schedule and fell only slightly behind. Mockups were ready in early 1944. Great effort was expended to keep weight down, although this was a challenge for a deck-landing aircraft. Following the contemporary trend, a bubble canopy without turtledeck provided unrestricted vision in the rearward quarter, and 169 pounds of armor was designed into the aircraft. The water-injected R-2800-22W, with two-speed supercharger, provided 2,100 hp via a four-blade Aeroproducts propeller. The second prototype was to have the R-2800-30W with variable-speed supercharger, rated at 2,250 hp, but this was dropped. An unusual feature was an articulated trunnion at the base of each main landing gear post that permitted the gear length to be shortened when retracting. Fuel was the minimum required and in just one fuselage tank. Only four .50s were placed in the wings.

The first prototype flew in August 1944, about a month behind schedule. It was soon evident the Grumman fighter was among the fastest and most maneuverable fighter in existence. The second followed in December but crashed in March 1945. During tests, it was found necessary to increase horizontal tail's span by a foot and add a dorsal extension to the vertical fin. Directional-stability deficiencies persisted, leading eventually to a taller tail on the postwar F8F-2 model. Internal fuel was expanded slightly, but the quantity (i.e., range) was one sacrifice for other performance measures. A rollover pylon was subsequently added behind the armored seatback.

The 2,100-hp R-2800-34W was selected for production, and internal fuel capacity was increased from 162 to 183 gallons at Navy insistence. Aircraft finish was exceptionally smooth because of flush riveting, spot welding, and tight production tolerances. Instead of Grumman's signature "sto-wing," the Bearcat wings folded up, and dive recovery flaps were featured just behind the gear doors. Four .50-cal. machine guns with 300 rpg were placed in the wings. A 150-gallon drop tank could be carried on the centerline and two 100-gallon tanks on the wing hardpoints. Alternatively, two 1,000-pound bombs, 11.75-inch rockets, or other stores could be carried under the wings. With the 201st aircraft, two posts for rockets were added under each wing, these also accommodating 100-pound bombs.

Flight testing had barely begun when an order for 23 developmental F8F-1 Bearcats was placed in June 1944, followed in October by a contract for 2,000. This number was doubled in April 1945, and plans were laid to completely replace the F6F on the Bethpage production lines by March 1946. Plans were also introduced on 5 February 1945 to place an order with Eastern Aircraft for 1,876 as the F3M-1.

The first F8F-1 was accepted in February 1945, and it was clearly a big step up in performance from the Hellcat. Its rate of climb exceeded all other piston-powered fighters of the war. The Navy moved fast to qualify it aboard ship and deploy initial squadrons. The fighter's fast climb and high speed were possibly going to be crucial in combating kamikazes in the final battles of the conflict. Two squadrons were working up the Bearcat, and the first had just shipped out aboard USS *Langley* (CVL-27) when Japan surrendered. Nearly 150 had been completed by that time. Orders were then greatly cut back with the one to Eastern eliminated entirely. Grumman went on to build more than 1,000 of the fighters in the immediate postwar years. It was the end of a breed, and among the best.

The F8F-1 entered service in the last months of the war (this image from 15 July 1945) and just missed the action. Grumman combined power and exceptional engineering into a light airframe capable of outstanding performance. It was among the pinnacle of piston-powered fighters, but was quickly eclipsed by jets. (Naval Aviation Archives)

Although four .50-cal. machine guns had been shown to be plenty of punch to bring down most adversaries, especially the lightly built Japanese airplanes, the Navy wanted heavier armament. Adding two more guns turned out to require a significant design change, so substituting 20mm cannons with 205 rpg was chosen. This was done as a modification to F8F-1 Buno. 94803 in June 1945 to become the F8F-1C. The B suffix was originally intended as lend-lease aircraft to Britain. When these plans were dropped, the cannon-armed Cs took on the F8F-1B designation for postwar production.

Grumman F8F-1 characteristics:			
span	35.8 ft	weight empty	7,070 lbs
length	27.5 ft	gross	9,386 lbs
height	13.7 ft	maximum	12,947 lbs
wing area	244 ft²	speed, max. (19,700 ft)	421 mph
fuel capacity (int. + ext.)	183+350 gal	cruise	163 mph
service ceiling	38,700 ft	range, normal	1,105 mi
best climb rate	4,570 fpm	maximum	1,965 mi

Chapter 3

The U.S. Army Air Forces' "family tree" of fighters is represented by mid-war models in a 27 December 1943 inspection at Wight Field, Ohio. From front to back is a P-39N, an A-36A (representing the Mustang), a P-40K-15, a P-47C-5, and a P-38. (Dennis Jenkins Collection)

ARMY FIGHTER CLAN

The only fighters available to the U.S. Army Air Corps when World War II broke out were models that were clearly second-rate and few in number compared with what Germany and Britain were developing and fielding. However, the die had already been cast to correct these shortcomings. The P-35 and P-36 exemplified a new standard for U.S. pursuit aircraft with all-metal construction, retractable gear, and enclosed cockpits. The spin-offs from these basic designs through 1942 saw speed increase almost 100 mph in the span of just a few years, and it would increase markedly very soon. The U.S. Army Air Corps continued to buy such aircraft into 1940 to fill out its order of battle while more competitive designs were prepared, these being the P-38, P-39, and P-40. On their heels would come even more superior warplanes, the P-47 and P-51. Taken together, these aircraft offered a spread of capabilities and numbers that played a vital role in the Allied defeat of the Axis forces.

The Seversky P-35 was among the first of America's modern fighters. Although exported, by 1940 it was far behind the standard of the day, slow and under-armed. The type was indicative of the Army Air Corps' marginal preparedness as war loomed and it struggled to re-equip with more modern equipment. (San Diego Aerospace Museum)

Gene Pool

Breed for Speed (P-35, XP-41, YP-43, P-44)

The P-35 (Model AP-1) from Seversky Aircraft Corp. of Farmingdale, New York, entered service in 1938. At 282 mph top speed, 2,500-fpm climb, and a 1,134-mile range, it was a tremendous step forward in American pursuit performance. Its 850-hp R-1830 began a long military association with this Pratt & Whitney product. The P-35 also introduced the first reflector gunsight to U.S. pilots. Armament for the pursuit type was the Army standard of one .50- and one .30-cal. machine gun, or 500 pounds of payload. The landing gear retracted aft into deep wheel fairings. The 77-aircraft order was typical of the small production numbers in America's prewar period. By 1941, the airplane was already dated and relegated to operational training duties.

Fighters based on the P-35 and associated Seversky racers or civil aircraft were exported in modest numbers. The largest sale was the EP-1 (Export Pursuit) for Sweden, with the 1,050-hp R-1830-45 and an additional pair of each machine gun. The last 60 of these aircraft were shanghaied into the Army Air Corps as P-35As in October 1940 by edict of Gen. Arnold who felt they were urgently needed to replace the last Boeing P-26s in the Philippine Islands. These were still on the front line when the Japanese attacked and were quickly chewed to bits.

Alexander de Seversky, company president, designer, and test pilot, proposed P-35 performance enhancements, which were reflected in his AP-2 (Advanced Pursuit) racer, and the last of the 77

Seversky continued incremental improvement of its basic fighter design. One of these designs got closer Army Air Corps examination with the last P-35 built as the more advanced XP-41. The fully retractable landing gear, flush riveting, and supercharger were steps forward but gave only marginal improvement in performance. (Jay Miller Collection)

Thirteen Republic YP-43 service test aircraft were acquired to gather experience with turbosuperchargers and high-altitude interceptors. The fighter evokes the lines of the early Seversky and Republic fighters that would soon yield the outstanding P-47. (San Diego Aerospace Museum)

P-35s was so altered. The changes included substituting a 1,150-hp R-1830-19 with two-stage/two-speed supercharger, flush riveting, and landing gear that retracted inboard to lie flat within the wing. Known as the XP-41 (Army serial number 36-430), it was first flown in March 1939. The 6,600-pound gross weight aircraft demonstrated 323 mph at 15,000 feet, a 37,000-foot ceiling, and a maximum 1,860-mile range, but retained the standard weaponry. The incremental improvements did not warrant production.

The Republic Aviation Corp. Model AP-4 was a recognizable development of the P-35, XP-41, and other Seversky/Republic testbeds, with an air-cooled radial engine, barrel fuselage, and elliptical wing.* However, this design had a B-1 turbosupercharger under the aft fuselage, an R-1830-35 of 1,200 hp, a flush-riveted airframe, self-sealing tanks, improved rearward vision, and guns matching the P-35A. Although promising, the Army Air Corps was looking at a number of such aircraft during this period and hesitated to place an order too quickly. However, Gen. Arnold felt a handful of service test examples would provide experience with high-altitude interceptors.

Thirteen of these YP-43 Lancers (39-704/16) were ordered on 12 May 1939 with a guaranteed 351 mph at 20,000 feet and with hardpoints for small bombs. The turbosupercharger intakes were moved from the wing roots to the lower portion of the cowling. Although this made for a deeper fuselage, it avoided the far-aft cockpit of the YP-37 (which see). It was originally to have a broad, pointed spinner blending into a tight-fitting cowling for reduced drag, but inevitable cooling issues forced a redesign. Delivery ran from 13 September 1940 through 31 March 1941. Among the Navy's first experiences with turbosuperchargers was the loan of an Army YP-43 (39-706) on 25 May 1941.

* *Seversky became Republic in October 1939.*

Soon after the YP-43s were placed on contract, an Army competition was held for a pursuit aircraft suitable for high-altitude intercept with a speed range between 360 and 420 mph at altitudes ranging from 15,000 to 20,000 feet. A further evolution of the Lancer, the AP-4J, developed by designer Alexander Kartveli, with a turbo-supercharged Pratt & Whitney R-2180-1 Twin Hornet of 1,400 hp, won out over inline designs. The AP-4J was expected to top 386 mph and to be armed with a pair of .50-cal. machine guns and four .30s. This design was slated to have the broad spinner and tight cowl originally intended for the YP-43, although this may have been dropped during detailed design. Eighty of these P-44 Rockets were ordered on 13 September 1939 without a prototype having been built. The AP-4L with 2,000-hp R-2800-7 and added fuel tank promised 422 mph at 20,000 feet, and 225 of this configuration were ordered as the P-44-2 on 19 July 1940, increased to 827 on 9 September.

Early war experience made clear the YP-43 and P-44 were second-rate before they were delivered. The P-44 specification was adjusted in June 1940 to add two more weapons, armor, and self-sealing tanks. However, with these weighty modifications the new R-2180 would not get the aircraft to the required speed. Fortunately, all the incremental design work at Republic bred a more advanced design that would become the P-47.

To keep the Republic production line occupied until the P-47 was ready, and because the R-2800 engines were not yet available, the P-44 contracts were converted on 13 September to an order for 54 P-43s in the YP-43 configuration (41-6668/721) and 80 P-43As (40-2891/970) with the 1,200-hp R-1830-49s and guaranteed 360 mph at 20,000 feet. The first turbosupercharged, air-cooled production fighter for the Army, the first P-43 was delivered in May 1941 and P-43A in September, production running through December 1941. The Army Air Forces also facilitated a lend-lease order for 125 P-43A-1s to China, produced through March 1942. These aircraft were fitted with R-1830-57s, four .50-cal. machine guns, self-sealing tanks, some pilot armor, and hardpoints for under-wing tanks and light bombs. A few were diverted to the U.S. Army. The P-43 only saw action in China but was not terribly successful. The manually operated turbosupercharger was a bit much for the pilots, leading to mishaps. Those remaining in the U.S. inventory were redesignated RP-43s in October 1942, R for "Restricted," indicating not for combat use.

The Republic P-44 was ordered during 1939 in the hundreds directly off the drawing board. However, the war made it apparent that the design was not up to the standards required to compete with foreign warplanes and could not be readily adopted. The contract was converted to buy more P-43s instead. (Author's Collection, Artist Laune)

Several hundred P-43s and P-43As ended up being built to keep the Farmingdale plant busy while awaiting start of P-47 production. The few improvements introduced were not sufficient to make the warplanes competitive. Some P-43As saw action in China, but with dismal results. (National Museum of the United States Air Force)

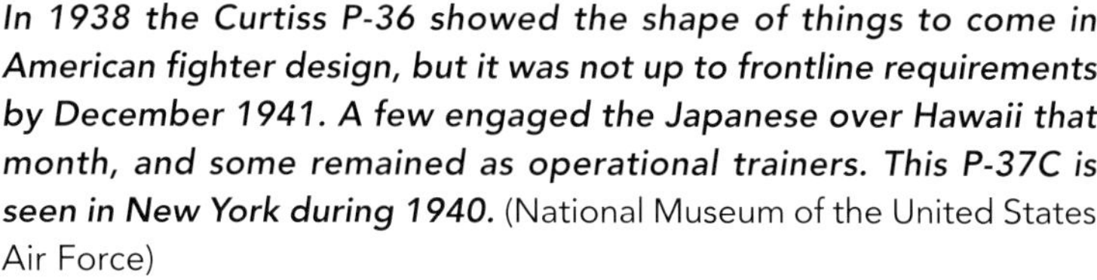

In 1938 the Curtiss P-36 showed the shape of things to come in American fighter design, but it was not up to frontline requirements by December 1941. A few engaged the Japanese over Hawaii that month, and some remained as operational trainers. This P-37C is seen in New York during 1940. (National Museum of the United States Air Force)

Trial installations of various engines and guns on the P-36 and Hawk 75 were instructive. This XP-36D (P-36A 38-174) was photographed at Wright Field on 2 October 1939, carrying four .30-cal. machine guns in the wings with 500 rpg and two .50s in the nose with 400 rpg (dummies only seen here). (National Museum of the United States Air Force)

One of 13 YP-37s is shown in flight. This was the Army's first comprehensive experience with an inline engine and turbosupercharging, and it was sometimes a frustrating experience. However, much was learned from the aircraft tested from 1939 through 1942. (National Museum of the United States Air Force)

Steady Pace of Progress (XP-36D, XP-36F, YP-37, XP-42)

The Curtiss P-36 (Model 75) was the most numerous Army fighter at the opening of the war, until displaced in 1941 by the P-40. When introduced in 1938, it was noted for achieving more than 300 mph and for a main landing gear that rotated 90 degrees when retracting aft to lie flat within the wing. However, its speed and weapons complement were badly outdated by December 1941. Yet, the P-36 was exported in the hundreds as late as 1942, allowing the design to become the first American fighter of the period to exceed 1,000 built. It fought in several theaters with many combatants as the Hawk 75, bearing a variety of engines, armament, and some with fixed landing gear. In France, on 8 September 1939, Hawk 75s achieved the first Allied kills of the war by downing a pair of Bf-109s. Their only actions with the Americans were a few engagements during the Pearl Harbor attack, achieving four of the 10 kills made on 7 December 1941. Experimental P-36 models were created into 1942 by adding guns and swapping engines, but no more were produced or deployed.

An advanced inline engine was first placed in an Army fighter during 1937, also having a turbosupercharger. This was a reworked Model 75 airframe (Model H75I) that was then sold to the Army Air Corps to become the XP-37 (37-375). It had the 12-cylinder, 1,150-hp Allison C-8 (later V-1710-11) with the turbosupercharger below and radiators plus fuel tank immediately behind. The arrangement forced the cockpit to be well aft of the wing for balance. The prototype was followed by 13 YP-37s (38-472/84) with a V-1710-21 engine and a General Electric (GE) B-2 turbosupercharger in the lower left side of the cowling. The first was delivered in March 1939. Although experimental (never armed), these remained in active service until 1942, albeit seldom flown. They became the first American production fighter to exceed 300 mph in level flight, although short of the guaranteed 340 mph. Although the engine and turbosupercharger combination proved cranky and the far aft cockpit was unsuitable, the aircraft served their experimental purpose.

Another reworked P-36 (38-004) had the 1,050-hp R-1830-31 in a tight cowling that narrowed to a broad, pointed spinner, the narrow fuselage bulging out to match engine diameter. The installation sought to reduce the drag penalty of the wide radial. The engine case and propeller shaft extended forward 18 inches to permit the narrowing of the cowling. It was felt the volume ahead of the engine within the cowling would become pressurized with ram air and provide more even cooling to the engine. With inline engine development slow despite considerable investment, this avenue of investigation appeared fruitful.

This P-38 rework, the XP-42 (Model H75S) delivered in March 1939, underwent nearly a dozen variations in cowl, cowl flaps, spinner, propeller cuffs, carburetor inlets, and air scoops with and without fans, during testing over several years at Curtiss, Wright Field, and NACA's Langley Research Center, Virginia. The long cowling was gradually reduced to more common dimensions as the test team battled elevated engine temperatures, extension-shaft vibration, and problems with carburetor ducting. Any potential gain in performance was lost to the added weight of the engine modifications and balancing tail ballast. After much effort, the XP-42 pushed the P-36's speed up more than 30 mph to 344 mph at 14,500 feet.

The XP-42, with original long nose, is seen at Wright Field on 21 August 1939. This attempt at reducing the drag of a radial engine installation produced useful data over several years of testing by the Army and NACA, but the concept was operationally impractical. (National Museum of the United States Air Force)

Family Tree

Despite all the fascinating projects begun after the United States entered the war, the primary composition of the American fighter force was made up of aircraft that had their beginning before December 1941, the P-38, P-39, P-40, P-47, and P-51. Those begun in 1939 were designed to outdated tactics reflected in Army requirements that emphasized mid-altitude pursuit and ground attack with comparatively light weapons. Growing these initial fighters to meet the challenges posed by the enemy required progressive improvements while production was ongoing with more capable powerplants, heavier weapons, and refined aerodynamic design.

Older Brother (P-40)

The P-40 was the first of the new fighters available when the crisis broke, and so was produced in numbers exceeding all other U.S. types combined during the early war years. It quickly began appearing all over the world. It had some maturing to do, but was on par with most of the opposition and Allied fighters when ordered.

The XP-40 (Model 75P) was created in 1938 by installing a single-stage 1,160-hp V-1710-19 on a P-36A airframe (38-010), producing excellent mid-altitude performance. The aircraft won a January 1939 competition for a fighter capable of 360 mph at 15,000 feet, although it fell short of the objective top speed with 342 mph at 12,200 feet. With the assistance of NACA, the design was improved and flush riveting introduced. The liquid-cooled powerplant required a large radiator under the nose for a distinctive deep cowling. In April 1939, an unprecedented 524 P-40s were ordered in this configuration, the first of the major USAAC expansion effort. The aircraft then became the initial American fighter produced via a true assembly-line process.

The initial P-40 (Model 81) flew in April 1940 and began reaching Army units in significant numbers in the fall. The V-1710-33 delivered 1,040 hp at 14,300 feet for a respectable 357 mph. The fighter packed a pair of .50s and had provisions for a .30 in each wing, but lacked underwing stores, protected fuel tanks, and cockpit armor. Immediately, the armament proved deficient in light of combat experience abroad. Even as the U.S. Army was working furiously to meet its expansion goals, some of the P-40 production was diverted to lend-lease, with large numbers sold to the French as the H81 (France fell before taking delivery) and the British as the Tomahawk.

Addressing the P-40's shortcomings, British models introduced armor, self-sealing tanks, and four wing guns. As expected, speed suffered from the added weight. Such improvements were reflected

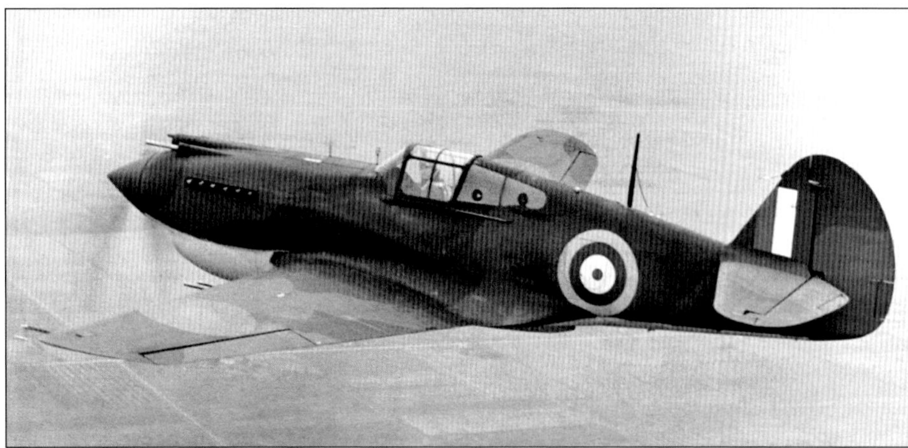

The Curtiss P-40C was exported as the Tomahawk, like this RAF H81-A2 seen on 14 November 1940. In the hands of a good pilot it could meet most of what the enemy had to offer on a competitive footing, but not top model fighters. Fortunately, the P-40 continued to evolve. (Jay Miller Collection)

Curtiss P-40E characteristics:			
span	37.3 ft	weight empty	6,079 lbs
length	31.7 ft	gross	8,122 lbs
height	12.3 ft	maximum	8,679 lbs
wing area	236 ft^2	speed, max. (15,000 ft)	362 mph
fuel capacity (int. + ext.)	148+52 gal	cruise	258 mph
service ceiling	29,100 ft	range, normal	700 mi
initial climb rate	2,100 fpm	ferry	950 mi

in the U.S. Army P-40Bs that featured a pair of .50-cal. machine guns in the nose and four .30s in the wings. Deliveries began in early 1941. These were quickly followed by the P-40C with self-sealing tanks, centerline external tank, and other refinements. Some of the original P-40s were upgraded to these standards as the P-40G. Lend-lease sales continued to expand, to include Turkey and the USSR. H81s shipped to China and operated by the American Volunteer Group provided direct combat experience.

The added power of the 1,150-hp V-1710-39 in the P-40D (Model 87, Kittyhawk to British and Commonwealth forces) gave back the lost speed and then some, despite introducing still more armor, tank protection, and weapons. For the Americans, this version included four .50s in the wings and hardpoints for under-wing stores. The P-40E upped the guns to six .50s in the wings, along with other changes, and these were on the line by fall 1941. Four Japanese planes fell to one Warhawk's guns on 7 December over Hawaii. Later, in the Philippines, the first Army Air Force ace gained the distinction in the P-40E

The single-stage supercharger in the P-40s limited high-altitude performance, but this had been an intentional choice to meet near-sighted January 1938 requirements and to speed development and production while turbosuperchargers got past their "teething" troubles. The opportunity to correct this shortcoming came with the two-stage British Rolls-Royce Merlin 28 inline engine, with single-stage/

The P-40E (H81 Kittyhawk) introduced more guns and under-wing hardpoints to the Curtiss fighter. These helped the design retain some relevance in the air war and allowed Americans to hold their own during the early years. However, it remained unequal to the best of the opposition. (National Museum of the United States Air Force)

two-speed supercharger. The Merlin powered the Hurricane and Spitfire fighters and was recognized as one of the finest aero engines in the world. Packard Motor Car Co. of Detroit produced Merlins under license in the United States as the V-1650-1 beginning in September 1940. Continental Motors followed the Packard lead at a plant in Muskegon, Michigan. To meet British demand for the Merlin, Rolls-Royce enlisted the Ford Motor Co. to undertake production in England. Manufacturing the English engine in the United States required plans to be completely redrawn and "Americanized." The first Packard-built Merlin was run in August 1941. This gave 1,300 hp at 12,000 feet and 1,120 hp at 16,500 feet. The company was granted license to manufacture 9,000 units, of which 3,000 could be sold to the U.S. Army, and the service scrambled to find suitable platforms.

The requirements of ferry overseas and the requirements of the air battle were sufficient to overcome Army resistance to drop tanks. This P-40E models enormous dirigible tanks on 24 October 1942 adapted to the fighter with wooden sway braces in an experimental configuration that did not become operational. (National Museum of the United States Air Force)

When the V-1650 was introduced during the first half of 1942 in the P-40F, it boosted top speed at 20,000 feet to 364 mph. The plane also had six .50s in the wings, additional weapon hardpoints and external fuel, and armor, and some had an aft fuselage extended 20 inches for enhanced directional stability in high-speed dives. A year later, the P-40L stepped back in weight by removing two guns and some fuel tanks, although the reduction of 250 pounds bought only 4 mph. However, the Packards were in short supply, and the performance improvement in the P-40 application was not considered tactically significant or vital. Consequently, 300 were yanked from stateside Warhawks for aircraft of greater potential (read: *P-51*). Substituting V-1710-81s in these "castrated" P-40Fs and Ls yielded the P-40R. This and the fact the P-40s were never given valuable cannons or turbosuperchargers illustrate the attitude that the P-40 was second-string even in 1942.

The late-model P-40s, like this P-40N, turned inexorably to the ground-attack role as more capable fighters displaced it in the air-to-air fight. Much effort was expended to improve the P-40's potency through the years, but it remained largely second-string. However, the type served through the end of the war. (San Diego Aerospace Museum)

Further development introduced the P-40K fitted with a 1,325-hp Allison V-1710-73 with automatic boost control, and the P-40M with the -81, both models possessing other minor changes, to keep production of fighters rolling into 1943. Some of these returned to the short fuselage and so received an extended rudder and dorsal fin fillet to help control takeoff swing. The N-model that year achieved production Warhawks' peak speed of 378 mph at 10,000 feet by, again, offloading guns and lightening structure. Other blocks of N production were given the guns back, various engine selections, and revised aft canopy and fuselage decking for improved rearward vision, and

The limited value of the Warhawk is graphically illustrated by these P-40Ns stacked like cordwood at the Walnut Ridge, Arkansas, disposal site. In truth, many thousands of aircraft of all types were junked in this manner after the war, but the Curtiss fighter was marginalized earlier than most. (National Museum of the United States Air Force)

some were winterized.[1] External stores capacity rose to 1,500 pounds, reflecting the increased dedication to the ground-attack role for a fighter clearly past its prime for air-to-air combat. Warhawk production peaked with the N at 463 delivered in August 1943, but the final contract in 1944 was truncated. Such second-line aircraft, ordered in the thousands, came to characterize the American war machine with proven types reflecting incremental changes retained in production to keep units at strength while superior new types were developed and production ramped up.

Warhawk production petered out in November 1944 on the N-model with a total of 13,738 P-40s delivered. Only the P-47 and P-51 surpassed this number. The P-40 was the most numerous U.S. Army fighter from 1940 through 1943, yet never ranked among the top world fighters in that period. They were gradually displaced in the main battle during 1943 by P-47s and P-51s. The type continued to serve on the fringes throughout the remainder of the war, although usually with foreign operators.* They were rugged, handled well, and remained effective. Eight foreign air arms eventually employed the P-40 in the thousands, with some provided to Britain shipped second-hand to others. For the Americans, the Warhawk was a symbol of the early tough fighting with weapons barely equal to the challenge.

Curtiss P-40N-20 characteristics:			
span	37.3 ft	weight empty	6,000 lbs
length	33.3 ft	gross	7,400 lbs
height	12.3 ft	maximum	8,850 lbs
wing area	236 ft^2	speed, max. (10,000 ft)	378 mph
fuel capacity (int. + ext.)	122+170 gal	cruise	288 mph
service ceiling	38,000 ft	range, normal (combat)	240 mi
average initial climb rate	2,239 fpm	ferry	1,400 mi

Stunted (P-39, P-63, P-400, P-45)

The P-39 was most unusual when introduced, having the liquid-cooled inline engine mounted behind a cockpit and the propeller driven via a long torque shaft, side automobile-style doors, roll-down windows, and tricycle landing gear. The rear engine simplified integration of the retractable nose gear and heavy fuselage armament, particularly the cannon, aided weight-and-balance, and made for a more streamlined nose for good pilot visibility. The higher approach speeds

** All remaining P-40 and P-40B, C, and D aircraft in United States service were redesignated with an R-prefix (e.g., RP-40) in early 1943, denoting "Restricted Use" or not for combat. In January 1945, the ZRP-40s and ZRP-40Bs designations were introduced to denote obsolete.*

An "undressed" P-39N reveals the Allison buried in the aft fuselage just behind the cockpit, the feed for 37mm cannon shells on the weapon whose barrel protrudes through the prop hub, and containers for the nose .50-cal. machine guns. Note also the cockpit side door and roll-down side window. (San Diego Aerospace Museum)

Tricycle landing gear was accepted by the Army before the war and by the end had become the standard, although nose-wheel steering remained rare during this period. Concern with nose-gear fragility did not prevent movement of this P-39D on a muddy field. (National Museum of the United States Air Force)

made possible by the tricycle gear permitted reduced wing area for lower weight and drag, although making for high wing loading that degraded flight maneuvering.

The Bell Aircraft Corp. Model 4 won a 1937 single-place fighter competition and one XP-39 Airacobra prototype was ordered (serial number 38-326), powered by a 1,150-hp V-1710-17 engine with B-5 turbosupercharger. This was the first single-engine fighter with tricycle gear bought by the U.S. Army. It was notably small and light by comparison with its rivals. A 37mm cannon with 30 rounds was to fire through the propeller hub and a pair of .50-cal. machine guns with 200 rpg were installed in the cowling above. Initial flight testing during April 1938 suffered power shaft vibration and excessive drag that cut top speed short of the guaranteed 400 mph. However, a contract had already been placed for 13 YP-39s (Model 12), and one YP-39A mounting a V-1710-31 with geared supercharger.

In spring 1939, the Army chose to drop the turbosupercharger for the -31's supercharger to save weight and reduce drag, this much to Bell's relief to be free of its inherent hazard and mechanical complexity. It was expected or hoped that upped engine power, weight reduction, and drag clean-up would help balance the loss of the turbosupercharger. However, the V-1710-31 never left the test stand and an engine more suited to lower altitude operations was ultimately selected. These circumstances reduced the Airacobra design altitude to 15,000 feet, which appeared acceptable in the context of 1939. The service then ordered an XP-39B with the single-stage V-1710-37 delivering 1,090 hp at 13,200 feet, reflecting all these changes. This aircraft began flight tests in November 1939, but weight growth prevented attainment of speed goals.

The evolution of the design was reflected in the YP-39s that began flying in September 1940, with an anticipated top speed of 375 mph. These 13 aircraft began introducing additional equipment to meet operational requirements, such as cockpit armor and a pair of .30-cal. nose-mounted machine guns joining the .50s. Production plans went ahead for a model powered by an improved V-1710-35, delivering 1,150 hp at 12,000 feet, the Army ordering 80 in August 1939. The Army Air Corps futilely anticipated 400 mph at 15,000 feet from this aircraft they designated P-45.

The P-45 production model designation was subsequently changed to P-39C (Model 13) to align the aircraft types, and deliveries began in January 1941. Weight growth, again, countered any benefits from eliminating the turbosupercharger such that performance remained anemic. However, the die was cast. The Air Corps had to expand tremendously and rapidly, so production needed to move forward immediately and at a high rate. The P-39 never recovered from these decisions. As little as a year before, this would not have happened, as the aircraft clearly needed further development.

The Army Air Corps next purchased 623 P-39Ds (Model 15) that added another pair of .30-cal. guns with 1,000 rpg, with all four .30s placed in the wings, and introduced self-sealing fuel tanks. The P-39D had its hub-mounted 37mm cannon replaced with a 20mm. The final 60 aircraft in the P-39C order were built to this new standard. Provisions for a 75-gallon belly tank or 600-pound bomb were also included. With weight inevitably growing, the block 2 aircraft (P-39D-2-BE) had the -63 engine rated at 1,325 hp. The block 3 and 4 aircraft had dual-armored oil and glycol coolers in the belly in view of the plane's likely ground attack role. These aircraft began arriving in May 1941. Ultimately 923 P-39Ds were delivered. Although more than 400 were completed by the end of 1941, cannons and propellers were too few to outfit all of these aircraft. An alternate propeller was substituted for the 229 P-39Fs toward the end of the year, and 25

The rate at which new fighters were being produced by mid-war presented new difficulties. Final work, like preparation for flight, was sometimes handled outdoors to free plant floor space, as exemplified by these Bell P-39D-1s in Buffalo. Sometimes airframe production ran ahead of engine, propeller, and delivery of other government-furnished equipment. (Air Force Flight Test Center)

Bell P-39D characteristics:			
span	34.0 ft	weight empty	6,300 lbs
length	30.2 ft	gross	7,650 lbs
height	11.8 ft	maximum	8,400 lbs
wing area	213 ft²	speed, max. (13,800 ft)	368 mph
fuel capacity (int. + ext.)	120+75 gal	cruise	213 mph
service ceiling	32,100 ft	range, normal	800 mi
average initial climb rate	2,632 fpm	ferry	1,545 mi

The Bell Airacobra, a P-39D shown, was available in comparatively large numbers when the United States entered the war. Prewar decisions greatly reduced its performance potential as an air-to-air fighter by the standards of 1941, but it remained potent in air-to-ground attack. (National Museum of the United States Air Force)

The P-400 was essentially a P-39D with a 20mm cannon and other changes to meet British requirements. However, the Americans came to operate hundreds after the Pearl Harbor emergency. This example is seen at Henderson Field, Guadalcanal, in fall 1942. (National Museum of the United States Air Force)

received the V-1710-59 with automatic boost control (rated at 1,100 hp at 15,200 feet) as the P-39J.

Further incremental changes generated orders for 1,880 P-39Gs (Model 26), but were altered during construction to other variants such that no P-39G models were actually fielded. The 1,325-hp V-1710-63 was fitted to the 210 Ks, and a change back to the original Curtiss 10-foot, 4.5-inch propeller marked the 250 L models. The 240 Ms beginning to emerge in November 1942 had water injection for the 1,200-hp V-1710-83s producing 1,420 hp at 9,500 feet in War Emergency power, yielding 370 mph at 15,000 feet. The 2,095 P-39Ns carried over the water injection with the -85 reaching 399 mph by reducing weight. A pair of .50-cal. machine guns in underslung gondolas on the 4,905 P-39Qs replaced the four .30-cal. wing guns, a few hundred with four-blade propellers, and some with fuel capacity and armor weight alterations. Some or all these received bottom armor for ground attack. Exactly 9,589 Airacobras were completed when production ended in July 1944.

Foreign sales of the Airacobra began with an April 1940 contract to provide 175 P-400 (Model 14) examples to France. Based on the P-39D, these substituted a Hispano-Suiza Mk 404 20mm cannon with 60 rounds and two .50s in the nose with 270 rpg. The order was taken over by Britain who increased the quantity to 675. However, performance was not what the RAF desired and they were almost immediately relegated to second tier duties. More than 200 were shipped off to Russia. The Army Air Forces took ownership of 196 P-400s still in the States as an emergency measure after Pearl Harbor. U.S. Army units in Britain operated another 179. A further 336 examples were already on order via lend-lease, but most of these ended up with the Americans and Soviets as P-39Ds, some with V-1710-63s. More than half the Ns and Qs were shipped to the USSR.* Indeed, most Airacobras went to lend-lease and most of those (5,578) to the Soviets. Other users included Australian, Free French, and Italian Co-belligerent forces.

The Russians were quite successful with the Airacobra, especially in close air support, but also made a good showing in air-to-air combat. The U.S. Army considered it of marginal value, but found work for it in ground attack when accompanied by fighter top-cover. In 1943, the P-39 was the most numerous fighter manufactured in the United States, with 511 rolled out in April. At its peak, the Army Air Forces fielded 2,105 of the type in February 1944, but these were rapidly being displaced by more capable aircraft. To that time, it was mostly in action in the Pacific and in the Mediterranean Theater of Operations (MTO).

In all its production forms, the Airacobra was possessed of lackluster performance in comparison with contemporaries that always seemed one step ahead. Bell's exuberant promotional campaign only enforced the impression of over-sold capabilities. This gave the fighter a bad reputation, but it was still potent at low altitude. The Airacobra displayed an admirable ability to absorb combat damage and return to base. However, the 37mm cannon was prone to jamming after firing a few rounds, gun fumes penetrated the cabin, and

Advanced models of the Airacobra, like this P-39J, made improvements consistent with the evolving requirements of air fighting, but it continued to be relegated to air support missions. Its contribution in this role was commendable, its cannon being quite effective against armored targets. (National Museum of the United States Air Force)

* *The P-39H and P variants were either unassigned or never realized. The I and O suffixes were not used as they might be confused as digits.*

The Bell P-63 Kingcobra improved on the P-39 as a new design, but its role was unchanged. The vast majority of the thousands produced went to the USSR, but a few served with the Army Air Forces stateside, like this P-63A-9. It was an under-rated fighter that contributed measurably to victory. (National Museum of the United States Air Force)

This Bell P-63C Kingcobra is en route to the USSR, operating from a frozen lake. More than a thousand of the models were delivered to the Soviet Union, where they were very successful. The principal mission was ground attack, but the Soviets did well with it in air-to-air operations. (National Museum of the United States Air Force)

spins could be tricky. Some operators preferred the faster-firing 20mm with more rounds. Wing loading continued to increase over this evolution with the P-39Q-20 grossing nearly 8,000 pounds compared with the XP-39's 6,100 pounds.

In answering some criticisms of the P-39, Bell offered the Model 24 with the goal of improving performance using larger wings with a laminar-flow section and two-stage engine, plus addressing maintenance and servicing complaints. The Army ordered two prototypes (41-19511/2) of the XP-63 Kingcobra (project MX-90) on 27 June 1941.[2]

Although identical in layout to the Airacobra, this was a new design sharing no common parts with the P-39. Bell's design called for the V-1710-47 engine, but the Army asked that it consider the two-stage, 12-cylinder Continental XIV-1430-1. By February 1942, the team stopped waiting for the Continental and went with the Allison that was already flying in the experimental XP-39E (which see). The -47's supercharger was driven by auxiliary hydraulic pressure. Also adopted from the XP-39E were the straight lines in the aft fuselage closeout and vertical tail. A longer fuselage sought to improve spin characteristics. Intended armament was the 37mm cannon with 30 rounds and a pair of .50s above with 270 rpg. The aircraft sported a four-blade propeller and was overall larger than the Airacobra (32.7-foot length and 38.3-foot span compared with the P-39D's 30.2 feet and 34.0 feet, respectively).

The XP-63 ship 41-19511 was taken up for the first time in December 1942. Unfortunately, both prototypes were lost in accidents. However, a contract for a production-representative example, the XP-63A (Model 24A), had been placed in September 1942. A production order did not await this airplane, or even flights of the prototypes, with 3,200 Model 33s ordered in October. The P-63 became the only type committed to full-scale production and to see combat, where the prototype flew after America's entry into the war. However, as will be seen, it saw very little service with the U.S. Army Air Forces. It was also only the second aircraft bound for production in the United States with a laminar-flow airfoil.

Bell P-63A-9 characteristics:

span	38.3 ft	weight empty	6,375 lbs
length	32.7 ft	gross	8,815 lbs
height	12.6 ft	maximum	10,416 lbs
wing area	248 ft²	speed, max. (24,450 ft)	408 mph
fuel capacity (int. + ext.)	126+225 gal	cruise	378 mph
service ceiling	43,000 ft	range, combat	450 mi
average initial climb rate	3,425 fpm	ferry	2,575 mi

The XP-63A (42-78015) flew in April 1943 with the 1,325-hp, two-stage V-1710-93, which attained 421 mph at 24,100 feet. This engine had a war emergency rating of 1,500 hp. However, combat weight diminished its performance. Added was 123 pounds of armor, a 75-gallon centerline drop tank or alternative 500-pound bomb, and two more .50-cal. machine guns – one under each wing with 250 rpg. Production of the P-63A saw first deliveries in October 1943, and some 1,725 were turned out by December 1944. Seven successive blocks of aircraft added more armor, hardpoints for fuel and weapons (including rockets), ammunition, and introduced water injection. Most of the P-63As went to the Soviet Union.

Production then shifted to the P-63C (Model 33C) with the V-1710-117 capable of 1,900 hp with water injection. Some had a ventral strake under the vertical stabilizer for improved spin characteristics, and added more armor. Again, almost all of the 1,227 aircraft produced during 1945, in the -1 and -5 blocks were shipped east. Free French forces operated more than 100 C models.

Although more suitable for air fighting above 15,000 feet, the role for the Kingcobras remained the same as the Airacobras. They were employed almost exclusively for ground attack and close air support. Still, many Soviet aces earned the distinction in the Bell fighters, including the second highest scoring Allied fighter pilot with 48 of his 59 kills in the P-39. The Americans' focus had shifted to other designs and had little interest in the Kingcobra. They flew limited numbers stateside in advanced training units.

Maverick (P-38, P-322)

Among the top three American fighters of the war, the Lockheed P-38 had its origins in a 1936 competition. It was the Air Corps' first multi-engine single-seat fighter, first production aircraft with turbosupercharger and tricycle gear, and first twin-boom airplane. It was also noteworthy as a twin-engine fighter without rear gunner. It employed the latest all-metal construction techniques (including control surfaces), with flush riveting and butt joints. The twin-boom layout was rare, and certainly new to American combat aircraft. This simplified incorporation of the inline, liquid-cooled engine with coolant radiators and turbosupercharger. By employing counter-rotation of the handed propellers, torque effects were cancelled to eliminate swing on takeoff. The raised canopy, promising all-around vision, dominated the center "gondola" fuselage pod.

The sole XP-38 (37-457) flew on 27 January 1939 with a 1,150-hp V-1710-11/15 – actually the only suitable liquid-cooled engine then available – and General Electric B-1 turbosuperchargers.* The aircraft soon demonstrated it was the fastest fighter in the United States achieving speeds in excess of 400 mph at 20,000 feet, getting to that altitude in 6.5 minutes, and with the longest range. However, it still had a way to go before entering service. Engine cooling was a battle and tail buffet was worrisome. A major setback was loss of the aircraft in February, 15 days after first flight. This experience emphasized the false economy of funding a single prototype, although budgets in the period permitted little more.

The military usually purchased a number of service test examples of new aircraft for operational evaluation and final adjustments in the design. The practice was largely suspended during the war, among the last being 13 YP-38s, five shown here at the Lockheed Air Terminal, Burbank, in 1941. (Jay Miller Collection)

Deliveries of 13 YP-38 (Model 122) service test aircraft, from September 1940 through June 1941, picked up the slack. These aircraft were powered by V-1710-27/29 engines and were provided with greater radiator cooling capacity accessed via larger inlets on the sides of the booms. Oil cooling was likewise improved with a fixed chin inlet vice the retractable scoop of the XP-38. The powerplants were matched with General Electric B-2 turbosuperchargers to maintain 1,150 hp at 20,000 feet. No weapons were fitted, but these were to be in pairs of .50s with 210 rpg and .30s with 500 rpg, plus an Oldsmobile 37mm cannon with 15 rounds. A framed windscreen was soon introduced to permit armored glass. A measure taken to address the tail buffeting was reversing the direction of the counter-rotating propellers, these now turning outboard at the top. External mass balance weights on the elevator were also introduced, and the horizontal tail area outboard of the verticals increased.

** The engine with suffix numbers separated by the virgules (/) denote paired engines (left to right) or like design but geared to turn in opposite directions. Twin-engine aircraft like the P-38 employed such pairs to drive counter-rotating propellers.*

Tail buffet continued to be an issue, especially after the first YP-38 (39-689) suffered catastrophic tail failure recovering from a dive. The second YP-38 was passed to NACA Langley for full-scale wind tunnel testing of the phenomenon. Large fillets were added between the center fuselage and wing, eliminating vortices shed from this interface, and tailplane incidence angle was increased slightly. These cured the tail buffet, and the corrections were soon introduced to the production line and retrofitted to earlier aircraft.

The world situation demanded the Army wait no longer, and a contract for 66 production P-38-LOs (Model 222) was issued in September 1939 before the Y-airplanes had been completed.* Weaponry was altered again to four .50s with 200 rpg and the 37mm. Deliveries began in June 1941 but, after 29 P-38-LOs, the rest of the initial production order became P-38Ds with delivery commencing in August 1941. These introduced the tail buffet solutions, added armor and leak-proof tanks, but some lacked the complete complement of weapons (the 37mm never fitted). Being the first P-38s considered combat worthy, a squadron of Ds were deployed to the Aleutian Islands in June 1942 in answer to the Japanese threat.

In June 1940, the Anglo-French Purchasing Commission placed an order for 667 of the Lockheed fighter. The order consisted of 417 Model 322-F variants for France and 250 Model 322-Bs for Britain. Weapons were a pair each of .50- and .30-cal. machine guns. The aircraft were to be simplified by deleting the turbosuperchargers and returning to Allisons without counter-rotation to standardize with RAF Curtiss Kittyhawks. The decision was not entirely the choice of the customers, as the turbosuperchargers were then restricted from export.

As with many other such *L'Armee de L'Air* contracts, the entire 322 deal was eventually assumed by Britain. They had the terms revised to 143 built to the original specifications as Lightning Is, and the balance of 524 Lightning IIs with more suitable engines and turbos. Evaluation of the first three Lightning Is, begun in December 1941, made clear the export model propulsion decisions considerably limited the fighter's usefulness. The remaining 140 "castrated" Lightning Is were taken on by the Army Air Corps, 20 as P-322-Is and 120 upgraded with -27/29 engines, but still without turbosuperchargers, as P-322-IIs. However, these were all devoted to testing and training and soon redesignated RP-322s. The RAF would not see any of the Lightning IIs as the U.S. Army retained all in the emergency following the opening of Japanese aggression against the United States and because the RAF lacked any enthusiasm for them. Only one of the aircraft was actually built to the Lightning II standard while the rest were completed as 150 P-38F and 374 P-38G aircraft.

This stack-up of P-38Fs emphasizes the unusual configuration of the Lightning and the turbosuperchargers atop each boom. Despite the generous transparencies, armor and supports actually gave poor rearward vision. The twin engines were greatly appreciated in the Pacific given the long over-water distances typical of that theater. (National Museum of the United States Air Force)

Lockheed P-38F characteristics:			
span	52.0 ft	weight empty	12,264 lbs
length	37.8 ft	gross	15,900 lbs
height (top of tail)	9.8 ft	maximum	18,000 lbs
wing area	327.5 ft²	speed, max. (25,000 ft)	395 mph
fuel capacity (int. + ext.)	300+300 gal	cruise	305 mph
service ceiling	39,000 ft	range, normal	350 mi
average initial climb rate	2,273 fpm	ferry	1,925 mi

By August 1940, the Army was convinced it had an important new aerial weapon to meet any coming crisis. It was, in fact, the only fighter then produced in the United States that outperformed foreign examples. That month the service placed an order for 210 P-38E (Model 222) with the V-1710-27/29. These were the most mature of the Lightnings, with more than 2,000 upgrades, and standardized armament of four .50-cal. machine guns with 500 rpg and a 20mm cannon with 150 rounds. The first E was delivered in November 1941

* *The first production P-38s lacked a suffix, so they have been differentiated here as elsewhere with the LO contractor identification.*

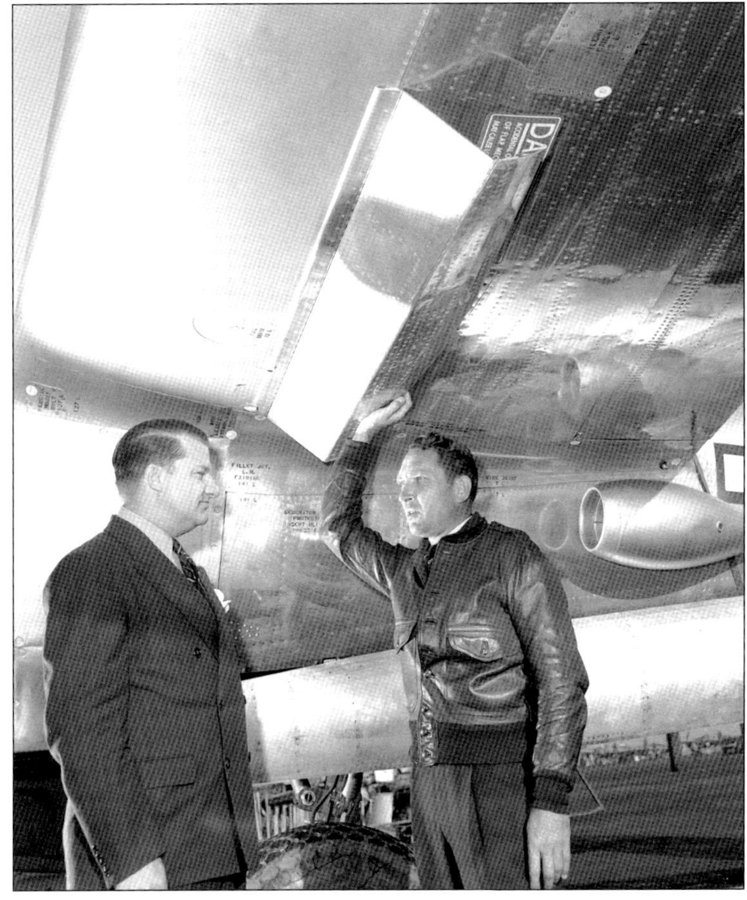

Lockheed designer Clarence Kelly Johnson and test pilot Milo Burcham (left to right) stand below the port dive flap on a P-38J-25. These two-piece, 4.8-foot wide "compressibility flaps" or "dive recovery flaps" were electrically actuated via switches on the control yoke. (Jay Miller Collection)

and was the first model to see combat, blooded in the Aleutians during August 1942. Many Es were later upgraded to G-standard, including the addition of external hardpoints.

Next up were the 377 P-38Fs with 1,325-hp V-1710-49/53s and B-13 turbosuperchargers compensating for weight growth. The "combat flap" or "maneuvering flap" was also featured on the P-38F-15 block, this simply an actuator modification permitting a quick 8-degree flap droop at high speed for greater lift and maneuverability (tightening a turn) to improve air combat agility. Of great importance was the pair of wing pylons under the inner wing panels for 1,000-pound bombs or external tanks. The standard 75-gallon drop tank eventually gave way to a specially designed 165-gallon laminar flow tank and pylon designed by Lockheed's Clarence "Kelly" Johnson. This low-drag tank soon began appearing on other fighters. It gave the Lightning about a 1,000-mile combat range. It extended ferry range from 1,300 miles to 1,900 miles, and Lockheed even demonstrated more than 3,100 miles. This range made the fighter desirable as a bomber escort.

The P-38F was the first Lightning considered ready for the main air battle and so was among the first fighters deployed to Europe. The larger external tanks allowed them to fly to the UK under their own power instead of via transport vessels subject to the German U-boat menace. The first dispatch of 200 P-38Fs required urgent modifications by Lockheed to permit carriage of 165-gallon drop tanks. These were the first single-seat fighters to make the crossing, guided by a bomber, and their twin engines offered a safety factor on the long over-water and over-ice mission.

The weapon hardpoints were retrofitted to P-38Es going abroad. Many of the earlier models were redesignated "Restricted," or RP-38, as early as 1942. The delivery rate of the more worthy models was frustratingly slow, and the program worked to accelerate production. Construction was complex and with close assembly tolerances. Efforts in Burbank included introducing a moving production line and establishing a Dallas modification center at Love Field to handle upgrades.

P-38Gs (excluding the former RAF models) were optimized for long cruise flight with 1,325-hp V-1710-51/55 engines, the B-13 turbosupercharger coming with the block 3 (P-38G-3). The last 200 P-38G-10s were fitted with 1,600-pound capacity hardpoints. This permitted a 300-gallon ferry tank, which increased the fighter's range to 2,300 miles. The block 10s also had provisions for a pair of triple-tube 4.5-inch rocket launchers mounted off the center fuselage under the wing. The 708 Gs were delivered between June 1942 and March 1943.

The P-38H substituted the new V-1710-89/91 engines with 1,425 hp and automatic B-33 turbosupercharger plus oil cooling shutters. Fleet deliveries of these 601 Model 222-81-20s commenced in March 1943. While this powerplant installation ostensibly permitted military power settings of 1,240 hp at 25,000 feet, and war emergency power of 1,600 hp, P-38Hs remained restricted because of insufficient cooling.

The cooling problem was finally corrected in August 1943 with the first P-38J (Model 422-81-14).* These featured revised cooling scoops at the chin of the booms that fed the supercharger intercoolers. Previously, the intercoolers, undersized for the more powerful

* *The I designation was skipped because of potential confusion with the numeral 1.*

This P-38L-5 exhibits the "tree" rocket launchers, each with five 5-inch HVAR rounds. These and up to 2,000 pounds of bombs under the inboard stations, matched with the nose weapons, made for an impressive ordnance delivery capacity for the air-to-ground missions. (San Diego Aerospace Museum)

engines, were moved from within the outboard leading edge of the outer wing panels. The radiators were also made more efficient with enlarged and more aerodynamic housings. These changes permitted 1,425 hp at military settings and five minutes of war emergency power at 1,600 hp (over-speeding the turbosupercharger). The aircraft reached 420 mph at the 25,000-foot design altitude as the fastest Lightning. Moving the intercoolers allowed recovery of the fuel quantity lost with incorporation of self-sealing cells, the space filled with 55-gallon tanks, although not in all P-38Js. Cabin heating and defrost were also greatly improved. The front armored glass was made integral as the windscreen. Also interesting was the fact that fuses were replaced with circuit breakers in the cockpit.

Lockheed P-38L characteristics:

span	52.0 ft	weight empty	12,800 lbs
length	37.8 ft	gross	17,500 lbs
height (top of tail)	9.9 ft	maximum	21,600 lbs
wing area	327.5 ft²	speed, max. (25,000 ft)	414 mph
fuel capacity (int. + ext.)	410+600 gal	cruise	290 mph
service ceiling	44,000 ft	range, 3,200 lbs bombs	450 mi
average initial climb rate	2,857 fpm	ferry	2,600 mi

The P-38G was among the first Lightning models ready to join the main fight. The turbosupercharged Allisons gave it a top speed near 400 mph, and four .50-cal. guns and 20mm cannon concentrated in the nose was a powerful punch. They possessed extraordinary range and had increased external stores capacity. (Air Force Flight Test Center)

The last block of the 2,970 J models, the P-38J-25s, introduced dive flaps to reduce the hazards of compressibility in high-speed dives. The Lightning was a noteworthy victim of this phenomenon, placarded at Mach 0.65 dive speed, with heavy buffeting and Mach tuck experienced around Mach 0.72 as a function of g loading. The flaps were also supplied as kits for retrofit in the field to earlier model Lightnings. The block 25s also had hydraulically boosted ailerons for lighter control forces and improved roll performance – among the first fighters so equipped.

The final Lightning production variant was the P-38L. These aircraft were fitted with V-1710-111/113 engines rated at 1,425 hp for takeoff and military power, 1,200 hp war emergency power at 28,700 feet. Initial deliveries of the 3,810 P-38Ls began in June 1944. The fuel system was improved with booster pumps and the external tanks were pressurized. Hardpoints were upgraded to carry 2,000 pounds. Notable were the outboard wing stations accommodating a five-round "Christmas tree" rocket launcher for 5-inch HVARs. Gun pods were also seen on these stations. These features were retrofitted to many P-38Js.

Consolidated-Vultee's Nashville plant was converted late in the war to produce 2,000 P-38L-5-VNs under a June 1944 contract, after previously building wing center-sections as a subcontractor. However, only 113 were rolled out before orders were cancelled at war's end. Likewise, 1,380 Lockheed Ls were cancelled. All others were built in Burbank, with peak production of 432 per month achieved in January 1945.

The P-38 aroused suspicion simply by its unusual design, and skepticism about its suitability for maneuvering in combat with single-engine types. The early trouble with tail buffet, engines, and compressibility, and disappointing initial roll rate at high speed, all colored the opinion of many. There were markedly diverse opinions regarding vulnerability. However, the Lightning had as many fans as detractors and left an indelible mark on the history of the air war.

The P-38Fs, appearing in Britain during mid-1942, made long-range fighter sweeps over the European continent. Lightnings flew the first American fighter mission over Berlin in a round trip from the UK. However, their capability in the bomber escort role was possibly more important. At the time, escorts were not felt to be essential and the P-38's early troubles left them largely unemployed. Instead, the Lightning squadrons were sent to the MTO where the teams initially had a tough time until becoming seasoned.

It was fall 1943 before the P-38 began operating as a large force in Western Europe. By this point, the requirement for a bomber escort capable of staying for the entire mission had become vital to continuing daylight raids. The long "legs" of the P-38F allowed them to stay with a bomber stream for more of the route to targets in Germany. However, the aircraft suffered engine problems related to British fuels, and the frigid cockpits left pilots in a poor state to engage in combat. Consequently, the Lightnings were replaced in the role at the earliest opportunity.

This 11th Air Force P-38E is undergoing maintenance on Adak Island in the Aleutians during mid-1944. The Lightning's twin engines and complex systems demand more attention than most other American fighters. Yet the airplane played a vital role throughout the war. (National Museum of the United States Air Force)

Because of the different circumstances, tactics, and opposition, the Lightning would leave its greatest mark in the Pacific and China-Burma-India (CBI) theaters. The safety factor of twin engines was particularly appreciated during the long over-water flights typical of Pacific combat. Initial difficulties operating the intercoolers in the tropics were quickly overcome. The P-38 dominated Army kill scores and downed more Japanese aircraft than any other fighter in the conflict. The two top American aces won the distinction in P-38s.

The total number of P-38s produced, 9,538 not counting more than 1,400 reconnaissance birds, appears small by comparison to other principal Army and Navy fighters. Mainly to blame were the two different engines and propellers, a hefty price of $95,000 apiece, maintenance complexity, and the logistical burden of fielding a multi-engine airplane. Very few were provided to Allied operators. It was the only American fighter in continuous production from the beginning to the end of the war.

Big Guy (P-47)

Pleased with the proposal that yielded the P-44, Republic also offered the AP-10 conforming to the prevailing criterion for a light, modestly armed, fast fighter. The smallest airframe that could be wrapped around the V-1710, it was to gross 4,900 pounds with a 115-ft-square-foot wing area seeking 415 mph and armed with two .50-cal. machine guns in the nose. Proposed in August 1939, it was ordered in November as the XP-47 (40-3051).

The changes in desired attributes that killed the P-44 lead inexorably to revision of the AP-10 into a much heavier aircraft with greater ordnance. The design was initially transformed into a 6,150-pound gross weight airplane with a 165-square foot wing area, four .30 caliber wing guns in addition to the cowl guns, and seeking 410 mph at 15,000 feet. The rapidly changing requirements were reflected in a request for a stripped-down variant, the XP-47A (40-3052), added to the contract in January 1940, to get an early look at the aircraft while the fully equipped example continued in assembly.

In May 1940, responding to reports from the war in Europe, the Air Corps realized even the greatly revised XP-47 would not have the combat potential originally expected. This prompted further changes in the requirements to a long-range escort fighter with ground attack capability, heavily armed and armored, with self-sealing tanks. The Air Corps chose the enormous, turbosupercharged R-2800 as the powerplant. The Navy's early success with the Pratt & Whitney unit on the F4U, and Republic's success with radials, was reason enough for the Army to make an exception to their drive for inlines.

The multitude of changes wrought an increment in designation to XP-47B with contract revisions in September 1940. However, even this was not enough, and the P-47C was conceived for simultaneous

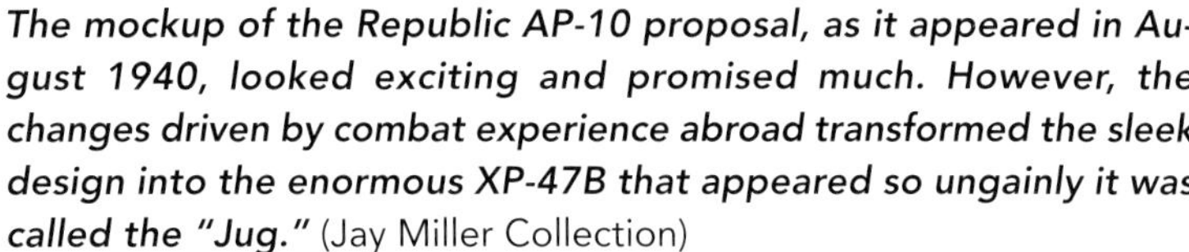

The mockup of the Republic AP-10 proposal, as it appeared in August 1940, looked exciting and promised much. However, the changes driven by combat experience abroad transformed the sleek design into the enormous XP-47B that appeared so ungainly it was called the "Jug." (Jay Miller Collection)

The Republic P-47 proved one of the most successful combat aircraft of the war and built in larger numbers than any other American fighter. Production focused on the D-model, an early model here typified by a block 23 airplane (42-28009) built in Evansville, Indiana. (National Museum of the United States Air Force)

development, raising the gross weight to 11,500 pounds and weaponry to eight .50s. In September 1940, 171 P-47Bs and 602 P-47Cs were ordered in the largest single fighter contract to that date, while the earlier efforts and P-44s were discarded. This was the only Army radial-engine fighter developed in the run-up to war that entered production, the first Army fighter reaching 2,000 hp, and the first with strategic range. It would become among the largest and heaviest single-seat, piston-powered fighter ever built.

A primary source of the aircraft's size and weight growth was the long and voluminous ducting for the turbosupercharger system. For balance reasons, the turbosupercharger was placed in the rear fuselage as in the P-43. Intake air to the turbine came via a large duct from an inlet under the engine and running more than a dozen feet aft within the belly. Twin exhaust ducts, from a collector ring on the engine, were laid on either side of the intake duct. Exhaust air was used to turn the turbine and then dumped out a shroud under the aft fuselage. The twin carburetor inlet ducts ran the same distance back to the engine to an intercooler above the turbosupercharger. Converting the tremendous power of the Double Wasp to thrust required a huge, 12-foot diameter, four-blade Curtiss Electric propeller. Providing adequate ground clearance for the propeller, yet keeping main gear strut length short enough for retraction into available wing volume, led to telescoping main landing gear struts that extended nine inches when lowered, and the reverse when raised. Eight .50-cal. wing guns with 267 rpg was the heaviest armament of any fighter then in production.

The XP-47B (40-3051) flew its maiden flight in May 1941, powered by the XP-2800-17. Much work remained, introducing numerous control system changes to improve handling qualities and to correct other operationally unsuitable features. Two of the earliest examples were lost in dives when the empennages separated, with tail flutter and compressibility suspected.[3] This caused a production change to metal-covered control surfaces versus fabric. The remedies greatly slipped the operational debut from 1942 to 1943. Performance, however, was most promising with rapid climb to altitude and more than 400-mph top speed that allowed it to dive away from a bad situation.

Production examples began rolling off the line in Farmingdale, New York, during March 1942, fitted with the R-2800-21 with C-1 turbosupercharger. P-47Bs were never considered combat-worthy and were eventually redesignated RP-47B. The C models began appearing in September with a slightly extended fuselage and further control system improvements. The P-47C-4 employed the R-2800-59 with water injection for 2,300 hp at 27,000 feet and 428-mph peak airspeed. The block 5s had provisions for a 75- or 110-gallon centerline drop tank or 1,000-pound bomb, and this was retrofitted to many earlier examples.

With the nation at war, production of the Thunderbolt ramped up sharply. This came to focus on the P-47D, ordered in October 1941, with initial deliveries beginning in early 1943. Production eventually exceeded 600 per month, almost one per hour, with a total of more than 12,600 delivered. To supplement New York production, a new plant was erected in Evansville, Indiana. It was up and running within five months. Even Curtiss manufactured 354 of this type in Buffalo, New York, as the P-47G-CU.

The P-47D had additional armor and, through consecutive blocks, progressively more under-wing hardpoints were added as

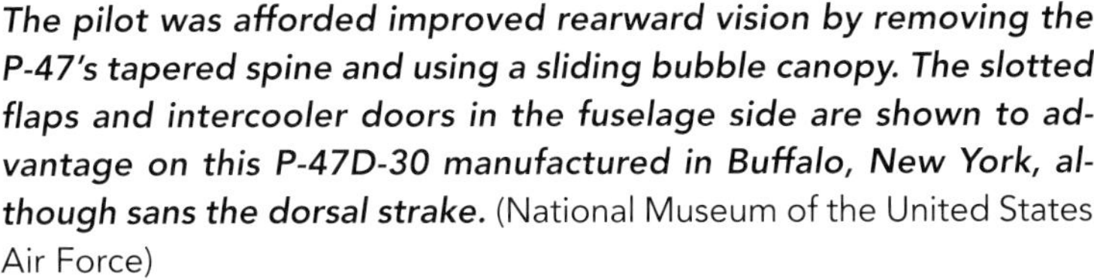
The pilot was afforded improved rearward vision by removing the P-47's tapered spine and using a sliding bubble canopy. The slotted flaps and intercooler doors in the fuselage side are shown to advantage on this P-47D-30 manufactured in Buffalo, New York, although sans the dorsal strake. (National Museum of the United States Air Force)

The P-47M was built in comparatively small numbers late in the war as a short-term means of dealing with German jet aircraft just appearing on the scene. It emphasized speed by removing features intended for air-to-ground work and mounted the most powerful engine and supercharger combination. (National Museum of the United States Air Force)

the ground attack mission increased in importance. Up to 1,500 pounds of bombs or tankage could be accommodated, and machine gun ammunition was increased to 425 rpg with the block 20's "universal wing." Some saw an engine change to the -63 and a paddle-blade propeller for more efficiency at war emergency power and greater rate of climb for better low altitude work. The bubble canopy was introduced with the block 25 in early 1944, with the aft fuselage cut back, improving all-important rearward vision. This block also had internal fuel capacity expanded by 65 gallons.

Under-wing capacity increased further, especially permitting 165-gallon drop tanks for greatly extended range, or two 1,000-pound bombs. Dive flaps were added with the block 30s in anticipation of compressibility issues; these folding down from the wing lower surface between the gear bays and landing flaps. Ten zero-length rocket launch stubs came in with the block 35s but were

Republic P-47D-22 characteristics:			
span	40.8 ft	weight empty	10,143 lbs
length	35.3 ft	gross	13,500 lbs
height	14.6 ft	maximum	16,200 lbs
wing area	300 ft²	speed, max. (30,000 ft)	433 mph
fuel capacity (int. + ext.)	305+330 gal	cruise	300 mph
service ceiling	40,000 ft	range, normal (combat)	640 mi
best climb rate	3,100 fpm	external tank	1,725 mi

retrofitted to many earlier aircraft. Some aircraft would also mount the trio cluster of 4.5-inch rocket launch tubes under each wing beginning in summer 1944. A dorsal fin extension was introduced with the block 40, and retrofitted in the field to improve directional stability degraded by elimination of the "razorback" spine.

The centerline drop tank on the C model permitted deep penetrations of German airspace, beginning in summer 1943, and this began American experience with external tanks. However, supply did not initially keep up with demand, and a flush 205-gallon ferry unit was unacceptable for combat. Fortunately, beginning in July 1943, the British hosts were able to provide a 108- to 200-gallon unit formed of pressed paper and glue. This gave a 350-mile radius of action, two tanks in later models extending this to 445 miles. With the greater internal fuel of the block 25 and 330 gallons of external tankage, combat radius went to 690 miles. A 375-gallon tank could be mounted on the fuselage station and 165-gallon units on the wings. By early 1944, this allowed P-47s to escort B-17s deep inside Germany and back. Weapons and tanks were mixed to match individual mission requirements.

A further upgrade to the Thunderbolt offered a stopgap interceptor in meeting the looming German introduction of jet-powered aircraft while American jets were still in development. The 130 P-47Ms were given the 2,800-hp R-2800-57 engine with CH-5 turbosupercharger combination of the experimental XP-47J (which see), along with some automatic engine controls. Speedbrakes for

The P-47N was optimized for late-war combat in the Pacific, demanding exceptionally long range for bomber escort and ground attack. The P-47N had a new wing, most easily recognizable by its squared tips and six guns. This example has the dorsal fin extension for improved directional stability. (San Diego Aerospace Museum)

Republic P-47N characteristics:			
span	42.7 ft	weight empty	11,132 lbs
length	35.3 ft	gross	16,300 lbs
height	14.6 ft	maximum	20,700 lbs
wing area	322 ft²	speed, max. (32,500 ft)	467 mph
fuel capacity (int. + ext.)	556+600 gal	cruise	350 mph
service ceiling	43,000 ft	range, normal (bombs)	800 mi
best climb rate	2,770 fpm	maximum	2,200 mi

rapid deceleration following a dive were added under the wings, and under-wing store provisions deleted to reduce weight. The sprint P-47Ms topped out at 473 mph at 32,500 feet and had a 3,500-fpm initial rate of climb, although range was down to 530 miles. Delivery began in December 1944 and, although hastily deployed, engine troubles kept them out of action until the last weeks of the war in Europe.

The final Thunderbolt variant was the P-47N that carried over the M features married to a new wing with expanded internal fuel capacity to meet demands of the vast Pacific Theater. This heaviest of P-47s, at 21,200 pounds maximum gross weight, still reached 467 mph and had a range of 2,200 miles, enough to escort B-29s to Japan and back from Pacific bases. Total fuel capacity, including external tanks, rose to 1,256 gallons, which supported a 1,000-mile combat radius. Alternatively, three 1,000-pound bombs and rockets could be carried. Beefed-up landing gear was necessary to match the higher weight. An autopilot and other automatic controls were introduced to ease the pilot burden and support escort missions that could last as long as nine hours. Later blocks saw the seat get armrests to reduce pilot fatigue as well as adding tail-warning radar. The block 25 featured the -77 engine.

The 1,816 P-47Ns brought total Thunderbolt production to 15,683 through December 1945 as the most numerous American fighter ever (eclipsed by three foreign types). More than 1,000 were sent to Britain, French units, the USSR, plus Mexican and Brazilian forces fighting abroad. Orders for 5,943 Ns were cancelled after VJ-Day.

The P-47 was tremendously successful in air-to-air combat and ground attack. The first Thunderbolt squadrons began operating during summer 1942 and they entered combat in Europe the following spring. The potbelly airplane was initially looked upon with skepticism, observers likening it to a milk container and christening it "Jug." However, the type soon earned respect. It offered both advantages and disadvantages compared with adversaries that its pilots were taught to exploit. The expanded external weapons load made the Thunderbolt one of the first fighter-bombers as its ground attack mission grew. Often, when returning from an escort mission, pilots dropped to the deck to attack ground targets, and the plane could take a lot of punishment from ground fire. This earned it the handle "Juggernaut," giving new meaning to the earlier nickname. The Jug quickly became the bane of anything moving on road or rail.

Over Achiever (P-51, XP-78)

The truly all-around standout American fighter airplane of the war was the P-51. From humble beginnings, the Mustang went through the usual gestation and maturation to rank among the top fighters from any nation.

In December 1939, Britain asked North American Aviation (NAA) to manufacture the Kittyhawk for RAF service because Curtiss was already working at capacity yet not meeting P-40 quantity demands of its American and foreign customers. North American responded with a proposal to place the Kittyhawk's V-1710-39 engine, already on order, into an entirely new and superior airframe. The British agreed to allow the Inglewood, California, firm a go at the task.

For the next few months, the conceptual aircraft was formulated and shared with the RAF until an April 1940 contract was inked to prepare a prototype. Unlike all other American fighters at the time, the new airplane was conceived from the start to meet the evolving requirements of air combat then experienced in Europe. North American's president, James H. "Dutch" Kindelberger, had toured aircraft manufacturing facilities in Europe during 1938, so his company was already in tune with the most current aspects of fighter design and had been working on suitable concepts. From the outset, the new aircraft included heavy armament, self-sealing fuel tanks, and armor. It would be the first fighter featuring a laminar flow airfoil for reduced drag, combined with slotted flaps. The engine coolant radiator was placed under the mid-fuselage with an exhaust formed to create thrust.

Despite North American's lack of experience developing high-performance fighters, the NA-73 was designed and built in an extraordinarily short period, flying in October 1940. By that time, the British had already placed an order for 320 of the aircraft, with two more going to the U.S. Army for testing as the XP-51.

The first production NA-73 was delivered to the RAF in spring 1941 as the Mustang I. The fighter was clearly among the fastest and most maneuverable in the world, and had a heavy punch with four .30-cal. and two .50-cal. machine guns in the wings with 500 rpg, and two more .50s in the lower cowling with 200 rpg. The very clean design and 1,150-hp V-1710-39 made the Mustang faster than the Spitfire V and all other British fighters below 25,000 feet, and range exceed all as well. However, the Spitfire could out-climb the Mustang and the Allison lacked high altitude performance.[4] Consequently, the RAF employed the Mustang in the tactical reconnaissance and ground attack roles. It went into action during May 1942 and fought its first air battle in August. Its excellent range was

The American aviation industry's readiness to support urgent national requirements was greatly aided by foreign orders and lend-lease prior to the United States joining the war. A notable accomplishment to emerge from these endeavors was the North American NA-73 developed for the RAF and first produced as the Mustang I. (American Aviation Historical Society)

The U.S. Army was slow in adopting the North American Mustang fighter, initially developed for the RAF. However, a portion of a lend-lease order was requisitioned and became P-51s. These were armed with four 20mm cannons in the wings, this example in American olive drab with few markings. (San Diego Aerospace Museum)

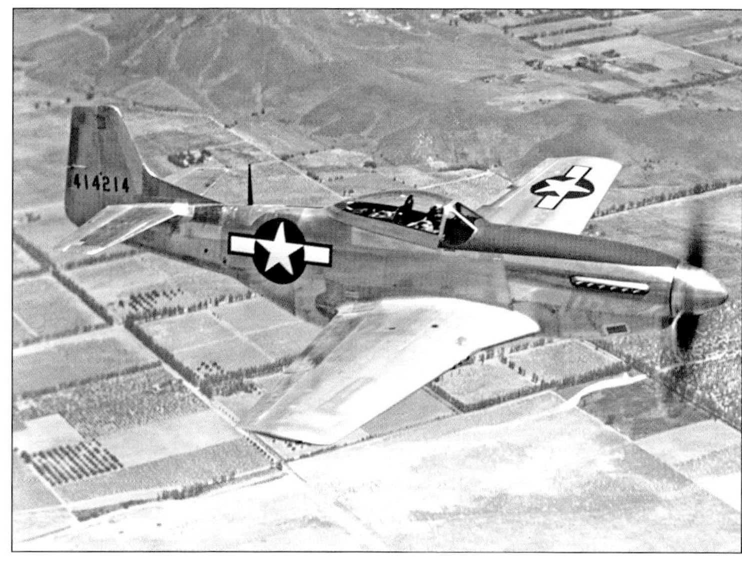

The speed, maneuverability, and hitting power of the North American P-51D Mustang was matched to extraordinary range to make its role as an escort fighter crucial to winning the war. The D and its antecedents knocked down more enemy fighters than any other American fighter. (National Museum of the United States Air Force)

demonstrated in October 1942 when it became the first fighter based in the UK to penetrate German airspace.

The RAF contracted for 300 more Mustang Is in October 1940, although introducing changes that produced the NA-83. A lend-lease order from the U.S. Army Air Forces followed in July 1941 for 150 Mustang IAs (NA-91) with four 20mm cannons and 125 rpg replacing the machine guns in the wings. To this point, preoccupied with its own development projects, only a few in the U.S. Army were paying attention to the XP-51s and seeking to establish the Mustang as an American fighter. Pearl Harbor and the intervention of Gen. Arnold changed all that. Starting in July 1942, the Americans retained 57 of the NA-91s on an emergency basis as P-51s, and some Mustang Is were also requisitioned.

This RAF Mustang III models the Malcolm Hood, a bulged canopy for greater headroom in a notoriously cramped cockpit. Some UK-based Army Air Forces units copied the feature. The bubble canopy of the P-51D offered the same increased comfort plus all-around vision. (Ray Wagner Collection)

The U.S. Army finally placed its own order in early 1942 for 500 dive-bomber variants of the Mustang as the A-36A (which see). Having then obtained funds for pursuit aircraft, 1,200 P-51As (NA-99) were ordered in August 1942. These were powered with the V-1710-81 of 1,200 hp, 1,330 hp with war emergency settings at a critical altitude of 11,800 feet. To lighten the fighter, the P-51As carried four .50-cal. machine guns in each wing, two with 280 rpg and the others with 350 rpg. They also had hardpoints for two 500-pound bombs or 75-gallon drop tanks, alternatively 150-gallon ferry tanks. Only 310 of this model were accepted by the Army Air Forces, beginning in March 1943 and 50 going to the RAF as Mustang II replacements for seized IAs, before switching to the next model.

Simultaneous and independent investigations on both sides of the Atlantic lead to Mustang-production shifting to the Merlin powerplant. The -3 model of the Merlin 60-series adapted to the Mustang had a two-stage, two-speed supercharger with intercooler yielding 1,380 hp at takeoff, 1,330 hp at 29,000 feet, and 1,600 hp in war emergency low blower. The final two NA-91s were fitted with V-1650-3s in fall 1942, and were redesignated NA-101s, which were evaluated as XP-78s (MX-278) before becoming XP-51Bs. The heavier engine with updraft carburetor and different cooling requirements required substantial changes to the airframe. The belly radiator was increased in size, the radiator intake moved from the brow

When the Army Air Corps finally began accepting large numbers of Mustangs as fighters, these were P-15Bs and Cs with Merlin engines. They were among the finest combat aircraft introduced by any nation, and their range made them ideal for bomber escort. The prowess of these aircraft and their pilots is legendary. (San Diego Aerospace Museum)

North American P-51A characteristics:

span	37.0 ft	weight empty	6,433 lbs
length	32.2 ft	gross	8,633 lbs
height (parked, prop down)	12.7 ft	maximum	10,300 lbs
wing area	235.57 ft²	speed, max. (10,000 ft)	390 mph
fuel capacity (int. + ext.)	180+300 gal	cruise	293 mph
service ceiling	35,100 ft	range, normal	700 mi
best climb rate	3,800 fpm	ferry	2,400 mi

of the cowling to the chin, and a four-blade propeller substituted. The ailerons were also modified and the bomb shackles streamlined, the latter capacity increased to 1,000 pounds.

As expected, high-altitude performance of the Mustang was dramatically improved with the powerplant change, gaining almost 50 mph in top speed at the rated altitude of 25,000 feet, and climb rate jumping 35 percent. It was the fastest fighter when it first entered combat and with "legs," making it the solution for Allied bomber escort in Europe.

Based on projected performance alone, prior to flight test, the Army Air Forces wasted no time taking advantage of the metamorphosis of the Mustang. The service ordered 400 P-51Bs (NA-102) as well as the nearly identical P-51Cs (NA-103). The latter were manufactured at a Dallas plant expanded for this purpose. The American contracts were soon increased to more than 3,725 airplanes, including 1,000 Mustang IIIs for the RAF. Approximately 100 B/C Mustangs were supplied to China. The aircraft carried four .50s with 280 rpg for the outboard guns and 350 for the inboard, and retained the wing hardpoints for bombs or tanks. Some later B and C blocks went to six guns. P-51B-15s and C-5s substituted the V-1650-7 rated at 1,490 hp sea-level takeoff, 1,720-hp war emergency low blower at 6,250 feet, and 1,505 hp at 19,250 feet in high blower. This became the standard Mustang powerplant installation.

As part of a Fighter Airplane Range Extension Program, via an urgent July 1943 request, an 85-gallon fuselage tank was introduced behind the pilot with the P-51B-7 and C-3 blocks, and subsequently retrofitted to many earlier aircraft. The added fuel gave a range of 1,300 miles, or 2,080 miles with a pair of 110-gallon drop tanks. However, it moved the center of gravity (cg) dangerously far aft such that squadrons were ordered to fill to only 65 gallons, and the pilot was left with unpleasant options in the event of an engine cut on takeoff or on entering combat with fuel remaining in the tank.[5] A control system modification was required to preclude control reversal and potential wing failure during dive pullouts.[6]

The escort role was perhaps the P-51's greatest contribution to winning the war against Germany, and arriving on the scene when needed most. It was only after the grave bomber losses suffered during the Schweinfurt raid on 14 October 1943 that fighter escort to the target and back was seen as essential if the daylight heavy bomber offensive was to succeed. The first of the B/C aircraft reached Army Air Force units in the UK during November 1943. Their range and altitude capabilities were immediately put to use in the critical escort mission, and permitted more than 1,000-mile accompanied raids. The first such operation into Germany occurred during January 1944. Within months, the new Mustangs were appearing in the CBI and Mediterranean theaters.

The British, dissatisfied with the cramped headroom and poor rearward vision within the Mustang III's cockpit, introduced the Malcolm Hood, a bulged, frame-less, sliding canopy also used on Spitfires. The Americans adapted this to some of their aircraft while engineering more suitable changes to the P-51 beginning in fall 1943. The Mustang took an approach similar to the Typhoon, the aft fuselage cut down and a blown-bubble canopy introduced, in addition to other refinements. The resulting fighter became the definitive Mustang, the P-51D (NA-109). Soon a dorsal fin was added to the vertical stabilizer to improve directional control degraded by shallowing the aft fuselage. The fin was also retrofitted to some Bs and Cs in an effort to correct endemic directional "snaking" with the Mustang.

During escort duties, the P-51D matched anything the enemy could put up until the advent of the Messerschmitt Me 262 jet fighter. The two hardpoints accommodated two 1,000-pound bombs or two of the lightweight compressed-paper 108-gallon tanks (or standard 75-gallon units). The 165-gallon drop tanks were introduced for the exceptionally long B-29 escort missions from Iwo Jima to Tokyo. The P-51D's extraordinary range was the longest of any Allied fighter.

With the all-important engine cooling system in the belly, and as such exposed to ground fire, the Mustang's vulnerability in the fighter-bomber role was carefully considered as it took on more and more such missions. The role was enhanced with a return of two additional .50-cal. machine guns. The installation was re-engineered to reduce the incidence of jamming during maneuvers. Ten rocket launch points were introduced – six with bomb racks installed. They could also carry two of the bunched trio of tubes for launch of 4.5-inch rockets.

Almost 8,000 of these airplanes emerged from California (P-51D) and Texas (P-51K) during the war. The 1,500 P-51Ks (NA-111) differed principally by a change in propellers. More than 600 D/Ks went to Britain as Mustang IVs. Commonwealth Aircraft in Australia tooled up to manufacture the P-51D as the CA-17 Mustang XX. Assembly began with 80 from 100 shipsets supplied by North American, but the war was wrapping up as the production line gathered steam to build their own CA-18s.

Production of the P-51 peaked at 857 in the month of January 1945, and the total ran to 15,486 aircraft. This and the combat record of the Mustang stand among the greatest American achievements of

North American P-51D and K characteristics:

span	37.0 ft	weight empty	7,125 lbs
length	32.3 ft	gross	10,100 lbs
height (parked, prop down)	12.7 ft	maximum	11,600 lbs
wing area	235.75 ft²	speed, max. (25,000 ft)	437 mph
fuel capacity (int. + ext.)	269+220 gal	cruise	363 mph
service ceiling	41,900 ft	range, clean (25,000 ft)	950 mi
best climb rate	3,450 fpm	tanks (10,000 ft)	2,300 mi

the war. In Europe alone, more than 213,873 sorties were flown – the second highest of any type. They brought down 4,950 enemy aircraft and destroyed a further 4,131 on the ground – the highest score of any type and more than half of all American victories in the theater. Hundreds continued in service for more than a decade after the war.

Misfits

Sharing Among Friends (Spitfire)

The Americans of the three RAF volunteer "Eagle" squadrons had been operating Spitfire IIs, Vs, and IXs, and carried on with these aircraft when they were absorbed into the U.S. Army Air Forces during September 1942. Two fighter groups deploying from the United States had worked up on P-39Fs, but these were judged unsuitable for Western European combat. Consequently, when they arrived in the UK during September 1942, they were given Spitfires under "Reverse Lend-Lease." The Spitfire Mk Vb had a normal loaded weight of 6,750 pounds, a maximum speed of 369 mph at 19,500 feet, maximum 4,750-fpm rate of climb, 36,200-foot service ceiling, and approximately 500-mile range on internal fuel. Armament was made up of two 20mm cannons with 120 rpg and four .303-inch machine guns with 350 rpg, all in the wing outside the propeller arc. The Yanks flew the Spitfire in the UK, North Africa, and Italy through April 1944, getting Mk VIIIs and Mk IXs as they went. The United States was the second largest user of the Spitfire besides Britain, and the Americans operating the fighter did very well by the British airplane.

A Spitfire Vb of the 334th Fighter Squadron, 4th Fighter Group, still wears the codes for its former incarnation as the Royal Air Force's No. 71 Squadron of American volunteers. Army Air Forces fighter groups operated Spitfires in Britain, North Africa, and Italy between fall 1942 and spring 1944. (National Museum of the United States Air Force)

For the Foreign Crowd

Nations across the globe began an enormous rearmament campaign in 1938 in the face of the burgeoning militarist threat from beyond their borders. The United States was their principal supplier. In some cases, customers ordered aircraft and engines already being acquired by the U.S. military, or with changes. In other cases, these were planes developed at the manufacturer's expense. Many were evaluated by the U.S. Army and given American designations.

Weak Sister (CW-21, CW-22)

An aircraft that attracted some attention was the light and comparatively inexpensive Curtiss-Wright CW-21 Demon single-place interceptor. This first flew in September 1938 and had a .30-cal. and .50-cal. machine gun firing from the cowling, and the 1,000-hp R-1820-G5 propelling the plane to a top speed of 315 mph. Four CW-21s were acquired by China, only to end in crashes. Plans to assemble 27 others in-country were overcome by the Japanese offensive.

The largest sale was 24 CW-21B Interceptors to the Netherlands in spring 1940. Unlike the earlier models with the main landing gear retracting aft into deep underwing fairings, the B had the gear fold inboard flush with the lower moldline. Armament was four .303-inch machine guns in the cowling. The aircraft used the R-1820-G5, weighed just 4,500 pounds loaded, and had a top speed of 314 mph with an attention-grabbing 4,500-fpm rate of climb. However, performance was achieved at the expense of ruggedness, armor, self-sealing tanks, and heavy armament. Consequently, it was unlikely to prevail against a true fighter. The Netherlands surrendered in the face of German aggression before the aircraft could be delivered, and the aircraft were diverted to the Netherlands East Indies. The Japanese

This Curtiss-Wright CW-21 Demon is seen following assembly in Rangoon, Burma, December 1941, in preparation for delivery to China. The CW-21 was inexpensive and appeared to have reasonable performance by virtue of its very light weight. However, it was of little tactical value against the superior Japanese fighters. (San Diego Aerospace Museum)

The CW-21B upped the Demon's armament to four .30-cal. guns, although these were rapidly being found inadequate to consistently knock down modern fighters. Two dozen of the light fighters were acquired by the Dutch and wound up in the East Indies colonies. There they fell easy prey to Japanese fighters. (National Museum of the United States Air Force)

The Curtiss CW-22 was a two-seat version of the Demon with rear gunner. This early U.S. Navy SNC-1 Falcon trainer derivative is unusual in having a gunsight and what might be a gun port in the cowling. (Naval Aviation Archives)

helped demonstrate the CW-21B's deficiencies by chewing up the aircraft during February and March 1942 in the capture of Java, although the Interceptors scored some successes.

The Demon was transformed again. The two-place CW-22 had one forward-firing .30-cal. gun and another on a flexible mount for a rear gunner. The Netherlands ordered 36, and these also found their way to the East Indies. However, the war again intervened—the aircraft diverted to Australia after Java fell. There they found useful work, and even the U.S. Army operated a dozen. Approximately 75 more of the aircraft were exported to Turkey and Latin America as the CW-22B.

Quick Change (NA models, A-27, P-64)

In early 1938, North American Aviation developed the NA-44, a light attack spin-off of the successful line of military trainers. With world air forces arming-up and modernizing, many variants of this aircraft were sold abroad in the hundreds as an inexpensive multi-role combat aircraft. These had various combinations of cowl and wing guns, under-wing racks for light bombs, some two-seat and some single-place, fixed and retractable gear. These sales began in 1939 and eventually included the NA-46 for Brazil, NA-50 for Peru, NA-56 for China, NA-57 and NA-64 for France (most taken up by Britain), NA-68 (redesignated NA-50As) and -69 (NA-44s) for Siam (later Thailand), -71 for Venezuela, -72 for Brazil, and the NA-74 for Chile. Australia manufactured a model under license as the more heavily armed Commonwealth Wirraway.

The Siamese shipment became subject of a political imbroglio when the U.S. State Department revoked the export licenses in October 1940. The military government in Siam was agitating for transfer of former territory under the colonial control of France and was moving ever more into the Japanese camp. The North American deliveries were prohibited to prevent use of the aircraft against the French that would further Japan's expansionist aims. The 10 NA-69s were intercepted in Manila, the Philippine Islands, on 10 October 1940 while awaiting transshipment. The U.S. government confiscated these on the grounds of urgent national defense need. Six NA-68s were held up in California before shipment.[7] The aircraft sat while the American and Siam governments argued fair compensation. On 5 March 1941, the U.S. Army formally requisitioned the impounded aircraft.

North American Aviation developed a broad family of light attack and fighter aircraft as variants of its very successful military trainers. These sold briskly all across the globe before the war as an inexpensive means of quickly rearming. This fixed-undercarriage NA-46, bound for Brazil, is a typical example. (San Diego Aerospace Museum)

Ten NA-69s were confiscated while in the Philippine Islands and taken on by the U.S. Army as A-27s. Two of these light attack aircraft are seen at Nichols Field in 1941, operated by the 17th Pursuit Squadron. All were destroyed in December fighting during the Japanese invasion of the islands. (National Museum of the United States Air Force)

The NA-69s were comparable with the Army's AT-6 trainers, but with additional weaponry. It had the 785-hp R-1820-75, two .30-cal. machine guns in the nose and one on a flexible mount in back, and could carry four 110-pound bombs below the wings and a 500-pound weapon in the centerline. It exhibited a maximum speed of 250 mph and a 575-mile range. The U.S. Army Air Corps operated the aircraft in the Philippines as the A-27 (41-18890/9). They were all damaged in the Japanese attack on Clark Field, 8 December 1941, but two were repaired and made a marginal contribution until the nation fell to the Japanese onslaught.

The impounded single-seat NA-68s weighed 5,990-pounds loaded and were powered by the 870-hp R-1820-77. They were armed with two .30s in the cowl and two more in the wings, two

This North American NA-50 export fighter was photographed in 1939. It is representative of the single-seat, light multi-role combat aircraft sold to many nations during the 1930s. The NA-50 was one of several variants offered for sale, tailored to customer requirements with numerous engine and weapons combinations, among other features. (American Aviation Historical Society)

20mm Madsen cannons in underwing housings, and could carry four 110-pound bombs. Top speed was 270 mph, and the NA-68s had a normal range of 635 miles. The U.S. Army stripped out the cannons and the aircraft were initially operated at Luke Field, Arizona, as P-64 advanced fighter trainers (41-19082/7). They eventually became headquarters hacks as attrition reduced their numbers.

Get What You Pay For (V-48, P-66)

Vultee Aircraft developed a family of easily manufactured aircraft in the late 1930s based on common engineering and a few like assemblies for economical production. Among the family was the Model 48 Vanguard single-seat fighter. While the Downey, California, company failed to gain American interest in the fighter, the design caught the attention of Sweden. That country ordered 144 Vanguards on 6 February 1940 in a new Model 48C configuration. This had the 1,200-hp R-1830-33, increased empennage area, and introduced compound wing dihedral. A pair of .50-cal. machine guns was placed above the engine along with provisions for two .30s or a 20mm in each wing, the cannons to be installed by the Swedes.

The first Model 48C flew on 6 September 1940. However, Sweden's support of Finland against the Soviet Union ran contrary to the Roosevelt administration's goals. Additionally, there was concern Germany might violate Sweden's neutrality and occupy the country, so any new arms could well fall into Nazi hands. This led the United States to embargo shipments to Sweden beginning in October. Britain took over the order, intending to employ the 48Cs as advanced trainers in Canada. However, finding the Vanguard's performance did not compare with other lend-lease aircraft and its lack of self-sealing tanks unacceptable, they bowed out of the deal.[8] The

Six NA-68 light attack aircraft bound for Siam were seized by the United States before departing California. These were operated in the States during 1941 and '42, mostly at Luke Field, Arizona, as P-64s. Their trainer role eventually devolved to station hack until they could no longer be sustained. (San Diego Aerospace Museum)

The Vultee Vanguard 48C was selected by Sweden, but the U.S. government would not permit delivery. They were eventually provided to China under lend-lease as P-66s, but only after serving some months in the Army Air Forces. The one shown has blanked off cowling gun ports for the pair of .50-cal. machine guns. (Ray Wagner Collection)

Chinese, on the other hand, found the 48Cs acceptable and a lend-lease deal was arranged on 19 June 1941.

As with all such lend-lease aircraft, the Vanguards needed an American designation and so became P-66s (42-6832/975). The .30s were placed in the wings and some cockpit armor was installed. Deliveries began on 24 October 1941 in preparation for shipment to the Orient. However, after the 7 December attack on Pearl Harbor, these and almost every other warplane within reach was pressed into service to oppose a possible Japanese attack on the mainland. Some P-66s were operated at West Coast fields while others were stored as operational reserve.

The first shipment of 48Cs/P-66s was finally permitted to leave for China in February 1942. The rest followed through August after the last aircraft rolled off the assembly line on 20 April. Only 96 left the States as 15 aircraft were destroyed while in American service, during factory test flights, or while being ferried to the East Coast for shipment. Some were lost at sea, victims of torpedo attacks. The aircraft were assembled in India and more were lost in accidents such that possibly fewer than 79 reached China.[9]

The Vanguard had weak landing gear that could mean a broken tail wheel or a ground loop that often ended very badly. It was somewhat fragile and was comparatively lightly armed and armored. However, it was very maneuverable and the engine was trouble-free. The 7,100-pound gross weight aircraft reached 340 mph at 15,100 feet, displayed 2,520-fpm initial rate of climb, and had a normal range of 850 miles. However, the Chinese were frugal in operating the aircraft, and their contributions appear to have been minimal.

The Vultee 48Cs made their way to China in early 1942, although little more than half the aircraft were ultimately delivered to combat units. The light main landing gear structure is evident, proving the bane for any inattentive pilot that permitted a ground loop to develop. (Military Aircraft Photographs)

Chapter 4

Three XP-40Qs (second aircraft shown) were a final attempt at modernizing the Warhawk and permitting the design to remain in production. Coolant radiators were incorporated into the wing leading edges, the engine supercharged, and the aft fuselage redesigned to accommodate the bubble canopy for improved pilot visibility. No production was ordered. (National Museum of the United States Air Force)

ARMY MISCREANTS

All of the Army's frontline fighters began life before the United States entered the war and had much maturing to do before they could meet the enemy on an equal footing. The designs also had to evolve with the changing character of the war and the opposition's capabilities. Some of the types were consigned to a second-rank existence while others received the most attention. Application of the newest production resources (weapons, engines, etc.) to upgrade an existing design had to be weighed against the likely combat potential derived. The risk of interrupting an ongoing production line and deliveries to introduce a new model had to be assessed against the perceived value of the additional capabilities. To a large measure, these goals were accomplished admirably. However, there were many such projects that fell by the wayside.

Missing Links (P-40A, YP-40F, P-40H, P-40J, XP-40K, P-40P, P-40Q)

The Warhawk production pedigree, as characterized by the model letter listing, had obvious gaps – beginning with the P-40A. This first model, after the Model 81 P-40, was to correct the deficiencies evident in initial aerial combat experience abroad, most specifically introducing armor, self-sealing tanks, and greater firepower. It was also to replace 324 aircraft from the original P-40 contract that were deferred to permit early deliveries to Britain and France. However, requirements were evolving so quickly that the P-40B configuration gained the production contract while the earlier A was passed over with none being built.

Other little-known P-40 variants included the unofficially named "YP-40F" (43-13602, third production F) that moved the Merlin radiator aft in various configurations, including a volume added within the wing roots. The first P-40F (41-13600) was employed to explore solutions to directional control issues that ultimately became the aft fuselage extension. It also included adding a dorsal extension and, separately, increased vertical stabilizer/rudder area and the lengthening fuselage. Introduction of a later model

The directional stability complaints with the P-40 were addressed during F-model production with a fuselage lengthened 20 inches. This was initially tested on the first production example, which was also modified with a larger vertical tail and rudder. Both features are seen here, but the enlarged tail was not carried forward. (Military Aircraft Photographs)

The third production P-40F was employed in experiments that relocated the Merlin radiator progressively aft. The photo of this so-called YP-40F shows one such configuration with the radiator fairing like a distended belly aft of the unusually narrow nose. (Ray Wagner Collection)

Merlin may have been intended for the P-40H, but this did not come about.[1] Adding a turbosupercharger to the V-1710 on the P-40E was to produce the high-altitude P-40J, but this remained conceptual. Another airframe used to find a lower-drag means of incorporating the coolant radiator for its V-1720-43, and other experimental improvements, was the XP-40K (42-10219), this featured the radiators distributed into a deepened wing centersection to leave a pointed nose, like the YP-40F configuration. The P-40P was another attempt to mount an uprated Merlin, but this was also nixed before being built, the order for 1,500 converted to P-40Ns.

The large frontal area represented by the radiator was a large contribution to drag of the P-40. Efforts to reduce this drag and achieve improved performance included the XP-40K that had the radiators under the wing/fuselage center section. While this left a notably pointed nose, it proceeded no further. (Ray Wagner Collection)

The XP-40Q (Model 87X) was a concerted effort to inject new life into the Warhawk and keep the production line open by significantly modernizing the airframe. This saw the cowling frontal area reduced by moving the ethylene glycol coolant radiator into the wing panels while the aft fuselage was shallowed to accommodate a bubble canopy. Within the cowling was a two-stage V-1710-121 rated at 1,425 hp, 1,100 hp at 25,000 feet, and turning a four-blade propeller. Armament was reduced to four .50 wing machine guns. Two prototypes were created from P-40Ks (42-29987 and 45722) and a third from an N (43-24571).

The reduced aft fuselage and bubble canopy was first tried on 43-24571 as the unofficially named "XP-40N" and "P-40XN," apparently before the Q program began. The first Q incarnation (42-29987) had the original canopy, but the radiators incorporated into the wing leading edges outboard of the landing gear, displacing the inboard guns, were such that the nose was very narrow. First flight of this XP-40Q-1 was on 13 June 1943. Aircraft 42-45722 was modified in 1944 with the bubble canopy and the radiators in the centersection, *a la* the XP-40K, although a radiator scoop was present under the engine (at reduced depth). The XP-40Q-2 configuration was eventually mimicked by 42-29987 before being damaged beyond repair in Buffalo on 27 January 1943. A final change gave the engine water injection for 1,800-hp (war emergency power), retained only the chin radiators, and clipped the wings to a 35.3-foot span. This configuration was applied to 43-24571 as the XP-40Q-3.

Curtiss XP-40Q characteristics:			
span (clipped)	35.3 ft	weight empty	6,400 lbs
length	35.1 ft	gross	9,000 lbs
height	10.9 ft	maximum	10,000 lbs
wing area	236 ft²	speed, max. (20,500 ft)	422 mph
service ceiling	39,000 ft	range, normal	700 mi
best climb rate	4,167 fpm		

The P-40Q was the heaviest Warhawk, yet also the fastest. Suggested production armament was six .50s or four 20mm cannons, although the prototype had just four of the machine guns.

Only one of the aircraft was delivered to the Army Air Forces for evaluation, probably 43-24571. However, no orders were forthcoming. Even this big step forward could not match the performance of the P-47 and P-51 to justify interrupting P-40 production.

Cross-Dressing (XP-46, XP-53, XP-60, XP-62)

Look Alike (XP-46)

The Curtiss team, after winning the January 1939 pursuit competition, did not rest on its laurels. Preparing for an Army design competition in mid-year, they incorporated some of the features appearing on advanced warplanes introduced overseas. Curtiss' Model 86 offered a smaller and lighter-weight airframe than the P-40, the 1,150-hp V-1710-39 having the radiator once more under the fuselage, and wide-track landing gear retracting inboard instead of aft. Automatic leading edge slats ensured aileron effectiveness at slower speeds. The radiator system included a hot air exit ramp designed to create thrust. While coming in third, the Army still approved development of two prototypes (40-3053/4) on 29 September 1939 as the XP-46.

Almost immediately, the service began requesting changes to the design. Although the heavier armament, self-sealing tanks, and armor were reasonable additions at the time, they undercut the intent of lightweight and high speed. Postulated armament was as much as the two .50s low in the nose and eight .30s in the wings. The second aircraft, the XP-46A, was to be completed first without weapons such that it could enter flight test quickly to establish performance potential.

The XP-46 mockup inspection commenced on 4 March 1940. Not long after this, production appeared certain despite no aircraft having flown. Under the 18 April Foreign Release Agreement, the P-46 would replace the aircraft diverted to European customers. Beyond this, an export variant, the H86A, captured a French order for 140 on 10 May and Britain was expected to follow suit.

It was not to be. The growing pressure to deliver more fighters faster made it desirable to keep the

The first XP-40Q (43-24571) was painted in Army olive drab and probably photographed in mid-1943. Even to the end, the P-40 retained the partially exposed landing gear with faired strut. Still, performance was respectable but not outstanding. (National Museum of the United States Air Force)

Curtiss XP-46 characteristics:

span	34.3 ft	weight empty	5,625 lbs
length	30.2 ft	gross	7,322 lbs
height	13.0 ft	maximum	7,665 lbs
wing area	208 ft²	speed, max. (12,200 ft)	355 mph
fuel capacity (int. + ext.)	103-156+0 gal	cruise	322 mph
service ceiling	29,500 ft	range, normal	325 mi
average initial climb rate	2,460 fpm	maximum	717 mi

The XP-46 shared heritage with the P-40, but had a smaller airframe and sought to incorporate advanced features. Although France placed an order for the type, the U.S. Army preferred Curtiss concentrate on expanding P-40 production. It was hoped progressive Warhawk upgrades would yield performance equal to the XP-46. (Ray Wagner Collection)

The unarmed Curtiss XP-46A was captured in this rare color image from 1941 showing the then-typical Army Air Corps markings. The P-40 origins are evident with the notable exception of the landing gear retracting inboard, wing leading edge slats, and a more complex radiator housing in the belly intended to extract thrust. (Ray Wagner Collection)

P-40 production line humming along without the interruption required to transition to the P-46. Incremental changes to the P-40 airframe might achieve the same performance targeted for the P-46. On 24 May, Curtiss proposed dropping P-46 production plans, instead offering what became the P-40D with the same engine. The service consented within a month, although construction of the XP-46s went on.

First flight of the XP-46A was performed on 15 February 1941 without all of the required equipment installed. Its fully equipped twin, the XP-46, soon followed. These were delivered to the Army on 22 September, but performance tests were discouraging. The guaranteed maximum speed of 410 mph at 15,000 feet was demonstrated in the lightweight configuration, but the equipped aircraft fell 55-mph short at 12,200 feet. Consequently, Curtiss suffered a financial penalty and lost money on the project. Of course, focus had shifted to higher altitudes where performance fell off even more because the Allison lacked a suitable supercharger. The aircraft was also criticized as being difficult to maintain.

Misdirection (XP-53)

The Curtiss Model 88 was a recognizable extension of the XP-46 and first offered to the Army Air Corps during April 1940 in response to Request for Data R40-C. The concept proposed using a laminar flow wing with experimental Continental XIV-1430-3, rated 1,600-hp (war emergency power) at 15,000 feet with turbosupercharger, radiators placed under the centersection, and employing the XP-46 landing gear and 11.2-foot Curtiss Electric propeller. The design appeared worth pursuing, and it was granted designation XP-53 (MX-4) preparatory to a 1 October 1940 contract for one prototype. However, under terms of the April 1940 Foreign Release Agreement, the XP-53 became Curtiss' advanced design offered at no charge to the government.*

Discussions arrived at a mutually agreeable specification in July 1940 and go-ahead followed in August. Soon after, the Army requested a change from four to six .50-cal. wing guns. The XP-53 detailed design and initial construction proceeded. The aircraft was to have an empty weight of 7,650 pounds and gross 9,975 pounds. Span was 41.4 feet, and wing area 230 square feet. Maximum speed was projected at 465 mph at 18,000 feet, service ceiling 30,500 feet, with an average 2,344-fpm climb rate.

Six weeks after contract signature, during a conference on 1 October, the Army expressed a desire to install one of the new V-1650-1 Merlin 28 clones in the second XP-53 in the event the troubled V-1430 program failed. The two prototypes were placed on contract 28 October. In November, the request was to explore the potential

* *Under the Foreign Release Agreement, the government consented to domestically produced sales overseas provided like aircraft delivered to the Army Air Corps contained the armor and self-sealing fuel tanks ordered by the foreign customers. Rooted in the 25 March Release of Aircraft Policy, this required foreign customers to share their combat experience and insights for modernization. It also contained a clause requiring manufacturers to develop an advanced type based on the technology at no cost to the government.*

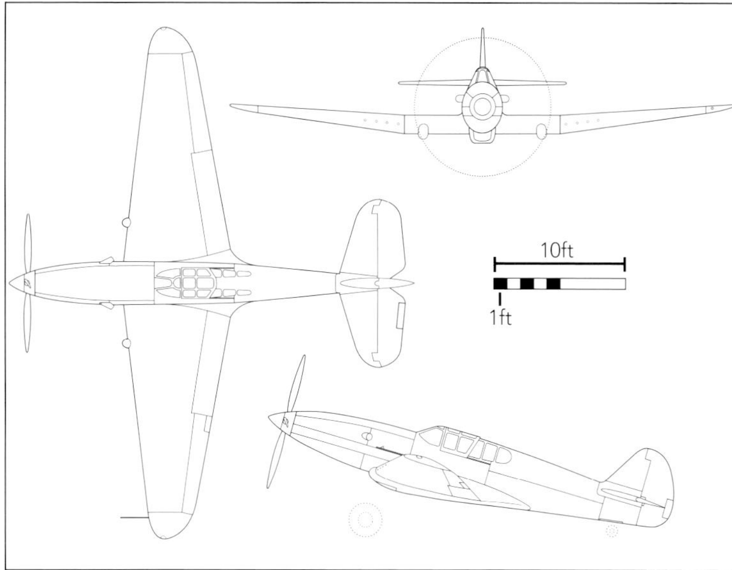

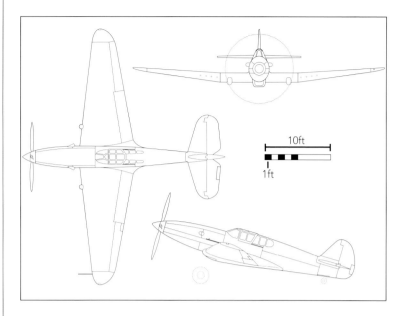

The XP-53 was to use the new Continental IV-1430 liquid-cooled engine in a clean cowling and under-slung radiator. However, long work on this powerplant eventually came to naught and the XP-53 was abandoned. The single airframe was used for ground loads testing, then scrapped. (Author)

for eight guns. However, the increase in wing area to 275 square feet raised the potential of pushing wing loading beyond the desired 35 psf. Top speed was also reduced to 430 mph.

It was quickly realized that the Continental was not coming together fast enough to allow a P-53 production run to leave its mark, and the design was falling short of expectations. On November 1941, the decision was made to put the first XP-53 (41-140) to use as a static test airframe supporting the Merlin-powered aircraft, by this time redesignated the XP-60 (MX-69). Anything useful to the XP-60 was removed and, after the test, the XP-53 scrapped.

Cavalcade (P-60)

The Curtiss preliminary design for the XP-60 (Model 90, 41-19508) was shown on 16 January 1941 and approved. The V-1650-1 was rated at 1,300 hp, 1,120 hp at 19,000 feet military power, and spun an 11-foot diameter Curtiss Electric three-blade propeller. Like the XP-53, the fuselage and empennage were derived from a P-40D, but with the radiator farther back under the nose, possessed a single-stage/two-speed mechanical supercharger, and employed P-46 landing gear. It was planned to mount eight .50s in the wings with 2,000 rounds.

The Air Corps was expecting the first of 1,300 P-60s to be delivered in July 1942. Consequently, eager for flight with the new engine, design changes were discouraged and nonessentials like armor, self-sealing tanks, and weapons, were left off the plane. In this way, taxi trials began in just 10 months, on 16 September 1941, with a British-built Merlin. Flight occurred two days later. The vertical tail was enlarged, along with some minor changes, to become the Model 90A. The aircraft was scheduled to have the self-sealing tanks and bulletproof windscreen installed from the XP-53. Military tests began in March 1942 and delivery occurred on 11 July.

Even as the XP-60 moved to assembly and test, Curtiss and the Air Force were looking beyond. Other programs farther along in development were employing the Merlin and there were doubts Packard could meet delivery numbers. It appeared more profitable to look at the V-1710-75 with General Electric B-14 turbosupercharger for 1,425 hp and 394 mph at 25,000 feet, an engine already proven reliable. This became the conceptual P-60A and a 29 October 1941 contract for 1,950 such fighters, valued at $107 million, was initiated with deliveries to begin in September the following year. This aircraft, again, shared a common layout with the P-40, but required an exceptionally deep cowling and more rounded, full-bodied fuselage to accommodate the turbosupercharger ducting. It was to mount six .50-cal. guns with 200 rpg.

In the meantime, XP-60 flight testing by the Army Air Forces had suffered delays from a pair of mishaps owing to landing gear failures. The engine was not delivering the promised power and the wing had not been finished within the manufacturing tolerance necessary to derive laminar flow benefits, so performance suffered. Top speed fell short of the guaranteed 387 mph.

The P-60A ran into its own problems. By 17 November, analysis made clear the fighter would be underpowered with the V-1710-75, the service seeking at least 1,500 hp. In addition, with the nation by then at war, it was more important to maintain high P-40 production rates without the interruption of introducing a new design into the Buffalo line. Consequently, a stop-work order on 20 December was followed by a 2 January 1942 decision to forego production preparations.

The program still had potential and so, at the same 2 January meeting, the move was taken to build a covey of experimental airplanes, each with different powerplants. These would include the XP-60A (Model 95A) powered by the V-1710-75 but with B-14 turbosupercharger, four-blade airscrew, Model 90 wing with increased dihedral, and six .50s in the wings with 1,200 rounds.[2] The XP-60B (Model 95B) would be similar apart from fitting a Wright SU-504-2 turbosupercharger. The XP-60C (Model 95C, MX-313) would get the inline Chrysler XIV-2220. All these aircraft employed the same basic XP-60 wing on fuselages of more rounded cross-section than the XP-60's Warhawk airframe. Additionally, Curtiss was tasked with building hundreds of P-47Gs to keep its assembly line workers occupied until P-60 production began.

The Merlin 28 engine is being installed on the XP-60 in this image. Note the bottom intake for the updraft carburetor. A supercharger was not part of the design. (National Museum of the United States Air Force)

Curtiss XP-60 characteristics:			
span	41.4 ft	weight empty	7,010 lbs
length	33.3 ft	gross	9,350 lbs
height	14.3 ft	maximum	9,961 lbs
wing area	275.4 ft²	speed, max. (20,000 ft)	380 mph
fuel capacity (int. + ext.)	135-228+0 gal	cruise	314 mph
service ceiling	29,000 ft	range, normal	800 mi
average initial climb rate	2,055 fpm	ferry	1,100 mi

As Curtiss resumed work, it quickly became clear the weight of the much-delayed XIV-2220 in the XP-60C would demand considerable fuselage changes or hundreds of pounds of ballast in the tail. Brought to the attention of the Army on 1 April 1942, it was August before the proposal came down to substitute an R-2800 with six-blade contra-rotating airscrew and four guns, promising more than 4,500 fpm climb. The parties agreed to the change in September.

By this time, the XP-60 had been passed back to the manufacturer to receive the V-1650-3 (Merlin 61) engine with two-stage supercharger and 11-foot diameter four-blade propeller, plus the enlarged vertical stabilizer of the XP-60A. Rated at 1,380 hp, the powerplant was expected to deliver 1,210 hp at 25,800 feet. In this guise, the aircraft became the XP-60D (Model 90B, MX-280) in August 1942 with 630 pounds more weight and an anticipated 390-mph peak speed. However, the aircraft was lost on 6 May 1943 at Rome Air Depot, New York, when its tail separated during a dive demonstration.

During XP-60A (42-79423) ground engine runs in late October 1942, a small fire began because of inadequate cooling to the shrouds surrounding the exhaust manifold. In order to move ahead quickly, standard exhaust stacks were installed and the turbosupercharger was removed along with all associated ducting. Although this permitted a maiden flight on 1 November, it prevented demonstrating the promised maximum speed. It is reported a revised turbosupercharger system was installed and tested.[3] Since the service wished to focus on the R-2800 approach, testing was spotty. Further work was halted on 6 November and the aircraft disassembled, some parts making their way into the other experimental aircraft.

Although Army interest was turning away from the multi-faceted experimental program, Curtiss' predictions for performance

The XP-60 used a P-40 fuselage but mounted the Merlin 28 and a new laminar-flow wing. The aircraft is shown late in its career (19 November 1941) after the vertical tail has been expanded and main gear doors added. (San Diego Aerospace Museum)

Curtiss XP-60A characteristics (performance estimated with turbosupercharger):			
span	41.3 ft	weight empty	7,806 lbs
length	33.7 ft	gross	9,616 lbs
height	10.8 ft	maximum	10,158 lbs
wing area	275 ft²	speed, max. (29,000 ft)	420 mph
fuel capacity (int. + ext.)	115-200+0 gal	range, normal	375 mi
service ceiling	32,500 ft	initial climb rate	2,560 fpm

Testing of the Curtiss XP-60 was disappointing when it was found the Merlin did not put out the expected power and the laminar-flow wing had not been finished to the fineness required to derive its benefits. The airspeed jump was meager, and the Merlins were needed by higher-priority programs. (National Museum of the United States Air Force)

with the two-stage, 2,000-hp R-2800-53 in the XP-60C was enough to win them a 27 November, $41 million letter contract for 500 P-60A-1s so configured, with intent for 2,500 more.* The first 26 were to be YP-60A-1 (43-32762/87) service test examples with R-2800-10 engines driving single-rotation propellers, the rest P-60A-1s (43-32789/3262) with contra-rotating propellers, requiring gearing changes to the Pratt & Whitney to be available in February 1944. All would have four .50-cal. wing guns with 300 rpg. Because these features would likely be unavailable for the first production aircraft, it was decided on 31 October to collect early data by putting a 2,000-hp R-2800-10 on the XP-60B (42-79425) with General Electric turbosupercharger and a four-blade propeller to become the XP-60E (Model 95D, MX-313).

Flight testing with the R-2800-53 and 12.1-foot diameter, six-blade dual-rotating propellers on the XP-60C (42-79424) began on 27 January 1943. The aircraft handled well except for high rudder and elevator forces.

A new element of urgency was added to the program when the Air Forces decided the XP-60E should join a fly-off of new fighters at Patterson Field, Dayton, Ohio, in order to determine the most promising designs to pursue into production. In late April 1943, the Army Air Forces requested the presence of the XP-60E at the event within four days. Since the aircraft had not even flown, the XP-60C was sent. However, just days prior, this aircraft had dropped a piece of cowling in flight and was undergoing repairs. It was quickly reassembled and sent off to Ohio.

The haste worked against a good showing by the XP-60C. A smoothing finish on the wing had flaked off the leading edge and

The XP-60D was the XP-60 reworked with a larger vertical stabilizer and plans to mount the Merlin 61 engine. However, testing after the tail modification, but before the engine change, proved its downfall, literally. The tail came off in flight. (San Diego Aerospace Museum)

* *Most wartime contracts began with a Letter of Intent (letter contract) under which work began immediately while full terms were negotiated. The formal contract usually followed months later. For simplicity, the Letter of Intent is treated as a contract in this text.*

Curtiss XP-60C characteristics:			
span	41.3 ft	weight empty	8,601 lbs
length	33.9 ft	gross	10,525 lbs
height	10.8 ft	maximum	11,836 lbs
wing area	275 ft²	speed, max. (20,350 ft)	414 mph
fuel capacity (int. + ext.)	178-360+0 gal	range, normal	315 mi
service ceiling	35,000 ft	best climb rate	3,890 fpm

The XP-60A incorporated the Allison V-1710-75 with turbosupercharger in a different fuselage. It is seen here on 14 October 1942 before engine runs that found the turbosupercharger a fire hazard, compelling its temporary removal. Flight in this configuration required standard exhaust stacks to be added, extending out the cowling. (American Aviation Historical Society)

prevented laminar flow formation, and the engine was not delivering full power. The opposition, such as advanced P-51 and P-47 models, was simply too far ahead in development. Another potential consideration for the War Department was concern with having Pratt & Whitney introduce the engines altered for the dual-rotation airscrew into its mass production scheme. Additionally, an analysis suggested the P-63 would be a superior warplane. Not surprisingly, the P-60A's production plans were shelved on 3 June 1943. The YP-60A-1s were killed on 19 July; the numbers reduced to 20, then just two YP-60A-1s with 2,100-hp R-2800-18s.

The lighter-weight propeller on the XP-60E installation mandated shifting the engine forward 10 inches. Following problems during initial engine runs that demanded an engine change, first flight of the XP-60E (42-79425) was delayed until 26 May 1943.

Testing of XP-60E (42-79425) continued until a January 1944 gear-up forced landing following an engine failure. Because of the

The contra-rotating propellers and enormous engine on the font of a beefy fuselage gave the XP-60C the appearance of power in this 24 February 1944 image. Only the canopy and wheels belie its Curtiss Warhawk lineage. (National Archives)

The 2,000-hp R-2800-53 put the enormous XP-60C in excess of 400 mph. However, the weight savings of a standard propeller appeared to equal the power benefits of the dual-rotation unit, and the program joined so many other Curtiss efforts on the shelf. (Jay Miller Collection)

This XP-60E was created from the XP-60B that never flew with its intended Allison powerplant. Instead, a R-2800-10 swung a four-blade propeller rather than the XP-60C's contra-rotating unit, but was still supercharged. (National Museum of the United States Air Force)

importance of the work, the engine was removed from the airframe and installed on the XP-60C to become another XP-60E (42-79424). Aircraft 42-79425 was eventually repaired, given the XP-60A's wings and the XP-60C's propulsion package, and assumed the latter designation. The new XP-60E (42-79424) was delivered to the Army Air Forces Proving Ground at Eglin Field, Florida, on January 1944. Official testing found the big fighter's performance had little to recommend it over existing late-war types, and the four guns were considered inadequate. In the air, it required close attention to trim in maintaining a steady flight condition.

Although Curtiss expressed a desire in May 1944 to be rid of the convoluted P-60 program, the service wanted at least one of the new YP-60A-1s, by then redesignated YP-60E since the contra-rotating propellers were out. The aircraft had a bubble canopy atop a fuselage that eliminated the turtledeck, and four wing guns. This aircraft (43-32763) finally flew on 15 July 1944. After one more test mission, the aircraft was delivered to Wright Field on 16 September where it received minimal attention. It was struck off charge 22 December without having been flown again.

A further reincarnated P-60 was to be the other YP-60A-1 with yet another R-2800 model as the XP-60F. This was quietly forgotten.[4] Thus ended the disappointing saga of the P-60s that cost taxpayers $8.88 million.

Curtiss YP-60E characteristics:			
span	41.3 ft	weight empty	8,285 lbs
length	33.9 ft	gross	10,270 lbs
height	10.8 ft	maximum	11520 lbs
wing area	275 ft²	speed, max. (24,500 ft)	405 mph
fuel capacity (int. + ext.)	178-368+0 gal	range, normal	315 mi
service ceiling	34,000 ft	best climb rate	4,600 fpm

End of the Line (XP-62)

Curtiss might have been accused of having "eyes bigger than its stomach," for it continued to pursue very ambitious fighter projects even with a full plate of work. Its biggest yet was begun with a proposal to Gen. Arnold, in his office, on 7 January 1941.[5] Curtiss wanted to build a fighter around the largest available radial engine, a turbosupercharged Wright R-3350 Cyclone 18. The aircraft, with pressurized cockpit, would have equally powerful armament with twelve .50-cal. machine guns or eight 20mm cannons. With Arnold's blessing, the XP-62 (MX-88) program was born on 16 January.

The long and frustrating P-60 program culminated in this one YP-60E. It was flown twice and then ferried to Wright field where it is seen in this photo. There it received scant attention and never flew again. (Author's Collection)

This Wright R-3350 Cyclone 18 was among the most powerful mass-produced engines in the United States. The 18-cylinder, two-row radial gained fame in the B-29 bomber, but also found its way onto several fighter prototypes. The R-3350-57 shown on 28 September 1944 delivered 2,200 hp from the 2,500-pound unit. (U.S. Government via Kim McCutcheon)

The 18-cylinder, twin-row R-3350 engine project was initiated in January 1936, but became plagued by troubles. It was a monster at more than 2,500 pounds, the heaviest engine installed on a fighter at that time. A new plant was built in Woodridge, New Jersey, and another by Dodge in Chicago, specifically to manufacture the engine while Wright facilities in Cincinnati also turned to R-3350 production. Despite enormous problems and delays, more than 30,000 of the powerplants were delivered during the war. Even in service, the engine was temperamental.

The selected R-3350-17 delivered 2,300 hp (2,250 hp in war emergency at 25,000 feet). Converting this power into thrust on the scale of a fighter mandated a contra-rotating propeller, and a 13.2-foot, six-blade Curtiss unit was selected. The Cyclone would provide excellent high-altitude performance, a guaranteed peak speed of 468 mph at 27,000 feet being specified. In the manner of the P-47, the turbosupercharger was placed under the mid-fuselage, requiring engine exhaust to be ducted back to the unit and pressurized air then run more than 10 feet forward to the engine. Maintaining 10,000-foot cabin altitude up to 35,000-feet made an upward-opening canopy hatch necessary. An engine-driven blower with armored ducting to reduce the risk of explosive decompression from battle damage provided pressurization. The latest laminar flow wing was also to be employed. The chosen weapons were four or eight 20mm cannons with 150 rpg.

Answering these unprecedented requirements, the formal Model 91 proposal was submitted on 29 April and go-ahead followed on 16 May. The $1.4 million contract was signed 27 June calling for an XP-62 (41-35873) and production-representative XP-62A, with first delivery in 15 months (28 September 1942) and the second three months later.

The program, housed in Curtiss' Buffalo facility, ran into immediate trouble. Within days of contract signature, it was learned the engine and propellers would not be ready in time to support the scheduled aircraft delivery. On 2 August, Curtiss requested a reduction in top speed to 448 mph, an increase in gross weight by 1,537 pounds, and the eight-cannon weapons package. These changes were approved, and the specification still pointed to a very capable fighter.

The mockup was inspected on 15-16 December 1941 with 90 major changes requested. However, a review on 1 January 1942, comparing the XP-62 with contemporaries at home and abroad, concluded that the 15,568-pound loaded weight should be cut to 14,000 pounds to remain superior. A concerted weight-reduction program was instituted with elimination of four cannons and propeller anti-icing gear recommended. Maneuvering flaps were later eliminated as contributing no benefit for the added weight.

On 13 January 1942, Curtiss proposed building 100 P-62As, with initial deliveries in May 1943 and production ramping up to 30 per month by October. This was approved by $4.2 million letter contract on 25 May. However, when it was realized Curtiss would have to slow its P-47G construction for Republic and the P-62 would not be competitive, the production contract was withdrawn on 27 July. Additionally, anything disturbing Curtiss production of the P-40 was undesirable and the R-3350 supply was

The notably small tail of the Curtiss XP-62 was acceptable given the contra-rotating propeller that eliminated torque effects. The dorsal extension to the fin was all too typical of American fighters during the war, usually added when flight testing found inadequate directional stability. (American Aviation Historical Society)

almost entirely consumed by the supremely important B-29 bomber program.

These were only the most overt signs that the program was losing steam. More than a year into the project, the first aircraft was 75 to 80 percent complete and still nine months from flying (estimated at April 1943), and more funds were required to finish. Then, the cockpit pressurization system, which would require powerplant modification, was delayed, pushing first flight out to 10 months beyond the original delivery date. The turbosupercharger source was changed for expediency. Curtiss suggested converting the second prototype to a low-altitude attack aircraft, but the Army Air Forces already had many such projects in development.

When the XP-62 finally flew on 21 July 1943, it was among the largest single-engine, single-place fighters built in America during the war. However, it still lacked pressurization and weapons were never installed. Other than collecting data on performance of the pressurization system, one of the first for a fighter, the program was of little further value. To focus on that goal, the XP-62A element of the contract had been cancelled on 21 September.

Curtiss XP-62 characteristics (performance estimated):

span	53.6 ft	weight empty	11,773 lbs
length	39.5 ft	gross	14,600 lbs
height	16.3 ft	maximum	16,651 lbs
wing area	420 ft²	speed, max. (27,000 ft)	448 mph
fuel capacity (int. + ext.)	245-384+0 gal	cruise	340 mph
service ceiling	35,700 ft	range, normal	1,300 mi
best climb rate	2,300 fpm	ferry	1,500 mi

After an initial battery of tests logging a few hours, the XP-62 stood down in February 1944 for pressurization system installation. However, priority dropped to such a level that by autumn the work was still in progress. By this point, the Army's fighter production program for the rest of the war was largely set, and the XP-62 was unlikely to contribute anything. The program was cancelled without the aircraft having resumed flight test, and it was scrapped.

When terminated, the XP-62 was the last of many Army fighter designs developed during the war by the hardworking Curtiss team, but none had "stuck" after the pre-war P-40. Contributing were shifting priorities within Curtiss and the War Department, the latter also shifting requirements, and engines that frequently did not materialize or had troubles of their own. These facts and the similarity of all these aircraft is testament to decaying vision and design talent.

Cobra Strikes (XP-39E, P-76, XP-63B, P-63D, P-63E, P-63F, XP-63H)

Coincident with Bell's Model 24 proposal of February 1941, which became the XP-63, was an offer to develop a refined Airacobra as the Model 23 with improved performance. By 26 February, the project moved ahead based on a Bell cost quote. The two XP-39E prototypes (41-19501/2) were ordered on 11 April for $510,000. The XP-39E prototypes had a larger wing, squared wingtips, redesigned empennage, and lengthened fuselage. The design incorporated greater fuel capacity, strengthened landing gear, the wing root radiator intakes were enlarged, and the carburetor intake behind the canopy revised. The Air Corps wanted the company to consider the upright V-1430-1 engine while Bell favored the inverted 1,325-hp V-1710-47.

A mockup and static test article were constructed. In the event, the V-1430 failed to materialize and the V-1710-35 was installed temporarily in the first prototype while awaiting the delayed two-stage -47, chosen for improved high-altitude performance. This aircraft also lacked the squared wingtips. The cannon, with 30 rounds,

The chunky appearance of the XP-62 belied potentially the most powerful single-seat, single-engine fighter built by the United States during the war. It was also the heaviest, was to carry a tremendous punch, and featured cabin pressurization. However, development ran so long that it was overcome by more urgent work. (National Museum of the United States Air Force)

The XP-39E program sought marked improvements in the Airacobra by introducing aerodynamic refinements and a two-stage engine. Although performance was somewhat improved, it was not sufficient to justify production of what was designated the P-76. This image of the second aircraft shows off the revised empennage. (Author's Collection)

was topped by a pair of .50s and another pair in each wing with 300 rpg. Consideration was given to installing maneuvering flaps on the test aircraft and the P-63. To this end, experimental maneuvering flaps were installed on a P-39 and flight-tested during the latter half of 1941. The outcome suggested the flaps were not beneficial and so were not carried forward.

The first XP-39E (41-19501) was devoted to handling qualities and armament trials while 41-19502 would work performance and powerplant tests. XP-39E 41-19501 flew on 21 February 1942 at the Niagara Falls Airport, but was lost in a 26 March spin after logging 14.9 hours in 35 flights. Bell's chief test pilot, Robert M. Stanley, attempted to deploy the spin parachutes that would pitch the nose down to break the stall, but instead pulled the handle to jettison the chutes. He was forced to abandon the aircraft. The automatic boost control and aftercooler within the engine were never installed.

By this time, production of the XP-39E was planned with 4,000 to be built as the P-76 at a new facility in Marietta, Georgia. These were ordered on 24 February 1942. However, by the time of 41-19501's crash, the Army was already convinced the model had no future. Although marginally faster than the P-39 (dive tests to limit speed were never performed) and with more high-altitude capability, it was the heaviest Airacobra yet and remained inferior by most other performance and handling indices. The 1,600-pound added weight compared with the P-39D was not suitably compensated by added engine power. It was also feared Bell was over-extending itself. P-76 production plans were cancelled on 20 May.

Owing to the importance of flight testing the V-1710-47, the XP-39E program continued with focus on engine cooling and performance trials. The second prototype took over testing on 4 April 1942, with the -47 and intercooler fitted. This aircraft had an engine failure and forced landing at Niagara Falls, sustaining serious damage on 15 May, the 27th flight after logging about 18 hours. It flew again only to suffer another accident on 8 February 1943. The nose gear failed in a forced landing owing to fuel exhaustion brought on by faulty gauges. Fortunately, a third prototype (42-71464) was authorized on 27 May 1942, created from the static test article for $270,000. This began flying on 19 September, logging 5.7 hours by mid-October.

Between 13 October 1942 and 7 March 1943, Allison used the third XP-39E at its plant in Indianapolis, Indiana, to optimize the supercharger installation and controls, putting 7.4 hours on the aircraft. Tests were also performed with various propellers seeking improved performance as well as to verify choice of propeller for the XP-63. A form-fitted external belly tank was also developed and flown.

Aircraft 41-19502 and 42-71464 were ferried to Wright Field on 9 and 12 June 1943, respectively. Both were also the subjects of further engine testing in Indianapolis. The Es became testbeds for altered vertical stabilizers and other changes that fed into the Kingcobra program; one tail squared all-around, one with the tip squared, and one "conical." The XP-39E effort appears to have been closed-out by the end of 1943 at a total cost of $920,000.[6]

Bell XP-39E characteristics:

span	35.8 ft	weight empty	7,631 lbs
length	31.9 ft	gross	8,918 lbs
height	9.8 ft	maximum	9,240 lbs
wing area	236 ft²	speed, max. (21,680 ft)	386 mph
fuel capacity (int. + ext.)	100-150+0 gal	cruise	205 mph
service ceiling	35,200 ft	range, combat	500 mi
maximum climb rate	2,800 fpm		

Other attempts to recover lost performance of the P-39 included methods of adapting a turbosupercharger or more capable supercharger with the least complexity. A proposal was to install the equipment in the decking behind the pilot's seat, the engine exhausts run up to it via external ducting. This was mocked-up on P-39D (40-6770) for flight testing. Another option, flight tested in fall 1941, placed a turbosupercharger and intercooler in a pod under the fuselage of 40-6770, an external pipe running back to the engine. The drag of these installations proved prohibitive.[7] None appeared to meet the criteria of simplicity, ease of integration, and effectiveness.

Extreme measures to improve the altitude performance of the P-39 are illustrated in this image. Placing a turbosupercharger and intercooler in a belly pod (dummy shown) on the P-39D increased drag to an unacceptable level, reducing top speed by 40 mph. (Jay Miller Collection)

A four-blade propeller on the P-39 was a rare sight. This one on a P-39C was apparently installed to flight test candidates for the XP-63. (Jay Miller Collection)

Another unsuccessful attempt at bumping up Airacobra performance had the supercharger and intercooler gear in a saddleback fairing atop the fuselage. This was mocked-up and flight tested, but experienced a 45-mph speed decrement. (Jay Miller Collection)

Bell P-63D characteristics:			
span	39.2 ft	weight empty	7,076 lbs
length	32.7 ft	gross	9,054 lbs
height	11.2 ft	maximum	11,044 lbs
wing area	255 ft^2	speed, max. (30,000 ft)	437 mph
fuel capacity (int. + ext.)	168+225 gal	cruise	188 mph
service ceiling	39,000 ft	range, normal	700 mi
average initial climb rate	2,500 fpm	ferry	2,000 mi

The improved P-39 configuration, in the form of the P-63, was itself subject to upgrade efforts. Attempts at fitting the Army's other successful inline engine, the V-1650, begat the XP-63B (Model 34, MX-436). The V-1650-5 engine was expected to yield 1,390 hp at 24,000 feet, 1,500 hp at 25,800 feet owing to the supercharger, and 426 mph at 23,400 feet, with a 40,000-foot service ceiling. The radiators where to be in a belly fairing, and XP-63A (42-78015) was chosen for this conversion. Empty weight was to be 7,206 pounds and gross weight 8,676 pounds. However, the modifications required torque shaft and gear changes that proved too bothersome, and it is unlikely the precious V-1650 would have been made available at the expense of Mustangs and other front-line types.

Instead of the Merlin, a 1,425-hp V-1710-109 was fitted to a P-63C as the sole P-63D (43-11718, Model 37) that had a sliding bubble canopy and a new wing with a 10-inch span increase. Adoption of the 37mm cannon permitted 48 rounds capacity. Performance was an improvement over earlier Kingcobras, but not over other production

The Bell P-63D showed the steady improvement in the Kingcobra design with increased wing area, new engine, and sliding bubble canopy. This XP-63D prototype was lost in a fatal accident, but the program rolled on to production as the P-63E. (Jay Miller Collection)

Bell P-63E characteristics:			
span	39.2 ft	weight empty	7,306 lbs
length	32.7 ft	gross	9,397 lbs
height	12.7 ft	maximum	11,033 lbs
wing area	255 ft^2	speed, max. (25,000 ft)	410 mph
fuel capacity (int. + ext.)	126+225 gal	cruise	188 mph
service ceiling	39,000 ft	range, combat	727 mi
average initial climb rate	3,290 fpm	ferry	2,150 mi

End of the line for the Kingcobra was the Bell P-63F in which configuration two P-63Es were completed. These were fitted with a 1,500-hp engine and redesigned vertical stabilizer. These changes were intended for later blocks of the E, but this never occurred. (Jay Miller Collection)

fighters. The aircraft was lost in a dive test, apparently owing to engine failure, with Bob Borcherdt still in the seat.

The P-36D, in turn, begat the P-63E (Model 41) with standard cockpit form intended for lend-lease. Orders for 2,943 of these aircraft were terminated at 13 (43-11720/1, -11725/35) with the end of the war.

Two of the P-63E orders were subsequently completed as P-63Fs (43-11719, -11722) with intent to demonstrate 449-mph maximum airspeed. Each was powered by a V-1710-135 at 1,500 hp and were distinguished by their notably larger and reshaped vertical tail and rudder, these changes intended for later blocks of Es. Coming so late in the war, nothing came of these plans.

A final Kingcobra design iteration was intended as a testbed for the Allison V-1710-127 turbocompound engine. This powerplant ported exhaust gases to a turbine that converted the energy to additional horsepower delivered via a direct drive into the reduction gearing and to the crankshaft. The powerplant was expected to realize 3,090 hp at 28,000 feet with water injection and 1,740 hp at

The P-63E featured the same changes as the XP-63D except for returning to the standard cockpit enclosure. This model actually entered production and 13 were completed before termination of hostilities ended the run. Relocation of the UHF antenna to the nose is a curious change. (National Archives)

33,000 feet dry.[8] One of the P-63Es was to be modified for the engine as the XP-63H (Model 45), and this was coming together at war's end. However, the program was cancelled in 1946, jet engines rendering further exploration of such technology moot.

Lightning Flashes (XP-38A, YP-38K)

An early Lightning was the XP-38A (Model 622, MX-6) that would have been the 13th P-38-LO (40-762). It featured a pressurized cabin to collect data supporting development of the XP-49 (which see). To partially compensate for the added weight of the modified cockpit, the 20mm cannon was to replace the 37mm, although no weapons were installed on the test aircraft. Developed under project engineer M. Carl Haddon, flight testing was conducted between May and December 1942 by pilot Joe Towle before being passed to Wright Field. A proposed Model 722 would have incorporated features of the 622 with those of the 222 and 322, and with P-38F or -G powerplants.[9] It was not pursued.*

The P-38K (Model 422, 42-13558) was a P-38G-10 airframe with 1,425-hp V-1710-75/77 engines and broad-blade, 12.5-foot diameter Hamilton Standard propellers. This was to provide improved high-altitude performance. The earlier XP-38K was the first P-38E rebuilt (41-1983). This may have had the same general modifications while 42-13558 was more production representative. In any case, the design failed to yield any marked improvement over the latest models and the engines were in short supply. Accommodating the new propellers would also have required raising the thrust line one degree, and this was considered too disruptive to the production line. The K was taken no further.

The first P-38E was modified to become the sole YP-38K optimized for high-altitude operations. Most noticeable are the broader propeller blades of greater diameter, turned by V-1710-75/77 engines. Performance was too little improved to justify the effort of converting production to this variant. (Author's Collection)

A number of P-38s were employed in armament trials. The RAF's Lightning Mk II (AF221, P-38F-13 43-2035) remained in the United States and was employed in aerial torpedo and smoke laying trials with weapons or tanks up to 1,900-pounds on inboard hardpoints. The test drops of the torpedoes were performed in December 1942. The earliest attempt to integrate rockets onto the aircraft had the usual zero-length launch stubs on the outer wing panels, seven per side. The P-38L-1 (44-24490) employed in these trials revealed that the firing produced wing skin deformation, prompting development of the launcher "tree."[10]

During 1945, P-38L-1 (44-24649) was given eight .50-cal. machine guns in the nose and pods under the outboard wing stations with twin-.50s for enhanced strafing effectiveness. Another test during the same period had three of the new .60-cal. machine guns in the nose of P-38L-1 (44-23601), the barrels protruding more than two feet from the skin.

The 13th P-38-LO was modified with a pressurized cockpit to become the XP-38A. This is evidenced by the heavy canopy framing bereft of the side roll-down window. It was flown in tests during 1942 without weapons. The data was valuable, but no pressurized Lightning was produced. (American Aviation Historical Society)

* *It is said the B and C designations were assigned to projects proposed by Lockheed in October and November 1939, but not developed. However, it has also been reported that with a collection of warplanes coming to maturity as D-models (B-24D, P-39D, etc.), the Air Corps had the idea of all new models in the period have D suffixes. Therefore, the P-38B and C may have been skipped to conform with this short-lived notion. "Lightning, Lockheed's Innovative Interceptor," Air International, May 1981, 238.*

A P-38 carrying torpedoes? Actually, it is a Lightning II employed in weapons carriage trials at the end of 1942, these also including smoke-laying tanks. Note the cables and braces stabilizing the torpedoes. Some other configuration was probably necessary for separation tests. (San Diego Aerospace Museum)

This P-38L, seen at Wright Field in the latter half of 1945, has been modified with eight .50-cal. machine guns in the nose instead of the usual four plus 20mm cannon. Four additional .50s are in pods under the outboard wing panels to increase the Lightning's ground attack lethality. (National Museum of the United States Air Force)

The .60 installation was tested at Eglin during 1946, but was found unsuitable owing to structural issues with the guns and links that failed under aircraft acceleration. Development of the .60-cal. gun began in 1939 and had a muzzle velocity superior to all other aircraft machine guns and round mass approaching that of the slower-firing 20mm cannon. It was entering production in 1943, but the 20mm had become so pervasive that the .60 was shelved. A concept for incorporating a 75mm cannon into an enlarged center fuselage of a P-38G was explored at Wright Field but did not advance beyond the drawing board.[11]

Numerous other field modifications for weapons and external stores were observed. Field modifications to the Fs introduced auxiliary pylons on either side of the production hardpoint for smaller bombs, the shallow mounts taking 100-pound projectiles, although this was seen in relatively small numbers. These required the weapon or tank on the primary rack to be released first.

Thunder Echoes (XP-47E, XP-47F, XP-47H, XP-47J, XP-47K, XP-47L)

The last P-47B, 171st aircraft retaining the original cockpit side-door, was given a pressurized cabin to improve support of the high-altitude bomber escort mission. Intake for the Eclipse-Pioneer cabin supercharger pressurization unit was placed in the root of the port wing. This XP-47E (41-6065, MX-146) was contracted for on 16 October 1941 and flew in September 1942 before the pressurization system was functional. Pressurization was achieved in July 1943, but much frustrating work remained owing to the immature system. The aircraft was finally sent to Dayton in July 1944 after changing to an R-2800-59 with a Hamilton Standard propeller. However, the Jugs seemed to be getting along just fine in combat without this added complication, especially as P-51s seemed destined to assume much of the escort responsibilities, and the growing air-to-ground mission was changing Thunderbolt emphasis. The aircraft still delivered invaluable data and experience with

This P-38L-1 was fitted with the typical distributed rocket launch points under the wings. However, tests showed firing caused wing skin deformations. This mandated development of the launcher tree shown with the insert on a P-38L-5. (San Diego Aerospace Museum and National Museum of the United States Air Force)

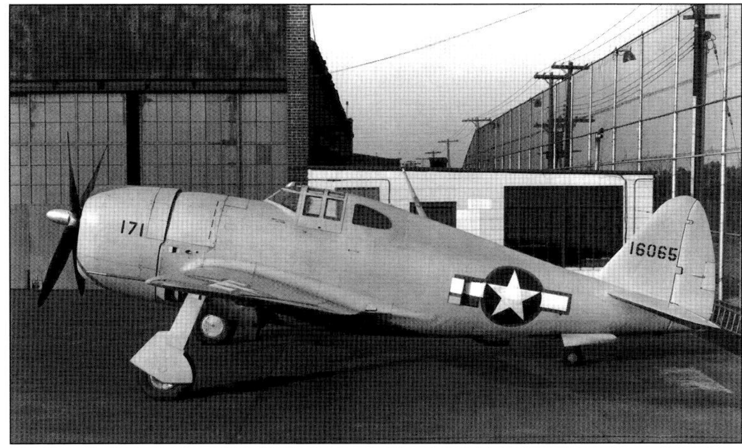

Use of the P-47 as a long-range escort was incentive to explore adding cabin pressurization. This was implemented with the XP-47E, seen here with the B-model's original cockpit door and a new "high-altitude finish." Pressurization was never introduced to production, although useful data was gleaned from the project. (San Diego Aerospace Museum)

With laminar flow airfoils all the craze after its demonstrated success on the P-51, it was only a matter of time before it was tried on the P-47. However, the resulting XP-47F showed little performance benefit. A long period of testing finally ended with its fatal crash. (National Museum of the United States Air Force)

cockpit pressurization systems that remained rare in fighters throughout the war.

Another almost inevitable experiment was mating a laminar-flow wing to the Thunderbolt, designated MX-116. Kartveli and project engineer Don Reed were principals on the project, but also with aerodynamicist Costas E. Pappas and NACA's Eastman Jacobs. This modified B, the 44th, became the XP-47F (41-5938) as completed on 25 June 1942. The wing planform differed in having straight trailing edges, 42-foot span, and 322-square foot area.

The XP-47F flew in July and was passed to Wright Field on 17 September where testing stretched into 1943, including a period at Langley between February and October. The design yielded 422 mph, an inadequate advantage to justify carrying it forward. The design possessed stability deficiencies that finally claimed the life of a pilot in a 14 October 1943 crash.[12] Republic had no enthusiasm for adopting the refined manufacturing techniques and quality control necessary to introduce the laminar flow technology to the production line.

Another sign of the times was an attempt to mate an inline, liquid-cooled engine to the P-47 airframe. The Chrysler XIV-2220 was rated at 2,500 hp and had 16 cylinders in a long inverted-V arrangement. It evolved from two automobile V-8s mated front-to-front such that the reduction gearing was in the middle of the engine. It employed hemispherical combustion chambers with spark plugs in the center for quicker, more uniform burning, and with integral two-stage supercharger and intercooler. It dated from June 1941 when automaker Chrysler shouldered its way into an Air Corps contract, and the equipment ran for the first time in December 1942. Plans for a flight test project were initiated in August 1943, but slow progress on the engine meant the airframe work did not begin until 1944. The project had always been simply a means of getting the experimental engine into flight, and was not aimed at any potential production.

Chrysler was to do the aircraft conversion in Detroit, but contracted it out to Republic's Evansville, Indiana, facility. Two P-47D-15s were extensively altered to take the XIV-2220, becoming XP-47Hs (42-23297/8). Due to wide cylinder spacing, the engine extended more than 10 feet in length. This gave the aircraft a startlingly long "proboscis" and a "beer gut" radiator fairing under the belly. The effort became moot in June 1944 when, soon after the XI-2220-11 was cleared to the full 2,500 hp, production plans for the Chrysler were set aside.* Consequently, Chrysler funded continuing work on the XP-47H in hope of salvaging something from the years of effort. The engine was mated to a CH-5 turbosupercharger after Chrysler failed in developing its planned axial-flow supercharger.[13]

The XP-47H looked fast but fell well short of the anticipated 490 mph in tests that began with a maiden flight on 26 July 1945. Engine

* *The V was dropped from powerplant designations by this time.*

The Chrysler XIV-2220-1 experimental engine is shown projecting nearly a dozen feet out from the firewall of the XP-47H. The 16 cylinders in inverted-V configuration were supposed to deliver 2,500 hp, but may have fallen short as the expected 490 mph was not even approached during flight test. (National Museum of the United States Air Force)

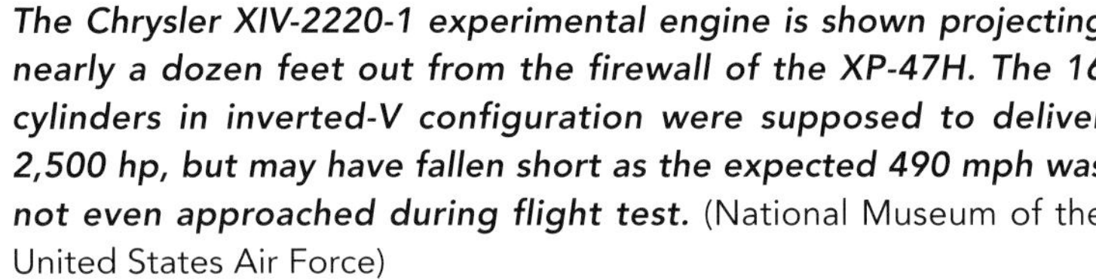

Republic XP-47H characteristics:

span	40.8 ft	weight empty	11,442 lbs
length	38.3 ft	gross	14,010 lbs
height	13.7 ft	maximum	15,138 lbs
wing area	300 ft²	speed, max. (30,000 ft)	414 mph
fuel capacity (int. + ext.)	205-295+0 gal	range, normal	770 mi
service ceiling	36,000 ft	economy	1,000 mi
best climb rate	2,740 fpm		

overheating required that the cooler-regulator doors be full open almost continuously, greatly increasing drag.[14] The engine had its share of other problems in test. On the 27th flight, with 18 hours on the aircraft, the test pilot executed a dead-stick landing after the propeller shaft failed. This brought the program to a standstill. As the government still owned the aircraft, it was decided to put a second test engine on the other aircraft and send it to Wright Field for evaluation. However, there was little enthusiasm for undertaking such tests, so the aircraft was instead ferried to Freeman Field, Indiana, in September 1945, where it was withdrawn from service. No weapons were ever installed. Performance with the Chrysler

The P-47 was selected as a testbed, if not potential production airframe candidate, for the IV-2220 inline engine. The result was the extraordinary looking XP-47H. By the time it flew in 1945, seen here over Evansville, Indiana, the combination had no future in any respect. (National Archives)

engine offered nothing special and, by this late date, no such exotic piston aero engine had a future.

An attempt by Republic to squeeze the most speed from the P-47 was initially conceived in a Wright Field meeting on 22 November 1942. After a Letter of Intent on 2 April 1943, a contract for two XP-47Js followed on 18 June 1943.* This was to include general design cleanup and a reversal of the creep in gross weight.

The first XP-47J (43-46952) had the water-injected, 2,800-hp R-2800-57 engine mounted slightly farther forward in a close-fitting cowling with intake fan for force cooling. The new 13-foot diameter propeller was fitted with a spinner. An exhaust ejection system sought to extract thrust from this flow. An intake under the nose provided air to the turbosupercharger. The canopy and rear decking were altered for lower drag, but also some improved visibility without going to a bubble. Guns were reduced to six .50s with 267 rpg in a wing revised for light weight. Fuel capacity was reduced and some radios eliminated.

When personnel were shifted to work the XP-72 project (which see) progress on the XP-47J was slowed . The first aircraft took flight on 26 November 1943. A test sortie in March 1944 touched 493 mph in level flight at 33,350 feet altitude. Afterwards, the General Electric CH-5 turbosupercharger and a larger diameter,

* *The suffix I was skipped.*

The Republic XP-47H was perhaps a look at things to come if the turbojet engine had not appeared in the late 1940s. The massive engine and turbosupercharger equipment made for an enormous and complex fighter that was stretching to the limit systems that could be maintained in an operational environment. (American Aviation Historical Society)

The XP-47J demonstrated 505 mph on 5 August 1944, a speed near the limits of what could be achieved with a piston engine and propeller aircraft. This remarkable accomplishment was all the more noteworthy in that it used a mass-produced engine and propeller at a time so much effort was being put into exotic technologies. (Air Force Flight Test Center)

A bit of work to clean up the P-47 design aerodynamically and lighten the airplane, and squeeze more power from the R-2800 with turbosupercharger, yielded the XP-47J. This was the fastest prop fighter of the war, but did not enter production. Plans to install a dual-rotation propeller were set aside. (National Museum of the United States Air Force)

Republic XP-47J characteristics:			
span	40.8 ft	weight empty	9,663 lbs
length	33.3 ft	gross	12,400 lbs
height	14.2 ft	maximum	16,780 lbs
wing area	300 ft²	speed, max. (34,450 ft)	505 mph
fuel capacity (int. + ext.)	287+0 gal	cruise	400 mph
service ceiling	45,000 ft	range, normal	765 mi
best climb rate	4,900 fpm	economy	1,070 mi

paddle-blade Curtiss Electric propeller were fitted. However, the XP-47J could still not be operated at full power owing to limitations of the special exhaust system. Nonetheless, a 5 August test achieved 505 mph at 34,450 feet under the hands of Mike Richie. The XP-47J was the first propeller-driven aircraft to exceed 500 mph in level flight and the fastest (unofficially) of the war – all without an "old-fashion" radial and single propeller. This earned 43-46952 the nickname *Superbolt* and it was adorned with a painting of the Superman cartoon character on the nose holding a lightning bolt.

Plans called for the second J to have a bubble canopy and R-2800-61 turning a contra-rotating propeller. However, the program was running well over budget, approaching half a million dollars, and the second plane was dropped in March 1944 before any assembly.[15] Tests with the dual-rotation unit on a P-47B "Double Twister" (possibly 41-6048) showed little benefit and Pratt & Whitney warned working out the remaining problems, which included reduction gearing, would not be simple.[16]

Production of the J was nixed in August 1943 in favor of the XP-72 that appeared even more promising, and there were the usual concerns with disrupting P-47 production for the changeover since the

The XP-47K was a P-47D block 5 airframe modified with a Hawker Typhoon bubble canopy and cut-down aft fuselage in place of the framed affair mated to the razorback spine. It took the Thunderbolt a step into what would be the future of fighter-bomber aircraft. (San Diego Aerospace Museum)

J had only about 30 percent commonality in tooling with the baseline design. The XP-47J configuration served as impetus for the more quickly realized P-47M.

The first Thunderbolt to be fitted with the bubble canopy was a modified P-47D (42-8702, the last block 5 aircraft). The rear decking was cut down and a late-model Typhoon canopy installed. Completed on 3 July 1943, this XP-47K was evaluated during that month. Another production change initially evaluated on an experimental model was expanded internal fuel capacity from 305 to 370 gallon in the wing destined for the P-47N. A P-47D was modified with this feature as the XP-47L (42-76614, last block 20).

Mustang Strays (XP-51F, G, H, J, L, M)

Concern was expressed with the steady weight growth of the Mustang during its maturation to the D/K models. Although an outstanding fighter, there were contemporaries with advantages, such as the Fw 190 that could roll nearly twice as fast and the Spitfire that possessed 1,200 fpm greater climb rate. At the request of the RAF, North American began examining the potential for a lightweight Mustang in early January 1943. Although ostensibly for the RAF, the lightweight Mustang was executed under an Army Air Forces contract and program management. Three prototype XP-51Fs (NA-105, MX-356) were ordered on 3 January 1943.* Notably, this was just prior to NAA's creation of the first P-51D. The goal was to get to 5,700 pounds basic empty weight from 7,000 – while ensuring maintenance access and no degradation of structural strength.

Edgar Schmued, principal P-51 designer at North American, traveled to Britain in spring 1943 to examine the Supermarine aircraft and hold discussions with RAF personnel for insights into its design and construction, in addition to examining captured or wrecked German aircraft. Lightweight construction was evident, permitted by the RAF's ultimate load factors that were lower than those specified by the U.S. Army. A structure designed to carry lower load factors would be light, but potentially less rugged and with less margin of safety than one designed to a higher load factor.[17] Building a P-51 to these standards promised a faster aircraft, but was essentially a new design in terms of structure and systems. The manufacturer also employed the new, high-strength, 75ST aluminum that allowed a reduction in skin thickness for a weight savings.

In June 1943, the XP-51F contract was amended to include five aircraft (43-43332/6) powered by the 1,380-hp V-1650-3. This was altered later to the 1,490-hp V-1650-7 engine while the aircraft were still under assembly. The British also agreed to deliver five 1,675-hp RM-14SM Merlins that would provide powerplants for the final two aircraft of the amended order as XP-51Gs (NA-105A). The Rolls-Royce engine employed fuel control metering versus a standard carburetor, with 25,000-foot critical altitude where it gave 2,200 hp in war-emergency burning-grade 150 fuel, and an 11-foot Rotol five-blade wooden propeller. The RAF requested one of each model for its own testing.

The Mustang airframe was extensively redesigned to eliminate unnecessary structure and substitute different materials to include plastics. Principal changes included removal of some equipment and substitution of small wheels with disk brakes on a lighter landing gear. So light was the gear assembly that a bungee cord served for ensuring downlock engagement with an emergency gear extension. A new and lower-drag wing with thinner section had a straight leading edge since the addition at the root was not needed to stow the smaller wheels. A revised radiator housing blended more smoothly

* *There is no clear evidence of a program with the E designation; it may have been simply skipped.*

The effort to cut weight from the Mustang and realize a jump in top speed began with the XP-51F. It succeeded in trimming 2,000 pounds from the airplane by careful redesign and materials substitution that produced a respectable increase in speed. The result looked like a Mustang with indefinable differences. (National Archives)

into the aft fuselage. The oil cooler was replaced with a heat exchanger. The longer bubble canopy reduced drag, but required hydraulics to move it and pilot seat adjustment. Maintenance considerations yielded a design with a demonstrated engine-change time of less than one hour. The fuel system was also reworked with two 102-gallon wing tanks. A three-blade, hollow-steel propeller was adopted for the F. This model had four .50-cal. machine guns with 250 rpg, the G six. Hardpoints were reduced from 1,000- to 500-pound capacity, with jettisonable racks. The result of all this work was roughly 2,000 pound shaved from the Mustang.

Bob Chilton flew the first XP-51F (43-43332) on 14 February 1944 from Mines Field, Los Angeles. Although the aircraft was limited to 475 mph and required full rudder by 480 mph to compensate for a yaw tendency, it eventually reached 493 mph. The next two aircraft followed 43-43332 into the air on 20 (43-43334) and 22 (43-43333) May. Aircraft 43-43332 remained a test aircraft at North American Aviation and later NACA Ames Aeronautical Laboratory, Moffett Field, in Sunnyvale, California. Aircraft 43-43333 was accepted by the Army Air Forces on 30 June and flown to Wright Field on 3 July. The third aircraft was sent on to the UK on 11 July for trials there as Mustang V, serial number FR409. A dorsal extension to the fin was added to the aircraft after a time.

North American XP-51F characteristics:			
span	37.0 ft	weight empty	5,635 lbs
length	32.2 ft	gross	7,340 lbs
height (parked)	12.7 ft	maximum	9,060 lbs
wing area	233 ft²	speed, max. (21,500 ft)	493 mph
fuel capacity (int. + ext.)	180+150 gal	cruise	379 mph
service ceiling	42,100 ft	range, normal (bombs)	650 mi
best climb rate	4,000 fpm	maximum	2,100 mi

Rework of the last two P-51Fs (43-43335/6) to take the RM-14SMs began in January 1944; the engine fitted the next month after arrival from Britain. The port wing tank had a 75-gallon capacity while the starboard had 105 gallons. Ed Virgin flew the XP-51G (MX-356) on 9 August. This and the next three flights were with a three-blade propeller. The Rotol was then substituted for a single flight by Chilton who found the aircraft directionally unstable. With the three-blade propeller reinstalled, the XP-51G appeared very similar to the Fs. Continued testing showed the RM-14SM was troublesome and not ready for production.

The last two of five XP-51Fs were reworked to take the Merlin RM-14SM engine with five-blade wooden propeller as the XP-51G. The propeller was unsatisfactory and replaced with a three-blade metal unit. However, the model was heavier than the F, offered little advantage in speed, and the Merlin was cranky. (Jay Miller Collection)

The XP-51G was limited to a 45,000-foot ceiling, as any more would have required cockpit pressurization. Best climb rate was nearly 6,000 fpm and highest speed 498 mph at 22,800 feet. Like the P-51F, North American worked hard to get the G over the 500 mph mark, but even a generous coating of wax failed to achieve this result. Aircraft 43-43336 was identified for shipment to the RAF as FR410, a Mustang IV with a four-blade propeller. However, it apparently never made the journey. Following the end of the war in Europe, the British lost interest and it was scrapped.

The second XP-51G was prepared for shipment to Britain, seen here with a four-blade propeller in this image dated 26 February 1945. The aircraft apparently never made it across the water, the RAF having lost interest, and it was eventually scrapped. (San Diego Aerospace Museum)

The lightweight Mustang work met with favor. However, the reduced armament and range was deemed too great a sacrifice and the lessened ultimate load factors undermined ruggedness. Consequently, the P-51H (NA-126) added 1,000 pounds back into the aircraft. It was ordered into production on 26 April 1944 without an experimental example, the contract eventually totaling 2,400 aircraft. The H had much in common with the F but with a smaller canopy, a dorsal extension, a four-blade propeller, and a 50-gallon tank behind the seat. The tank was vertically oriented and the fuselage lengthened 13 inches. These last two changes helped avoid the center of gravity issues experienced in the P-51B/C/D. The P-51H employed the V-1650-9 of 1,380 hp takeoff and 1,630 hp at 23,500 feet with water injection and burning 150 fuel. The cooling systems were considerably redesigned, with coolant and oil radiators in one unit. Choice of armament was six .50s with 390 rpg for the inboard guns and 260 for the others. Loading of the rounds was simplified with insertion of pre-loaded containers. It had the usual under-wing accommodations for six 5-inch rockets (10 with bomb racks removed) and two bombs up to 1,000 pounds.

Chilton initially flew the first of 20 P-51H-1s on 3 February 1945. The model achieved a maximum 487 mph at 25,000 feet, making it possibly the fastest production piston-powered fighter of the war. The 280 block 5s were followed by 255 -10s with minor equipment changes and an integral engine mount. A taller tail and rudder were introduced with the 13th aircraft. Some of the preceding Hs, and even earlier models, were fitted with a fin cap. Combined with the dorsal fin extension and lengthened aft fuselage, these changes finally resolved the long-standing dynamic stability problems endemic in the Mustangs and exacerbated with the redesign. Unresolved problems were wing skin buckling (usually due to overloading) and tail wheel downlock failures causing it to fold. The lighter main gear with small tires was suitable only for prepared fields.

Of the 370 P-51Hs delivered by mid-August 1945, none reached combat theaters before the end of hostilities. Orders for 1,445 more were cancelled after VJ-Day. Production wound down on 9 November 1945 with a total 554 constructed. Aircraft 44-64181 was provided to the UK as a Mustang IV, KN987, but it never left the States and was eventually absorbed by the Army Air Forces.

The P-51L (NA-129) was a variant of the H to be produced in Dallas and powered by the V-1650-11 engine with direct fuel injection.

North American XP-51G characteristics:			
span	37.0 ft	weight empty	5,750 lbs
length	32.2 ft	gross	7,265 lbs
height (parked)	12.7 ft	maximum	8,885 lbs
wing area	233 ft²	speed, max. (22,800 ft)	498 mph
fuel capacity (int. + ext.)	180+150 gal	cruise	315 mph
service ceiling	45,700 ft	range, combat (bombs)	510 mi
best climb rate	5,882 fpm	maximum	1,865 mi

North American P-51H characteristics:			
span	37.0 ft	weight empty	7,040 lbs
length	33.3 ft	gross	9,465 lbs
height (final)	13.5 ft	maximum	11,500 lbs
wing area	235.7 ft²	speed, max. (25,000 ft)	487 mph
fuel capacity (int. + ext.)	256+220 gal	cruise	380 mph
service ceiling	41,600 ft	range, clean (10,000 ft)	945 mi
best climb rate	3,333 fpm	tanks (10,000 ft)	2,400 mi

This late-model P-51H displays the lengthened vertical tail via the cap. The H was the offspring of the XP-51F and the last production Mustang. It was probably the fastest prop fighter to reach production during the war, but was too late to see operational deployment. (Tony Landis Collection)

Yet another of the late-war lightweight Mustang herd was the XP-51J. This returned to the Allison engines, mounting the V-1710-119. However, the immature powerplant caused many problems and the airplane was lent to Allison for continuing testing. The program died after the end of the war. (Jay Miller Collection)

An order for 1,699 was cancelled at the end of the war before any were completed.

Two more spin-off lightweight airplanes were also added to the F/G contract. The XP-51Js (NA-105B, 43-76027/8, MX-356) were to use the F airframe mated with a V-1710-119 engine.* Unlike earlier Allisons, the 119's two-stage supercharger helped delivered 1,500 hp at takeoff or 1,720 hp with water injection at 20,000 feet. The variable speed supercharger was regulated hydraulically by manifold pressure as commanded by throttle. The carburetor intake disappeared from the nose, moved to the belly radiator. The J kept the four guns of the F.

George Welch flew the first XP-51J on 23 April 1945. However, the engine was still immature and so prohibited from full power operation. The aircraft were eventually passed to Allison. The project appears to have expired like so many others with the end of the war. Testing never reached the stage to demonstrate predicted performance.

The Dallas plant was to manufacture yet another incarnation of the P-51D-30 as the P-51M (NA-124) with the V-1650-9A (water injection deleted) of which 1,629 were ordered. A single P-51M-1 was accepted in June 1945 and promptly ferried to a storage depot. This was followed by 64 more Ms completed in July and August as all contracts for Mustangs and V-1650 engines were being cancelled. All are believed to have been scrapped without being formally accepted by the Army. Not completed were 43 additional P-51Ms.

North American XP-51J characteristics (performance estimated):

span	37.0 ft	weight empty	6,030 lbs
length	33.0 ft	gross	7,550 lbs
height (parked)	12.7 ft	maximum	9,140 lbs
wing area	233 ft²	speed, max. (27,400 ft)	491 mph
fuel capacity (int. + ext.)	180+150 gal	service ceiling	43,700 ft
best climb rate	4,000 fpm		

* *The I designation was skipped.*

Chapter 5

Grumman performed a remarkable industrial feat in rapidly getting the new TBF-1 Avenger naval bomber into mass production in time to help arrest the Japanese bow wave of conquests. Although enormous for a naval aircraft, the Grumman TBFs and Eastern TBMs operated off all carriers. (Northrop Grumman History Center)

NAVY HEAVY LIFTING

Apart from the Navy and Marine Corps type-designated fighters, there were the numerous fighter-like carrier-based aircraft with "bomber" in their designation. As these operated in the same shipboard environment, were similar to aircraft intended for air-to-air combat, and with missions analogous to the Army's attack aircraft, they are reviewed in a like manner. Included are the scout-bombers and torpedo-bombers that reached their pinnacle during the war and evolved into multi-role fighters. This evolution found expression in the bomber-torpedo (VBT), the Department of the Navy's equivalent of the fighter-bomber (Chapter 8).

The Scout-Bomber Fades

Legacy

The Navy and Marine Corps kept dive-bombing viable in the inter-war years as an effective means of hitting point targets like moving vessels at sea or enemy forces engaged with Marines ashore. This role was combined with scouting, and bombs were replaced with additional fuel to create the scout-bomber type. At the outbreak of World War II, both services were still operating mostly biplane dive-bombers in the form of the Curtiss SBC Helldiver, Great Lakes BG-1, and Vought SBU. Filling nine squadrons, these were clearly obsolete aircraft by late 1939. The Navy was already replacing them with more capable monoplanes, although even these were quickly rendered outmoded by models introduced by warring nations abroad.

Two for One (SBC-4)

At the time of America's entry into the war, the Navy had two squadrons of Curtiss SBC-4 Helldiver biplanes at sea and the Marines had one squadron ready for action. Although this type dated from 1932, it was the final combat biplane produced in the United States with the last delivered in 1941. While the aircraft could carry 1,000 pounds of bombs, its top speed was just 237 mph and it ranged 590 miles with a 500-pound load.

Fifty Navy SBC-4 Helldiver biplanes were withdrawn and sold to France in early 1940. These were flown to Nova Scotia where all but six were loaded on the French carrier *Bearn*. Following the surrender of his nation, Adm. Darlan ordered the vessel, already at sea, to make for Martinique. Once there, the carrier and its aircraft played no further role in the war. Five of the SBCs remaining in Canada wound up in the UK where, dubbed Clevelands, their only useful purpose was as instructional hulks.

Last Legs (SB2U, V-156)

Among the new types on hand at the start of the war was the Vought SB2U Vindicator, the first metal-frame (albeit mostly fabric covered) monoplane scout-bomber with the fleet. It was also the Navy and Vought's first shipboard monoplane with folding wings and fully retractable undercarriage. The SB2U-1s and -2s carried a 1,000-pound bomb on the center sling or two 500-pound weapons on wing hardpoints. The centerline bomb-cradle swung the weapon down and clear of the propeller arc for the diving deliveries. A .30-cal. gun on a rear flexible mount and another in the wing provided for

This SB2U-2 of VS-9 takes the cable aboard USS* Charger *(CVE-30) on 29 October 1942. The fabric covering evident on the aft fuselage was by then archaic. Note the split flaps that were common high-lift devices of the time. (Naval Aviation Archives)

The Marines operated the Vought SB2U-3 as dive-bombers. This image shows off the centerline bomb crutch, under-wing hardpoints, and the pilot's telescope gunsight. The .50-cal. machine guns in the wing and for the rear gunner were too little by June 1942, when Zeros cut the Vindicators down readily. (Naval Aviation Archives)

defense against enemy interceptors. A 50-gallon tank could replace the centerline store. Attempts at wing dive brakes or employing propeller pitch for achieving the desired dive angle and speed proved unsuccessful. Consequently, the pilot had to lower the landing gear and accept a shallower dive. The SB2U-3 was developed principally as a Marine Corps dive-bomber with enlarged horizontal tail, added fuel load, plus other improvements. The .30s were replaced with .50-cal. weapons and with provisions for three more in the wings. The 825-hp Pratt & Whitney R-1535-02 Twin Wasp Junior powered the -3 model. This was the same powerplant as the earlier light models, so performance and handling suffered proportionally.

Having been ordered in 1934, the Vindicator was clearly second-rate by the standards of 1940 when it first entered battle. Between December 1937 and June 1941, 169 aircraft were delivered to the Navy department, representative of the low-quantity contracts of the period.

France acquired 40 Vindicators as V-156-Fs during 1939, these with "finger" dive brakes but without the bomb crutch that was not cleared for export. These aircraft were all destroyed fighting against German and Italian invaders. An unfulfilled 1940 French order for an additional 50 aircraft was taken up by the UK. These arrived during the first half of 1941 as V-156-B1 Chesapeakes. These aircraft had all four wing guns, added armor, and other equipment changes. It was found that at their heavier weights they could not be operated from the shorter decks of Royal Navy carriers with any useful war load. Instead, they served training and target tow functions before being discarded.

The Navy aircraft spent most of their time in the Pacific on submarine scouting duties. The Marines took the SB2U-3 into battle at Midway, but the slow speed, weak armament, lack of armor, and non-self-sealing wing tanks were acute deficiencies – not counting inadequate fighter cover during the battle. The aircraft did not match the valor of their crew. The remaining American Vindicators had exceeded their useful combat value, and were cast to training and other mundane roles until they had all been consumed by the end of 1943.

In the Way (SBN-1)

In December 1941, the Navy was still accepting the last of 30 Naval Aircraft Factory SBN-1 monoplanes with the 950-hp Wright R-1820-38. These had begun as the SBA-1 from newcomer Brewster. It had the usual aft gunner, perforated split dive-flaps, and a bay for a 500-pound bomb. The slow-moving program had originated in a 1934 competition and so the aircraft did not measure up to the standards of 1942 when they were required to fight. The aircraft saw only brief service as a front-line asset before being relegated to operational training. They were withdrawn early in the war.

Vought SB2U-3 characteristics:

span	41.9 ft	weight empty	5,634 lbs
length	33.9 ft	gross	7,474 lbs
height (parked)	14.3 ft	maximum	9,421 lbs
wing area	305.3 ft²	speed, max. (9,500 ft)	243 mph
fuel capacity (int. + ext.)	370+50 gal	cruise	152 mph
service ceiling (combat)	23,600 ft	range, combat (bomb)	1,120 mi
best climb rate	1,070 fpm	ferry (tank)	2,450 mi

Naval Aircraft Factory SBN-1 characteristics:

span	39.0 ft	weight empty	4,503 lbs
length	27.7 ft	gross	6,245 lbs
height (parked)	12.4 ft	maximum	6,759 lbs
wing area	259 ft²	speed, max. (15,200 ft)	254 mph
fuel capacity (int. + ext.)	136+0 gal	cruise	117 mph
service ceiling (combat)	28,300 ft	range, combat (bomb)	1,015 mi
initial climb rate	1,970 fpm	scout	1,110 mi

The Brewster SBA-1 was manufactured in small numbers and at low rates by the Naval Aircraft Factory as the SBN-1. Started in 1934, the program was delivering the last of 30 aircraft when the United States was shoved into the war. The mid-'30s-era warplane was of little value. (Ray Wagner Collection)

This SBD-1 Dauntless dive-bomber shows off the perforated split flaps, the upper outboard dive brake also visible. The Marine Corps operated these aircraft early in the war, its sister SBD-2 equipping Navy squadrons. They performed suitably despite being under-armed and with inadequate fuel in vulnerable tankage. (Jay Miller Collection)

Ol' Faithful (SBD)

The U.S. Navy's principal SB type during most of the war was the SBD Dauntless built by Douglas Aircraft Co. The SBD had fully retractable main gear and an R-1820-32 with 1,000-hp rating turning a constant-speed, three-blade propeller. The non-folding wing featured leading-edge slots and perforated split dive-flaps (segments separating to rotate up and down). Deliveries began in September 1940. The SBD-2 had a rear machine gun, armored windscreen, rubber-lined tanks, and hardpoints for tanks and bombs. Since the SBD-1 lacked these features, they were not considered fully combat capable. Consequently, the first 57 of 144 ordered on April 1939 were passed to the Marines while the remaining 87 went to the Navy as SBD-2s.

The SBD-2 armament consisted of a .30-cal. drum-fed machine gun on a rear flexible mount and a pair of .50-cal. machine guns in the cowling, although one nose gun was commonly removed for weight savings. The centerline cradle swung a 1,000-pound bomb, and hardpoints under each wing accommodated one 100-pound bomb each. The SBD-2 was also the first carrier aircraft equipped with an autopilot. Despite being a dated design by the standards of 1942, SBDs served well during the early, difficult period of America's involvement in the war where they played pivotal roles during the battles at Coral Sea and Midway.

The French ordered 174 Dauntless dive-bombers with the -52 engine for its Navy, requesting the introduction of armor and self-sealing bladder tanks and two guns, now belt-fed, fitted in the rear. A move to lighter Alclad aluminum from dural and deletion of floatation gear kept weight growth to around 500 pounds, such that performance was not terribly impacted. After the fall of France, the U.S. Navy took on these undelivered aircraft as SBD-3s, and increased the order by 410 after the declaration of war against the Axis powers.

Douglas, like so many others, had to shift to mass-production techniques in its El Segundo, California, plant. The -3s began reaching the fleet in June 1942. The SBD-4 began arriving in October 1942 with a number of internal enhancements,

This SBD-6 provides a fine study of the Douglas dive-bomber that served so well during the war. The centerline and outboard bombs are shown, as well as the twin .30-cal. guns with the radio operator/gunner. The barrel of one cowl-mounted .50-cal. gun is visible. (Naval Aviation Archives)

The last SBD was delivered in July 1944. It contributed to all major battles in the Pacific, sinking more Japanese vessels than any other aircraft and shooting down many enemy aircraft. Despite plans to replace it with the SB2C, the delays in that program meant the "Slow But Deadly" SBDs carried on through the end of the war, although off attack carriers or land bases after July 1944. In the Atlantic, the type sailed on escort carriers before being displaced by Avengers. A small number of SBDs went to foreign operators.

including a 24-volt electrical system supporting new gear. Of the 780 SBD-4s, most went to the Marines and many to the Army as A-24s (which see).

The SBD-5 finally increased power with the 1,200–hp R-1820-60, but this yielded little improved performance owing to the steady increase in aircraft weight. Two 58-gallon drop tanks were accommodated under the wing to extend scouting range. The centerline cradle then carried a 1,600-pound weapon and 325-pounds of bombs were mounted outboard. The old-fashion telescopic gunsight finally gave way to a reflector unit. The Navy took 2,409 of this model beginning in February 1943, manufactured at Douglas' new plant in Tulsa, Oklahoma. The SBD-6 used the R-1820-66 at 1,350 hp and had self-sealing bladder tanks. Deliveries began in February 1944, but the order was truncated with 451 produced. The Holmberg automatic dive pull-out device was introduced to the fleet at about this time, but looked upon with suspicion by the crews and generally ignored.[1]

Tough Row (SB2C)

The Curtiss SB2C Helldiver (Model 84) was intended to displace the SBDs and populate the new Essex-class carriers early in the war. The prototype SB2C was powered by the 1,700-hp R-2600-8 with two-speed supercharger and turning a three-blade Curtiss Electric propeller. The aircraft was to have two .30-cal. guns in the nose and a .50 in an aft powered turret. Capacity of the enclosed bomb bay was 1,000 pounds, with swinging bomb-cradle or a 130-gal auxiliary fuel tank. Two wing hardpoints could each take a 325-pound store or 58-gallon drop tank. The wings folded upward, were fitted with split dive flaps, and introduced automatic leading edge slats. Much of the movement of heavy elements was via an extensive hydraulic system. The SB2C was possibly the most complex single-engine aircraft to that time.

A single prototype was ordered in May 1939 following an August 1938 competition, but development complications stretched out the work. The XSB2C-1 made its maiden flight in December 1940, and was subsequently damaged in an accident the next February. It returned to flight test only to suffer a collapsed gear in July. While being rebuilt, substantial modifications were introduced to address

Douglas SBD-1 characteristics:

span	41.5 ft	weight empty	5,903 lbs
length	32.1 ft	gross	8,138 lbs
height (parked)	13.6 ft	maximum	9,190 lbs
wing area	325 ft²	speed, max. (16,000 ft)	253 mph
fuel capacity (int. + ext.)	180-210+0 gal	cruise	142 mph
service ceiling (combat)	29,600 ft	range, combat (bomb)	860 mi
best climb rate	1,730 fpm	scout	985 mi

Douglas SBD-5 characteristics:

span	41.5 ft	weight empty	6,533 lbs
length	33.0 ft	gross	9,352 lbs
height (parked)	13.6 ft	maximum	10,700 lbs
wing area	325 ft²	speed, max. (15,700 ft)	252 mph
fuel capacity (int. + ext.)	254+116 gal	cruise	153 mph
service ceiling	24,300 ft	range, combat (bomb)	1,115 mi
best climb rate	1,550 fpm	scout (tank)	1,565 mi

This July 1941 gear collapse mishap with the Curtiss XSB2C-1 was indicative of the Helldiver's myriad development problems that much-delayed the program. The aircraft is shown as it existed before extension of the forward fuselage to move the engine forward to assist in balance. (Naval Aviation Archives)

Wing leading-edge slats were a feature adopted by some designers. This Curtiss SB2C-1, photographed on 9 July 1943, shows off its extended slats and flaps during an approach with tail hook down. The slats energize the flow behind, in this case over the ailerons to maintain suitable roll authority at low speed. (Naval Aviation Archives)

stability issues. These included increasing the area of the vertical stabilizer and rudder, extending the forward fuselage and the engine mount each one foot. Cowling alternations and propeller cuffs sought to improve engine cooling. The bomb bay was also lengthened. The aircraft was then lost in December 1941 due to catastrophic in-flight structural failure while recovering from a dive. Testing resumed in summer 1942, to include service trials, but things did not progress smoothly as more and more problems were uncovered.

The first production SB2C-1 broke up in a fatal dive during January 1943, prompting a crisis to restore confidence in the plane and ensure combat suitability. Strengthened tails were already in work, but in the interim, the aircraft was prohibited from making clean-wing dives to limit speed. A planned power turret was discarded early, leaving a .50-cal. machine gun on a hydraulically rotated ring and frame mount. The turtledeck between the rear canopy and tail collapsed down to improve the field of fire for the gunner. As a consequence of all the design changes, the guaranteed empty weight of 7,868 pounds was exceeded by more than 2,225 pounds, promised maximum speed fell short by more than 30 mph, and landing speed was 10 mph high. These were only the most prominent of the program's many setbacks that greatly delayed delivery and fleet entry.

Mired in development hell, the slow progress of the SB2C brought criticism from within the service and from Congress, and nearly spelled its extinction. Certainly many other programs were terminated for less justification. However, the Navy had a big stake in the Helldiver. They had dictated very demanding requirements to take a dramatic step up in performance and were intending to wind down SBD production. The service was also responsible for some of the major design changes introduced to an already exceedingly complex airplane, contributing to delays.

Nearly 900 major design changes were introduced, along with thousands of additional minor ones that slowed production. Among the problems being addressed were persisting stability inadequacies, unsatisfactory handling qualities, high stall-speed that resulted in a disappointingly high approach speed, structural deficiencies, and lingering propulsion system issues. The tail area was increased further to unusually large dimensions proportional to the rest of the aircraft. Drawing upon lessons from combat abroad, armor plating was introduced, fuel capacity was expanded and self-sealing tanks substituted, and the number of guns doubled with the pair of .30s in the nose giving way to four .50s in the wings with 400 rpg and a reflector sight replacing the telescope. The .50 in back was replaced with a pair of .30s and 2,000 rounds, but this was soon reversed.

Production of 370 Helldivers had been ordered on 29 November 1940, even before first flight. First delivery was expected by the end of December 1941 and a monthly rate of 85 aircraft thereafter. Prior to initial delivery, the backlog increased to 3,865 units owing to the war coming home to America. While SB2C development was underway, the government built a new plant in Columbus, Ohio, to supplement the St. Louis production line, although with an inexperienced workforce. Even this did not meet demand, and so examples were built in Canada by Fairchild Aircraft in Longueil, Montreal (SBF designation), and Canadian Car & Foundry Co. in Fort William, Ontario (SBW). The first production SB2C finally took to the air in June 1942, but only around 50 had been delivered by the end of the year when fleet introduction occurred. Even after deliveries began, changes had to be introduced to cure remaining "childhood diseases" and poor workmanship. Aircraft were being rotated back to the factories for modification programs through the 601st SB2C.

After just 200 SB2C-1s were manufactured, production shifted to the SB2C-1C that incorporated most of the earliest modifications. In addition, the wing machine guns were replaced with a pair of belt-fed 20mm cannons with 200 rpg, and hydraulic flap actuators were installed to combat asymmetric flap conditions that caused several fatal accidents. The cannons and two .30-cal. rear machine guns with 2,000 rounds became the standard Helldiver armament. The 778 SB2C-1Cs, 50 SBF-1s, and 38 SBW-1s began flowing to the fleet at the end of 1943.

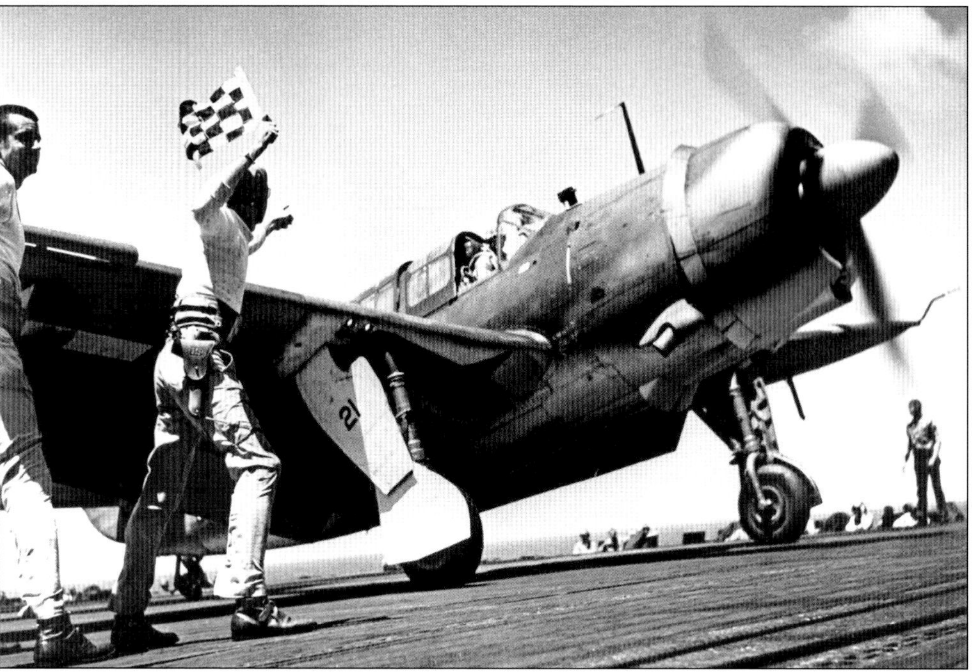

The SB2C-1 was a long time coming, and proved underwhelming when first introduced. A plethora of design and manufacturing issues had to be overcome before a warplane suitable for deployment was available. The Helldiver eventually filled its role, contributing substantially during the final year of the war in the Pacific. (Naval Aviation Archives)

Curtiss SB2C-1C characteristics:			
span	49.8 ft	weight empty	10,114 lbs
length	36.7 ft	gross	14,720 lbs
height (parked)	13.2 ft	maximum	16,607 lbs
wing area	422 ft²	speed, max. (12,400 ft)	281 mph
fuel capacity (int. + ext.)	320+246 gal	cruise	158 mph
service ceiling	24,700 ft	range, combat (bomb)	1,110 mi
best climb rate	1,750 fpm	maximum	1,895 mi

The type was so beset by lingering technical issues and the first carrier qualifications so problematic, that it was another 11 months before the initial units deployed. The experience was so discouraging as to bring new doubts that the aircraft could be effective, renewing suggestions that the entire enterprise be abandoned. The Helldiver missed its planned sailing with the USS *Essex* (CV-9) in March 1943 and later the USS *Yorktown* (CV-5), both taking SBDs instead. The SB2C finally went to sea in August 1943 and first saw action in November, although it offered few advantages over the Dauntless. Such are the consequences of concurrent development and production under the pressures of war.

The 1,112 SB2C-3s, 150 SBF-3s, and 413 SBW-3s were introduced at the beginning of 1944. These used the R-2600-20 powerplant at 1,900 hp, turning a four-blade propeller without spinner, which was omitted in an effort to recover lost performance. The retractable tail

This SB2C-4 reveals several features of the late-model Helldiver. The perforated dive flap is evident, as are the zero-length rocket launchers under the outboard wing panels. The under-wing bomb rack was also fitted. (American Aviation Historical Society)

This XSB2C-6 is most readily identified by the flattened cowling lip at the top and "paddle-blade" propeller, and less evident is the lengthened fuselage. The cowling encloses an R-2600-22 delivering a bit more horsepower than previous models. The model came too late to have any future as the war closed. (Ray Wagner Collection)

wheel feature was deleted, among numerous smaller improvements. The 2,045 SB2C/SBW-4 variant had wing hardpoints for up to 1,000 pounds of external stores, including up to eight 5-inch rockets, and introduced perforated flaps for improved handling in the dive and reduced tail buffet.

The Royal Navy was interested in acquiring 450 SB2C-2B Helldivers at the earliest possible date. In the event, only 26 of the SBW-1s were shipped to the UK by February 1944 as SBW-1Bs, the U.S. Navy giving its needs priority. These were so delayed and of such small initial quantity as to be rendered inadequate for combat deployment, and the British dropped the remainder of the order.

The final production variant, the SB2C-5, featured increased fuel capacity, a lengthened bomb bay, and an improved cockpit layout. The first of 970 -5s and 85 SBW-5s came off the line in February 1945, too late to see action. As early Helldiver models were replaced at sea by later models, the former became trainers and some were even scrapped before the end of the war. The cessation of hostilities prompted termination of contracts for 2,500 more SB2C-5s and 165 SBW-5s, the last of more than 6,200 delivered to the Navy by the end of October 1945 – the most produced dive-bomber of the war.

Curtiss SB2C-4 and SBW-4 characteristics:			
span	49.8 ft	weight empty	10,547 lbs
length	36.7 ft	gross	14,189 lbs
height (parked)	13.2 ft	maximum	16,618 lbs
wing area	422 ft²	speed, max. (16,700 ft)	295 mph
fuel capacity (int. + ext.)	320+246 gal	cruise	158 mph
service ceiling	29,100 ft	range, combat (bomb)	1,165 mi
best climb rate	1,800 fpm	maximum	1,920 mi

The Navy was so convinced they had the right airplane that there were eventually two dozen active dive-bomber squadrons operating the Helldiver as the standard bomber, at least one on each of the 20 large carriers and three shore-based Marine squadrons. The SB2C finally displaced the last Devastators at sea in summer 1944, even though small-deck carriers were unsuitable for the SB2C. Yet, the Helldiver retained many unpleasant stability and control characteristics that made it a difficult airplane to fly, and it was hard to sustain. Many who maintained and operated the troublesome early examples wondered at BuAer's devotion to the type they nicknamed "The Big-Tailed Beast," others attributing the SB2C designation to "SonovaBitch2ndClass." Few who flew even the later models were fond of the airplane. However, by the end of the war the Helldiver made good. The character of the war had changed by this time, and more Helldivers were lost in operational accidents than to enemy action.

Helldiver Miss (XSB2C-6)

A pair of production SB2C-1Cs (18620/1) were modified with 2,100-hp R-2600-22 engines within an altered cowling, paddle-blade propellers, and added fuel as the XSB2C-6 (Model 84H). To correct the endemic stability issues, the wingtips were squared and the fuselage lengthened. Carrier elevator dimensions had dictated the length of the original aircraft; two to fit in an area of 40x48 feet with a one foot margin all around. However, Curtiss had not used the full allowance, and the resulting short distance between wing and tail had been a principal cause of stability problems. The XSB2C-6 was ordered on 9 February 1944 and flown in August 1945, too late to be taken further. They subsequently became test-beds for other projects.

Sour Brew (SB2A)

Brewster's dive-bomber pedigree continued with the SB2A, which the company preferred to call Blaster. Emerging from a 1938-39 VSB (scout bomber) competition, it was a clear growth of the SBA-1 and promised a marked improvement over planes then in fleet service. The SB2A was developed in parallel with the SB2C in the event Curtiss failed to deliver.

The salient specifications of the VSB were 1,000-pound internal payloads carried to a 1,000-mile range. To meet this, Brewster conceived a single-place Model 340 airplane powered by the 1,700-hp R-2600-8. Apart from the bomb bay capacity of 1,000 pounds, one 250-pound bomb could be slung under each wing. It was to be armed with two .30-cal. machine guns firing through the propeller, with four more in the wings. A powered turret was to be equipped with twin .50s. This was originally to be a remote turret operated by the pilot before a more reasonable manned turret was pursued.

The Brewster SB2A was originally to have a gunner in a powered rear turret. The XSB2A is shown here at the Newark, New Jersey, flight test site, with a mockup turret and original small tail. Note the lack of greenhouse aft of the cockpit that later became standard. (National Archives)

A single XSB2A Buccaneer (Buno. 01005) was ordered on 4 April 1939. The mockup was inspected in Long Island City during August. A production contract for 441 planes was placed in December 1940 prior to first flight as compelled by the naval expansion bill. The French had expressed intent in July 1940 to buy the SB2A-1 as the Model 340F. This never gelled into a contract before France fell under the Nazi yoke. The Netherlands placed an order in June 1941 for 162 aircraft, which they named Bermuda (Model 340-17). The U.S. Navy aircraft (340-20) were to be equipped for carrier operations, while the French and Dutch orders were land planes.

Attempting to accommodate the requirements of all these customers into a single aircraft proved exceedingly difficult and, at one point, the designers simply had to start over. Delay followed delay as efforts were made during 1940 to introduce armor and self-sealing fuel tanks. The XSB2A-1 finally flew, well behind schedule, on 17 June 1941, under control of Woodward Burke. With an empty weight of 7,208 pounds, the aircraft achieved 313 mph at 18,000 feet. Development problems included aileron design issues that were positively hazardous until resolved, and roll response was never as desired. Buffeting with the dive-brakes out lead to these being perforated.

A principal source of concern was the turret. Flight with a mockup turret induced heavy buffeting and reduced rudder effectiveness due to blanking, prompting several consecutive increases in vertical tail size. Anticipated weight of the turret increased to more than 600 pounds, compelling the designers to extend the nose, placing the engine 10 inches farther forward for balance. Brewster's chief engineer, Dayton T. Brown, favored a partially retractable Maxson turret with hydraulic power, while the Navy pushed a Tucker turret with electric drive.

Despite the continuing evolution of the design, the prototype was accepted by the Navy as the SB2A-1 and re-serial numbered as Buno. 1632. It was flown to Anacostia for the first time in April 1942. Service testing found weight growth of more than a ton had reduced the top speed to just 275 mph against the expected 304, and maximum range was 1,750 miles. In July 1942, the Navy finally agreed to eliminate the turret. Its order was reduced to 203 SB2A-1s in the new configuration. The turret had already been abandoned by the Europeans, requiring a significant redesign to a long "greenhouse" from the pilot aft to a rear gunner station with a pair of .30-cal. machine guns.

The prototype had been built in Long Island and assembled at the Newark, New Jersey, test site. Production expanded to the new Johnsville plant, built by the government expressly to expedite Brewster production. However, productivity continued to be slow, aggravated by persisting design issues and the late arrival of engines.

The changes and design problems added up to substantial production delays. The last of the Dutch airplanes were supposed to be delivered in December 1941, but six months later only 25 had been produced. To speed delivery, the Navy had agreed to take a

The XSB2A-1 continued to be tested by the Navy after the turret shape had been removed and the aft fuselage faired over. This was to investigate performance and system fixes for the Buccaneer. However, the -1 model was abandoned as changes seeking an operationally suitable naval warplane continued. (Ray Wagner Collection)

shore-bound variant, the SB2A-2 (Model 340-26) to supplement the carrier-based SB2A-3 (340-27) with folding wings and arresting gear, among many other differences. The original SB2A-1 configuration was abandoned. These 202 aircraft had four .30s in the wings, two .50s in the cowl, and twin .30s at the rear. The French interest had been assumed by the UK in November 1940, these now to be Model 340-14 with 750 aircraft ordered. They were to have eight .30-cal. machine guns in the wings (as did the Dutch airplanes), two in the cowling, and two for a rear gunner (later reduced to a single weapon). Each wing could mount three 100-pound bombs or two 250-pounds weapons. The internal load was reduced to a single 500-pound bomb to ensure adequate performance. The Dutch aircraft emerged in March 1942, by which time the Netherlands had been occupied by Germany and their East Indies possessions overrun by Japan. The U.S. Navy took up these airplanes as SB2A-4s beginning in November 1942.

In 1942, Brewster had also become another supplier of the F4U Corsair. However, the Navy Department lost confidence Brewster could meet any reasonable production schedule for any of its obligations. By Presidential order, the Navy took over operating Brewster on 20 April 1942 because of low production rates, Navy discontent with quality control, strife among management, and press stirrings over an apparent history of fiscal malfeasance.

The new Naval Air Test Center (NATC) at NAS Patuxent River, Maryland, took up the testing of Buno. 1632 on 9 November 1943 as a single-seat aircraft with the turret area faired-over to continue rectifying design problems. "Pax River" was established to relieve the congestion at Anacostia in the crowded Washington, D.C. area. The SB2A-4s gave the Navy an early taste of what to expect from the -2s and -3s, and it was sour. The first SB2A-2 was flown in September 1942 and the initial -3 in May 1943. Testing showed performance fell well short of the specification, even with the weapon load reduced to a single 500-pound bomb, and control forces remained heavy. The SB2B-3 failed its shore-based carrier acceptability tests in the later half of 1943 and no sea trials were conducted.

The SB2A, in all its incarnations, was poorly suited for its intended role and not worthy to stand in the front ranks. The Buccaneer held little promise of contributing significantly to the war effort, yet was continued in the event the similarly delayed SB2C failed to materialize. However, by mid-1942 it was clear the Navy was committed to making the Curtiss plane the principal fleet bomber. Therefore, the Navy order was reduced to 80 SB2A-2s and 60 -3s to be delivered by October 1940, although only a handful were on hand by that date. After receiving 21 SB2A-4s, the Navy was trying to decide what to do with the worthless aircraft. The Marine Corps specifically sought them to train a night fighter squadron. However, their enthusiasm faded quickly. Apart from all the other deficiencies, spares were few and the brakes grabbed dangerously when wet. Several groundings ensued for propeller issues and after a vertical tail failed during a dive, severe flight restrictions were imposed until modified. The SB2A-2s and -3s were also consigned to training.

Considered useless as they were being delivered, Buccaneers were never employed in their intended role in any formal capacity, and never operated from a ship. In November 1943, any thought of using the aircraft operationally or in training was abandoned. They were flown far and wide as hacks. The last -4 was finally delivered in January 1944 after the Navy had accepted around 150. By this point, the aircraft were going directly to storage or deposited on gunnery ranges as targets. All were cast aside in June 1944 and soon scrapped.

The RAF, having requested many changes, began taking the aircraft in August 1942 and was immediately disenchanted with the handling and performance. At this point, the RAF felt it simply did not need a dive-bomber, and especially one of this ilk. Some 468 were

Brewster SB2A-4 characteristics:			
span	47.0 ft	weight empty	9,785 lbs
length	39.2 ft	gross	12,663 lbs
height (parked)	15.4 ft	maximum	13,811 lbs
wing area	379 ft²	speed, max. (12,000 ft)	275 mph
fuel capacity (int. + ext.)	174-421+0 gal	cruise	155 mph
service ceiling (combat)	25,400 ft	range, combat	750 mi
best climb rate	2,190 fpm	scout	1,750 mi

The SB2A was developed for European nations as the Bermuda and for the U.S. Navy as the Buccaneer (SB2A-3 shown). However, the final product did not measure up as a fieldable weapon. They proved of limited value as trainers, thus hundreds were stored and scrapped, or employed as targets. (San Diego Aerospace Museum)

The Douglas XSB2D-1 dated from 1940 as a large-capacity torpedo and dive-bomber with exceptional range. Typical of the period were remotely controlled gun turrets and dive brakes. Development ran long and requirements shifted such that the aircraft was no longer the optimal solution when production was contemplated. (San Diego Aerospace Museum)

accepted before further RAF production was cancelled. Hundreds were scrapped without leaving the States and only a few of the 206 or so aircraft reaching the UK were ever flown in service. Most were stored until discarded. Some were also provided to Canada as trainers, but similarly ignored. Attempts to employ Bermudas in towing targets proved futile, inadequate even in this role.

Including U.S. Army A-34 production (which see), final Buccaneer/Bermuda output totaled 771, none ever seeing combat. With the last delivered in early 1944, an exasperated Navy threw in the towel and Brewster was shuttered forever that July.

Near Miss (XSB2D-1)

With the Navy decision in summer 1940 to build Essex-class carriers, the service expanded orders for fleet aircraft and initiated development of new types. A design competition saw Douglas submit a concept on 3 February 1941 for a two-place scout-bomber that was a leap ahead in this category, seeking to make the aircraft equally suitable for torpedo delivery as well as dive-bombing. A 30 June 1941 contract for two XSB2D-1s (Bunos. 03551/2) followed.

Designer Ed Heinemann's team had to integrate principal features dictated by the Navy. These included the first laminar flow airfoil on a Naval aircraft, double-slotted flaps, and a pair of remotely controlled defensive gun power turrets, each with a .50-cal. machine gun supplied with a total of 800 rounds. The gunner sat in a revolving seat with a telescopic periscope sight top and bottom. More significant was the tricycle gear for an aircraft destined for a carrier.[2] Douglas adopted the inverted gull wing to allow for the bomb bay and to meet Navy-mandated wingspan without excessive gear strut length, but retaining essential area. A 20mm cannon and 200 rpg was placed in each wingfold where they were readily accessible. The Navy insisted on the 2,300-hp, supercharged R-3350-14. This turned a 12.7-foot diameter three-blade propeller. A weapons load up to 4,200 pounds included 3,200 in the bomb bay and two 500-pound weapons on wing hardpoints outboard of the gear posts. Two 1,947-pound torpedoes could be carried under the fuselage after the bomb bay doors were replaced with a fairing. Two 100-gallon drop tanks could be hung from the hardpoints and a long-range fuel cell could be installed in the bay.

With all the projects underway in El Segundo and the complexity of the design, progress on the XSB2D-1 was slow. The first was to be delivered 12 months after contract award, but this slipped substantially. The mockup was presented in August 1941. As with many early war developmental aircraft, production contracts were let before the first aircraft had substantially taken form. Thirteen service test examples (Bunos. 04959/71) were ordered on 9 April 1942.

The first prototype was completed on 17 March 1943 with dummy turrets and LaVerne "Tommy" Brown performed the maiden flight on 8 April. An effort was made at introducing dive brakes that did not disrupt the laminar flow of the wing. The "hat" type dive brakes, emerging from top and bottom of the outer wing

Douglas XSB2D-1 characteristics:			
span	44.6 ft	weight empty	12,458 lbs
length	38.6 ft	gross	16,273 lbs
height	16.2 ft	maximum	19,140 lbs
wing area	375 ft²	speed, max. (16,100 ft)	346 mph
fuel (int. + ext.)	350+200 gal	cruise	180 mph
service ceiling	24,400 ft	range (1,000-lbs load)	1,480 mi
initial climb rate	1,710 fpm		

panels, were replaced on Buno. 03551 with "picket fence" dive brakes of greater area that were supplemented with four perforated panels in the aft fuselage.

Flight testing showed the promise in the design, with marked speed and payload advantages on the competition. Hence, a production contract for 345 SB2D-1s (Bunos. 09048/392) was signed on 31 August 1943, delivery to be between November 1943 and February 1945. Assembly began on the first aircraft; however, the aircraft was overweight, complicated, and would likely be a budget-buster to manufacture.

About this time, the Navy revised its aircraft needs in response to war trends. Heavy defensive armament and multiple crewmembers were out so that speed and mission flexibility could be emphasized. Douglas was allowed to examine possible alterations to the SB2D-1 to meet the new trend, but production was no longer in the cards. The aircraft then evolved into the BTD-1 (which see). While the BTD-1 design was underway, the second XSB2D-1 was completed and flown on 11 August 1943. The June 1944 cancellation was expected. Soon after this, the aircraft were moved to NACA Ames to support research.

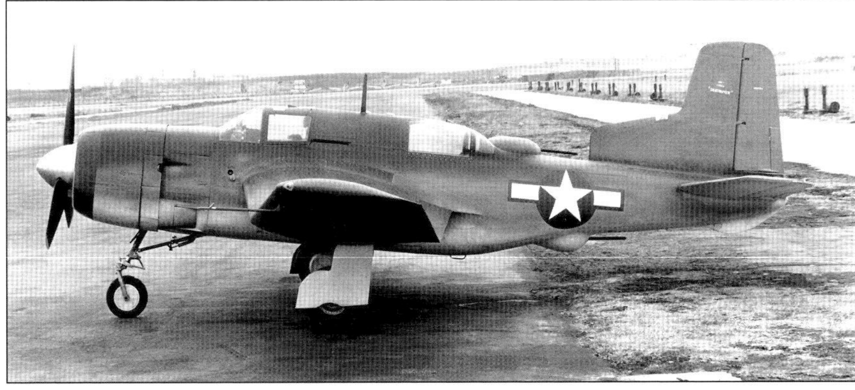

Weighing in at more than six tons, the XSB2D-1 employed double-slotted flaps on the laminar flow wing to achieve suitable approach speeds for a carrier landing. A 2,300-hp engine allowed a top speed of nearly 350 mph. Its tricycle landing gear was still unusual for a naval fighter. (Ray Wagner Collection)

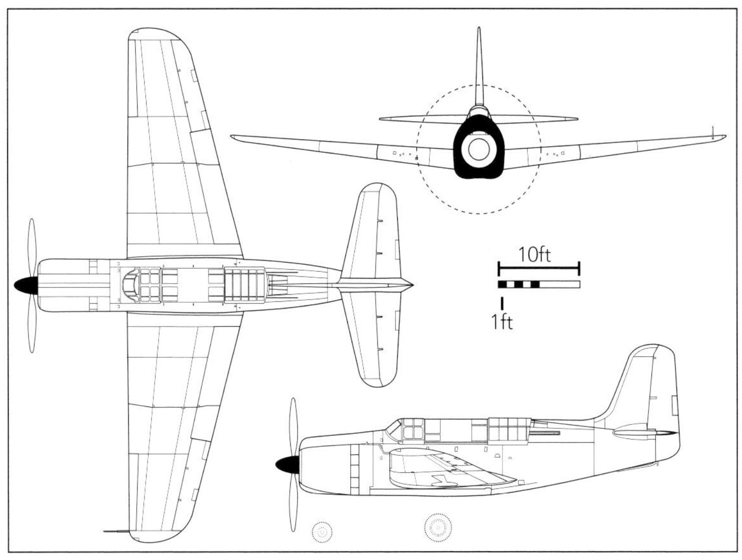

Growth of the Helldiver into the Curtiss XSB3C-1 was envisioned even before the first production SB2C emerged. The much-enlarged airplane would have carried more weapons as enabled by a more powerful engine, but the program did not extend beyond a December 1941 mockup. (Author)

Infant Mortality (XSB3C-1)

The Curtiss XSB3C-1 dive-bomber answered a Navy design requirement of 3 February 1941 and competed with the Douglas XSB2D-1. A further evolution of the Helldiver, the concept featured the 2,300-hp R-3350-8, an aft gunner, and had tricycle landing gear. It was to be heavily armed with six .50-cal. machine guns or four 20mm cannons in the wings. The wings also had hardpoints for two 500-pound bombs. The bomb bay could handle 4,000 pounds of bombs or two partially submerged torpedoes.

Two XSB3C-1 prototypes (03743/4) were ordered. The mockup, inspected in December 1941, emphasized the enormous size of the proposed aircraft. Certain aspects of the design, such as taller and higher aspect ratio tail with dorsal extension, revised horizontal stabilizer planform, and blunted wingtips compared with the SB2C, were tested on the XSB2C-6 aircraft.[3] Also to be featured was a power turret. However, as the design developed further during 1942, it was not measuring up to the Douglas XSB2D-1 and so the Navy terminated the XSB3C-1. Another factor was the design's requirement for the 115/145 aviation fuel that the Navy would have found difficult accommodating aboard ship or at remote shore bases.[4]

Torpedo-Bomber Saga

Sparse Stable Old School (TBD-1)

As with fighters, the Navy sought to move beyond the biplane for torpedo delivery in the mid 1930s. Concerns were that only one wing would mean a high stall speed and therefore fast approaches to the carrier and long takeoff runs. Wing flaps were, of course, the answer. Out of this came the new TB designation and the three-place Douglas TBD-1 Devastator as the Navy's first carrier-based monoplane. Typical of the period, the undercarriage was semi-retractable and the semi-recessed torpedo was carried under the belly. Up to 1,200-pounds of bombs could also be delivered from the centerline station, or up to a dozen 100-pound bombs from outboard wing mounts for horizontal bombing. Unusually, the TBD had corrugated skin over most of the wings and, like its sibling the SBD, possessed perforated split flaps. It was also among the first carrier planes with wheel brakes for improved deck maneuvering and the first with hydraulically powered wing folding.

The TBD-1 proved very worthy at the time and 129 were purchased, the last delivered in November 1939. These were the only torpedo-bombers in service when the country was drawn into the war. By that time, the 100 remaining Devastators were badly dated. The 900-hp R-1830-64 pulled the plane through the air a bit faster than 200 mph and combat radius was a little more than 200 miles. At the slow speed and atrocious climb rate, with just one .30-cal. machine gun in front and back, plus no crew or fuel tank protection, it was easy prey for Japanese fighters and shipboard gunners. These deficiencies were tragically demonstrated at Midway with 90 percent losses. Little was gained by these sacrifices owing to the limitations of the Mk 13 torpedo.

Douglas TBD-1 Devastator torpedo-bombers crowd the deck of USS Enterprise (CV-6), in the company of F4F-3 fighters, during April 1942. The Devastator was a significant advance when introduced in the mid 1930s, but was growing increasingly ineffective by the time it was committed to battle and was quickly replaced with TBFs. (Naval Aviation Archives)

Douglas TBD-1 characteristics:			
span	50.0 ft	weight empty	5,600 lbs
length	35.0 ft	gross	9,289 lbs
height (parked)	15.1 ft	maximum	10,194 lbs
wing area	422 ft^2	speed, max. (8,000 ft)	206 mph
fuel capacity (int. + ext.)	180+ 0 gal	cruise	128 mph
service ceiling	19,500 ft	range, combat (torpedo)	435 mi
best climb rate	720 fpm	(bomb)	716 mi

Although the Devastator had successes elsewhere, its day had clearly passed. It was out of production and lacked growth potential, and the replacement was in the wings. The greatly reduced force was withdrawn to the beach as trainers, test birds, and station hacks. The last was scrapped in November 1944.

Rough 'n Tumble (TBF and TBM)

A competition began in March 1939 to replace the TBD with a 300-mph airplane flying 1,000 miles with a torpedo in its bomb bay. Unusually, the perennial fighter maker Grumman won an April 1940 contract for two XTBF-1 torpedo-bombers. Its design (G-40) bore strong family resemblance to the company's F4F fighter, with the mid-wing on a thick fuselage and high-seated crewmembers. It was also enormous, becoming among the largest single-engine aircraft to serve in the war, especially for a carrier-based aircraft.

The general arrangements of the TBF-1 were typical of Navy bombers: a long greenhouse for the pilot, bombardier/ventral gunner, and radio-operator/dorsal gunner. Dorsal defense was a single .50-cal. machine gun with 400 rounds in an electrically powered dorsal turret developed by Grumman – the first on a Navy aircraft. A .30-cal. machine gun was placed in a ball mount at the bottom of the aircraft in a fuselage step, and a forward-firing .30 was fixed in the cowl, each gun with 500 rounds. The bomb bay took one "fish" or 2,000 pounds of bombs. Armor and self-sealing tanks were standard from the beginning. A rare aerodynamic feature was the fixed leading edge slots ahead of the ailerons. The aircraft was powered by the two-speed R-2600-8 with three-blade Curtiss Electric propeller.

Initially flying in August 1941, changes to the XTBF-1 were soon introduced addressing stability concerns, while work also was underway to remedy its poor engine cooling. An increase in tail area came in the form of a dorsal fin extension, and the engine mount

The Eastern TBM-3 fitted a more powerful engine to the Avenger airframe, but increasing weight of the type meant performance was virtually unchanged. Capability improvements included additional external fuel and ordnance capacity. This pair from VMTB-233 overflies the invasion fleet at Okinawa on 9 July 1945. (Naval Aviation Archives)

was extended a foot. The first XTBF-1 was subsequently lost to an in-flight fire during November. However, the second prototype soon took over the testing.

As a sign of the growing sense of urgency, a contract for 286 TBF-1 Avengers was placed in December 1940, well before the aircraft had left the ground. The first production aircraft was delivered in January 1942. By mid year, 145 more had been delivered, then 645 by year-end. With the country then at war, the first squadron quickly became acquainted with its aircraft and shipped out to meet the enemy. The Japanese gave them a thorough drubbing in the first encounter at Midway on 4 June. However, matters improved and the Avenger became the principal Navy torpedo-bomber for the remainder of the conflict.

Unlike the SB2C, the TBF could readily operate on escort and light carriers. The Avenger was versatile enough to serve as an attack aircraft and with the Marine Corps. Although the suspect torpedoes were less frequently carried after 1942, level bombing was again shown to be ineffective against shipping. Consequently, the Norden bombsight was removed and low-altitude skip- or glide-bombing tactics adopted. The Avenger also performed the U.S. Navy's first aerial mine laying during the night of 20 March 1943 at Palau.

A new TBF-1C model replaced the cowl machine gun with two .50-cal. wing guns and 300 rpg, had additional armor, featured wing hardpoints for 58-gallon drop tanks and bombs, and a 275-gallon long-range ferry tank could be fitted in the bomb bay. The Navy added zero-length launch studs under the outer wing panels for up to eight 5-inch rockets on many -1 and -1C aircraft. The cockpit behind the pilot, with seat and instruments, was deleted to make space for more electronic gear.

To more quickly ramp up production, Eastern was contracted in March 1942 to build the Avenger as the TBM, with assembly in Trenton, New Jersey. They had the first flying by November. Grumman manufactured 2,293 of the TBF-1s and -1Cs through the end of 1943, after which they focused on fighters. Eastern carried on, producing 1,000 Avengers in their first year of production and eventually turned over a total 7,546 – with a peak of 400 in March 1945 and the last in September of that year.

Grumman TBF-1 characteristics:

span	54.2 ft	weight empty	10,080 lbs
length	40.0 ft	gross	13,667 lbs
height	16.4 ft	maximum	15,905 lbs
wing area	490 ft²	speed, max. (12,000 ft)	271 mph
fuel capacity (int. + ext.)	335+60 gal	cruise	145 mph
service ceiling	22,400 ft	range, combat (torpedo)	1,215 mi
best climb rate	1,430 fpm	scout	1,450 mi

Eastern TBM-3 characteristics:			
span	54.2 ft	weight empty	10,960 lbs
length	40.0 ft	gross	16,940 lbs
height	16.4 ft	maximum	18,440 lbs
wing area	490 ft²	speed, max. (16,500 ft)	272 mph
fuel capacity (int. + ext.)	335+475 gal	cruise	163 mph
service ceiling	28,900 ft	range, combat (torpedo)	1,065 mi
best climb rate	1,480 fpm	scouting	1,065 mi
		ferry	1,510 mi

The weight growth of more than 2,500 pounds was detracting from performance and threatening the ability of the aircraft to operate from smaller carriers. This prompted an upgrade in engine to the two-speed R-2600-20 delivering 1,900 hp for the TBM-3s. Yet, the model was also loaded with more armor, the hardpoints upgraded for 100-gallon drop tanks or 1,000 pounds of ordnance, and the rocket launchers became standard. Hence, actual performance was little changed. More than 4,660 TBM-3s were delivered, the first in April 1944, as the last production variant.

Every carrier, regardless of size, had at least some Avengers onboard and the aircraft participated in every major engagement after summer 1942. They were instrumental in changing the character of naval warfare to one dominated by airpower. The Marine Corps operated the aircraft ashore and both branches performed level bombing of enemy emplacements. They were less effective in hitting ground targets directly with rockets or gunfire as their long line-up driving into the target made them vulnerable to ground fire.

Numerous changes were introduced to the Avenger during the war, some on the production line and some following delivery. The size, systems, and versatility of the Avenger made it an ideal choice for special equipment installations supporting its role or ancillary missions. Some early production aircraft were modified for operations in Arctic conditions, these TBF/M-1Js given boosted cabin heaters and other equipment.

Nearly 1,000 TBF-1Bs (export TBF-1), TBM-1Cs, and TBM-3s were sent to Britain beginning in 1943, initially named Tarpon, and 48 TBF-1s and -1Cs to New Zealand.

Avenger Theme (XTBF-2, XTBM-4, XTBM-5)

The missing model number between the TBF/M-1 and TBM-3 was an experimental aircraft. The XTBF-2 was ordered concurrent with the initial TBF-1 production contract and was a modification of the 21st TBF-1 (Buno. 00393). It had the XR-2600-10 and initially flew on 1 May 1942. Eastern then built an example production aircraft, TBM-2 (Buno. 24580). However, the two-stage engines were better directed to those aircraft with high-altitude missions, and the project was not carried forward.

A 2,000-hp R-2800-20 or -27 engine with Hamilton Standard 13.2-foot propeller from the F6F-3 was to be installed in the 200th

The Avenger was rugged, versatile, and operated off every carrier in the fleet. As torpedo delivery became rare, it moved to level bombing of shore targets. The workhorse airplane helped change the character of naval warfare to one dominated by airpower. (Naval Aviation Archives)

The XTBF-2 was created from an early TBF-1 (00393) by substituting a two-stage R-2600-10. Since the Avenger's mission did not require the altitude performance gained from the powerplant, which was in demand by other projects, the model was not carried forward. (Northrop Grumman History Center)

Another early variant of the Avenger explored without a unique model number would have seen many alterations in armament and propulsion system. The only change that actually appears to have been tested is the Martin turret with twin-.50-cal. machine guns shown here installed on the 200th TBF-1 (01746). (Northrop Grumman History Center)

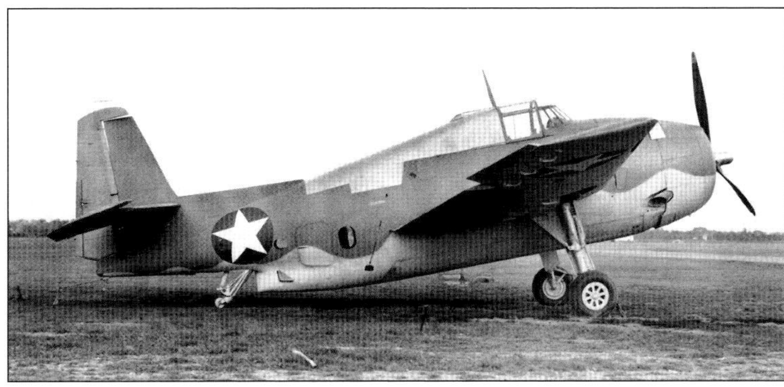

An early attempt at creating a specialized ground attack aircraft generated a startling conversion of a TBF-1 (00550), seen here on 26 July 1942. Removal of the turret and greenhouse still left a rotund bomber that performed little better than a standard Avenger. The unusual "FTBF-1" went no further. (Northrop Grumman History Center)

TBF-1 (Buno. 01746) along with a twin-gun Martin turret as the G-56. Other modifications were to delete the cowl .30 for two .50s in the wings, upgrade the tunnel gun to .50-cal., and increase fuel capacity. All this would have added 800 pounds to the aircraft. Tests with the turret were conducted in fall 1942, but the engine does not appear to have been flown, and few, if any, of the other modifications were performed.[5] The R-2800 was considered for the TBF-3/TBM-3, but there were many higher priority demands for this powerplant and so it was rejected in favor of an upgraded R-2600. The turret was also rejected. With firing interrupted twice as frequently to avoid hitting the tail, defense was actually less effective.

On 26 July 1942, Grumman flew a TBF-1 (Buno. 00550) converted in less than a month to a long-range, single-seat attack aircraft. This deleted the rear guns and crewmen, the greenhouse truncated behind the pilot and faired into the aft fuselage, while adding a pair of wing guns. However, the "FTBF-1" was still a deep-bellied bomber weighing only 100 pounds less than a standard Avenger, and at only 10 mph higher top speed, lacked any advantages for the fighter-bomber mission. It went no further. However, a TBM-3E (Buno. 69465, see Chapter 10) was modified with the same aim, although with a fighter-type canopy and greenhouse removed to allow the aft fuselage to be faired over.[6]

In answer to the evolving use of the warplane, the XTBM-4 was created from a partially completed TBM-3 to facilitate dive-bombing at up to 16,000-pounds gross weight. The airframe was strengthened for five-g loading, with particular attention given to the wing center-section and folding hardware. The first of three prototypes (Bunos. 97673/5) underwent ground static testing to verify the strength and began flying in June 1945. Also ordered were 900 TBM-4 production examples. However, only the first was completed before the end of the war halted further work.

The final wartime model of the Avenger was two XTBM-5s converted from TBM-3Es by the NAMU at Johnsville (former Brewster plant). Again, this focused on meeting the growing demand to more effectively attack land targets by improving performance through weight cutting and reduced wing loading. The ventral step was faired into the fuselage, the wing slots sealed, gear doors installed to fully enclose the wheels, and jet augmentation exhausts added to the engine. The third crewmember was eliminated and twin .30-cal. machine guns in a flex mount replaced the dorsal turret. Finally, wingspan was extended by three feet. Flight testing began in June 1945, but the project was terminated after VJ-Day.

The Almost-Ran (XTBU-1, TBY-2, -3)

The 1939 torpedo-bomber competition also saw a 22 April 1940 contract awarded to Vought for one XTBU-1 prototype (Buno. 2524). Powered by the 2,000-hp XR-2800-6 with three-blade 13.3-foot propeller, the aircraft was typical of the period. A long dorsal greenhouse enclosed the three crewmen while the mid-wing made room for a bomb bay. A .30-cal. machine gun fired forward from above the engine, a .50 machine gun fired aft in the dorsal power turret with 400 rounds, and another .30 was in a ventral ball. The bomb bay accommodated a torpedo or 2,000 pounds of other ordnance, while two inboard wing hardpoints took up to 500 pounds each of bombs or tanks. The wing had spoilers, slats, and aileron droop for enhanced low-speed lift. A Master Flight Control

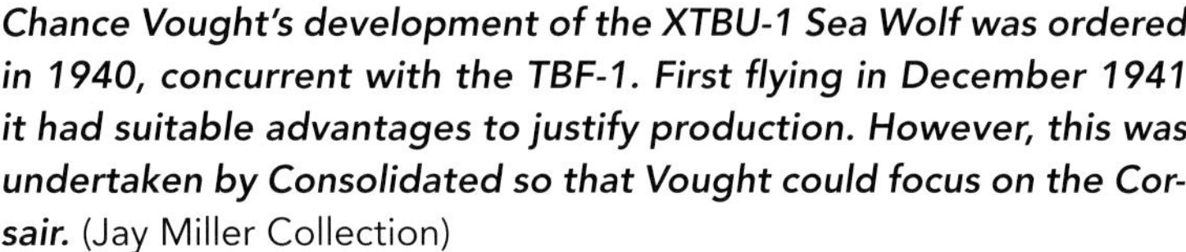

Chance Vought's development of the XTBU-1 Sea Wolf was ordered in 1940, concurrent with the TBF-1. First flying in December 1941 it had suitable advantages to justify production. However, this was undertaken by Consolidated so that Vought could focus on the Corsair. (Jay Miller Collection)

In preparing the Sea Wolf for production, Consolidated altered the designed sufficiently to justify a designation change to the TBY-2. These efforts took an exceptionally long period. By the time aircraft began rolling off the line in suitable numbers the war had passed it by. (San Diego Aerospace Museum)

System lever adjusted all control surfaces, landing gear, propeller, and engine for taxi and landing instead of adjusting everything individually. This feature was roundly met with suspicion.

The XTBU-1 Sea Wolf first took to the air at Vought's Stratford facility on 22 December 1941 and went on to Anacostia for service testing in March 1942. Although the TBF was doing very well, the Vought aircraft promised some performance advantages, despite being heavier. This was merit enough to plan a production run of 1,100 units as a backup should Grumman stumble.

Vought was so saturated with F4U work that much of the production engineering for the TBU-1 was subcontracted. In December 1942, the decision was made to have Vultee manufacture the aircraft as the TBY-1. That company established the production line at a converted Mack truck plant in Allentown, Pennsylvania. It eventually assumed full responsibility for engineering and manufacture while Vought remained involved in flight test as the aircraft evolved. Changes were mandated after an entire tail section was torn away during cable engagement trials. Immediately after being rebuilt over four weeks, with the tail wheel moved forward and the tailhook aft, the empennage was chewed up by the propellers of a trainer after an aviation cadet lost control of his aircraft. While rebuilding the tail a second time the opportunity was taken to install the R-2800-20 engine after its selection for production.

Further evolution saw the main landing gear redesigned, two-piece bomb bay doors replaced with one-piece doors, and the ventral gun turret revised. A load of bombs, mines, or depth charges up to 3,200 pounds could displace the Mk 13-2A torpedo in the bay. Hardpoints in the wings accommodated two 1,000-pound bombs or drop tanks, and stubs existed for eight rockets. Additional machine guns were added, with a pair of .50 cals in two under-wing fairings with 220 rpg, plus Douglas Mk 2 gun pods with twin .50s (340 rpg) could also be installed on the hardpoints. Some 390 pounds of armor were installed for crew protection. Consequently, weight went up approximately 1,000 pounds.

Work in Allentown progressed slowly in both plant conversion and personnel retraining. Owing to the delays, then-Consolidated Vultee chose to adopt the R-2800-22 at 2,100 hp for production of what then became the TBY-2.[7] It was mid-1944 before the first aircraft (Buno. 30299) was completed, flown from Convair Field on 20 August by Phillip M. Prophett. Testing and problem resolution in Allentown and Pax River went on for a year. The first delivery to the Navy (Buno. 30301) was on 7 November, almost three years after the first flight of the XTBU-1. Yet, it would be another year before a Sea Wolf unit was trained and in the fight against Japan.

The revised schedule had been for 504 TBY-2s delivered by the end of 1944, but the inexperienced workers rolled out only two. The initial squadron was training to ship out aboard USS *Leyte* (CV-32) on 1 November. Some examples were used for flight training of

Consolidated Vultee TBY-2 characteristics:

span	56.9 ft	weight empty	11,336 lbs
length	39.2 ft	gross	17,491 lbs
height	15.5 ft	maximum	18,940 lbs
wing area	440 ft^2	speed, max. (17,700 ft)	312 mph
fuel (int. + ext.)	317+200 gal	cruise	156 mph
service ceiling	29,400 ft	range (torpedo)	1,025 mi
initial climb rate	1,770 fpm	scout	1,615 mi

Aesthetics were not a defining factor in design of the TBY-2. The locations of the dorsal turret and ventral ball gun are revealed. There appeared plenty of room under the long greenhouse for the three crewmen. (San Diego Aerospace Museum)

The Vultee V-72 Vengeance dive-bomber was sold abroad before being picked up by the U.S. Army as the A-31 and then A-35A (V-88), an example of the latter seen here. The Navy briefly expressed an interest in turning the type into the TBV-1 Georgia (V-57) torpedo-bomber, then dropped the idea. (San Diego Aerospace Museum)

night fighter units. By mid 1945, production reached seven aircraft per day. However, the discouragingly long time getting to this point meant the type would clearly contribute nothing to the war effort, and the aircraft had little to recommend it over the TBM-3. An R-2800-34 was flight tested on the seventh aircraft, exploring the potential of a TBY-3 of which 600 were planned.[8]

On 6 July the Navy order was cut to 250 units, and on 14 August the program was shutdown completely. A total 180 TBY-2s were built, the last aircraft delivered on 24 August. All Sea Wolfs were broken up in 1947.

Clean Miss (TBV-1)

The Navy explored the potential for employing the Army Air Force's Vultee A-35 dive-bomber (which see) as a torpedo aircraft. The concept, evaluated in spring 1942, was identified as the TBV-1 Georgia (Model V-57) and the aircraft was to deliver a 22-inch torpedo from a "crutch" under the fuselage. This type was likely intended for shore basing, as converting a landplane to shipboard operations is exceedingly problematic. However, the project was dropped as the ship-based TBU-2 was selected for production. Additionally, the utter unsuitability of the A-35 became clear by this time.[9]

Good in Concept (XTB2D-1)

When the big Midway-class carrier was initially planned, the Navy was free to seek larger, more capable aircraft to fill these decks. The Battle of Midway also emphasized the desire for a torpedo-bomber with more weapons load and range, launching from shore installations. BuAer initially judged a twin-engine design most suitable, with delivery of multiple torpedoes, level bombing from high altitude, and long-range scouting as potential missions.

Douglas was given a go-ahead in November 1942 to begin designing such an aircraft.[10] The firm leaned toward a single-engine aircraft from the outset, the original concept including a bomb bay and a tail gun at the aft end of a bottom bombardier gondola. Large dive flaps would extend from flush stowage in the wing upper and lower surfaces. However, the project was soon slowed as the Midway was delayed. When initial construction of the USS *Midway* (CV-41) commenced, the program was revived four days later, 31 October 1943, with a contract for two XTB2D-1 Skypirate prototypes (Bunos. 36933/4) and a static article. Lead designer was the prolific Ed Heinemann and chief engineer was Bob Donovan.

The final concept was for the ultimate torpedo-bomber with the most powerful engine available able to carry two torpedoes off a Midway deck or four from shore. Converting the 3,000 hp of the XR-4360-8 with supercharger to thrust with a propeller of practical dimensions meant adapting an eight-blade, 14.3-foot diameter, fully

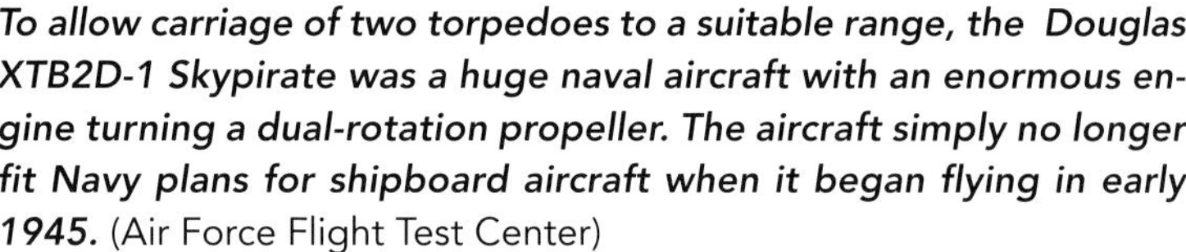

To allow carriage of two torpedoes to a suitable range, the Douglas XTB2D-1 Skypirate was a huge naval aircraft with an enormous engine turning a dual-rotation propeller. The aircraft simply no longer fit Navy plans for shipboard aircraft when it began flying in early 1945. (Air Force Flight Test Center)

This image of the XTB2D-1, probably on landing, shows the full-span slotted flaps. The "rollflaps" on the outboard wing panel are just one of the advanced features of this very large carrier-based airplane. Two wing-pylons are also visible on the port side . (San Diego Aerospace Museum)

feathering, Hamilton Standard contra-rotating system. This also gave ground clearance for tricycle landing gear, the level attitude simplifying weapon loading. Unusually, the bomb bay was eliminated and the four fish were carried externally on a low-mounted wing. The hardpoints were stressed for 2,100 pounds to take Mk 13-2 torpedoes or bombs for a total capacity of 8,400 pounds. Alternatively, 300-gallon tanks could be mounted under the outboard stations. Four .50-cal. machine guns in the wings with 400 rpg were complemented by a pair of .50s in an upper Firestone power turret and another remotely fired from a bottom fairing. The three crewmen were protected by 527 pounds of armor.

The XTB2D-1 had a number of innovations. The Navy specified a unique engine exhaust system whereby exhaust ports from cylinders in alternating rows were combined to reduce the effects of backpressure. The wing had full-span slotted flaps, the outboard segments also deflecting as ailerons (rollflaps) and the center segments serving as dive flaps. The flaps could be drooped slightly for more efficient cruise, and they would blow back as speed or turning loads increased to relieve stresses and produce an optimal configuration without pilot intervention. This innovative flap design was proven in flight test on another airframe during the Skypirate design phase.[11] The rudder controls could be interconnected with roll control for automatic adverse yaw compensation as the control wheel was turned.* On approach, the incidence of the horizontal tail could be set to an angle that maintained a more suitable nose attitude. To reduce the length of the nose gear for retraction, a telescoping strut was included. A three-axis autopilot was intended for use during horizontal bombing for greater accuracy. An anti-icing system was to circulate hot air to the wing and tail leading edges, while the heaters in the wing centersection and at the base of the vertical stabilizer burned aircraft fuel.

Mockup inspection occurred in March and May 1943. An order for 23 service test aircraft (Bunos. 89097/119) was placed in March 1943 and tooling prepared for building 100 aircraft per month. Delays were suffered with late delivery of the engines and propellers. However, by mid-1944 it was evident no TB2D-1 production would be forthcoming. With first flight still at least six months away, the Midways only sailing postwar, and the Japanese naval threat sunk to impotence, the need for the Douglas aircraft receded. The advent of fast multi-role attack aircraft operable from earlier carriers bespoke a desirable mission flexibility lacking in the Skypirate. The service test aircraft were cancelled and the XTB2D-1 slowed as higher priority projects took precedence.

The first XTB2D-1 was rolled out on 18 February 1945 at El Segundo, completed on 13 March, and flown on 8 May. The dorsal turret and ventral gun fairing, by then anachronisms, were never installed. Consideration was also given to an experimental installation of a jet booster engine in the aft fuselage of Buno. 36934, but this

** Adverse yaw is the tendency of the aircraft to yaw away from the direction of a roll, reducing turn rate and increasing drag. This is due to differing orientations of the lift vector on each wing. It is normally countered by applying rudder to bring the sideslip to zero (rudder in direction of the turn).*

was ultimately set aside.[12] The scout mission was given some consideration, and provisions for a fixed mapping camera were included in Buno. 36933. This aircraft had reduced outer wing dihedral and a 10.5-foot tall vertical tail, while Buno. 36934 had an 8.6-foot tail, probably to address hangar deck clearance concerns.

Flight testing was slowed by engine difficulties. A flight in June had the inboard flap segments depart the aircraft, although the pilot brought the plane down safely. Propeller problems cropped up in August, halting flight test until well after the war. Work continued into early 1947 at a slow pace and with costly changes before the program was closed out.

Douglas XTB2D-1 characteristics:			
span	70.0 ft	weight empty	18,405 lbs
length	46.0 ft	gross	28,545 lbs
height	22.6 ft	maximum	34,760 lbs
wing area	605 ft²	speed max. (15,600 ft)	340 mph
fuel (int. + ext.)	774+600 gal	torpedo	312 mph
service ceiling	24,500 ft	cruise	168 mph
initial climb rate	1,390 fpm	range (torpedoes)	1,250 mi
		maximum	2,880 mi

Carriage of weapons externally on the four weapons stations, including up to four torpedoes, permitted a comparatively shallow fuselage for the Skypirate. Planned dorsal turret and ventral gun position were never fitted, and the XTB2D-1 was rendered an obsolete aircraft by the time it flew in May 1945. (San Diego Aerospace Museum)

The Skypirate was a giant of a carrier-based plane, among the largest considered for shipboard operations during the war, with weights similar to the Army's twin-engine B-25C medium bomber. Compared with other torpedo bombers, its performance was exceptional. The war and Navy requirements had simply moved beyond the TB2D. Some thought was given to turning the airplane to electronic warfare and possibly anti-submarine warfare, but nothing came of this. By the end of the war there were simply too many aviation projects to sustain as the country moved to a postwar economy.

Miscues (XTB2F-1, XTSF-1)

Add-ons to the TBF/TBM drove up aircraft weight and affected performance, prompting consideration of a replacement. It was also worth exploring the potential for replacing the TBF, SBD, and SB2C with a single type. The Navy initially considered a twin-engine attacker intended for Essex and Midway carriers, and BuAer turned to Grumman for ideas. A preliminary design for the G-55 was offered on 21 December 1942 and a detailed proposal followed on 19 March 1943 promising initial delivery by May 1945. Approval to proceed was issued on 6 August 1943 with intent to build two prototypes (Bunos. 84055/6).

The XTB2F-1 was to stand on tricycle landing gear and be powered by two 2,100-hp R-2800-22s driving 14-foot, three-blade Curtiss propellers. Top speed was projected to be 335 mph at 20,500

The TBF Avenger's weight growth prompted the Navy and Grumman, in March 1943, to explore a twin-engine shipboard bomber as the XTB2F-1, seen here in mockup form on 11 June 1944. However, by this point in the war, fighter-type attack aircraft appeared more suitable, and the project was cancelled. (Northrop Grumman History Center)

This angle on the partial XTB2F-1 mockup shows the nose blister for the 75-mm cannon, the dorsal turret, and radar pod under the port wing. The vast expanse of transparency over the cockpit would likely have made for an uncomfortable greenhouse effect on sunny days. (Northrop Grumman History Center)

feet, with a 29,000-foot service ceiling, and combat range of 1,137 to 2,063 miles, 3,700 miles ferry. It would have 960 gallon of internal fuel and two 300-gallon drop tanks. The bomb bay would accommodate two torpedoes or up to 8,000 pounds of other weapons. A 75mm cannon with all of six rounds was to project from the starboard nose, complemented by two .50-cal. machine guns in the port side, four .50s or a 20mm cannon in the wings, and a pair of gun turrets with twin .50s.

Inspection of the mockup in early May 1944 brought home the sheer size of the XTB2F-1. It possessed a projected empty weight of 23,650 pounds and 45,700-pounds maximum, with 74-foot wingspan, 36 feet folded. The aircraft was approximately the size and weight of the Martin B-26 Marauder medium bomber and simply too large and heavy even for the CVB. More of the smaller attackers could fill the space taken up by these mammoth aircraft and deliver more firepower. Instead of working to shrink the design, the Navy wished for Grumman to concentrate on more practical projects. BuAer cancelled the XTB2F-1 on 14 June 1944.

More practical appeared to be turning the two-seat F7F-2 Tigercat twin-engine fighter into a torpedo-bomber with the addition of a TBF bomb bay. On termination of the XTB2F-1, BuAer requested Grumman submit such a proposal. The concept design (G-66) was offered in late June 1944 and, responding to BuAer comments, a revised design submitted on 21 July. Believing conversion of an existing fighter to the torpedo-bomber mission would yield rapid results and also allow scouting, the Navy moved on 17 August to revise the XTB2F-1 contract to cover development of two torpedo scout XTSF-1s (Bunos. 84055/6).

Grumman moved smartly to have a partial mockup ready in October and was proceeding with detail design. The lovely Tigercat lines were distorted to fit the enclosed torpedo bay. The fuselage was lengthened by just 5.5 inches, but the nose was swollen for an AN/APS-3 or APS-4 radar. The outer wing panels were extended to a span of 59.3 feet and total area of 501.5 square feet. The area of the vertical tail and rudder was also increased, and span of the horizontal tails and elevators lengthened 28 inches per side. Guns were reduced to a pair of .50 cals and 300 rpg in each inboard wing segment with potential of change to 20mm cannons and 200 rpg. The design retained the F7F-2's R-2800-22W engines, but empty weight was expected to go up more than 1,600 pounds to 17,533 pounds and gross to as much as 25,936 pounds. Performance was still expected to be respectable with a 389-mph top speed, maximum 4,410-fpm rate of climb, and up to a 419-mile radius of action, all dependent on fuel and weapon load.[13]

Once again, the service judged the new conceptual bomber too heavy for operations from escort carriers and felt Grumman's

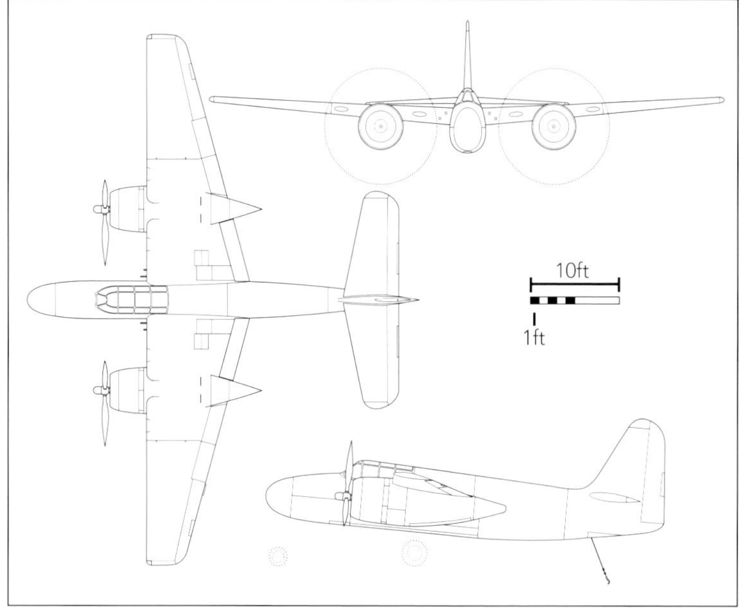

Another attempt at replacing the Avenger with a twin-engine aircraft of reasonable dimensions was the XTSF-1. Grumman modified the F7F-2 design with a TBF torpedo bay, air-to-surface radar in the nose, and changes to wing and tail dimensions. The Navy judged even this aircraft too large for escort carriers. (Author)

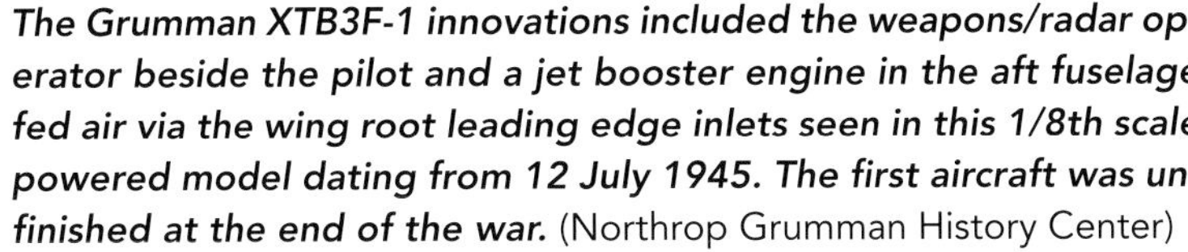

The Grumman XTB3F-1 innovations included the weapons/radar operator beside the pilot and a jet booster engine in the aft fuselage fed air via the wing root leading edge inlets seen in this 1/8th scale powered model dating from 12 July 1945. The first aircraft was unfinished at the end of the war. (Northrop Grumman History Center)

This mockup of the XTB3F-1 was photographed on 30 March 1945, the background subsequently removed. It is substantially complete with Wright R-3350 engine, landing gear, and canopy over line abreast seats. The jet power unit (JPU) exhaust is evident under the tail. (Northrop Grumman History Center)

engineering staff was over-extended. The Navy jettisoned the XTSF-1 in January 1945.

Last Gasp (XTB3F-1)

Grumman began working in July 1944 along a different track to supply the TBF/M replacement. The G-70 proposal submitted on 18 September was for an aircraft representing natural growth evolution of the Avenger, a two-place TBF without the tunnel gun. Two 20mm wing cannons with 200 rounds supplemented the turret machine gun. It was to be stressed for dive-bombing and have a general aerodynamic cleanup. Performance improvement would come via an R-2800-22 with four-blade propeller. Proposed guarantees included an empty weight of 10,661 pounds, 340-mph maximum speed, and 32,500-foot service ceiling.

Grumman was encouraged by BuAer to take the design further. Alternatives were substituting engines and introducing a jet power unit (JPU) as a "booster" in the aft fuselage. At first a 2,700-hp R-3350 was chosen (G-70A), then an R-4360 with General Electric remote-controlled turret (70B), an R-2800-24 with a 3,000-pound force thrust (lbf) Westinghouse 24C turbojet (70D), an R-2800-22 with General Electric I-20 (70E), and finally an R-3350-26 with 24C jet and deleting the turret (70F).[14] Overall dimensions had increased about seven percent. The promised advantage of the 70F with the jet operating for bursts of speed made the turret unnecessary, consistent with current thinking. The baseline design placed a weapons/radar operator (beginning of the later Weapons Systems Operator) side-by-side with the pilot. The engine became the two-speed R-3350-24 at 2,800 hp with the 24C delivering 3,000 lbf. Empty weight grew to 13,627 pounds and gross 21,200 pounds. The aircraft was expected to reach 428 mph and climb 4,850 fpm. Scouting radius would be 788 miles.

The G-70F's November 1944 proposal was green-lighted as the XTB3F-1 on 25 October and assigned high priority. Three prototypes (Bunos. 90504/6) and a static article were ordered on 19 February 1945. First flight was projected as July 1945.

A mockup inspection in February 1945 was followed by another in March, with wing alterations to carry larger external stores and replacing the two new .60-cal. machine guns with 20mm cannons. Soon the TBF weapons bay was altered to one accommodating two fish or 4,000 pounds of other ordnance. The JPU was fed air via wing root inlets and internal ducting, and exhausted under the tail. It was accessed by removal of a fuselage panel above the compartment. The aircraft spanned 60.0 feet with a 549 square-foot wing area. Empty weight was kept in check at 13,306 pounds, with 19,065 pounds loaded and 21,465 pounds maximum. Normal range was to be 1,280 miles. It was perhaps one of the last new military aircraft with fabric covered flight control surfaces.

By January, there were concerns over availability of both the reciprocating and jet engines because of delivery delays. Consequently, BuAer directed the contractor to examine the performance implications of changing to the 2,100-hp R-2800-34W turning the four-blade propeller and 1,600-lbf Westinghouse 19XB jet unit. Top speed was expected to be reduced to 367 mph and takeoff distance to go from 205 to 330 feet. These numbers were considered acceptable and the change in powerplants was authorized. However, in July, BuAer directed that Buno. 90505 have the R-3350-26W and 24C-4B. These changes pushed first flight beyond the end of the war to December 1946.

The program survived the postwar budget cutting and eventually entered production for the anti-submarine warfare role as the AF Guardian with the R-2800 but without the JPU.

Chapter 6

For the service test models of the Airacuda, YFM-1, the side blisters gave way to gun ports and a belly tunnel for a bottom, rear-firing gun was added as well as a dorsal extending turret. The turbosuperchargers were also relocated. A periscope and gunsight protrude under the nose. (Author's Collection)

ARMY ABERRATIONS

The war years saw some Army fighter development projects that were a significant departure from convention, either by intent or circumstances. These addressed the categories of bomber-destroyer (a prewar concept), escort fighter, and single-seat twin-engine fighter. The efforts were generally slowed by higher-priority programs and suffered any number of problems. All but one was cancelled before the end of the war. They are, nonetheless, a fascinating look at how such work sought to keep pace with shifting priorities, combat requirements, and available resources. They also illustrate the rapid maturing of the American aeronautical industry with increasingly sophisticated and capable aircraft.

Misbegotten – Bomber-Destroyers

First Out the Gate (XFM-1, YFM-1, YFM-1A, YFM-1B)

At the start of the war, the Air Corps had an experimental "strategic" fighter capable for long-endurance bomber intercept, long-range bomber escort, or supplemental ground attack. This was then in vogue, foreign examples being the Fokker G.I. in The Netherlands and the Messerschmitt Bf 110 in Germany. These were heavy aircraft, with two engines for safety on the long mission beyond the border, carrying a great quantity of fuel, and were heavily armed to pound all-metal bombers from the sky or strike ground targets. These characteristics were merged into what the Army Air Corps designated Fighter, Multi-place (FM). The first and only entry came as Bell Aircraft's first airplane and set the company's reputation for unusual designs with the first American pusher fighter.

The XFM-1 Airacuda (Model 1, 36-351) derived from a 1936 competition for a B-17 bomber escort and bomber-destroyer. Its maiden flight was in September 1937. This was the first airplane designed around the V-1710, using two -9s at 1,090 hp with GE F-10 turbosuperchargers. Each of these engines was placed at the back of a large nacelle and turned a three-blade propeller via a 5.3-foot extension shaft. In front of the engine was a compartment for a gunner operating a 37mm cannon in a hydraulic ball mount for limited 25-degree field of fire. These were provided 110 rpg in five-round clips. A coaxial .30-cal. machine gun was intended principally to fire tracers aiding in cannon aiming. The gunners could gain the fuselage via a crawlway within the wing leading edge. Within the fuselage were the pilot, copilot/navigator, and a rear radio operator/gunner with a .50-cal. machine gun on each side of the aft fuselage mounted in blisters and providing 600 rpg. As with other aircraft of the period, twenty 30-pound fragmentation bombs could be dropped from the belly onto aircraft formations below. All this made for an extraordinary five-man crew in a fighter the size of a medium bomber. Bell accepted a guarantee for 300 mph, climb to 15,000 feet in 10 minutes, 30,000-foot ceiling, and 3,000-mile range.

The Allisons were soon upgraded to the V-1710-13 at 1,150 hp, attempting to compensate for weight growth from a proposed 16,300 pounds to more than 18,000 pounds. Testing revealed many areas for improvement, and the aircraft quickly earned an unpopular reputation among maintenance personnel. The fire from the .30s was worthless in adjusting cannon aim, as the range and ballistics of the two weapons were widely different. Instead, the design added a Sperry Instruments "Thermionic" remote fire control system coupled to a gyro-stabilized autopilot and telescopic rangefinder sight. When fitted, this innovation permitted the copilot/navigator to aim the cannons via electrically actuated servo motor valves using a hand controller, while the gunner merely loaded the clips.

Toward the end of 1939, the aircraft was returned to Buffalo for alterations that included a larger rudder, smaller spinners and propeller blade cuffs, and replacement of the waist blisters with flat hatches possessing integral gun ports with extending air blast shields. The XFM-1 had shown enough promise for Bell to earn another contract in May 1938 for 13 YFM-1 (Model 7) service test examples (38-486/98).

The YFM-1s were given 1,150-horsepower V-1710-23s with B-1 turbosuperchargers moved from the side to beneath the nacelles. The fuselage and nacelles were reconfigured and flush riveting introduced. The side guns were still .50s with 1,200 rpg, and the .30s with 500 rpg moved to a retractable dorsal turret and a ventral tunnel mount. The gunsight hung under the nose with a periscope that provided a

The first Bell aircraft, the XFM-1 Airacuda, was innovative in design and mission, and an enormous twin-pusher fighter for bomber intercept and escort. The heavy weaponry is evident in the two 37mm cannons in the nacelles with coaxial .30-cal. machine guns, and .50-cal. machine guns in the waist blisters. (National Museum of the United States Air Force)

The three YFM-1As featured tricycle landing gear, the main gear retracting inboard. This greatly improved pilot forward visibility on takeoff and landing while improving the ease of ground maneuvering. Airacuda engine cooling was so critical that the aircraft was taxied very little, usually being towed to and from the runway. (San Diego Aerospace Museum)

means of detecting attack from the bottom rear quarter. The bomblets gave way to hardpoints for 600 pounds of standard-size weapons. Bell still assumed a guarantee for 305 mph at 20,000 feet.

The YFM-1 engineering and construction ran late, the first flying on 28 September 1939. The starboard turbosupercharger turbine bucket disintegrated on the second flight, causing shrapnel damage to the fuselage. This aircraft was finally passed to the Army 23 February. Nine aircraft (38-486/8, 491/5) were built to the basic YFM-1 standard, the last delivered on 30 July 1940. Two aircraft (38-489/90) were built in the YFM-1B (Model 7B) configuration during March 1940, delivered on 30 July, with 1,090-hp V-1710-41 engines without turbosuperchargers. The final three aircraft (38-496/8) were finished in August through October with tricycle undercarriage, the main gear redesigned to retract inboard fully into the wings vice partial retraction rearward into the nacelles. This YFM-1A (Model 8) conversion did not come without difficulty as Bell battled nose wheel shimmy.

One of the YFM-1s (38-492) was lost near Buffalo during testing, unable to recover from a spin when the rudder locked hard over. After shutting down the engines, company test pilot Brian Sparks jumped from the ship. He struck the empennage, breaking both legs, but painfully settled to earth via parachute. The other Bell pilot, John F. Strickler, found the impact freed the rudder and he was able to recover from the spin and make a dead-stick landing that damaged the ship beyond repair.[1]

The balance of the YFM-1s underwent service trials through the end of 1941. An A model, 38-497, was written off in an accident in January 1942. Funds were programmed to purchase FM-1s sufficient to fill two fighter groups, but never appropriated.

Performance of the Airacuda never matched its exciting looks, given a typical 2,000 hp from the two Allisons. None of four V-1710 models fitted delivered the power expected in the original design, and so never pushed the airplane fast enough to keep up with a B-17 bomber. Climb rate fell well short at 10 minutes to 15,000 feet, and ceiling was deficient. Engine cooling was such a problem in warm weather that the aircraft was usually towed to and from the runway. Most of the Airacuda's

Bell YFM-1A characteristics:			
span	70.0 ft	weight, empty	13,962 lbs
length	45.9 ft	gross	19,000 lbs
height	19.5 ft	maximum	21,625 lbs
wing area	686 ft²	speed, max. (12,600 ft)	270 mph
fuel capacity (int. + ext.)	400-800+0 gal	cruise	200 mph
service ceiling	30,500 ft	range, normal	940 mi
average initial climb rate	1,456 fpm	ferry	1,800 mi

ancillary equipment and cockpit instruments were electrically powered by a full-time gasoline motor auxiliary power unit (APU) within the fuselage. The APU drove not only an alternator, but also a hydraulic pump and compressor. If the motor failed, which it occasionally did, all auxiliary systems were severely impaired. This included the engine fuel pumps. When the APU quit, simultaneous engine fuel starvation quickly followed! Additionally, the aircraft was unstable in pitch, making for high pilot workload.[2] Bell never cleared the aircraft for aerobatic maneuvers typical of fighters. The bailout hazards from the pusher propellers were evident to every aviator who approached the plane. The big ship was expensive to buy and costly to maintain.

The Airacudas were shunted aside in January 1942, some with as little as 15 hours in the log. This happened despite fear of enemy bombers appearing over the United States being at its height that very month. The aircraft was simply a poor example of what bomber-destroyers could achieve. By 1942, the FM-1's top speed was meager by comparison with the adversaries. Experience in Europe showed aircraft such as the Bf 110 to be too slow and vulnerable mixing it up with lighter, more maneuverable single-engine fighters, often needing an escort themselves. Similar aircraft were developed later, with more powerful engines, for ground attack and night fighting, but it seems there was no champion for the Airacuda within the Air Forces. The Lockheed P-38 was coming along and appeared exceedingly more promising, and Bell had more important work. The $3.6 million expended on the FM-1 project proved valuable in gaining experience and providing data on the fire-control system and cannons.

Swings of the Pendulum (XP-58)

Lockheed's XP-58 Chain Lightning had a curious origin. The aircraft was to be provided to the Army at no charge under terms of the April 1940 Foreign Release Agreement. Lockheed was to develop an improved Lightning model suitable as a bomber escort and deliver it in 16 months, or 15 August 1942.

The subsequent L-121 proposal, developed under project engineer James Gerschler, was offered in single-seat and two-seat variants. The concept employed two 1,500 to 1,600-hp Continental IV-1430 powerplants in a 20,000-pound airplane with a projected maximum speed of 450 mph and at least a 1,600-mile range. Armament for the single-seater was to be the same as the P-38; a 20mm cannon supplemented by four .50-cal. machine guns. The two-seat version added a remote-controlled .50 at the end of each tail boom. In a 6 May 1940 meeting at Wright Field, the Army chose to pursue the two-seat version as the XP-58 bomber escort (MX-2).

After the initial agreement, a dismaying series of redirections occurred that greatly extended development and undermined any intended commonality with the P-38. As preliminary design got going, it was readily apparent the Continentals would likely render the XP-58 underpowered. Instead, the 1,800-hp Pratt & Whitney XH-2600-3/5 liquid-cooled inline, augmented with turbosuperchargers, were on a short list by July 1940. A second 20mm was added in the nose and the rearward-firing .50s joined into an Air Arm remote-controlled dorsal turret. In this configuration, a single prototype (41-2670) was ordered on 16 October 1940. With weight increased dramatically to 24,000 pounds, the guaranteed peak speed was lowered to 402 mph at 25,000 feet.

The 24-cylinder XH-2600 was aimed at 2,000 to 2,200 hp with sleeve valves that were to prove problematic. Translating sleeves within the cylinders uncovered intake and exhaust ports at appropriate moments in the piston stroke. This was being attempted on both sides of the Atlantic, with prodigious resources expended during the war in a failed effort to make sleeve valves viable. However, epic engineering problems and Navy withdrawal from the program caused the entire endeavor to be abandoned so Pratt & Whitney could concentrate on improving and producing proven radial designs.

Within a month of selection for the XP-58, the XH-2600 was cancelled. New XP-58 project lead Neil Harrison then prepared studies exploring three powerplant options. Lockheed recommended a pair of the 1,850-hp R-2800s, but provided data with Continental XH-2860s and Lycoming XH-2470s. The R-2800s would bring gross weight to 26,000 pounds and provide only 418-mph top speed at 25,000 feet. This appeared inadequate given the timeframe, two or more years hence, when the aircraft would likely enter service. By March 1941, the unusual Wright XR-2160 Tornado at 2,350 hp was short-listed to get projected top speed back to 450 mph. In May, the Army added cabin pressurization and a ventral turret mated to the dorsal unit.

With the spring 1941 alterations, gross weight rose again to 31,000 pounds, then 34,242 pounds by May, and 35,250 by 10 October. Mockup inspection occurred on 24 August 1941. More changes ensued, including introducing the latest radios and swapping propellers. The Air Forces had to accede to reducing the guaranteed speed to 445 mph and range fell to 1,300 miles.

The design team reached a peak of 187 personnel in October 1941. The country's entry into the war then greatly shifted resources

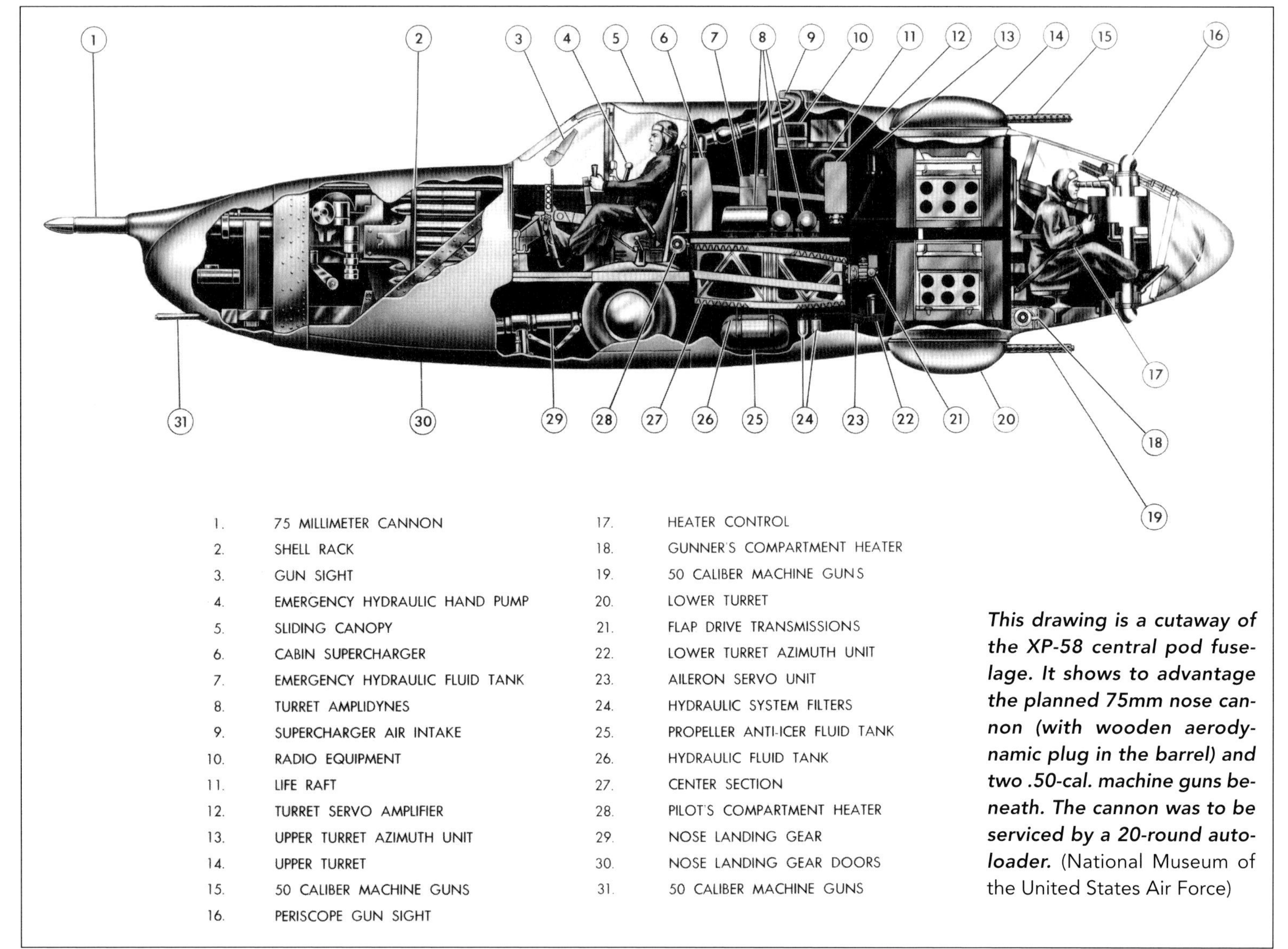

This drawing is a cutaway of the XP-58 central pod fuselage. It shows to advantage the planned 75mm nose cannon (with wooden aerodynamic plug in the barrel) and two .50-cal. machine guns beneath. The cannon was to be serviced by a 20-round autoloader. (National Museum of the United States Air Force)

and the XP-58 work slowed considerably, the team dropping to just a dozen after the new year. Lockheed proposed building a second prototype as insurance against loss of the first in test. The Army consented in May 1942 as long as the aircraft was also used to explore options for regaining range and even extending it to 3,000 miles with added fuel tanks and other improvements.

In early 1942, thought was given to changing the P-58's role to bomber-destroyer by adding a 75mm cannon to the aircraft with 20-round magazine and auto feed. This was expected to be markedly superior to the hand-fed 75mm in the North American B-25H employed in ground attack, and so potentially suitable for aerial engagement.

As the attack mission gained priority, consideration turned to employing the XP-58 with its 75mm cannon for low-altitude ground attack and tank busting. With the weight gain in the design and continuing concern over engine availability, lingering doubts existed over the competitiveness of the design as a fighter in any mission. It might itself need fighter escort! The low-altitude role could see the turbosuperchargers and pressurization deleted. Two .50-cal. machine guns would join the cannon in the nose, the turrets retained with at least the lower unit allowed to fire forward on boresight, and under-wing store options would be expanded. Consideration was also given to six 20mm cannons for a concentrated forward barrage or emphasizing bombing with a bomb bay and

The Lockheed XP-58 Chain Lightning was greatly delayed and suffered tremendous weight growth as a consequence of numerous changes in intended powerplants and mission. Performance was lackluster and progress of the war had rendered its bomber-destroyer mission moot. It was dead upon arrival. (American Aviation Historical Society)

The XP-58 had a wingspan of 70 feet, and fully loaded was nearly 20 tons. Yet, the two 24-cylinder Allison V-3420s, delivering 2,600 hp each, could get the big plane to 435 mph. The dummy shape for the top turret is visible. The turrets and other armament were never installed. (Tony Landis Collection)

bombardier in a glass nose. Preliminary estimates suggested a weight of 36,000 pounds and top speed of 355 mph at 5,000 feet. This proposal was forwarded to Washington and the change in mission was approved on 16 September 1942. The second prototype was no longer seen as necessary.

By late October 1942, the Army changed its mind again. The Douglas XA-26 Intruder and Beech XA-38 (which see) were assessed as adequately addressing the heavy ground attack mission. In addition, 90 percent of the prototype's components were already completed and airframe assembly 25 percent complete, making a major redirection costly and time-consuming. The confusing signals finally resolved into direction turning the XP-58 into a bomber-destroyer retaining the 75mm cannon, pressurization, turrets, and turbosuperchargers. However, the cannon system was still in test and so likely unavailable before aircraft completion. Consequently, the decision was codified on 3 November 1942 that the prototype be assigned four 37mm cannons in the nose with 100 rpg and the second aircraft retained to get the 75mm matched with a pair of .50s at 300 rpg.

The flurry of changes left the XP-58 even heavier at 37,900 pounds for the first aircraft and 38,275 pounds for the second. This knocked top speed down to 414 mph at 25,000 feet and reduced range to 1,150 miles. However, the first aircraft was too far along for rework to carry the maximum loads at the projected gross weight, so accommodations would have to be made in flight test. This program then suffered another blow when the Tornado engine program was cancelled. With Army concurrence, by June 1943 the Allison V-3420-11/13s was substituted, this at 2,600 hp, 3,000 hp at 28,000 feet, with single-stage/single-speed turbosuperchargers. The engine was developed as two V-1710s V-12s arranged around a common crankcase with the crankshafts geared together at the propeller end. It was the most powerful liquid-cooled engine available and turned four-blade, 14.7-foot diameter propellers (15.2-feet expected for production).

Of all the U.S. fighter projects of the war, the XP-58 was most affected by advanced and failed engine programs and shifting mission priorities. However, after two years of vicissitudes, the aircraft was allowed to proceed to completion in the final configuration. The second airplane was begun in May 1943 with delivery specified as 31 December. The performance guarantee had been revised to 430 mph at 30,000 feet with a 1,150-mile range. The first aircraft was expected to come in at 38,874 pounds and the second 39,149 pounds.

Delays continued to intrude with as few as 30 personnel working on the aircraft when higher priority tasks pulled the rest away. This situation and the notion of interchangeable nose weapon sections finally justified cancelling the second aircraft in April 1944 when it was 65 percent complete.

Lockheed XP-58 characteristics:

span	70.0 ft	empty, weight	31,624 lbs
length	49.4 ft	loaded (gross)	39,192 lbs
height	13.7 ft	maximum	43,000 lbs
wing area	600 ft^2	speed, max. (25,000 ft)	436 mph
fuel (int. + ext.)	656-760+930 gal	cruise (25,000 ft)	274 mph
service ceiling	38,400 ft	range, normal	1,150 mi
initial climb rate	2,290 fpm	ferry	2,650 mi

End of a project – the solitary XP-58 sits neglected on a snowy winter day in Ohio. The Lockheed development was wracked with vacillations from changes in mission and engine choices. After about 26 flights and 25 hours logged, it was delivered to the Army Air Forces, but never flown again. (William T. Larkins photo via Jay Miller Collection)

As the XP-58 finally took shape, it had become the heaviest U.S. fighter of the war. Although the lines resembled the P-38, it was considerably larger. The weight increase demanded "beefy" landing gear that had two wheels on each strut, including the nose gear. The gunner occupied a transparent enclosure at the end of the center pod where he would direct fire of the twin turrets, each fitted with two .50-cals (300 rpg). Underwing stores could include four 1,000-pound bombs or fuel tanks. Control surfaces, doors, and hatches were plywood, and the rudder and ailerons had hydraulic boost.

Given the long and convoluted development history and fading of the bomber-destroyer mission, it is surprising the XP-58 survived to first flight. Cannons above 20mm had already been dismissed as impractical as a fighter weapon.[3] However, the Chain Lightning did fly, briefly. After completion in January 1944, the maiden flight on 6 June was a 50-minute ferry from Burbank to Muroc Army Air Base (AAB) under the hands of Joe Towle.* The test program moved slowly due to higher priority work and trouble with torching from the turbines that scorched the booms and tails. Longitudinal stability issues required a larger metal elevator with spring tabs to replace the wooden unit.

After 25 flights at Muroc, the XP-58 was ferried to Wright Field on 22 October for acceptance trials. However, the aircraft received scant attention by the Army test personnel, and maintenance issues kept it on the ground. The pressurization, guns and turrets, armor, and fire control systems had not yet been installed. Two noses with the different gun installations were delivered separately. The aircraft would clearly not be required in bringing the war to a satisfactory conclusion. With only about 25 hours in the log, the aircraft was not flown again. The multitude of contract changes had cost the Army Air Forces $1.89 million, most for the unrealized second prototype.

Escort Reach

A Good Try (XP-75)

General Motors Corporation's Eastern Aircraft Division was providing essential and commendable service manufacturing Grumman aircraft. However, GM desired to contribute more overtly to the war effort by producing an aircraft of its own design and employing the V-3420 built by its Allison division. This would also more fully employ its Fisher Body Division. Consequently, in January 1942, GM hired chief designer Donovan R. Berlin of Curtiss P-36 and P-40 fame.

The principal idea of GM and Berlin was to use assemblies from other aircraft already in production to shorten development time such that their first airplane could be flying within six months and mass production begin soon after. However, it was 10 September 1942 before the proposal was first presented to Materiel Division. After some discussions and changes, the Fisher proposal met with favorable response. Approval to proceed with two XP-75-GMs (43-46950/1, MX-317), for an estimated $410,000, was given on 10 October with the first aircraft to be delivered within six months (May 1943).[4] However, it would be more than a year before a definitive contract was signed.

The V-3420 was expected to produce an interceptor possessing impressive climb performance – although the XP-75 would be the first airframe to mount the experimental powerplant. Maximum speed was specified at 440 mph at 20,000 feet, 5,600-fpm initial climb rate, and a service ceiling of 38,000 feet.

Berlin placed the 2,600-hp V-3420-19 amidships for favorable balance, driving a six-blade, 13-foot diameter Aeroproducts contra-rotating propeller via long, coaxial shafts and reduction gearing, and with a two-stage, variable-speed supercharger. The original design borrowed a Douglas SBD empennage, Vought F4U undercarriage, P-51 outer wing panels in an inverted gull configuration, P-40E canopy and instrument panel, and featured 177 pounds of cockpit armor. The wing was soon simplified to a straight centersection with P-40E outer wing panels at a slight dihedral and with modified tips. Selected weapons were four .50-cal. machine guns with 300 rpg in the nose and six more with 235 rpg in the wings. Wing hardpoints for two 1,000-pound stores were included.

The very idea of mating disparate assemblies to create a first class fighter in six months must have caused furrowed brows if not outright ridicule from some quarters of Materiel Division. It sounded much

** The Muroc Bombing and Gunnery Range became Muroc Army Air Base on 23 July 1942. The remote location in the Southern California Mojave Desert simplified security. However, the principal attraction was the vast Rogers Dry Lake surface that was a natural runway miles long. Favorable weather permitted year-round flying.*

The XP-75 began as an idea by General Motors Corp. to build its own aircraft. This would use an experimental engine from Allison and airframe assemblies from other aircraft to speed up development and early delivery of production examples. This is an image of the first prototype Eagle. (Tony Landis Collection)

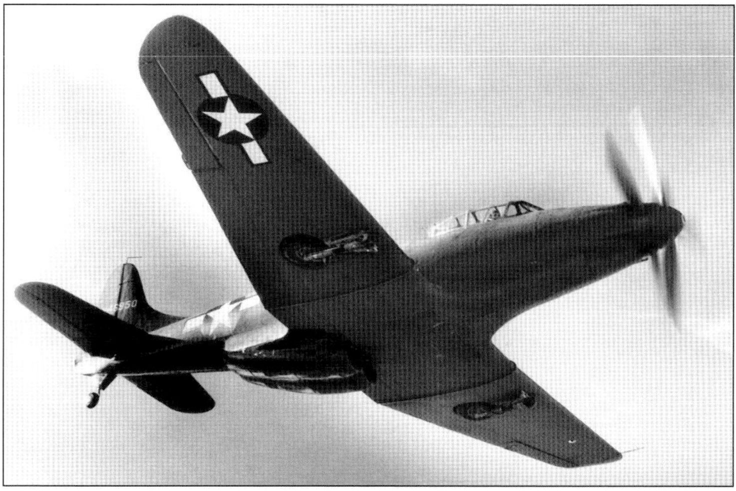

The large airscoops for the buried propulsion system had to contribute markedly to XP-75 drag. The landing gear was never fully enclosed, but at this point the first prototype also lacked the fairing around the forward end of the landing gear struts. (Tony Landis Collection)

simpler than it would be in reality. Not having been designed from the outset to work aerodynamically or structurally as an integrated airframe, the approach had to smell like trouble to experienced engineers. Adding an experimental, liquid-cooled engine, long power shafts, and dual-rotation propellers was just going to increase the challenges. However, at that stage of the war the Americans were quite anxious about fielding warplanes to meet the enemy on equal or superior terms. If someone of Berlin's stature thought it could be done, and if GM thought it could be done quickly, it was worth a try.

Mockup inspection occurred in spring 1943 after which the contractor was asked to explore switching back to P-51 wings but with four 20mm cannons installed under MX-455. Ultimately, the P-40 wings were retained. However, things were about to change equally substantially.

As concern grew about the lack of suitable long-range bomber escorts, the Army Air Forces explored the potential for the heavily armed XP-75 to meet this urgent need. A 6 July 1943 meeting in Washington between Fisher and Wright Field personnel, and the Chief of Materiel Command, Gen. Oliver P. Echols, yielded a decision to build six pre-production XP-75-GCs (44-32161/6) with expanded wing tank fuel capacity and production variant 2,885-hp V-3420-23 engines. The P-75 then became insurance against the P-51 or P-47 failing to be suitable for long-range escort. An additional $1.53 million was allocated for the new work; this after the initial effort had already escalated to $1.36 million. A definitive development contact was finally signed on 1 October 1943 for $2.91 million and included a static test article. The first of the two original XP-75s was to be ready for flight by 30 September 1943 (a five-month slip) and the first escort model delivered by December 1943.

As this restructuring was made before the original XP-75s had moved under their own power, and further undercut the intent of employing existing assemblies, it was even more remarkable when a letter of intent was issued on 8 July to buy 2,500 P-75A-1 Eagles (44-44549/7048). The first production aircraft was expected in May 1944. General Motors projected first delivery of 586 production aircraft by the end of October 1944, and deliveries ramping up to 250 per month. Considering the rate at which GM was producing Navy aircraft, this did not seem outlandish.

All aircraft were to be manufactured at the Fisher Body Division plant in Cleveland, Ohio, although the first two prototypes were assembled in Detroit. A new plant had been built at the Cleveland Airport in 1942, originally for B-29 component assembly by Fisher.

As detail design and construction began, difficulties began to intrude. It was not a simple matter to combine the assemblies from different aircraft and manufacturers into a coherent whole. Changes required adjustments to jigs, fixtures, and other tools, and also engineering on items for which the original design analysis had been performed by other companies. The swapping of assemblies required major alterations to the newly designed structure. It would probably have been more efficient for Berlin to design a new aircraft from scratch.

On 17 November 1943, Russell Thaw performed the first flight of the XP-75. Soon after this, GM came to understand how much there was to making airplanes than just mass-producing them. Evident were the adverse effects of time pressures, inexperienced staff,

The P-75 entered production after eight X-planes had been built. This P-75A shows the revised tail assembly and bubble canopy as the most obvious changes from the earliest XP-75. It was a commendable effort, but came too late and without much to recommend it. (National Museum of the United States Air Force)

The GM Fisher XP-75A was exciting in appearance if not performance. The long forward fuselage with far-forward cockpit placement is emphasized in this photo. Note the contra-rotating propeller, transitional canopy design, external tanks, three wing-guns per side and fairings for four nose-guns, and the many protrusions. (Jay Miller Collection)

and problems inherent in the engineering personnel being physically separated (Detroit) from the production personnel. Most serious were longitudinal stability issues resulting from an incorrect estimate of the aircraft's center of gravity location. The airplane also had excessive aileron forces at high speeds resulting in a low roll rate, and spins were unfavorable. These were quite significant problems for an aircraft that was supposed to see the first production unit delivered in six months. Even the Allison engines gave trouble with power loss and inadequate cooling.

The team steadily worked through the problems, and the data were employed in some redesign of the escort models still in assembly. The ailerons were altered several times, to include by increasing their span and eventually adding hydraulic boost among other changes. The tail was tinkered with before being completely redesigned. A dorsal extension was added later and a ventral strake improved spins. The much-enlarged empennage shifted the center of gravity aft, requiring the nose to be extended forward several inches to compensate. A 12.6-foot diameter propeller also appeared on some of the later airplanes. The canopy was substituted with a bubble arrangement, among many other changes. Analysis was re-accomplished, new drawings prepared, jigs and tools reworked. All this proved contrary to the promise of rapid assembly using pre-existing assemblies. The contract was reportedly adjusted for the first 25 production aircraft to be modified with the fixes as P-75A-5s and the remainder built as P-75A-10s.[5]

The first escort XP-75 began flying in February 1944. The third of these (44-32163) crashed on 8 April 1944, killing the pilot who may have been performing unauthorized low-level aerobatics.

Although matters were running quite long and advanced models of the P-51 and P-47 were filling the escort role quite respectfully, the program continued. Cost overruns due to engineering changes

This lineup of Eagles has the remaining prototype in the company of four of six pre-production examples. The changes in canopy and empennage are evident. Ultimately, 13 XP-75s and P-75As were completed and flown, but plans to produce 2,500 were dropped. (National Museum of the United States Air Force)

eventually exceeded twice the value of the original contract. Government officials began commenting on resources expended for a program that did not appear destined to contribute anything to the war effort. Furthermore, a Fisher employee sent letters to the military, law enforcement, and legislative officials charging the company with enormous fraud against the government. Although an investigation failed to substantiate the allegations, the bad press did not help.

An attempt at official performance trials was made in June 1944. It yielded questionable results owing to improper engine operation. Although the third aircraft (44-32161) had demonstrated 418 mph at 21,600 feet and 2,990-fpm climb rate with perhaps only 2,210 hp, the production airplanes had gained more than 1,300 pounds and performance suffered accordingly.

Another blow fell on 5 August 1944 when an explosion and fire at altitude forced a pilot to abandon 44-32161. The first P-75A flew on 15 September 1944 and the initial two aircraft were soon sent to Eglin Field for tactical suitability trials. There, 44-44549 was lost in a fatal crash on 10 October. However, speed runs had already shown the aircraft fell short of the guarantee by 30 mph. An experimental intercooler for the first stage of the supercharger installed on 44-44551 might have recovered some of the performance, but the chance to show its stuff had passed.

The opinion of Materiel Command officers was that the aircraft still had six more months of work before it met expectations. The Air Forces had decided by summer 1944 not to undertake large-scale production of any new types unless they could be deployed quickly in large numbers and their performance warranted the effort. Neither was the case with the P-75.

The production contract was cancelled on 6 October 1944 at 20 aircraft. This ultimately resulted in five P-75As being completed (44-44549/53) and a sixth (44-44554) delivered incomplete to serve as a spares source. Airplane 44-44550 was sent to NACA Ames for experimental work in the full-scale wind tunnel to reduce drag and perform propeller tests. The experimental program was terminated on 8 November. The four operational aircraft continued flying for a time as testbeds for the V-3420 under a new $250,000 contract. This was closed-out on VJ-Day and most aircraft were soon scrapped. Aircraft 44-44551 was bailed to Allison for flight trials with the new intercooler, but it was not flown.

Some $9.37 million had been expended on the X-plane contracts and more than $40.75 million on the abortive P-75A production. This did not sit well with Congress, but such are the gambles of war. Considering the experience level of the engineering and production staff, the P-75 team did remarkably well. Certainly many "clean-sheet" designs from well-established aeronautical firms had taken longer and had more trouble than the P-75.

General Motors/Fisher P-75A characteristics:

span	49.3 ft	weight empty	11,255 lbs
length	41.4 ft	gross	17,875 lbs
height	15.5 ft	maximum	19,420 lbs
wing area	347 ft²	speed, max. (22,000 ft)	404 mph
fuel (int. + ext.)	210-638+220 gal	cruise	250 mph
service ceiling	36,400 ft	range, normal	1,100 mi
initial climb rate	4,200 fpm	max. combat	3,150 mi
		ferry	3,850 mi

Radical but Practical (XP-82)

Sometimes even the strangest aeronautical incarnations can be successful. This is true of the North American Aviation P-82 Twin Mustang that began as a sketch on 21 October 1943 by chief designer Edgar Schmued. It showed two P-51 fuselages joined like Siamese twins via a constant-chord center wing section and rectangular horizontal tail. This, it was estimated, might provide the long range sought for B-29 escort to Japan and back, launched from Saipan or other remote islands. The "Twin" – as it was known around North American Aviation – would provide a relief pilot in one of the cockpits during the very lengthy missions in addition to the over-water safety of two engines. Propellers would turn in opposite directions to cancel torque effects. The preliminary design group then prepared a proposal for what became NA-120. It was shown to Gen. Arnold when he visited the plant on 7 January 1944, and he approved it on the spot![6]

The Materiel Division staff then had to follow-up on the general's autocratic decision. Nevertheless, they found the NAA design had high potential to solve the nagging escort problem. The two cockpits addressed the physiological problems of such long missions with a single pilot. It could also be equipped for ground attack duties. After Arnold's impromptu go-ahead, two XP-82 prototypes (44-83886/7, MX-485), a pair of XP-82As (44-83888/9), and a static test article were formally ordered on 8 February 1944. The XP-82 would be powered by 1,380-hp V-1650-11/12s with 2,270 hp (water) at 4,000 feet. The XP-82As would use 1,500-hp V-1710-119s. A production contract for 500 P-82Bs (NA-123, 44-65160/659) followed on 8 March, a year away from first flight, with 1,380-hp V-1650-19/21s and outboard wing hardpoints for up to 4,000 pounds of tanks and bombs, and more rockets.

Ultimately, the P-82 had almost no parts in common with the P-51. The fuselages bore a resemblance to P-51F bodies, although extended 57 inches aft of the air scoop, but with almost entirely new structure that included a dorsal fin extension and ventral strake. It actually ended up with V-1650-23/25s with counter-rotation. A main gear strut under each fuselage, ahead of the cooling intake, retracted inboard into the fuselage and center wing. A tail wheel retracted into each aft fuselage. The outboard wing halves were similar to the

P-51H but with slightly larger chord lengths. The inboard laminar-flow section was fitted with a flap. Aero surfaces had the latest thermal de-icing features.

The idea was for the relief pilot to occupy the starboard cockpit, with only essential instruments and controls, who would also assisted with navigation duties. There was initial concern that pilots seven feet off centerline would suffer spatial disorientation during high-rate rolls. A ground rig was constructed to explore this potential, and the fears were shown to be unfounded.[7] Systems were installed to permit all-weather operations. Six .50-cal. machine guns in the center wing had 400 rpg. A pod with eight .50s mounted on the centerline of the center wing was also tested.

The work proceeded under project engineer George Gehrkens. The first XP-82 was completed in May 1945. First flight was attempted on 15 April, but this and other tries through June found the aircraft refused to leave the ground. Only by off-loading fuel to reduce weight did the aircraft reluctantly takeoff for a brief first flight from Mines Field on 16 June with Joe Barton at the controls. The engineers suspected an adverse flow phenomenon that stalled the inboard wing section with the propellers turning inboard. Only when the prop rotations were reversed by swapping the engines side-to-side (-23 on port side, -25 starboard) did the aircraft behave properly, as demonstrated on 26 June by Bob Chilton. The second XP-82 flew on 30 August. Only the first XP-82A was completed, hampered by backfiring problems with the Allison. Oddly, those engines all turned in the same direction.

At war's end, the remaining XP-82A was cancelled and the P-82B order was reduced to 20 (44-65160/79). However, production was eventually resumed as the last new propeller-driven and tail-wheel fighter bought by the Air Forces. A very fine postwar night fighter and attack aircraft resulted.

Missed Goal: Single-Seat Twins

Left Behind (XP-49)

An 11 March 1939 Army requirement sought a high-altitude, turbosupercharged interceptor to counter advanced designs emerging overseas. The Circular Proposal 39-775 welcomed developments

North American XP-82 characteristics:

span	51.3 ft	weight empty	13,402 lbs
length	38.1 ft	gross	19,170 lbs
height	13.5 ft	maximum	22,000 lbs
wing area	408 ft²	speed, max. (22,800 ft)	468 mph
fuel (int. + ext.)	600+445 gal	cruise	227 mph
service ceiling	40,000 ft	range, normal	1,390 miles
initial climb rate	4,900 fpm	maximum	2,600 miles

Developed for the escort mission, the Twin Mustang design included wing hardpoints for vital fuel drop tanks and ordnance. The first XP-82 is shown with a pair of 1,000-pound bombs on the center wing panel below the six .50-cal. machine guns, two 500-pound weapons outboard, and 10 HVARs. (National Museum of the United States Air Force)

of existing aircraft in order to accelerate the acquisition process. Consequently, Lockheed offered the L-106 Tornado design, an improvement on the P-38 that had only recently begun flight testing and had suffered a crash. The company wanted another avenue to ensure success of the program. Although the Air Corps was supposed to be moving quickly, evaluation of the proposals ran through 3 August 1939. The Lockheed design placed first and was given a go-ahead on 14 October with the $560,300 contract following on 22 January 1940. One XP-49 (Model 522, 40-3055) was to be delivered in March 1941.

The new aircraft was to have more powerful engines with counter-rotating propellers, heavier armament, and higher-capacity landing gear. The Pratt & Whitney XH-2600 at 2,000 to 2,200 hp was selected, although production aircraft might be fitted with a pair of the 2,300-hp R-2160 Tornado. Lockheed predicted the Tornado would allow 500-mph top speed at 20,000 feet while the Pratt & Whitneys would give 473 mph at the same altitude. Turbosuperchargers would enhance high-altitude performance and Royalin fuel cells would provide greater capacity than those installed in the P-38. Four .50-cal. machine guns with 300 rpg would be matched with two 20mm cannons at 60 rpg. This armament combination was tested aboard P-38G 42-12866.

Although the aircraft was seen as a rework of the P-38, the project moved slowly at Lockheed due to higher priority Lightning efforts. Detail design finally began in earnest on 23 December 1940 under project engineer M. Carl Haddon. It was quickly realized the proposed powerplants were not going to be available in the near future. The Continental XIV-1430-9/11 with single-stage, single-speed GE B-33 turbosuperchargers was the only reasonable alternative, despite delivering less power. The substitution was made by March

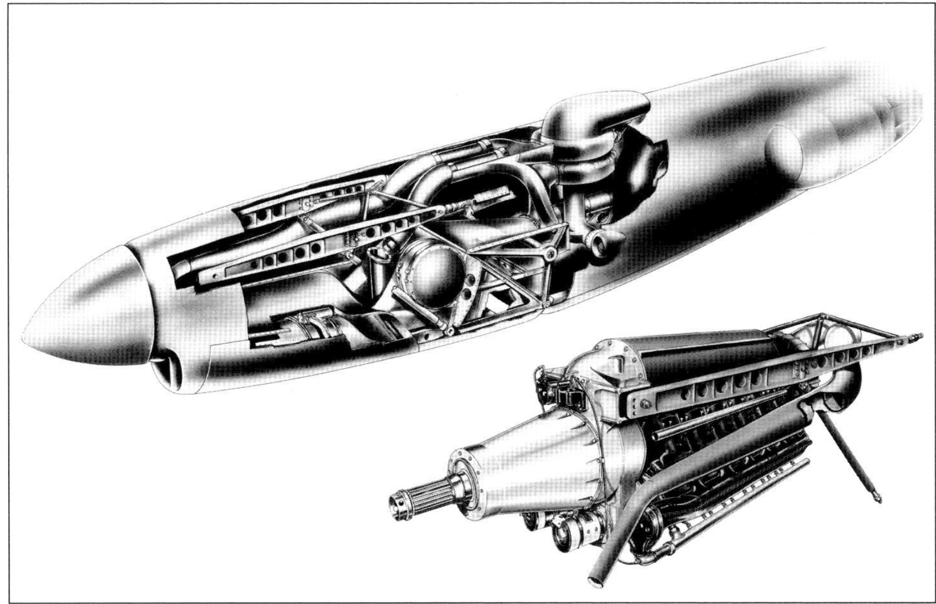

A drawing of the Continental IV-1430 accompanies another showing the internal arrangement of the XP-49 nacelles. The engine never reached production, despite the tremendous resources expended. The turbosupercharger and associated ducting is evident within the nacelle, although the hood on the turbosupercharger exhaust was apparently not installed in actuality. (National Museum of the United States Air Force)

1940. The specification was suitably altered to 458 mph at 25,000 feet top speed, and 372 mph at 5,000 feet, and delivery slipped to January 1942.

The IV-1430 was one of several high-performance (Hyper) aero engine projects begun in the 1930s by the Army and Navy. A rough aim was achieving 1 horsepower per cubic inch with a liquid-cooled engine, as racers had demonstrated. The Continental evolved from a protracted experimental effort under Army direction and funding, initially with horizontally opposed cylinders. It finally emerged from the test stand in 1939 as a liquid-cooled, inverted V-12 with reduction gearing giving 1,600 hp with 27 percent less frontal area than the P-38's V-1710s. An entire plant was built in Muskegan, Michigan, to manufacture the engine.

An XP-49 mockup was ready by summer 1941 and inspection was performed from 25 August through 4 September. Some two-thirds of the airframe was common with the P-38, so it is not surprising that prototype construction ran ahead of powerplant availability. The engines were not delivered until 22 April 1942. The most readily identifiable differences from the P-38 were a revised center pod profile and rework of the nacelles. In the interest of expediency, the weapons were left for later installation and test. A change in August 1942 required the introduction of a pressurized cockpit, but this was also left for later. Lockheed was gaining experience and data with pressurization on the XP-38A. Additional measures to speed-up development were to substitute other material for the armor plates that were in short supply.

The XP-82 (second prototype shown) was created by conceptually mating two P-51 Mustangs in a design that must have seemed at first too simplistic to yield a useful fighter. Yet, the aircraft very nicely filled the long-range escort and ground attack roles. It went on to a meritorious postwar career. (San Diego Aerospace Museum)

The XP-49 cockpit pressurization drove changes to the gondola fuselage and canopy that most readily identify the plane as the one-off sibling of the P-38. The nacelles were also altered, enclosing the IV-1430 engines and pressurization gear. (Author's Collection)

The Lockheed XP-49 sought a quick increase in performance with an existing design by re-engining the P-38 and adding heavier armament and cockpit pressurization. However, the 1939 project did not see the prototype delivered to the Army Air Forces until mid-1943. By this point, it was overcome by events and went no further. (National Archives)

Lockheed XP-49 characteristics:			
span	52.0 ft	weight, empty	15,410 lbs
length	40.1 ft	loaded	18,750 lbs
height (initial tail)	9.8 ft	maximum	22,000 lbs
(revised tail)	10.4 ft	speed, max. (15,000 ft)	406 mph
wing area	327.5 ft²	max (sea level)	347 mph
fuel (int. + ext.)	300+425 gal	cruise	372 mph
service ceiling	37,500 ft	range, normal	680 mi
initial climb rate	3,280 fpm	maximum	1,800 mi

Joe Towle took the XP-49 up for its first flight on 11 November 1942 from Burbank. It flew well enough, but after a week and three more flights the aircraft was put down on 20 November for modifications. To cure fuel system issues, the Royalin cells were replaced with standard self-sealing tanks then used in the P-38. The engines were swapped out with XI-1430-13/15 models rated at 1,350 hp for takeoff and 1,600 hp at 25,000 feet. A second seat and test instruments were added behind the pilot for a flight test engineer to support evaluation of the I-1430s. When flying resumed in December, the aircraft was plagued with hydraulic problems. This culminated on 1 January 1943 with dual hydraulic and electrical system failures prompting shutdown of an engine and an emergency landing at Muroc AAB. It ended with a collapsed port main gear and airframe damage.

During the repair period, the vertical stabilizers were replaced with surfaces 7.75 inches taller. The aircraft flew again on 16 February (11th flight) and, following a few more sorties, was ferried to Wright Field on 25 June 1943. There it was flown a few times, but fuel leaks required fabrication and installation of metal tanks that, owing to low priority, took until May 1944. This delayed commencement of official performance testing.

Being some 18 months behind schedule, the XP-49 had been outpaced by other programs. The Continentals never delivered the specified power, and aircraft top speed was well below predictions with 406 mph at 15,000 feet and 361 mph at 5,000 feet. The McDonnell XP-67 (see later) offered a predicted 14-mph advantage, more than twice the range, and heavier armament. Even the P-39J, already being delivered, did better with 414 mph at 25,000 feet. Furthermore, the V-1430 engines, which proved difficult to maintain, had not been selected for production. It was clear the XP-49 was going nowhere.

By September 1943, the decision was made to use the aircraft as a testbed for the Continentals and possibly "stratospheric research" testing of pressurization systems above 40,000 feet. Consequently, accoutrements suitable for a fighter were never installed. The aircraft was flown in May 1944, but failure of the port engine required a change-out that took until August. A flight that month found another fuel system problem that took until December to resolve. By this point, the Air Forces had had enough. It accepted the aircraft on 11 December and permanently grounded it on the 22nd. Total program cost had been $587,700.

The XP-49 ended its life by being repeatedly dropped by a hydraulic lift to investigate the results of hard landings. What remained after this abuse was scrapped.

Army Dance (XP-50, XP-65)

Grumman submitted its G-41 design, leveraging off its Navy XF5F-1 Skyrocket work (which see), against the Army requirement for which the XP-49 was developed. The updated Skyrocket was to get two turbosupercharged R-1820s. Although not selected, the Army encouraged Grumman to incorporate improvements in the design, yielding the G-45. The Army Air Corps contracted for one XP-50 Skyrocket on 25 November 1939 as a counterpart to the Lockheed aircraft. Project engineer Bill Schwendler and his team for Grumman's first Army contract transformed the naval fighter with a nose extending past the propeller arcs to accommodate different armament choices and a nose gear, and revised the nacelles to fit the 1,200-hp R-1820-67/69 with turbosuperchargers and three-blade propellers. It was to carry two .50-cal. guns with 500 rpg and two 20mm cannons with 60 rpg, plus two 100-pound bombs under the fuselage. Weight increased further with pilot armor and self-sealing fuel tanks.

Changes in the design ensued, prompting a revision to the contract on 17 January 1940. The mockup was inspected on 22 April. More changes were requested and Grumman fell behind schedule. The XP-50 (40-3057) flew initially from Bethpage on 18 February 1941, with Robert L. Hall at the controls, and displayed improved handling over the XF5F-1.

The Army's interest in a twin-engine interceptor led them to contract with Grumman in late 1939 for a variant of the XF5F-1 they had developed for the Navy. The sole XP-50 flew in early 1941, but only briefly before being destroyed in an accident. There was no follow-up. (Northrop Grumman History Center)

The XP-50 was powered by two turbosupercharged Wright R-1820 radials at a time the Army was pushing inline engines. The long nose was to accommodate two 20mm cannons and two .50-cal. machine guns. The tricycle landing gear was atypical in 1940 but greatly improved ground handling. (Northrop Grumman History Center)

Although the aircraft was scheduled to be delivered to the Air Corps, Grumman insisted on performing more tests as a number of problems cropped up. It was damaged on 14 March after a main gear collapsed, but returned to flight. The prototype was then destroyed on 14 May after the right turbosupercharger exploded, disabling the engine and hydraulic system. Hall was compelled to abandon the aircraft with just 20 hours logged. By this point, Army needs had evolved beyond the original intent of the program and the service chose not to pursue the type.

Grumman's sole product for the Army, the XP-50, appeared a good airplane but was short-lived. Its loss emphasized the false economy of buying just one experimental prototype. This image reveals the poor pilot visibility in the forward lower quarters owing to cockpit placement aft of the wing and nacelles. (Northrop Grumman History Center)

Grumman XP-50 characteristics (performance estimated):			
span	42.0 ft	weight empty	8,307 lbs
length	31.9 ft	loaded	10,558 lbs
height	12.0 ft	maximum	13,060 lbs
wing area	304 ft²	speed, max. (25,000 ft)	424 mph
fuel (int. + ext.)	217+0 gal	cruise	317 mph
service ceiling	40,000 ft	range, normal	585 mi
best climb rate	4,000 fpm	maximum	1,250 mi

Grumman continued concept development of twin fighters based on its XF5F-1 and XP-50. The experience gleaned was put to use in its G-46 design begun in October 1939, refined further as the G-49 and then G-51. The latter possessed a more conventional cockpit location, the wing moved up and a single vertical tail employed, and so was much removed from the Skyrocket. The G-51 featured turbo-supercharged R-2600-22Ws of 2,100 hp, and was to be armed with four .50-cal. machine guns and four 20mm cannons. It was expected to span 52.5 feet, weigh 21,425 pounds loaded, and fly to 427 mph at 27,000 feet, possess 4,400-fpm climb rate with a service ceiling of 36,000 feet and be capable of an 825-mile range.

The G-51 layout appeared so promising that the Army used residual XP-50 funds to pay for studies of the aircraft, designated the XP-65 (MX-138). The service was then authorized on 16 June 1941

The Grumman G-51 became the XF7F-1 for naval service and the XP-65 for the Army Air Forces in a rare joint program. Unfortunately, the differing requirements made coincident development difficult and the Army terminated its interest before the XP-65 advanced much beyond the G-51 model shown here. (Northrop Grumman History Center)

to procure two prototypes, just a month after loss of the XP-50. The G-51 had also been submitted on 24 March for Navy evaluation and that service ordered the Grumman twin on 30 June as two XF7F-1s. This presented the unusual spectacle of the two American air arms jointly developing a combat aircraft, and the programs proceeded in parallel.

Although the joint design path appeared economical, the sister services were soon at loggerheads over conflicting requirements that was adding to Grumman's already prodigious workload. The Army wanted turbosuperchargers, a pressurized cockpit, and several 37mm cannons, while the Navy chose mechanical superchargers, had no use for pressurization, and wanted 20mm weapons. The carrier gear would be excluded from the Army Air Forces version, yet the P-65 would still suffer some weight penalty, as would the Navy plane with elements of the Army variant. The result would be little better than existing types. Continuing was potentially contrary to either's interests, and the services soon became concerned Grumman would find it difficult filling all essential requirements of both specifications. They agreed Grumman was traditionally a Navy supplier and should focus on naval types. The Army bowed out and the XP-65 was cancelled on 16 January 1942.

Appearances Can Be Deceiving (XP-67)

Newcomer McDonnell Aircraft Corp. had only formed in 1939 and was providing valuable services as a subcontractor. However, the St. Louis, Missouri, company had bigger plans to build its own designs. It sought an Army contract and consulted with Materiel Division on several fighter concepts. The single-engine, twin pusher propeller Model I, with extensive wing-fuselage blending, failed to win the R40-C competition of early 1940, but the Army Air Corps was intrigued enough to purchase the engineering data. McDonnell continued to refine the design with feedback from Materiel Division engineers. The Model II-A reached a stage where it was granted project code MX-16 in spring 1941.

The Model II-A was to employ two 1,350-hp XIV-1430-1s with General Electric D-2 turbosuperchargers. The fighter was to have a pressurized cockpit (yet with sliding canopy) for one pilot, 760 gallons of fuel in the fuselage, plus six .50-cal. and four 20mm weapons. McDonnell accepted a guarantee for 472 mph at 18,600 pounds, and maximum climb rate was expected to be 3,200 fpm. A late change was the substitution of six 37mm cannons and compensating gunsight. This would test the value of such heavy but slow-firing weaponry to destroy bombers and permit comparison with a single 75mm cannon then being tested on other platforms. These and other changes drove the design gross weight up to 20,000 pounds.

A $1.51 million contract was finalized on 29 October 1941 covering development of two XP-67 prototype (42-11677/8, MX-127) bomber-destroyers, the first to be delivered on 29 April 1943. Mockup inspection occurred in mid-April 1942. Changes resulting from this event included extending the nose for improved gunsight vision, an engine change to the XI-1430-17 in the right-hand nacelle and a -19 in the other, both with D-23 turbos for 1,600 hp (war emergency) at 25,000 feet. Following this, the Army also revised its standards, requiring the main landing gear to retract into the engine nacelles instead of the wing and entailing substantial redesign of both aspects of the aircraft. Such changes from the government continued through late July 1942. Extensive wind tunnel testing yielded other design revisions, including increasing tail height. Many aspects of the aircraft were tested in full-scale mockups, including a nacelle with engine to optimize cooling which resulted in radiator cooling duct changes.

The XP-67 had a number of innovations that were a challenge for the St. Louis team led by Garrett C. Covington. They had never before designed and built any aircraft, much less an advanced, high-performance fighter. It retained the blended wing-body character of the Model I, had the latest laminar flow airfoil, split flaps, and tricycle landing gear with non-steerable nose wheel. The wheels and tires were unusually large to meet the original rough-field requirement. As a survivability measure, dual cable controls were employed throughout, replacing an intended pushrod single system. The I-1430 engines were tightly cowled and turned four-blade, 10.7-foot diameter propellers. The radiator cooling intakes consisted of troughs along the nacelles to openings in the wing leading edges. The turbines were mounted axially aft of the engines such that their exhausts, and those of the engines, were carried to the end of the

The McDonnell XP-67 was intended to be a bomber-destroyer, carrying heavy armament and considerable fuel. The extensive wing-fuselage blending and tightly cowled, liquid-cooled engine was unusual for the period. However, the project ran long, had its share of problems, and its mission ceased to be vital. (National Museum of the United States Air Force)

McDonnell Aircraft's first fighter and self-designed product was exceedingly ambitious. It is not surprising that it was behind schedule and performance was lackluster, but the XP-67 was still an impressive initial effort. (National Museum of the United States Air Force)

long nacelles and emerged in pipes designed to extract thrust from the flow. Self-sealing tankage for 735 gallons of fuel was provided. The six Oldsmobile M-4 cannons, three in each wing, were placed inboard of the propeller arcs with 45-rounds each. Aileron droop was to assist takeoff and landing performance.

Not surprisingly, the project ran substantially behind schedule and over budget. Because wind tunnel data foretold potential aerodynamic problems, in October 1943 the Army suspended construction of the second ship. Early flight test data and evolving Army needs were expected to guide any changes to yield a more production-representative design.

Taxi testing began with 42-11677 in early December 1943 and quickly showed the engines would be a problem. Fires in both nacelles were experienced during a run-up on 8 December. Following required changes, the aircraft was trucked to nearby Scott Field, Illinois, for flight testing. Ed E. Elliott finally performed first flight on 6 January 1944. It lasted all of six minutes as poor engine performance revealed overheating. Further nacelle changes followed. The fourth flight on 1 February ended dramatically with a tachometer failure and overspeed of the engines, the crankcase bearings burned out, and separation of the canopy from the aircraft. Since the project had to wait for replacement engines, it was a good point to stop for modifications. The aircraft was hauled back to St. Louis. Rework included further changes to the engine/nacelle cooling arrangement and raising the horizontal tail a foot. The intake troughs gave way to ducts.

Flying resumed on 23 March at Lambert Field, St. Louis, although the engines still had to be nursed to avoid overheating. The program seemed to be over a hump and productive testing was performed over the next few months. However, the experimental engines gave 300-hp less output than promised and gross weight had crept up to 25,400 pounds. Army pilots got their turn beginning on 11 May and they were underwhelmed. The aircraft was felt to be underpowered, with unimpressive acceleration and climb performance. Takeoff runs were overly long and the expected 76-mph landing speed became 93 mph. There were dynamic stability issues and the aircraft was generally less maneuverable than some existing fighters.

An attempt to address lateral stability concerns included adding a dorsal fin and increasing stabilizer dihedral from five to seven degrees. A drag reduction program was undertaken that included removing scoops and altering fairings. The overweight aircraft eventually demonstrated 405 mph at 25,000 feet and 22,000 pounds weight – still well below guarantee. The pressurization, oxygen systems, and drooped ailerons were never fitted. The cannons were also left out, although mockup installations were the subject of firing trials at Wright Field.

During 1944, several discussions explored possible changes to the second prototype to improve performance and suitability. Water injection was considered to provide 2,000 hp. McDonnell proposed substituting Curtiss dual-rotation propellers, matched with suitable engines, to increase ceiling plus adding 7- to 10-mph to its top speed and 400 fpm to climb. However, it was later found that 150-octane fuel could produce 2,100 hp in war emergency without the complexities of water injection, and that an 11-foot Aeroproducts propeller could suitably convert this power to thrust without heavy contra-rotating units. With availability of the Continentals in doubt, and delivering only about 1,060 hp, developers considered installing two-stage engines, such as the V-1710 or V-1650, with a jet unit in the rear of each nacelle, possibly the 2,040-lbf General Electric I-20 replacing the turbosuperchargers.

A decision was made to complete performance trials on 42-11677 and then test the contra-rotating propellers on that aircraft while final judgment was rendered on the powerplant installation for 42-11678. Construction of those aspects of 42-11678 not affected by

The extensive blending between the fuselage and nacelles to the wing of the XP-67 is evident in this shot. Also visible are the exhausts from the engine nacelles that sought to produce additional thrust. (Jay Miller Collection)

the pending propulsion decisions was finally permitted to begin on 10 April 1944.

Aircraft 42-11677 was written off following an accident on 6 September 1944 after logging 43 flight hours. An engine malfunction caused a fire that forced an emergency landing after which the plane was damaged beyond repair before the flames were extinguished. Sister-ship 42-11678 was then only 15 percent complete. The contractor's progress had been slow on the four-year-old contract, the aircraft would clearly not be essential in resolving the war, the I-1430s were not going into production, and the advent of jet fighters suggested aircraft like the XP-67 would have short careers. The program was suspended on 13 September and formally terminated on 24 October after expending $4.63 million.

Size Does Not Matter (XP-71)

As Americans watched the progress of the war during 1939 through 1941, anxiety about potential bombing attacks on the United States grew. A number of fighter projects were accordingly initiated. One was an enormous aircraft intended to take a large cannon to high altitude to bang away at enemy formations, yet also serve as an escort for friendly bombers. Curtiss submitted six concepts in April 1941, followed by two complete proposals on 2 November. One configuration was agreed upon and the XP-71 (MX-147) was born on 28 October 1941 with an order for two prototypes. A $3.2 million contract was delayed until 6 March 1942 because of concern over deliveries dates of 2.3 and 2.8 years.

The Curtiss airplane (Model CW-29) would have been the largest fighter developed in the United States had it been completed. It was to span 82.3 feet, gross 39,950 pounds, and carry 900 to 1,940 gallons of fuel. It was to climb to 25,000 feet in 12.5 minutes, make 428 mph once there, and its ceiling would be 40,000 feet with 3,000-mile range. The armament was two 37mm cannons with 60 rpg and a 75mm cannon with 20 rounds in an automatic feed, all firing from the nose. Two wing-mounted R-4360-13s were to deliver a combined 6,900 hp wet with GE turbos. To convert this to thrust, Curtiss planned to employ a pair of eight-blade, 13.5-foot diameter Hamilton Standard contra-rotating propellers in a pusher configuration. This mandated tricycle gear. The pressurized cockpit would accommodate the crew of two.

Mockup of the XP-71 was inspected in St. Louis on 16 November 1942, at which time the change was made to a single-place

The blending to reduce drag on the XP-67 also produced this unusual planform. The tightly cowled engines tended to overheat as one of numerous problems McDonnell struggled to resolve. (National Archives)

McDonnell XP-67 characteristics:

span	55.0 ft	weight empty	17,745 lbs
length	44.8 ft	gross	22,114 lbs
height	15.8 ft	maximum	25,400 lbs
wing area	414 ft²	speed, max. (25,000 ft)	405 mph
fuel (int. + ext.)	735+0 gal	cruise	270 mph
service ceiling	37,400 ft	range, normal	700 mi
initial climb rate	2,600 fpm	ferry	2,385 mi

This wind tunnel model of the Curtiss XP-71 emphasizes the twin-engine layout with contra-rotating propellers. When proposed in 1941, the tricycle landing gear arrangement was becoming accepted. The wide canopy suggests the original side-by-side seating for the two crewmen. (San Diego Aerospace Museum)

aircraft. As detailed design continued into early 1943, the aircraft was shaping up as one of the most complex aircraft of the war. During ground trials of the gun installation in early February 1943, the sample nose section failed dramatically. Development of a range finder for the fire control system was suffering its own woes, with radio and optical approaches investigated as separate efforts. The former was selected.

By the latter half of 1943, it was clear only the Allies would be putting up long-range bomber formations during the remainder of the war, and the XP-71 was without a mission. The Army gave some thought to using it as a photoreconnaissance bird, but without commitment. The program was terminated on 23 October with $2.3 million expended and first flight anticipated in June 1944. Curtiss may have followed-up with a variant suggested for convoy fighter or anti-shipping duties. A wind tunnel model that may have been of this iteration possessed swept outboard wing panels.[8] However, the design was quite unsuitable for either role and Curtiss needed to focus on more vital projects.

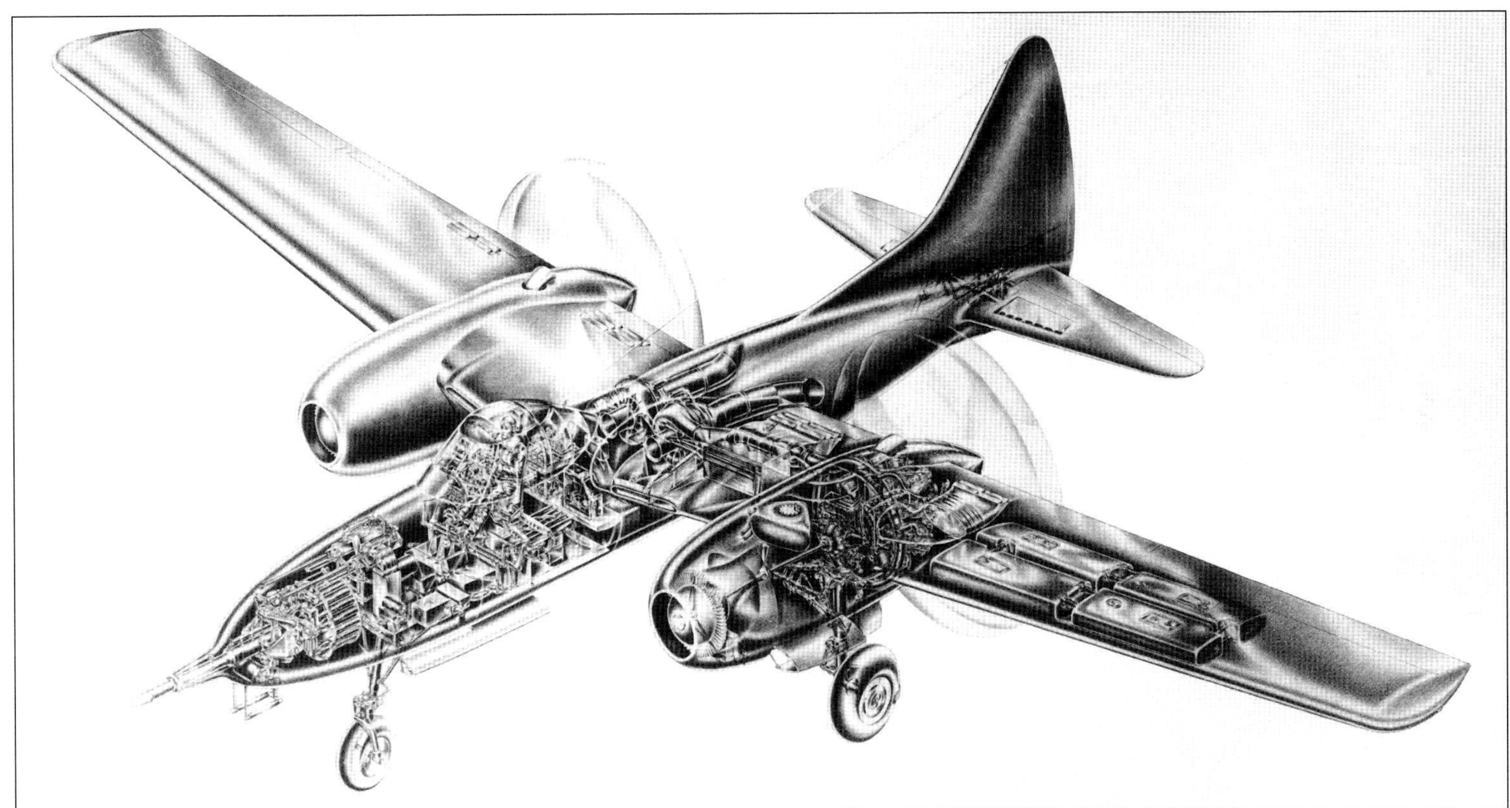

This Curtiss cutaway illustrates the complexity of the proposed XP-71. Note the fans to promote cooling flow within the nacelles, turbo-superchargers within the fuselage, and the large 75mm cannon in the nose with twin 37mm above. This drawing dates from 16 December 1943, after cancellation, and shows the single-seat cockpit. (National Museum of the United States Air Force, artist G.L. Flanders)

Chapter 7

Ostensibly a reasonable stretch of technology, the XP-54 came in overweight and late, sealing its fate by the time the second prototype flew (shown here wearing an incorrect 41-1211 serial number; the actual number was 42-108994). It ended as among the largest single-seat, single-engine fighters ever built. But performance fell well short of requirements. (Gerald Balzer Collection)

ARMY EXPERIMENTALS

In the pre-war and early war years, threats abroad demanded rapid expansion of the Air Corps. Fighter designs emerging overseas and new tactics evident in air fighting had to be answered or matched quickly should the United States find itself drawn into the conflict. The Army reassessed its approach to combat aircraft acquisition and the underlying assumptions. This was evident in a number of projects that truly challenged convention and the state of the art. Although few reached prototype owing to a number of factors, and none were taken to production, they were invaluable learning experiences for both the service and aviation firms involved.

Queer Company

The clearest indication of change came with issuance of Pursuit Specification XC-622 on 14 November 1939. This was America's attempt to leap ahead in fighter performance by encouraging innovation. The lofty aim was a single-seat, single-engine aircraft capable of reaching 20,000 feet in 7 minutes, attain 425 mph at 15,000 to 20,000 feet, and 525 mph desired (believed to be the theoretical limit for propeller-driven flight). It was to possess a minimum 1.5-hour endurance operating from a 3,000-foot rough field surrounded by 50-foot obstacles. Armament was to be four guns or cannon and six 20-pound bombs. These were extraordinary goals in light of what had been produced until recently, and given available engine power. The Army Air Corps favored the liquid-cooled, 1,800-hp Pratt & Whitney H-3130. This had initially been developed for the U.S. Navy as a 24-cylinder with sleeve valves and liquid cooling. It soon evolved into the H-3730 with the immediate goal of 2,000 to 2,200 hp, and hopes of eventually achieving 3,000 hp.

Rather than the common Circular Proposal, the 1940 fighter competition was kicked off on 20 February 1940 with release of the Request for Data R40-C. This, too, marked a rare and still new approach to aircraft development in that it informally solicited concepts from many manufacturers and then weighed them in a competitive fashion. The service expected to proceed with two revisions of existing designs capable of achieving 425 mph at approximately 15,000 feet and quickly entered into production for 1941 fielding. Three would be more far-reaching designs capable of meeting all specifications and entering production in 1941 for service in 1942. The Phase 1 proposal would be followed by Phase 2 of preliminary design and wind tunnel testing to clarify proposal potential. Phase 3, construction and flight test of one or two prototypes, depended on satisfactory results of Phase 2 and availability of funding. Of the two prototypes, the first might be without all tactical equipment to permit the earliest possible look at performance and handling.

Innovation was welcomed from the R40-C respondents, and those working with the new laminar flow airfoils were particularly sought out. The specifications forced designers to make radical departures from convention in order to reduce drag and realize the most speed from available engine power. Moving the engine to the rear of the aircraft eliminated slipstream drag on the airframe and adjacent wing, especially helping ensure benefits from a laminar airfoil. This would also allow a streamline nose with easier weapons integration. Dispensing with tails for flying wing designs further contributed to drag reduction. Inline, liquid-cooled engines promised less cooling drag.

The Air Corps selected the five designs for development, and another (the XP-67) eventually emerged. These were pursued to various levels of effort over the next few years. Three designs from the R40-C competition from Vultee, Curtiss, and Northrop eventually flew. These were fascinating experimental tricycle gear, pusher types that included swept-wing and tail-less designs that expanded the state of the art. However, development was long and painful with mixed results. This odd troika, too, was outpaced by the war and ended on the shelf.

In Limbo (XP-52, XP-59)

Bell's initial proposal against R-40C, the Model 13, was similar to its P-39C but with potentially more powerful engines including the XIV-1430-1 and -3, and further models of the V-1710 at 1,500 hp. Discussions with the Air Corps also explored the V-1430-5, all models reversed from inverted to upright and adding a two-stage supercharger, the H-3130, and Lycoming XH-2470, seeking 1,600 to

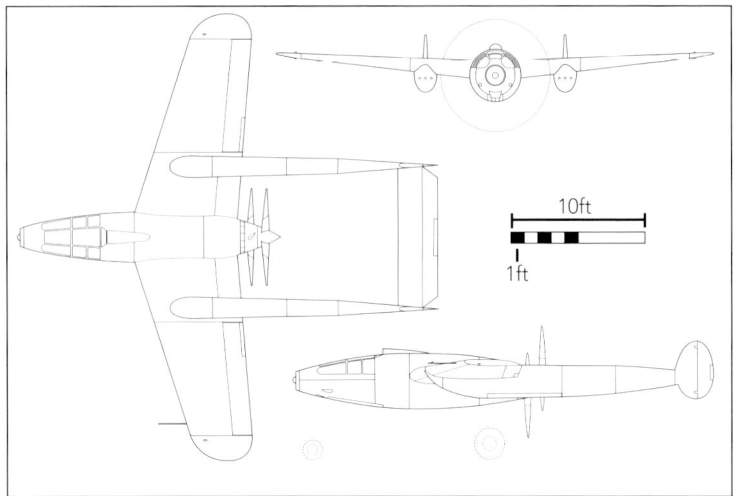

Among the unusual designs coming out of the R40-C competition was Bell's Model 16 twin-boom contra-rotating pusher proposal, developed at no cost to the Air Corps. However, the IV-1430 engine for the XP-52 was too long reaching an airworthy stage and the project was terminated. (Author)

The Bell Model 19, pitched to the Navy, was very similar to the Model 20. This was given form in a mockup built in Buffalo. It shows the six-blade pusher propeller, two 20mm cannons in the nose, and trio of .50-cal. machine guns in the front of each tail boom. (Jay Miller Collection)

1,800 hp from the selection. All of these were experimental engines requiring changes to adopt them to the P-39-like installation, potentially consuming more time than acceptable. Consequently, Bell moved to a more radical design in July 1940.

The Model 16 was a twin-boom pusher, single-seat fighter powered by a 1,250-hp liquid-cooled XIV-1430-5 turning a nine-foot diameter, six-blade Hamilton Standard contra-rotating propeller between the booms. A nose intake for the radiator gave a gapping maw appearance. Added to these unusual aspects was the tricycle undercarriage, essential given the pusher layout, and laminar flow wing. Span was to be 35.0 feet, length 34.8 feet, height 9.3 feet, and loaded weight 8,200 pounds, 6,480-pounds empty, with maximum speed of 425 to 435 mph at 19,500 feet. A service ceiling of 40,000 feet was expected, with climb to 20,000 feet in just 6.3 minutes. With 270-gallons of fuel, range would be 960 miles at 420 mph. It was to pack two 20mm cannons with 100 rpg in the nose and a trio of .50-cal. machine guns at the front of each boom with a total of 3,000 rounds.

Although Bell was new to the business and there was some hesitation to engage them, the Army was intrigued and gave the project a tentative designation of XP-52 (MX-3). This was the Air Corps' first pusher pursuit aircraft program. Risk to the Air Corps was minimized, as this was the chosen design Bell was to pursue at minimal cost to the government in exchange for releasing the P-39 for foreign military sales. Since the 1430's prospects were marginal, the government encouraged Bell to also consider the R-2800-19 already configured for a buried pusher installation.

In October 1940, the Army began preparing a contract with Bell for one V-1430-powered prototype XP-52 and a second with the R-2800. The latter aroused concerns due to the substantial changes to the Model 16, like increased frontal area, that would degrade performance. Late in October, before the contract was codified, the service decided the 1430 approach was simply too slow in reaching a producible state. The XP-52 died at that point.

The XP-52 layout with the air-cooled Double Wasp was continued as the Model 20. The R-2800-23 was of 2,000 hp, and an enlarged nose intake fed cooling air to the rear-mounted engine via ducting. The design was overall larger than the XP-52, its swept wings spanning 40.0 feet, fuselage length was 37.3 feet, and it was 12 feet to the top of the tail. Loaded, the aircraft weighed 10,463 pounds, and 7,960 pounds empty. Maximum speed was predicted at 450 mph at 22,000 feet, 6.3 minutes to reach 20,000 feet, and its service ceiling was 38,000 feet. Cruising at 380 mph, a range of 850 miles was afforded by 270 gallons of fuel. The same weapons layout was planned, but the .50s given 300 rpg, and 70 rpg for cannons.

Go-ahead was given on 2 October 1940 for what the Army Air Corps named the XP-59 (MX-45). With a satisfactory design offered in January 1941, a pair of prototypes was ordered on 26 February. Unfortunately, the project was overcome by higher priority work demanding the lion's share of engineering and shop manpower, and Bell was judged as over-stretched. The XP-59 was terminated on 21 November 1942 as the mockup was coming together.[1]

The XP-52 was taken up again with an R-2800 powerplant as the XP-59 (Model 20) as depicted by this wind tunnel model. Only the more rounded fuselage for the radial engine differentiated the two designs, but they suffered the same fate. Bell was simply overcome with more vital work. (Jay Miller Collection)

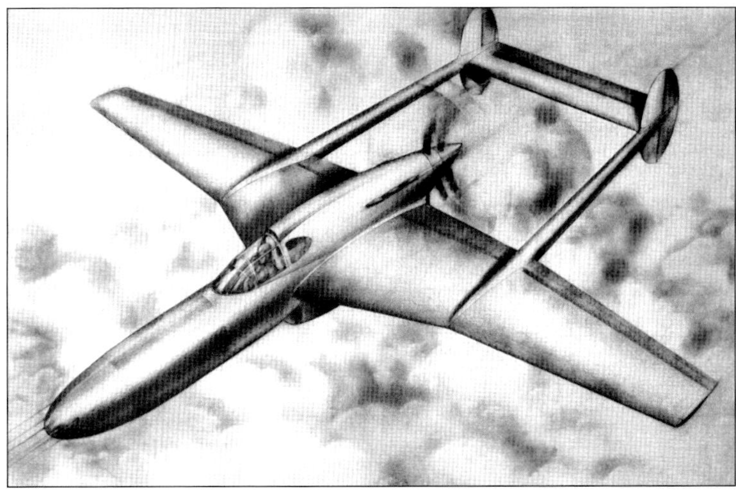

This drawing is of the XP-54 as originally placed on contract, dated 11 December 1940. The photos that follow give appreciation for the marked increase in aircraft size that occurred during development. Note the original tail design, turtledeck aft of the cockpit, and belly cooling intake that were all eliminated. (Jay Miller Collection, artist W. Fritz)

Weight Gain (XP-54)

The proposed Vultee Model 70 appeared to be a reasonably conventional design, although the twin-boom layout was still unusual at the time. More unusual was the pusher layout, double-tapered inverted-gull wing, and tricycle landing gear. It was to span 40.0 feet, be 37.5-feet long, and gross 9,055 pounds. The 10.0-foot diameter, six-blade, contra-rotating propeller was to be turned by the H-2600-1 at 1,850 hp with two-speed, gear-driven supercharger. Armament was to be two .30- and two .50-cal. machine guns, plus a pair of 20mm cannons, all in the nose. Vultee expected 525 mph at 15,000 to 20,000 feet with military power.

Program go-ahead was given on 31 May 1940. The first contract, dated 22 June, covered preliminary design and wind-tunnel testing, and was coded MX-12. The prototype contract came on 8 January 1941. Vultee was to deliver the single XP-54 (41-1210) on 1 July 1942. At that time, armament became six .50s in the nose while performance estimates were 510 mph at 20,000 feet and 6.3 minutes to reach that altitude. A second prototype (42-108994) was added on 17 March 1942, delivery specified for 1 October.*

The H-2600 engine was cancelled on 4 October 1940. At the urging of the Air Corps, Vultee substituted the 24-cylinder Lycoming XH-2470-1, promising 2,300 hp at 25,000 feet from a heavier unit. This engine was created by the merging of two 12-cylinder opposed, 1,000-hp O-1230 "Hyper" engines. This conglomerate powerplant first ran in July 1940. Its 2,300 hp came from a 2,430-pound unit with single-stage supercharger. Lycoming was only just beginning to

Vultee settled on the Lycoming XH-2470 to power the XP-54 when the Pratt & Whitney XH-2600 was cancelled. They also jettisoned the contra-rotating propeller. These and numerous changes requested by the Army dug a deep hole from which the design (first prototype shown on 2 November 1942) never emerged. (National Archives)

* *Serial 42-108994 was assigned to the second XP-54, but it carried the number 41-1211 in practice.*

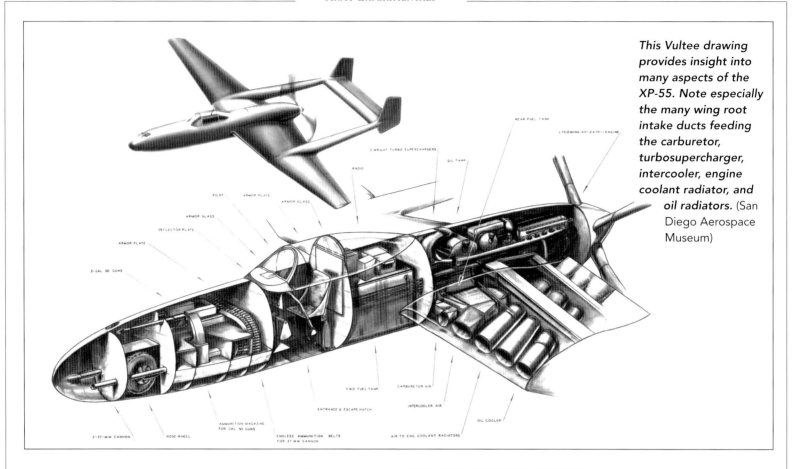

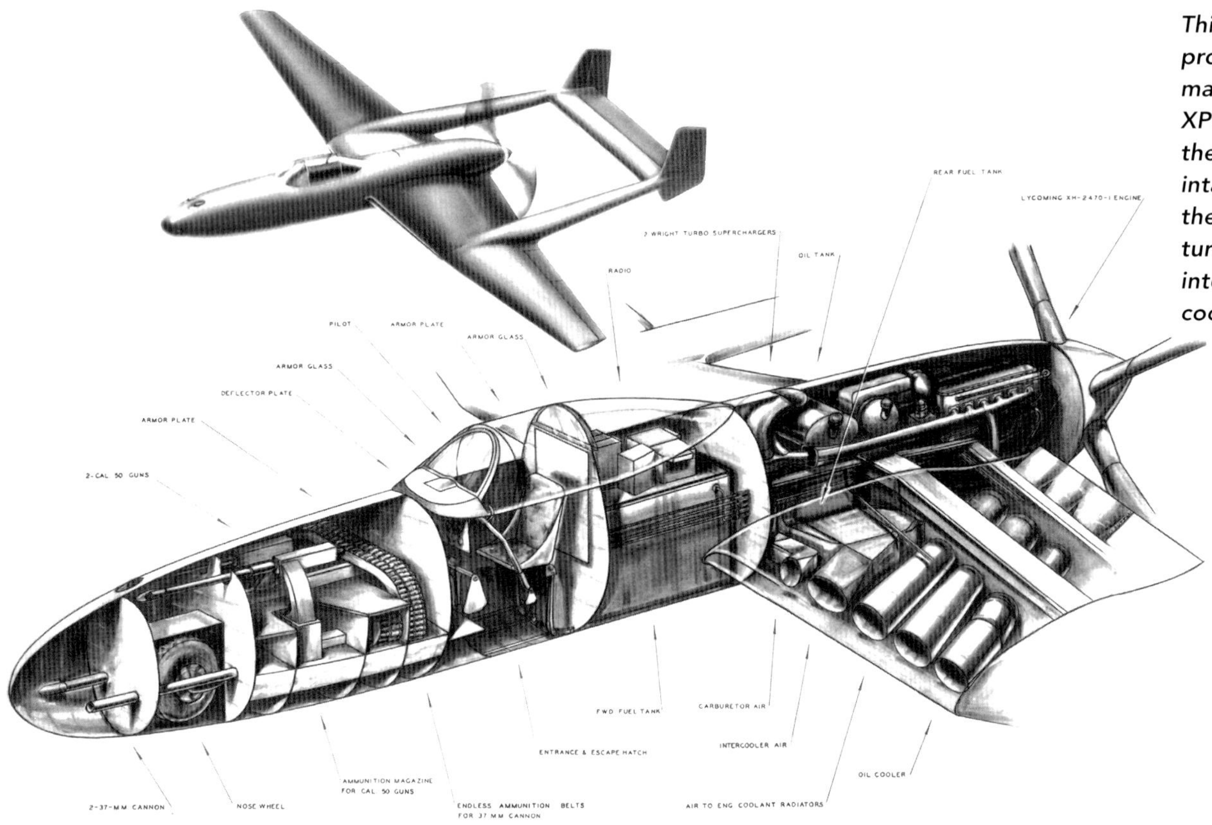

This Vultee drawing provides insight into many aspects of the XP-55. Note especially the many wing root intake ducts feeding the carburetor, turbosupercharger, intercooler, engine coolant radiator, and oil radiators. (San Diego Aerospace Museum)

study changes in the engine to interface with dual-rotation propellers. Vultee was compelled by schedule to go with a single propeller, leaving the contra-rotating unit as a future option. Furthermore, the Air Corps could not guarantee output of the experimental engine would meet expectations.

Responding to the rapidly changing requirements of aerial combat as observed abroad, mission emphasis changed to high-altitude intercept with a 30,000-foot design altitude and 40,000-foot service ceiling. Even as the XP-54 mockup was inspected on 23 May 1941, the Army Air Corps was calling for numerous changes along these lines. Added were cockpit pressurization (still new and without industry design standards) and a turbosupercharger. The inevitable self-sealing tanks and armor had to be inserted. The service also requested heavier armament, favoring the 37mm cannon.

The development team was formed under chief engineer Richard W. Palmer, eventually replaced by A. P. "Jack" Fontaine. This changeover, higher priority work, and uncertainty engendered by Army Air Corps requirements changes contributed to substantial XP-54 delays. The upshot was three Vultee model specifications in the span of 15 months that made the original delivery dates unattainable. The considerable divergence from the original intent of the Model 70 came with a 20-percent increase in size and a weight growth of more than 100 percent, making it among the largest single-seat fighters ever flown to that time. Lacking the contra-rotating

The high stance of the XP-54, cabin pressurization, and bailout hazard posed by the pusher prop, compelled this unusual pilot entry. The seat was lowered on a panel and then raised after the pilot strapped in. On bailout, the panel and seat pivoted down below the arc. (San Diego Aerospace Propeller Museum)

props, guaranteed top speed dropped to 479 mph at 27,000 feet, and the service ceiling was reduced to 37,000 feet. It was doubtful that these figures could be met and the aircraft suitable for the new or old mission.

The H-2470-1 engine was tightly cowled and turned a four-blade, 12.2-foot diameter Hamilton Standard propeller. Aircraft 41-1210 had two Wright Type B turbosuperchargers in parallel while 42-108994 had the higher capacity experimental GE XCM turbo, all under the aft fuselage. All propulsion system air came via openings in the leading edge of the wing inboard segments. This NACA "ducted wing" design fed the turbosupercharger intake and intercooler air inlets, engine coolant radiator, and oil cooler. Radiators were within these inboard wings, and the associated inboard split flaps had a segment that served to regulate the airflow out the exhaust opening. An opening under the cowling was still necessary to assist in cooling the engine compartment. All fuel was in a fuselage tank, 140 gallons for 42-108994. Outboard flaps were the double-slotted type and the wing featured laminar flow airfoil technology.

Because the aircraft stood with the bottom of the fuselage nearly six feet off the ground, the cockpit situated well forward of the wing and its pressurization negating canopy entry, a unique pilot entrance was necessary. The seat was lowered on a fuselage bottom hatch/escape door via electric motor, and then lifted the pilot into the cockpit. The design simplified cockpit sealing for pressurization. In an emergency, the hatch and door pivoted open, the seat sliding down and pilot was automatically released clear of the propeller. The turtledeck behind the cockpit in the Model 70 concept was eliminated in favor of a canopy with no rearward obstruction.

The weapons complement evolved to two 37mm cannons with 60 rpg plus a pair of .50s with 500 rpg. A new computerized compensating gunsight was integrated with a nose assembly that could be elevated and depressed hydraulically to adjust for the widely different ballistics of the two types of weapons without changing aircraft attitude. Rotating on the nose landing gear pivot axis, the nose and cannons raised three degrees of elevation and could be depressed six degrees, while the pair of .50s were attached to separately moving mounts. This permitted the machine guns to be fired to ensure range and aim before engaging with the cannon. Operation of gunsight functions was via controls on the yoke and throttle, values and symbology projected onto the combiner glass.

Vultee XP-54 characteristics:			
span	53.8 ft	weight empty	15,262 lbs
length	54.7 ft	gross	18,233 lbs
height	14.5 ft	maximum	19,377 lbs
wing area	455.5 ft²	speed, max. (28,500 ft)	381 mph
fuel capacity (int. + ext.)	223-395 +0 gal	with cleanup	403 mph
service ceiling	37,000 ft	cruise	328 mph
best climb rate	2,300 fpm	range, normal	500 mi
		ferry	850 mi

All the innovative features added weight, 16,145-pounds gross was estimated, such that projected peak speed degraded to 476 mph at 30,000 feet for what was relabeled the Model 84. Eventually, the specification was revised to 403 mph for the Model 84E.

With the first aircraft completed and flight approaching, the XP-54 Swoose Goose was disassembled and trucked from Downey's Vultee Field to Muroc AAB for initial testing. The aircraft was temporarily equipped with a Curtiss propeller that reduced performance. It also had one of the first data telemetry systems for transmitting engineering data to the ground. The 31-minute maiden flight occurred on 15 January 1943, Frank Davis doing the honors. After five flights, the aircraft was flown to Ontario AAB, California, and testing continued there and at Vultee Field. The experimental engine proved temperamental, but the aircraft handled well. Changes introduced included enlarged vertical tails to combat fin stall by extending the top leading edge forward, a revised exhaust behind the cockpit, and steel cowls added aft of the turbo exhausts to prevent overheating of the structure. Ship two began flying on 24 May 1944.

Without much surprise, performance of the overweight aircraft did not measure up to expectations. Top speed was just 381 mph. Only by rigorous cleanup of the design and surface polishing was the aircraft able to reach 404 mph at 28,000 feet, but was still woefully inadequate. Takeoff at gross weight was 3,020 feet over a 50-foot obstacle.

The aircraft's performance shortfall and its late development date were not the only factors working against the XP-54. The H-2470's lackluster performance in the XP-54 (military power was actually 2,200 hp), the only platform that flew it, contributed to its demise after a long and costly development. Consideration was given to adapting the design to the Allison V-3420, but schedule and cost appeared prohibitive. The Air Forces told Vultee on 25 May 1943 there would be no production of the P-54. Although, work continued to glean potentially valuable engineering data, everyone seemed to have lost heart.

Aircraft 41-1210 was delivered to Wright Field on 28 October 1943. On the next flight, following an engine modification, backfiring damaged the Lycoming. The unit was removed for repair, but this was too costly. The aircraft was grounded after having logged 63.2 hours in 86 flights. It provided parts to 42-108994 for which the union of the Lycoming engine and General Electric XCM turbo was not a happy one. Ship two flew 10 flights for 10.7 hours through 2 April 1945, the last a delivery flight from Vultee Field to San Bernardino Air Depot.[2] There it was stripped of useful parts. The nose assembly was cut off and shipped to Eglin Field for gunfire trials. The XP-54 contract was closed-out at a total cost of $1.3 million.

Just Out of Reach (XP-55, CW 24-B)

Curtiss-Wright Corp., St. Louis Airplane Division, submitted proposals for an aircraft with three potential engines. The evaluators selected the P-249C with the 1,600-hp, two-stage Continental IV-1430-3 turning a contra-rotating propeller. This was another pusher design, but with an aft-mounted swept wing possessing vertical surfaces at the tips. An all-flying elevator at the nose, controlled via tabs, gave it the appearance of a tail-forward concept, although it technically was not a canard as it had no fixed surface and the elevator trailed in trimmed flight. Proposed weaponry was one .30-cal. machine gun, two .50s, and a 37mm, all in the nose. Curtiss expected 507 mph top speed at 5,674 pounds gross weight. It would be the Army's first swept wing fighter, the concept spanning 32.3 feet, with a length of 25.5 feet.

The initial contract for the XP-55 (Model CW 24, MX-13) preliminary design and wind tunnel testing was signed 22 June 1940. Curtiss agreed to performance guarantees that included a top speed of 507 mph at 20,000 feet and five-minutes climb to get there, 1.5-hour endurance, and 2,000-foot takeoff plus 2,900-feet landing over a 50-foot obstacle. During wind tunnel tests, particular attention was paid to the choice of wing sweep and dihedral angles, and leading edge down twist toward the tip (washout) to combat an outboard spanwise flow of air when approaching stall angle of attack.* Such a pattern promoted flow separation at the tip first that degraded roll control nearing stall.

Wind tunnel results revealed potentially poor stability and control characteristics, particularly at stall. Design changes to address these and meet evolving tactical requirements had the potential for substantially impacting performance and schedule. The Air Corps hesitated to proceed further. Consequently, Curtiss chose to use its own funds to build a proof-of-concept full-scale flight article to collect additional data. This Model 24-B precursor was in the final stages of construction when Wright Field issued a 28 November 1941 contract covering the project.

The CW 24-B fuselage was constructed of welded steel tubing with fabric covering. The wing was made entirely of wood and spanned 36.6 feet with 191.5 square foot area, and possessed 26.5-degree sweep at the quarter-chord line. Overall length was 27.4 feet and it grossed 3,604 pounds. Unlike the P-249C proposal, the 24-B had the vertical surfaces and rudders installed approximately mid-span. The wing had slots about mid-chord in the outer wing panels, along with washout in this area, to help ensure airflow over the ailerons remained attached well into stall. It had fixed undercarriage with wheel pants. Crew stations for the pilot and a flight test engineer were included. Flight instruments and systems were extremely basic. The 24-B was given a 275-hp Menasco C6S-5 and two-blade propeller. The aircraft was desperately underpowered, achieving only 180 to 200 mph.

The CW 24-B (42-39347) was sent to Muroc by rail and first flown on 2 December 1941 by J. Harvey Gray. The first portion of the flight test program sought a suitable aircraft configuration through modifications. Nose gear strut length was increased to optimize

Curtiss-Wright's proposal for an unusual high-speed fighter had some worrying potential flying qualities that caused the Air Forces pause. Consequently, the corporation built the CW 24-B demonstrator. This photo shows the aircraft in its original configuration, as well as revealing the spartan accommodations at Muroc AAB in 1942. (Gerald Balzer Collection)

Readily altered to test new configurations and control solutions in flight, the CW 24-B provided valuable data to the XP-55 designers. This image is of the aircraft in its final configuration with the vertical surfaces moved far outboard, wingtip extensions added, and vertical surfaces above and below the engine compartment. (Gerald Balzer Collection)

* *Angle of attack is the angle between the wing mean chord line (line between the leading and trailing edges of the airfoil or wing cross-section) and the incident airflow.*

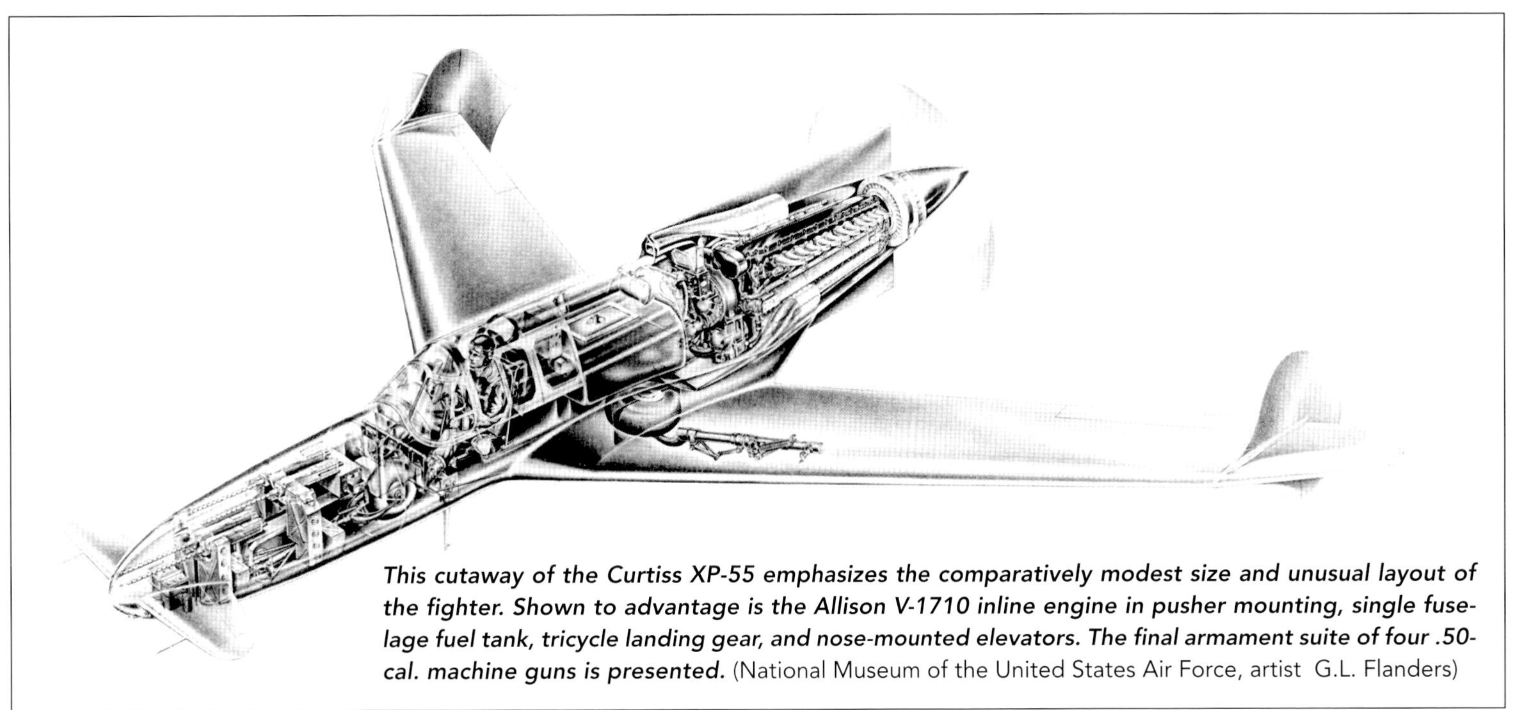

This cutaway of the Curtiss XP-55 emphasizes the comparatively modest size and unusual layout of the fighter. Shown to advantage is the Allison V-1710 inline engine in pusher mounting, single fuselage fuel tank, tricycle landing gear, and nose-mounted elevators. The final armament suite of four .50-cal. machine guns is presented. (National Museum of the United States Air Force, artist G.L. Flanders)

incidence angle for takeoff roll. Elevator area was increased by 25 percent (span lengthened) for greater longitudinal controllability. Several control system changes were made for optimal trimming and control forces.

The mid-span vertical surfaces and rudders proved inadequate, with directional stability leaving something to be desired as previously suggested by tunnel data. Efforts to improve matters included trying several sizes and shapes of vertical stabilizers and rudders, as well as adding these at the wingtips, and finally moving the original surfaces four feet further outboard. This ultimately converged on vertical stabilizers at the tips and with shallow fins installed at the top and bottom of the engine cowling. Wing extensions outboard of the vertical surfaces were added later to improve longitudinal behavior at low speed. The slots were eventually sealed.

Testing of the CW 24-B then moved to collecting performance and controllability data supporting design of the XP-55. In total, 169 flights were conducted through May 1942, some of these by Army and Navy pilots. Spin tests were delayed because a 1/16th scale model of the design showed hazardous behavior in free-spin tunnel tests.* Although the rotation could be stopped, the model stabilized in a level descent that could not be broken. The 24-B stalls, while occasionally unusual and unpredictable, were recoverable and safe. In some respects, the stalls were considered superior to conventional aircraft, with exceptionally slow speeds and high angles of attack achievable. It exhibited no tendency to unintentional spin entry. However, no spins were attempted because of the low ceiling of the aircraft owing to meager power. The 24-B was then shipped to Langley for full-scale wind tunnel tests.

Based on the 24-B test results, the Army ordered three XP-55 prototypes (42-78845/7) on 10 July 1942 for $1.22 million. By this time, the IV-1430 engine program had foundered, thus the powerplant was switched to the 1,250-hp Allison V-1710-F16 originally proposed with the P-249A. The Allison was chosen on the basis of availability and reliability, with the expectation that a more advanced and powerful model would likely be used for production. Curtiss accepted revised performance guarantees of 419 mph top speed at 19,300 feet, 7.1 minutes to reach 20,000 feet, 1-hour endurance, and 1,950-foot takeoff and landing distance over a 50-foot obstacle.

Design of the XP-55 proceeded under chief engineer George Augustus Page, Jr., and chief designer E. M. "Bud" Flesh. Tunnel tests included checking results with a laminar airfoil. Results indicated a more conventional NACA airfoil was most suitable. However, the Air Forces continued to favor the laminar flow wing, and additional testing finally settled on a suitable selection. A full-scale nose section with elevator was also constructed and tested in the Wright Field and Moffett Field wind tunnels preceding dive tests.

* *The free-spin tunnel is a vertically oriented wind tunnel into which a model can be launched with a spinning motion to fly free and the dynamics observed.*

The first XP-55 is shown on jacks in St. Louis on 28 October 1943 with the original wingtip and a mid-wing fence. The Ascender had unfortunate stall and spin characteristics that caused the loss of one aircraft, a lengthy test program, and redesigns that did not satisfy the Army. (San Diego Aerospace Museum)

This image is a fine study of the aft fuselage and propulsion segment of the third prototype XP-55. Although fitted with an inline engine, air scoops at top and bottom plus the aft cowl flaps were required for compartment cooling and to the feed oil cooler and carburetor. (Air Force Flight Test Center)

The XP-55 Ascender followed the lines suggested by the 24-B. The wing incorporated ailerons and split flaps with 28.5-degree quarter-chord sweep (45-degrees at the leading edge). The ailerons automatically biased up 10 degrees when the flaps were extended to compensate for the nose-down pitching moment of landing flap and gear extension. Vertical surfaces above and below the engine incorporated an engine bay cooling duct at the bottom and a coolant radiator intake at the top. Carburetor air was derived from either duct or the engine compartment. Cowl flaps and a fan attached to the propeller shaft assisted in regulating compartment and coolant temperature. Wing hardpoints were included for two 50-gallon external tanks. A single 10-foot diameter three-blade Curtiss Electric propeller replaced the dual-rotation unit of the proposal. An electrically actuated link and compressed air charge was added to the propeller shaft to release and separate the propeller in the event the pilot had to bail out. The weapons were also altered, settling on four .50s and a pair of 20mm cannons.

Mockup inspections in the latter half of 1942 yielded even further changes in the XP-55. Weapons were revised again to just the four .50s with 250 rpg. Fuel capacity was lowered and the powerplant changed once more to the 1,275-hp V-1710-95 without supercharger, again owing to availability. Weight had grown 40 percent to 7,931 pounds.

The first XP-55 was rolled out on 26 June 1943. On 7 July, it was trucked to nearby Scott Field, where the longer runway afforded greater safety. It began engine runs and taxi tests on 11 July and was flown two days later by J. Harvey Gray.

Initial testing revealed a long takeoff roll, the aircraft reluctant to get airborne. The elevator area was subsequently increased 15 percent (span extension) to provide additional pitch authority for earlier rotation. The elevator interconnection with the flaps was revised to provide some up elevator trim when the flaps were lowered. The ventral intake was redesigned twice in an effort to achieve suitable cooling – although this was never satisfactory. The engine was prone to overheating during ground operations. A fence was installed inboard of each aileron to preclude spanwise flow at high angles of attack.

Testing continued at Lambert Field, showing good performance and maneuverability, although some handling characteristics were disquieting. Leading-edge stall strips (spoilers) were also attempted to induce stall about mid-wing before the tips. During stall tests on 15 November, the 27th flight, with gear and flaps down, the aircraft pitched over onto its back. The deep stall produced a stable vertical descent like that observed with the spin model. The engine quit from fuel starvation, preventing the pilot from accelerating out of the condition. After a 16,000-foot descent with no indication of imminent recovery, Gray abandoned the aircraft.

Considerable additional work was necessary to recover from this event, and a new campaign of wind tunnel investigations began in Langley's free spinning tunnel and at Wright Field. These included numerous potential configurations, including horizontal surfaces added to the engine cowlings. The conclusion was that additional area in the wingtip extensions and elevator travel increased to 70-degrees up and down would be beneficial. Added to the expanded tips were "trailerons" in the surfaces, linked to the ailerons, to ensure against degradation in roll rate with the span increase. A fuel system change provided a few minutes of fuel with the aircraft inverted. These features were introduced on the third aircraft, 42-78847, still in fabrication.

Ship two flew on 9 January 1944, but under restrictions until the spin problem was resolved. It had the elevator span increase and trim mechanism improvements. The fairings around the upper and lower intakes were also revised to reduce drag.

Aircraft 42-78847 took up the testing on 25 April. On the very first takeoff, an undesirable outcome of the changes was evident when the high-elevator angle on the roll caused the surface to stall, extending the liftoff distance. Consequently, an elevator travel stop was introduced that restricted down travel to the original 17 degrees except when the aircraft was inverted. Pilots also complained of inadequate longitudinal feel at low speed, such as approach and landing, with tendency to over-control.

Ship three soon entered stall tests. Stall warning was nonexistent. The stall was abrupt, usually characterized by a roll and sharp pitch down such that the aircraft almost reversed direction and suffered an excessive 3,000- to 4,000-foot altitude loss during recovery.

Curtiss XP-55 characteristics (final configuration):			
span	41.1 ft	weight empty	6,354 lbs
length	29.6 ft	gross	7,931 lbs
height	11.6 ft	maximum	8,805 lbs
wing area	217.2 ft²	speed, max. (19,300 ft)	390 mph
fuel capacity (int. + ext.)	110+100 gal	cruise	296 mph
service ceiling	35,800 ft	range, normal	635 mi
best climb rate	2,460 fpm	ferry	1,440 mi

The third XP-55 flew with two 50-gallon external tanks. It also exhibits the modifications mandated by the design's unsatisfactory stall characteristics, visible here the expanded wingtips with trailing edge surface. Pilot bailout was problematic, although a jettisonable propeller was intended to help ensure a safe outcome. (Gerald Balzer Collection)

A pressure sensor driving a stick shaker was provided and was among the first artificial stall warning systems, but there were no ready solutions for the altitude loss.

Aircraft 42-78846 was modified with the same changes as ship three to permit Army performance testing in St. Louis during fall 1944. Test pilots reported many good aspects of the aircraft, but also much that still required work to be operationally suitable. It was ferried to Dayton on 25 October for further testing. Aircraft three was flown to Eglin on 5 November for weapons trials. This proved short-lived when the weapon mounts failed and blast tubes collapsed during ground firing. The aircraft was then taken to Wright Field in mid-December. It crashed during a slow roll at an aerial display on 27 May 1945, killing the pilot and a motorist while gravely injuring others.

The Army considered the stall characteristics of the Ascender unacceptable, even with artificial warning. The takeoff distance over the 50-foot obstacle was an excessive 5,000 feet without flaps. Being 1,000 pounds overweight, maximum airspeed was considerably below the guarantee and engine cooling was wholly inadequate. Any benefits of the unusual design paled in the face of these deficiencies. With its development schedule running well beyond expectations, no production was forthcoming. The program was cancelled with $3.5 million expended.

Monstrosity (XP-56, N-1M)

More aerodynamically and structurally innovative and challenging than the Vultee and Curtiss R40-C fighters was Northrop's design. However, winning the competition is where the firm's fighter triumph ended. The XP-56 was the least successful of any American World War II fighter to reach the flying prototype stage.

The N-2B proposal was for a tailless aircraft, almost a flying wing with short "crew nacelle" for the engine, pilot, and weapons. Despite a laminar flow wing spanning 40.4 feet, overall length was to be just 22.9 feet, height 9.5 feet, and it was to gross 9,046 pounds. The only thing resembling a tail was a short ventral surface under the engine compartment primarily serving to prevent over-rotation and propeller strike. The pusher installation mandated tricycle landing gear. The H-2600 with turbosupercharger was to turn the contra-rotating propellers via extension shafts. Armament was to be two .50-cal. machine guns and a pair of 20mm cannons.

As with the other R40-C winners, Northrop received a 22 June 1940 contract for initial design and tunnel testing. Northrop Aircraft Inc. had only just opened its doors, but was blessed with excellent talent and visionary leadership. John K. "Jack" Northrop had pursued flying wing aircraft for nearly 20 years. His firm was then completing the N-1M flying wing experimental light aircraft.

The order for a single XP-56 (MX-14) prototype (41-1786) was issued on 26 September 1940, the aircraft to be delivered one year

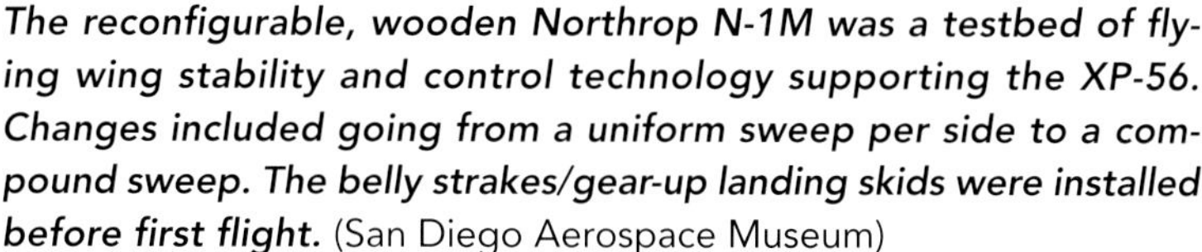

The reconfigurable, wooden Northrop N-1M was a testbed of flying wing stability and control technology supporting the XP-56. Changes included going from a uniform sweep per side to a compound sweep. The belly strakes/gear-up landing skids were installed before first flight. (San Diego Aerospace Museum)

The final configuration of the N-1M eliminated the wingtip anhedral. Other changes from the original were the three-blade props turned by more powerful Franklin engines. The N-1M lent confidence to the ability to fly an all-wing airplane, but the XP-56 was too great a step up from the underpowered N-1M. (Gerald Balzer Collection)

later. With the H-2600 cancelled just days later, the most immediate task was settling on a replacement engine. Northrop and the Army Air Corps jointly selected the 2,000-hp R-2800 with two-stage/two-speed supercharger on 12 March, approved on 21 July 1941. Not all were happy with this choice. It would mean a 2,000-pound increase in weight, a 14-mph loss in top speed at critical altitude, and a delay of 5.5 months. It was going to be a tight fit even with redesign, and Pratt & Whitney had work ahead creating the new -29 model. This had to accommodate the 9.7-foot Curtiss Electric six-blade contra-rotating propeller with extended concentric shafts and two-speed remote gearbox. A gearbox and cooling fan also had to be integrated into the engine. To facilitate safe pilot bailout, an explosive chord had to encircle the gearbox to blow off the propeller. The XP-56 may have been the first with a dual-rotation propeller as a pusher and the first with a buried, air-cooled radial engine.

Mockup inspection occurred on 15 July 1941. Aircraft delivery was now to be March 1942. Northrop accepted a performance guarantee of 467 mph at 25,000 feet against a specified 425 mph, 1.5-hour endurance, 7.2-minutes climb to 20,000 feet versus the specification's 7.0 minutes, plus 1,860-foot takeoff and 2,500-foot landing over a 50-foot obstacle vice a required 3,000 feet. The risk of proceeding with just one prototype finally compelled the service to order a second (42-38353) on 5 December 1941, approved 13 February 1942.

During development, the XP-56 underwent notable changes from the proposal. The fairing aft of the canopy now ended in a shallow vertical surface to supplement the dorsal fin. Wing leading edge sweep was 26 degrees and the trailing edge was now swept as well. The laminar flow airfoil was apparently dropped. The wing had inboard "elevons," functioning both as elevators and ailerons, with split flaps beneath the inboard wing segment. The rudder pedals deployed scoop rudders that rotated out the bottom of the drooped outer wing panels, and a top flap rudder that also served as a pitch flap. Augmenting these was a top yaw trimmer or "ailerudder" scoop. Engine and oil cooling employed air ducted from the wing root intakes and out through the suction fan at the rear with a perimeter of cowl flaps. Carburetor air was also drawn in through the root openings, through an intercooler and then up into the supercharger. Weapons were to be two 20mm cannons with 100 rpg and four .50-cal. machine guns with 400 rpg. An unusual aspect of this was that spent cartridges had to be collected instead of ejected overboard and passing back into the propeller. Weight rose 21 percent to 11,350 pounds gross.

The XP-56 was the first all-magnesium, all-welded aircraft. The relatively thick magnesium offered light weight and high tensile strength, and the selection leveraged off Northrop's pioneering work in heliarc welding. The choice must also have pleased the War Department since magnesium was not listed as a strategic material. It certainly made for a smooth, low-drag surface. However, the welding process was fraught with problems in its first large-scale production application, greatly slowing assembly.

While the N-2B program progressed, Northrop continued the N-1M Jeep (M for mockup) as a risk-reduction sideline. The project had begun in 1939 to build and fly the world's first and truly successful flying wing airplane (as opposed to glider). The small aircraft had only the two pusher propeller extension shaft fairings and rear over-rotation strut/wheel fairing as vertical stabilizing surfaces. The wing closely resembled that proposed for the XP-56, with "elevons" inboard and "split rudders" at the wingtips. It was built almost entirely of wood and with fully retractable tricycle undercarriage. There was no fuselage, only the bubble canopy and cooling air passages for the buried engines. It was underpowered with two 65-hp Lycoming O-145 engines turning two-blade propellers on 10-foot shafts. It was readily modified to try new configurations, including revising sweep from single to compound angles, altering dihedral and tip anhedral, plus changing control surface area and layout. Span was 30.0 feet, length 17.0 feet, and area of 300-square feet.

Registered NX-28311, the N-1M first flew on 3 July 1940 under the control of Vance Breeze, on one of Southern California's desert lakebeds. However, this was a brief hop in ground effect. Later, with Moye Stephens at the controls, the envelope was expanded further. On one such flight, there was a propeller strike that broke the rear spar. During repair back in Hawthorne, the Lycomings were replaced with two 117-hp Franklin 6AC-264-F2s and three-blade propellers. Lacking propwash and running beyond limits at all times, elevated engine temperatures were a severe problem until baffling was improved and airflow through the engine compartments was increased.

At 4,000 pounds gross, the N-1M could fly to 200 mph and 4,000 feet. It was soon successfully exploring the stability and control potential of the XP-56. Although the aircraft was flown with only modest maneuvering, the results were encouraging. The aircraft was stable about all three axes. It flew well without the wingtip anhedral, but this feature was retained in the XP-56. It completed some 50 flights through January 1943. These included a spin by John W. Myers. The Army took interest in the testing, Air Corps pilots flying the N-1M and national markings applied after the nation went to war.

Delivery of the XP-56's new model R-2800 was late. A propulsion rig had been assembled to test the integrated engine/propeller and airframe, especially to ensure suitable cooling. Once the engine was fitted to the airframe, ground vibration tests were performed and installation changes made to avoid potentially destructive resonances. Such work was delayed by Northrop engineering manpower shortages and the construction difficulties. These factors contributed to costs rising precipitously above the $1.24 million value of the amended contracts.

The first XP-56 was finally completed in March 1943. Engine runs quickly revealed a roughness that required a month of adjustments and rework. Initial taxi runs at Hawthorne on 12 April were punctuated by sharp and hazardous yaw excursions, particularly at high ground speeds, that were attributed to "grabby" brakes. Manual hydraulic brakes were substituted. Other powerplant issues required an engine change and gearbox mounting changes, and more months were lost awaiting the replacement from Pratt & Whitney.

The aircraft was moved up to the vast expanse of Rogers Dry Lake on 3 September. When taxi testing resumed, elevated engine temperatures became a persistent problem. A "high-lift door" had been added at the base of the forward nose, on both sides, opening level on final approach to help reduce anticipated nose-down pitching moment from lowering the gear and flaps that exceeded trim authority. However, this was deemed inadequate, so the flaps could not be employed with the gear down.

First flight on 6 September 1943 by John Myers was to a cautious four or five feet above the ground and 130 mph for a short but uneventful 30 seconds. Very little maneuvering was attempted, but some nose heaviness was observed. On a second flight the same day, to 25 to 50 feet and 170 mph, Myers tried a bit more and got an education. The aircraft displayed uncommanded yaw, roll, and nose-down

The first of two Northrop XP-56 fighters is shown on Rogers dry lakebed in its original configuration. It would soon get an addition to the dorsal vertical stub tail in an effort to improve directional stability. Flight would also be performed without the landing gear doors. (Gerald Balzer Collection)

The second XP-56 had a number of significant changes compared with the short-lived first aircraft, but still flew poorly. A prominent dorsal tail surface was installed from the outset of testing, wingtip drag rudders were enlarged and provided more power via the wingtip venturi ducts. (Air Force Flight Test Center)

Aircraft 786 was destroyed in a taxi accident after only about a minute of flying time in four brief hops. A blown tire caused loss of control during high-speed taxi and the aircraft tumbled across the lakebed. Fortunately, the pilot was thrown clear. (Gerald Balzer Collection)

The XP-56 flew less than six hours because of the many changes necessary to produce just tolerable and marginally safe flying qualities. The little performance data indicated capabilities were well short of expectations. The program continued to extract useful data, but was simply not worth the cost and risk. (Gerald Balzer Collection)

pitch excursions, requiring much of Myers' skill and strength to get it back on the ground safely. It set down so heavily that the tail bumper was torn away.

After reviewing flight and wind tunnel data, directional instability with the landing gear down was suggested, especially with the nose gear doors open. An extension was fitted to the shallow upper fin, adding about 11 to 12 square feet, and the nose gear doors were removed. Testing resumed on 8 October with Myers performing several high-speed taxi runs and two brief but low hops over the lakebed. On one run to 130 mph, the left tire blew out and the aircraft swerved sharply before going out of control. The aircraft tumbled backwards across the lakebed and was destroyed. Myers was thrown clear, suffering a ruptured vertebrae and broken ankle.

When ship two emerged in January 1944, it had some significant differences from the first XP-56 that increased empty weight by 1,180 pounds. The center of gravity was shifted forward with ballast and a larger dorsal fin was added, approximately the shape of the ventral surface but of greater area. It also featured wingtip "aero boost ducts" to provide ram air pressure power for enlarged split or drag rudders. Pedal input diverted the air through the venturi into bellows that pushed the surface segments apart. A small wheel was installed in the tip of the ventral fin, replacing the bumper.

On 23 March 1944, Harry Crosby flew 42-38353 for the first time, with the nose gear doors removed. He reported extreme nose heaviness, only able to rotate above 160 mph. He did get off and circled the desert site, climbed to 2,500 feet and accelerated to 180 mph, but was working hard against the very high stick forces and rudder sensitivity. Crosby ended the flight after just 7.5 minutes.

The center of gravity was moved back to its original location for the next flight on the 31 March. On this second sortie, the pitch response during takeoff was improved markedly. The undercarriage was retracted after liftoff, but the aircraft entered an incipient stall and the gear was quickly extended. Crosby took the XP-56 to about 7,800 feet, but the aircraft did not control well and suffered a severe vibration that precluded flight above 250 mph. After 35 minutes of gingerly flying, Crosby brought the aircraft down, noting control reversal just before touchdown (pushing the stick forward to get down the last few feet).

Four similar flights were conducted, some with the gear doors reinstalled. Speeds up to 320 mph were achieved, but overall control and trim authority indicated much work remained to be done. Considerably more power was required than expected; suggesting performance would fall well short of predictions. On its seventh flight, 12 May, Crosby complained of wing heaviness and stability issues that appeared to be worse than recent flights. The engineers were puzzled by the degradation and could not isolate the cause.

The very long development of the XP-56 made any hope of production unrealistic. In late May, Materiel Command deemed the aircraft a lost cause, beset by profound stability and control problems and showing no attributes greater than aircraft already in service. Based on slim flight test data, predicted peak speed was just 340 mph at 19,500 feet, considerably below requirements. Weapons were never installed, and clearly the aircraft's suitability as a fighter was in grave doubt.

There was value in continuing the testing given the aircraft's unusual character. It was recommended NACA Ames assist in the flight program to gain more insight. Instead, it was judged best to send the aircraft to Ames for full-scale wind tunnel testing in order

Northrop XP-56 characteristics (final configuration, performance figures projections):			
span	43.1 ft	weight empty	9,879 lbs
length	23.6 ft	gross	12,588 lbs
height	13.2 ft	maximum	13,272 lbs
wing area (projected)	311 ft²	speed, max. (19,500 ft)	340 mph
fuel capacity (int. + ext.)	215-320+0 gal	range, normal	445 mi
service ceiling	33,000 ft	ferry	660 mi
best climb rate	3,100 fpm		

to understand the controllability and speed issues that failed to match extensive scale model tunnel data, and then conduct follow-up flight testing.

Since it would be fall before an opening was available in the tunnel schedule, three further flights were performed. The ventral fin was damaged on the ninth landing, requiring the aircraft to be trucked back to Hawthorne for repairs. On its tenth flight, an 11 August ferry back to Muroc, the aircraft felt tail heavy during ground operations, low on power in flight, and experiencing excessive fuel consumption. After landing, the fuel mixture was found too rich and a pitch change linkage between the two propellers had failed, allowing one set to go to full low pitch. The latter fault had occurred twice before in flight and twice in ground operations. To continue flying with this potential failure mode was considered unsafe.

The aircraft, with 5.9 hours logged, remained grounded and was placed in flyable storage. It was eventually transported to Ames, but, with a low priority, the XP-56's tunnel entry was repeatedly slipped. The moribund project was soon closed-out. The dismaying $12.3 million spent, many times the original contract value, having rendered no discernible contribution to the war effort.

Stretching

Largess (XP-61E)

The exceptional range and maneuverability of the P-61 night fighter (see Chapter 10) made it a natural choice as the basis for a very long-range (VLR) day fighter suitable for bomber escort. The concept was first suggested by Northrop chief test pilot John Myers to several senior field officers during a trip around Pacific bases in summer 1944, and then followed up at Wright Field upon return. His discussions may have reflected a design study already underway at Northrop. One of the officers Myers engaged was Gen. George Kenney, Fifith Air Force commander, who endorsed the project in a letter to Gen. Arnold. The Army Air Forces consequently gave Northrop a go-ahead to build two XP-61E prototypes (MX-563), although some senior officers in the service resisted the move.

The new aircraft had the P-61's center pod redesigned, cutting it off above the wing, new structure used forward of the wing with a

The Northrop XP-61E altered the center fuselage of the Black Window to serve as a long-range escort fighter, accommodating two crewmen under a bubble canopy and replacing the nose radar with quad .50s. This second prototype (42-239549) had a side-hinged canopy and the nose guns in a box arrangement. (Gerald Balzer Collection)

The second XP-61E, shows off the ample volume under the canopy and the ventral cannon tub. Although of great potential value in the vast Pacific Theater, the war's terminus ended the program, although there was plenty of competition for the mission. (National Museum of the United States Air Force)

cockpit for two crewmen under a bubble canopy, and streamlined close-out structure aft of the trailing edge. The cockpit was narrower and rearranged for improved forward vision, moving everything below the canopy sill, plus adding a second set of instruments and controls for the relief pilot. Four .50-cal. machine guns with 300 rpg replaced the radar in the nose and the ventral cannons were retained. A fuel tank replaced the turret for increased overall fuel capacity.

Two P-61B-10s (42-39549 and 42-39557), still with R-2800-65 engines, were heavily modified as XP-61Es. First completed in January 1945, 42-39557 had the canopy sliding aft on tracks and the nose guns arranged along a horizontal line. Aircraft 42-39549 followed in March with a canopy hinged to port and the guns in a box

The first XP-61E displays the elegant center pod closeout aft of the wing. Not being fitted with the turbosupercharger and engines of the P-61C, the low altitude evident in the photo would have been the P-61E's operating regime if produced like the prototypes – appropriate at that point in the war. (Ray Wagner Collection)

Northrop XP-61E characteristics:			
span	66.0 ft	weight empty	21,350 lbs
length	49.6 ft	gross	31,425 lbs
height	13.4 ft	maximum	40,180 lbs
wing area	662 ft²	speed, max. (17,000 ft)	376 mph
fuel capacity (int. + ext.)	1,157+1,240 gal	cruise	200 mph
service ceiling	30,000 ft	range, normal	2,250 mi
initial climb rate	2,500 fpm	ferry	3,750 mi

arrangement. First flight occurred on 3 January 1945. Aircraft 42-39577 was written off following an 11 April accident. During a maximum-performance takeoff test, the pilot retracted the gear a bit too early and the aircraft settled back onto the runway. It suffered propeller strikes that kept it down, sliding off the runway on its belly.

Some may have expected the Es to have C-model engines with turbosuperchargers, but performance was still impressive at nearly 4,000-mile range and speed a respectable 375 mph. Even before the end of the war, the program was overcome by selection of the P-82 for the escort mission. Aircraft 42-39549 entered modification for conversion as the XF-15 reconnaissance platform for which its performance was more suitable.

Engine Bottleneck (XP-68, XP-69, XP-72)

A number of experimental engines under development during the war stretched the state of the art beyond what could be delivered on a reliable schedule. One such was the liquid-cooled Wright R-2160-3 Tornado with 42 cylinders, expected to deliver 2,350 hp from the 2,400-pound powerplant or 2,500 hp with turbosupercharging. This was based on seven-cylinder radial "modules" with small 51-cubic inch "jugs" and required reduction gearing. Six of these modules made up the Tornado, but as many as 10 (70 cylinders) were contemplated. The complexity of this approach can be imagined, but the promise was small diameter for less aircraft frontal area and reduced drag. The first Army contract for the development dated from June 1939.

The Army began two concurrent projects to exploit the new powerplant. During the confusion about engine selection for the XP-54 and its redesign, consideration was given to building one aircraft for the Tornado, or both constructed with the means to accommodate the engine at a later date. The former was pursued with the Vultee Model 78 concept. This was to have a 46-foot wingspan, 48-foot length, and a gross weight of 8,500 pounds. Radiator intakes were placed under and atop the fuselage. Six .50-cal. machine guns were to be installed in the nose, and it was said to have retained the XP-54's originally intended six-blade dual-rotation propeller.

Discussions had Vultee developing the Model 78 as the XP-68 Tornado under a September 1941 agreement. Drawings of the Model 78 had nine gun ports in the nose and a three-blade propeller. Due to different gearing ratios between the R-2160 and primary H-2470, initial predictions showed the Tornado would require a single propeller too large to swing between the twin booms of the Vultee airplane. Consequently, the XP-54s were built with the potential to take a Tornado at a future date provided the engine was fitted with

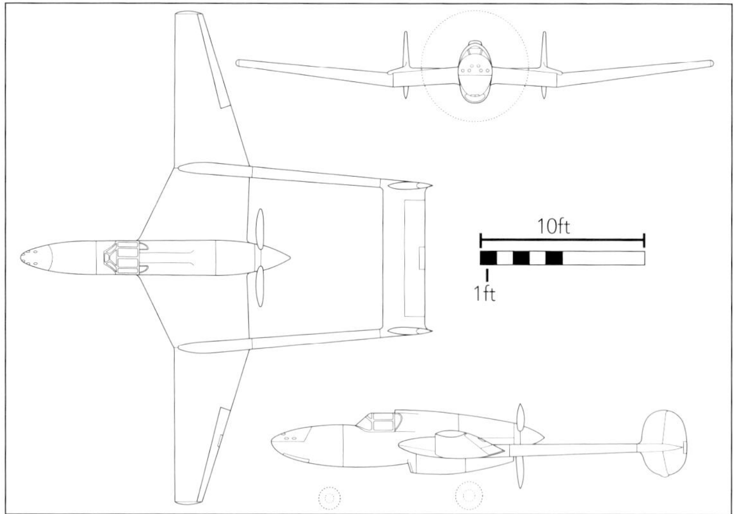

A proposal to mount the Wright R-2160 engine in the XP-54 airframe was briefly pursued under the XP-68 Tornado project. This illustration is based on the Vultee Model 78 drawing but with the proposed six versus nine guns and single propeller of practical diameter. (Author)

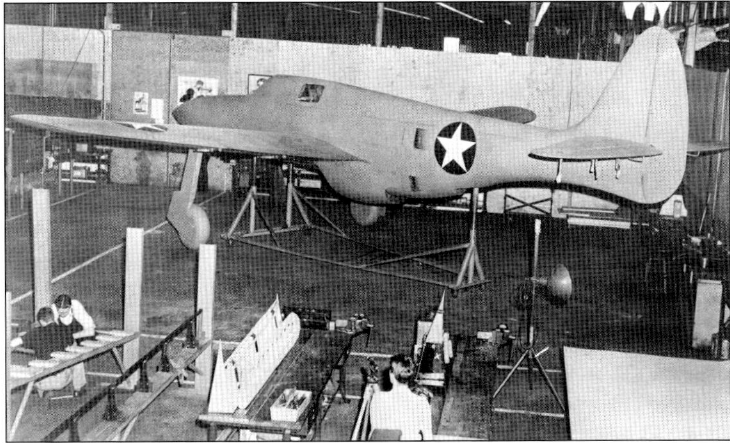

This three-quarter-scale wind tunnel model of the Republic XP-69 does not have the later bubble canopy introduced to the design. The bottom intake and aft fuselage vents reveal the location of the engine that was to turn a contra-rotating propeller via a long shaft. (Tony Landis Collection)

This image of the XP-69 shows the model in the Langley tunnel with contraprop and emphasizing the narrow fuselage and low aspect-ratio wings with what were going to be sealed-gap ailerons. The program floundered when the engine failed to mature and other promising designs took center stage. (San Diego Aerospace Museum)

two-speed gearing and dual-rotation propellers.[3] The XP-54 developed far beyond the interim Model 78 and all company resources were engaged with this and its other priority projects. Consequently, the XP-68 project was terminated on 22 November 1941.

Republic submitted designs in July 1941 for a fighter with either the Tornado or the Wasp Major. The intended mission was a high-altitude, high-speed interceptor that could also defend critical locales from enemy bombers. As the Tornado was expected to be available sooner and the Army wanted to move quickly, they contracted with Republic to build two single-seat prototype XP-69 (MX-162) fighters around the R-2160-3 at 2,500 hp with turbosupercharger. The December 1941 contract was valued at $1.5 million and called for one aircraft with single-rotation propeller and the other with contra-rotating propellers. Republic's Model AP-18 was derived from the earlier AP-12 Rocket concept, with the engine mounted within the aft fuselage turning the dual-rotation propellers via extension shafting. The Hamilton Standard unit would have been an enormous six-blade unit at 13.7-feet diameter. The aircraft was to be equally large with a 51.7-foot span for the laminar-flow wing and 18,655 pounds gross weight. Calculated performance was 2,750-fpm initial rate of climb, 450 mph at 35,000 feet, service ceiling of 48,900 feet, and range of 1,800 miles on 500 gallons of fuel. The cockpit was, by necessity, to be pressurized. Planned armament was four .50-cals with 1,280 rounds and a pair of 37mm cannons with 80 rounds, all within the wings and outside the propeller arc.

Only a three-quarter-scale wind tunnel model of the XP-69 was built as the mockup, inspected in June 1942. Construction of the first airplane began in November, but by early 1943 it was evident the problems with the engine would not soon be overcome. The Tornado was dropped with none of the 11 engines on contract ever flown. Republic also found itself swamped with work that slowed progress on the XP-69. Additionally, its XP-72 project (see next) was shaping up as an aircraft that might fulfill the XP-69's missions. Other Army aircraft entering production also appeared suitable for the tasks. Consequently, the XP-69 was cancelled on 24 May 1943 after expending $810,000 with engineering approximately 75 percent complete and fabrication still in the early stages.[4]

Even as the Thunderbolt began to show its stuff in flight testing of the XP-47B, Alexander Kartveli's design team was already reaching for the next evolution in the design. Studies beginning in July 1941 sought a considerable performance jump by adopting the most powerful production aero engine of the war. The R-4360 promised 3,450 hp at 25,000 feet. Persistent work on the Model AP-19 paid off when the Army ordered two examples of the XP-72 (MX-189) on 18 June 1943. This came as the XP-69 effort was dumped. With the Wasp Major at hand, the XP-72 appeared a good prospect.

The wing and empennage were very similar to the P-47, including dive flaps and strengthened undercarriage. Like the XP-47J, the radial was within a close cowling with intake fan for forced-air cooling. Weight was cut by turning a centrifugal supercharger and intercoolers behind the cockpit using fluid coupling drive shafting,

The Republic XP-72 was a growth of the P-47 with the most powerful aero engine of the war. It used an enormous four-blade propeller with the 3,000-hp Pratt & Whitney R-4360-13 four-row, 28-cylinder radial engine with a cooling fan behind the spinner. The aircraft was very fast, pressing 490 mph. (National Archives)

The second of two XP-72s used 3,450-hp R-4360-19 to spin a contra-rotating prop of such size the pilots had to takeoff and land in a three-point attitude. The XP-72s were the pinnacle of piston-engine fighter technology and speed during 1944, but were soon eclipsed by jet-powered aircraft. (Jay Miller Collection)

and speed was controlled by gearing instead of exhaust ducting.[5] However, this blower was itself large at nearly five feet in diameter. The designers expected to realize 504 mph with this combination, and up to 540 mph later as further work was planned to raise power to 4,000 hp. The turbosupercharger inlet was placed farther back, parallel with the wing leading edge. Another stage of supercharging was integral to the engine. It was to be armed with six .50-cal. wing guns with 267 rpg, and two hardpoints for 1,000-pound weapons or tanks.

The first prototype (43-36598) was finished on 29 January 1944 and took to the air on 2 February. Because the engineers were still chasing down problems with the dual-rotation propeller and centrifugal compressor, 43-36598 flew with the 3,000-hp R-4360-13 turning a conventional four-blade propeller and with only the integral single-stage supercharger. Nevertheless, the aircraft roared to 480 mph on the deck. Its twin (43-36599) followed on 26 June with the intended R-4360-19 engine and 13.5-foot diameter, six-blade, Aeroproducts unit. The remote turbosupercharger may never have been installed.[6] The propellers on both aircraft were so large that the pilots had to takeoff and land in a three-point attitude to avoid propeller strikes. There were problems with the contra-rotating propeller, suffering jumps in RPM to over-speed levels. Aircraft 43-36599 was written-off following a fire and gear-up landing early in its test career before it could demonstrate the maximum anticipated airspeed.

Testing showed the XP-72 Ultrabolt to be "hot," rapidly accelerating to 490 mph at 25,000 feet. It could perhaps deal with the emerging German jet aircraft threat until Allied equivalents were ready. An initial production contract of 100 P-72s was inked, these to have the R-4360-3 and an optional change to four 37mm cannons replacing the wing guns. However, the evolving requirements of the war worked against this worthy design. The Army then needed long-range escort fighters while the P-72 was intended as a fast interceptor, and jets were rapidly maturing as the means to high speed.

Republic XP-72 characteristics:			
span	40.9 ft	weight empty	11,375 lbs
length	36.7 ft	gross	14,760 lbs
height (parked)	12.3 ft	maximum	17,492 lbs
wing area	300 ft^2	speed, max. (25,000 ft)	490 mph
fuel capacity (int. + ext.)	370+300 gal	cruise	300 mph
service ceiling	42,000 ft	range, normal	1,200 mi
best climb rate	5,280 fpm	ferry	1,530 mi

Quest for the Light Fighter

The idea of a lightweight, inexpensive fighter seized the imaginations of many around the world in the years leading to the war and during the conflict. Especially as a point-defense interceptor to attack bombers, the concept appeared to have merit...provided the bombers did not arrive with fighter escort. Gen. Arnold had shown an early interest in such an approach when he requested the small but fast Caudron racer from the 1938 speed competition be examined for its potential as a fighter. Army Air Corps engineers calculated that the addition of military accoutrements would have yielded an aircraft closely matching the P-36 in performance, and so a project was not pursued.[7]

Less Filling (XP-48)

Douglas initiated a light-fighter project in 1939 with an unsolicited proposal to the Air Corps for the Model 312. This was to employ the air-cooled Ranger XV-770 inverted 12-cylinder engine fitted with a two-stage supercharger. It would deliver 525 hp to a three-blade, 9.5-foot diameter propeller. The Army assented to the proposal and gave a contract to a Santa Monica company that had no recent fighter development experience. The XP-48 specification was dated 5 August 1939.

The single-seat XP-48 was to weigh just 3,400 pounds gross, carry 50 gallons of fuel, and have a length of 21.8 feet. A tricycle undercarriage had the main gear within the aft fuselage. The wing was of unusually high aspect ratio with a 32.0-foot span and 3.0-foot mean chord, for a 92-square foot wing area. Proposed armament was one .50-cal. with 200 rpg and one .30-cal. with 500 rpg, all above the engine. The numbers Douglas offered as likely performance included 350 mph top speed. This and other figures were apparently met with such skepticism that the Army cancelled the project by February 1940.

This Douglas concept art shows the racer-like lines of their diminutive XP-48. However, translating such performance to a combat aircraft could prove challenging. Douglas offered such unlikely performance with the 525-hp engine that the Army dropped the project. (Author's Collection)

Sales Job (XP-57)

Preston Tucker was another American afflicted with the lightweight fighter notion. He ran a family owned machine parts company in Ypsilanti, Michigan. Motivated to expand and win some of the lucrative government rearmament contracts, Tucker generated a conceptual design for the Model AL-5. The persuasive salesman then won backers to form the Tucker Aviation Co., incorporated in May 1940 in Detroit. Astonishingly, he then managed to get an audience with Gen. Arnold during May and convince him the fighter was worth initial seed money. Wright Field was so ordered, and issued a contract to Tucker Aviation in July 1940 for a single XP-57 prototype (41-4, MX-20) to cost not more than $40,000.

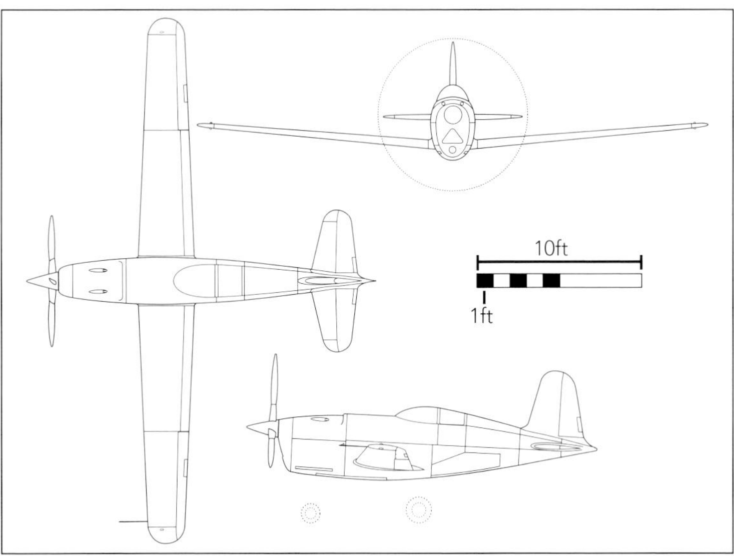

The Douglas XP-48, dating from 1939, was intended to be a lightweight, point-defense fighter of just 3,400-pounds gross weight. It would have been quite small at just 21.8 feet in length and powered by a V-12 inverted inline engine, the main gear housed in the aft fuselage as the drawing indicates. (Author)

Like the Bell P-39, the new aircraft was to have tricycle undercarriage and an engine mounted within the fuselage. With few options from the over-stretched aero engine industry, the powerplant chosen for the XP-57 was the little-known Miller L-510-1 Double turning an 8-foot two-blade propeller via the extension shaft. This was a V-12 liquid-cooled powerplant of 720 horsepower. Tucker predicted 308 mph and 1,700 fpm initial climb rate. His aircraft was to weigh 1,920 pounds empty and have a maximum gross weight of 3,000 pounds, with a wingspan of 28.4 feet and a 120-square foot wing area. Armament was to be three .50-cal. machine guns with 488 rounds, or a single .50 and 400 rounds with 20mm cannon and 60 rounds firing through the long power shaft. The wing was to be wood and fabric, the fuselage steel tube frame with aluminum skin.

The Tucker XP-57 design would not accommodate the evolving requirements for fighter aircraft, such as survivability, armor, additional armament, and greater speed. Besides, little Tucker Aviation did not have the wherewithal to bring its dream to reality. After some XP-57 detailed design and initial fabrication at the Detroit City Airport, the firm went bankrupt in February 1941. The Army Air Corps let the matter lay where it fell.

Overcome by Events (XP-77)

As war loomed, strategic materials for weapons manufacturing became carefully regulated in the United States for fear of debilitating shortages. This brought forth a desire to use less traditional materials

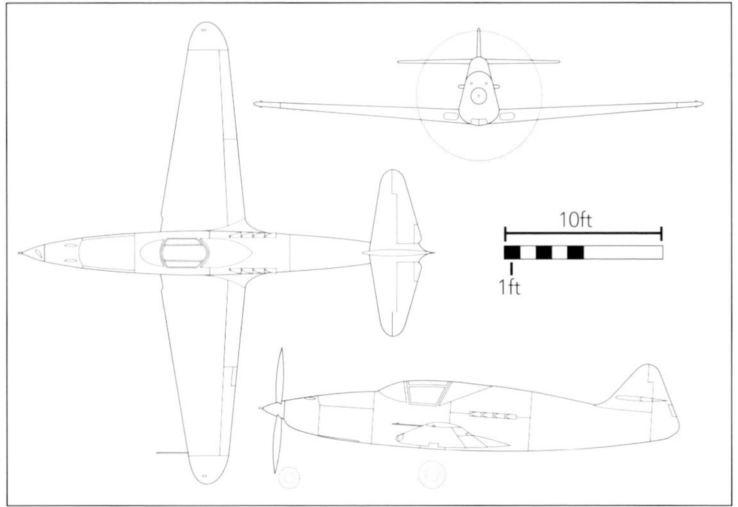

The lightweight Tucker Aviation XP-57 was to be built cheaply and quickly in large numbers. This concept and the sleek design won the start-up company an Air Corps contract in 1940. However, the project was beyond the means of tiny Tucker and fighter requirements that moved beyond such simple solutions. (Author)

for some projects, as expressed in October 1941 at a Wright Field conference with aircraft manufacturers. Use of such material as wood and magnesium in a small fighter offered the potential to reverse the trend to ever more complex and heavy aircraft that was detracting from performance. The notion of a purpose-built prototype emphasizing these design priorities was posed to Bell on 30 October. The specification required 346-mph top speed, 3,050-fpm climb, and 3,700-pound gross weight. The very light interceptor was expected to have maneuverability potentially superior to opponents of more conventional construction. By 1942, this equated to meeting the vaunted Mitsubishi A6M Zero on equal terms.

Bell was given the go-ahead by Gen. Arnold on 16 May 1942 to develop the XP-77 (Model 32, MX-272) to be built inexpensively and quickly, predominately of wood. The mockup was inspected in September 1942. The chosen powerplant was the air-cooled 520-hp Ranger XV-770-7. The 10 October 1942, $700,000 contract was for a static test article and six examples (43-34915/20) with the first to be available in six months. Initial intent was to have 25 of the aircraft built, reflecting the belief that development was low risk and construction time brief. However, this many of the Rangers were not then available.

The aircraft took shape as a tiny tricycle gear airplane with laminar flow wing and unusual triangular fuselage cross-section matching the inverted V-12 engine. The powerplant was in a long cowling and the cockpit unusually far aft. The principal structural material was laminated Sitke spruce resin-bonded as a stressed skin. Armament was to be two .50s in the forward fuselage with 200 rpg and a 20mm cannon firing through the propeller hub. Bell's designer, Robert J. Woods, sought symmetry with 400 hp, 400 mph, and 4,000 pounds gross weight ("Tri-4"). Expected climb rate was 3,200 fpm. A top speed of 410 mph might be achieved with the XV-770-9 fitted with the unique French Planiol supercharger for 670 hp, although this engine was still in development.

Bell found itself with too few resources for all the military projects it was juggling, and the XP-77 took a back seat. The wood construction design and fabrication and use of magnesium were all new to Bell. Project engineer Sam Treman found the learning process cost unanticipated time and money, even when contracting out much of the work. Despite initial expectations that the woodworking industry was underutilized in war production, by mid 1942 it was heavily engaged in producing Army gliders. Furthermore, the wing subcontractor had to be changed late in the process due to inferior workmanship. Cooling problems with the Ranger became known and Bell had to expend extra effort to avoid these. This yielded unusual side flaps at the center of the cowling, opposite the middle cylinders. A late change was made from manual to electrical landing gear actuation.

The Air Forces decided the aircraft must be capable of carrying a 300-pound bomb or 325-pound depth charge. Provisions for this were made on the centerline, also accommodating a 37-gallon tank. Something had to go to make this possible in this very light aircraft, so the

The Ranger XV-770-7 chosen for the XP-77 generated 520 hp from 12 cylinders in an inverted V configuration. Bell much preferred the supercharged -9 model engine, but this never materialized. The engine was attached to the airframe without shock mounts and so produced unacceptable vibration at some power settings. (San Diego Aerospace Museum)

The wooden Bell XP-77 was to reduce use of strategic materials and dramatically reduce weight for enhanced maneuverability. The diminutive fighter looked peculiar with the triangular fuselage cross-section, long cowling, and cockpit aft of the wing. (San Diego Aerospace Museum)

While the XP-77 flew, it impressed no one, especially after the second prototype crashed. Weight had crept up and performance fell well short of expectations. Besides, the late program simply did not fit the air war requirements when it finally reached fruition. (Jay Miller Collection)

The exceptionally small size of the Bell XP-77 is demonstrated by the one man towing the airplane manually. Also evident is the triangular fuselage cross-section, forward cowl details, and very clean lines from the laminated wood construction. (San Diego Aerospace Museum)

cannon was deleted. Weight was creeping up, so a drastic reduction program was enforced. Costs also rose sharply and Bell requested an increase in contract price to $2.55 million.

The delays and cost rise caused the Army Air Forces to rethink the program. By the latter half of 1943, the supply of aluminum and other aircraft construction alloys was looking secure and deliveries less critical than a year before. Furthermore, the prospects for a lightweight fighter were appearing dim in the face of air combat trends where a single-task interceptor faded from importance. Consequently, the Army Air Forces' interest in the program waned. Instead of outright cancellation, the service reduced the scope on 3 August 1943 to two prototypes, the first expected on 31 January 1944, and price adjusted to $1.85 million. The plan to install the V-770-9 was set aside, Bell having called this the Model 35 and "XP-77A."

Still, Bell ran into trouble meeting terms, and costs continued to creep to $2.65 million. It was 1 April 1944 before Jack Woolams took up the first aircraft at Niagara Falls. Although the rudder was inadequate, the aircraft proved largely trouble-free and Bell was able to deliver it to Wright Field on 2 May. Tests were also performed at Eglin Field during the summer with the second example.

By this late point in the war, the aircraft were only useful for collecting engineering data. Overall, the XP-77 was disappointing, as partially expected given the engine model fitted. It came in heavy at 3,857 pounds gross and only did 316 mph at 5,000 feet, managing 2,900 fpm climb. At war emergency power, the little aircraft delivered 330 mph at 4,000 feet and 3,630 fpm climb. These numbers did not even come up to fighters then being operated by the Army Air Forces. The engine was rigidly hung on the airframe without shock-mounts and so produced excessive vibrations at some speed settings. Pilots also complained of high cockpit noise and inadequate heating.

Aircraft 43-34916 crashed at Eglin on 2 October 1944 when it entered an irrecoverable flat spin, compelling the pilot to take to his parachute. This event, the poor performance, and general unsuitability of such a design were cause on 26 October to conclude the program, and it was closed-out on 2 December. The XP-77 was the last new single-seat, reciprocating-powered prototype developed by the Air Forces (and later Air Force), and the only American fighter built of wood.

Bell XP-77 characteristics:			
span	27.5 ft	weight empty	2,855 lbs
length	22.9 ft	gross	3,671 lbs
height	8.2 ft	maximum	3,989 lbs
wing area	100 ft²	speed, max. (4,000 ft)	330 mph
fuel (int. + ext.)	52+38 gal	cruise	274 mph
service ceiling	30,100 ft	range, normal	305 mi
initial climb rate	3,630 fpm	ferry	550 mi

Chapter 8

A Navy contract with Bell sought a light fighter and a vehicle for gaining experience with inline engines. The XFL-1 shared much in common with the P-39, and had its own share of problems, especially with the landing gear. These and general suspicion of the design sounded its death knell. (San Diego Aerospace Museum)

NAVY EXPERIMENTALS

The U.S. Navy undertook several experimental fighter projects during the war years that stretched the technology and its own institutional tendency to hesitant, incremental change. That the resulting aircraft did not enter production and fleet service was due in part to that hesitancy and temporizing, but also the deficiencies of these designs and demonstrated adequacy of upgraded existing models already in service.

Reaching

Four projects were among the boldest departures from conventional naval aircraft of the period. They display willingness to attempt new approaches and reach for potentially revolutionary fighter designs – at least within the Bureau of Aeronautics. Perhaps they reached too far at a time the war demanded potent new capabilities while also requiring caution at introducing anything so radical as to disrupt the momentum built-up in sustaining combat operations. At the same time, BuAer was duty-bound to explore, in at least an experimental capacity, technologies with potentially superior naval fighter applications.

Crossbreed (XFL-1)

At the outset of war, the Navy was testing a fighter that employed an inline, air-cooled engine. The service had always hesitated to adopt such equipment because of the added hazard of storing the inflammable glycol coolant aboard ship. However, with the growing number of advocates for this technology, it was judged worthy of closer examination. More unusual was the layout of the aircraft, with the engine placed mid-fuselage. This was the Bell XFL-1 developed in parallel with the Army's P-39 and sharing many traits. However, at the time, the U.S. Navy judged tricycle gear unsuitable for carrier operations and so, unlike the Airacobra, the Airabonita was a tail-dragger.

The program was born in a January 1938 competition for a high-performance, lightweight fighter, with a $125,000 November contract for one prototype (Buno. 1588) delivered in 300 days. The Model 5, designed by Bob Woods, looked like the XP-39 but was virtually a new design. A tail wheel was installed and the main gear posts moved forward to the wing's front spar. A tailhook was added at the end of a fuselage strengthened and shortened to withstand the stresses of catapult and arrestment. The empennage had to be redesigned as well for suitable stability. The wing area was expanded and three-segment flaps installed, one segment under the fuselage, to facilitate reduced approach speeds. The pilot seat and canopy were raised to improve visibility during approach. Wing folding was not included in the prototype. The supercharged 1,150-hp XV-1710-6 was selected, spinning a three-blade 10.4-foot propeller of new hollow steel design. The Prestone engine coolant was circulated through radiators relocated to under the wings by the wheel wells.

A 37mm cannon with 30 rounds was to fire through the airscrew hub and two .30-cal. machine guns in the nose firing through the propeller. Non-availability of the cannon meant a .50-cal. machine gun was substituted. Only the .30s were fitted as ballast, but the gun ports were never cut. Most peculiar was a Navy requirement for underwing bays, five per side, to carry twenty 5.2-pound anti-aircraft bombs, to be dropped on a bomber formation by sighting through a window at the pilot's feet.

The mockup of the XFL-1 was inspected on 19-20 December 1938. During development in Buffalo, under project engineer Paul Burr, weight went up eight percent beyond the goal without the recourse of fitting a more powerful engine. This and other problems, including late delivery of the Allison, meant first flight planned for fall 1939 slipped to 13 May 1940.

The maiden flight was actually an unplanned end to what was supposed to be a high-speed taxi test when a wind gust got the ship airborne with insufficient runway remaining. Bryan Sparks took the plane around and setup for an approach when floatation bags in the wing upper surfaces suddenly popping out and inflated. Despite violent shaking until the bags tore away, Sparks managed a safe landing. The second flight ended abruptly when the engine quit at liftoff, the airplane coming to rest in a ditch with minimal damage. On 29 June, Bob Stanley took the airplane up and encountered yaw oscillations that stalled the fin and resulted in a spin. Recovery was possible only

This 1 October 1940 image emphasizes the tricycle undercarriage and under-wing radiators of the XFL-1's inline engine. With other programs promising advanced, albeit heavy fighters, coming along, the Navy perhaps did not work hard enough to bring the Airabonita to a satisfactory state. (Naval Aviation Archives)

This view of the Bell XFL-1 shows the original radiator cooling ducts that exhausted through slots atop the wing, near the trailing edge (see photo page 160). These proved inadequate, leading to a straight-through design. The glycol coolant for the radiators was not welcome aboard ship. (Author's Collection)

Bell XFL-1 characteristics:			
span	35.0 ft	weight empty	5,161 lbs
length	29.8 ft	loaded	6,651 lbs
height	12.8 ft	maximum	7,212 lbs
wing area	232 ft²	speed, max. (12,000 ft)	333 mph
fuel capacity (int. + ext.)	200+0 gal	cruise	160 mph
service ceiling	30,900 ft	range, normal	1,072 mi
initial climb rate	2,630 fpm	combat	965 mi

after the Plexiglas panel at the apex of the canopy failed and altered the flow over the rudder. The test program was proving more exciting than desired.

Flight testing at Bell revealed significant shortcomings. Air passing out the radiator ducts was originally expelled atop the wing, but this provided inadequate cooling. Several alterations to duct size and exit scheme were attempted, resolving to a straight-through design. Handling was initially poor in all three axes but especially directionally, with rudder reversal experienced. Enlarged "tail feathers," already built in anticipation of problems, were fitted in June 1940. With further alterations and generous fillets, these changes showed positive results. The program was then well behind schedule and had run over budget to the extent Bell operated in the red after 5 December 1940.

The XFL-1 was delivered to NAS Anacostia on 27 February 1941 with about 35 hours logged. Testing there and at the Naval Aircraft Factory, Philadelphia, found suitable stability and control. However, this had only been achieved with the addition of hundreds of pounds of ballast to the nose. The overall weight increase meant the guaranteed 339-mph top speed was just 333. The minimum speed of 78.6 mph versus the guaranteed 70 rendered it unfit for shipboard landings. The prototype was passed back to Bell in December for corrective actions.

By the next February, with the F4U shaping up nicely, the service made clear there would be no production of the FL-1. The program was shelved and, a year later, the XFL-1 became the subject of destructive armament tests.

The U.S. Navy's attitude toward tricycle undercarriage was changing in some quarters, and this sparked interest in reexamining a tricycle Airabonita-like aircraft. This was communicated to Bell via a BuAer missive of 12 October 1939, and the company began exploring a navalized P-39B with armor, folding wings, and potential alternate engine. This was not a trivial task and the Model 21 was finally offered on 17 February 1941. By that point it was met with indifference.[1]

First Twin (XF5F-1)

At the beginning of the war, the U.S. Navy was preparing to evaluate an unusual Grumman design for a carrier-based twin-engine fighter, the XF5F-1 Skyrocket. This had stemmed from a 1935 requirement for a fighter competitive with land-based warplanes. A specific focus was rate of climb to reach a bomber formation approaching an anchorage. Although a twin-engine fighter was indicated given the existing powerplants, none had ever successfully been adapted to shipboard operations and the concept was met with suspicion.

A competition in 1937 failed to yield suitable designs for prototyping. Another Navy attempt in 1938 was not specific to a twin, the

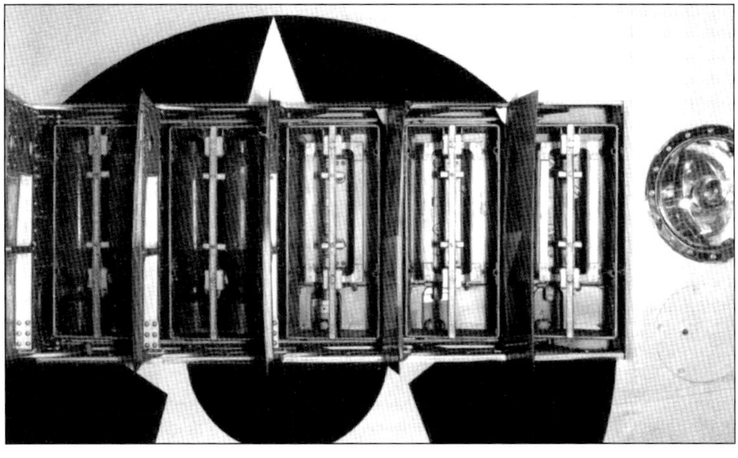

Many aircraft designs of the mid and late 1930s were fitted with anti-aircraft bomblet bays like these in the Grumman XF5F-1 with retracting doors. Ten weapons were accommodated in five small bays in both outer wing panels. The 5.2-pound stores (four shown) were to be dropped above bomber formations. (Northrop Grumman History Center)

The XF5F-1 remains a bizarre sight after decades. It was a clever if unusual design, the propwash over the wings enhancing low-speed lift and interacting with the twin tails to improve directional control in a single engine operating condition. The close-spaced engines also reduced asymmetric thrust with one engine out. (Northrop Grumman History Center)

requirement stating a maximum speed greater than 350 mph, minimum power-on speed 73.5 mph, 32,000-foot service ceiling, and 210-foot takeoff ground roll in 25-knot headwind. Out of these efforts, the Navy gave the award to Grumman for an XF5F-1 twin.

Dick Hutton headed-up the Grumman design team. They placed the wing far forward on the fuselage such that the engines could be placed closer together and propeller arcs swing in front of the fuselage. This helped reduce width for carrier stowage with wings folded, although the aircraft would still be the largest considered for shipboard operation to that time. The unobstructed nose was to give excellent approach visibility and a simplified gun installation. Counter-rotating propellers were to eliminate propeller-induced torque effects on takeoff. Propwash over the wings would enhance low-speed lift, even without flaps, while also interacting with twin vertical tails/rudders for good directional control in single-engine operation. The close-spaced engines also reduced asymmetrical thrust in the engine-out scenario.

Grumman initially sought the Navy-preferred 750-hp R-1535-96 Twin Wasp Junior with two-stage supercharger, but Pratt & Whitney declined to pursue the combination. The subsequent choice of 1,200-hp R-1820-40/42 and 3-blade Curtiss propellers of 10-foot diameter was largely schedule-driven. The single-row Cyclone layout might have improved visibility in the forward quarters but the comparatively large diameter affected drag and demanded heavier propellers. However, the prototype airframe was designed to accommodate the R-1535 as a future option, even considering flying one engine of each type.

The Model G-34 won the Navy's approval and a June 1938 contract for a single XF5F-1 (Buno. 1442). The 1939 mockup included a turtledeck behind the canopy, but this gave way to a sliding canopy without rearward obstruction. Weight rose during detailed design 750 pounds above specification, due in part to BuAer-requested changes. Initial plans to employ twin 23mm cannons were set aside. The design armament (never fitted) was a pair of .30- and .50-cal. guns, with 500 and 200 rpg, respectively. A pair of 165-lb bombs was to be carried under the fuselage. Again, the Navy inserted its requirement for ten 5.2-lb anti-aircraft bombs distributed among five containers in each outer wing panel lower surface.

The Skyrocket was rolled out in late March 1940. R. A. "Bud" Gillies performed the maiden flight on 1 April. The team struggled with high engine temperatures that required oil cooler modifications. Flying qualities and handling were good, and a top dive speed of 505 mph was demonstrated. Improvements were introduced, including altered gear doors, segmented exhausts for reduced backpressure, and rudder balancing that altered the hinge lines. The aircraft went to Anacostia on 22 February 1941 for Preliminary Demonstrations.

The aircraft was returned to Bethpage on 28 April for rework and major modifications. A lengthened nose allowed for increased gun ammo or change to cannons while also improving balance. Engine nacelles were extended aft of the wing trailing edge and the landing gear was fully enclosed. Wing/fuselage fillets were added for improved airflow and engine cooling. Spinners were added, the canopy height reduced, and the rudders revised again.

The longer nose produced more abrupt stalls and required higher landing speeds, and the over-weight margin rose to 817 pounds. The

Derived from a 1938 fighter competition, Grumman won a contract for the first Navy twin-engine fighter, the XF5F-1. Shipboard space limitations pushed the two engines close together, the props swinging in front of the fuselage. The nacelles degraded pilot vision during landings. (Naval Aviation Archives)

The sole XF5F-1 Skyrocket prototype was reworked to address design issues and test results, most noticeably getting a lengthened nose. Although a worthy airplane, development had been slow and there were lingering Navy concerns about carrier compatibility with a twin-engine fighter. The program faded away. (San Diego Aerospace Museum)

aircraft still exceeded all performance requirements when sent back to Anacostia on 24 July. Especially in climb rate it bested the other competitors by a wide margin. Among the remaining issues was inadequate longitudinal stability in approach and high-power dives. Only

Grumman XF5F-1 characteristics (final configuration):

span (spread)	42.0 ft	weight empty	8,107 lbs
length	28.7 ft	loaded	10,138 lbs
height	11.3 ft	maximum	10,892 lbs
wing area	303.5 ft^2	speed, max. (17,300 ft)	358 mph
fuel capacity (int. + ext.)	178+0 gal	cruise	210 mph
service ceiling	34,500 ft	range, normal	780 mi
maximum climb rate	4,000 fpm	maximum	1,170 mi

shore-based carrier landing trials were performed and, as expected, visibility in the forward quarters was criticized. Sight of the Landing Signals Officer (LSO) might be lost in the final seconds of an approach as he disappeared behind the nacelles.*

The XF5F-1 was included in an evaluation of advanced fighters held in summer 1941. A half dozen highly experienced naval pilots each flew the Skyrocket, F4F, XF4U-1, F2A, XFL-1, P-39, P-40, plus British Hurricane and Spitfire. The Skyrocket was a favorite in terms of speed and handling.[2]

Regardless of the encouraging results, Navy enthusiasm was waning as development stretched out. Further design changes to achieve Navy goals, including a difficult self-sealing tank installation, portended additional weight growth with performance impact. The service was concerned with the added shipboard logistical burden of a twin. Besides, the single-engine F4U was already achieving speeds in excess of 400 mph and the F7F twin was in gestation. With production prospects dim and much other work pressing, Grumman expressed its desire on 31 March 1942 to be rid of the project. It was 4 September before the service assented.

Despite a series of landing gear mishaps, the Skyrocket flew on until 11 December 1944 when a final gear-up landing ended its career after accumulating 155.7 hours in 211 flights.

Flash in the Pan (XF14C-1, -2, -3)

With liquid-cooled engines appearing in high-performance land-based fighters, the Navy decided to explore this technology again. A competition for a new fighter gave them the opportunity via a 30 June 1941 contract to Curtiss for two prototypes (Bunos. 03183/4). The XF14C-1 (Model 94A) would use the new inline, Lycoming XH-2470-4 with 2,000 hp at 4,500 feet, 2,200 hp in Mil, and a hoped-for 3,000 hp. This was to yield 374 mph at 17,000 feet and 2,810-fpm initial climb rate. The original armament of four to six .50-cal. machine guns was altered to four 20mm cannons with 664 rounds.

The Navy sponsored the XJ-2470 development and built a production plant in Toledo, Ohio, specifically to support F14C-1 production. However, it was not long before Lycoming ran into trouble with

** The LSO stands astride the landing threshold and observes the approach of each aircraft, signaling for corrections with paddles (in that period) or waving-off the pilot for another attempt.*

The Navy explored the potential of inline, liquid-cooled engines in the Curtiss XF14C-1, but this evolved to the Wright R-3350-16 radial in the XF14C-2. The ungainly looking aircraft was slow coming together and performance proved disappointing. The program was shelved so that Curtiss could focus on more hopeful efforts. (Naval Aviation Archives)

Converting the R-3350's 2,300 hp to thrust required a contra-rotating propeller that was only one aspect of the propulsion system that seemed to dominate the XF14C-2 with the enormous cowling, many intakes, and large exhaust pipe. The long fairings around the four 20mm cannons were also peculiar. (Naval Aviation Archives)

the H-2470 and the aircraft's projected speed at altitude fell short of Navy expectations. This was reason enough for the Navy, still leery of liquid cooling, to terminate the XF14C-1 in December 1943.

With substantial construction completed on the XF14C-1, Curtiss petitioned for the program to continue with the R-3350-16 with turbosupercharger. Commonalities of this XF14C-2 with the earlier Curtiss XP-60 and concurrent XP-62 airframes were evident, the latter using the same R-3350. To exploit the 2,300 hp, Curtiss turned to one of its six-blade dual-rotation propellers. Apart from the enormous cowling and large exhaust pipe under the fuselage, the aircraft was unusual in having a short aft fuselage and small vertical tail because the contra-rotating propellers eliminated torque effects. An intake at the base of the cowling fed the turbosupercharger. The interceptor was armed with four 20mm cannons in the non-folding portion of the wings and 166 rpg.

The XF14C-2 (Buno. 03183) was flown in July 1944 and delivered on 2 September. However, performance was lackluster, perhaps measuring only 398 mph versus the guaranteed 424. The R-3350 was still maturing and this or the propeller in combination produced objectionable vibrations in the fighter. After three years, the urgency for a high-altitude interceptor had faded and the B-29 program demanded all R-3350s. The program was cancelled in favor of more promising work.

Curtiss XF14C-2 characteristics (performance estimated):			
span	46.0 ft	weight empty	10,582 lbs
length	37.8 ft	gross (loaded)	13,405 lbs
height	17.0 ft	maximum	14,582 lbs
wing area	375 ft²	speed, maximum (32,000 ft)	424 mph
fuel capacity (int. + ext.)	230+150 gal	cruise	172 mph
service ceiling	39,500 ft	range, normal	950 mi
initial climb rate	2,700 fpm	ferry	1,355 mi

At Curtiss' suggestion, BuAer funded a feasibility study of incorporating a pressurized cockpit for operations up to 40,000 feet and 400 mph as the XF14C-3. This effort carried on into 1945 before also being dropped.

Odd Balls (V-173, XF5U-1)

Charles H. Zimmerman conceived an unusual "flying wing" design for a fighter or light plane. This was essentially an aircraft with nearly circular, very low aspect ratio planform truncated with a straight leading edge for propeller clearance. The two large tractor propellers at either end of the leading edge would blow propwash over the wing for exceptional lift, allowing short takeoffs and landings at low speed. The counter-rotating propellers would turn opposite the wingtip vortices to reduce induced drag that would normally render such low aspect ratio wings inefficient.* This was especially

** The high pressure on the bottom of the wing flows around the tip to the low-pressure zone on top, creating a swirling vortex of air as the aircraft moves forward that generates induced drag. For a normal aspect-ratio wing, this is generally not dominant. However, a low aspect-ratio wing would generate considerable induced drag from the tip vortices.*

Vought explored the potential for a low-drag flying wing design with the propeller wash enhancing lift and reducing wingtip vortices. This innovative design was demonstrated in the proof-of-concept V-173 that initially flew in 1942, seen here in the early configuration with large trailing surfaces on the ailevators and no wing flaps. (Jay Miller Collection)

important near stall where countering the powerful vortices could prove essential to ensuring suitable lift. Zimmerman's original intent was for rudders on two vertical tails, but elevator and ailerons to be combined as elevons. Zimmerman was also determined to employ a prone pilot position to reduce drag further by eliminating a protruding canopy.

Another benefit of the low drag for high speed and blowing for low speed was an increase in the ratio of top speed to landing speed from a typical 4:1 to 10:1 or more. With sufficient power, the large propellers could also generate more lift than weight of the aircraft for vertical takeoff and landing. The expectation was that the blowing over the wing control surfaces would allow the pilot to pitch the aircraft straight up for a vertical takeoff or approach, and readily pitch forward for landing or transition to forward flight. Propeller articulation like helicopter rotors would facilitate control at such low speeds and hover.

Zimmerman and associates worked on flying scale models and a light-plane testbed (never flown) on their own before he became a consulting engineer with Vought in 1937. There a 3-foot diameter model of the aircraft, the V-162, was constructed and operated during 1937. It was powered by two electric motors and flown on a tether, controlled remotely in hover and translation by two pilots. The entire aft "fuselage," with fins and rudders, was hinged to act as an elevator.

The V-162 caught the attention of the U.S. Navy, which finally found minimal funding in 1939 for a demonstrator aircraft. This became the V-173, but the small budget, careful preparatory testing, and higher priority projects slowed development.

The V-173 possessed a wood frame with fabric covering, spanning 23.3 feet, with a 26.7-foot length, and 427-square foot area. Two three-blade, 16.5-foot diameter propellers were driven by a pair of 80-hp Continental A-80 horizontally opposed engines. The powerplants were connected via shafting to ensure both propellers turned in a single-engine out scenario that would otherwise prove uncontrollable. Shafting then ran outboard and turned 90 degrees via gearboxes to the propellers. The large propellers demanded a high ground attitude of 22.3 degrees, requiring long, fixed landing gear. Repeated laboratory trials demonstrated that prone piloting was impractical. Discomfort rapidly built up and vision to the rear was almost nil – a non-starter for a fighter. The compromise was a reclined seat that also proved unsuitable as the pilot developed back pain leaning forward to operate the aircraft.

Careful preparatory work included placing the entire airplane in NACA's full-scale wind tunnel at the end of 1941. It was found the trailing edge elevons were inadequate and so "ailevator" surfaces were added outboard. The propulsion system was tested on a ground rig during the first half of 1942. Three-blade propellers were chosen over the original two-blades to prevent dangerously exciting structural oscillations.

The V-173 (Buno. 02978) first flew on 23 November 1942 under the control of Boone T. Guyton at Stratford, Connecticut. For the 3,050-pound gross airplane, the small engines not only precluded vertical flight but also produced exceedingly poor single-engine performance that contributed to two forced landings. It cruised at a mere 75 mph and the maximum achieved was 120 mph level, 138 mph diving. However, its short-field performance was readily evident. In calm conditions, the plane lifted off in 200 feet, and with 25-mph headwind it levitated and alighted with no ground roll. Additionally, it could not be induced to spin nor fully stall. Sustained flight at 45-degrees nose-up attitude and 34 mph power-on was demonstrated.

The incidence of the V-173's outboard ailevator surfaces could be adjusted as ailerons while trailing elements served as elevators. This proved less than ideal, so the surfaces were made all-moving with trailing edge tabs. Balanced, free-floating wing flaps were also added to reduce a nose-down pitch trim change during landing. Dangerously high stick forces had to be corrected, and propeller blade angles and engine power output were varied for improved handling. The "Flying Pancake" also suffered heavy vibrations from asymmetric disc loading generated with the propellers at high incidence angles to the freestream flow.

After seeking a proposal on 19 January 1942, delivered on 30 June, the Navy gave Vought go-ahead on 17 September for a prototype fighter, the XF5U-1, based on the V-173. The light plane subsequently became a vital testbed. It was flown 131 hours during some 200 flights

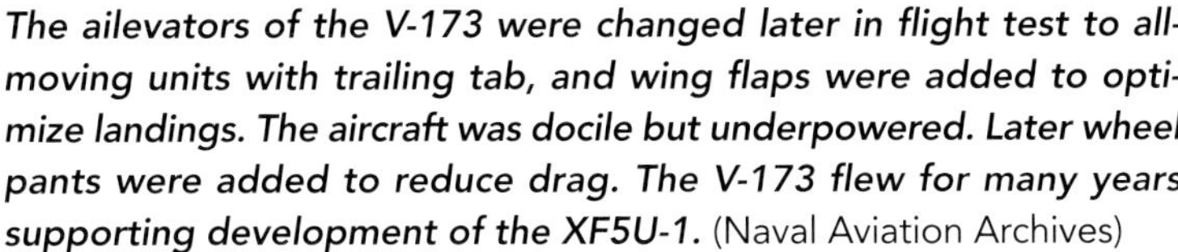

The ailevators of the V-173 were changed later in flight test to all-moving units with trailing tab, and wing flaps were added to optimize landings. The aircraft was docile but underpowered. Later wheel pants were added to reduce drag. The V-173 flew for many years supporting development of the XF5U-1. (Naval Aviation Archives)

A naval fighter program based on the V-173 concept was initiated in 1942. The XF5U-1 concept is shown in mock-up form with three-blade props. Visible are the wing root gun ports and cooling intakes for the buried radial engines with fans near the front to accelerate the flow. (Jay Miller Collection)

through 1947 by several pilots and provided valuable engineering data. However, the step up to explore the vertical takeoff and landing (VTOL) flight capabilities, that would have required a major redesign and development testing, was never undertaken.

The Navy contract for the XF5U-1 (VS-315) called for a static test article and a single-flight model, designed under project engineer E. J. Greenwood. A wooden mockup was inspected on 7 June 1943, although with three-blade 16-foot propellers versus the final four blades. The planform and wing area closely matched the V-173, but the airframe was metal with Vought's Metalite skin.* The retractable landing gear gave the XF5U-1 a deck angle of 18.7 degrees. The goal was 500 mph top speed, 40 mph landing, and 1,000-mile range. Undersurface hardpoints were included for two drop tanks or two 1,000-pound weapons. Originally conceived with six .50-cal. guns in the wing, four 20mm cannons were considered later.

Two 1,350-hp Pratt & Whitney R-2000-7 Twin Wasps were selected for the XF5U-1, the buried radials accommodated within bulges in the wing. These were air-cooled via fans within intakes at the wing leading edge. The engines were interconnected by shafting and via speed-reduction gearing to the propellers. These turned the power from each engine 90 degrees, providing overrunning clutch protection while reversing the rotation of one engine, permitted speed reduction for phases of flight, and turned the shafts 90 degrees again to the propellers. A change to a more powerful engine was planned, this the turbosupercharged XR-2000(D)-2 at 1,600 hp still in development. However, even more power would be necessary to explore the vertical flight regime. A top speed of perhaps 425 mph could be expected of the initial installation, 460 with water injection added. Turboshaft engines (see Chapter 11) might yield 550 mph, but these were still struggling to maturity.

Problems inevitably intruded during development. Each propeller had to be transformed into two pairs of teetering blades, one in front of the other, to permit flapping action for reduced loads and vibration at high angles of attack with the asymmetrical disc loading. Unfortunately, the flapping action produced destabilizing pitch and yaw moments that required automatic dampers added to the control system, these still experimental in 1945.[3] After further research, the prone piloting position was dropped as impractical. It also does not appear much effort was expended at developing a VTOL flight capability. Success in this regime was exceedingly remote given the technology of the period.

Construction of the XF5U-1 "Flying Flapjack" (Buno. 33958) at Stratford was completed on 25 June 1945 and the war ended as the aircraft was preparing for engine runs. With the teetering wooden propellers unavailable until 1947, initial work employed F4U airscrews. Engine overheating was an early problem. However, the

* *Metalite was a pre-curved sandwich of thin aluminum sheets with balsa wood between. Eliminating rivets, joints, and stiffeners, it was also more rigid and lighter than single sheet skin, and gave a particularly wrinkle-free and smooth surface. However, it was considered more difficult to maintain.*

The sole XF5U-1 is shown being positioned onto jacks, possibly for a ground vibration test. The Plexiglas nose dome encloses a landing light and gun camera. The large leading-edge intakes give the appearance of a jet engine, but are actually passages for cooling air to buried radial engines. (Jay Miller Collection)

Progress on the XF5U-1 was slowed by more urgent wartime work and complexity of the gearbox and propeller articulation design. Construction was completed just as the war wrapped up (this photo dated 20 August 1945), seen here with F4U Corsair propellers substituted. However, the aircraft was fated never to fly. (Naval Aviation Archives)

Vought XF5U-1 characteristics (performance estimates with R-2000(D) engines):

Width (elevon tips)	32.5 ft	weight empty	14,000 lbs
(prop tips)	36.3 ft	gross	16,802 lbs
length	28.6 ft	overload	18,917 lbs
height	14.8 ft	speed, max. (28,900 ft)	504 mph
wing area	475 ft^2	cruise	235 mph
fuel capacity (int. + ext.)	261+300 gal	range	910 mi
service ceiling	32,000 ft	initial climb rate (water inj.)	3,950 fpm

heavy and complex gearboxes were the biggest headache. Two gearboxes failed in rapid succession during initial runs.[4] These appeared to be pressing the state of the art, and operation of more than 90 minutes risked a failure that would be catastrophic in flight.

Ultimately, the struggles with propellers, gearboxes, shafting, stability augmentation elements, and cost overruns proved the XF5U-1's undoing. With the advent of jets, this peculiar airplane was not worth pursuing. It may have become airborne briefly during a taxi run in March 1947, but the program was cancelled on the 17th and the prototype promptly scrapped.

Mixing Missions

The Pacific naval air battles made clear many longer range fighters would be needed to defend torpedo- and dive-bomber attack formations. However, carriers would be hard-pressed to accommodate another type among their complement of aircraft. The best answer appeared to be a fighter that could also serve in the attack role. With sufficient speed, the aircraft could be operated by a single aviator, dispensing with the weight and complexity of a manned gun turret that experience had shown was minimally effective against a superior fighter. The vast majority of casualties by the end of 1943 came from ground fire, suggesting armor and speed were better insurance. For the Navy, this combination spelled a multi-role carrier-based fighter with range to strike targets ashore, such as the Japanese home islands during a potential future invasion, while the carriers remained beyond the reach of land-based attackers.

The growing air-to-ground mission of fighters, with superior precision attack capability compared with level bombing, was another impetus to pursue the multi-role fighter. This emergence of the fighter-bomber was a natural outcome of evolving aeronautical technology. The power inherent in new engines, high-lift devices making possible slow carrier landing approaches of even heavy aircraft, expanding internal and external stores mixes, and electronic gunsights that enhanced weapons delivery accuracy, all bespoke the potential of a new kind of fighter. Of concern was the increased pilot workload. All such late-war combat aircraft were also enormous aircraft for single-seat carrier planes and represented a significant further step down the path of growing complexity in systems and structure.

From 1942 through the end of the war, the U.S. Navy had several projects running to develop what would soon be known as fighter-bombers. One was formulated under the fighter rubric while

Efforts to evolve a multi-mission attacker included developing a means for the SB2C-1 (actually an Army A-25 shown) to carry a torpedo. A framework within the bomb bay covered by a fairing provided the external mounting points. The capability was never employed in service. (Ray Wagner Collection)

the rest fell under a new designation "torpedo-bomber" (VTB), defined in a January 1942 requirement, that could turn and fight when necessary. This sought a single-seat aircraft combining the scout-bomber and torpedo-bomber missions, and a single aircraft to replace the TBF and SB2C.

Singularity from Seattle (XF8B-1)

The Navy's desire for a long-range fighter with substantial weapons load was made known, but evidently no formal competition was undertaken. Surprisingly, a proposal from the Boeing Aircraft Co., who had not built a fighter in more than a decade, was selected. The eventual Navy specification sought an airplane possessing a 262-foot takeoff roll with 25 mph wind over the deck, 3,760 fpm sea level rate of climb, 342-mph top speed and no more than 79 mph minimum, and at least a 30,000-foot ceiling. Range was apparently not specified, perhaps leaving it to Boeing to do the best possible. The contract for three test aircraft and a static test article was awarded on 10 April 1943. The result would be the largest and heaviest single-seat, single-engine piston aircraft developed in the United States, especially for a carrier.

The $3.6 million contract was unusual in giving Boeing full decision authority of the project. Ed Wells initially led the XF8B-1 development team as head engineer, followed by Lyle A. Wood. The Seattle company dubbed its Model 400 the "Five-in-One" fighter because of the intent for it to serve as a long-range escort fighter, interceptor, dive-bomber, torpedo-bomber, and level bomber all rolled into one. The design was wrapped up on 7 October 1943, and the mockup inspected early that month. The first example was completed a year later, more than six months behind schedule owing to the press of bomber work and engine delivery delays.

The three prototypes were powered by the enormous XR-4360-10 of 3,000 hp Mil, and 2,500-hp max continuous, with two-stage supercharger. This was the most powerful piston engine then available and the largest ever coupled to a fighter. The "corn cob" engine reduced frontal area but was long and complex. When selected by Boeing during the first half of 1944, it had already flown on the F4U-1WM and the XP-72, the latter also operating the Aeroproducts contra-rotating propeller chosen for the XF8B-1. The 13.5-foot diameter, six-blade propeller was selected to keep the arc within practical dimensions, avoid supersonic tip speeds, and allowed landing gear height to remain reasonable. The propellers also eliminated torque effects on control – a surprise for almost all pilots initially operating the powerful aircraft. The engine unit, with associated accessories, was designed for easy removal and replacement. As a Navy aircraft, it naturally had folding wings. Range was expected to exceed 1,300 miles.

Other notable features of the XF8B-1 were rearward retraction of the main gear into the wing after pivoting 90 degrees (leaving the gear partially exposed), a retractable tail wheel, and Fowler flaps. The wings were constructed with extensive use of spot welding for a cleaner surface. As a safety feature, integral control surface locks would automatically disengage when the throttle was advanced should they still be locked. The rapid acceleration during a wave-off made it necessary to introduce an automatic flap retract feature, activated at 150 mph. The pilot control column moved forward and aft, but only the top portion with grip moved side-to-side to reduce cockpit width requirements and potential interference. A bomb bay with fast-acting doors was incorporated, although the Navy expressed reservations about its suitability. This accommodated four 500-pound or two 2,000-pound bombs, or a 288-gallon drop tank, and weapons up to 1,600-pounds could be carried on two inboard wing stations, making for a total 5,200-pounds of stores. The wing stations could also carry 285-gallon drop tanks while a 270-gallon long-range fuel tank could be fitted in the bay. Choices of internal armament (never fitted) were six .50-cal. machine guns with 400 rpg or six 20mm cannons at 200 rpg with the .60-caliber machine gun considered later. These were in the wings, beyond the propeller arc.

The first aircraft (Buno. 57984) made its maiden flight on 27 November 1944 under the control of Bob T. Lamson. Testing was slowed by some minor mishaps, but the design appeared sound if lacking

The U.S. Navy's reach for a multi-role fighter included a contract with Boeing for what would be the largest single-place, single-engine prop aircraft emerging in the United States during the war. The XF8B-1 (57984 shown on 30 January 1945 with engineer in improvised rear seat) was propelled by the most powerful engine hung on a fighter, and turning contra-rotating propellers. (Jay Miller Collection)

The Pratt & Whitney R-4360 Wasp Major was a massive four-row, 28-cylinder monster that powered a number of American fighters during the war years. The arrangement made for a relatively small frontal area, but a long piston-studded powerplant, likened to a corn cob, which typically delivered 2,500 to 3,000 hp. (U.S. Government via Kim McCutcheon)

standout performance. The oil cooler scoop under the fuselage and the cowl flaps, among other features, underwent improvements while the team struggled with high control forces. The XF8B-1 was ferried on 10 March 1945 to Patuxent River. There it underwent exhaustive service trials running through 9 April. By this point in the war, the Navy could be thorough and insistent on remedying hazardous or especially objectionable characteristics. However, the fighter met or surpassed all requirements and, overall, was praised. Still, the Navy found room for improvement, especially lightening the control forces (aileron boost was added) and improving the brakes. They noted the contra-rotating propellers created a stroboscopic effect at certain sun angles that, it was feared, could be distracting or even hypnotic on long cruise legs.

The second aircraft was completed in January 1945, but waited almost 11 months for an engine. The third followed soon after. The aircraft was more than 1,400 pounds overweight and the program was more than 100 percent over-budget.

The Navy had considered a production contract during spring 1945 to get things rolling, but Boeing felt the proposed delivery schedule would jeopardize meeting Army bomber quotas.[5] The Navy did not ask again. The service was turning to jets, and missions still dominated by "prop jobs" were well served by other types. Consideration was given to converting the plane to an attack torpedo type, two-seat attacker, or night fighter. However, there was simply no longer a need for the XF8B-1 in any guise, especially in the postwar budget squeeze.[6] Boeing itself was losing interest as they saw the war wrapping up and looked ahead to peacetime markets where its fortunes appeared to lay with commercial transports and strategic bombers. It began repositioning personnel and assets appropriately, negatively influencing the XF8B-1.

The impressive XF8B-1 joined others as among the most powerful piston aircraft developed anywhere, but was the end of their line as jets soon displaced almost all propeller-driven fighters. It was the last new piston design evaluated by the Navy.

Boeing XF8B-1 characteristics:

span	54.0 ft	weight empty	14,190 lbs
length	43.3 ft	gross	20,508 lbs
height	16.3 ft	maximum	22,960 lbs
wing area	489.4 ft^2	speed, max. (26,500 ft)	432 mph
fuel capacity (int. + ext.)*	395+570 gal	cruise	190 mph
service ceiling	37,500 ft	range, normal	1,305 mi
initial climb rate	3,660 fpm	maximum	2,300 mi

* *includes bomb bay droppable tank*

The XF8B-1 prepares for a run of the R-4360 four-row engine under the long cowling. This powerplant delivered 3,000 hp from 28 cylinders, the most powerful piston engine hung on a fighter. The engine and airframe were among the pinnacles of World War II fighter technology, but about to be rendered anachronisms. (Jay Miller Collection)

The U.S. Army also evaluated the XF8B-1 (57984 photographed) as a potential fighter-bomber. The aircraft was an exceptional piece of American aeronautical engineering and construction, but had much competition at the end of the war in a field challenged by the emergence of jets. (Naval Aviation Archives)

Near-Run Thing (BTD-1, XBTD-2)

The Navy's first foray into the bomber-torpedo realm was a conversion of the Douglas XSB2D-1 into a single-seat variant called the BTD-1 Destroyer. This was initiated with a 9 April 1942 contract, prior to first flight of the XSB2D-1 and well before America's war fortunes had turned for the better in the Pacific and Asia. Ed Heinemann provided the principal design while Reid Bogert served as project engineer in El Segundo.

The gun barbettes and gunner were deleted, more pilot armor added, the cockpit enclosure faired into the aft fuselage, and the fin dorsal extension carried forward. An additional internal fuel cell was installed, the outer wing dihedral reduced 10 degrees from 14 degrees, and empennage area expanded. The upper and lower "picket fence" wing dive brakes and revised fuselage dive brakes tested on the XSB2D-1s were chosen, although the first few BTD-1s had to be retrofitted with the fuselage panels. All these changes ensured there was essentially no weight savings.

Continuing the SB2D-1 search for dive brakes that did not disrupt the laminar flow wings, six long fuselage "banana peel" panels were tested in combination with modified inner flap segments, eliminating the wing brakes. Trials of reverse thrust via propeller reversal were conducted as well as a braking parachute for deceleration. A four-blade propeller was also fitted.

With satisfactory progress on the BTD-1, production contracts for the SB2D-1 – 13 service test examples and 345 production articles – were converted over on 7 September 1943. The airframes under assembly were modified on the line to the BTD-1 standard. The first (Buno. 04959) was completed on 15 February 1944, and Tommy Brown flew it on 5 March. It performed well enough with the flaps allowing a mere 300-foot takeoff roll.

Seeking a single-seat aircraft combining the scouting, torpedo attack, and dive-bombing missions into a carrier-suitable type, Douglas converted the Douglas SB2D-1 along these lines. This image of the BTD-1 shows the four-blade propeller that was tested as well as open bomb bay doors. (Air Force Flight Test Center)

The project was truncated by the decision to pursue the entirely new BT2D design. Only 26 BTD-1s were completed (Bunos. 04959/61, 04963, 04965/71, 09048/62), delivered between June 1944 and 8 October 1945. The new-design bomber-torpedo airplanes, with their mission flexibility in a smaller airframe, were the wave of

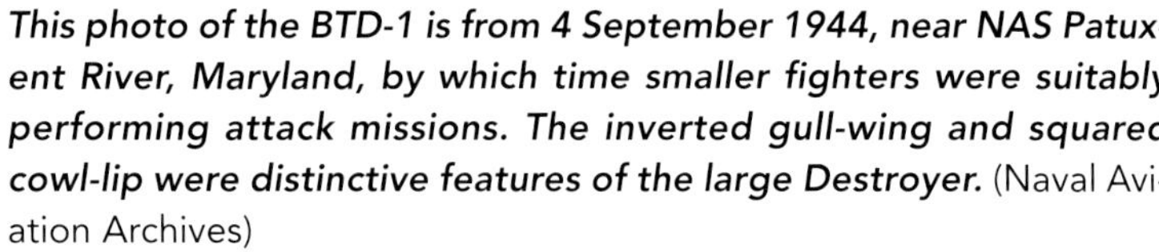

This photo of the BTD-1 is from 4 September 1944, near NAS Patuxent River, Maryland, by which time smaller fighters were suitably performing attack missions. The inverted gull-wing and squared cowl-lip were distinctive features of the large Destroyer. (Naval Aviation Archives)

With aircraft weight growth during the war, drive brakes became larger, exemplified by the enormous banana peel surfaces on the BTD-1. They had the advantage of avoiding the airflow disturbances of wing-mounted brakes. Note also the more common three-blade prop. (Naval Aviation Archives)

the future, leaving no place for the enormous Destroyer. The balance of the contract – 330 aircraft (Bunos. 09063/392) – was cancelled. The delivered airframes served various flight test functions.

Two other BTD-1s became the first composite engine Navy aircraft to fly, combining reciprocating and jet engines in one airframe. The idea was to apply a jet booster engine to an existing design in hopes of quickly creating a fast attack capability. This resolved as incorporating a turbojet into the Destroyer, yielding the XBTD-2. The Douglas aircraft already possessed the tricycle landing gear necessary to reduce the jet blast hazard and featured a cavernous aft fuselage that might accommodate the engine and inlet ducting.

The chosen engine was the 1,600-lbf Westinghouse WE-19XA (later 19B and then J30) axial flow turbojet of 19-inches diameter. Fitting the powerplant into the aft fuselage required removing the new fuel cell and permanently installing the bomb bay tank to feed kerosene to the jet. The aft portion of the canopy was truncated more abruptly and the air inlet installed directly behind. Inlet ducting length

Douglas BTD-1 characteristics:			
span	45.0 ft	weight empty	12,900 lbs
length	38.6 ft	gross	18,140 lbs
height	16.2 ft	maximum	19,000 lbs
wing area	373 ft²	speed, max. (16,100 ft)	344 mph
fuel capacity (int. + ext.)	460+180 gal	torpedo	340 mph
service ceiling	23,600 ft	cruise	188 mph
initial climb rate	1,650 fpm	range (torpedo)	1,480 mi
		maximum	2,140 mi

and turns could adversely affect engine performance, and a horizontal engine installation risked heating effects on the bottom of the aft fuselage. Consequently, the 19B was tilted 10-degrees nose up, reducing the longitudinal thrust vector. The exhaust pipe extended below the moldline of the fuselage bottom, adding to drag already exacerbated by the open inlet rising up on top.

BTD-1s 04962 and 04964 were converted during production to XBTD-2s. Ground runs in March 1944, behind screens at Los Angeles Municipal Airport, were followed by first flight in May. This became the Navy's first "jet" aircraft and the first for Douglas. However, the results were disappointing, the anticipated 50 mph speed increase failing to materialize. It is reported the turbojet became inoperable above 200 mph. Consequently, only 04962 was completed.[7] The later XBT2D-1 successfully filled the speed gap without a jet and so the XBTD-2 was cancelled soon after VJ-Day.

Try and Try Again (XBTC-1, XBTC-2)

BuAer sought the first original bomber-torpedo aircraft from the Navy's long-time supplier, Curtiss. On 9 February 1942, it requested a single seat airplane with 1,000-mile range while hauling a 1,000-pound bomb and 1,500-mile range with drop tanks supplementing the self-sealing internal cells. It was also to mount a 1,600-pound torpedo or two 1,000-pound bombs internally or a Mk 13-2 torpedo beneath the bomb bay, supplemented by four 20mm cannons. Wing fold and pilot armor were also necessary. Curtiss proffered preliminary designs including an aircraft with the 2,300-hp R-3350 with three-blade and another with the 3,000-hp XR-4360-14 matched to a six-blade contra-rotating propeller and larger wing with duplex flaps.

A jet booster engine was added to the Destroyer to create the XBTD-2. The Westinghouse WE-19X in the aft fuselage was fed air via a serpentine duct from atop the fuselage. The sharp cant of the jet and the separate fuel tank in the bomb bay contributed to non-optimal results. (Steve Ginter Collection)

The Navy gave a go-ahead on 26 June 1942 for both designs, the first with an R-3350-8 as the XBTC-1 (Model 96) and the larger the XBTC-2 with R-4360-8. The Wasp Major was fitted with a single-stage, variable speed supercharger and water injection. Mockups were ready by December. These aircraft were continuing developments of the SB3C, and the Army bought into the XBTC-1 as the XA-40. However, Curtiss began to over-extend itself and the R-3350 program was troubled in addition to being heavily committed to priority Army projects. Consequently, by December 1943 the Navy had terminated the BTC-1.

A contract was let the last day of 1943 for two XBTC-2 prototypes (Bunos. 31401/2). The Navy stretched out the effort to reduce the Curtiss workload. The lengthened development period meant the first example did not fly until 20 January 1945. It had four 20mm cannon with 200 rpg, a bomb bay for a single weapon up to 1,600 pounds, two external mounts for up to 1,000-pound bombs, or a torpedo under the bay. The first aircraft had a standard wing (Model A) with Fowler flaps behind upper and lower dive brakes. Buno. 31402 had the Model B wing with duplex flaps plus revised sweep and taper in the outer wing panels. This latter added outboard Fowler flaps under lengthened ailerons, behind an additional pair of dive brakes, and leading edge slats in the outer wing panels.

Testing was slowed by mishaps and prop issues, making little progress by war's end. By this time, the competition had established their capabilities and some had won production contracts. More of the same in a peacetime Navy was too much.

Near Miss (XBTM-1)

The Navy pursued other "clean-sheet" designs for the bomber-torpedo aircraft in the first half of 1944, seeking lighter weight aircraft for the escort carriers. They did not mandate a bomb bay and all had conventional landing gear. Over seven months, three such aircraft were placed on contract, again without any clear competition.

The Curtiss XBTC-1 was the first formal program seeking a multi-role naval attack aircraft on the scale of a fighter. Powerplant choices had the design reach flight as the XBTC-2. Aircraft 31402 is seen with the Model A wing. The airplane found no place in a crowded postwar field. (Jay Miller Collection)

Another product of the prolific if unsuccessful Curtiss team, the XBTC-2 had a 3,000-hp engine and hefty weapons load with bomb bay, but apparently little else to distinguish it. Aircraft 31402 is seen with the Model B wing. Note the cut-down upper cowl lip for improved pilot field of view forward. (Jay Miller Collection)

Curtiss XBTC-2 characteristics:

span	50.0 ft	weight empty	13,947 lbs
length	38.6 ft	gross (loaded)	17,910 lbs
height	16.7 ft	max. (13-2 torpedo)	21,660 lbs
wing area	406 ft^2	speed, max. (16,900 ft)	374 mph
fuel capacity (int. + ext.)	540+150 gal	torpedo	322 mph
service ceiling	26,200 ft	cruise	188 mph
initial climb rate	2,250 fpm	range (torpedo)	1,245 mi
		maximum	1,835 mi

The next bomber-torpedo project went to the Glenn L. Martin Co. for what became the XBTM-1. They were given a Letter of Intent on 15 January 1944. Following mockup inspection in February, a contract was let on 31 May 1944 for a static article and two test aircraft.

The two Model 210 prototypes (Bunos. 85161/2) were powered by the 2,975-hp XR-4360-4, capable of 2,400 hp at 13,500 feet, turning a four-blade propeller. In spring 1944 this was still the most powerful engine readily available. Four 20mm cannons with 200 rpg were fitted in the wings. The wings and fuselage had a remarkable 15 hardpoints for approximately 4,500 pounds of distributed weapons carriage that made a bomb bay unnecessary. A centerline station could accommodate a 2,000-pound torpedo while inboard wing stations carried 1,000-pound weapons or 150-gallon tanks. The 12 remaining stations were for rockets or 250-pound bombs. The picket-type dive brakes also served as flaps, deflected together closed with intermeshed "toothcomb" fingers or splitting to open as brakes. This was supplemented with a fuselage "Swiss-cheese" perforated dive flap. Armor, retractable tail wheel, and provisions for the APS-4 radar pod were other features.

Because engineering work on its B-26 Marauder was winding down, the Martin staff was able to concentrate on the Navy project. Consequently, they had the first example ready in an astonishing seven months. Buno. 85161 took to the air for the first time on 26 August 1944 with O. E. "Pat" Tibbs piloting. Changes during the course of testing included vertical stabilizer and rudder alterations, and addition of a spinner. These were represented on 85162, which flew on 20 May 1945.

Service trials at the NATC, starting on 11 December 1944, found the aircraft showed much promise. In light of later events, it seems the testers overlooked much or were excessively optimistic. A production contract for 750 BTM-1s was placed on 15 January 1945. Delivery from the Baltimore company did not begin until after the war, 15 December 1945.

Martin XBTM-1 characteristics:			
span (24.0 ft folded)	50.1 ft	weight empty	14,500 lbs
length	40.6 ft	gross (bomber)	19,000 lbs
height (folded 16.5 ft)	11.8 ft	maximum	23,386 lbs
wing area	496 ft²	speed, sea level	342 mph
fuel capacity (int. + ext.)	510+300 gal	max. (16,000 ft)	367 mph
service ceiling	26,800 ft	cruise	189 mph
initial climb rate	2,780 fpm	range, attack	1,200 mi
		maximum	2,350 mi

Production was initially truncated to 99 at war's end, but 50 more were eventually added. These went on to serve as the AM-1 Mauler with mixed reviews. Significant design refinements and extensive modifications were required, including control changes and structural beef-up, suggesting the rapidly developed wartime airplane would not have been found operationally suitable.

Out of Left Field (XBK-1, XBTK-1)

A 1943 requirement for a light (compared to the SB2C), single-seat dive-bomber for escort carriers was met with a January 1944 proposal from Kaiser-Fleetwings. The Bristol, Pennsylvania, Fleetwings had primarily built trainers and other light aircraft, plus performing subcontract work. Henry J. Kaiser's Kaiser Cargo Co. had been building ships, but was expanding into other war production, and acquired Fleetwings in March 1943. Approval to proceed with two XBK-1 prototypes (Bunos. 44313/14) powered by R-2800-22W engines was given on 23 February 1944. The 31 March contract raised the number of aircraft to five (adding Bunos. 90484/6) with static article. The concept aircraft accommodated

Martin took a shot at the attacker concept with the XBTM-1. The team had the aircraft flying in mid 1944 and production was ordered early the next year (this image from 28 September 1945). None of these aircraft, establishing the trend toward multi-role fighter-attack aircraft, were available until after the war. (Naval Aviation Archives)

The large XBTM-1 could carry 4,500 lbs of external stores on 15 hardpoints, supplementing the four 20mm cannons in the wings. Facilitating bombing, the flaps split to act as dive brakes and a perforated flap extended from the belly. (Naval Aviation Archives)

stores on three stations rated to 1,000 pounds. The mockup was inspected in fall 1944 and 17 service test examples (Bunos. 90487/503) were ordered on 7 October 1944.

The decision to pursue the bomber-torpedo category had Kaiser-Fleetwings strengthen the fuselage hardpoint to 2,000 pounds for a Mk 13-2 torpedo and a total war load of 4,890 pounds. A pair of 20mm cannons was included in the wings with 200 rpg and eight rocket mounts on the folding wing panels. The designation changed to XBTK-1 on 9 February 1945.

Other features of the XBTK-1 were self-sealing fuel tanks and 230 pounds of cockpit armor. The landing flaps include a bottom split "picket fence" dive brake while "finger" brakes rose out of the wing upper surface ahead of the flaps. Bomb shackles and sway braces were integral with the wing and normally lay flush. Likewise, the centerline station bomb-displacing arm for dive attacks lay flush when not engaged. Longitudinal trim was via electrical pitch incidence change of the "flying" horizontal tail, a feature derived from inspection of captured German equipment and passed along through design conferences.[8] A yaw-only autopilot was included as well as provisions for the AN/APS-4 radar. Fuel was contained in a single fuselage tank. Most unusual was the innovative engine exhaust system. Based on BuAer research, this sought to turn the cooling drag into thrust by mixing the exhaust with air flowing out the rear of the cowling. This "exhaust pump" directed the air into steel ducts within the forward fuselage sides where it mixed with exhaust gases and exited out duct flaps aft of the cockpit.

The "Victory Plane" project fell six months behind schedule, first flight finally occurring on 12 April 1945. The engine was soon switched to the superior 2,100-hp R-2800-34W with supercharger. The team struggled with engine overheat and airframe vibration exacerbated by the exhaust pump. Apart from cooling issues, it was evident the exhaust design mattered little to aircraft performance and made cockpit ingress/egress dicey given the hot skin. Consequently, a trio of cowl flaps was added on each side of Buno. 44313 and the duct exhaust faired over. Engine cooling remained marginal.

Another attempt at the attack aircraft role was the Kaiser-Fleetwings XBTK-1, ordered in March 1944. With an April 1945 first flight, the project was still in progress when the war came to an end. The exhaust pump within the fuselage beneath the cockpit is visible in this image. (Jim Hawkins Collection via Dennis Jenkins)

Although from a source new to fighter development, the XBTK-1 was a very sound design with four ultimately flying. Among the advanced features was electric-pitch trim adjusting incidence of the horizontal stabilizer. However, like so many other worthy efforts, there were insufficient postwar resources to carry the program forward. (Naval Aviation Archives)

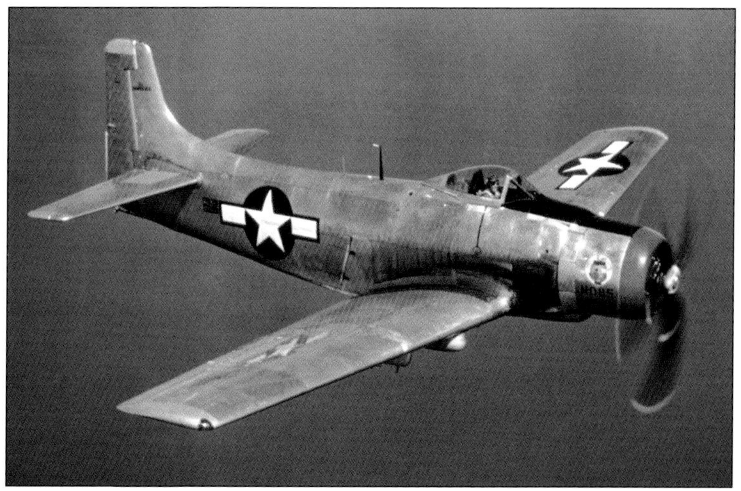

The big winner in the transition to fighter-attack aircraft in naval aviation was the XBT2D-1 Dauntless II. A proven engine and simplicity in the airframe yielded a rugged airplane with extraordinary payload capacity. Ordered into production early, these only reached the fleet following VJ-Day and eventually became the AD-1 Skyraider. (Naval Aviation Archives)

Kaiser-Fleetwings XBTK-1 characteristics:			
span	48.7 ft	weight empty	9,959 lbs
length	38.9 ft	gross	12,728 lbs
height	15.7 ft	maximum	15,782 lbs
wing area	380 ft²	speed, max. (18,000 ft)	373 mph
fuel capacity (int. + ext.)	275+100 gal	(torpedo)	258-297 mph
service ceiling (scout)	33,400 ft	cruise	158 mph
initial climb rate	3,550 fpm	range, max. (torpedo)	1,250 mi

The aircraft was passed to the Navy for service testing soon after the war where the evaluators found plenty of room for improvement. Although work was undertaken to address the deficiencies, including fitting leading-edge slats, the biggest obstacle to success of the worthy airplane was evolving requirements and too little growth potential owing to the light design. The Navy was also hesitant to proceed with a company possessing so little production history. Henry Kaiser had muscled his way into the naval aviation business and so made few friends in the Bureau. The XBTK-1 passed into history with only four completed.

Longevity (XBT2D-1)

Douglas undertook one of the "clean-sheet" bomber-torpedo designs. Poor prospects for the XBTD-1 and XTB2D-1 potentially left Douglas without a Navy program, and they felt this unacceptable if they hoped to keep their foot in the door as a Navy supplier. In a June 1944 meeting with its customer, the company recommended dumping the BTD-1 and replacing it with a more practical aircraft. A team of senior engineers made up of Heinemann, Leo Devlin, and Gene Root generated a conceptual design literally overnight that answered the Navy's criticisms and evolving requirements. BuAer reacted so positively to the proposal that on 6 July what funds remained on the BTD-1 contract was converted to a new development program. This was followed on 21 July with an order for 15 XBT2D-1s, later increased to 25 (Bunos. 09085/109).

Although the XBT2D-1 concept departed from the Navy's earlier edicts as to aircraft features, experience had taught them to give design teams more leeway. Company representatives were visiting combat units in the field to gain firsthand knowledge as to what did and did not work, and what the warfighters felt they really needed. In this case, the process paid off handsomely. Heinemann had been advocating this type of warplane for years, and the free hand allowed the chief engineer to excel.

Given the lead of the other bomber-torpedo aircraft design competitors, Douglas had to sustain a fast pace throughout the development. For this reason, the company intentionally kept things simple and employed many existing components. The El Segundo team had the mockup ready in mid-August and the prototype rolled out a remarkable eight months later. This was four months ahead of schedule and they came in 1,628 pounds under the specified weight, both extraordinary achievements in aircraft development.

In order to convert structural weight to ordnance carriage capability, Douglas did not incorporate the bomb bay so many competitors had adopted. Instead, 15 weapons stations under the wings and fuselage accommodated an impressive 6,000-pounds of stores. The team did not hesitate to design new ordnance fittings and even new weapon shapes for reduced weight, drag, and improved delivery. These would become standard U.S. military equipment. A pair of 20mm cannons with 200 rpg was fitted in the wings. Chosen powerplant was the 2,300-horsepower R-3350-8 with supercharger turning a 13.5-foot four-blade propeller. All internal fuel was in one fuselage tank. External fuel tanks could be carried on two wing stations and the fuselage centerline. A distinguishing feature was the large dive brakes folding out of the unusually faceted aft fuselage sides and base. A bubble canopy covered the cockpit that included 208-pounds of armor.

Tommy Brown made the maiden flight of the XBT2D-1 on 18 March 1945 from Mines Field, and a few more flew before the end of the war. The fast-paced company testing, and Navy trials at Pax River beginning on 7 April, showed the design to be sound and possibly the best of the new attackers in development. Consequently, a contract for 548 BT2D-1 Dauntless IIs was let on 5 May, just weeks after first flight, reflecting the service's faith in Douglas.

Termination of hostilities saw production numbers trimmed to 277; still a large order given the numerous programs axed outright. Testing revealed problems with landing gear and associated wing structure, and propeller vibration, which required remedy. Still, it was the big winner of the bomber-torpedo designs initiated in the late war years, going on to meritorious service as the AD-1 Skyraider and then A-1 in many models and roles for both the Navy and Air Force.

Last Roll of the Dice (XBT2C-1)

Curtiss responded to a Navy requirement issued on 29 January 1945 with what would be the last bomber-torpedo design. This was a further development of its SB2C Helldiver and bore similarities to the XBTC-2. Indeed, the Model 98 had approximately 50 percent commonality with the SB2C-5, incorporating many changes long advocated by Curtiss in a number of unsuccessful proposals.[9] Among the most obvious carryover was the basic wing, wing fold, perforated split dive flaps, and bomb bay. The wingtips were clipped to reduce folded height of the taller aircraft. The new airplane would pack a more powerful engine on a lengthened fuselage with revised tail. This commonality allowed the design and later construction to move quickly given that the competition had a substantial calendar lead. The Navy responded with an order on 27 March 1945 for 10 XBT2C-1 service test aircraft (Bunos. 50879/88). Such late-war contracts that moved directly to multiple prototypes reflected confidence in the then highly experienced national aircraft industry.

Although similar to the XBTC-2, the XBT2C-1 had a smaller engine and single propeller, while adding a radarman in the fuselage aft of the pilot. The 2,500-hp R-3350-24 with single-stage, two-speed supercharger, drove a four-blade 13.7-foot diameter propeller. An unusual feature was the propeller shaft/engine-cooling fan at the front of the cowling on some examples. Some also had a water injection system (-24W engine). The 100-gallon drop tanks could be supplemented with such a tank in the bomb bay. The longer main gear struts compared

Curtiss XBT2C-1 characteristics:

span	47.6 ft	weight empty	12,268 lbs
length	38.7 ft	gross (scout)	15,975 lbs
height	16.4 ft	maximum	19,022 lbs
wing area	416 ft²	speed, max. (scout 17,000 ft)	349 mph
fuel capacity (int. + ext.)	410+300 gal	torpedo	313 mph
service ceiling	28,100 ft	cruise	175 mph
initial climb rate	2,590 fpm	range, torpedo	1,435 mi
		maximum	2,220 mi

Brought to fruition just days before Japan's surrender, the XBT2C-1 had little chance for success, yet was one of Curtiss' finest efforts. The program continued delivery of service test examples. Curiously, it added a separate radarman within the fuselage (window visible) instead of the pilot handling these tasks. (Naval Aviation Archives)

Developed at an extraordinary pace, the XBT2D-1 appeared a winner from early in flight test. Visible in this image is the dive brake in the right side of the fuselage, another opposite, and one in the belly. Weapons included a pair of 20mm cannons and 6,000 pounds of external stores. (Naval Aviation Archives)

Another Curtiss attempt at meeting the attack requirement was an aircraft sharing commonality with the SB2C-5, the XBT2C-1. Although a worthy effort, other types were selected for the smaller postwar production contracts. The bomb bay and cowl cooling fan are evident in this image. (Jay Miller Collection)

with the SB2C-1 were devised to hydraulically telescope to shorter dimensions to allow gear retraction into essentially the same gear wells. The aircraft structure was stronger to offset some of the Helldiver's deficiencies, although adding weight. The AN/APS-4 radar was pod-mounted under the starboard wing. Why a separate radarman was felt essential when single-seat fighters were already being produced with this radar is unclear. Armament consisted of two 20mm cannons, up to 2,000 pounds of bombs or a Mk 13-3 torpedo in the internal bay, and two 1,000-pound-capacity wing hardpoints, as well as eight rocket stations. The cockpit had 182 pounds of armor.

Robert W. Fausel took the XBT2C-1 up for its first flight on 7 August 1945 (before the earlier XBTC-2). Deliveries were made through October 1946 as the last Curtiss aircraft for the Navy. Compared with the SB2C-1, the XBT2C-1 could fly approximately 40 mph faster and carry about 1,000 pounds more with better takeoff performance. Yet, extended service trials found plenty to criticize, including insufficient reserve power in combat configuration. The competition was just too far out ahead of the Curtiss plane that appeared to possess too little growth potential.[10]

Douglas XBT2D-1 characteristics:

span	50.0 ft	weight empty	10,093 lbs
length	39.48 ft	gross	13,500 lbs
height	15.7 ft	maximum	17,500 lbs
wing area	400 ft²	speed, max. (13,600 ft)	375 mph
fuel capacity (int. + ext.)	365+750 gal	torpedo	303 mph
service ceiling	33,200 ft	cruise	185 mph
initial climb rate	3,680 fpm	range, clean	1,554 mi
		torpedo	1,427 mi

Chapter 9

After Pearl Harbor, the Americans shanghaied more than 100 Vengeance dive-bombers already bought by the United Kingdom. These Vultee aircraft were called V-72s and A-31s, offering a ready means of creating a dive-bomber force. The A-31s shown were manufactured by Northrop, still bearing RAF colors and code. (Gerald Balzer Collection)

ARMY ATTACK DIVERSION

Saga Defined

Until the mid 1930s, attack aviation was considered secondary to the primary aim of gaining air superiority. This branch of the Air Corps was small and its aircraft typically obsolete. This neglect ended as war loomed overseas and attack aircraft were sought during the rearming surge. The new aircraft were still in development or small in numbers at the outbreak of war, leaving the Air Corps without effective attack aircraft in the event the country was drawn into the conflict. This precipitated a scramble for suitable types since observations of recent combat abroad made clear this class of combat aircraft was essential.

Prewar, the U.S. attack aircraft had evolved as single-engine monoplanes for low-level bombing and strafing. Some had weapons bays and usually two or three crewmen. Many of these types were exported and saw action before America entered the war. Twin-engine attackers were resisted throughout the 1930s because of cost and complexity. However, addition of bombsights for medium altitude bombing with heavier weapons loads, plus the need for extended range and armor, was cause to seek twins for attack. The results came to be known more as light bombers. Many of these airplanes had yet to enter production or were still maturing as the Army hastened to reequip. Consequently, single-engine types diverted from other roles were acquired before and during the war.

At the beginning of the conflict, the frightening success of the Junkers Ju 87 Stuka dive-bomber gained worldwide notice, and elements within the U.S. Army felt a similar capability was needed. The Air Corps was expected to support the ground forces' two new armored divisions in a manner like that of the Luftwaffe, with close air support such as dive-bombing. Army Chief of Staff Gen. George C. Marshall insisted the Army Air Corps procure dive-bombers. The Navy and Marine Corps had been employing dive-bombing with suitable single-engine aircraft for more than a decade. Certainly, the large twins being developed by the Army were inappropriate for diving attacks and other close support missions. However, the move to dive-bombers and other single-engine attackers was not embraced

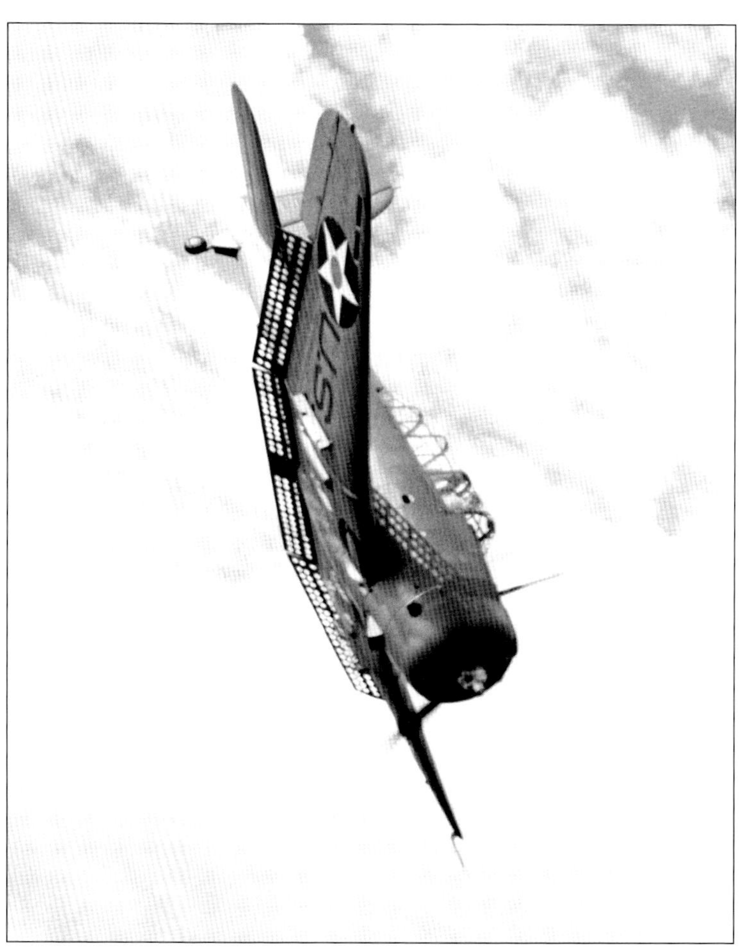

The close air support example set by the Luftwaffe created pressures for the Army Air Corps to adopt dive-bombers. The most expedient means to comply was to adopt Navy types such as this SBD Dauntless. However, neither the Army nor the RAF had much enthusiasm for dive-bombing. (National Museum of the United States Air Force)

by all within the Army. Hap Arnold was convinced pursuit aircraft could perform the role as an adjunct mission. It was noted the RAF also resisted adopting dive-bombers.

Many development projects for new aircraft were begun, as single-seat, single-engine models and as swift twins, while thousands of Navy models were purchased as interim solutions for the attack role. However, before the airplanes in production could be committed to battle in a big way, the war passed them by. A 22 March 1943 report from a board of officers evaluating dive-bomber procurement recommended ceasing all such acquisitions as soon as practicable. The Battle of Britain in summer 1940 and fighting in the Western Desert the following year revealed dive-bombers to be much too vulnerable in the absence of absolute air superiority. The war was compelling such rapid change in aircraft requirements that the attack mission demanded greater speed and firepower than extant dive-bombers could deliver. The board suggested production of the twin-engine A-20 and A-26 be accelerated as substitutes. The underemployed pursuit aircraft were also getting by as improvised multi-role fighter-bombers without a steep diving attack. Subsequently, in spring 1943, the Army discontinued seeking dive-bombers. Considering the great success the Navy and Marine Corps enjoyed with their dive-bombers, and mid-war examples by other air arms, one might conclude the Air Forces leadership never embraced the role with sufficient enthusiasm.

Although dive-bombing was curtailed, ground attack in general remained a vital mission and the Army Air Forces performed the mission admirably. Several attack projects continued, but the single-engine types were dropped with the decision to focus on twins. Yet, none of the twins ever entered production. The entire program proved largely a misdirection, with enormous resources expended for marginally useful combat airplanes and fruitless programs.

Might Have Been

Old Reliable (A-17 and A-33)

When war broke out, the Army was operating what remained of 110 Northrop A-17s and 129 Douglas A-17A all-metal monoplanes, delivered between 1936 and 1938. These siblings were among the first warplanes representing the character of those that would be taken to war in a few short years. The two-place A-17s were powered by one 750-hp Pratt & Whitney R-1535-11. The A-17As employed the R-1535-13 at 825 hp and introduced retractable landing gear. The aircraft had a gross weight of 7,550 pounds and a top speed of 220 mph. They had four .30-cal. wing guns and another on a flex mount for the rear gunner. They could carry four 100-pound bombs or twenty 30-pound anti-personnel bombs in a small fuselage weapons bay.

With focus shifting to twin-engine attackers, the effective A-17s and A-17As were considered surplus. Between 19 and 20 June 1940,

During the mid 1930s, the A-17A was judged the most effective attack aircraft ever produced in the United States. A large number of the Northrop aircraft were given to France at the beginning of the war but ultimately taken on by the UK. (National Museum of the United States Air Force)

The Douglas 8A-5, derived from the A-17A, was one of a family of attack aircraft that garnered export orders. Thirty-six were bound for Norway, but 31 of these were pressed into service by the U.S. Army as A-33s, the one shown photographed at Moffett Field, California, on 7 March 1942. (Jay Miller Collection)

93 of the As were returned to the manufacturer for reconditioning and resale to France. The engines were changed to the 825-hp R-1535-S2A5-G. The aircraft were then flown to Halifax, Nova Scotia, to await transport. The fall of France saw the aircraft taken on by the UK and Canada as trainers and target tugs, naming them Nomads. Of the 61 for Britain, only two traveled to that island while the

rest went to South Africa. By then considered obsolete by the Air Corps as well, those remaining in the United States were employed as trainers and hacks before the last was cast off in October 1944.

Douglas had continued development of the A-17 as the Model 8A, which won brisk export orders. Thirty-six 8A-5Ns, with 1,200-hp R-1820-87s, were purchased by Norway in early 1940. By October, when the aircraft were ready to ship, Norway had fallen under Nazi occupation. The aircraft went to the "Little Norway" training center in Canada, although the owners wished to sell 18 to Peru. The U.S. government had imposed an embargo on Peru and so requisitioned the 18 airplanes on 9 December 1941 for the U.S. Army (42-13584/601). The remaining 13 aircraft (42-109007/19) were likewise taken up in June 1943. These served as A-33s for training and liaison transport through September 1944. The aircraft grossed 8,600 pounds and possessed a maximum speed of 248 mph. They were armed with four .30-cal. wing guns, two .50s in under-wing sponsons, and twin .30s in a flexible mount for the rear gunner. Up to 1,800 pounds of bombs could be carried.

No Future (A-18)

At the beginning of the war, the U.S. Army was experimenting with a small number of two-seat, twin-engine attack aircraft. These 13 Curtiss Y1A-18 service test airplanes (Model 76A, 37-52/64) had been ordered in 1936 on the strength of the predecessor XA-14. These were powered by two R-1820-47s at 850 hp with three-blade propellers. Bombs were distributed in two cavities within each wing with a capacity of 200 pounds each. However, four 116-pounds bombs could also be carried on under-wing racks. Deliveries occurred between July and October 1937 and they were placed with an operational squadron. By 1940, these were being employed in training as A-18s. The last was retired in 1943.

The Curtiss airplane showed potential, although the diminutive horsepower of its engines made for meager weapons delivery capability. At a unit price of $104,640 they were costly aircraft for the

Curtiss A-18 characteristics:			
span	59.4 ft	weight empty	9,410 lbs
length	42.3 ft	gross	12,849 lbs
height	11.5 ft	maximum	15,016 lbs
wing area	526 ft²	speed, max. (2,500 ft)	247 mph
fuel capacity (int. + ext.)	287-639+0 gal	cruise	217 mph
service ceiling	28,650 ft	range, combat	1,445 mi
best climb rate	2,273 fpm	ferry	1,700 mi

Several Vultee YA-19 light bombers were being operated by the Army Air Corps at the beginning of World War II. They were badly dated and not the basis for a suitable combat aircraft meeting potential threats. Vultee sold a modest number of like V-11 and V-12 aircraft during the immediate pre-war years. (National Museum of the United States Air Force)

The Curtiss A-18 had its origins in the mid 1930s and so was modestly powered, its weapons load capacity and speed meager. Still, results of testing encouraged development of more advanced and larger twin-engine attack types. The 13 A-18s continued in service as operational trainers until 1943. (San Diego Aerospace Museum)

time. The company offered a Model 76B with R-1830s, but neither the U.S. Army nor a foreign power showed any interest. Nevertheless, the results were encouraging enough to spur the development of larger attack aircraft like the A-20 and A-26 that could deliver more ordnance, becoming essentially light bombers.

The Few (A-19)

At the beginning of the war, the Army Air Corps was operating a handful of Vultee YA-19s. These were the V-11GB variant of a light bomber that had seen pre-war sales of 102 airframes in six variants to China, Brazil, Turkey, and to the USSR where it was manufactured under license. The V-11s were built in two- and three-man versions. The Army's purchase of seven YA-19s (38-549/55) in June 1938 was more to establish a relationship with Vultee than to truly evaluate a potential combat aircraft. An upgraded model, the V-12, saw modest sales in China, and was built there under license.

YA-19 deliveries were slow, stretching from June 1939 to May 1940, since airplanes were essentially hand-built given the small orders of the period. After a brief evaluation, most of the aircraft were employed in diplomatic air attaché liaison flights between U.S. embassies in Central America. The aircraft was powered by the 1,200-hp R-1830-17. It carried four .30-cal. machine guns in the wings with 600 rpg, plus one each in ventral and dorsal rear flexible mounts with a total 1,200 rounds. The ventral gun was within a deployable "dustbin." Bomb capacity was 1,080 pounds with the weapons partially submerged within a fairing attached to the belly or six 30-pound bombs released from cells within the center wing box.

Vultee A-19 characteristics:			
span	50.0 ft	weight empty	6,452 lbs
length	37.9 ft	gross	10,421 lbs
height	10.0 ft	maximum	16,285 lbs
wing area	384 ft²	speed, max. (6,500 ft)	230 mph
fuel capacity (int. + ext.)	311-330+0 gal	cruise	207 mph
service ceiling	20,400 ft	range, combat	1,110 mi
best climb rate	1,320 fpm	ferry	1,385 mi

Dressing for the Party

Keeps Going (A-24)

In seeking an immediate solution for its neglect of dive-bombing, the Army borrowed several Marine Corps SBD-1s in July 1940 for evaluation. They appeared suitable, so the Dauntless was adopted by the Army as the A-24 Banshee. This would serve as a stopgap until specialized land-based types were developed. The Army acquired its first A-24s by adding 78 airplanes to a Navy SBD-3 contract on 2 July 1940.

The Army adopted the Navy's SBD Dauntless as an interim dive-bomber, but ended up buying hundreds. These A-24s (A-24B-15 shown) were quickly judged marginally suitable and devoted mostly to training and other non-combat duties. Their few combat uses had decidedly mixed results. (San Diego Aerospace Museum)

The Army Air Forces experimented with a mechanical siren to generate the terrifying scream that accompanied a Stuka dive. The system shown here beneath a Douglas A-24 was built by Chrysler but not produced, as far as is known. (National Museum of the United States Air Force)

The first of the Douglas A-24s (SBD-3A in Navy parlance) was delivered in June 1941 and the last in October. The equipment for carrier operations had been removed, a pneumatic tire replacing the solid rubber on the tail wheel, and Army radios installed, in addition to other minor alterations. Otherwise, it was a typical Dauntless with the 1,000-hp R-1820-52, perforated dive-brakes, self-sealing

This 13th Air Force A-24B was photographed on 1 January 1945 on Morotai Island in present-day Indonesia. By that point it had been downgraded to non-combat roles and so was more formally an RA-24B. (San Diego Aerospace Museum)

Douglas A-24B characteristics:			
span	41.5 ft	weight empty	6,330 lbs
length	33.0 ft	gross	9,250 lbs
height (parked)	12.9 ft	maximum	10,250 lbs
wing area	325 ft²	speed, max. (15,000 ft)	254 mph
fuel capacity (int. + ext.)	260+0 gal	cruise	180 mph
service ceiling	27,000 ft	range, 1,000-lbs payload	950 mi
best climb rate	1,700 fpm	scout	1,250 mi

fuel tanks, and armor. The .30 on a flex mount in the rear complemented two .50-cal. nose guns supplied with 360 rounds. A 500- or 1,000-pound bomb was slung off the centerline "crutch," or a 100-pound weapon could be carried under each wing. The Army even conducted tests of a system to generate a frightening scream like the sound accompanying a Stuka's dive enhanced with sirens.

These dive-bombers equipped three squadrons of a light bombardment group at the start of America's active participation in World War II. They were en route to the Philippines when Japan's attack on the islands began. The immature force eventually joined the fight, but came away having achieved little for its losses. Compared with A-20 bombers, they were judged under armed, lacking range, and too slow to operate without what little fighter support was available.

Despite the poor initial showing, further A-24s were procured by the Army with a July 1942 order because the A-25 (which see) was delayed. Douglas' El Segundo factory delivered 90 more A-24s. By this point, the Army had 13 dive-bomber groups, but inadequate aircraft. The Dauntless was a fine airplane, but limited by the standards of mid-1942 land planes. Yet, the Navy and Marine Corps operated the type fruitfully well beyond this point.

A further 170 Dauntlesses were diverted from Navy procurements and delivered through March 1943 as A-24As (SBD-4As). Bomb capacity went to 1,600 pounds on the centerline and 325 pounds outboard, and the gunner now had two machine guns and 2,000 rounds. A big step was taken on 1 December with an Army contract for 1,200 A-24Bs (SBD-5), powered by the R-1820-60 at 1,200 hp, from the new Tulsa plant. Deliveries of the B commenced in March 1943, but the order was cancelled on 30 October as the Army was divorcing itself of dive-bombers. The last of 615 aircraft were handed over in December, and that month also marked the only other time in which Army Air Force A-24s were employed in combat. One squadron engaged Japanese strong points in the Gilbert Islands with good results. Yet, the Army Air Forces had already decided the fate of the Banshee.

Sixty A-24Bs were passed directly to the Marine Corps. Twenty-eight were transferred to Mexico for Caribbean submarine patrol and Chile received a dozen. Some 40 to 50 A-24Bs went to Free French forces that employed them in the liberation of their country.

Tough (A-36)

The RAF orders for Mustangs dried up and production was running down toward the end of 1941. Although the U.S. Army was interested in the type, they had funds on hand only for dive-bombers, and the service urged North American to consider designing such a variant. The process resulted in the NA-97, powered by the V-1710-87 with 1,325 hp at 3,000 feet, or 1,500 hp in combat power. It had four .50-cal. machine guns in the wings and two in the nose, with a total 1,200 rounds. The Army followed up with an order for 500 of the A-36A dive-bomber models in April 1942. The type first flew in September 1942 and deliveries ran from October through March 1943.

The A-36A featured hydraulically operated wing dive brakes and shackles for two 500-pound bombs or 75-gallon tanks. The brakes reduced dive speed from around 350 mph to a maximum 250 – still considered too high by some–the aircraft so clean that speed built up quickly. However, the brakes were found to create lateral controllability problems owing to pressure differentials side-to-side during asymmetrical dives, and they could overstress the airframe. Crews were initially ordered to reduce their dive angles by 20 degrees and not employ the dive brakes. The brakes were eventually wired closed, although this was not met with uniform adherence. Additionally, the nose guns were often removed to save weight.

The A-36A was the first Army Air Force Mustang variant to see combat, this during summer 1943 in the Mediterranean and CBI

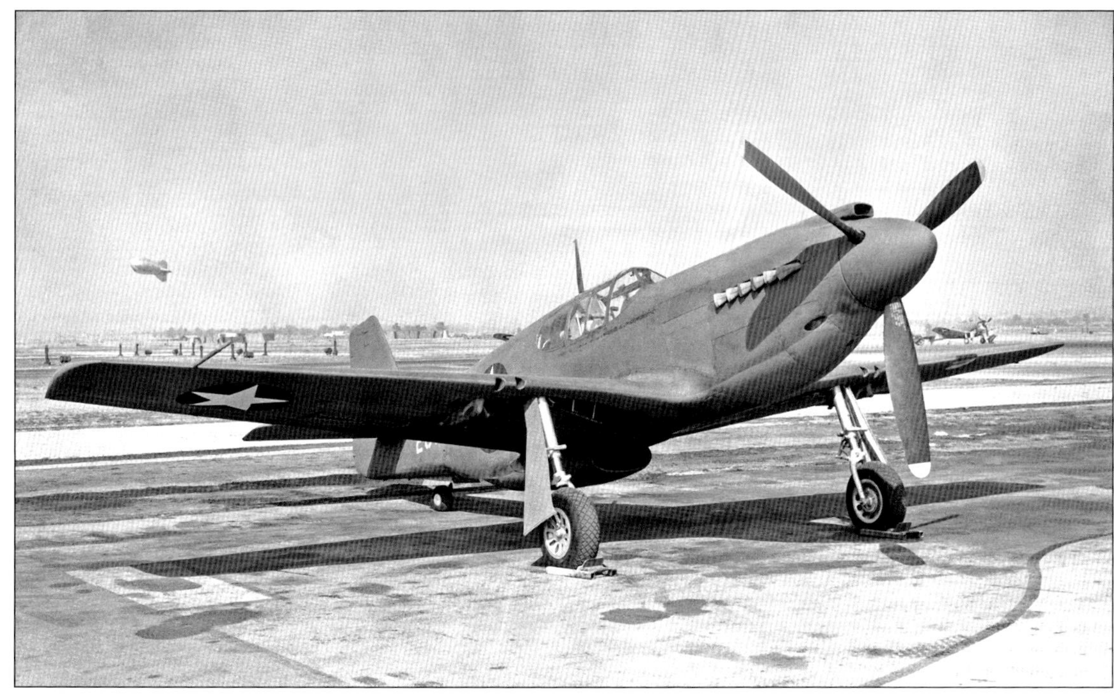

The North American A-36A was the harbinger of fighter-bombers to come. A single-seat aircraft of great speed, it began with the dive brakes evident on other dive-bombers of the period, but these were usually locked-out. The A-36 served well, the last Army Air Forces type to occupy the passé dive-bomber role. (American Aviation Historical Society)

North American A-36A characteristics:			
span	37.0 ft	weight empty	6,650 lbs
length	32.3 ft	gross	8,370 lbs
height (parked)	12.7 ft	maximum	10,700 lbs
wing area	235.75 ft²	speed, max. (5,000 ft)	356 mph
fuel capacity (int. + ext.)	180+300 gal	cruise	250 mph
service ceiling (combat)	25,100 ft	range, combat	550 mi
best climb rate	2,700 fpm	ferry	1,290 mi

theaters. After all other Army dive-bombers were withdrawn, the very effective A-36A remained as the last in the Army Air Force, and the only one with a liquid-cooled engine.

Misfires

The Unwanted (A-31 and A-35)

In the run-up to war in Europe, France contracted with Vultee for 300 Model 72 dive-bombers while the aircraft was still in design. Deliveries of the aircraft were to commence in October 1940, thus the occupation of France left the V-72s without a customer. The UK stepped forward to take 200 of the aircraft they named Vengeance under a 3 July 1940 contract; increased to 300 Vengeance Is on 2 December.

The V-72 carried a pilot and rear gunner. The latter operated a pair of flexible .30-cal. machine guns with 500 rpg in addition to the four fixed in the wings with 750 rpg. Two 500-pound bombs filled the bomb bay, with room for two more 250-pound weapons in an overload capacity. The R-2600-A5B-5 at 1,600 hp swung a three-blade propeller. The tough airframe was stressed for 12 g and incorporated armor plus self-sealing fuel cells. The main landing gear retracted aft, turning through 90 degrees for the wheels to lie flat in the wings. The "lattice" dive brakes were hydraulically deployed from the top and bottom of the outer wing panels. The first V-72 had vertical surfaces with rudders at the tips of the horizontal stabilizer. However, following dismaying characteristics uncovered during initial taxi trials, the single vertical tail on the second prototype was adopted for the first flight that occurred in March 1941.

Vultee's Downey facility was already saturated with BT-13 trainer production. Its Stinson plant in Nashville, Tennessee, purchased to produce the Vengeance, was still being converted. Consequently, Northrop was subcontracted in September 1940 to manufacture the first 200 Vengeance Is.

In spring 1941, RAF orders were increased with 400 more from Vultee as Vengeance IIs, and 200 from Northrop as Vengeance IAs. This was the largest RAF order for dive-bombers and, combined with the Bermuda (Brewster SB2A-1) and Chesapeake (Vought SB2U) aircraft, meant that all dive-bombers for British and Commonwealth forces were produced in the United States. When the 1941 contracts became lend-lease orders in April, the aircraft received the American designation A-31. A further RAF order was placed for 100 Nashville-built A-31Cs or Vengeance IIIs (Model 73). The late

The U.S. Army and Vultee worked long and hard trying to make the Vengeance suitable for combat, but were ultimately unsuccessful. Multiple customers and the exigencies of war worked against them. The distinctive planform of the airplane, an A-35A pictured, marked it as a Vultee product. (San Diego Aerospace Museum)

A-31s introduced minor equipment changes and the engine bore the military designation R-2600-19. The Army Air Forces then placed its own order for 400 A-31s on 16 January 1942, with ongoing production proportioned between the RAF and the U.S. Army.

The first production aircraft emerged from Hawthorne on 30 November 1941 and deliveries commenced in January. Northrop delivered its last A-31 in May 1943 as it turned its attention to P-61 production. Nashville turned out its initial aircraft in March 1942. With America's entry into the war, the U.S. Army requisitioned more than 100 Vengeances, flying in RAF colors and markings. These were from the British "cash and carry" orders, and so just a handful of the original orders reached the island nation.

Evaluations of the V-72 in the UK, and during February 1942 at Wright Field, were disappointing. The aircraft fell about 20 mph short of the specified top speed in combat configuration and it tended to sink as speed fell below 140 mph. The rear pair of machine guns was prone to frequent jams and the .30-cal. armament was generally considered too light. Range was marginal and, fully loaded, the Vengeance required around 6,000 feet to get off the ground. Operators were soon complaining of extraordinarily high oil consumption, as much as 8 to 16 gallons per flight hour, and enormous maintenance demands. On the positive side, the Vengeance was rugged and easy to fly. With the brakes out and the aircraft trimmed, it dove at a steady 290 to 310 mph that made targeting a breeze. There seemed no middle ground. The airplane was either detested or appreciated. Nonetheless, the airplanes were needed until more potent types could be deployed, and so orders continued.

The Army Air Corps came away from its testing with a long list of engineering changes required to make the Vengeance a suitable combat aircraft. The wide separation of production facilities and engineering staff suggested this process would be long, with spring 1943 the earliest the Army could expect to get deployable warplanes. From this moment, there were officers agitating to have the Vengeance contract cancelled.

Trying hard to respond to customer requirements as quickly as possible, design changes were introduced on the two production lines willy-nilly such that earlier aircraft were delivered with outstanding work remaining and with little uniformity in configuration. The Army also learned that many parts or assemblies manufactured in Hawthorne and Nashville were not interchangeable. Consequently, the Americans accepted only Nashville-built airplanes while the rest from Tennessee and those from Northrop were passed to foreign operators.

Efforts to improve the Vengeance and stabilize the design still left many senior officers judging the aircraft unworthy for combat and likely unsuitable as even an operational trainer. However, Gen. Arnold intervened and insisted the aircraft be supplied to the dive-bombing squadrons then forming. The first 140 or so unmodified Army Air Force aircraft were called V-72s. The other 24 or so with more of the design changes were labeled RA-31s, already restricted in their use.

Vultee proposed a single seat Vengeance, the V-86, that attracted no interest.[1] Instead, the airplane was revised in July 1942 as the A-31A or A-35 (Model 88) to meet Army Air Force requirements. These replaced the .30-cal. wing machine guns with .50s at 425 rpg, and one .50 for the gunner at 400 rpg. Wing incidence was raised four degrees to improve pilot visibility during level flight and landing – the latter previously requiring a turning approach. The bomb bay could now accommodate a 1,000-pound weapon.

The first A-35 emerged belatedly in September 1942, and an order for 400 was placed on the 22nd before testing at Eglin Field had been completed. The number was upped to 2,730 aircraft on 17 December, but design and production problems placed deliveries far behind schedule.

The first 99 V-88s of the American order were built in Nashville as A-35As, delivered through May 1943. All subsequent aircraft were built as A-35Bs. These had an additional pair of .50s in the wings plus hardpoints for two 500 pounders or ferry tanks. Substituting the 1,700-hp R-2600-13 compensated for the weight increase.

The A-35B introduced under-wing stores, generally a 500-pound bomb or 162-gal ferry tank beneath each wing. A second pair of .50-cal. machine guns was added, making three in each wing. Even these changes and a slightly more powerful engine failed to bring the Vengeance to a useable state for combat. (San Diego Aerospace Museum)

Vultee A-35B characteristics:			
span	48.0 ft	weight empty	10,300 lbs
length	39.8 ft	gross	16,400 lbs
height (parked)	15.3 ft	maximum	17,077 lbs
wing area	332 ft²	speed, max. (13,500 ft)	279 mph
fuel capacity (int. + ext.)	300+325 gal	cruise	230 mph
service ceiling	22,300 ft	range, combat	530 mi
average initial climb rate	1,327 fpm	ferry	1,900 mi

Britain was provided 562 of the A-35Bs as Vengeance IVs while Brazil received 29. The Free French forces in North Africa received 29 A-35As and 37 A-35Bs in late summer 1943. Many of these French aircraft were seen with extended exhaust pipes, probably to move the hot gases well clear of an already overly warm cockpit.

An Army Air Force evaluation in March 1943 indicated the A-35B model was still unsuitable for combat and less desirable as a trainer than existing types. The decision was firm that they would not be deployed. Other aircraft appeared more promising to transform in keeping pace with the evolving needs of war, thus the Vultee aircraft quickly faded from importance. Outstanding orders for 2,035 A-35s were cancelled on 20 May, leaving some remaining to be built.

To keep the trained Nashville workers occupied until retooling for another type, an order for 250 A-35s was reinstated. However, this was finally suspended with the last 300 cancelled and final delivery in June 1944. The additional aircraft were clearly unwanted and the waste had become intolerable for any reason. This brought the total Vengeance production to 1,931. Of 930 A-35s, the U.S. Army had taken on at least 20 As and 240 Bs.

The RAF had early judged the aircraft unsuitable for the "main act" in Western Europe. Most were shipped directly to Australia and India. They continued to buy the aircraft for enforcement of these Commonwealth units at the outer fringes of the war in the Far East where the Japanese had fewer counter-air assets and fighters could accompany the dive-bombers. The "VDBs" (Vengeance Dive-Bombers) shipped to India and operated by British and Indian squadrons, contributed significantly when it was found their vertical dives could deliver weapons onto targets within dense Burmese forest more effectively than level bombing. Likewise, the Aussies, who took on 122 VDBs, used the aircraft to good effect in the jungles of New Guinea. The aircraft fought through summer 1944 when fighter-bombers became available.

The Far East combat was the exception. The French never placed its examples in combat, refused further deliveries, and grounded the Vengeances within less than a year. The RAF and Royal Navy, Royal Australian Air Force (RAAF), and Army Air Force all turned many VDBs into unarmed tugs, fitted with a winch for towed drogue targets. Many of the aircraft in the United States and elsewhere, especially the last few hundred, were simply parked as an operational reserve and allowed to deteriorate.

Wrong Path (A-25)

Casting about for dive-bombers during 1940, the Army chose to benefit from the Navy's latest scout-bomber effort, the SB2C-1. On 31 December 1940, they placed a cautious order for 100 of the aircraft, which had only just flown, under the Navy contract as SB2C-1As. The initial plan was that these A-25A Shrikes (Model S84, later 84B) would be largely identical to the Navy Helldivers. However, during 1941 the Army made clear its intention to greatly expand the purchase of Helldivers and introduce essential configuration changes. The Navy saw this as interfering with an already troubled program, and it was unlikely the enormous demand would be met within the Curtiss-Wright plants already engaged. The firm followed Army direction and began converting its St. Louis facility to A-25 production. After America found itself at war, the Army raised its contract by 3,000 airplanes on 18 February 1942 under its own contracts with Curtiss-Wright.

The Shrike retained the SB2C-1's engine, the 1,700-hp R-2600-8. Armament was likewise the same, with two .50-cal. machine guns in the wings and another for the rear gunner. The bomb bay accommodated 1,000 pounds of weapons and the two under-wing stations could handle 500-pound bombs or external tanks.

The U.S. Army adapted the Navy's SB2C-1 Helldiver to its dive-bombing requirements as the Curtiss A-25A Shrike. Plans included procuring 3,100 of the airplanes, but disappointing performance and a decision to drop specialized dive-bombers from combat units spelled the demise of the A-25. (National Museum of the United States Air Force)

The A-25s were quickly rendered second rank assets, unfit for combat. These A-25As received the prefix R denoting "Restricted" usage. They performed glider tow at South Pines Army Air Field, Lubbock, Texas. Hundreds of such airplanes were given to the Marine Corps where they were similarly restricted to stateside training. (National Archives)

Curtiss A-25A characteristics:			
span	49.7 ft	weight empty	10,363 lbs
length	36.7 ft	gross	15,076 lbs
height (parked)	16.9 ft	maximum	17,162 lbs
wing area	453 ft²	speed, max. (12,400 ft)	285 mph
fuel capacity (int. + ext.)	320+246 gal	cruise	155 mph
service ceiling	24,500 ft	range, 1,000-lbs payload	1,130 mi
best climb rate	1,580 fpm	ferry	2,020 mi

The first 10 A-25As kept the Navy's folding wings but with the slats locked shut, had larger main gear tires for rough field operations (subsequently adopted by the Navy), a pneumatic tail wheel tire, and 474 pounds more armor was installed in the crew compartments. Eliminated were the arrestment and catapult gear, the radar, the telescopic gunsight giving way to a ring-and-bead sight, and Army radios were substituted. Beyond these 10 airplanes, the wing fold and slats were eliminated entirely. Changes became so numerous that attempts at standardization between the Navy and Army models were moot. St. Louis created its own drawings and the Army took over managing these contracts. This switchover introduced more delays. An Australian lend-lease order for 150 Shrikes in 1942, with its own set of changes, further complicated matters.

The problems suffered with the Navy SB2C-1 development were shared by the Army. Maiden flight of the A-25A was repeatedly delayed until it finally occurred on 29 September 1942, three months following the flight of the first production SB2C-1. Deliveries began in December, and it was 22 March of the following year before the 10 making up the first block were completed.

The A-25s were probably the Army's best dive-bombers in terms of bombing accuracy. However, excessive weight and comparatively poor performance – having gained more than a ton in weight and losing 28 mph off its promised top speed, too slow to evade enemy fighters – made it less than ideal. In any event, by this point the Army no longer needed or wanted specialized dive-bombers.

The A-25 order was reduced to 900 aircraft on 12 June 1943, the last delivered in March 1944, before the outstanding balance was cancelled. The Marine Corps took 410 of the aircraft as SB2C-1As, but employed as advanced trainers. Airplanes bound for the Marine Corps had to pass through modification centers for alteration to meet unique Marine circumstances. The RAAF's 150 A-25 were cancelled following a decision by the theater commanders that they were unsuited to their needs. Ten had already been delivered in November 1943. Those A-25As that remained with the Army Air Forces at the end of 1943 were redesignated RA-25A. They were employed for general training, utility hacks, and target tow. No A-25As or SB2C-1As ever saw combat.

No Way (A-34)

The Army also looked to the Brewster SB2A as a possible means of filling its dive-bomber "gap." The development history of the type was as discouraging as that of the SB2C. Nonetheless, the Army Air Forces accepted approximately 108 examples of unwanted British Bermudas as the A-34s.[2] These could carry a 500-pound weapons load in the bay and were armed with two .30-cal. machine guns firing through the propeller, four more in the wings, and a pair for the gunner.

It was not long before Army pilots developed the same distaste for Brewster's "Blaster" as all other users. The aircraft were almost immediately redesignated RA-34s and never assigned Army serials. Their value was virtually nil as a trainer. They were flown far and wide as hacks, but so disliked many were abandoned wherever they broke down, simply parked out of the way to rot, or pushed onto artillery ranges as targets. In all, a most discouraging experience.

This A-34 was photographed as accepted, still in RAF color and markings as the Brewster Bermuda. Army pilots soon learned why the Bermudas were so disliked, and the airplanes were quickly shuffled aside, having contributed practically nothing to the war effort. (National Museum of the United States Air Force)

Brewster A-34 characteristics:			
span	47.0 ft	weight empty	8,173 lbs
length	39.2 ft	gross	12,700 lbs
height (parked)	15.4 ft	maximum	13,062 lbs
wing area	379 ft²	speed, max. (12,000 ft)	304 mph
fuel capacity (int. + ext.)	174-271+0 gal	cruise	161 mph
service ceiling	27,230 ft	range, 500 lbs bomb	750 mi
best climb rate	1,807 fpm	no bomb	1,150 mi

Attacker cum Bomber

The Army let contracts for development of single-seat/single-engine attack aircraft with weapon bays that could serve as dive-bombers. These yielded four programs but only two flying prototypes before the Army Air Forces chose, in spring 1943, to acquire only twin-engine attack types.

Trying Hard (A-32)

Another spin-off of Brewster's SB2A was the Model 341 dive-bomber offered to the U.S. Army on 15 May 1941. This immediately sparked interest and a 6 September 1941 requirement for a Close Support Army Cooperation Airplane (Dive-Bomber) resulted, substituting armor for a rear gunner and able to fight respectably air-to-air.[3] Subsequently, two XA-32 prototypes (42-13568/9, MX-136) were ordered on 31 October as Brewster's only Army Air Forces contract, delivery promised for September 1942.

The aircraft was to follow the XSB2A-1 design but as a single-place airplane under the supposition that higher speed and a hefty 650 pounds of armor (among the heaviest of any fighter) would make up for the lack of rear gunner. Speed came via an R-2800-37 at 2,100 hp swinging a four-blade Curtiss propeller. A top speed of 331 mph at 10,000 feet was anticipated along with 500 miles range with 3,000 pounds of bombs. Like the SB2A, the A-32 had split flaps for dive brakes, but sans the perforations. The airplane would be heavily armed with four 20mm cannons and 120 rpg, plus six .50-cal.

Brewster built two dive-bombers for the U.S. Army, but delays, problems with manufacturing, and evolving requirements rendered the type surplus to Army Air Forces needs and the prototypes fell short of performance goals. This XA-32 has two 20mm cannons and ports for four of the three .50-cal. machine guns in each wing. (National Museum of the United States Air Force)

The four large 20mm cannons in the wings of the XA-32A are evident in this 15 August 1944 image. The multiple exhausts ringing the cowling, instead of using a collector ring, produced distracting flame during night flight at low power settings, contributing to the conclusion it was unsuitable without further development. (National Archives)

This photo of the XA-32A emphasized the portly character of the Brewster design, derived from the Navy SBA and SB2A designs. It was also unusual in being a single-seat attacker when most of its counterparts had a rear gunner. (Ray Wagner Collection)

Brewster XA-32 characteristics:			
span	45.1 ft	weight empty	11,820 lbs
length	40.6 ft	gross	15,512 lbs
height (parked)	12.7 ft	maximum	19,960 lbs
wing area	425 ft^2	speed, max. (13,200 ft)	311 mph
fuel capacity (int. + ext.)	200+330 gal	cruise	236 mph
service ceiling	26,000 ft	range (3,000 lbs bombs)	300 mi
average initial climb rate	1,754 fpm	maximum	approx. 960 mi

machine guns with 400 rpg, all in the wings and outside the propeller arc. The second example, relabeled the XA-32A, would have four 37mm cannons with 120 rpg. Bomb-bay capacity was to be 1,000 pounds with the ability to carry a 1,000-pound bomb or 165-gallon external tank under each wing.

The mockup was inspected in May 1942 and optimism was running high for the promised capabilities of the new attacker. However, the Army soon shared the Navy's frustrations with Brewster. By summer, it was clear A-32 development had fallen behind schedule. The firm's production problems with its Navy and foreign commitments were legion, boding ill for meeting A-32 contract terms in any meaningful manner. By first flight on 22 May 1943, the Army Air Forces had essentially abandoned any hope the A-32 would be fielded, and never generated a production contract.

At the time the aircraft was passed to Eglin for testing, fighter-bombers were already filling any perceived requirement. In any event, Brewster proved true to its reputation. The XA-32 did very well until loaded to fight. It then fell short of speed and range specifications, and had handling issues while bombing. The XA-32 lacked current features such as a bubble canopy and retractable tail wheel, and was unsuitable for combat without considerably more development. The project withered.

Infanticide (XA-39)

The single Kaiser-Fleetwings XA-39 (MX-300) was to have been powered by the R-2800-27 at 2,000 hp with four-blade Hamilton Standard propeller. The armament of two 37mm cannons with 60 rounds and four .50-cal. machine guns with 1,600 rounds was

The mockup of the little-known Kaiser-Fleetwings XA-39 reveals a large attacker of conventional layout. The 2,000-hp R-2800 engine was to give 357-mph top speed and permit a heavy load of 5,000 lbs of bombs, two 37mm cannons, and four .50-cal. machine guns. It faded away as the Army turned to twins. (Jay Miller Collection)

probably all in the wing. Mention is made of a weapons bay for six 500-pound bombs or two 1,600-pound bombs. However, at least two wing stations for 1,000-pound bombs or tanks were included for a total capacity of 5,000 pounds. Suitable armor and leak-proof tanks were included. Gross weight was to have been 21,772 pounds, with a span of 55.8 feet and length of 43.8 feet. Top speed was projected as 357 mph at 16,600 feet, climb rate 2,040 fpm, and 27,800-foot service ceiling, with a 1,400-mile normal range. The XA-39 did not progress beyond mockup because of the Army's shift in emphasis to twins.

Never Mind (XA-40)

The Army variant of the Curtiss XBTC-1 under development for the Navy was tentatively designated XA-40 (MX-305).[4] With the same R-3350-8, top speed was an estimated 358 mph at 16,000 feet. Ordered in fall 1942, it was to combine six .50-cal. machine guns with 2,400 rounds and four 20mm cannons with 480 rounds. Wing hardpoints for two 500-pound bombs complemented a bomb bay for a 2,000-pound torpedo or 1,000-pound bomb. The Army bird would have increased armor while eliminating carrier gear. Gross weight was to be 17,120 pounds with a wingspan of 48.0 feet and length 36.4 feet. In October 1943, after the mockup had been completed, the Army shelved its contribution following the decision to concentrate on twin-engine attackers.

The Vultee XA-41 was designed and built expeditiously specifically for the attack mission and with an experimental engine. It was an excellent American aircraft, but by the time it was evaluated the Army no longer needed a new aircraft to fill the role. (San Diego Aerospace Museum)

Fine Specimen (XA-41)

In September 1942, the Army requested Vultee perform a study of a single-place dive-bomber powered by one of the most powerful engines then in existence, the 3,000-hp XP-4360. Pleased with the Vultee's Model 90 design, a contract was let on 10 November 1942 for two XA-41 prototypes (43-35124/5, MX-312).

Despite a successful mockup inspection in March 1943, the Army Air Forces abruptly changed the mission to low-altitude attack. Responding to this caused a delay, and a new contract was signed on 30 April that also including a static test article. Vultee development still proceeded quickly and by the end of September 1943 the first XA-41 was nearly half completed. At this point, the Army concluded its existing fighters were adequately performing ground attack missions and a specialized platform was not needed. Instead of terminating the contract, Maj. Gen. Oliver P. Echols, Chief, Materiel Division, who had initially championed the effort, pushed that one aircraft be finished to demonstrate the latest attack aircraft technology and serve as a testbed for the Wasp Major. This decision was affirmed in a 20 November contract change with the first aircraft then 75 percent complete and with $2.3 million expended. A study to convert the design to a long-range fighter did not arouse any interest.

The XA-41 ultimately mounted the R-4360-9, four-blade Hamilton Standard propeller, and all the

The Navy-developed XBTC-1 was to be similar to the XBTC-2 except with R-3350 engine turning a four-blade propeller and three .50-cal. machine guns joining the two 20mm cannons in each wing. The Army set aside this XA-40 when it turned to twin attackers, and the Navy ultimately cancelled the project. (Ray Wagner Collection)

The XA-41 was to be heavily armed with four 37mm cannons, four .50-cal. machine guns, and up to 6,500 pounds of stores under the wings and in a shallow bomb bay. It would likely have been an exceptional ground attack aircraft. However, the Army had turned to multi-role and twin-engine attackers. (San Diego Aerospace Museum)

This angle on the XA-41 emphasizes the utilitarian yet clean character of the airplane. Note the missing tail-wheel doors, spinner, outline of the bomb bay, and dorsal extension ending at the ADF antenna. (Tony Landis Collection)

fuel was in two tanks. The aircraft featured a cockpit well forward on the fuselage and the seat raised up to provide excellent visibility. The wide landing gear, retracting inboard, made for outstanding ground handling. The airplane was given four .50-cal. machine guns in the outer wing panels with 400 rpg, and four 37mm cannons in the inboard wings with 30 rpg, all outside the propeller arc. The shallow bomb bay could accommodate up to four 500-pound bombs, two 1,600-pound weapons, a torpedo, or additional fuel cells. Mention is made in the literature of 1,100 pounds external load capacity under each wing and 6,500 pounds total weapon load capacity. At some point during the development, Vultee found it necessary to add a dorsal fin.

Frank Davis took the XA-41 up for the first time on 11 February 1944 from Vultee Field, and landed at nearby March Field. Subsequent test flights were from the Army base. The manufacturer had done a fine job as evidenced by the aircraft flying frequently, with both company and Army pilots, but experienced a few problems. After a time, tail wheel doors were installed as well as a spinner.

Vultee XA-41 characteristics:			
span	54.0 ft	weight empty	13,400 lbs
length	48.7 ft	gross	18,800 lbs
height (parked)	14.5 ft	maximum	23,359 lbs
wing area	540 ft²	speed, max. (15,500 ft)	353 mph
fuel capacity (int. + ext.)	350+790 gal	cruise	270 mph
service ceiling	27,000 ft	range, (3,000 lbs bombs)	800 mi
average initial climb rate	2,326 fpm	ferry	3,000 mi

The aircraft was accepted by the Army on 25 June and ferried to Eglin Field on 16 July, the airplane's 60th flight. The XA-41 had many good attributes, including a turn rate that exceed the P-51B, and carried an impressive array of weapons. However, it was felt a ground attack aircraft must also respond suitably if challenged by enemy fighters. The speed of the XA-41 at around 350 mph maximum, among other factors, made it unsuitable in this regard when compared with fighters then in service.

The XA-41 went on to a brief evaluation by the Navy at Patuxent River as that service was interested in similar aircraft for carrier basing. It was then passed to Pratt & Whitney, in East Hartford, Connecticut, on 22 August 1944, to support development of a variable speed supercharger and other R-4360 work. The company purchased the aircraft on 9 October and registered it as NX60373N. It served well for many years.

Swift Twins

The return to focus on twins for the attack mission found two aircraft already being pursued. Unlike the early war twins that were essential light bombers, these attackers were to be fast and maneuverable. Only one yielding very good results albeit too late to be of value in the war.

Forget It (XA-37 and XP-73)

The Hughes Aircraft Co. XA-37 design may have begun as early as 1937 when Hughes submitted the Model D-2 twin-boom design in the two-engine fighter competition announced on 8 January 1937. This ultimately produced a contract to Lockheed for the XP-38, while the Hughes design was found deficient in speed and climb rate. This outcome and later disappointing interactions with the Air Corps led company owner Howard R. Hughes, Jr. to suspect a bias against his business, and this attitude would color his future dealings with Materiel Division.

Hughes continued the D-2 development into 1938 with his own funding, possibly as an aircraft by which Howard Hughes could best his own around-the-world speed record. The twin-boom layout was retained, although it may have initially been a "tail-dragger" and with a crew of as many as five. Hughes had already obtained rights to the Duramold process in order to greatly reduce aircraft weight and create an ultra-smooth exterior finish. This is a construction technique wherein a wood laminate is cured under pressure and temperature into compound shapes. However, the changing world situation made obtaining the high-power aero engines and other components for such an aircraft exceedingly difficult, as well as making an around-the-world flight nearly impossible. Interesting the Air Corps in the D-2 would allow him to obtain the Wright XR-2160 Tornado engines he desired as well as finally allowing his firm to sell an aircraft. Hughes Aircraft, which would occupy a new Culver City, California, plant in spring 1940, had devoted most of its efforts to specialized aircraft designs and modifications to permit its wealthy owner to satisfy his aviation aspirations.

In a 5 December 1939 letter to the chief, Materiel Division, Hughes sought a nominal $50 and Army cooperation in obtaining necessary equipment in developing his "pursuit-type airplane," then under construction. In exchange, Hughes Aircraft would provide data and drawings for the aircraft. After incorporating any changes felt necessary to meet Army Air Corps requirements, Hughes would follow-up with a report of estimated performance. After several months delay, Hughes' contacts throughout the government and military finally led Materiel Division to state it had no opposition to the endeavor, suggesting the R-2160 engines would be forthcoming. The Army also prepared a contract under the terms Hughes had proposed in December. In doing so, Materiel Division sought details of the aircraft and a potential delivery date for the proffered report. Although Hughes failed to fully satisfy this request, the contract was signed on 22 May 1940.

The contract referred to a "Hughes Duramold bombardment airplane." At 37,000 pounds normal gross weight and a crew of five, the aircraft was to carry more than 4,000 pounds of bombs with a top speed exceeding 300 mph. This was one of several transmogrifications the D-2 would undergo. It changed again by March 1941 into a two-place long-range fighter, essentially duplicating the XP-58 with seven .50-cal. guns and Tornado engines with General Electric B-2 turbosuperchargers turning four-blade Hamilton Standard propellers. At a gross of 31,000 pounds and top speed of 450 mph, it was to reach 2,600 miles range. In May 1941, the design was mentioned with respect to bomber escort. In correspondence, the aircraft was alternately referred to as the DX-2, XD-2, D-2A, and DX-2A, and the military derivative concept may have had the Hughes designation D-3. By 30 June 1942, it was being called a fighter and the XP-73 designation was apparently reserved. On 2 July, it was identified as the XA-37 with 430-mph maximum speed fully loaded. This was clearly an airplane in search of a mission. The state of affairs persisted only because of the war and the fact Hughes was paying the bills.

While Hughes Aircraft continued the D-2 development with its own money, it occasionally sought a proper contract. Yet, Howard Hughes resisted sharing much information with the Army who was concerned about the suitability of plywood construction for a high-performance aircraft. Following an inspection of the Culver City facility and the state of the D-2 project, one Army officer assessed the entire endeavor a "hobby" of the management, the engineering personnel and plant not employed to full advantage.[5] The Duramold process did interest Materiel Division, especially in its potential to replace aluminum assemblies on other aircraft. Hughes was also contracted to build a P-51-like aircraft with V-1710 employing the Duramold process under MX-176. Although P-51 data was transferred to Hughes, nothing is known of the outcome.[6]

After a year being stonewalled, the exasperated Materiel Division leadership had about given up on the effort. Still, Hughes' contacts allowed him to reach Gen. Arnold who personally intervened, apparently acting upon a query from the President, to maintain Army support for a potential production contract and reimbursement of development costs. By mid-July 1942, the Army was prepared to give the firm a development contract with a reimbursement clause, but little more than a week later Howard Hughes reversed himself and insisted on proceeding without government oversight. Convinced the Army was determined to ignore Hughes Aircraft, its president set out to build an aircraft that could not be ignored.

Hughes had many subcontract projects and was performing valuable defense work. However, Howard Hughes insisted on inserting himself into details such that he was indispensable. Yet, his eccentricities were an annoyance, often being difficult to locate and fostering unorthodox business practices. The secrecy surrounding the D-2 was so severe that even Hap Arnold was turned away by armed guards when he showed up seeking a look at the airplane. The company's aircraft projects were eventually reduced to the lowest priority rating. Thus, Howard Hughes' paranoid impression that the Army Air Forces resented him became self-fulfilling.

Hughes Aircraft continued the D-2 development at its own expense. Assemblies were built in Culver City and the aircraft assembled at a remote and secretive location at Harpers Dry Lake, near Muroc. Development difficulties with the Tornado and an unknown delivery date caused Hughes to again seek government assistance for replacement powerplants. In March 1942, the firm received three 2,000-hp R-2800-49s. These turned three-blade propellers, although four blades were seen in some concept drawings. Primary flight controls were hydraulically boosted. The tricycle landing gear retracted aft, the nose wheel turned 90 degrees to lay flat in its bay. Hughes had designed its own turbosupercharger installation for the engines.

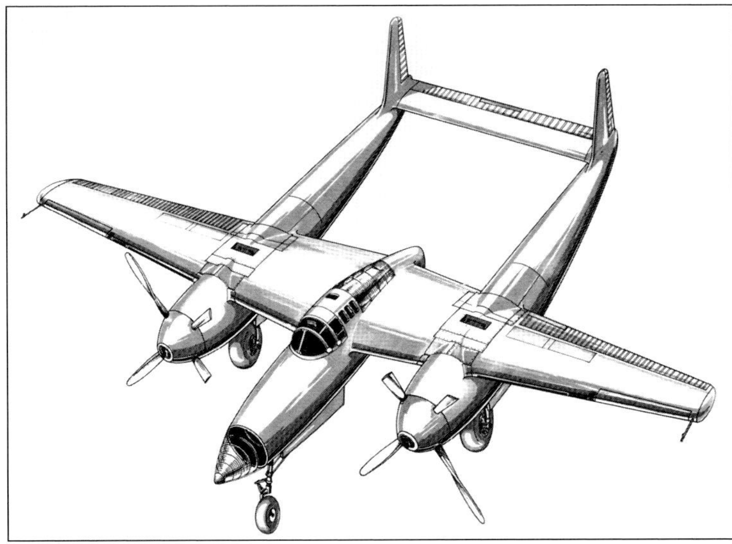

This Hughes artist concept shows the XA-37 as it might have appeared if completed with full military accoutrements. The aperture in the spinners provided air via "blower" to the engines. Howard Hughes surrounded his D-2 project with such a veil of secrecy that no photos of the aircraft are available. (U.S. National Archives via Kimble McCutcheon)

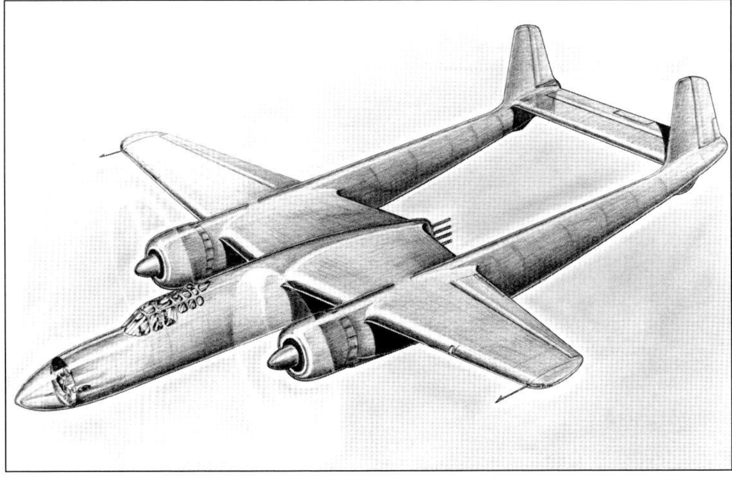

The D-2 was recast several times as the Army sought an application for the plywood airplane championed by the well-connected Howard Hughes. This concept is that of a fast, long-range light bomber with a crew of three and 4,000-pound load. The curious placement of the defensive rear-firing guns is noteworthy. (U.S. National Archives via Kimble McCutcheon)

This, however, was never installed, nor was an intended cabin pressurization system. A crew of two or three was apparently envisioned. The aircraft was then expected to gross 23,900 to 36,000 pounds, and top 446 mph at 25,000 feet, carrying 2,200 pounds of bombs to a 1,000-mile range.

Taxi testing on the lakebed in spring 1943 piloted by Howard Hughes, with brief hops, immediately revealed inadequate roll control authority and even roll reversal. This may have been due to deficient torsional rigidity with the plywood structure. Modifications were introduced to include increasing aileron chord by 40 percent. Excessive control friction also had to be overcome.

Howard Hughes flew the aircraft for its first flight on 20 June 1943. Roll control continued to be a problem, with high stick forces and a tendency to roll with throttle advance, in addition to pitch stability issues. Wingspan was increased to permit the ailerons to be moved farther outboard, although shortened on the inboard ends to get them out of the propwash. Outboard flaps were installed in the vacant space. An investigation showed that air over the laminar flow wing was separating and even reversing ahead of the ailerons. Further changes included extending the wing trailing edge about 10 inches. Testing of these changes through a total nine hours of flight time were still not encouraging.

A change in airfoil appeared warranted, if not a complete redesign of the wing with greater area and aspect ratio. Furthermore, taking the experimental aircraft without weapons bay, bombardier windows, turrets, or guns the next step to meeting specific military mission requirements would also entail considerable work. A redesign of the wing spar carry through structure in the center pod would be required to accommodate a bomb bay.

Hughes had continued lobbying for a production contract covering a military variant of the D-2. After spring 1943, the airplane would be without the R-2160 that had been cancelled. One incarnation of the variant tentatively identified as the D-5, was a three-place light bomber with 4,000-pound weapons capacity and a remotely controlled rear turret of four .50-cal. guns.* The second design was a two-place escort or "convoy" fighter with the same turret combined and six 20mm cannons in the nose. The third was to be a two-place long-range photoreconnaissance aircraft without weapons possessing legs of 3,600 miles and a peak speed of 488 mph at 30,000 feet. The third concept had caught Arnold's attention in June 1943 because of his concern the Army lacked sufficient high-speed reconnaissance aircraft.

** Oddly, the four aft machine guns on the D-2 appeared to sweep only laterally, within the very restricted field of fire between the tail booms, and without direct gunner vision.*

Following an inquiry, Hughes reported it could have the first production article delivered within a year and eventually reach production rate of two per day within 18 months on a contract for 200 aircraft. All it needed was an infusion of $7.25 million to expand its facility. When asked to provide the D-2 for evaluation, the company reported the aircraft was in rework. It proposed building a D-5A wing for the D-2 for demonstration purposes. Still concerned over Duramold, the true production capabilities of Hughes Aircraft, skeptical of provided performance data, and frustrated with Howard Hughes, the Army decided on 13 August 1943 against further involvement on the D-2/D-5.

By this time, Howard Hughes was disappointed and did not bemoan loss of the D-2 in an 11 November 1943 hangar fire started by a freak lightning strike – or so it was claimed. However, the matter would not die and the irrepressible Hughes would not go away. The design soon found renewed life as the all-metal XF-11 reconnaissance aircraft prototype.

This cutaway of the Beech XA-38 reveals the heavy nose gun installation with automatic loader and 20-round magazine. The twin turrets amidships were controlled remotely from the gunner station farther aft, equipped with top and bottom periscopes. The large fuselage and wing tanks supported impressive range. (National Museum of the United States Air Force)

Pinocchio (XA-38)

A late-war twin-engine attack prototype from Beech Aircraft Co. began as a bomber-destroyer concept, packing a 75mm cannon in the nose. However, the XP-71 appeared to have this mission tied up. The Model 28 was then offered as an attack aircraft in a proposal dated 23 September 1942. This found favor and two prototypes (43-14406/7) and a static test airframe that were ordered on 2 December as the XA-38 (MX-297).

The choice of Beech was unusual considering that the firm had produced only light twins for transport and training for the military, all derived from commercial products. The two-seat XA-38 was dubbed "Destroyer," but nicknamed "Grizzly" by Beech employees. It was to be rugged, maneuverable, and carry a heavy punch. Project engineer Bill Cassidy led the development team and construction began in 1943. The Wichita, Kansas, company employed the latest all-metal construction techniques, with flush riveting and butt joints.

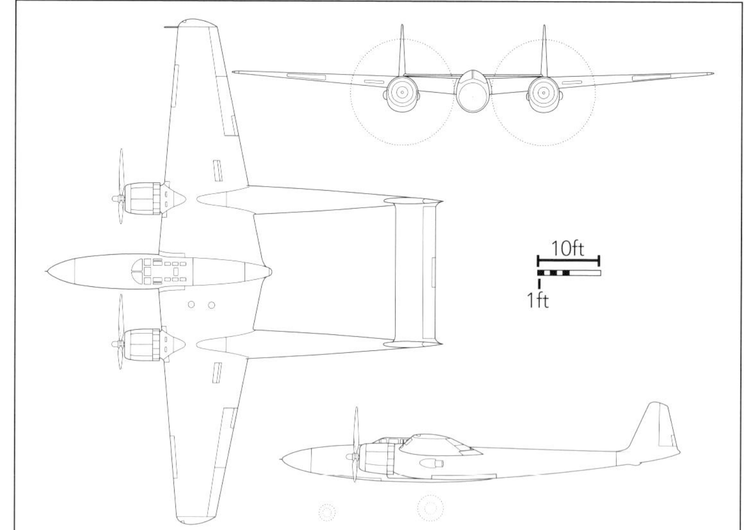

This drawing is a representation of the Hughes XA-37 as it likely appeared at the end of its brief flight-test career. The rear guns have not been installed, wing chord has been extended slightly, and the span increased with the dual-segment ailerons moved outboard. (Author)

Hughes D-2 (XA-37) characteristics in its final form (performance figures estimates):

span	60.0 ft	weight, gross	31,672 lbs
wing area	616 ft²	speed, max. (25,000 ft)	433 mph
service ceiling	36,000 ft	cruise	274 mph
best climb rate	2,620 fpm	range, (2,200 lbs payload)	1,000 mi

The second XA-38 shows off its 75mm cannon and .50-cal. guns, and the dorsal turret with twin .50s matched to an identical ventral turret. Note the periscope protruding from the rear gunner station. This very worthy aircraft was a victim of late engine delivery and the end of the war. (National Archives)

Beech XA-38 characteristics:			
span	67.3 ft	weight empty	22,480 lbs
length	51.8 ft	gross	31,250 lbs
height	15.5 ft	maximum	35,265 lbs
wing area	625.9 ft²	speed, max. (5,800 ft)	376.5 mph
fuel capacity (int. + ext.)	825+600 gal	cruise (16,000 ft)	344 mph
service ceiling	27,800 ft	range, combat	1,070 mi
best climb rate	2,170 fpm	ferry	1,960 mi

The Beech attack aircraft is a fine example of what the American aircraft industry could generate by the mid 1940s. It simply was not required by the Army at the time it was flown. Note the low-drag NACA cowlings with oil cooler intake just outboard in the wing leading edge. (San Diego Aerospace Museum)

The selected powerplant was the R-3350-43 at 2,200 hp, with two-speed supercharger, turning 14.2-foot diameter, three-blade Hamilton Standard props. Oil coolers were placed in the XA-38's wings, which had slotted flaps. The self-sealing fuel tanks included submerged fuel pumps. An auxiliary power unit was a supplemental source for electrical power, and exhaust air could be ducted into the wing leading edges for deicing. The Grizzly was armed with a 75mm cannon protruding from the nose. The gun was fed by a 20-round magazine, possessing an autofeed firing rate of 50 rounds per minute. This gun system alone was a 1,138-pounds installation. Two .50-cal. machine guns were installed under the cannon with 500 rpg. The entire nose was hinged to swing open for ease of maintenance, or removed entirely and another with different armament suite installed. There were also a pair of low-profile General Electric turrets amidships, one dorsal and one ventral, each with a pair of .50s and 500 rpg. These remote-controlled turrets were directed by the gunner at a rear station using a periscope. The lower turret could be locked forward and fired by the pilot for straffing. There were four wing stations for fuel or weapons, with total capacity up to 2,362 pounds.

The static test article was sent to Wright Field for trials, but the flight aircraft were delayed awaiting engines. Even the cannon ran long, being initially fired on 1 July 1944. Vern L. Carstens finally took up aircraft 43-14406 on 7 May 1944 from Beech Field. Early testing looked very promising, with few problems and a speed of 376.5 mph at 3,100 feet measured on one flight. With a landing speed of 97 mph at 45-degrees double-slotted flap setting, the aircraft could operate from a 2,500-foot strip, taking off and landing over a 50-foot obstacle. The Army had a look during 38 flights at Beech in October 1944, and came away impressed. The first XA-38 was passed along to Dayton on 7 July 1945, still with dummy turrets. Carstens flew 43-14407 for the first time on 22 September 1945, this one with full armament. The aircraft eventually went to Eglin Field, Florida, where it was flown for 38 hours on armament trials.

The XA-38 and its gun system were advanced yet operated very well. However, the Army was loath to divert any R-3350s from B-29 production and the turrets were also assigned to A-26s and P-61s, so the Beech program was probably a lost cause by the time the first aircraft reached Wright Field. By the time the full-up XA-38 was available, the war had passed it by.

Chapter 10

The second P-70 night fighter (39-737) carries the ventral pannier of four 20mm cannons as the sole armament. The modification sealed the bomb bay that was filled with a long-range fuel tank. It was this configuration that was first deployed to Guadalcanal, but proved largely ineffectual. (National Museum of the United States Air Force)

NIGHT FIGHTING

Emerging from the Lab

This photo reveals the components of the 5.4-foot-long AN/APS-4 radar pod carried by thousands of U.S. Navy aircraft during World War II. The 14-inch parabolic antenna and vacuum tube technology are evident. Western Electric manufactured 3,100 of these units during the conflict. (Jay Miller Collection)

Americans observed the emergence of ground-based and airborne radar in Europe as night fighting evolved in the early years of World War II. The United States had its own radar development efforts and contributed to the maturation of the technology. However, the military programs truly took off in summer 1940 when Britain and the United States established a technical exchange of information. The Americans combined all such research activities while also setting about to manufacture the RAF's air intercept (AI) Mk IV aircraft radar as the AI-4, later SCR-540, for British and American use. Concurrently, the Radiation Laboratory was established at the Massachusetts Institute of Technology, Boston, closely collaborating with British scientists, to develop more advanced sets for various missions.

The SCR-540 was a 1.5-meter wavelength unit requiring large external antennae on the aircraft. The newest innovation was a set based on microwaves (centimeter wavelength) with a single concave antenna under a radome. It would be more sensitive for target discrimination among "clutter" and possess shorter minimum range. The British developed the first such radar with the Americans right on their heels. The United States flew its first microwave AI unit in a Douglas B-18A bomber. This was then evolved for air-to-surface vessel (ASV) units and the SCR-582. An optimized American AI set became the AI-10 or SCR-520, with pre-production units manufactured in early 1941 for testing. Airborne trials included flights in the United States aboard a Douglas A-20 Havoc medium bomber and in the UK on a modified Boeing 247 airliner. The British provided the Americans with a Beaufighter IF (RAF serial X7610) on 10 October 1941 and another (X7718) on 2 January 1942, to serve as AI radar testbeds.[1]

Series production SCR-520 units incorporated some British circuits to improve jamming resistance. Only 108 SCR-520A sets were produced before transitioning to a further evolved design, the SCR-720. This radar could detect airborne targets within 8 to 10 miles and landmasses on the ocean to 100 miles. Deliveries began in November 1942, and soon thousands were flowing to Britain as the AI Mk X where it became the standard AI set. The SCR-720 has been described as the finest AI radar deployed during the war.[2]

The U.S. Navy was also keenly interested in airborne radar, including surface search as well as air intercept sets. For carrier-based aircraft, radar installations had to be accommodated on single-engine aircraft, possibly with only the pilot as operator. Night operations aboard carriers, alone, were rare and hazardous. The Naval Research Laboratory worked with the Radiation Laboratory on microwave radar for naval fighters. Project *Affirm* was begun in April

1942 at NAS Quonset Point, Rhode Island, to oversee equipment development and training, and establish tactics for night fighters. From the first, the intent was for the AI fighter to be able to make a blind firing pass on a target, requiring demanding minimum range performance.

By early 1941, the Naval Research Laboratory developed the first ASV search radar suitable for carrier aircraft. The air-to-surface Type B (ASB) was first introduced to the fleet in May 1942. The unit was characterized by its rotatable Yagi "comb" antennae under each wing.* The 60-cm system could detect a capitol ship at 46.0 miles and a submarine at 6.6 miles, and more than 20,000 units were produced. Efforts to reduce the size of ASV radar to a podded system yielded the ASD (AN/APS-3) 3-cm radar with 18-inch parabolic antenna. A large vessel could be detected at 57.5 miles (34.5 miles more typically) and a surfaced submarine at 11.5 miles. The ASD was followed by the ASH, redesignated the AN/APS-4, that was carried as an under-wing pod on fighter-size aircraft. This was also a 3-cm unit capable of detecting a large vessel at 57.5 miles and a submarine at 17.3, and thousands of these were deployed. The APS-4's small wavelength also supported (with difficulty) air-to-air search, detecting a fighter at 3.5 miles and bomber at 5.8.

A project was kicked off in January 1941 to create a 3-cm AI radar. This emerged on 2 November 1941 as the SCR-537 (AI-3, AIA or AI type A). The radar was initially flight tested in April 1942 with the unit in the nose of a Navy JRB (militarized Twin Beech). This combination was turned to training at Quonset Point in June. Although radar range was just 2 miles to 500 feet, resolution was good enough to make a blind firing pass. The radar could also be employed for ground mapping in support of night attack missions. A photograph of the screen showing coastline contours was taken and then prints used later as a reference for the radar-equipped attackers.

The AIA was taken further to create the much lighter AN/APS-6 centimetric radar, kicking off the project in January 1943. Another podded system, the pressurized waveguide of the AIA was eliminated. It could detect a bomber at 4.5 miles and a fighter at 4.0, and to a minimum range of less than half a mile and as little as 360 feet. Coastline contours could be discerned at 40 miles. The APS-6 was first flight tested in October 1943 aboard a modified Beech SNB-1 Kansan.[3] Some 2,160 were delivered between April 1944 and the end of the war to become the standard wartime naval AI radar.

By the end of the conflict, many more advanced American AI radar systems were in development or initial production, but no more reached combat. One that came close was the centimetric AN/APS-19, perfected near the end of the war to replace the APS-6. The unit was about half the weight and possessed greater reliability, with a 6.9- to 11.5-mile detection range. This emphasized the Navy's success in developing and fielding naval fighter radar to a measure far beyond any other navy.

The instrument panel of the Grumman F6F-3E shows the APS-4 radarscope dominating the center. Making a fighter suitable for night missions required changes in the cockpit and windscreen for suitable lighting (red) without distracting reflections. Also usually mandatory were exhaust flame dampers to prevent degrading pilot night-adapted vision. (Jay Miller Collection)

The Identification Friend or Foe (IFF) radar beacons and VHF radios, so important to effective night operations, were also manufactured by the Americans and fielded in 1943 – also owing much to technical exchange with Britain. The AN/APS-13 tail warning radar was introduced in mid-1944, equally valuable during daylight, with a 4,000-foot range aft. Ground Control Intercept (GCI) radar, for detecting enemy "bogies" and vectoring fighters were also developed and produced, these among the best in the world. Radar and ancillary gear was a field wherein the United States clearly lead its adversaries.[4]

Army Hustle

Scrambling

In September 1941, before the United States had become a belligerent, it agreed with Britain to manufacture 1,687 night fighters while the UK built 4,380. This would leave the RAF as the dominant wartime night fighter operator, particularly in North Africa and Europe.

* *Interestingly, the Yagi antenna was named after a Professor Yagi in Japan who did pioneering pre-war work on directional antennae.*

Immediately after Pearl Harbor, the Japanese flew reconnaissance missions over the Hawaiian Islands to assess damage and locate American carriers. This and concern over potential attacks on the western seaboard and Panama Canal compelled the Air Corps to form a night fighter squadron equipped with P-26, P-36, and P-40B day fighters. Equipped only with the "Mk I eyeball" and with performance of these aircraft only marginally suitable for the role, they had little hope of being effective. This was followed by a unit trained for night intercept and coordination with searchlights and, where available, GCI radar and controllers. This amounted to little more than staggering about in the dark, with more risk to the American fighters than enemy airmen.

Once American forces began offensive operations in the Asia and Pacific theaters, Japanese night raiders became a concern. The Army had initiated the P-61 Black Widow program in 1940 to develop a specialized, radar-equipped interceptor, but this would clearly not bear fruit for at least two years. An interim night fighter was required. Operations across the Atlantic also demanded night interception capabilities.

Ersatz Solution (P-70)

As the Air Corps contemplated developing a stopgap, an interim, rapidly fielded night fighter during 1940, it followed the British example in employing large, twin-engine aircraft for this role. Radar-equipped night fighters in Europe were then converted medium bombers because of the bulky electronics gear weighing hundreds of pounds plus an added radar operator. These were adequate because maneuvering combat was not expected and most early targets were bombers. These aircraft also had the endurance for what could be a prolonged search and closure process. Heavy firepower was advised for assurance of destroying targets on what might be the one and only pass. A twin-engine airplane was considered most suitable for the safety benefits in the event of an engine failure.

The A-20 with experimental SCR-520 radar was employed on patrols in California immediately following the Japanese attack in Hawaii.[5] The British had already accomplished such conversion of exported A-20s, or DB-7s. The bombardier's "glass" nose was replaced with a "solid" nose carrying a battery of .303 machine guns and AI radar gear, and the engine exhausts were fitted with flame dampers. The Americans took a similar course, naming the incarnation the P-70 Nighthawk, to serve as the interim night fighter and trainer. Adaptation of turbosuperchargers to the A-20 with 1,700-hp R-2600-7s had run into severe cooling difficulties. Conversion of these bombers already coming off the Santa Monica, California, production line to the night attack role seemed a good purpose. All P-70s resulted from such rework, the first delivered almost a year from inception of the program.

The engines were changed to -11s of 1,600 hp, and fitted with exhaust flame dampers. Some armor was removed to lighten the aircraft and because a night fighter was not expected to be engaged from behind. The electrical system was upgraded from 12 to 24 volts. The XP-70 carried the SCR-540 radar in the nose, the radar operator (RO) working from the former rear gunner's compartment. The transmit antenna protruded from the nose, azimuth receivers on the fuselage sides beneath the cockpit, and elevation receivers on the top and bottom of the outer wing panel. Radar range at the P-70's operating altitude was two to three miles, but it was readily disrupted by ground clutter and disturbed by low pressure at altitude. The A-20's glass nose was painted over for the XP-70 but solid for "production" examples. Four 20mm cannons with 60 rpg were installed in a pannier under the sealed bomb bay, and the rear ventral gun deleted. Two .50-cal. machine guns were installed in the lower nose to assist in laying the cannon fire. Armed mostly with tracers, the pilot was to see the rounds splashing off the target before engaging with the 20mm and their fewer shells. A 300-gallon long-range fuel tank was installed in the bomb bay.

Only the prototype XP-70 had been flown by the time the United States entered the war, although go-ahead for more examples had been given on 15 October 1941. Deliveries of the 59 P-70s began

This P-70A-2 is seen at Magenta AB in New Caledonia on 13 November 1943. The six-gun nose installation and radar antennae are shown to advantage, including antennae on the wing. The low ceiling of these aircraft meant they could seldom reach the Japanese night intruders. (National Museum of the United States Air Force)

The singular P-70B-1 was created from an A-20G-10 (42-54053) by filling the nose with an SCR-720 centrimetric radar, displacing the six .50-cal. guns into three-pack cheek fairings. This gun installation was not adopted as the fairings generated unacceptable tail buffeting. The aircraft was eventually painted standard flat black. (National Museum of the United States Air Force)

Douglas P-70 characteristics:			
span	61.3 ft	weight empty	16,031 lbs
length	47.6 ft	gross	21,264 lbs
height	17.6 ft	maximum	24,500 lbs
wing area	464 ft²	speed, max. (14,000 ft)	329 mph
fuel capacity (int. + ext.)	600+0 gal	cruise	270 mph
service ceiling	28,250 ft	range, combat	1,060 mi
average climb rate	1,500 fpm	ferry	1,460 mi

in April 1942. Thirty-nine P-70A-1s were converted from A-20Cs during 1943. These had either six or eight .50-cal. guns with 350 rpg in the nose, the radar gear moved to the bomb bay and gunner's compartment, and R-2600-23 engines. They could carry 2,000 pounds of bombs in the bomb bay. These were followed by 65 A-20Gs that became P-70A-2s with a six-gun nose, some also possessing rear flexible-mounted .50s. Most of these were created at modification centers and a few others by field units. Other gun installations were also seen, with a pair of .30s in the rear gunner's station and a .50-cal. firing out the lower hatch for this station.

After the invasion of Guadalcanal in August 1942, night fighters were desperately needed to deal with Japanese night raiders. However, the low availability of the radar sets meant only 59 P-70s had been created between April and September 1942 and crews were only just graduating from training. The R-2600-11s gave the aircraft respectable speed for the period, but the lack of supercharging meant they could not get much above 20,000 feet, or reach any altitude with alacrity. Although there was hesitation to deploy them, the need was great.

A squadron of P-70s finally reached Henderson Field at the end of February 1943. Others were stationed in Hawaii and the Panama Canal Zone. Standing patrols or scrambles were flown. Although the deployed P-70s soon scored America's first night fighter victory, they were largely ineffectual as the enemy normally operated above the P-70's ceiling. Efforts to improve performance included stripping out armor and the aft guns, plus fitting P-38 fuel boost pumps and substituting B-17 bomber propellers. Little was gained from these field improvisations.

The P-70s remained in the theater, moving with the front and operating with P-38s in some areas. Their missions evolved to weather reconnaissance and night intrusion, executing strikes where the radar helped guide the aircraft across the island-dotted sea. They also served as PT boat escort, protecting them against attack by Japanese float planes.[6] This mission, at low altitudes, was more befitting the capabilities of the P-70. Only one more confirmed kill was recorded for the P-70. The advent of the P-61 night fighter in summer 1944 permitted the P-70s to be withdrawn and devoted exclusively to training. Only at this point did the night fighters begin to seriously blunt the Japanese night intrusions.

The Army's night fighter force expanded considerably during the war from its humble beginnings. Enabling this was 105 P-70B-2 trainers (later TP-70B) with SCR-720 or -729 centimetric radar fitted to A-20Gs and Js. The plastic noses for some of these were unsuccessful, as they tended to cave in at high speed and required the aircraft to be limited to 300 mph. These aircraft sometimes had the belly tray or ventral turret, or six-gun nose, but were usually unarmed. The P-70's primary claim to fame was facilitating the training of 485 night fighter crews for 19 squadrons.

Making Do (B-25, P-38)

A North American B-25 medium bomber was modified with a Navy AN/APS-4 radar pod, presumably under a wing, and three radar scopes for RO training.[7] The night fighter units had been using the Mitchell without radar as a night intruder, benefiting from their pilots' excellent instrument training.

From the moment it reached the Pacific Theater, the P-38 was employed as a night interceptor, working with GCI and searchlights. They were important adjuncts to the few P-70s and that aircraft's poor altitude performance. The P-38's first nocturnal kill was on 16 June 1943. The Army did not follow the Navy example of giving existing single-seat fighters radar for some night-fighting capabilities. However, the twin engines and high performance of the Lockheed P-38 Lightning suggested it might be suitable for such a conversion and further improve night fighting capabilities while awaiting P-61s. Field units in the Pacific attempted several such conversions.

Two P-38Fs were modified in early 1943 by the Fifth Air Force with the P-70's SCR-540 AI radar and VHF radio within a drop tank. The antennae were fixed on the wings and to either side of the nose. They operated from Henderson Field, Guadalcanal, to answer the

Several field modifications included placing a seat behind the P-38 pilot for a radar operator and the AN/APS-4 radar beneath the plane. One of these lash-ups is seen at Hammer Field on 2 September 1944 in the company of a P-61B, an RAF Mosquito NF Mk 30, and a YP-59A. (National Archives)

A Beaufighter Mk VI of the 417th Night Fighter Squadron shares a field with a P-61. The Americans operated a force of these British aircraft from early 1942 through the end of hostilities. The aircraft did well enough in night fighting, but was a bear to handle on the ground. (Warren Thompson Collection)

This de Havilland Mosquito NF Mk 30 was operated by the Army Air Forces in the last seven months of the war in Europe. It was the RAF's top night fighter and compensated for the Americans' paucity in such equipment. However, the aircraft were principally employed in night interdiction strikes. (National Museum of the United States Air Force via Norman Malayney)

Japanese night raiders and compensate for the P-70's inadequacies while awaiting the long-promised P-61s. Two P-38J-20s (44-23544 and -23549) were also modified as single-seat night fighters in April 1944, although by Western Electric at a depot in Townsville, Australia, and fitted with an AN/APS-4 pod under the starboard wing. One of these Js shared a kill with a P-61 over Leyte on 9 January 1945.

Two-seat conversions of the P-38 were also created by squeezing the RO into the space behind the pilot vacated by moving the radios and other equipment, and a seat placed atop the wing center section. Even a small man found the accommodations cramped. During October 1943, two P-38Gs were subject of the "piggyback" modification in New Guinea, each with an SCR-540 unit within a drop tank. While not entirely practical or effective, these efforts by deployed squadrons revealed the potential and need for a night fighter akin to the Lightning.

Strangers in a Strange Land (Beaufighter, Mosquito)

Initial U.S. combat operations during 1942 found it still without a practical night fighter. The P-70 was deemed unsuitable for European combat and the P-61 was still in gestation. Hence, when U.S. forces prepared for operations in North Africa, they were compelled to adopt British equipment. This came in the form of more than 100 Bristol Beaufighters from the RAF. Top speed was 333 mph at 15,600 feet. It carried four 20mm cannons and six .303-inch machine guns. The airmen were first introduced to the aircraft during training in Britain during early 1942. This was not the Americans' first choice of night fighter, but it was the RAF's first choice of airplane to give away. On the ground, the "beast" was a handful with its vicious swing and lack of steering tailwheel. It proved an education for many inexperienced GI pilots.

Four Army Air Forces night-fighter squadrons began operating Beaufighters in early 1943. These were Beaufighter Mk VIs with Mk VII or VIII radar in the thimble nose, but some still with Mk I units in the original nose. The early sets were easily confused by "window" – metal foil strips ("chaff" or "gizmos" to the Americans) deployed by the enemy. The Americans deployed to North Africa in the summer and eventually made their way to Italy. Although some of the squadrons transitioned to Mosquitos and P-61s, the "Beau" remained in the U.S. order of battle through the end of the war with squadrons claiming 32 kills.

By spring 1944, with the much-anticipated P-61 becoming available, some in the Army Air Forces still favored the RAF night fighters. A fly-off between a Black Widow and Mosquito on 5 July 1944 found the American plane the better performer.[8] Still, a single Army Air Forces unit, the 416th Night Fighter Squadron, received the Mosquito NF Mk 30s between early December 1944 and June 1945 in Italy to replace Beaufighters and while awaiting "Widows." They operated just a dozen aircraft at any one time, although individual airframes came and went as attrition claimed some. The night fighter Mk 30 was equipped with an AI Mk X radar. It possessed a top speed of 407 mph, initial climb rate of 2,850 fpm, and carried four 20mm cannons. The exceptionally high 39,000-foot ceiling of this aircraft was an advantage for the mission. However, by this point in the war, enemy night activity had fallen off dramatically and the aircraft were used principally for dusk or moonlight interdiction of ground traffic.

Loose End (XA-26A)

From the earliest stages of the Douglas A-26 Intruder gestation, in spring 1941, the Army funded development of a night fighter variant in concert with the light bomber. This seemed natural as Douglas had created the P-70s from its A-20 bomber, and the lessons from that experience could be readily applied. What was unnatural was that it never received its own Pursuit "P" designation. The project would provide insurance against a Northrop failure to deliver on the P-61 contract. Assembly began at El Segundo during summer 1941.

The XA-26A night fighter (41-19505) was powered by the same R-2800-27 engines, at 2,000 hp, as its bomber siblings and included propeller spinners. One pilot and an RO manned the aircraft. The latter was forward of the cockpit, behind the SCR-540 radar mounted in a nose lengthened 1.5 feet. The pilot had a small radarscope as well. Initial design had the RO provided with a bubble observation port overhead, but this did not survive to the final configuration. However, Plexiglas blisters above and below the former gunner's compartment, aft of the turret, were apparently intended for an observer. The ventral turret was deleted, but four .50 machine guns were placed in the upper turret vice the normal two guns. Lacking a gunner, the turret was fixed to fire forward only. This was supplemented by a tray of four 20mm cannons mounted on the belly with ammo feeding from the bomb bay. The tray could be removed to permit loading of 2,000 pounds of bombs for night intruder missions. The XA-26A was 5 mph slower than the bomber variant.

The Douglas XA-26A night-fighter variant of the Invader light bomber, shown in test on 2 July 1943, was an unproduced alternative to the P-61. The elongated nose was to contain an SCR-540 radar, but lack of external antennae suggests the gear was not installed at this time. (Jay Miller Collection)

Douglas XA-26A characteristics:			
span	70.0 ft	weight empty	20,794 lbs
length	51.4 ft	gross	25,300 lbs
height	18.5 ft	maximum	28,893 lbs
wing area	540 ft²	speed, max. (17,000 ft)	365 mph
fuel capacity (int. + ext.)	440-800+0 gal	cruise	264 mph
service ceiling	25,900 ft	range, combat	700 mi
average initial climb rate	1,961 fpm	ferry	1,420 mi

The XA-26A suffered from the same delays that slowed the Intruder program as a whole.Testing began with first flight on 27 January 1943 and continued until the USAAF accepted the aircraft in September. The program was successful. However, progress on the P-61 was satisfactory and Douglas needed to focus on pumping out bombers. It went no further.

Better Late Than Never (P-61)

The Air Corps provided several airframe manufacturers a look at an AI Mk IV radar set to start them thinking of suitable platforms. Northrop was already working on a night fighter concept at the instigation of the RAF, and the Army Air Corps had its eye on this company to take the project forward. In October 1940, the Army formally requested Northrop develop a night fighter equipped with the radar. Preferred design features were based on RAF experience and as considered for the P-70.

Northrop's preliminary design was presented in December, and the Army ordered two XP-61 prototypes in January 1941 for $1.4

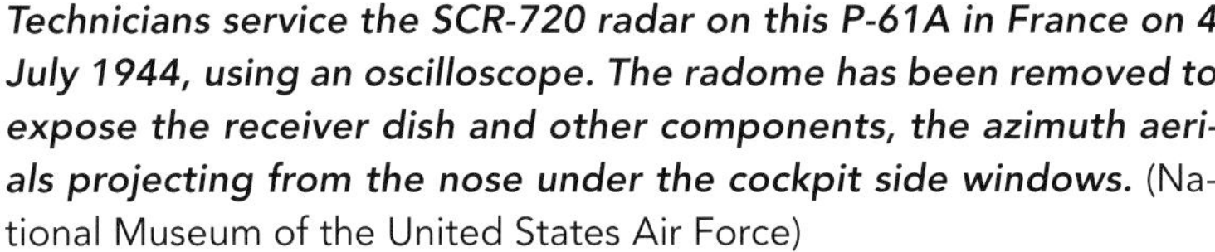

Technicians service the SCR-720 radar on this P-61A in France on 4 July 1944, using an oscilloscope. The radome has been removed to expose the receiver dish and other components, the azimuth aerials projecting from the nose under the cockpit side windows. (National Museum of the United States Air Force)

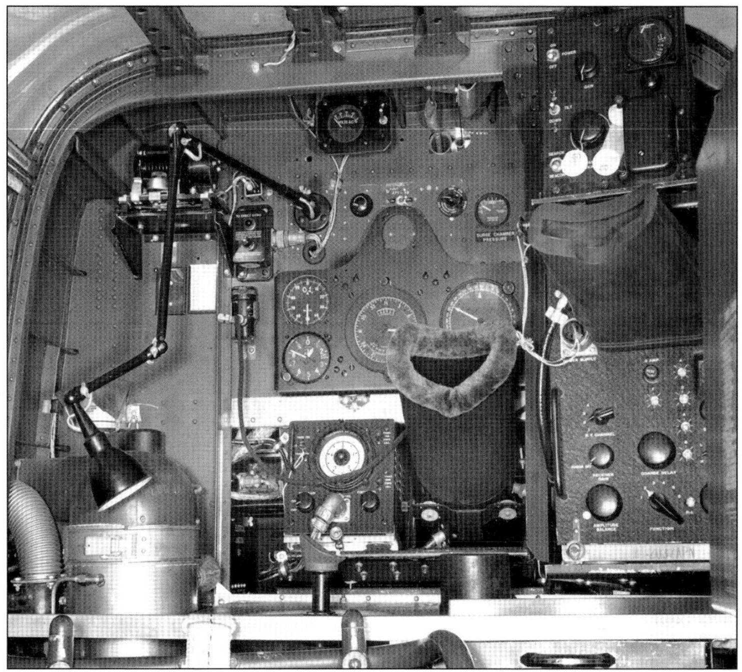

The radar operator (RO) station in the P-61A, relocated to the previous gunners station, is illustrated here. Facing aft, the two scopes are separate azimuth and elevation indicators typical of the SCR-720. (Jay Miller Collection)

million. The ink was hardly dry on that contract when the Army ordered 13 YP-61 service test examples and a static test article in March. Then, even before first flight of the Black Widow, a production order was placed in September for 150 P-61As, this increased by another 410 in February 1942, the first scheduled for delivery in April 1943. The objective maximum speed was 375 mph with 450 mph desired.

The P-61 was the first aircraft anywhere, and the only one of the war, designed from the beginning for the night fighter role. It was also the largest production fighter of the war and Northrop's first large-scale design and production challenge.

The Black Widow design was contrary to prevailing convention for fighter aircraft. The size of airborne radar demanded an enormous twin-engine aircraft with three crewmembers. A gunner sat behind the pilot and the nav/radar operator in a glazed enclosure at the aft end of the central pod where he would be undisturbed by the flash of gunfire. Each R-2800-10 engine generated 2,000 hp with a single-stage, gear-driven supercharger. Top and bottom wing spoilers, augmented by tiny ailerons, gave very fast roll and turn rate to allow the pilot to avoid losing sight of a maneuvering target. The P-61 could turn inside most fighters and decelerate surprisingly quickly to avoid overshooting the target. It frequently took a demo ride with a company pilot to convince line officers of the remarkable speed and maneuverability of the aircraft. It also possessed a powerful punch with four forward-firing 20mm cannons in the belly with 200 rpg as well as a dorsal remote-controlled turret with four .50s, 560 rpg, for defensive fire or to shoot at the passing target if the P-61 overshot. This was the most intense and hard-hitting volume of fire of any American production fighter of the war. The General Electric top turret could also be fired by the RO, or fixed to fire forward when triggered by the pilot. The nearly full-span slotted flaps reduced landing speeds to 93 mph, allowing the big plane to operate from forward fields.

The XP-61 had the SCR-520 radar, but the YP-61s and initial production aircraft had the SCR-720. The unit's oscillating antenna was within a dielectric nose cone made initially of Plexiglas – first transparent then frosted, later painted before being replaced with fiberglass. Azimuth readings were via the dipole antennas on either side of the cockpit.

Development of the aircraft proved frustratingly long and arduous. The XP-61 first flew from Hawthorne on 26 May 1942, and the

The Northrop P-61 Black Widow was the first aircraft developed from inception as a night fighter. Its gestation was long, and it was summer 1944 before it was deployed and scored its first kill. This P-61A shows the size of the three-place aircraft as it normally appeared, without the dorsal turret. (Gerald Balzer Collection)

The dorsal turret with its four .50-cal. machine guns was reintroduced in the P-61B-15. Along with added underwing store stations this aircraft supported long-range operations and air-to-surface attack. The B airplanes had a lengthened nose for the more advanced SCR-720C radar. (San Diego Aerospace Museum)

YP-61s were delivered between August and September 1943. Weight had grown with the addition of armored windscreens and the replacement of welded magnesium components with conventionally assembled aluminum alloy. The horizontal tail was redesigned to improve pitch control. The aircraft originally flew without the final flaps and aileron design as these continued to be perfected in the wind tunnel. Tail buffeting from the turret, when rotated or the guns elevated, was investigated through a series of turret shape changes and flight testing. Firing any of the weapons initially caused structural damage until corrected. The Plexiglas tail cone tended to collapse at high speed until reinforced. Nose-gear collapses would be a lingering albeit minor problem throughout the war.

The first P-61As began leaving the factory in October 1942. The RAF was to get 50 of the first production order, but the long wait made the aircraft nonessential and the transfer never occurred. Since the turret was still the source of worrying tail buffeting, and the B-29 had priority for the unit, only the first 37 P-61As were completed with this feature, but with the guns fixed in the forward firing orientation. The remaining As had the turret removed and the gunner station omitted, cutting 1,600 pounds and improving performance. In many of these, the RO station was moved forward to the former gunners position. On other aircraft, the vacant space was filled with a field-improvised long-range fuel tank.

After 45 P-61A-1 aircraft, the 35 block 5s introduced the R-2800-65 powerplant with 2,250 hp war emergency and a two-speed/two-stage supercharger. The 20 block 11s possessed hardpoints for two 1,600-pound bombs, or 165- or 310-gallon drop tanks, this indicating a desire to use the P-61 for night interdiction and daylight attack operations.

The 163 B-1s and -10s added 8 inches to the length of the nose with a one-piece radome to accommodate the more capable SCR-720C. The P-61B-10s, initially delivered in July 1944, included four hardpoints put to use with tanks for long missions or ordnance for ground attack, and also had four 5-inch rocket stub mounts per wing outboard of the propeller arc. Numerous system improvements were also introduced with the Bs. A radar repeater scope in the cockpit improved pilot situational awareness, especially when the radar was used for navigation. Since the reflector gunsight in the A tended to be too bright and obscure the target (leading some crews to paint out the top portion), 5.8-power night binoculars connected to the gunsight were added to the B. These were on an articulated arm such that they could be folded aside, yet were gimbal-mounted and showed an illuminated horizon line with "tick marks" for ranging. The dorsal turret reappeared on the 286 P-61B-15 and -20s with improved fire control for the latter.

The Army Air Forces acquired 674 P-61s before the end of the war and 32 more after. These received the full complement of advanced

Northrop P-61B-20 characteristics:			
span	66.0 ft	weight empty	20,000 lbs
length	49.6 ft	gross	29,700 lbs
height	14.7 ft	maximum	38,000 lbs
wing area	664 ft²	speed, max. (20,000 ft)	366 mph
fuel capacity (int. + ext.)	640+1,240 gal	cruise	318 mph
service ceiling	33,100 ft	range, combat	410 mi
best climb rate	2,090 fpm	max. external fuel	1,900 mi
		ferry	3,000 mi

communication and navigation radios and indicators, autopilot, and blind-flying instruments, including radar (or radio) altimeter, tail-warning radar, IFF, and IFF/beacon locator that could also serve as a navigation aid. The Widow handled very well, with plenty of excess power, and had no significant vices. It was an outstanding aircraft, showing well the state of American aerospace technology in the last phase of World War II.

The P-61As entered combat in the Pacific, CBI, and European theaters in late spring 1944. Although fielded late in the war, they still contributed valuable night fighting capabilities as they discouraged night attacks on bomber bases. A P-61B crew scored the last aerial kill of the war. By this point, the Allies had virtual air superiority, and few enemy aircraft were venturing deep into Allied areas on night raids. Total confirmed kills for the P-61 was 128 of the total 158 Army Air Forces confirmed night victories. Given the 900 night fighters produced, the thousands of sorties flown, and dozens of losses, this indicated the high workload/low yield nature of the mission. The Black Widow also accomplished some respectable daylight engagements, dusk and moonlight interdiction, and could fly in weather that kept other fighters on the ground. Its armament was so heavy that it was invaluable in ground attack, with more than half its missions so devoted. Bombs, however, were seldom carried.

Spider Bites (P-61C, XP-61D, XP-61F, P-61G, P-61H)

Seven P-61B-25 aircraft, the last variant of this model, were created with conversions of airplanes from other blocks to incorporate the APG-1 gun-laying radar. This permitted automatic aiming of the GE turret via signal from the radar. Northrop performed the modifications that included a high-capacity generator. Although the aircraft were tested, they were too late to be fielded.

The P-61A and B had fallen short of the specified peak speed at the design altitude, and field experience made clear the original 375-mph number had not been an unrealistic operational requirement. The Japanese flew their bombers at maximum altitude and just above where the P-70s and P-61As could consistently reach them, although the Bs helped. Responding to these deficiencies, plus adding greater endurance, the P-61C came into being. Plans were

One of two P-61As converted by Goodyear with turbosupercharged R-2800-57 engines shows off the revised cowling and bottom intake. The work was in support of the P-61C program, but substituting R-2800-57 engines for the delayed -77s prompted a designation change to XP-16D. (Ray Wagner Collection)

Turbosuperchargers were added to the Black Widow with R-2800-73 engines. The P-61C was a better performer, although with even heavier weight that some pilots felt compromised maneuverability. None of the aircraft left the States before the end of hostilities. (American Aviation Historical Society)

laid in November 1943 to use the R-2800-77s with General Electric CH-5 turbosuperchargers, especially since added fuel in later blocks would make up for the higher burn rate.

Because of excessive workload at Northrop, two new P-61As (block 5 42-5559 and block 10 42-5587) were modified at Goodyear's Akron, Ohio, facility. The R-2800-77s were not immediately available, so 2,100-hp R-2800-57s were installed and the aircraft designated XP-61Ds. The turbosuperchargers, fed by boom bottom intakes, boosted performance to 2,800 hp. Four hardpoints, common in late-model aircraft, were also added. After a long delay for redesign work addressing maintainability desires and because of manpower issues at Goodyear, initial flights commenced in late November 1944. The aircraft were soon passed back to Hawthorne for detailed testing. The turbo exit was reworked as hot exhaust gases heated the boom structure excessively. The two aircraft remained in flight test past the end of the war.

The turbo installation was found sound and beneficial. Consequently, P-61C production commenced and deliveries followed during July 1945. The 2,100-hp R-2800-73 was employed, delivering 2,800 hp war emergency and turning a new Smith electric, paddle-blade, fully feathering propeller. Despite coming with an additional 2,000 pounds empty weight, the C model raised the service ceiling to 41,000 feet and top speed to 430 mph at 30,000 feet. However, some pilots judged the added weight a detriment to maneuverability. None of the Cs had an opportunity to contribute during the war. The end of hostilities truncated an order for 517 P-61Cs to just 41 aircraft (42-8321/61), most finished after the war.

"Picket fence" speed brakes in the wing upper and lower surfaces of the P-61C were to help prevent overshooting a target, especially with the extra power in the C. These were planned very early on with intent to introduce them with the 201st production Black Widow. To this end, the third P-61A (42-5487) was bailed back to Northrop for initial testing of the feature. However, if actually tested on that aircraft, the speed brakes did not make it into the line until advent of the Cs. Then, during C-model flight testing on 29 August 1945, when the speed brakes were deployed at maximum permissible airspeed and load factor, the outer wing panels and empennage separated from the aircraft. Test pilot Max R. Stanley survived, but the speed brakes were locked out from that time forward.

Plans were in place by mid 1945 to create 18 two-place XP-61F day fighters through modification of P-61Cs. Aircraft 43-8338 was held in Hawthorne for conversion to this standard. However, the end of the war appears to have halted work with little accomplished, and the program was dropped on 24 October 1945. Characteristics of the F are unclear.

The range and radar of the Black Widow made it suitable for a new wrinkle in the weather reconnaissance mission that verified conditions for impending operations. Sixteen P-61B-20s (43-8275, -8278/82, -8290/4, -8298, -8300/1, -8303/6) were modified by Douglas Aircraft at its Tulsa mod center to the P-61G standard for this role with all armament and combat radios removed for increased speed of about nine mph. The AI radar was to be replaced with General Electric APS-10 radar optimized for detecting weather cells, in addition to air sampling gear and specialized radios. Work began in summer 1945 and this program was sustained for a time postwar before also falling to the budget axe.

A P-61H appears to have been a proposal to remove the dorsal turret, permanently install a fuel tank in the vacant space, and also add a "dome tank" atop the fuselage. A wind tunnel test of the external change was performed, but little else seems to have come of the concept.

Late Arrival (P-38M)

The early success with the field-modified P-38s generated a test program back home. Wright Field, in concert with Lockheed, converted a P-38J-5 (42-67104) in summer 1943 with the AN/APS-4 behind the nose gear on a converted bomb rack. The radar pod was found susceptible to damage from material kicked up by the nose wheel and ejected shell casings, and so moved under the starboard wing. This conversion was tested at the USAAF Tactical Center in Orlando, Florida, during early 1944. The engine nacelle was found to interfere with a portion of the scan. The evaluators recommended a radar operator be used.

Concurrently, the night fighter training team at Hammer Field in Fresno, California, was flying converted P-38Js with the APS-4 during 1944. At least one P-38 was flown as a single-seater and the rest as piggybacks. The radar unit "bomb" was placed in three positions. Mounting under the fuselage and under the outboard wing meant

After field modifications demonstrated the need and potential for an Army Air Forces night fighter on the true scale of a "fighter," the P-38M was developed with an AN/APS-4 radar pod under the nose and radar operator in the rear. Although practical, and 75 were built, the P-38M did not reach theaters before hostilities ended. (National Archives)

some obstructions. Only the under-nose location was judged suitable. Both single-seat and a P-38J piggyback with RO were evaluated. A single-seat P-38J-20 (44-23336) was sent on to the Pacific Theater in early 1944 for field trials. The impression was that it was inferior to the P-61 without an RO. Another radar-equipped P-38J, but with piggyback RO, was later sent to the Philippines where its cramped conditions were understandably found unsuitable. Again, the concept held promise.

The Air Forces embarked on a formal P-38 night-fighter program in September 1944. One P-38L-5 (44-25237) arrived in Dallas on 26 October 1944 for modification under Chief Engineer Robert C. Pote and Project Engineer Harry Schuhart. The AN/APS-4 unit was placed under the nose on a revised under-wing pylon, and an RO station installed behind the pilot but under a raised hood. Only a slender RO under 5.5-feet tall found the arrangement comfortable. A radar and AN/APN-1 radio altimeter were added and flash suppressors fitted to the gun muzzles. The complete modification first flew on 5 February 1945 and demonstrated a 36-mph speed advantage on the P-61. On the sixth flight, the test aircraft was destroyed in a takeoff accident following an engine failure. Nonetheless, the modification appeared to provide a suitable P-38 night fighter.

Work was successful enough to see 74 P-38M-5 "Night Lightnings" created via conversion of P-38L-5 airframes under an October 1944 contract. The work was performed at Lockheed's Dallas Modification Center. The aircraft were painted gloss black and the alteration added 500 pounds to each aircraft. The first flew on 5 January 1945 and comprehensive testing continued at several sites.

Training was undertaken at Hammer Field as the aircraft accumulated in summer 1945, although this had begun earlier in the year with a few piggyback Js fitted with radar. Specifics for the P-38M are essentially the same as for the P-38L, except top speed was reduced by about 20 mph to 391 mph. Although they had a speed advantage, range was considered marginal for the mission and the Lightning was more lightly armed than the P-61. The radar was also less capable (including inferior range) compared with the Black Widow. One limitation of the P-38 as a night fighter was that the entire exhaust system atop the nacelles glowed with radiant heat, and shielding this area was impractical.

Although the P-38M appeared capable, and the initial combat team was trained and ready to deploy, they did not leave the States before the war gratefully ended. Reportedly, not all 75 mods were completed.[9]

Navy Course

Sea Change

The U.S. Navy, usually assumed to be tradition-bound and resistant to change, readily adopted radar technology as an advantage or necessity. The Japanese naval and air power and German U-boat threat left little room for argument. Japanese night raiders were a persistent annoyance to frontline forces. Ashore in the Pacific, the Navy and Marines contributed the same sort of stopgap assets as the Army possessed to help suppress the nightly forays of "Bed Check Charlie." These efforts met with some success, but high altitude bombers still got through until AI-equipped fighters appeared in fall 1943.

The American island-hopping campaign brought carriers close in on the objective to provide fighter cover and ground attack assets. This made the carriers more easily located by the enemy, and nearly coincident with the enemy's loss of air superiority. Consequently, the Japanese airmen took to dusk and night attacks on high-value shipping to avoid American fighters. This meeting with some success, the U.S. admirals were agitating for better means of countering the threat with shipboard night fighters.

Japan fielded only a very limited airborne radar capability. What the Japanese lacked in technical assets she made up for in determination and skill. Night aerial attacks, on land and sea, were quite troubling to U.S. forces. By December 1943, more than 90 percent of all enemy attacks were prosecuted at night. Beginning in May 1943, Japanese night-intruder formations would occasionally drop chaff to confuse night fighter and GCI radar operators. They also sometimes flew these missions with old wood and fabric biplanes that were largely undetectable by radar. Evasive techniques included diving toward the nearest land mass to add clutter to radar displays.

In November 1943, during landings on Tarawa and Makin Atolls in the Gilbert Islands, the Navy began its first night operations to help protect its vessels from attack by experienced Japanese night bomber pilots. The need was emphasized on 20 November 1943 when the carrier *Independence* (CVL-22) was severely damaged by a dusk attack. This was followed by damage to the *Lexington* (CV-2) on 4 December and *Intrepid* (CV-11) on 8 February. Yet, the AI-capable fighters were still in the pipeline. Any arguments against limited-use night fighters and the strain of night carrier operations fell by the wayside.

The first night intercepts were flown in November 1943 with standard Hellcats vectored by shipboard search radar to the proximity of raiders. Although this yielded some success, it had already been demonstrated in Europe that it amounted to little more than stumbling about in the dark. Another attempt the same month had two Hellcats flying formation with an Avenger torpedo-bomber fitted with surface search radar that could paint airborne targets for closing after the initial steer. This, too, was far from optimal and at best a hazardous stopgap (the first kills on 22-23 November were by the TBF-1C while the Hellcats avoided collisions). It was a poor substitute for real AI intercept technology and techniques.

The F6F and F4U fighters equipped with AI-radar finally began appearing in January 1944 aboard ship and ashore. In the next few months, the night victories began to mount and the enemy intrusions were blunted. These fighters were deployed as night squadrons that month with small detachments aboard *Enterprise* and *Intrepid*, mixed with standard aircraft within squadrons. The first squadrons retained as coherent night fighting units formed in fall 1944 and shipped out in January 1945 aboard *Enterprise*.

Four carriers, *Independence* (CVL-22), *Saratoga* (CV-3), *Bon Homme Richard* (CV-31), and *Enterprise* (CV-6), were eventually designated "night carriers," embarking night-fighting air groups (fighters and torpedo-bombers), although their daylight operations remained more common than night. The first night-carrier attack was 17-18 February 1944 with TBF-1Cs from *Enterprise* hitting Japanese shipping at Truk. By late summer, an air group aboard *Independence* that included TBF-1Ds began operating, executing night bombing of shipping and shore targets. Detachments of six night fighters and bombers continued to operate from most larger carriers. This, again, became the norm in spring 1945 as the kamikaze threat prompted shifting the aircraft complement aboard ship to emphasize day fighters. Throughout this period, the Marines continued to operate night fighters from land bases. The eight Marine Corps night fighter squadrons alone accounted for 106 enemy aircraft destroyed in nocturnal combat.

American night attackers employed radio countermeasures (RCM) as early as 1944 to jam Japanese radar, as well as dumping "window" out the aft door of Avengers.[10] These techniques became more prevalent in the final months of the war, including during initial naval air attacks against the Japanese home islands that began on the night 16 February 1945.[11]

Air-to-Air Assets

Better Than Nothing (PV-1)

The parallels between the U.S. Navy and Army during the initial period of American involvement in the war are understandable. The lack of night fighters was felt immediately as the enemy exploited the weakness. Attempts at night intercepts with standard day fighters were, as usual, more hazardous to the defending pilots than the attackers. When the Department of the Navy cast about for an interim night fighter while more capable AI systems wound their way through development, they hit on something like the British had used. The Lockheed Vega PV-1 Ventura medium maritime patrol and attack aircraft appeared a suitable stopgap.

When initially acquired in December 1942, the PV-1 already had ASD-1 radar in the nose, so it could be readily adopted with an AI modification. At least 14 of the aircraft were given AI Mk IV radar in the nose in addition to VHF radios and IFF, and shielded exhausts. Four .50-cal. machine guns were installed low in the nose to complement the two at the top and a pair in a dorsal turret. The crew of three included an RO/radio operator and gunner.

The first naval night fighter squadron, the Marine Corps's VMF(N)-531, took on these PV-1s in April 1943 and had barely become proficient in the mission when ordered to the South Pacific. They arrived in September to meet the persistent Japanese night raiders. Although useful, the PV-1 was hardly ideal for the mission. The top speed was modest as was the service ceiling (usually just 15,000 feet at combat loading), although these could match many night intruders. Most frustrating was the lack of speed brakes to help slow the aircraft during an intercept and prevent overshooting. Nonetheless, the Marines claimed six bombers downed by the Venturas through May 1944 at which point all the PV-1s had been consumed.[12]

Lockheed PV-1 characteristics:

span	65.5 ft	weight empty	20,197 lbs
length	51.8 ft	gross	26,500 lbs
height	13.2 ft	maximum	31,077 lbs
wing area	551 ft²	speed, max. (13,800 ft)	312 mph
fuel capacity (int. + ext.)	981+790 gal	cruise	166 mph
service ceiling	26,300 ft	range, torpedo	1,360 mi
best climb rate	2,230 fpm	depth charges	1,660 mi

This Lockheed PV-1 configured as a night fighter was photographed in January 1944 at Bougainville, Solomon Islands, property of the Marine Corps' first night-fighter squadron, VMF(N)-531. Like the Army's P-70, the Ventura was a fighter in name only and, although useful, was gratefully traded for single-engine, high-performance fighters. (Naval Aviation Archives)

Late Start (F4U-2, F4U-4N)

Progress in creating radar sets small enough for a single-seat night fighter prompted the suggestion on 7 August 1941 to integrate such equipment on the new F4U. In September, BuAer had Vought begin exploring options. This was well before the first production aircraft had flown, although the Navy expected it to be the next hot fighter. The emergence of the AIA project in November prompted immediate action, the Navy tasking Vought on the 8th with early integration concepts for the Corsair.[13] The firm submitted a proposed design on 6 January 1942, and the XF4U-2 mockup was presented on the 28th. The company modified its first production example F4U-1 (Buno. 02153) to the new standard and began testing it on 7 January 1943.

The Corsair was selected for installation of the APS-6 air intercept radar. An F4U-4 (97361) was selected for modification with the unit in a wing pod, becoming the F4U-4N shown here. However, it did not become a standard model before the end of hostilities, instead providing data for postwar projects. (Naval Aviation Archives)

While Vought's progress on the F4U-2 was favorable, the firm was simply too busy to take on the production tasks and the Navy hesitated to disturb the production line. Instead, the Naval Aircraft Factory in Philadelphia performed the modification of 32 F4U-1s to the F4U-2 standard. Deliveries began in spring 1943. Two additional examples were created as field modifications from F4U-1As.

The F4U-2 had the AIA radar pod merged into the starboard wingtip, although this contained only the scanner. Most of the electronics were behind the pilot seat and a waveguide ran out through the wing to the pod. This necessitated removal of the starboard outboard gun, although it was also done for balancing reasons. The other guns were fitted with flash dampers and the electrical generator was upgraded. A 3-inch radarscope was added to the instrument panel. To accommodate night flights, an autopilot was integrated into the control system, cockpit changes made such as lighting, a radar beacon transponder installed, a radar altimeter added, and the HF radio replaced with a VHF set.

Two F4U-2s await takeoff from the USS* Enterprise *(CV-6) during a strike on Truk. The F4U-2 was the U.S. Navy's first night fighter, employing the AIA radar in the starboard wing pod and a small display in the cockpit. The results were sufficiently successful to encourage further night-intercept programs. (Author's Collection)

The F4U-2s were quickly sent to the fleet where the Navy's first night-fighter squadron, VF(N)-75, was formed on 1 April 1943. After months of training they were sent to war, although restricted like all Corsairs to land-based operations. A second Navy squadron and a Marine Corps unit also flew the model in combat. The first Navy squadron arrived on New Georgia in early October 1943. On 31 October, one of these aircraft became the world's first single-seat fighter to perform a combat radar intercept kill. The first Marine Corps unit arrived on Tarawa in early January 1944, but was soon sending detachments to other islands harassed by Japanese "washing machine Charlie" night raiders.

While the F4U-2s joined other Corsairs aboard ship beginning in January 1944, it is not surprising that only the initial batch of 32 F4U-2s was acquired. The airplane was difficult enough to bring aboard in daylight, much less in the dark.

An F4U-4 (97361) was selected for conversion with the larger and much-improved APS-6 radar installed farther inboard and without sacrificing armament. Designated the F4U-4N, this was completed after the war on 3 March 1946.

This F6F-3N is shown on USS **Block Island** ***(CVE-106) late in the war, apparently after engaging the barrier. It shows well the prominent APS-6 pod protruding from the starboard wingtip. More than 200 of these variants were created as modifications.*** (Northrop Grumman Historical Society)

This F6F-5N of VF(N)-107 shows off the AN/APS-6 airborne intercept radar-pod integrated into the starboard wing leading edge during a flight from NAS Quonset Point in August 1945. Note the 20mm cannon barrels protruding from the inboard of three gun ports on each wing. (American Aviation Historical Society)

An illustration from the F6F-5 flight manual shows the instrument panel of the -5N night fighter. The scope for the APS-6 radar is prominent in the center. The instruments are sunken to aid lighting while reducing reflections. (Naval Aviation Archives)

Prime Time (F6F-3N, F6F-5N)

Still seeking a night fighter that could immediately move to the boat, unlike the F4U, the Navy asked Grumman in early 1943 to study integrating an AI radar into the F6F-3. A design was in hand by spring that had the APS-6 unit in a starboard wing leading-edge pod, an AN/APN-1 radar altimeter, IFF transponder, flat windscreen to reduce distracting cockpit reflections, and instrument panel optimized for night work to include red lighting and the radarscope. The first modified aircraft was flown on 26 June 1943 and passed to the Project *Affirm* team that month. Eighteen more followed through September when the radar units were finally available for installation.

A total 229 F6F-3Ns were created, all via modifications, and they began operations aboard ship in May 1944. These night Hellcats were successful enough for more to be sought based on the F6F-5 model that appeared in mid 1944. Grumman built 1,432 F6F-5Ns in the same configuration as the F6F-3Ns, some with the APS-6A. Late in this production run the inboard .50 machine guns were replaced with 20mm cannons to increase probability of first-pass kill and some also had exhaust flame dampers.

The night fighting Hellcats commonly operated alongside standard models within deployed Navy and Marine squadrons. With formation of specialized night squadrons and night carriers, they operated in conjunction with Avenger bombers. The F6F-5Ns also

The Grumman F7F-1 was the first single-seat fighter with nose radar incorporated from the outset. With the nose radome removed, the AN/APS-6 radar is revealed in the front of this F7F-1. This was definitely the shape of things to come in fighter design. (Northrop Grumman History Center)

flew from carriers in the Mediterranean to support the invasion of southern France. The Royal Navy took on night fighting Hellcats to operate from their carriers.[14]

Too Late to Place (F7F-1, F7F-2N, F7F-3N, F8F-1E)

Almost all new fighter projects after mid-1943 required accommodations for radar, at a minimum the APS-4 pod and associated cockpit gear. Of those reaching production, the F7F-1 had the distinction of being the first single-seat aircraft produced with radar integrated into the nose as standard equipment. This was also a

The instrument panel of the F7F-1 had the display for the APS-6 radar centered directly in the pilot's forward line of sight. The screen is covered to prevent damage during maintenance. There are knobs for **Signal Level** ***and*** **Wing Calib.*****, while the knobs for*** **Intense** ***and*** **Focus*****, have been removed.*** (Northrop Grumman History Center)

The rear cockpit of the F7F-2N contained radar-system controls and display, and some basic flight instruments. The display is usually enclosed on a sighting hood to reduce extraneous light spill. The overhead canopy had a bulge added, the few inches enough to ease operator neck strain. (Northrop Grumman History Center)

The performance of the Tigercat suggested it would be a superb night fighter. A second seat for a radar operator was added to improve night intercept effectiveness, becoming the F7F-2N. The Grumman aircraft reached the Pacific Theater as a Marine Corps asset on literally the last day of the war. (Northrop Grumman History Center)

Late-war Tigercat production continued to emphasize night fighting with a two-seat variant of the F7F-3. The F7F-3N had an SCR-720 radar added in an extended nose. This image from early 1944 shows the 300-gal centerline tank, the Mk 9 rocket launchers, and an integral boarding ladder left extended. (Naval Aviation Archives)

source of confusion, as many seemed determined to append an N to the aircraft designation. Indeed, when the Marines first took on its 35 aircraft and the AN/APS-6 radar in spring 1944, these were soon redesignated F7F-1N.

The Tigercat's outstanding rate of climb and heavy armament made it more than suitable in dealing with Japan's very light fighters, and so a desirable night fighter. However, efficiency as a night fighter would be improved with a dedicated radar operator, and so development of a two-seat model was begun in January 1944. Reducing fuselage fuel tank capacity provided space for the crewman aft of the pilot. The Plexiglas canopy over the station soon had a bulge added to give the RO more headroom. One F7F-1 was completed as an XF7F-2 (Buno. 80261) and 65 F7F-2N production examples (Bunos. 80294/358) followed between on 31 October 1944 and 8 March 1945. Weight went up about 400 pounds and range was trimmed about 150 miles. These had the four .50-cal. nose machine guns removed, leaving the four wing

An APS-4 pod hangs under the wing of F8F-1 Buno. 90445 at Bethpage, making it the one and only F8F-1E. The light weight and considerable power of the Bearcat promised a formidable night fighter with a true AI radar, but none reached combat and its like were soon displaced by jets. (Northrop Grumman History Center)

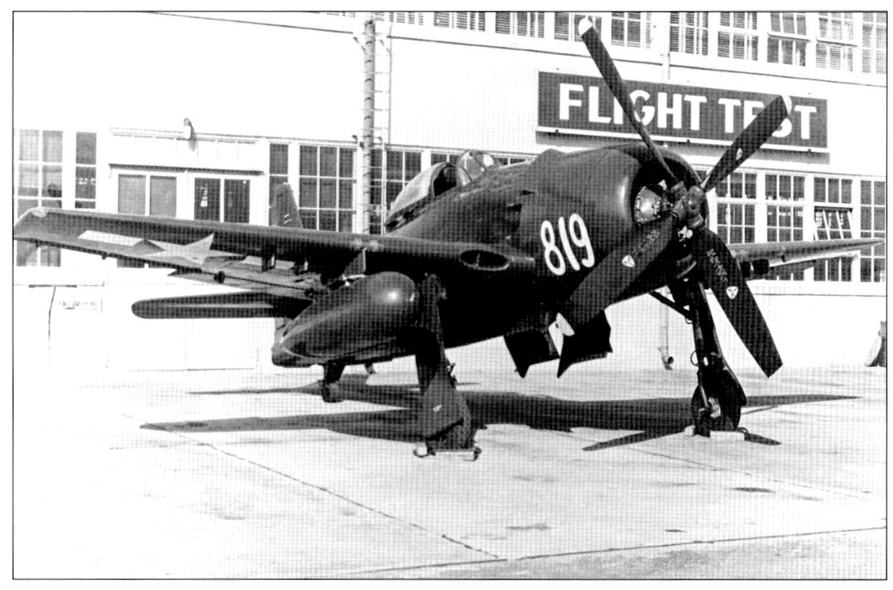

The large AN/APS-19 pod added under the wing of the Bearcat denotes 94819 as one of the first two XF8F-1Ns. The configuration was accepted for production, but these appeared only after the war. The large pod in the asymmetrical layout created drag and handling issues that were unwelcome. (Northrop Grumman History Center)

20mm cannons. A Marine F7F-2N unit, VMF(N)-533, landed on Okinawa one day prior to Japan's surrender.

The F7F-3 also came as a two-seat version, the F7F-3N. Its SCR-720 radar with 21-inch diameter antenna, versus 17 inches for the APS-6, required removal of the nose guns and elongation of the nose with an added bottom bulge. The first F7F-3N emerged on 15 May 1945 and a few were on hand at close of the war.

During 1945, an F8F-1 Bearcat (Buno. 90445) was fitted with an APS-4 pod beneath the starboard wing. This F8F-1E led to trial installations and testing of an AN/APS-19 "rabomb" pod under the starboard wing of two F8F-1s (Bunos. 94812, 94819) during the summer 1945. The aircraft also had an autopilot and exhaust flame dampers. The -1E work generated 12 F8F-1Ns, but only postwar. The drag and adverse handling produced by the pod made the configuration undesirable.

AEW Appears (TBM-3W)

One key to countering anti-shipping attacks was to place search radar at altitude, in an aircraft, to provide earlier detection beyond the surface vessels' radar horizon. The night-fighter radar commonly installed on shipboard aircraft possessed inadequate range for this task, but an aircraft devoted exclusively to the mission could carry aloft a much more capable unit. This was the beginning of what is today called Airborne Early Warning (AEW).

The Radiation Laboratory explored the requirement under a February 1942 Navy contract codenamed Project *Cadillac*. The solution involved installing an 8.3-foot wide antenna for the AN/APS-20 S-band radar specifically designed to fit under the belly of an Avenger, and with the necessary electronic equipment and operator within the voluminous fuselage. From 20,000 feet, the system could monitor airspace with up to a 100-mile radius, two to four times the range of shipboard radar depending on the target. It possessed adequate discrimination to detect low-flyers. The radar image could then be relayed via data link to the Combat Information Center of a surface ship for appropriate action.

The first aircraft converted with the APS-20 was originally the XTBM-3 (Buno. 25700), becoming the XTBM-3W. The modification was performed during spring 1944 at NAMU.

Extending the radar-detection range of a naval task force beyond the horizon required a powerful radar on an airborne platform. This gave birth to the TBM-3W, the first shown here, with an AN/APS-20 radar in an enormous radome under the belly and vertical stabilizers added to the tail. (Northrop Grumman History Center)

This Douglas SBD-5 is equipped with the air-to-surface vessel (ASV) radar as evidenced by the Yagi rotating antenna beneath the wings. With the two antennae, the operator could identify the range and azimuth of a surface contact beyond visual range in day or night conditions. (San Diego Aerospace Museum)

The enormous radome nearly filled the space between the landing gear and deck. The fact the Avenger's main landing gear retracted outboard was one factor in choosing this aircraft. Additional vertical surfaces were installed on the horizontal stabilizers to maintain suitable directional stability, and all armament was removed. The RO, the only crewman besides the pilot, was housed in the fuselage with the aft greenhouse and turret replaced with a housing for electronic gear.

The XTBM-3W first flew on 5 August 1944 and the program took on new urgency when the kamikaze threat emerged in fall 1944. Deliveries began in March 1945 with 27 TBM-3s converted at Johnsville. The first TBM-3W teams were training, including shipboard ops, during May and June 1945 aboard USS *Ranger* (CV-4). They were preparing to ship out when the war came to a close. After the war, the -3W found greater value in anti-submarine warfare.

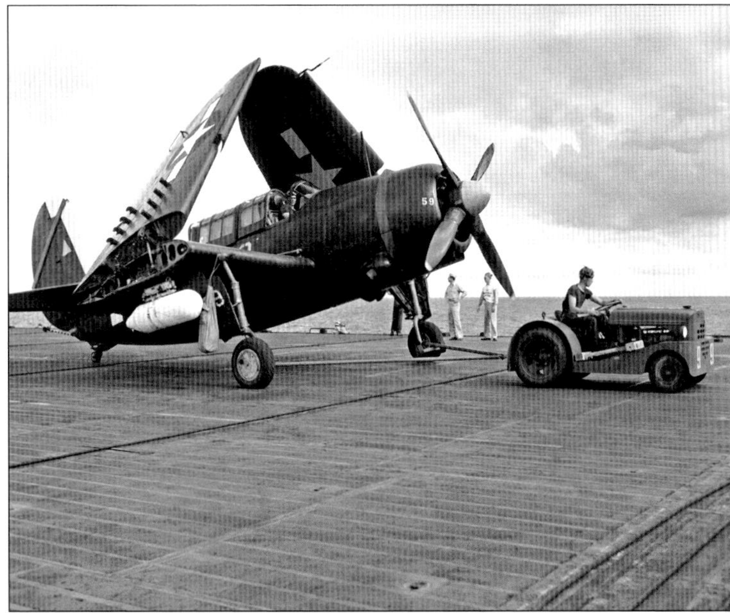

This SBW-4E displays the ASH radar pod under the starboard wing. Hundreds of these installations were made to the late-model Helldivers, yet earlier Yagi surface search radar was almost standard equipment from the beginning of SB2C production. This set the stage for postwar practice. (Naval Aviation Archives)

This TBF-1C is typical of mid-war Avengers sprouting antennae. The rotatable Yagi antennae under each outer wing was for the air-to-surface Type B (ASB) surface search radar. The aerial under the fuselage received signals from sonobouys during antisubmarine operations. (San Diego Aerospace Museum)

Perhaps to avoid taking up under-wing store stations, TBF-1D 01733 had the ASH radar installed in a pod atop the canopy greenhouse. One can imagine the blind spot the airframe created within the radar field, reducing its effectiveness. This remained a one-of-a-kind configuration. (Northrop Grumman History Center)

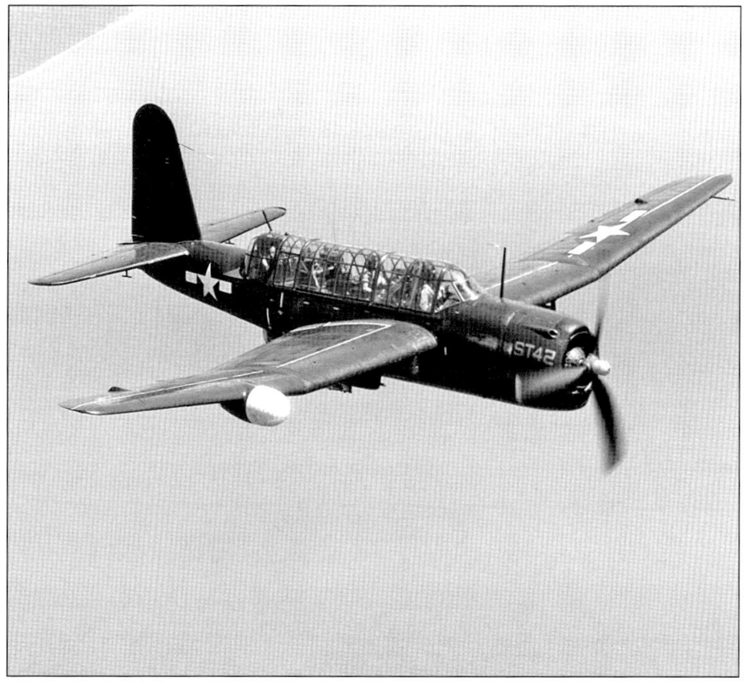

Radar became such a common asset on naval aircraft, particularly attack aircraft, that it was often incorporated in new production deliveries instead of as a retrofit. So it was with the abortive TBY-2 that received an APS-3 radar pod grafted into the starboard wing leading edge. (San Diego Aerospace Museum)

The AN/APS-4 radar pod is visible under the starboard wing of this TBM-3E and it passes over the bow. The ventral gun appears to have been removed to reduce weight. Radar-equipped Avengers were a step toward a true night surface attack capability that remained exceedingly challenging without guided weapons. (Northrop Grumman History Center)

Air-to-Surface Assets

Raptors (SBD, SB2U, SB2A, SB2C, TBF/M, TBY, F6F-3E, F6F-5E)

Five Douglas SBD-4s were modified with the ASB-3 search radar starting in October 1942, concurrent with five Grumman TBFs, to create the Navy's first capability to locate vessels in the dark via aircraft. The engine exhausts were fitted with flame dampers. The radar addition, plus navigation radios and other electronic equipment, required the aircraft electrical systems to be upgraded from 12 to 24 volts. Subsequently, many SBD-4s, -5s, and -6s had radar installed as field modifications or in the factory.

The Vindicator may have been considered for radar as a SB2U-1 was fitted with a mocked-up radar pod in the starboard wing in February 1942. However, events would soon show the Vindicator to be of little further operational value and the modification does not appear to have been taken further.[15]

A few Marine SB2A-4s for night training were seen fitted with ASB radar. A least one SB2A-2 Buccaneer (Buno. 00811) was modified with a radar pod in fall 1943.[16]

The earliest models of the Curtiss SB2C had ASB radar installed virtually as standard equipment. The SB2C-3E and SB2C-4E, plus

A more practical air-to-surface radar integration for the Avenger is typified by this TBF-1D (Buno. 47670) captured on film on 3 November 1943. The starboard wing pod contains the AN/APS-3 (ASD-1) system ideal for anti-submarine warfare (ASW). Both the pilot and radar operator were provided scopes. (Northrop Grumman History Center)

The versatile TBF/M Avenger was a favorite platform for modifications facilitating night fighting. The number of variants is unclear, but can be characterized as a comparatively small number of aircraft.

Some TBF/M-1s and -1Cs were modified after delivery with ASB-3 radar. First appearing in October 1943, it soon became standard equipment. Some TBF/M-1Cs were given APS-3 radar, the pod integrated into the starboard wing leading edge. The operator was in the radio compartment and the pilot had a repeater scope. These TBF-1D and TBM-1D aircraft were intended for dedicated night operations. Some retained the ASB gear and they usually had zero-length rocket launchers. The guns and armor were frequently removed, in whole or in part, to lighten the aircraft. This sometimes entailed removing the turret entirely. A least one TBF-1D (Buno. 01733) was seen in Philadelphia during early March 1944 with the APS-3 pod mounted above the greenhouse.

One of 18 such aircraft, this F6F-5E (Buno. 70678) was photographed at NAS Patuxent River on 18 October 1944. The AN/APS radar "bomb" is evident under the starboard wing. Less evident are the cockpit and system changes to create this night intruder modification of the Grumman Hellcat. (Naval Aviation Archives)

Competition for the TBF, the Vultee TBY Sea Wolf, did not reach series production until mid 1944. By that time, it was a natural decision to integrate an APS-3 radar pod into the starboard wing leading edge. The radarscope and controls were in the rear cockpit. As already related, this airplane never went to war (see Chapter 5). Almost all naval-attack aircraft projects after 1942 had provisions for radar, the XTB2D-1 being an example with an AN/APS-4 in the starboard wing, and AN/APS-6 in the port wing of the XTB2F-1.

The addition of an APS-4 pod under the Avenger's starboard wing outer panel brought forth the TBM-3E. However, Eastern also took the opportunity to trim weight and prevent an adverse performance impact. Among the things to go was the ventral gun, wing and tail de-icing components, and armor plate in the back was replaced with flak curtains and vests. Altogether, the developers cut 300 lbs from the aircraft. The APS-4 was substituted in the wing pod for the TBF/M-1F

100 SBF-4E and 270 SBW-4Es, had APS-4 radar installed on the starboard wing when supporting night ops. However, this installation was also made as modifications of other models. All SB2C-5s had the APS-4 as standard equipment, with a scope for the pilot and observer. It is unclear how many of these aircraft were fielded.

This Avenger, in colors suggesting an Atlantic ASW patrol role, reveals the shielded exhaust that was evident on some of the night fighting variants. Although the exhaust appears to be well outside the crew's field of vision, the flame could reveal the aircraft's position to enemy aircraft and ship gunners. (Northrop Grumman History Center)

The AN/APS-4 pod hangs under the wing of a F6F-5E in a photograph from 22 August 1944, likely at Bethpage. This was surface search radar for locating vessels at sea or revealing shorelines in the dark. The pod was easily removed and the aircraft could operate as a day fighter. (Northrop Grumman History Center)

modifications to late-production -1Cs. The TBM-3Ds were similarly modified and occasionally with the turret removed and opening faired over. The Yagi antennae, if retained, were seen above the wing if rockets were carried. Some of the night fighting-equipped Avengers were given shielded exhausts.

A few TBM-3s with a special search radar were designated TBM-3H. The effort to create a night torpedo attack capability was undertaken at NAS Norfolk, Virginia, with further modifications to the TBM-3. This TBM-3N had the turret removed and canopy extended over the space to create an RO station.

Attempts were made at employing fighters for surface attack. For surface search and night intruder work, the F6F-3 was given the night treatment but with an APS-4 pod hung under the starboard wing. The combination was less suited for a fighter, so only 18 of these F6F-3Es were delivered by January 1944. A small number of F6F-5Es were manufactured in the same configuration as the -3Es.

ASW Contribution (TBM-3D, TBF/M-1L, TBM-3L, SBD)

In the Atlantic, the focus was anti-submarine warfare – ASW in postwar parlance. Shore-based airplanes or flying boats performed the ASW mission almost exclusively. However, in the early years of the war there was a mid-Atlantic "gap" beyond the range of these large aircraft. The introduction of the escort carrier for convoy duty in March 1943 permitted small, shorter-range aircraft to search for and attack German submarines. From this point, the U-boat scourge began to recede. The big Avenger's ability to operate off these small carriers was a tremendous advantage, especially at night, and it contributed to sinking subs in both oceans. For them, ASW initially consisted of searching visually for surfaced submarines and attacking with bombs, rockets, or gunfire. For submerged subs, the chance sighting of a periscope or snorkel, or sonar detection by a surface ship, could allow attacks by dropping depth charges. The Avenger could execute long patrols where its mere presence hampered U-boats from shadowing convoys and closing for attack. Some of the aircraft were stripped of nonessential gear and one crewman left behind, with bomb-bay auxillary tank and drop tanks installed, to permit launch at dusk and recovered at dawn in 13- to 14-hour "Night Owl" missions.

The Avenger's air-to-surface radar soon became the best means of locating submarines. At night, radar allowed detection of boats surfaced to recharge batteries or the planes overhead discouraged them from surfacing. TBM-3Ds were seen carrying podded searchlights under the port wing. A few TBF/M-1Ls and TBM-3Ls were

This TBM-3D is configured for ASW with both APS-3 and ASB radar, a searchlight under the port wing, and enhanced 3.5-inch rockets on zero-length launchers for attack of surfaced and shallow submerged subs. Note the lack of guns and the Yagi antennae moved to the top of the wings. (San Diego Aerospace Museum)

produced with retractable searchlights in the bomb bay (another British ASW innovation) or under the port wing. A few SBDs were given searchlights, and conversion of other types to ASW was in development. These lights were met with mixed feelings as they tended to attract fire from the submarine's gunners. At least one F6F-3N (Buno. 65950) was given a trial installation of a searchlight pod under the port wing to explore suitability for anti-submarine warfare. At least two F6F-5Ns (Bunos. 70729, 79139) were given searchlights in the opposite leading edge from the radar for trial purposes.

Rockets and Mk 54 depth charges were weapons of choice for attacking submarines, once found. The Mk 54 had 300 pounds of explosives and sank at 8 fps, but they had to be placed very close to the boat to create heavy or fatal damage. The American aircraft rockets were originally developed as ASW weapons following the example of the British three-inch rail-launched rocket. Weighing 55 pounds, the projectile had a solid steel head, reached 1,175-fps velocity, and could penetrate 50 feet of water (soon extended to 130 feet). The aim point was to be just short of the boat because the head of the rocket was shaped to flatten the trajectory on water penetration such that it impacted below the waterline.

Development of a Navy night torpedo attack capability had begun in July 1945 with the Avenger a principal component, but this did not reach fruition before conclusion of the war. A capability that did see combat was the new Mk 24 "Fido" passive acoustic homing torpedo. This added another dimension for engaging submerged submarines. It was a comparatively small weapon at 680 pounds with 92-pound warhead. It was so secret it was labeled a "Mine" and was to be fired only against a solitary target to ensure a second boat did not escape to "tell the tale."

The Avenger also deployed the first air-dropped sonobouys, developed in the United States, that detected sounds of submerged boats and relayed these to the aircraft via radio for assessment. The CRT-1A was a 12- to 14-pound unit 36 inches long by 4 inches in diameter. It descended via parachute and then floated with a hydrophone hanging 30 feet below. During its four-hour battery life, it detected sounds in the 100 to 10,000 cycles band and transmitted the data on six radio frequencies. The CRT-4 was a sonobouy providing the directional data lacking in the CRT-1A. This was evaluated in 1945 but not produced.

Several Avengers were tested with a magnetometer commonly referred to as magnetic airborne detector (MAD). This system sensed the disturbance in the Earth's magnetic field by the presence of the dense ferrous metallic mass of the submarine. The breakthrough that made MAD possible was the 1940 invention of the saturable-core magnetometer by an American researcher.[17] The first

Sailors struggle to right an Avenger that has ended up with one wheel in the side catwalk of the USS* Bogue *(CVE-9) during June 1943. The shot shows well the four 3.5-inch rockets on launch rails under the starboard wing. (U.S. Government)

experimental sets were flown in tests during early 1942. The earliest American production set, the ASQ-1, had a range of just 600 feet and was used in an effort to verify a sonar or sonobouy contact. This meant the aircraft had to pass almost directly over a submerged submarine at just 100-feet for positive detection.

The short ASQ-1 range required a weapon to be dropped instantly if a hit was to be expected. Consequently, the retrobomb was developed during 1942. Rocket motors were fired forward to cancel the horizontal velocity imparted by the aircraft such that the weapon tipped over and fell straight down to strike the submarine from directly overhead. Retrobombs of seven-inch diameter with 35-pound warheads developed by Caltech had three choices of motors matching different aircraft speeds. These were fielded at the end of 1942 and employed briefly in 1943 with some success.[18] However, the German submarines then chose to engage aircraft with deck guns rather than submerge. As an aircraft had to pass over the target at 100-300 feet, the German tactic effectively rendered the retrobomb defunct.

An improvement in MAD was to place the magnetometer in a boom that could be extended aft, placing the magnetometer away from the magnetic disturbance of the aircraft. Such was attempted on the Avenger, the boom extended in flight from the ventral tunnel formerly used by the bottom gunner. This does not appear to have been fielded during the war.

Chapter 11

The Lockheed concept for the L-133 with L-1000 turbojet engines was well ahead of its time in early 1942. The L-1000 (mockup shown) was to be an axial-flow turbojet engine first conceived in 1940. It engine design incorporated intercoolers that would not ultimately be a feature in jet engines. The U.S. Army finally funded development of the L-1000 in 1943 as the XJ37-1. (Jay Miller Collection)

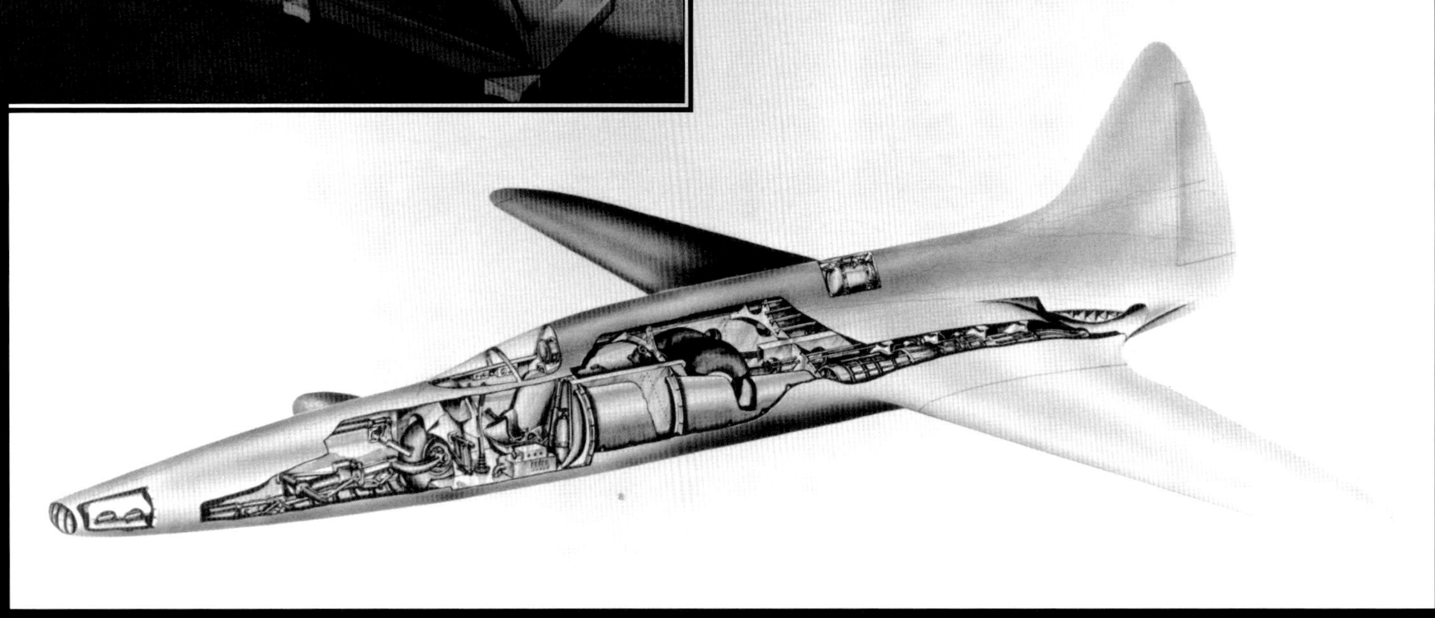

The L-133 cutaway reveals the long intakes running from the nose on either side of the fuselage, and main landing gear that nestle together within the fuselage centerline when retracted. The 18,000 pounds gross weight airplane was to be made of steel and have four 20mm cannons in the nose. (Tony Landis Collection, artist J.E. Davis)

JETS – FIRST BLUSH

Engine Facilitators

Mother of Invention

As discussed in Chapter 1, jet engines and jet-propelled aircraft were being pursued before World War II. Most such work occurred in Europe, but some efforts were undertaken in the United States. War and the realization that America was behind in this technology spurred an acceleration of such development.

Some U.S. firms were already doing preliminary design studies of jet engine hardware and jet-powered aircraft. Pratt & Whitney had a test engine running in 1940 that had a propeller turned by a turbine that was fed by eight free-piston diesel gas generators. Northrop conceived the Turbodyne turboprop engine and unsuccessfully sought War Department funding in 1940. That same year, Lockheed performed preliminary design work for the 5,100-lbf L-1000 axial-flow turbojet engine.

Lockheed also submitted the L-133 fighter design proposal featuring two L-1000s to the Army Air Forces on 30 March 1942. This was to be a single-place, tricycle gear jet aircraft of 18,000 pounds gross weight with predicted maximum level flight speed of 612 mph at sea level, 710 mph in a dive. The L-133-02-01 was a "tailless" design with forward canard or "trimmer." The wing had slats, and the boundary layer was sucked off ahead of the slotted flaps to keep the flow attached over the flaps and enhance lift.* All controls were hydraulically boosted. The L-133 was too big a step for the Army in spring 1942.

As the United States directed more resources to military expansion during 1939-41, research and development for advanced powerplants was not neglected. In a 25 February 1941 letter, Gen. Arnold requested NACA form a group under the direction of Professor William F. Durand to investigate jet propulsion. The group included representatives from the Army Air Corps, BuAer, the National Bureau of Standards, academia, and three manufacturers. None of the industry representatives had previously built aircraft powerplants (Arnold had forbidden aero engine manufacturer participation), but this ensured fresh thinking in a virtually new field and avoided weighing down aero engine firms already working to capacity. At that time, the United States had little knowledge of European turbojet development, but knew of Germany's rocket-propelled aircraft and rocket booster work.[1] Although Arnold's intent was investigation of rocket propulsion, the group quickly converged on gas turbines as the most promising avenue of exploration.

One recommendation of the Durand Special Committee on Jet Propulsion was that the three principal forms of reaction propulsion be developed under War Department contracts by the three firms represented. Westinghouse Electric Corp. would take on the turbojet, General Electric the turboprop, and Allis-Chalmers the ducted fan (turbofan). All three firms possessed prior experience with industrial turbines or high-pressure/high-temperature rotating elements. General Electric came with tremendous experience in compressors and high-temperature alloys, bringing its turbosuperchargers to a state superior to all others. This proved a good jumping off point for the turboprop, funded under a 7 July 1941 Army contract. The Navy sponsored the others: a July nod to Westinghouse for the turbojet, the contract on 8 December, and an October 1941 go-ahead to Allis-Chalmers for the turbofan, with the contract following in January.

Old World Examples

The first true gas turbine engine was developed in England under the motivation of engineer Frank J. Whittle, and run during April 1937. However, it was the end of 1940 before a practical aero powerplant from Whittle's firm Power Jets was operating under official funding. In May 1941 it took aloft the first British jet aircraft, the Gloster E28/39. The 623-pound flight-worthy W.1 of 855-lbf possessed a single stage, double-sided centrifugal compressor surrounded by a diffuser leading the air through a 180-degree turn to 10 combustion cans and through another 180-degree turn to a single

* *Reducing the thickness of the boundary layer by sucking it away reduces friction drag created by the air passing the aircraft surface.*

Apart from multi-stage, axial-flow jet engines, the blended wing-body and canard layout of the Lockheed L-133 concept were very innovative. Predicted speed was an almost unthinkable 612 mph at sea level. (Tony Landis Collection)

Britain flew its first jet aircraft on 15 May 1941. The Gloster E28/39 was powered by the centrifugal-flow Power Jets W.1 delivering 855 lbf from the 623-pound unit. It caught the attention of the Americans who moved immediately to buy an example and exploit the technology. (Jay Miller Collection)

turbine stage. The Whittle engine matured further as the Power Jets W.2B delivering no more than 1,200 lbf from an 860-pound, 43-inch diameter unit. The time-between-overhauls (TBO) was set at 180 hours. Gloster developed the F.9/40 Meteor airframe to take two of the turbojets.

There were soon competing engines from a collection of projects across the UK, including axial-flow designs and those with reheat.* The centrifugal de Havilland H.1, developed under Frank B. Halford, produced 3,010 lbf when first run in April 1942. Soon known as the Goblin, this 49.9-inch diameter engine featured a single-sided compressor and straight-through combustion. It was an H.1 that powered the first Meteor into flight in March 1943.

The initial production Meteor F.1 model was powered by the Rolls-Royce RB.23 Welland I, an improved W.2B delivering 1,700 lbf from an 850-pound unit with 100-hour TBO. The Meteor boasted a gross weight of 11,800 pounds with a 2,155-fpm initial rate of climb and 1,340-mile range. Maximum speed of the F.1 at sea level was 385 mph, and 410 mph at 30,000 feet. Approximately 40 Meteors were delivered during the war of which perhaps half entered squadron service and the rest were employed on trials. The de Havilland D.H. 100 Vampire was designed for a single 2,700-lbf H.1 turbojet and first flew in September 1943. Slowed by more urgent commitments, the initial production example did not fly until April 1945.

Less evident to the Allies were the accomplishments in Germany. There the new gas turbine engine technology was readily embraced and matched to advanced airframes for potentially war-altering weapons. The first jet aircraft, the Heinkel He 178, was flown in Germany during August 1939 with an engine possessing a centrifugal compressor and annular combustion chamber. A year later, axial-flow engines were running and production established during 1942. The Jumo 004B turbojet had such advanced features as hollow turbine blades for cooling and an adjustable nozzle exit area. However, fast production and lack of suitable materials meant an engine requiring an inspection after 10 hours of operation and overhaul after another 15 hours, although eventually reaching a TBO of 30 hours. This was adequate as the average life of a German fighter airplane by late 1944 was less than 15 hours. Many other engines were under development, some with features like afterburning.

The swept-wing Messerschmitt Me 262 twin-jet was the primary fighter benefactor of German jet engine development. The aircraft was years reaching maturity, and was still deployed prematurely. It retained many vices but achieved 500 to 540 mph depending upon altitude and with 3,937-fpm initial rate of climb. However, the engines deteriorated quickly, degrading this performance. The advanced aerodynamic design of the Me 262 as well as its engines gave it an approximate 150-mph speed advantage over Allied fighters and

** Also known as augmentation, afterburning, and secondary combustion, reheat is the injection of fuel into the hot exhaust of the turbine, forward of the nozzle, to produce additional thrust. The early engines typically ran slower than their best efficiency owing to cooling concerns, and so emitted excess oxygen to support further combustion aft of the turbine. Because of the high fuel flow rate, afterburning is generally reserved for short or heavy takeoff and for added engagement speed. An extended tailpipe is required and introduces additional airframe heating and weight issues.*

The first jet fighter was the German Messerschmitt Me 262. Although a tremendous advance in aircraft design, the Me 262 had many weak design points in its airframe and engine. This captured Me 262A1 was photographed at NAS Patuxent River on 2 February 1946. (National Museum of the United States Air Force)

was faster than the first American and British jets in some portions of the flight envelope. It was also designed largely as a point-defense asset. Excessive perfectionism and poor decisions ensured these were too few, too late, and too poorly performing to reclaim air supremacy for the Luftwaffe. Still, the Schwalbe was the greatest advance in fighter design for a fielded World War II warplane. While very worrying to the Allies, the Me 262 was never employed in decisive numbers. The type may have accounted for 150 enemy aircraft destroyed while 100 or so were lost to Allied fighters.[2]

Germany also shared turbine and rocket engine and aircraft technology with Japan. However, the resources to bring these to any meaningful production and combat late in the war were lacking.

America Steps Up

After setting the Durand Committee into motion, Arnold was in England during April and May 1941. He witnessed early tests of the E.28/39 with the Whittle turbojet and observed design work on the Meteor. Upon returning home, the general wasted no time in energizing the Army Air Corps's Materiel Command and the State Department in securing an agreement to build the engine in America. During a meeting in his office on 5 September, Arnold asked General Electric to produce the engine as project MX-398 under a "Most Secret" classification. Only the Manhattan Project had a higher level of security.[3] A cadre of American propulsion specialists, including GE personnel, visited Britain in late summer to gather information and establish details of the exchange. Originally, 15 engines were ordered from Power Jets, but instead GE signed on to build all the 1,650-lbf W.2Bs. A request for one of the two E.28/39s to serve as a testbed was later rescinded as the first American jet airplane was coming along well.

Power Jets personnel, the 1,250-lbf W.1X non-flightworthy unit, and drawings of the W.2B, were secretly flown to the United States aboard a B-24 on 1 October 1941. Within weeks, GE had the engine running under the code name "Type I Supercharger." It was not as straightforward as expected, and the firm was permitted to make only specifically approved changes. Nonetheless, they immediately began introducing improvements while developing their own variant, the I-A, under the guidance of Donald F. "Truly" Warner. They added an automatic control system and worked to resolve Whittle's compressor surge problem. The American unit was completed in March 1942 but did not run successfully until 18 April. However, the "clone" never matched the expected performance of the W.2B, GE only later learning they had been given the wrong thrust curves.[4]

The final 44-inch diameter I-A yielded 1,250 lbf, flying eight months before the British W.2B. It was further refined as the 1,460-lbf I-14B that ran in February 1943. By April, improvements produced the 804-pound I-16 at 1,650 lbf and 49.3-inch diameter, finally realizing the thrust originally expected of the local W.2B, and reaching an eventual TBO of 50 hours. Twenty-one of these

The General Electric variant of the Power Jets W.2B, the I-A, was quickly built and tested before entering limited production. This engine powered America's first jet aircraft, yet was just the first of a series of jet powerplants that appeared in rapid succession at the end of the war. (Air Force Flight Test Center)

The General Electric I-40 was a development much beyond the original Whittle design, featuring straight-through combustion in 14 chambers. Soon known as the J33, it exceeded 4,000 lbf in January 1944, suitable for a single-engine jet fighter. The Army moved quickly to apply this powerplant. (Jay Miller Collection)

developmental engines were built, some rebuilt to later models. The I-16 was a more practical product and hundreds were built as the J31.*

By January 1944, GE had squeezed out 1,800 lbf as the I-18 and in April was generating 2,040 lbf from the much-revised Whittle design as the 950-pound I-20 (J39 then J31-GE-5). However, the Army sought 4,000 lbf suitable for a single-engine aircraft. As a result, the centrifugal I-40 project began in May 1943 and was tested on 13 January 1944. At 50.5-inch diameter, it included many changes in materials, tolerances, and 14 straight-through combustors. More than 300 of these J33s were produced by war's end.

The first J33s had a turbine life of just five hours. Such limitations were common early on with any new engine but also characteristic of new technology maturation and simply the fast pace required to field a weapon system under the pressures of war. At the beginning of the conflict, high-performance American reciprocating aero engines had 200- to 300-hour TBOs, although rising to as high as 1,000 hours by mid 1945 for some models.[5] Therefore, expectations may not have been very high. The reliability of Allied jet engines rose quickly with each new model, and the Americans lead the way in achieving this outcome.

The turboprop project, General Electric's TG-100, reached maturity with a 14-stage compressor and nine combustion cans followed by a single-stage turbine. It ran on 15 May 1943, but with gearbox and propeller only in May 1945 as the T31 Prop-Jet. The long development was proving disappointing with the anticipated 2,300 shaft horsepower (shp) eventually falling to 1,650 to 1,700 shp.

A parallel GE program began in summer 1941 to create a 4,000-lbf axial-flow turbojet derived from the TG-100 under MX-414. It ran in April 1944 as the TG-180 with an 11-stage compressor, eight burner cans, and single-stage turbine in a 37-inch-diameter unit. This J35 and the J33 were essentially unique designs far removed from the Whittle engine. The J35 initially had a TBO of just 10 hours, eventually raised to 35 hours.

Allis-Chalmers did not do well with the axial-flow turbofan project and the Navy cancelled it in June 1943. Instead, the service asked the company to produce the Goblin under license. However, deliveries were so slow that, after accepting eight J36s, the Navy cancelled further work as the I-40 came along.

Westinghouse began construction of its 1,000-lbf axial-flow turbojet under a November 1942 contract the Navy hoped might produce a "booster" for piston-powered fighters. The team, under R. P. Koon, had the 827-pound prototype X19A running on the stand in Philadelphia on 19 March 1943 and passed a 100-hour endurance trial in July. This 19-inch diameter unit had a six-stage compressor, annular combustor, and single-stage turbine delivering 1,200 lbf. It flew on 21 January 1944 under an FG-1 Corsair. This was the first American-designed jet engine and only the second axial-flow turbojet outside Germany. Further refinement yielded the 19XB "Yankee," (later just 19B) at 1,600 lbf from a 10-stage compressor. It was first run on 14 March 1944 and test flown under a JM-1 (Navy B-26). Westinghouse and Pratt & Whitney manufactured some 261 of these J30s.

The 19A was scaled up and down for a family of engines. The 275- to 340-lbf, 9.5-inch 9.5A was for airplane applications while the 9.5B "Baby" (both J32) was intended to power a missile. The 24-inch diameter 24C (J34) boasted 3,000 lbf from the 1,220-pound unit with an 11-stage compressor, annular combustor, and two-stage turbine.

Other wartime U.S. engine programs failed to leave a mark before the end. Pratt & Whitney acquired the U.S. production rights to the 5,000-lbf Rolls-Royce Nene (J42). The firm was also contracted by the Navy in June 1945 to develop the PT2 (T34) "propeller-turbine," ultimately delivering 5,700 shp. Turbo Engineering Corp. won an initial Navy contract in June 1941 for turbojet development with a centrifugal turbine aimed at a 1,100-lbf booster. Slow progress and higher priorities compelled cancellation in September 1944. Northrop finally won initial funding in June 1941 for study of the Turbodyne. This eventually developed into America's first turboprop at 3,800 hp, operating successfully in December 1944 but

* *The uniform engine designation system for turbine engines was introduced on 10 April 1945. It is used predominantly in the text from this point.*

This FG-1 Corsair served as a flight testbed for the 1,000-lbf Westinghouse X19A turbojet during 1944. This axial-flow jet was only the second to run outside Germany and the first gas-turbine aircraft engine developed and flown in the United States. (Jay Miller Collection)

remaining developmental. Lockheed was placed on contract 19 June 1943 to develop the L-1000 engine for the Army Air Forces. It was by that time projected to produce 6,700 lbf from a 1,235-pound unit 24 inches in diameter, but also ultimately withered.

Turn 'n Burn

As with the push to develop American jet engines, the eagerness for matching airframes was no less energetic. The Army and Navy both kicked off a number of projects seeking different jet fighter capabilities.

Incipient

Army Leads Off (P-59A, XP-59B, P-80)

With the Whittle engine secured, the Army sought an American airframe. Although this would be the first step into jet aircraft, if successful there was every intention that the result would be fielded as a combat fighter. GE's facilities were situated in Schenectady, New York, and Lynn, Massachusetts, and Bell Aircraft was conveniently located in nearby Buffalo. All three facilities were remote enough to make tight security practical. Bell also had excess engineering and production capacity. The day after Arnold asked GE to participate, 6 September 1941, in another meeting in his office he asked Bell to begin work immediately on MX-397. A date of 30 May 1942 was set for first delivery. Expectations were for an aircraft of at least 480 mph, with a twin-engine configuration suggested by the thrust of the W.2Bs. The contract followed on 30 September for three XP-59As.

Initial design of the three Bell Model 27s started with a team of just six men under E. Rhodes, isolated under great secrecy. So severe were the security measures that even the designation was a smokescreen; the XP-59 designation reused and the serial numbers (42-108784/6) not assigned until after the aircraft had flown. Among the earliest XP-59A concepts was a P-39 with an engine embedded in each wing, *a la* the Meteor. The final concept had the engines mounted close to the fuselage in the armpits of the mid-mounted wings to shorten inlet and exhaust duct lengths, reduce yaw in an engine-out case, and allow easier maintenance access. However, the configuration was not ideal with respect to drag.

The concept was submitted to the Army Air Forces two weeks after beginning, and approved days later. Detailed design led to construction beginning in January 1942 off the plant grounds at a more easily secured site. Because Bell was restricted from using NACA Langley's full-scale wind tunnel for security reasons, the engineers did not get all the engineering data they desired. The XP-59A featured flush riveting and was the first fighter in the United States with a fully pressurized cockpit.[6] Yet, the rest of the aircraft was largely typical for the period, down to the fabric covered control surfaces.

The first two I-A engines were delivered to Bell on 20 August 1942 and the aircraft was moved by train to Muroc the following month. Since many of the early jet engines lacked airstart capability, the vast landing expanse of the dry lakebed could be crucial to saving an aircraft in distress. The engines were run installed for the first time on 26 September, and the maiden flight, performed by Robert M. Stanley, occurred on 1 October. Thrust was initially limited by

Early ideas for quickly creating an American jet fighter included converting an existing airframe with turbojets. Bell conceived a P-39 with the two engines in wing pods, much like the British Meteor, as seen in this art. However, this was passed over for an entirely new design. (Jay Miller Collection)

GE and the engines had to be pulled after just three hours. The pilots got into the habit of shutting down and landing dead-stick just to save test time on the engines.

The XP-59A testing soon revealed a number of airframe and engine discrepancies, particularly inadequate engine bearing cooling airflow. These and other factors caused the program to fall behind schedule by several months.

On 26 March 1942, the Army Air Forces approved production of 13 YP-59A Airacomet service test examples (42-108771/83), the first flying on 18 August 1943. Since assembly and test of the intended I-16 engines was lagging, these were also flown with I-As and some with I-14Bs. It was October 1943 before I-16s were installed.

Regardless of engine, flight trials found the Airacomet's speed disappointing, considerable rudder compensation was required at high yaw angles, and a directional snaking made it a poor gun platform. The snaking, possibly attributable to flow separation within the inlets alternately side-to-side, might have been predicted given suitable wind tunnel data.[7] Mock combat trials in February 1944 against the P-38J and P-47D found the YP-59A had few advantages over the frontline U.S. fighters and possessed poor rearward vision to boot. Even by the end of 1943, the engines still required inspections every 10 to 12 hours and overhaul after 20 to 25 hours of operation.

An order for 100 P-59As with the I-16 engine had been placed on 9 October 1943, and another 250 planned. Armament consisted of one 37mm cannon with 44 rounds, three .50-cal. guns with 200 rpg, two 1,000-pound bombs or eight 60-pound rockets. However, while the P-59 beat the Meteor into test and was generally comparable, it was not judged a suitable combat aircraft. As there appeared little ready means of mending these deficiencies, and another jet project was yielding promising results, Gen. Arnold decided the P-59 would be used only as a jet lead-in trainer, and as engine and systems testbeds. The orders were reduced to 50 on 30 October 1944, eventually made up of 20 As (44-22609/28) and 30 P-59Bs (44-22629/58). The first of the latter flew in December 1944 and incorporated 66 gallons of additional fuel, a ventral strake running the length of the aft fuselage to improve spin characteristics, plus squared wingtips and vertical tail. The production lot was delivered through 27 August 1945, some Bs receiving the I-20.

Many of the Airacomets went to test organizations while the first Army Air Forces jet squadron took on 18 Bs. The 412th Fighter Group was formed on 30 November 1943 with a mission to train the initial operational jet unit and conduct exercises with existing reciprocating fighter units.

Three single-engine XP-59Bs (Model 29, MX-398) were ordered on 26 March 1942 to be powered by the I-16. The design looked like a P-63 with a jet engine exhausting under the aft fuselage and intakes buried in the wing root leading edges. The mockup was inspected on 3-4 July 1942 but, by December, the Army Air

The two General Electric engines powering the XP-59A were accessed as shown. The exhaust pipe has been removed, revealing the turbine exhaust surrounded by the 10 combustor cans with fuel injector lines to each. A segment of the fuel line from the fuselage to the engine has also been removed. (Jay Miller Collection)

The Airacomet was placed into limited production to provide introductory trainers for those transitioning to jets. The P-59B is identified by the ventral strake under the aft fuselage and guns in the nose. Note the splitter plate in the inlet. (National Museum of the United States Air Force)

Upgrades from the XP-59A to the YP-59A included squared-off wing tips, which reduced the span to 45 feet, 6 inches and wing area to 386 square feet, squared-off vertical fin and rudder, relocation of the pitot-static tube to the top of the vertical stabilizer, metal-covered flaps and ailerons, a strengthened aft fuselage, and mechanically operated main landing gear up-locks (controlled from the cockpit). (Air Force Flight Test Center)

The Army Air Forces's first jet fighter unit was the 412th Fighter Group, formed on 30 November 1943 and operating P-59B Airacomets. Examples of those production aircraft, with 150-gallon drop tanks, are at Bell's plant in Buffalo, New York. Armament is a 37mm cannon and three .50-cal. machine guns in the nose. (Jay Miller Collection)

Forces had decided to revise the design to reduce weight. This was accomplished by 18 January 1943, cutting 400 pounds. Performance figures remained discouraging, particularly climb rate, given expected I-16 thrust. The service wanted to see how the I-16 actually

Bell P-59A characteristics:

span	45.5 ft	weight empty	7,950 lbs
length	38.8 ft	gross	10,822 lbs
height	14.3 ft	maximum	13,000 lbs
wing area	385.4 ft²	speed, max. (30,000 ft)	413 mph
fuel capacity (int. + ext.)	290+300 gal	cruise	375 mph
service ceiling	46,200 ft	range, normal	400 mi
initial climb rate	approx. 3,200 fpm	ferry	850 mi

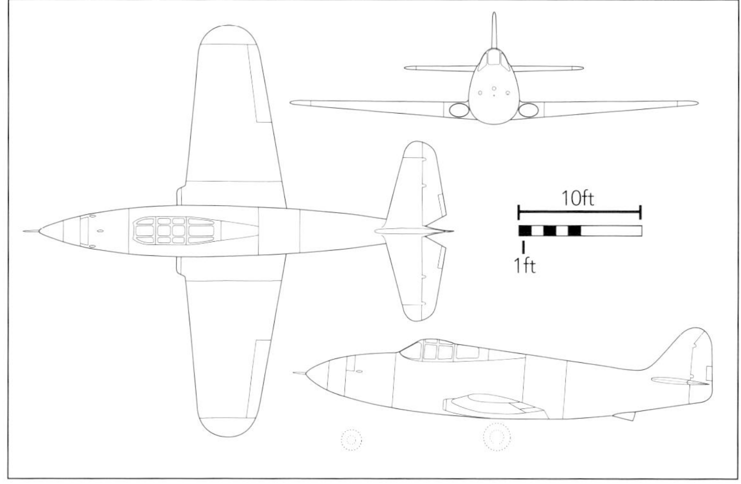

Conceived early in 1942, the XP-59B was to be a single-engine fighter intended to employ the General Electric I-16 engine. However, the anticipated thrust of the unproven engine was still marginal for a single-engine fighter. Given Bell's other important work, it was thought best to set the project aside. (Author)

did before proceeding much further, and work was idled. By summer, with Bell's heavy workload and continuing I-16 disappointments, and given progress on an alternative project, XP-59B work was suspended on 15 June. Cancellation followed on 31 August, long before metal was cut.

The first Meteor F.1 (EE210/G with W.2B engines) was sent to the United States in February 1944, for evaluation under MX-505, in exchange for a YP-59A shipped to Britain (42-108773 becoming RJ362/G) in September 1943. The first flight of the Meteor in March 1943 powered by two H.1Bs clearly marked this as one of Britain's most powerful jet engines at 3,000 lbf. This suggested to the Americans the Goblin might be suitable for a single-engine, high-performance fighter. The Army Air Forces felt an urgency to move beyond the XP-59 that had flown in the fall and was proving lackluster. Therefore, on 24 March, details of the de Havilland turbojet and the XP-59B studies were shared with Lockheed. This was followed on

17 May with an invitation for the firm to submit a proposal for a fighter equipped with a single H.1B.

Lockheed promptly went to work with a team headed by Kelly Johnson. On 15 June the L-140 proposal was handed to the Army Air Forces and approval to proceed granted on the 17th. The $520,000 contract followed on the 24th. This swiftness became characteristic of the entire effort. Project MX-409 was to deliver a single flying prototype (44-83020) in just five months. This unprecedented short time to design and construct a new advanced combat aircraft forced Lockheed to create a unique experimental shop under Johnson with a dense team of less than 130 persons, cutting red tape and middle managers. Everyone labored 10-hour days, six-day weeks, under secrecy and spartan working conditions.

The mockup of the XP-80, only the forward fuselage, was ready on 20 July. Aircraft construction proceeded rapidly, but the engine was late arriving from de Havilland. Finally, the powerplant was flown to Burbank from Britain aboard a B-24, the unit installed, then the aircraft disassembled and trucked to Muroc. Reassembled on 17 November, the engine was run installed for the first time. The next day the inlet ducts collapsed under suction of a high-power run. Upon inspection, the engine compressor wheel was found cracked due to a manufacturing flaw.

Acquiring a replacement engine took until the end of December; the Goblin removed from the second Vampire prior to flight and shipped to the United States. After XP-80 taxi tests on 3 January 1944, the first two flights were made on the 8th. The honor went to Milo Burcham as he took the ship to 470 mph and performed aileron rolls. Even though the installed thrust was limited to just 2,460 lbf, the XP-80 soon became America's first aircraft exceeding 500 mph in level flight (502 mph at 20,480 feet). There was plenty to optimize, however, with obvious external changes including adopting rounded wing and tail tips, an added elevator tab, horizontal tail incidence increase, plus adding wing root leading edge fillets to cure adverse stall behavior. A persistent elevated tail pipe temperature defied resolution.

The de Havilland H.1B Goblin turbojet engine is shown in the prototype Lockheed XP-80 in preparation for a test run at Muroc AAB. The engine retained the centrifugal compressor and individual burner cans of the Whittle engine, but the cans fed directly into the turbine to eliminate another flow turn. (Tony Landis Collection)

The first Meteor F.1 (EE210/G), fitted with W.2B engines, was provided to the United States in February 1944 in exchange for a roughly comparable YP-59A. It is shown in U.S. markings on 22 August 1944. The Meteor was just on the verge of large-scale production in Britain when Germany capitulated. (National Museum of the United States Air Force)

The Lockheed XP-80, photographed on the dry lakebed at Muroc AAB, is being prepared for its first flight on 8 January 1944. Another project executed at breakneck speed, this aircraft proved almost immediately to be a winner. It quickly demonstrated more than 500 mph in level flight. (San Diego Aerospace Museum)

Also developed under an extraordinarily short schedule, the pre-production XP-80A was initially flown on 10 June 1944 (seen here over the Muroc test site). These aircraft were significantly larger than the prototype and packed the more powerful I-40 engine. The P-80A appeared a weapon capable of countering the German opposition. (San Diego Aerospace Museum)

At the end of August 1943, the Army Air Forces and Lockheed agreed to a pair of follow-on prototypes that substituted the slightly larger I-40 engine then in development and promising 4,000 lbf. The Army Air Forces was concerned de Havilland would never meet the projected schedule for H.1 production, and the Vampire was competing for the Goblins. The service gave Lockheed 120 days and $930,000 to deliver the XP-80As (44-83021/2), MX-409A – the clock starting on 24 January 1944.

Intended to be a production-representative aircraft, the jet (L-141) entailed a general enlargement and overall improvement to the design such that it was almost an entirely new aircraft. The airframe was strengthened and 25 percent heavier with boosted controls, intakes of greater area, cockpit pressurization, fuselage dive brakes, and an engine water injection system.* Range was extended with more internal fuel and drop tanks mounted at the wingtips where they reduced drag and did not occupy weapons stations. Armament consisted of six .50-cal. guns with 1,200 rounds and two 1,000-pound bombs or eight 5-inch HVARs.

The first XP-80A was flown on 10 June 1944 by Tony LeVier and it was soon evident the jet had its share of problems. Inlet flow instability was created by air separation on the walls producing a "rumble" and snaking instability. The cure was boundary layer splitter plates added in the intakes.† Compressibility produced aileron "buzz" that was corrected with greater control cable tension.‡ Top speed was soon demonstrated at more than 550 mph.

Thirteen YP-80As service test prototypes (44-83023/35) were ordered on 10 March 1944 and the first flown on 13 September, packing a 3,850-lbf J33-GE-11. The YP-80As immediately set new speed standards and, with the more powerful American engines, were clearly competitive with the Meteor and probably the Me 262. The government had spent approximately $5.7 million over a year to get to this point, and it appeared money well spent.

The Me 262 was evidently about to enter the fray in a big way, and U.S. exercises with its few jets against existing fighters and bombers showed a jet interceptor to have enormous advantages. This compelled a P-80A fast-track to production, given the same production priority as the B-29 bomber.[8] An order for 500 P-80A Shooting Stars had already been placed on 4 April 1944, and the first were delivered on 12 February 1945. The order was supplemented with another 500 and then 2,500 near the end of the war, with plans

** Injecting a metered flow of water (usually a water-alcohol mixture) into the combustion chamber(s) helps reduce turbine inlet temperature, allowing more fuel to be burned in the combustor and the turbine to be run at high speed for greater exhaust mass flow and thus more thrust. Because of the limited supply of water, injection is typically only employed on takeoff.*

† The splitter plate or boundary layer diverter separates this flow from that entering the engine, typically dumping the air overboard.

‡ Buzz is the high frequency, low amplitude rotational oscillation of a control surface usually induced by unsteady airflow or shock wave repetitively moving over the surface.

One of 13 service trials YP-80As flys over the California desert. Four of these airplanes were shipped to Europe to acquaint fighter squadrons with such aircraft so they could improve tactics against German jets. (Tony Landis Collection)

Lockheed P-80A characteristics:			
span	38.8 ft	weight empty	7,920 lbs
length	34.5 ft	gross	11,700 lbs
height	11.3 ft	maximum	14,500 lbs
wing area	237.5 ft²	speed, max. (sea level)	558 mph
fuel capacity (int. + ext.)	425+330 gal	cruise	410 mph
service ceiling	45,000 ft	range, normal	540 mi
initial climb rate	4,580 fpm	maximum	1,440 mi

for North American to contribute 1,000. The Army Air Forces expected deliveries to reach 30 aircraft per day in 1946.

Tests at Muroc in July 1944 helped establish defensive tactics. These employed the P-59s and P-80s attempting to engage a bomber formation defended by P-38s, P-47s, and P-51s. In mid December 1944, a pair of YP-80As (44-83028/29) were shipped to Italy and two others (44-83025, 83029) to Britain – just 18 months from conceptualization of the aircraft. Operation *Extraversion* was an operational evaluation and to assist squadrons in developing tactics to deal with German jets.[9] By war's end, 16 or more Shooting Stars were flying of more than 30 produced. The Me 262 still had performance advantages on the P-80, but other factors such as pilot training and handling qualities would likely have leveled the playing field.

Unlike the XP-59 experience with two aircraft lost in mishaps, a high rate of attrition was being suffered by the P-80 – including one of the birds in England. By 7 August 1945, the Army Air Forces briefly grounded the Shooting Stars after seven aircraft were destroyed, six damaged, and half dozen pilots killed. Consequently, for a time the P-80 had a bad reputation that clouded its future. This was overcome. The faults lay partially with development being pushed too fast and partially with the aircrew. Everyone had much to learn about operating jet aircraft.

Cautious Navy Steps (YF2L-1, XFD-1, FR-1)

The Navy was at the forefront of American jet engine development from the first, and followed with great interest the associated U.S. Army and British aircraft projects. It was keen to reap the benefits of jet speed and in the eventuality it met jets in combat. It took immediate notice of the Army Air Forces' accomplishment when Bell flew the XP-59 in October 1942. The following month the Navy tasked Westinghouse with developing the X19A axial-flow turbojet. Within three months, a specification was released, a competition held, and a contract let to build the first U.S. Navy jet fighter.

The Navy's eagerness for jets was balanced by what they saw as potential difficulties introducing these to the carrier environment. It was clear that tricycle landing gear would be essential for jet aircraft to reduce the jet blast effects on wooden carrier decks, yet the Navy lacked experience operating tricycle-gear aircraft on its carriers.* Even so, jet blast could still be exceedingly hazardous and disruptive to flight operations on the confined deck. Existing jets were notorious for slow response to throttle and had a low thrust-to-weight ratio making a bolter (go around) extremely hazardous, in contrast to the piston-powered aircraft with rapid response and associated increase in propwash over elevator and rudder. The jet's throttle levers had to be moved slowly to avoid surges and flameouts with engine damage. These concerns were especially true for the powerplants with centrifugal compressors, but affected all turbojets, as the inlet mass flow (ram effect) was low at slow airspeed. For example, Allied fighters had adopted the tactic of "bouncing" Me 262s while on landing approach because they knew the enemy pilot was usually committed to a landing below a certain altitude. The poor acceleration also made for high approach speeds and long takeoff rolls, the latter suggesting catapults would be mandatory. The flush deck catapults in the Essex-class carriers were used only infrequently. Earlier carriers, plus the light and escort ships might be unable to accommodate jets. Additionally, fuel consumption rates were discouragingly high and endurance correspondingly short.

All these limitations gave Navy planners pause. The Navy saw itself faced with three present or future choices for powerplants: the pure turbojet, the turboprop (or prop-jet), and a mixed configuration of a reciprocating powerplant paired with a jet engine

* *The nose gear also tends to counterbalance the engine mounted aft in the aircraft and assist in attaining a suitable center of gravity location.*

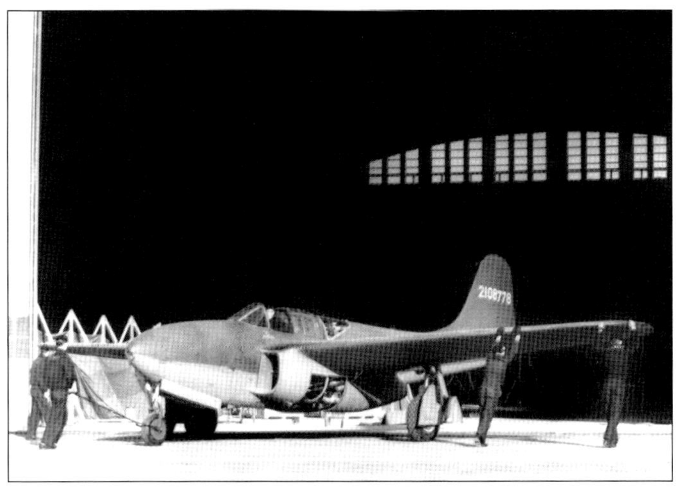

The U.S. Navy was keen to take advantage of the new technology, but had serious concerns about its suitability for carrier operations. Their first experience with jets was gained with several Airacomets loaned by the Army Air Forces. This YP-59A is seen at NAS Patuxent River on 20 June 1944. (Naval Aviation Archives)

One of the Navy's two McDonnell XFD-1 Phantom prototypes displays the exhaust of the X19B turbojet engine. The wing root installation had the advantage of minimal inlet and exhaust duct lengths. Evident is the advantage of the jet aircraft in its low and level stance. (National Archives)

as a stopgap. During the next three years, the service pursued projects in each area. However, powerful propeller-driven fighters like the F8F were also financed in the event the gamble did not pay off.

The service acquired two YP-59As in November 1943 (42 -108778/9 becoming 63960/1) and later three P-59Bs (44-22651, -22656/7 as 64100, 64108/9) for evaluations and pilot familiarization flights. Designated YF2L-1s, they were technically the Navy's first jet aircraft. They were flown at NAS Pax River, and much was learned.

BuAer, under the leadership of RAdm. John S. McCain, sent an RFP to nine firms, with design packages due in January 1943, for a fighter employing the X19A. Recognizing the great uncertainty in the undertaking, performance and armament were not specified.[10] The winner was McDonnell, then still a young firm only lightly engaged in War Department work, never having produced an aircraft in quantity, and new to naval projects. However, all this suggested a company potentially well suited to tackling new ideas. It had already done some conceptual design work on jet fighters.[11] Its Navy project was designated the XFD-1, two (Bunos. 48235/6) ordered on 7 January along with a static-test airframe.

The St. Louis development team, led by Kendall Perkins, chose a conservative approach to reduce program risk and borrowing from the company's XP-67. The tricycle landing gear and tail dihedral – keeping the surfaces out of the jet exhaust – were the only unusual aspects, apart from the turbojets with wing root intakes. Designing an airplane around engines that did not yet exist was a decided source of anxiety. Perkins initially had to consider using the Westinghouse 9.5B, with six embedded in the wings, but predicted performance was discouraging. Other concepts with more of the smaller or fewer large engines made clear a twin with the 19B was the only practical fighter. However, it was evident takeoff thrust would generally mandate catapult launch. Each intake included a butterfly shutoff valve to block the passage and reduce drag for envisioned single-engine cruise. Armament was to be four .50-cal. guns with 1,650 rounds.

Mockup of the XFD-1 was ready at the end of May 1943, but it was after the new year before the detailed design was finalized. Although construction proceeded rapidly, the Westinghouse engines were late in arriving. Only one of the WE-19XB-2B (J30-WE) powerplants was on hand by October 1944. Therefore, systems tests and taxi trials proceeded with this sole engine delivering just 1,165 lbf. Even a brief hop off the runway was possible on 26 January 1945 at Lambert Field, piloted by Woodward Burke.

Fitted with two J30s still delivering 1,165-lbf each, the XFD-1 Phantom performed a proper first flight a few days later, again with Burke in the seat. Testing was slowed by engine problems, but a BuAer pilot had a look in July and noted some deficiencies, including slight directional oscillations at high speed. Changes had to be made to the horizontal stabilizer. The Navy had seen enough though and, with the uncertainties of the continuing war, did not hesitate to

McDonnell's XFD-1 possessed the wing-root leading edge inlets so common in early jet fighters. The aircraft first flew on 26 January 1945 with the fairings covering the openings for the four nose-mounted .50-cal. machine guns. Flight test was still moving slowly by the end of the war. (National Archives)

McDonnell XFD-1 characteristics:

length	37.3 ft	weight empty	6,156 lbs
height	14.2 ft	loaded	8,625 lbs
span	40.9 ft	maximum	9,531 lbs
wing area	276 ft²	speed, max. (30,000 ft)	506 mph
fuel capacity (int. + ext.)	260+140 gal	cruise	250 mph
service ceiling	43,700 ft	range, normal	540 mi
initial climb rate	4,960 fpm	maximum	750 mi

place an order for 100 FD-1s (Bunos. 111749/848) on 7 March with J30-WE-20s. A night fighter version, the FD-1N, was being planned. This was the state of the program when the war concluded.

The FD-1 program continued, albeit at a slower pace. Still, McDonnell lost one prototype and Burke to an accident in the latter half of 1945. The jet went on to modest production and service as the FH-1, a good entry-level trainer for aviators new to jets.

Although the XFD-1 was a bold step forward, the possible difficulties introducing jets to the carrier-led aviation leadership to choose a parallel development path. This was the composite aircraft integrating a turbine powerplant with an aircraft also possessing a reciprocating engine and propeller. With the X19A developed initially as a booster for propeller aircraft, the Navy applied the concept to several large attack aircraft. A purpose-built fighter exploiting the advantages of the jet for rapid climb, high ceiling, and high-speed engagement, yet able to operate comfortably from escort carriers, was a logical step. The quick thrust response and comparatively modest fuel consumption of the reciprocating engine eased concern with carrier integration and endurance. The jet would be started airborne and shut down prior to landing.

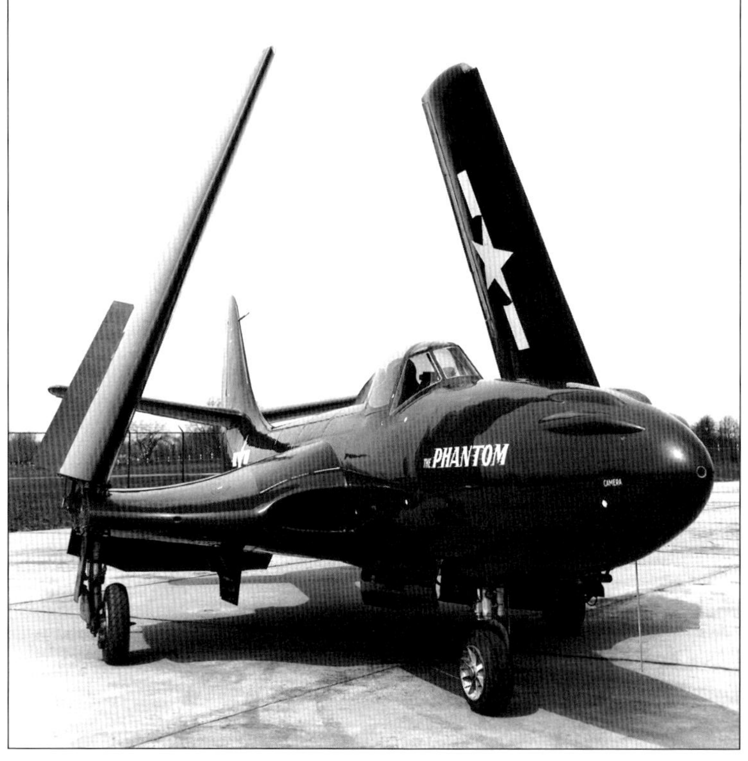

The second XFD-1 displays exceptional wartime workmanship, a fine finish, and a flashy nose logo. The wing flaps, fold mechanism, and tail plane dihedral are also evident. The canopy framing was typical to allow insertion of an armored windscreen. Changes to come would include squaring the fin tip. (National Archives)

RAdm. McCain released requirements to industry for the mixed-propulsion fighter in December 1942. Of nine respondents, the Ryan proposal won a go-ahead on 11 February 1943. This was not only Ryan's first Navy aircraft, but also its first combat type. Designated the XFR-1 Fireball (Model 28), it fit the 1,610-lbf I-16 turbojet (J31). The 45-inch diameter of the engine buried behind the cockpit made for an unusually wide fighter fuselage. The air to the compressor was fed via inlets in the wing root leading edges, and the I-16 was serviced by removing the entire aft fuselage and empennage on a trolley. In front, a comparatively modest R-1820-56 of 1,350 hp was an acceptable match with the turbojet. Being a fast-paced wartime contract, Ryan was to deliver a static test article in one month and the first of three prototypes (48232/4) in 14 months.

The first XFR-1 models the original tail with jet exhaust beneath. Tail surfaces were increased in size, the horizontal stabilizer moved down, and the vertical stabilizer moved forward with the rudder trailing edge just forward of the exhaust. This aircraft was later lost in a fatal accident in flight test. (Military Aircraft Photographs)

Developed under chief engineer Ben T. Salmon and project engineer William T. Immenschuh, the XFR-1 represented several notable firsts for the Navy. Although conventional in layout, the aircraft was the service's first tricycle gear fighter, had a laminar flow wing, flush riveting, and all-metal control surfaces. It also featured improved, heat-treated aluminum for thinner gauge and lower weight construction material. The wing design sought for the entire surface to reach its critical Mach number at the same speed to reduce tuck-under. The forward-placed cockpit with bubble canopy gave superb pilot visibility.

The Ryan XFR-1 represented the Navy's cautious approach to introducing naval jet fighters, using the turbojet for added power during combat while the reciprocating engine was the full-time propulsion system. The turbojet in back was fed air via ducts from the wing leading edge root. Note the original tail surfaces. (San Diego Aerospace Museum)

Japan's efforts to duplicate the German jet and rocket fighter accomplishments came to naught. Instead, they sacrificed young men in suicide attacks against Allied warships using such aircraft as this Yokosuka MXY7 Ohka. Its speed and size made it an exceptionally difficult target. (National Museum of the United States Air Force)

Each XFR-1 engine was operated independently, with separate power levers, the jet started with a single button push. The jet was expected to be used for just 11 minutes up-and-away with the reciprocating engine shut down. However, pilots habitually used both powerplants during takeoff (it could not takeoff on the jet alone).[12] Both engines burned the same fuel to avoid system complexity. Armament consisted of four .50-cal. machine guns with 300 rpg and two external weapons up to 1,000 pounds each or eight 5-inch rockets.

Robert Kerlinger flew the first XFR-1 on 25 June 1944, although the I-16 was not installed. When rectified, flight testing progressed rapidly. Electrically actuated cowl flaps had to be retrofitted to cure the R-1820's cooling problems. It was clear from wind tunnel data the aircraft would suffer inadequate longitudinal stability.* Consequently, an enlarged tail unit was already in design. Two or three configurations of the empennage were tested when retrofitted to the prototypes, characterized by the taller fin with added rudder throw, and the horizontal stabilizer similarly increased in area and lowered from near the base of the fin to top of the fuselage. Double-slotted flaps proved disappointing, with high sink rates at approach speeds and contributing to a tendency for the fighter to roll over. The final design had a single slot and reduced flap travel, but slotted ailerons. It was also learned that a low battery charge when it came time to unfeather the propeller and restart the reciprocating engine could produce disappointing and potentially grave consequences.

The XFR-1 test fleet suffered several accidents. Kerlinger lost his life in Buno. 48232 on 13 October 1944. It was initially believed he had exceeded the dive speed limits and suffered compressibility over the outer wing panels until these failed. However, Mickey McGuire was killed in Buno. 48233 on 25 March 1945 during a dive that may also have suffered compressibility problems that prevented recovery. The string of bad luck continued when the last XFR-1 had to be abandoned on 5 April when the canopy blew off during high-speed flight. Although pilot Dean Lake jumped to safety, he also had to abandon Buno. 39647 on 10 October 1945 when a fuel cell ruptured and flooded the cockpit. It was then suspected the wing bottom skin was pulling free of the leading edge as the edge of the dimpled skin holes cut through the countersunk rivets with wing flexure. The resulting gap allowed ram air to rupture the fuel tank and blow off the canopy. A restriction to 5 g versus 7.5 g normal load factor was imposed until outer wing panels with twice the number of rivets were introduced.

These and other accidents were due in part to a fast pace of development while production aircraft were already being rolled out and the first squadron training. As was common during the war, a

* *The original tail design had been based on the Wildcat. Most wartime projects moved to prototyping while detailed wind tunnel testing continued. As already demonstrated in early portions of the text, this frequently precipitated changes in the flight test aircraft based on later data.*

production contract was issued before the test aircraft had even flown to ensure capacity was in place to start turning out fighters as soon as the word was given. Therefore, 100 FR-1s, the world's first production composite aircraft, were ordered on 2 December 1943, and increased by 600 on 1 January 1945, the same month the first aircraft of the initial order began delivery. A preliminary Navy evaluation was performed in September 1944 and comprehensive testing followed in late October. Carrier suitability trials began on New Year's Day 1945. Changes were being introduced to production aircraft as flight testing progressed. Approximately a dozen FR-1s were on hand at the end of hostilities.

The FR-1 Fireball's mixing of jet and reciprocating propulsion is evident with the propeller feathered. Aircraft 39651 cruises near NAS Patuxent River in June 1945. Other than being a bit thick in the middle and with oil seeping from unlikely spots, it appears a conventional late-war fighter. (Naval Aviation Archives)

The Fireball possessed high-speed maneuverability and turning radius second to no production aircraft at the time it was introduced. The vastly different performance profiles of the two engines allowed it to engage enemy aircraft at any altitude with confidence. Consequently, the Navy wanted to get the fighter to the fleet as quickly as possible. It was the only aircraft expected in the near future that could intercept the Japanese Ohka suicide aircraft or engage the radar-equipped aircraft that located surface vessels before it directed kamikaze fighters to targets.[13]

Squadron VF-66 began working up on the type in March 1945 with a cadre of combat veterans. Their first sea experience with the new aircraft was on 1 May aboard USS *Ranger* (CV-4), but two of the three aircraft were damaged. They found the nose gear marginally suitable for carrier operations. Other operational mishaps were suffered as well.

VF-66 was to deploy in October 1945. However, the end of hostilities halted all preparations before any of the pilots completed carrier qualifications with the FR-1. Production was truncated to 66 examples (Bunos. 39647/712) on 15 August. Four FR-1s (Bunos. 39689/90, 39713/4) were supplied to the Army Air Forces for evaluation.[14] The type continued in service until structural issues compelled the Navy to withdraw the FR-1 in summer 1947.

Ryan FR-1 characteristics:

span	40.0 ft	weight empty	7,689 lbs
length	32.3 ft	gross	9,958 lbs
height	13.9 ft	maximum	11,652 lbs
wing area	275 ft²	speed, max. (17,800 ft)	404 mph
fuel capacity (int. + ext.)	180+200 gal	recip. only (sea level)	287 mph
service ceiling	43,100 ft	cruise	160 mph
initial climb rate	4,650 fpm	range, normal	930 mi
		maximum	1,620 mi

Plans were afoot to substitute the 1,450-hp R-1820-74W to create the FR-2, with one FR-1 flying in this configuration for testing.[15] Substitution of the 2,000-lbf I-20 would have wrought the FR-3. Ryan received an order on 31 January 1945 for 600 FR-2s (Bunos. 104576/5175), but both projects were cancelled outright on VJ-Day.

Chapter 12

Reaching for greater speed and more options in dealing with the emergent German jet threat, the Army Air Forces contracted with Republic in November 1944 for a fighter wrapped around the TG-180 delivering nearly 4,000 lbf of thrust. The resulting XP-84 is shown outside the Farmingdale plant prior to first flight. (Naval Aviation Archives)

JETS – FULL BORE

Pubescence

Army Follow-up (XP-84, XP-86)

With the initial appearance of the Me 262 in combat in fall 1944, the Army Air Forces looked for more expeditious means of getting a competing fighter into action than the projects already in hand. One idea was for Republic to replace the R-2800 with a J31 in its P-47, already one of the fastest and most potent American fighters in Europe.[1] This would have had a nose intake and exhaust under the tail, with the guns moved to the nose. Since the large-diameter engine could not fit inside even the barrel fuselage of the P-47 without major structural changes, and there were potential balance issues, the axial-flow J35 was substituted. However, preliminary design made clear this approach was simply impractical and little additional speed could be realized from the P-47, already experiencing compressibility problems.

The Air Forces were compelled to seek its jet through normal processes. The 11 September 1944 requirement sought a mid-wing aircraft giving 600-mph top speed, 850-mile range, and packing eight .50-cal. guns. However, the service also stated they simply wanted the best speed and range attainable given the available choice of jet engines.[2] The choice was still the J35 at 3,750 lbf. The axial-flow design offered a low frontal area and thus potentially less airframe drag, with nose instead of wing root inlets. Republic's chief engineer, Alexander Kartveli, and his team quickly drew up the smallest and cleanest airplane they could wrap around the engine. Flush riveting would further assist in drag avoidance. The engine would be readily accessible by removing the aft fuselage on a dolly.

The AP-23 concept documents were delivered on 2 November and the Army Air Forces gave a go-ahead on the 11th for three XP-84s (45-59475/7, MX-578). Republic kept up the pace and had a mockup ready in February 1945.

The first XP-84 was well along when the Empire of Japan capitulated. The straight-wing jet spanned 36.4 feet with 260-square-foot wing area, was 37.2 feet long, and had a gross weight of 13,400 pounds. On a more reasonable schedule, the fighter was completed in December and took flight for the first time in February 1946. In test, the Thunderjet demonstrated 611 mph top speed and 1,300-mile range. It had an illustrious postwar career.

In seeking the shortest route to a fast, single-engine jet fighter, the Army Air Forces asked Republic to explore installing a turbojet within a P-47 airframe. One resulting concept is shown in this concept art of a J35 in a distended belly and the guns moved to the nose. (via Renaud Mangallon)

North American's work on the Navy's XFJ-1 Fury jet fighter led the firm to conceptualize improved variants with less rotund lines. Four such designs were discussed with the Army Air Forces from February through April 1945. The most promising design (NA-140) employed the same J35 engine, had 32.8-foot straight wings featuring dive brakes on the upper and lower surfaces, boosted controls, cockpit pressurization, and an ejection seat. For the 14,000-pound gross weight jet, North American would accept a guarantee for 582 mph at 10,000 feet, predicted 750-mile range, and 46,500-foot ceiling. Armament was a battery of six .50-cal. machine guns in the nose. Although the Air Forces were seeking more than 600 mph, and the North American design was not markedly different from the XP-84, it addressed some problems with the early

North American reworked its Navy XFJ-1 Fury jet fighter with sleeker lines to meet a 1944 Army Air Forces requirement. However, predictions suggested the straight-wing XP-86 (concept model shown) offered little over what was already in development elsewhere. Substitution of swept surfaces promised markedly improved performance, as pursued post war. (San Diego Aerospace Museum)

jets and moved them another step forward as multi-role combat aircraft. It was worth an investment and so the Army contracted on 18 May 1945 for two XP-86 prototypes (MX-673) and a static article.

The XP-86 mockup inspection occurred in June 1945 and detailed design was progressing rapidly. However, North American understood the aircraft offered little over the XP-84 and saw bleak production prospects. In June, NACA contacted NAA and urged examination of the swept-wing research data then becoming available from captured German documents and personnel interviews.[3] This was provided in July and August, and project aerodynamicist Larry P. Greene quickly perceived a means of delaying compressibility effects and achieving 652 mph.

The Army Air Forces consented on 14 August to a four-month delay for new design studies. The XP-86 wing was soon changed with 35-degree leading-edge sweep back and outboard automatic leading-edge slats to reduce adverse stall effects associate with sweep. The Me 262 had 18.5-degrees sweep with slats, although the sweep was initially introduced to address center of gravity concerns and offered few compressibility benefits.[4] The resulting Sabre flew in October 1947 and would become the new U.S. Air Force's first swept-wing fighter, the first to achieve supersonic speeds in a dive, and went on to fame in Korean combat as the F-86.*

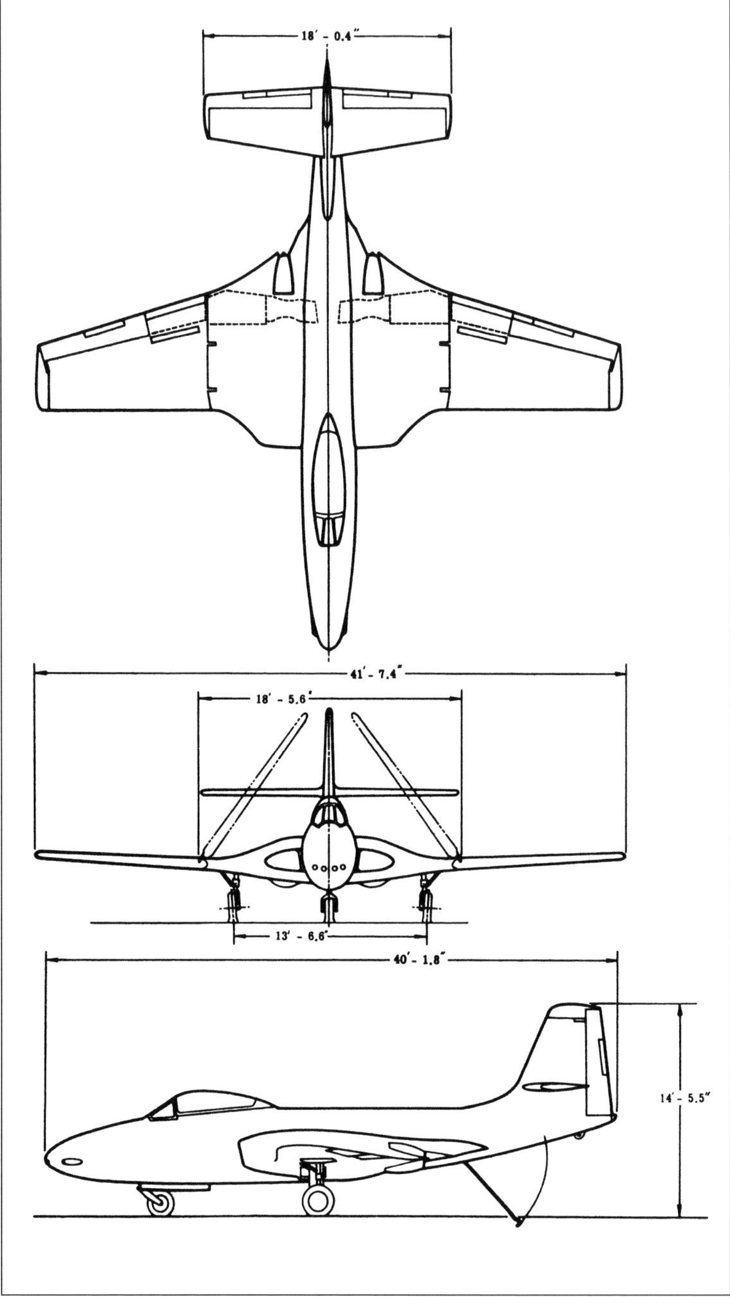

To keep jet fighter development progressing, the Navy sought another design in fall 1944. McDonnell responded with an evolution of the Phantom with J34 engines. The XF2D-1, shown here in a program 3-view, came together only after the war. (U.S. Navy)

** The Pursuit "P" prefix was supplanted by the Fighter "F" within the Air Forces on 11 June 1948.*

Literally in the last days of the war, the Army Air Forces drafted requirements for a penetration fighter of 630 mph maximum speed and 2,000-mile reach. The velocity bespoke a jet with swept wings that would make the range a challenge to attain. The McDonnell XP-88 and Lockheed XP-90 projects were begun in answer to the Invitation to Bid that emerged only after the end of hostilities.

Navy Strides (XF2D-1, XFJ-1, XF6U-1)

While the XFD-1 was coming together, the Navy decided to pursue a second design to offer an alternative in the event the McDonnell aircraft did not pan out. It also offered an opportunity to get

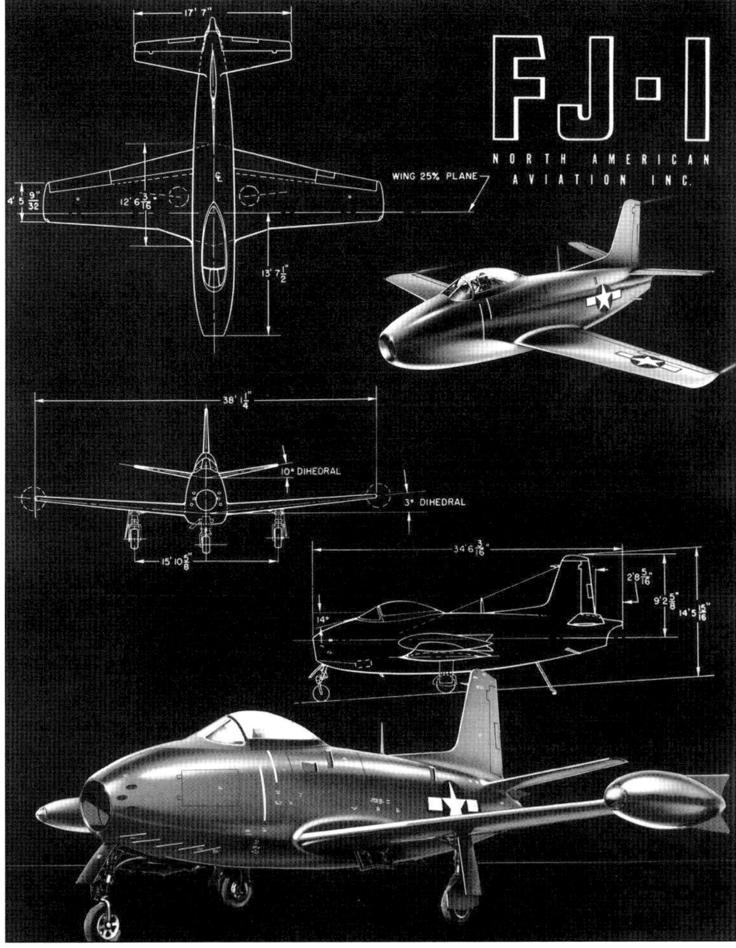

Another of the late-war Navy jet fighter projects was the North American FJ-1 Fury with the J35. Showing an evolution in design, the nose intake appeared with this model. It was ordered into production in the last months of the conflict, but metal was cut only afterwards. (San Diego Aerospace Museum)

other manufacturers involved in the new challenges of jets and provide a reservoir of talent for future naval aircraft development. Consequently, BuAer issued a new RFP on 5 September 1944 to eight firms for a carrier-based fighter with proposals due by October. Concepts were to employ the 3,000-lbf J34. There were four respondents.

One respondent to the new RFP was McDonnell, offering an advanced version of the Phantom it had barely begun testing. This looked too good to pass up, and a 22 March 1945 order went out for three XF2D-1s (Bunos. 99858/60). Project Engineer Herman D. Barkey's team essentially enlarged the Phantom with J34 turbojets. The mockup was inspected toward the end of April. The postwar slow-down meant construction did not begin until January 1946 and the aircraft flew in January 1947. The design was eventually produced as the very successful F2H-1 Banshee. In its initial mature form, the jet had ranging radar in the nose, a top speed of 586 mph at sea level, 7,300-fpm rate of climb, and 1,278-mile range.

North American's October 1944 proposal included the NA-134 with the 3,820-lbf J35-GE-2. The Navy favored this design as insurance against the J34 not measuring up. Three XFJ-1 Fury prototypes (Bunos. 39053/5) were ordered on New Year's Day. The Navy placed an order for 100 FJ-1s (NA-141) on 28 May 1945 before construction, and the war ended well before a prototype had taken shape. The quantity was subsequently trimmed to 30. A squadron would go to sea with the type as the service's first jet unit serving under operational conditions.

Dimensions of the FJ-1 included a 32.3-foot span, and 34.4-foot length. Gross weight was 14,386 pounds and a maximum sea level speed of 535 mph was eventually demonstrated. With its nose intake, the aircraft appeared much like the second-generation jets that were to follow. Speedbrakes in the non-folding wing were moved to the fuselage bottom in production examples. Addressing engine removal, North American opted for top extraction with a crane after a large fuselage panel was set aside. This was cumbersome aboard ship. Armed with six .50-cal. "hole punchers," this was the last use of machine guns in any U.S. Navy fighter.

Vought offered its V-340 in the fall 1944 competition. The Navy ordered the development of three prototypes (Bunos. 33532/4) as the XF6U-1 Pirate on 29 December with the J34-WE-22. The mockup was inspected in mid-January 1945. As originally envisioned the jet spanned 32.8 feet and of equal length, grossed out at 9,306 pounds, and with expected top speed of 530 mph.

Project Engineer Russ Clark and his team started with a fairly conventional design, but cutting-edge features were soon introduced. Wing-root intakes fed the engine that exhausted under the aft fuselage. With maintenance simplicity a goal, the initial engine installation was accessed by removing aft fuselage bottom panels and lowering the engine onto a dolly via a pulley system at the top of the engine bay. The unusually short span wings did not need to fold,

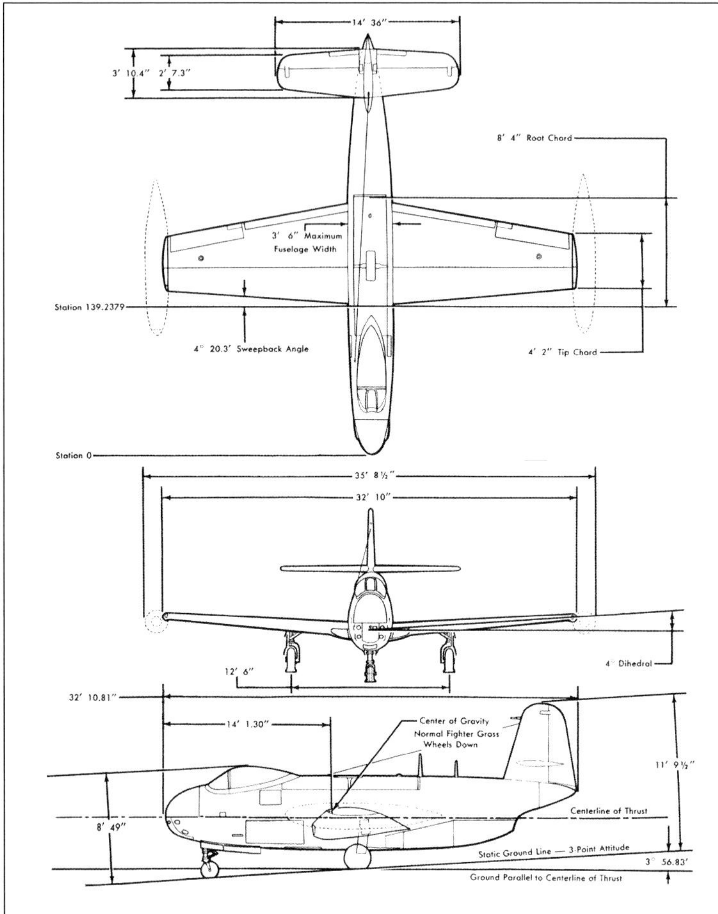

The third naval jet fighter project initiated in the last year of the war was the Vought XF6U-1 with the J34. Note the intent from the first to install wing tip tanks, but many other changes would intrude before the aircraft entered fleet service. (Vought Aircraft Heritage Foundation)

The XF6U-1 also had wing root inlets and a conventional full-bodied layout. It is seen here in mockup form on 17 January 1945. It flew only after the war, but had a frustrating battle with weight growth and deficient power. (Naval Aviation Archives)

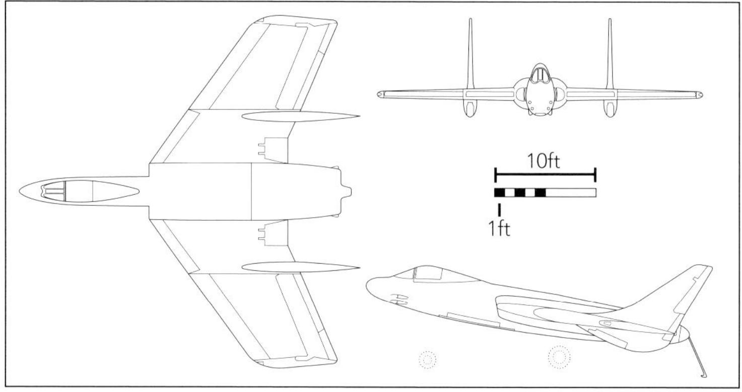

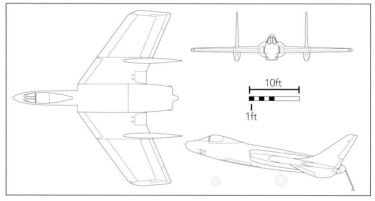

The Navy's reach for a 600-mph jet fighter in the final months of the war brought compressibility concerns to the foreground. Vought's solutions included a tailless, swept wing design with twin J34s fitted with afterburners. The design won funding after the war and came to fruition as the XF7U-1. (Author)

these with slotted Fowler flaps and hydraulically boosted ailerons. The horizontal stabilizer was mounted a third of the way up the fin to avoid the jet efflux. Armament was four 20mm cannons coupled to a Mk 6 Mod 1 fire control system with gyroscopic lead computing sight. The fuselage skin was Vought's innovative Metalite. A fiberglass/balsa sandwich called Fabrilite was employed in the empennage and molded fiberglass for the intakes.

On VJ-Day, the first XF6U-1 was still in gestation and did not fly until October 1946. It was February 1947 before the Navy ordered 30 F6U-1s, but the design continued to evolve. Among the most noteworthy changes were automatic dive brakes to preclude entering Mach buffet, cockpit pressurization and ejection seat, and the first afterburner on an American jet.[5] However, with a 2,000-pound weight growth, the Pirate was still underpowered. It ultimately proved a disappointment with 518 mph at sea level and 429 mph at 22,000 feet, and possessed some remaining hazardous flight characteristics. It so lacked adequate power that several ran off the end of runways during hot-day takeoffs.

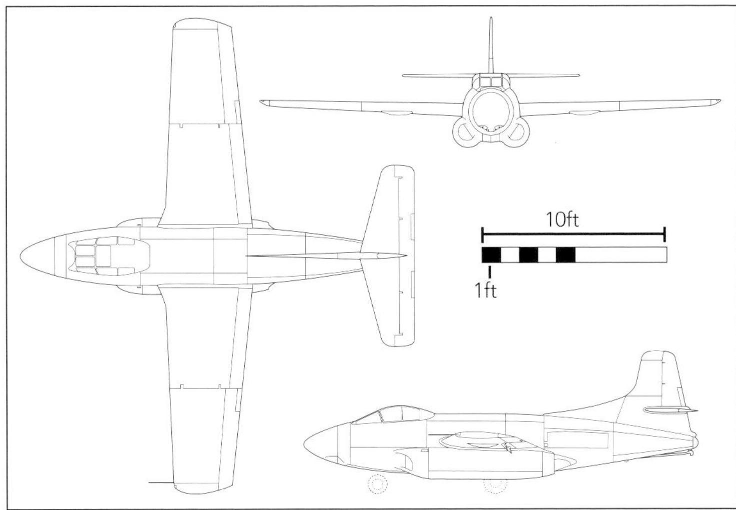

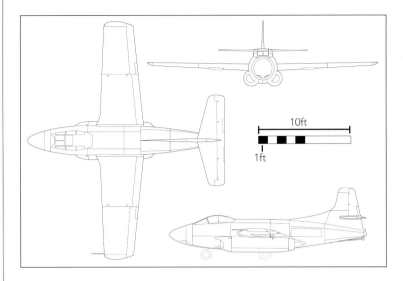

This large, two-seat night fighter was conceived by Douglas for the U.S. Navy as the war wrapped up. Carrier-based, it was to operate up to 40,000 feet and 500 mph while carrying a capable radar. It came to fruition postwar as the XF3D-1. (Author)

Both Vought and its customer learned much from the F6U-1 experience, and this would be applied to the company's next naval jet. A design team began work in June 1945 to meet a Navy requirement for a fighter capable of 600 mph at 40,000 feet. All concepts had swept wings addressing compressibility. Most startling was the V-346A's tailless configuration with low aspect ratio wing, leading edge slots, and twin afterburning J34s. Vought arrived at the design before German swept-wing research data had reached the U.S. aeronautical industry.[6] The Navy was leery of swept wings, fearing they would require higher takeoff and landing speeds incompatible with early war carriers. However, by the time the Vought concepts were first shown to BuAer in October 1945, the German research material lent the service enough confidence in swept-wing technology and they went for Vought's tailless concept during a 1946 competition.

The aircraft came to fruition as the F7U-1 Cutlass and was produced in quantity as the F7U-3. Its record would be a mixed one, but its beginning in summer 1945 showed the readiness of American designers to innovate even with the new jet technology, and the willingness of the armed forces to accept such risks.

In the closing days of the war, the Navy formulated a need for a carrier-based, all-weather, night fighter capable of detecting enemy aircraft at 125 miles and engaging at a maximum 500 mph at 40,000 feet. This suggested a large aircraft and second crewman as operator for the radar equipment of the period. Responses to this requirement were only forwarded after the war and led to the Douglas XF3D-1 Skyknight.

Over-Exuberance

Beating & Mixing (XF15C-1, XF2R-1, XP-81)

Two years after the FR-1 program was initiated, the Navy sought another composite fighter. The desired combination was the 2,700-lbf J36 and R-2800-34W delivering 2,100 hp with single-stage supercharger turning a four-blade Hamilton Standard propeller. The chosen proposal was the Curtiss Model 99, a design dating from the last quarter of 1943.

By mutual consent, the Navy cancelled the moribund XF14C-2 and Curtiss began the new project. Working long hours, Project Engineer Fred Steele and his design team submitted their design by Christmas. A trio of prototype XF15C-1s (Bunos. 01213/5) were ordered on 7 April 1944.[7] The development work had continued during negotiations, allowing the mockup to be ready for inspection the day after contract award.

Much larger than the FR-1, the XF15C-1 was intended for the new Midway-class carriers. The aircraft was of fairly conventional design, save for the jet engine installation in the belly. The short exhaust duct ended under a shallow aft fuselage that extended as a boom to the tail, reducing weight. Advanced features included the latest NACA low-drag cowling and laminar flow airfoil wing, double-slotted flaps, bubble canopy, and optimal cockpit layout with side consoles based on Navy research. BuAer also pressed Curtiss to utilize the new 75ST aluminum alloy, which the manufacturer did in the interest of weight savings. Armament would be four 20mm cannons in the wings.

Like the Fireball, the intakes for the turbojet were in the wing-root leading edges, the air following two serpentine paths to the bifurcated compressor face. Also like the FR-1, a common petroleum-based fuel fed both engines, ensuring operational flexibility and helping meet range requirements. There were reportedly plans to substitute a different engine should production be approved, probably because of J36 delivery concerns.

Because the jet engine was new to Curtiss and would rely upon airstarts while burning fuel other than kerosene, the company sought an engine testbed. The Navy lent the firm the XTBF-3 (Buno. 24141) to be modified in spring 1944 with the J36 in a belly nacelle for flight tests. Two inlets under the forward fuselage fed the engine. The first Goblin engine was delivered from Britain and operated satisfactorily in ground tests on the Avenger during November 1944, flight following in December.

After taxi and short hops on 27 February 1945, Lloyd Child flew the XF15C-1 the following day in Buffalo. The flight was made without the turbojet, as planned. Unplanned was the substitution of an R-2800-22W for the delayed -34W. From the beginning, it was clear work was required to optimize the flight controls. The turbojet was first flown on 3 May. Tragically, the aircraft was lost with

The Curtiss XF15C-1 began in the last months of 1943 to provide the Navy a powerful composite aircraft, mixing turbine and reciprocating engines as a step beyond the Fireball. It became enormous in size for a single-seat, carrier-based aircraft. (Naval Aviation Archives)

From the first flight of the XF15C-1 on 28 February 1945 it was evident there was much work to be done. Combating controllability difficulties, the horizontal stabilizer was moved to the top of the fin, a dorsal extension added, the tail boom deepened, and the rudder extended down. (San Diego Aerospace Museum)

pilot Charles Cox five days later, during its 23rd flight, from fuel starvation owing to a faulty valve.

The second XF15C-1 prototype took up testing on 9 July with the intended Pratt & Whitney and Allis-Chalmers-delivered J36. Work continued in resolving the control issues and, in line with this, Curtiss introduced a revised empennage configuration with a dorsal extension and moved the horizontal stabilizer to the top of the enlarged tail.

Curtiss XF15C-1 characteristics:

span	48.0 ft	weight empty	12,648 lbs
length	44.0 ft	overload	18,698 lbs
height	15.3 ft	speed, max. (25,300 ft)	373 mph (Recip.)
wing area	400 ft^2	(25,300 ft)	469 mph (both eng.)
fuel capacity (int. + ext.)	368+150 gal	cruise	163 mph
service ceiling	41,800 ft	range, normal	635 mi
initial climb rate (both engines)	5,020 fpm	maximum	1,385 mi

The XFR-4 improved on the Fireball by substituting a J34 and replacing the wing-root inlets with the flush NACA inlets seen in the forward fuselage (postwar photo). The shape of the inlet induced flow into the opening. Ryan designed doors that could close-off the inlets for drag reduction. (San Diego Aerospace Museum)

The Curtiss project continued after VJ-Day with the third aircraft added, but things were already looking grim given the intractable control problems and the tail retrofit. A Navy Preliminary Evaluation during October-December still found much room for improvement despite continuing changes to the design.

Although the fighter showed promise and even the Army Air Forces evaluated the XF15C-1, time ran out for Curtiss. The smaller Fireball had already been produced and entered service. Pure jet designs were by then clearly the way to go, and the project was cancelled in October 1946.

Another experimental Fireball incarnation was an FR-1 with 4,200-lbf J34 in back and the wing-root intakes replaced with new NACA-designed flush inlets in the forward fuselage. This XFR-4

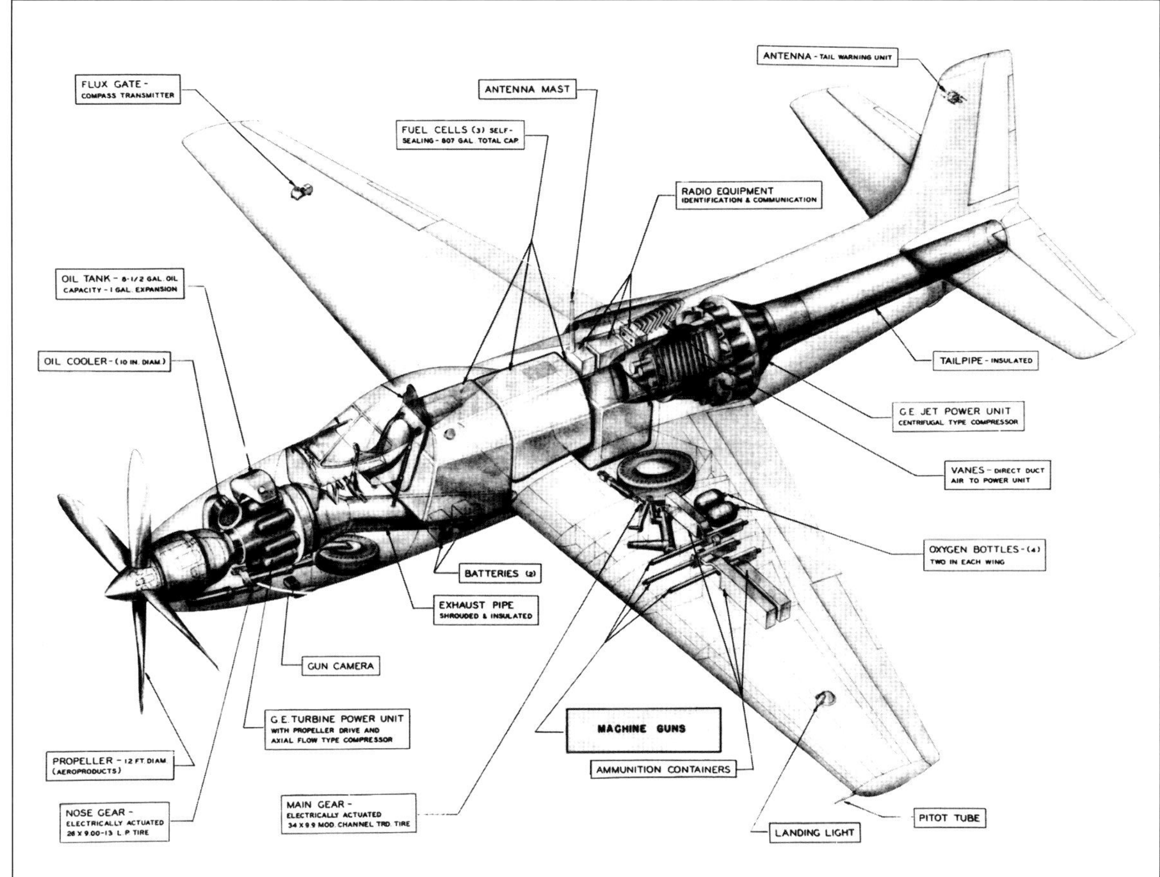

The Air Force sought its own composite fighter to extend range for escort duties. They contracted in early 1944 with Consolidated-Vultee to build the XP-81 with the T31 in the nose and J33 in the tail. This drawing emphasizes the features of the design. (San Diego Aerospace Museum)

(Model 28-5, Buno. 39665) had a fuselage lengthened 8 inches, the exhaust diameter increased, a taller tail introduced, and the wing leading edge straightened from tip to fuselage after eliminating the FR-1 intakes. The flush inlets could be closed by electrical doors to reduce drag, opening when the J34 start sequence was initiated. These were initially tested on an FR-1 in the Ames full-scale wind tunnel.[8]

With the General Electric turboprop finally emerging from the test cell, the Navy sought a single-place research aircraft with the turboprop in the nose and turbojet in the tail. Ryan won this contract and modified FR-1 39661 to create the XF2R-1 Darkshark (Model 29).* Still with the J31-GE-2 in back, the XT31-GE-2 in the nose gave 1,700 hp with an 11-foot diameter four-blade Hamilton Standard propeller plus 550-lbf exhaust thrust. The nose was lengthened four feet and the ventral extension increased.

Neither the XFR-4 or XF2R-1 reached the hardware stage until postwar.†

The Army Air Forces sought two XF2R-1s (Bunos. 39713/4, never consummated), possibly intended as contrast against a fighter with like propulsion layout the service already had in test.[9] This project stemmed from efforts to develop fighters with the range to

The turboprop proved more difficult to perfect than the turbojet, and it was near the end of the war before the General Electric TG-100 was ready for flight. Ryan converted a Fireball, with J31 still in the rear, to take the XT31 in the nose and become the XF2R-1 Darkshark. (Air Force Flight Test Center)

* *Although frequently referred to as "Dark Shark," the official form is uncertain.*

† *Several sources state the XFR-4 flew initially in November 1944. This appears too early in relationship to the FR-1 schedule, availability of the J34, and ongoing Ames tunnel testing. However, no official source has yielded a definitive date for the first flight.*

When General Electric fell behind in the T31 turboprop development, Convair turned to the V-1650-7 Merlin as a short-term substitute for the XP-81. This permitted the aircraft to begin flight test and uncover any general airframe issues. The Merlin installation is seen in this photo at Muroc. (San Diego Aerospace Museum)

The XP-81 initially flew in February 1945, and again at the end of the year with the T31. It exhibited the normal developmental problems. However, these were exacerbated by low power and high maintenance of the turboprop. The steady pace of changes and testing without getting a satisfactory state caused the program to flounder. (Tony Landis Collection)

escort B-29s to Japan and back. It was set forth in a summer 1943 requirement for a single-seat aircraft boasting 250-mph cruise and 500-mph maximum speed combined with 1,250-mile range, 37,500-foot ceiling, and 2,500-fpm climb at 27,500 feet.

To meet this extraordinary challenge, Consolidated-Vultee offered its Model 102 "twin" in September. This combined a 3,600-lbf J33-GE-5 turbojet in the tail with an XT31-GE-1 in the nose, its exhaust under the belly. This was a daring choice given the immaturity of the turbine engines at the time, particularly the "prop-jet," and their notoriously poor fuel economy. However, the turboprop was expected to give good cruise efficiency while the turbojet would be operated only for engagement speed and power. Six .50-cal. machine guns with 2,400 rounds or six 20mm cannons with 1,200 rounds were planned for wing installation. The Army Air Forces gave the firm a $3.7 million contract on 11 February 1944 for two prototype XP-81s (44-91000/1, MX-480 and later MX-796).

At the end of 1944, the first XP-81 was coming together under Downey engineers Charles R. Irving and Frank W. Davis. It had a loaded weight of 19,500 pounds, span of 50.5 feet, and 425-square-foot area. It also featured a pressurized cockpit, ejection seat, laminar-flow wing, and 752 gallons of internal tankage. Slipper tanks under the wing were tested and large tip tanks were considered.

With the GE "propeller turbine" lagging, Consolidated-Vultee (soon Convair) substituted a V-1650-7 of 1,490 hp up front, with a radiator duct under the forward fuselage. They could proceed with flight test and deal with any general airframe issues. The change was made in little more than a week. In this guise, Frank W. Davis initially flew the XP-81 on 7 February 1945. This permitted control system improvements and a directional stability problem to be addressed through extending the vertical stab and added ventral strake. The J33 tests included airstarts.

When the XT31-GE-1 was delivered on 11 June 1945 and flown in December 1945, the horsepower deficit already described meant it delivered little more than the Merlin. Although improvement got the J33 to 3,750 lbf, the aggregate was still disappointing. Oil cooling of the T31 was inadequate, the turbine wheel had to be replaced frequently, and the engine/propeller combination had a substantial lag in throttle response. The twin-turbine combination realized 492 mph against the predicted 507 at 30,000 feet, but had a range of 1,740 miles. The second aircraft featured some aerodynamic refinements that included NACA inlets in place of straight troughs ahead of the shoulder-mounted turbojet intakes, but propeller vibration and oil leaks plagued the testers. The XP-81 had no future.

In literally the last days of the war, 13 August 1945, the Navy initiated a project as a first step toward defining a nuclear attack role. It was to develop an attack aircraft with a 10,000-pound payload to carry one of the early atomic bombs. The winning postwar project became the North American AJ-1 Savage with an Allison J33-A-19 in the aft fuselage for the heavy weight takeoff and high-speed phases of flight, and should one of the two R-2800 piston engines fail. Once high thrust-to-weight turbojets and turboprops became available, this composite design option lost its few merits.

The XP-83 is shown at Bell in Buffalo on 8 February 1945. Note the original exhausts before they were lengthened and angled outboard. The alteration was done because this original design allowed the jet efflux to heat the aft fuselage excessively, requiring firemen to hose down the structure during engine runs. (National Archives)

Struggling to find a fast fighter capable of escorting B-29s over thousands of miles led Bell to offer what looked like a bloated P-59, stuffed with fuel cells. Ordered in early 1944, the XP-83 flew a year later. It came up short of desired performance and fell by the wayside. (Tony Landis Collection)

Bell XP-83 characteristics:			
span	53.0 ft	weight empty	14,105 lbs
length	44.8 ft	gross	24,090 lbs
height	15.3 ft	maximum	27,500 lbs
wing area	431 ft^2	speed, max. (15,660 ft)	522 mph
fuel capacity (int. +ext.)	1,150+600 gal	cruise	441 mph
service ceiling	45,000 ft	range, maximum	2,050 mi
initial climb rate	5,650 fpm		

Escort Challenge (XP-83, XP-85)

A large jet with layout similar to the P-59 was offered by Bell on 29 March 1943 as an interceptor, but revised in April to meet the Army Air Forces's B-29 escort need addressed by the XP-81. A second approach to the problem appeared wise, and two XP-83 prototypes (44-84990/1, Model 40, MX-511) were ordered on a $2.2 million contract issued on 24 March 1944.

The mockup was inspected in early June 1944. Its heritage with the P-59 was evident but had a bubble canopy, twin J33-GE-5 engines of 4,000 lbf, and greatly expanded fuel capacity. Refinements introduced by the team led by Bob Woods and Charles Rhodes included flush riveting, a laminar flow wing, horizontal stabilizer rotation for trim, and cockpit pressurization. Armament was to be six .50s with 300 rpg and external stores on two 1,000-pound capacity hardpoints. Hydraulic aileron boost and Fowler flaps were also adopted.

Initial engine runs found the jet efflux heated the aft fuselage and caused buckling, requiring the fire department to constantly spray water onto the structure. Jet pipe extensions were soon fitted to direct the flow slightly outboard. Jack Woolams conducted the maiden flight of the XP-83 at Niagara Falls on 25 February 1945. The second example flew in October with revised windscreen and canopy. The nose had been extended 8 inches for six .60-cal. machine guns, and the vertical stabilizer and rudder were extended 18 inches to improve directional stability. Data found the renamed XF-83 fell short of maneuverability expectations and performance, the latter due partially to J33 thrust deficiencies and 1,500 to 2,000 pounds overweight structure. The Air Forces had lost interest by the end of 1945.

The problem of escort fighters for long-range bombers appeared intractable when it came to the intercontinental behemoths being conceived at the end of 1942. For missions potentially lasting more than a day, a fighter might be so heavy with fuel and the pilot so fatigued, even at the mid-point, that engaging in aerial combat was unreasonable. The poor fuel economy of the early jet engines worked against the desire to employ a jet escort.

The Army Air Forces examined the problem under project MX-472 Unconventional Fighter Escort beginning in December 1942. This concluded a "parasite" fighter was the best solution.[10] The idea envisioned launching a few small, remotely controlled drones powered by ramjet engines, but this was beyond the state of the art. Only a manned aircraft seemed potentially feasible. The bomber could carry its escort with it as a small aircraft that would detach from and then return to the "mother ship." With the XB-36 intercontinental bomber growing close to realization, the parasite fighter requirement was finally issued on 20 January 1944.

Only McDonnell Aircraft responded in autumn 1944 with four Model 27 concepts. To partially nestle the tiny fighter within the bomb bay of the B-29, B-35, and B-36 required an unusual design. The Army Air Forces then decided the aircraft must fit entirely

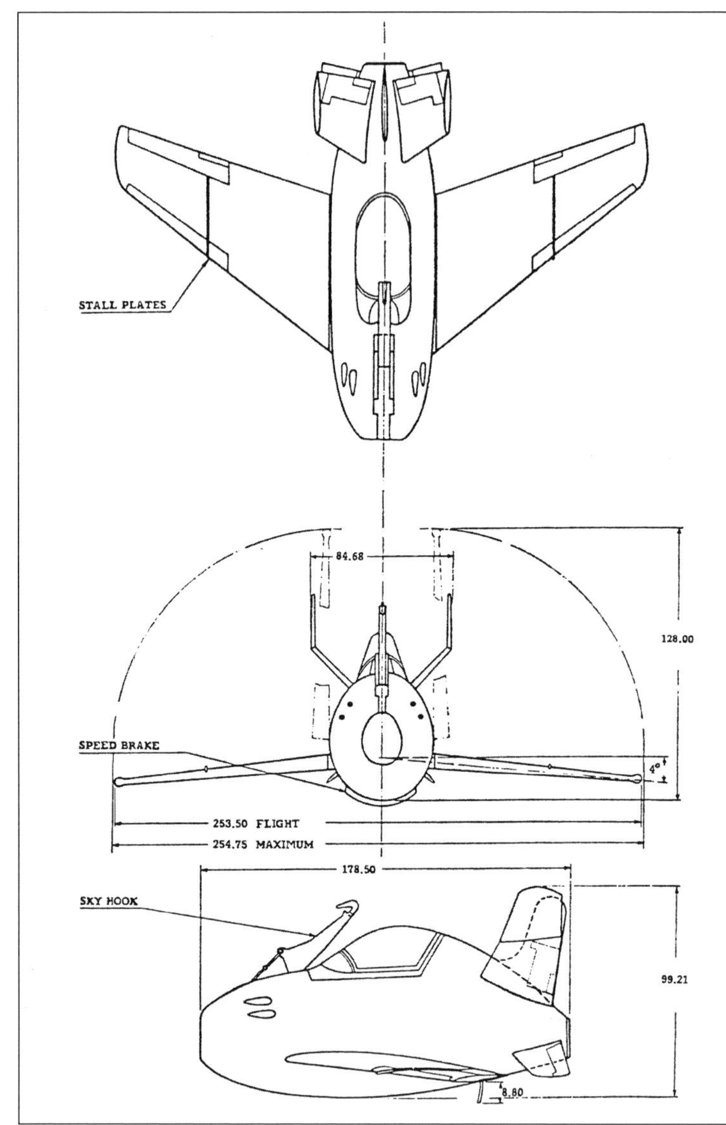

Facing a daunting problem in creating a long-endurance escort capability for the intercontinental B-36, the Army Air Forces conceived a parasite fighter that would fit in the bomb bay. The tiny XP-85 jet, sans undercarriage, featured folding wings and nose hook as shown in this program drawing. (National Archives)

within the B-36, dictating dimensional limits of just 15 feet in length and 5.5 feet in width, sending the McDonnell team back to the drawing board in January 1945. They returned on 19 March with the Model 27DE, which looked much like the final design.

The tiny egg-shaped fuselage packed four .50-cal. guns, compact multi-element tail surfaces, and a folding wing swept at 37 de-

The "parasite fighter" for bomber escort protection is seen in mockup form in June 1946. McDonnell's XP-85 solution had folding wings (seen here prior to addition of wingtip vertical surfaces) and is suspended on a hook and trapeze extending from the mocked-up B-36 bomb bay. (Tony Landis Collection)

grees – another swept-wing American design that had not relied upon German research. The envisioned powerplant was the 3,000-lbf J34-WE-7 axial-flow turbojet for the little aircraft that ultimately grossed 5,600 pounds and could fly to 581 mph at 35,000 feet, albeit with fuel for only 32 minutes. It was to have an ejection seat and pressurized cockpit, a perforated speedbrake under the fuselage, and an enormous hook projecting from the nose substituting for landing gear. The aircraft would be lowered from the bay, engine started, and then unhook to engage the enemy. At the end of the combat, the fighter would rejoin and hook onto the trapeze arrangement, shutdown, and be raised into the bomber.

Although the Army Air Forces were pleased with the design they labeled the XP-85 (MX-667), little more was done before the end of hostilities. However, interest remained and McDonnell received a contract in October 1945. The very inventive design was eventually carried to flight test as the XF-85 Goblin, the first sortie in August 1948, detaching from and recovering to a trapeze rig under an EB-29B. However, a combination of pilot difficulties engaging the trapeze, funding shortfalls, and continuing evolution of air warfare tactics led the curious project to be shelved.

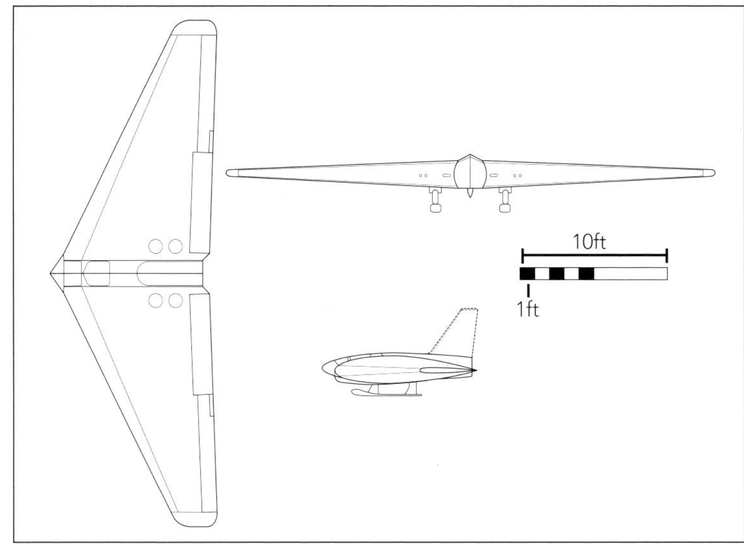

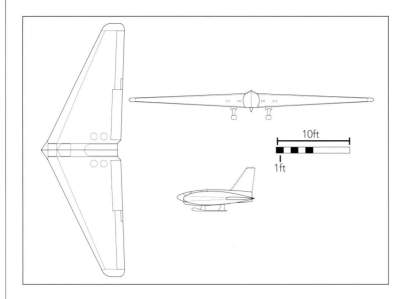

This three-view drawing of the XP-79 combines features of the original proposal drawing, the mockup, and how it might have been envisioned at the time of cancellation. The vertical tail would ultimately have been necessary. Note the skid landing gear and gun ports of the four .50-cal. machine guns. (Author)

Rocket Option (MX-324, MX-334, XP-79, XP-79B)

American firms developed rocket motors suitable for aircraft propulsion during World War II. These had the advantage of performance being independent of altitude in that they carried their own oxidizer for combustion. Solid propellants for artillery rockets were well established during the war, but solid or liquid propellant engines for aircraft propulsion required considerably more refinement.

Aerojet Engineering of Azusa, California, pursued solid propellants. The company grew from a group of academics investigating booster rockets that would assist the takeoff of overweight aircraft or affect a normal-weight takeoff in a shorter distance. The team included respected aerodynamicist Dr. Theodore von Kármán who had previously discussed booster rockets with Gen. Arnold.[11] The endeavor had some Army funding and soon yielded the 1,000-lbf 12AS-1000 D-1 Jet-Assisted Take-Off (JATO) motor. The Army wanted the team to produce these units, so they incorporated in January 1942.

Aerojet soon delved into liquid-propellant motors mixing monoethylaniline (aniline) and red fuming nitric acid oxidizer that combust spontaneously. Initially tested during February 1942, it was first developed as a booster pack. Aerojet also sought throttleable motors that could serve as aircraft propulsion. The XCALR-2000A employed two primary combustion chambers of 750 lbf each and a pair of auxiliary chambers generating 250 lbf each. The chambers of the "Rotojet" were oriented about the horizontal axis, but canted

The XP-79's prone-pilot flying wing required cautious analysis and testing, prompting a test program with flying mockups. The MX-334 glider with skids and trolley is seen on the Muroc lakebed with towlines attached. Also evident are the support wires for the simple fin added to improve stability. (Gerald Balzer Collection)

such as to rotate as a unit and contribute propellant pumping action through centrifugal force.

With the Army Air Forces' interest in high-speed interceptors well known, Jack Northrop offered a tailless rocket plane on 15 September 1942 as an unsolicited proposal. The earliest idea was for the Model 14 Jet-Driven Interceptor as an expendable point-defense fighter. Once the rocket and kinetic energy had been expended, and the mission completed, explosives would blow the ship apart and the pilot recovered via parachute. The concept included a novel prone pilot position that research suggested would permit the pilot to tolerate greater maneuvering g-forces than a conventionally seated pilot. It also allowed for smaller aircraft frontal and side area to reduce drag and vulnerability to enemy gunners. The aircraft was expected to achieve 540 mph and take 6.1 minutes to reach 40,000 feet, with a 454-mile range. Probably with some sponsorship of Northrop's friend Dr. von Kármán, who had the ear of Gen. Arnold, the Army Air Forces showed interest.

The concept was so radical that Materiel Division insisted three MX-324 mockups be created for wind tunnel and flight testing, collecting data to reduce technical risk. Northrop was so saturated with work that, beginning on 1 November 1942, the Engineering Division at Wright Field assumed responsibility for much of the analysis and drawing preparation. This ran a bit late and the project fell behind schedule. Northrop built these Model N-12 aircraft primarily of plywood over a steel tube centersection frame. Testing of the MX-324 would include glides and flight propelled by rocket motor.

Much to Jack Northrop's frustration, analysis and full-scale wind tunnel testing of the MX-324 made clear the aircraft required a stabilizing vertical surface. The offending appendage was added without rudder, held erect with guy wires. The aircraft possessed the basic flying wing controls. Elevons operated symmetrically with

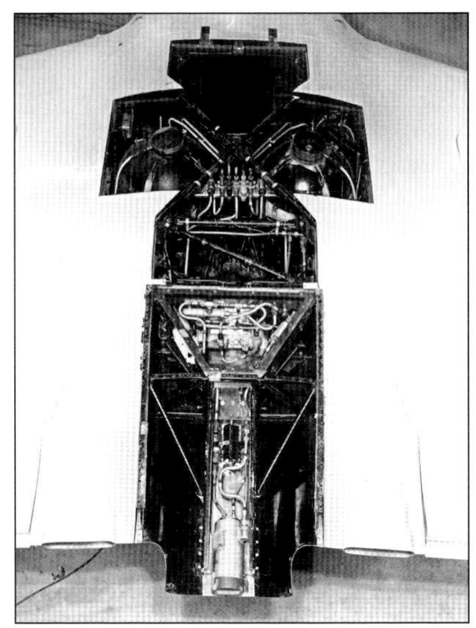

The Rotojet rocket motor was to deliver 2,000 lbf for the XP-79. For initial flight trials, only one of the four thrust chambers was installed as the XCALR-200A seen installed in the MX-324. The pilot couch is visible, his legs extending back on either side of the engine's centerline components. (Gerald Balzer Collection)

The MX-324 fixed landing gear had broad pants adding to directional stability. Inserted is the only known image of the aircraft under power – a lot of action for a little push. The meager 200 lbf was enough to reduce rate of descent and to check handling qualities with thrust. (San Diego Aerospace Museum and Gerald Balzer Collection)

fore-aft motion of the pilot's control bar producing pitch, and asymmetrically with differential motion of the bar for roll. Leading edge slats were added near the tips to improve elevon roll effectiveness as stall was approached. Further inboard, combination rudders/speedbrakes ("brudders") split to rotate both above and below the wing for directional control. Force to deploy the brudders was provided by bellows fed by ram air from intakes under the wing root leading edges and modulated by pilot pedals. Even means of supporting and counterbalancing the pilot's head under g-loading had to be devised. The MX-324's wings spanned 36 feet with 252 square feet of area and a 21.8-degree sweep, had a root chord of 11.3 feet (aircraft length), and flight weights of 2,600 to 2,800 pounds.

The MX-324 gliders began flight testing, towed aloft by a modified P-38, on 27 August 1943 from dry lakes in the Mojave Desert. The unpowered craft were soon redesignated MX-334. It was an instructive and eventful program. Starting with landing skids, the team installed a droppable undercarriage, and finally fixed gear. The flights found stability and controllability problems that were addressed through a number of design changes, including eliminating the slats. Three different fin sizes were flight tested. The MX-334s completed 13 flights through 19 May 1944 with speeds reaching 300 mph in dives, most free-flight lasting five to eight minutes of busy test maneuvers. Accidents claimed one glider and the others were damaged.

Because the Aerojet motor was not ready, the number two MX-324 "Rocket Wing" was modified with just one 200-lbf chamber (designated XCALR-200A) that was secured with the pilot's legs straddling the unit. It was not throttleable and had just a five-minute burn time. The installation of propellant cells, pressurization tanks, and electrical gear added 427 pounds to the glider's weight. The propellants were separated by the cockpit, one component in each wing. Accidental mixing of these fuels or contact with the pilot had to be prevented at all costs, so neoprene shields separate the center section from the tanks.

Harry Crosby first employed the motor in flight on 5 July 1944 after a tow to 15,000 feet, becoming America's first rocket plane. The modest thrust simply extended the glide. Eight glide and seven powered flights through 27 July were conducted, the highest weight being 3,476 pounds and the aircraft towed aloft each time.

The main fighter development project, three prototype XP-79s (43-52437/9, MX-365), was initiated on 12 January 1943. The XP-79 mockup was inspected in June 1943. At a loaded weight of 11,400 pounds, the aircraft was to be powered by the 2,000-lbf Aerojet motor with 8,400 pounds of propellant onboard permitting 35.5-minutes endurance. The aircraft was expected to be assisted aloft with two to six JATO units, dropped after takeoff, providing near-zero takeoff distance. Retractable landing skids were planned, so takeoff would have used a droppable trolley or other means. The XP-79 was to be armed with four .50-cal. guns and 200 to 250 rpg.

Because of the belief that the prone pilot could withstand high g-forces, the aircraft was stressed for ±18 g. The wings were to contain rocket engine fuel tanks, aniline and oxidizer tanks in each semi-span, and separated by gun bays. Any tank penetration by an enemy round could have proven catastrophic. Consequently, the tapered-wing skin thickness was as much as three-quarters of an inch, with one-quarter-inch steel armor plating behind the leading edge. The wing was particularly clean as it was made of welded magnesium – chosen as a non-strategic material.

The prone pilot position planned for the XP-79 created control system design challenges. The pilot had to lie comfortably, chin resting on a pad, the legs and arms free (yet not tiring) to maintain on the controls. The XP-79B cockpit is shown with the chin rest removed. (Gerald Balzer Collection)

With the Aerojet rocket motor failing to materialize, the XP-79 was redesigned as a jet fighter with twin J30 engines. The airframe was revised to a conventional aluminum aircraft structure but retained the control methodology developed during the MX-324 and MX-334 testing. The aircraft is seen at Northrop's Hawthorne facility. (Gerald Balzer Collection)

The XP-79B was completed and being prepared for flight when the war ended. Visible is the quadracycle landing gear, twin fins, and wingtip cavities for the "brudder" bellows. The first flight ended in a fatal crash that terminated the project. (San Diego Aerospace Museum)

Because of the aircraft's great structural strength, someone at Wright Field or in Northrop marketing conceived the notion of the XP-79 being employed as a "flying ram." This would have had the pilot intentionally colliding with enemy aircraft to cut through light aluminum empennages with the XP-79's tough wing. It was impractical and never seriously considered, although there was a project MX-78 with such an objective.[12]

The XP-79 was not to be. Aerojet had difficulties perfecting the XCALR-2000A motor. Delivery slipped repeatedly from 30 September 1943 to a first flight no earlier than 15 April 1945. By June 1944, Aerojet confessed its problems would not be solved anytime soon. Consequently, this aspect of the program was terminated in September 1944. The need for a point-defense interceptor had long passed.

An alternative was already in the works. With good progress being made on the Westinghouse 19B turbojet, the contract was altered in March 1943 to have the first prototype fitted with a pair of these engines as the XP-79B (NS-14, MX-365). Working with thick magnesium had proven very difficult, so the XP-79B was changed to a more conventional aluminum structure. It retained the general layout of the MX-324, but engine nacelles were buried in the wing roots on either side of the pilot compartment, and quadracycle landing gear retracted into the nacelles. The brudder bellows were enlarged and placed in wingtip cavities. The flying wing spanned 38.0 feet with 278-square foot of area, yet was just 14 feet long and stood just 4.8 feet to top of the fuselage. Gross weight was 8,559 pounds with 300-gallons of fuel, and it was expected to have a top speed of 547 mph at sea level, 508 mph at 25,000 feet, and 993-mile range.

The XP-79B was completed in June 1945 and trucked to Muroc where the J30 engines were installed in mid August. Following taxi trials, preparations for flight were well in hand when Japan surrendered. The maiden sortie was made on 12 September. The aircraft flew normally for 15 minutes and Crosby appeared to grow confident. He entered a slow roll that steepened into a vertical spin. Crosby bailed out at 2,000 feet but was struck and killed by the aircraft during descent and never opened his parachute. The Army Air Forces cancelled further XP-79B work.

The Navy had also performed early work with booster rockets. By January 1945, seeking an answer to the kamikaze threat and with access to early information on Germany's Me 163 rocket fighter, BuAer had performed preliminary design work for two rocket fighters and was shopping around for prospective manufacturers. The matter did not advance far before the end of the war.[13]

Chapter 13

The enormous production capacity of the United States was ramped up to a war footing and the country eventually manufactured 100,000 fighters. The busy production and test flying activities across the country was unprecedented, an example being this North American Aviation operation in Los Angeles with P-51Ds. (National Museum of the United States Air Force)

CONCLUSION BUT ADVANCEMENT

Transformation

At the start of World War II, the United States ranked with the world leaders in aviation design, development, and manufacturing. However, it had some catching up to do in matching foreign fighter aircraft. The run-up to war and the first two years during which America remained on the sidelines allowed rapid growth in the industry to meet this challenge as the economy and infrastructure was mobilized for total war. This process was still underway when the nation joined the fight, with superior fighters just emerging. However, the quantity and technology gap was rapidly closing.

In just a few short years, American production capacity exceeded that of any other combatant nation. Plant floor space, tooling and other capital investment, and personnel grew manifold with 1.25 million people employed in aviation by 1945. The move to aircraft mass-production was remarkable by contrast to prewar capacity. By the close of hostilities, half the country's industrial output was supporting the war effort. This was not without a few impediments, despite careful management of resources. The United States was also advantaged in not being bombed, relying on slave labor, being embargoed to any significant extent, or being led by irresponsible leaders. The prodigious industrial capacity, backed by strong national will, produced generally excellent weapons in an astonishingly short time and in overwhelming numbers. The United States built nearly 300,000 warplanes during the war, including 100,000 fighters; more than all other countries combined. The results were excellent if not elegant. They greatly facilitated resolving a war that changed the course of world history.

The experience level of the military agencies and industrial teams increased tremendously during the few years of war. Compared with prewar activities, aviation development projects were accomplished in a fraction of the time. By the end, new and advanced models were being created quickly and with greater likelihood of success owing to the considerable expertise. Lockheed's performance on the P-80 contracts is a sterling example.

The war accelerated trends already evident, such as expanded subcontractor work and international sales. The industry also tended to become divided between "Army contractors" and "Navy contractors," a state of affairs that would persist for decades. The industry expanded with new manufacturers and spin-offs of large concerns. There were also "casualties" such as Brewster, with Curtiss following close behind.

By the latter half of 1944, it was clear that persistence and the weapons at hand or in the pipeline would decide the war's outcome. Consequently, many of the more ambitious fighter projects began to be cancelled or substantially reduced in scope. The close of hostilities found the United States with far more fighters than would be needed in peacetime, and many more on the way. Orders were slashed and hundreds of brand new aircraft immediately disposed of. Within weeks of VJ-Day the axe had fallen on most of the remaining aircraft development projects. Just a few continued as research efforts or in sustaining postwar defense, but at a much slowed paced.

Influence

The United Kingdom had a significant influence on the American aviation industry and technology insertion in new military projects throughout the course of the war. Having been at the tough struggle two years before the United States came aboard, the Brits had much advice and examples to share. A close relationship was fostered between the nations that soon became allies in the mammoth struggle.

British cash and lend-lease aircraft orders were enormous, greatly bolstering the remarkable growth of the American industry. All told, deliveries totaled approximately 40,000 aircraft. The Americans also acquired a considerable portion of Great Britain's liquid wealth, helping fund its own war production. The industry's readiness to support urgent national requirements, when the United States entered the conflict, was aided through infusion of hard-won Anglo combat lessons into American designs.

The technological exchange was invaluable to both nations. This was especially evident in radar, anti-submarine warfare, and jet engines. The Americans initially followed the British lead in tactics and required systems, building on British technology as required to suit particular requirements or for improvement. The Allies avoided duplication of effort where practical, and each combatant faced their own unique set of circumstances and needs. The American manufacturing capacity was again invaluable in providing British advanced systems, even with equipment built under license. Much of the hybrid technologies and American tactics became standard equipment and missions by war's end. Hence, the United States scored advances in meeting its commitments in some areas while its partner enjoyed other successes.

The willingness of Great Britain to share among its most advanced and secret aeronautical advances with the United States, during the period when each jet engine and radar was precious, was a symptom of the time. That country sought to cement a close commercial relationship with the nation providing ever more war resources that helped ensure its very survival. It also wanted to solidify the strategic partnership when the Americans inevitably entered the war. However, the interchange was mutually beneficial.

Evolution

The evolution of fighter aircraft in the few years of war was remarkable. Speed, range, ceiling, weapon load, and lethality increased tremendously. American types reflected this evolution as much as any nation's fighters, more so in some areas as the circumstances of United States combat needs dictated. As these requirements became clear and then morphed, changes were introduced into the aircraft at the factory and in the field, and then through development of entirely new types. The war years were particularly noted for rapid changes in design, with many remarkable aircraft coming and going in quick succession, and some missions and types disappearing altogether.

Changes in the course of the war and evolving tactics had an effect on the fortunes of many fighter projects. Among these were the combining of naval roles in new aircraft to reduce the number of types aboard aircraft carriers, and the demise of Army bomber-destroyers and dive-bombers. Rear gunners faded and powered turrets came and went during the few years of war. The importance of heavy and costly torpedoes dimmed, and were seldom carried by the last year of the war because of a paucity of targets and growing effectiveness of bombing. Most notably, both Navy and Army fighters began to take on more of the new fighter-bomber roles of close air support and interdiction. The bomber escort role rose to supreme importance, but its eventual demise was also seen by the end of the war with the advent of super bombers that promised flights beyond the practical limits of fighters and fighter pilots. Even the adoption of the other service's types and joint development programs was pursued; something that would have been unthinkable in pre-war.

Despite the remarkable evolution, lesser types had a role to play. As with air arms around the world, the Americans possessed first-, second-, and third-tier fighters. Types and models shifted within these tiers and all reflected changes over time to meet the shifting requirements of war, meeting enemy challenges, and seeking superiority. Most changes were incremental and introduced as missions evolved. For example, gun heaters or heated gun bays had to be added when aircraft began operating at very high-altitudes, preventing the freezing of oil and solenoids. More commonly evident themes included the introduction and then standardization of armor, self-sealing fuel tanks, computing gun sights, and the increasing number and caliber of guns. Cannons became more common, with 20mm and 37mm weapons introduced before the former appeared most practical by the end of the conflict. The quantity of internal and/or external stores progressively expanded, with a mix of fuel tanks and ordnance. Air-to-surface rockets were introduced and standardized, again following examples overseas.

Experience and evolving mission requirements bred marked improvements in communications, pressurization, oxygen and escape systems, and required greater emphasis on high altitude physiology. The need for night fighting and long-range navigation drove further instrument and avionics maturation, in addition to radar and fire control systems. The fighter aircraft and fighter pilot's job grew much more complex and challenging.

As was true with all the combatants, only a handful of engine models were the heart of the American fighter propulsion systems. Yet, engine power continued its increase. The signature radial engine was displaced in some types by inline powerplants, but this "competition" was becoming moot by the end of the war. Skills in cooling either species of engine had grown progressively, as had the improvements in altitude performance with the enhanced capabilities of supercharger and turbosupercharger systems, and with direct fuel injection. Twins slowly found a place among the single-engine fighters, although shipboard twins remained an elusive goal to the end. Yet, the push for greater speed had topped out. New and advanced engine designs continued to be problematic in the United States as elsewhere. All this indicated the pinnacle had been reached for reciprocating engines and propeller propulsion, with the Americans in the vanguard.

The growing American capabilities were adequate to the evolving tasks and rapidly became the best in many areas. By mid 1942, the country was beginning to field competitive and superior fighters with well-trained personnel who were growing in experience, all in increasingly large numbers that soon turned the tide of battle. These also tended to be large airplanes by comparison with counterparts friend and foe. American planes were known for their ruggedness and safety.

Revolution

A great number of American advanced fighter design and development programs were initiated during the war. The evolution of established designs and new development projects took turns that as often lead to dead-ends as yielded a weapon of increased potency. Some reflected "advances" that came and went during the course of the war. The idea of heavy cannons like 75mm, for example, blossomed and as quickly wilted, as did other "good ideas" proven impractical in test or combat. Conversely, innovative flap and roll control surfaces were pioneered, as was the laminar flow airfoil, these all having vital roles to play. Likewise, materials innovations took another step forward.

The services were open to ideas from all quarters, including captured enemy systems. Prewar, government aeronautical organizations had evolved such that pursuit of theoretical innovation was unintentionally stymied.[1] This was quickly overcome. Expansion and reorganization of service development and test organizations greatly extended the professionalism and capabilities of these teams. The emergency allowed the services to move quickly in approving and pressing ahead with new programs. Although generally showing restraint, some very radical ideas were funded with very few progressed to production. There were plenty of misses: developmental aircraft that simply did not measure up or projects that were no longer required and were discarded. Some of those cast aside projects were continued for their research value. This was unusual in that few research efforts were conducted during the war unless they were expected to yield results in the short term that could benefit the war effort. By late 1944, the armed services leadership was already looking beyond the war. Still, all such efforts had their benefits. Advanced features and growing complexity were challenging design elements to incorporate, and experience progressively grew. In a short time these all became familiar and their integration was less fraught with problems.

Engines were a key pacing item in aircraft development projects. Tying new fighter designs to emerging engines was always a hit-and-miss proposition. Some new engine designs did not pan out, and this spelled the end of many airframe projects. With so little excess engine development capacity, such failures could be costly in missed opportunities. Again, all this provided valuable engineering and manufacturing expertise. For example, Americans appeared to have experimented with contra-rotating propellers more than other nations, and this found some postwar applications.

Consolidated-Vultee's XP-81, ship 2, reveals the NACA inlet trough ahead of the left shoulder-mounted inlet for the rear J33 turbojet. This hybrid also had one of the new XT31 turboprop engines in the nose. The T31 was too immature and the overall aircraft performance too lackluster to justify continuing. (Tony Landis Collection)

The greatest facilitators for revolutionary fighter design were the secret jet-propulsion projects. While America played catch-up in the field of turbine propulsion at the beginning of the war, at the end it was neck-to-neck with Britain and perhaps 18 months behind Germany, and closing rapidly. While Germany fielded larger jet engines earlier and in greater numbers, the Allies had lighter, more efficient engines with longer service lives.[2] However, even the jet booster engine idea faded quickly after the war as primary turbine engine powerplants improved in power-to-weight ratio and fuel economy.

The wartime jet-aircraft projects by the United States appear, in hindsight, conservative by comparison with some of the German jet projects of the period. However, the American efforts were generally more successful. They all displayed the willingness to embrace new technologies, especially given wartime urgencies, with the understanding that progress is best gained by undertaking experimental projects and accepting the attendant risks of failure. American jets in production and development were as innovative as those in Germany, yet within the reach of the technological capability of the period. By 15 August 1945, the United States had built approximately 140 jet fighters in seven models including shipboard aircraft. Three types were in production and nine other designs were in active development, including one of the first turboprops, and six official projects more were at the conceptual stage. Orders for more than 3,000 jet fighters had been let. The first Air Forces squadron was operational and the first naval squadron was approaching combat readiness. The U.S. Navy was the first naval power to move decisively toward adopting jets. A handful of American jets had just arrived in Europe as the war closed in that theater. These and others in development were competitive with the Me 262 and Meteor. However, the American and British jet fighters did not have the opportunity to contribute.

American work on throttleable rocket motors for aircraft propulsions was less successful during the war, although coming together soon after. This, however, had no future other than for missiles and launch vehicles. Germany's attempts at adapting throttleable rocket motors to fighter aircraft went farther with production of the Messerschmitt Me-163 Komet tailless, swept-wing fighter. This point-defense aircraft could climb at an extraordinary 16,000 fpm and dive at 590 mph. However, it was barely practical and potentially a greater hazard to its crew than the enemy. For the tremendous resources expended, the more than 370 aircraft accounted for perhaps no more than 16 Allied aircraft downed. By this and other examples, it was evident to many at the end of the war that rocket propulsion for combat aircraft was a chimera.[3]

Dealing with compressibility and other high-speed phenomena compelled new research and new design options. The depth of American under-appreciation for the importance of swept wings for high-speed flight is readily evident in their first generation of jet aircraft. These aircraft were intentionally pursued to build beyond the speed limits of piston-engine/propeller-driven combat aircraft. Yet, until the last months of the war all of them were conceived with straight wings. This was partially an intentional effort to introduce a limited number of major new design features into aircraft that had to enter production and service quickly, yet were already radical in fundamental aspect.

Swept wings were employed in the United States on some experimental aircraft, but for pitch stability reasons in unusual configurations. Leading aerodynamicists understood the swept wing benefits of delaying compressibility effects for higher critical Mach number and lower drag. However, such surfaces complicated structural design. They moved flow separation at stall to the wingtips and ailerons for degraded roll authority and with a pitch-up tendency; hence the outboard slats on the XP-86. In dealing with these problems, too little analytical or empirical information was available to support fast-paced wartime design programs. The U.S. military made no effort to specifically direct the use of swept wings on advanced aircraft projects and, consequently, NACA did not give priority to such research. For that matter, no one else in the world made any appreciable investigation or use of swept surfaces except Germany.

The introduction of airborne radar was another revolutionary development wrought by the war. From virtually a standing start, the United States rapidly developed and deployed a night fighting capability meeting Army and naval fighter requirements. Collaboration with the United Kingdom greatly aided such efforts by both nations. American manufacturing prowess allowed it to supply a significant measure of its allies' fighter radar needs. Like so much else, the radar-equipped fighters and ground control intercept assets were not on hand when the United States was plunged into the conflict. However, they arrived at a vital time when the enemy was compelled to adopt night tactics to avoid growing Allied air dominance. Still, the dawn of night raiding against land targets met with mixed effectiveness given that the technology still required visual attack once the force had safely navigated to the target. Navy attacks against shipping at night were similarly a seldom-employed capability of limited effectiveness. All this may have been different had these capabilities been introduced a year or more previously when targets where more plentiful.

Radar came to play roles in navigation, weather detection, gun laying, and rear warning in addition to night intercept and long-range detection. While the Army night fighters followed the theme established in Europe, the Navy and Marine Corps faced other challenges. The development of radar suitable for single-engine, single-seat, carrier-based aircraft, working in concert with ship-based GCI radar and combat information centers, pressed the technological advance and created a unique capability. Not even the Royal Navy took this course until acquiring radar-equipped American fighters. Ultimately, the U.S. Navy may well have placed more radar on aircraft, becoming standard equipment, than all other World War II combatants combined, leading the way to postwar interceptors. All this laid the groundwork for much more to follow as the Americans led the world in this field. The impact of the commercial spin-offs of the technology would be profound.

Wartime fighter development projects, successful and otherwise, yielded many other technological innovations that expanded the state of the art and facilitated further revolutionary change. Experimental stall warning systems, ejection seats, autopilots, and stability augmentation pointed to the future. Subscale demonstrators and flying testbeds were established as design tools. New ground-test facilities were built. The industry rose to these challenges, with assistance from service and NACA laboratories, as the aircraft became more complex aerodynamically, structurally, and systems-intensive, demanding finer tolerances and closer testing. The services became more demanding of workmanship, flying qualities, and adherence to specifications.

Unlike some comparable agencies in other countries, the services generally knew when to terminate a project and had the authority to do so. Most of the German advanced projects contributed little or nothing to the war effort yet were protectively promoted by a Nazi hierarchy enamored with secret weapons. Their numerous projects that never reached any substantive or operationally practical hardware stage only sapped the energy of a hard-pressed nation. Conversely, the United States could afford to try many things through multiple projects provided it could be done quickly. With the goal of defeating the enemy expeditiously and with the least cost of American lives, economy and refinement took a backseat. Yet, the surviving projects were generally reasonable and restrained, and set the stage for a postwar era of continuing rapid aeronautical advances.

Despite all the work, no new American fighter or high-performance aero engine development project initiated after the country entered the war was fielded in time to affect the outcome. It was with more conventional yet worthy fighter aircraft that the Allied team defeated the Axis powers.

Perceptions

The early Japanese successes emphasized the ill preparedness of the U.S. military to deal with the foes and weapons arrayed against it and its allies around the world. American losses during the first year of gains by Japan and initial battles with the Axis forces in Europe and North Africa were bitter pills to swallow while the nation expanded its capabilities and experience. Yet, even in 1942, the numbers show the Americans with a markedly superior fighter combat exchange rate over the Japanese. This only improved as the war continued, eventually including engagements against European Axis forces. The fighters extant in 1942 were competitive, and by 1945 then current aircraft were generally superior to all adversaries worldwide. Quantity went hand in hand with quality. By late 1944, the course of the war was clear and victory almost certain. The Americans, and Allies in general, had overwhelming air superiority in every battle in the Pacific and were eliminating Japanese naval and air strength with workman-like steadfastness. The Luftwaffe had been reduced to a shadow of its former self as Allied fighters ranged far and wide over enemy territory. The costs for all this were high in terms of national treasure and lost lives. American may have come late to the fight, but it paid its dues.

The new freedom of funding, war urgency, and national will allowed many avenues of fighter technology to be explored. The United States developed all manner of types exemplifying extremes in all performance and mission measures. "Yankee ingenuity" and perseverance was facilitated by broad talent brought to the game via added millions in uniform, in design office, and on shop floors. All services overcame long-standing biases, notions, and inertia, as exemplified in these advanced fighter development projects. For example, the Navy took big steps toward introducing twins, tricycle, and jet aircraft to their carriers. Night combat became more common albeit still challenging, especially aboard carriers. America was determined never again to yield the night to the enemy. All this set in motion technological advances that are still reflected in aircraft and missile designs today.

All the combatant powers took a large step forward in aviation technology during the war, but perhaps none so much as the United States as it began from a position of greater inferiority. It also started with possibly greater latent capacity and talent. The demands of the air war forced a phenomenal growth of American military air power. It was probably in part intentional that the numbers and variety of aircraft designed and built during the war, and engagement of technological challenges, exceeded that required to win the deadly contest. America emerged with the largest Army and naval air components in the world after expanding many-fold in just six years, even given the dramatic drawdown following VJ-Day. These services looked ahead to the postwar era of jets, contemplating how their air fleets would morph in the nuclear age.

The revolution in aeronautical sciences, airpower, and human ambition emerging from the war marched along parallel paths – although perhaps more grave than ever given the world-spanning capabilities and staggering destructive capability of nuclear weapons. America's good fortunes at the end of the conflict, a consequence of its industries remaining unharmed and with a favorable commercial environment, allowed it to exploit this new aeronautical power more than others, and with a momentum that would last several decades. The power exemplified by the enormous airplane fleets encompassing so much combat power, with so many sought by nations around the world, left Americans proud of their perceived role as the "Arsenal of Democracy" and world-spanning purveyors of peace. This proved important as it had a role to play in resolving or stabilizing many world disputes and conflicts that were left in the wake of the cataclysmic struggle. America was also well poised in terms of airpower for the new Cold War competition with the communists. At the end of the war, the world seemed a much smaller place, and Americans felt a sense of their place in it.

The growing complexity of fighter aircraft, with greater electronics content that was so accelerated by the war, has carried on to this day, with the Americans still leaning heavily on such attributes. The real or perceived contribution of airpower and the awe inspired by these fighters spawned generations of Americans willing to put their continued security in the faith of such complex weapons. While the aircraft have seldom faltered, strategy and leadership have occasionally proven disappointing. The fighter has still not lost much of its luster, but it has grown a bit tarnished by escalating cost and a few disappointments resulting perhaps from excessive expectations.

ENDNOTES

Chapter 1

1. B. S. Kelsey, *The Dragon's Teeth?*, 100.
2. J. McAuliffe, *AAHS Journal* Winter 2002, 317.
3. D. Daso, *Airpower Journal*, 113 n. 59. The USAAC Chief of Staff, Gen. Arnold, imposed a two-year timeline on this consideration.
4. W. F. Trimble, *Wings for the Navy*, 206.
5. G. Robbins, *The Aircraft Carrier Story 1908-1945*, 165.

Chapter 2

1. R. J. Francillon, *Grumman Aircraft since 1929*, 119.
2. N. Friedman, *U.S. Navy Weapons*, 95.

Chapter 3

1. The block system was introduced to differentiate groups of aircraft under the same model letter designation with changes that did not warrant identification as a separate model. These appeared as, for example, P-40L-20 for block 20. As it evolved, the numbers usually increment by 5, leaving the intervening digits to indicate depot or field modifications.
2. Secret Army projects were routinely given such code numbers during the war years; MX meaning Materiel, Experimental.
3. Flutter is an unstable oscillation of a portion of the aircraft or control surface that can grow to catastrophic levels. The instability is induced by unsteady air loads interacting with elastic deformation of the structure or control surface rotation at like frequencies.
4. B. Gunston, *Wings of Fame*, No. 1, 65.
5. Center of gravity (cg) is the point at which the aircraft would balance if suspended from that location, or the center of gravitational attraction acting on the mass of the aircraft. The distance of the cg from the center of pressure, the point at about which all aerodynamic forces acting on the aircraft can be considered to act, is a vital consideration for control. A cg too far forward or too far aft could make the airplane uncontrollable.
6. Control reversal is a phenomenon of control sense reversing, such as displacing the control column right producing a left rolling acceleration instead of the normal right roll. Reversal is normally the result of structural deformation under airloads (wing twist in the example of roll reversal) or the action of compressibility shocks on control surfaces.
7. E. M. Young, *AAHS Journal*, Fall 1980, p. 195. Several sources state the NA-68s were seized in Hawaii while awaiting follow-on shipping to Thailand, and sent back to the mainland following the Japanese attack on the islands.
8. Great Britain had actually assigned serials BW208 through BW307 to only 100 of these aircraft, and three aircraft were painted in British camouflage and markings as BW208, BW209, and BW210.
9. R. Martin, *AAHS Journal*, Summer 1984, 105. Most accounts mistakenly claim 15 aircraft were retained in American service as advanced trainers. A number of 104 is given in some sources as reaching China, but this is almost certainly too high. Mr. Martin relates that 79 received Chinese serial numbers.

Chapter 4

1. R. Wagner, *American Combat Aircraft of the 20th Century*, 303.
2. The original Model 95 was an entirely different design, so the XP-60-series aircraft utilizing the designation all had letter suffixes. P. M. Bowers, *Curtiss Aircraft 1907-1947*, 441.
3. F. H. Dean and D. Hagedorn, *Curtiss Fighter Aircraft*, 331.
4. ibid, 336.
5. *Case History of the XP-62 Airplane*, summary entry 1. Most substantiating information is derived from this source.
6. C. L. Hall, *AAHS Journal* Spring 1982, 69. This source was the substantiating document for the XP-39E data.
7. B. Matthews, *AAHS Journal* Winter 2001, 297, and *Cobra!*, 104-5.
8. B. Matthews, *Cobra!*, 365.
9. R. J. Francillon, *Lockheed Aircraft Since 1913*, 166 and 173.
10. R. P. Peczkowski, *Lockheed P-38 J-L Lightning*, 15.
11. R. J. Francillon, *Lockheed Aircraft Since 1913*, 167, mentions this 75mm concept.
12. J. Stoff, *The Thunder Factory*, 53.
13. W. M. Bodie, *Wings*, Special No. 1, 26.
14. J. Lake, *International Air Power Journal*, No. 7, 153.
15. F. A. Johnsen, *Republic P-47 Thunderbolt*, 31.
16. W. M. Bodie, *Wings*, Special No. 1, 29.
17. Load factor is a measure of acceleration in the vertical axis of the aircraft defined as units of gravitational pull on the surface of the Earth (1 g). This is a primary criterion for structural design to ensure the airframe can withstand maneuvering airloads and inertia, plus a factor of safety. The Brits required a positive limit load factor of 6 g versus 7.33 g for the Americans, and the original Mustang wing had been designed for 12 g (probably including a 50 percent factor of safety). Likewise, the RAF called for landing gear stressed to a 4 g landing whereas the Army Air Forces required 7 g. The intent of making the aircraft less "durable" may also have reflected actual combat usage, which chewed up aircraft in a matter of months regardless of ruggedness. The lighter airframe may have been intended for only 90 to 300 flight hours.

Chapter 5

1. P. C. Smith, *Dive Bomber!*, 107.
2. B. Kowalski and S. Ginter, *Douglas XSB2D-1 & BTD-1 Destroyer*, 4.
3. R. Stern, *SB2C Helldiver* in Action, 48-49. Aspect ratio is the span of the wing divided by the average chord length (width). For example, a high aspect ratio wing would be long and narrow.
4. P. C. Smith, *Curtiss SB2C Helldiver*, 142.
5. Notes on Design 56 found in TBF-1 file at the Northrop Grumman History Center.
6. M. H. Goodspeed, *Wings of Fame* No. 13, 42 and 60.
7. The Vultee enterprise became part of Consolidated Vultee Aircraft (Convair) after 17 March 1943.
8. J. M. Andrade, *U.S. Military Aircraft Designations and Serials 1909 to 1979*, 207-208, 227.
9. J. Thompson, *Vultee Aircraft 1932-1947*, 109 and 128, and J. Wegg, *General Dynamics Aircraft and their Predecessors*, 164, and P. Smith, Vengeance.
10. *Naval Aviation News*, January 1982, 20.
11. *Ibid.*
12. *Ibid.*
13. Design 66 file containing Estimated Weight Report dated 14 June 1944, Detailed Specification undated, blueprints of exterior elevations, and numerous memoranda, via Northrop Grumman History Center.
14. R. J. Francillon, *Grumman Aircraft Since 1929*, 274-5, and notes found in Design 70 file at the Northrop Grumman History Center.

Chapter 6

1. B. Matthews, *Cobra!*, 53. Loss of this aircraft and later 497 seems to be the source of erroneous reports that only 12 of the 13 YFM-1s were built.
2. T. McKelvey Cleaver, *Flight Journal*, December 2005, 26.
3. F. H. Dean, *Report of Joint Fighter Conference*, 5.
4. The P-74 designation was reserved but never assigned.
5. B. Gunston, *Aeroplane Monthly*, April 1980, 203. The authoritative *Army Aircraft Characteristics, Production and Experimental* also refers to block 5 and 10 aircraft, but without specifics.
6. R. Wagner, *American Combat Aircraft of the 20th Century*, 523.
7. N. Avery, *North American Aircraft 1934-1998, Volume 1*, 144.
8. F. H. Dean and D. Hagedorn, *Curtiss Fighter Aircraft*, 338.

Chapter 7

1. The clearest accounts of the XP-52 and XP-59 are found in S. Pace, *Bell P-59 Airacomet*, 15-16, and A. Pelletier, *Bell Aircraft Since 1935*, 202, B. Matthews, *Cobra!*, 370-375, and R. P. Swofford, Jr., *History of XP-52 Airplane Project.*
2. Most sources state the one and only flight of the second XP-54 was the final journey to San Bernardino. However, details of the 10 flights reported are provided by G. H. Balzer, *AAHS Journal*, Spring 1996, Vol. 41 No. 1, 50.
3. P. B. Smith, *Final Report on XP-68 Airplane.*
4. W. R. Rankin, *Final Report of History, Estimated Performance, and Cancellation of Airplane Model XP-69.*
5. W. M. Bodie, *Wings*, Special No. 1, 48.
6. J. Lake, *International Air Power Journal*, No. 7, 154.
7. B. S. Kelsey, *The Dragon's Teeth?*, 132.

Chapter 8

1. B. Martin, *AAHS Journal*, Fall 1993, 207-208.
2. D. Lucabaugh and B. Martin, *Grumman XF5F-1 & XP-50 Skyrocket*, 16.
3. W. O. Breuhaus, *AAHS Journal*, Spring 1991, 33.
4. H. Chrystie letter, 25 July 1988.
5. R. Koehnen, *Boeing XF8B-1*, 37.
6. *Naval Aviation Confidential Bulletin*, No. 4-46, 30.
7. B. Kowalski and S. Ginter, *Douglas XSB2D-1 & BTD-1 Destroyer*, 43.
8. B. Kowalski, *Kaiser Fleetwings XBTK-1*, 9.
9. R. Wagner, *American Combat Planes of the 20th Century*, 442.
10. B. Kowalski, *Curtiss XBT2C-1*, 2.

Chapter 9

1. J. Thompson, *Vultee Aircraft 1932-1947*, 109.
2. F. Gemeinhardt, D. Lucabaugh and B. Martin, *AAHS Journal*, Spring 1987, 58-73. Most sources insist the A-34s were never taken up. However, this extensively researched source provides evidence to the contrary.
3. W. Boyne, *Wings* or *Airpower*, date unknown, 13.
4. Some sources refer to the XA-40 as the Army counterpart to the Navy XSB3C-1. The authoritative *Army Aircraft Characteristics* makes clear this is erroneous.
5. *Case History of Hughes D-2, D-5, F-11 Project*, summary entry 25.
6. G. Cully and A. Parsch, *Designation of U.S. Air Force Projects*, MX-176 entry.

Chapter 10

1. J. Scutts, *Bristol Beaufighter*, 102.
2. B. Gunston, *Night Fighters*, 68.
3. Ibid, 129.
4. T. von Kármán, *Where We Stand*, 75.
5. B. Gunston, *Night Fighters*, 74.
6. J. G. Taylor, *Development of Night Air Operations 1941-1952*, 34.
7. G. R. Pape and R. C. Harrison, *Queen of the Midnight Skies*, 236 and 236.
8. S. L. McFarland, *Conquering the Night*, 14.
9. J. M. Andrade, *U.S. Military Aircraft Designations and Serials 1909 to 1979*, 146.
10. M. H. Goodspeed, *Wings of Fame* No. 13, 54.
11. R. F. Francillon, *Grumman Aircraft Since 1929*, 178.
12. T. E. Doll, *Night Wings*, 9.
13. M. Spick, *Air Enthusiast* No. 54, Summer 1994, 60. Some sources suggest 9 November to be the date, or overlook the date entirely.
14. Ibid, 63.
15. Annotation printed on poor quality photographs found in the Vought history archives. The prints bear the date 2-12-42.
16. S. Ginter, *Brewster SB2A Bermuda/Buccaneer*, 47 and 53.
17. A. Price, *Aircraft Versus Submarine*, 104.
18. Ibid, 104.

Chapter 11

1. R. Schlaifer, *Development of Aircraft Engines*, 459.
2. J. Ethell and A. Price, *World War II Fighting Jets*, 50.
3. D. Whitney, "General Electric "Type I Supercharger," Part II" in *AAHS Journal* Summer 2000, 96.
4. J. O. Young, *Riding England's Coattails*, 17.
5. D. Whitney, *AAHS Journal*, 96.
6. J. O. Young, *Lighting the Flame*, 22.
7. J. O. Young, *Riding England's Coattails*, 21. Most of the earliest jets experienced directional snaking. In many cases, this appeared to be due to flow separation off the vertical tail and rudder oscillation from the periodic pressure change. The lack of propeller slipstream uncovered these deficiencies. More careful design and tighter manufacturing tolerances were the solution for some while others introduced electric yaw dampers – among the first stability augmentation systems.
8. Dr. R. P. Hallion, "Lockheed P-80… The Story of a Star" in *Air Enthusiast* No. 11, 59.
9. J. Ethell and A. Price, *World War II Fighting Jets*, 175-176.
10. R. J. Francillon, *McDonnell Douglas Aircraft Since 1920: Volume II*, 63.
11. Ibid.
12. R. Wagner, *American Combat Planes of the 20th Century*, 475.
13. S. Ginter, *Ryan FR-1 Fireball and XF2R-1 Darkshark*, 49.
14. Ibid, 32.
15. No author stated, *Naval Aviation News*, July 1980, 21.

Chapter 12

1. J. Stoff, *The Thunder Factory*, 82.
2. R. Wagner, *American Combat Planes of the 20th Century*, 525.
3. Ibid, 533.
4. E. W. Constant II, *The Origins of the Turbojet Revolution*, 231.
5. Wagner, 618.
6. J. Winchester, *International Air Power Review* Volume 15, 100.
7. This was actually the designation and associated Bunos. from an earlier project that had been cancelled. P. M. Bowers, *Curtiss Aircraft 1907-1947*, 507.
8. B. Wagner, Correspondence, 2.
9. The unused P-73 designation may have been intended for the USAAF's XF2R-Is. J. M. Andrade, *U.S. Military Aircraft Designations and Serials 1909 to 1979*, 191.
10. R. K. Smith, *Flying Review International*, December 1967, 1060.
11. AeroJet Engineering Corp., *Report from AeroJet*, no page number.
12. G. Cully and A. Parsch, *Designation of U.S. Air Force Projects*, MX-78 entry.
13. G. Israel, "Summary of Investigation of Jet Propelled Fighters," Correspondence, 3.

Chapter 13

1. E. W. Constant II, *The Origins of the Turbojet Revolution*, 244.
2. Dr. T. von Kármán, *Where We Stand*, 44.
3. P. Jarrett ed., *Aircraft of the Second World War*, 86.

Bibliography

Books

Anderson, Fred, *Northrop, An Aeronautical History*, Northrop Corp., Los Angeles, California, 1976.

Andrade, John M., *U.S. Military Aircraft Designations and Serials 1909 to 1979*, Midland Counties Publications, Leicester, UK, 1997.

Avery, Norm, *North American Aircraft 1934-1998, Volume 1*, Jonathan Thompson, Santa Ana, California, 1998.

Barton, Charles, *Howard Hughes and His Flying Boat*, Aero Publishers, Inc., Fallbrook, California, 1982.

Bowers, Peter M., *Boeing Aircraft Since 1916*, Naval Institute Press, Annapolis, Maryland, 1989.

Bowers, Peter M., *Curtiss Aircraft 1907-1947*, Naval Institute Press, Annapolis, Maryland, 1987.

Bowman, Martin W., *Vought F4U Corsair*, The Crowood Press, Wiltshire, United Kingdom, 2002.

Breihan, John R., Piet, Stan and Mason, Roger S., *Martin Aircraft 1909-1960*, Jonathan Thompson, Santa Ana, California, 1995.

Brigman, Leonard, ed., *Jane's All the World's Aircraft, 1945-46*, Sampson Low, Marston, and Company, Ltd., London, England, 1946.

Cassagneres, Ed, *The Spirit of Ryan*, Tab Books, Inc., Blue Ridge Summit, Pennsylvania, 1982.

Constant, Edward W., II, *The Origins of the Turbojet Revolution*, The Johns Hopkins University Press, Baltimore, Maryland, 1980.

Dann, Richard S., *F4F Wildcat in Action*, Aircraft No. 191, Squadron/Signal Publications, Carrollton, Texas, 2004.

Dann, Richard S., *P-40 Warhawk in Action*, Aircraft No. 205, Squadron/Signal Publications, Carrollton, Texas, 2007.

Daso, Dik Alan, *Hap Arnold and the Evolution of American Airpower*, Smithsonian Institute Press, Washington, 2000.

Davis, Larry, *P-38 Lightning in Action*, Aircraft No. 109, Squadron/Signal Publications, Carrollton, Texas, 1990.

Davis, Larry, *P-47 Thunderbolt in Action*, Aircraft No. 208, Squadron/Signal Publications, Carrollton, Texas, 2007.

Davis, Larry, *P-51 Mustang in Action*, Aircraft No. 45, Squadron/Signal Publications, Carrollton, Texas, 1981.

Dean, Francis H., *America's Hundred-Thousand: U.S. Production Fighters of World War Two*, Schiffer Publishing Ltd., Atglen, Pennsylvania, 1997.

Dean, Francis H. and Hagedorn, Dan, *Curtiss Fighter Aircraft, A Photographic History 1917-1948*, Schiffer Publishing Ltd., Atglen, Pennsylvania, 2007.

Dean, Francis H., ed., *Report of Joint Fighter Conference, NAS Patuxent River, MD, 16-23 October 1944*, Schiffer Publishing Ltd., Atglen, Pennsylvania, 1998.

Dial, J. F., *The Chance Vought F4U-1 Corsair*, Profile No. 47, Profile Publications, Ltd., Leatherhead, Surrey, England, 1965.

Doll, Thomas E., *Night Wings, USMC Night Fighters, 1942-1953*, Squadron/Signal Publications, Carrollton, Texas, 2000.

Ethell, Jeffrey and Price, Alfred, *World War II Fighting Jets*, Airlife Publishing Ltd., Shrewsbury, England, 1994.

Friedman, Norman, *U.S. Naval Weapons*, Conway Maritime Press Ltd, London, England, 1983.

Francillon, René J., *Grumman Aircraft Since 1929*, Naval Institute Press, Annapolis, Maryland, 1989.

Francillon, René J., *Lockheed Aircraft Since 1913*, Naval Institute Press, Annapolis, Maryland, 1988.

Francillon, René J., *McDonnell Douglas Aircraft Since 1920: Volume I*, Putnam Aeronautical Books, London, England, 1988.

Francillon, René J., *McDonnell Douglas Aircraft Since 1920: Volume II*, Naval Institute Press, Annapolis, Maryland, 1990.

Ginter, Steve, *Chance Vought F7U Cutlass, Naval Fighters Number 6*, Steve Ginter, Simi Valley, California, 1982.

Ginter, Steve, *Chance Vought V-173 and XF5U-1 Flying Pancakes, Naval Fighters Number 21*, Steve Ginter, Simi Valley, California, 1992.

Ginter, Steve, *Consolidated Vultee XP-81, Naval Fighters Number 214*, Steve Ginter, Simi Valley, California, 2006.

Ginter, Steve, *Early Banshees, The McDonnell F2H-1, F2H-2/2B/2N/2P, Naval Fighters Number 73*, Steve Ginter, Simi Valley, California, 2006.

Ginter, Steve, *Ryan FR-1 Fireball and XF2R-1 Darkshark, Naval Fighters Number 28*, Steve Ginter, Simi Valley, California, 1995.

Ginter, Steve, *Brewster SBA Bermuda/Buccaneer, Naval Fighters Number 76*, Steve Ginter, Simi Valley, California, 2007.

Ginter, Steve with Chana, Bill and Prophett, Phil, *XTBU-1 & TBY-2 Sea Wolf, Naval Fighters Number 33*, Steve Ginter, Simi Valley, California, 1997.

Green, William, *War Planes of the Second World War Volume Four: Fighters*, Doubleday & Co., Garden City, New York, 1967.

Gunston, Bill, *Night Fighters, A Development & Combat History*, Charles Scribner's Sons, New York, 1976.

Gunston, Bill, *World Encyclopedia of Aero Engines*, Patrick Stephens Ltd., Wellingborough, UK, 1987.

Heron, S. D., *Development of Aviation Fuels*, Harvard University, Andover, Massachusetts, 1950.

Hughes, Kris and Dranem, Walter, *Douglas A-1 Skyraider, WarbirdTech Series Volume 13*, Specialty Press, North Branch, Minnesota, 1997.

Jackson, Robert, *Air War at Night, The Battle for the Night Sky Since 1915*, Howell Press, Inc., Charlottesville, Virginia, 2000.

Jarrett, Philip, ed., *Aircraft of the Second World War: The Development of the Warplane 1939-45*, Putnam Aeronautical Books, London, 1997.

Johnsen, Frederick A., *Republic P-47 Thunderbolt*, WarbirdTech Volume 23, Specialty Press, North Branch, Minnesota, 1999.

Jones, Lloyd S., *U.S. Fighters*, Aero Publishers, Inc., Fallbrook, California, 1975.

Jones, Lloyd S., *U.S. Naval Fighters*, Aero Publishers, Inc., Fallbrook, California, 1977.

Kelsey, Benjamin S., *The Dragon's Teeth?: The Creation of United States Air Power for World War II*, Smithsonian Institute Press, Washington, D.C., 1982.

Kinzey, Bert, *F4F Wildcat*, In Detail & Scale Volume 65, Squadron/Signal Publications, Carrollton, Texas, 2000.

Kinzey, Bert, *F4U Corsair*, In Detail & Scale Volume 55, Squadron/Signal Publications, Carrollton, Texas, 1998.

Kinzey, Bert, *F6F Hellcat*, In Detail & Scale Volume 49, Squadron/Signal Publications, Carrollton, Texas, 1996.

Kinzey, Bert, *P-38 Lightning, Part 1*, In Detail & Scale Volume 57, Squadron/Signal Publications, Carrollton, Texas, 1998.

Kinzey, Bert, *P-38 Lightning, Part 2*, In Detail & Scale Volume 58, Squadron/Signal Publications, Carrollton, Texas, 1998.

Kinzey, Bert, *P-39 Airacobra*, In Detail & Scale Volume 63, Squadron/Signal Publications, Carrollton, Texas, 1999.

Kinzey, Bert, *P-40 Warhawk Part 1*, In Detail & Scale Volume 61, Squadron/Signal Publications, Carrollton, Texas, 1999.

Kinzey, Bert, *P-40 Warhawk Part 2*, In Detail & Scale Volume 62, Squadron/Signal Publications, Carrollton, Texas, 1999.

Kinzey, Bert, *P-47 Thunderbolt*, In Detail & Scale Volume 54, Squadron/Signal Publications, Carrollton, Texas, 1998.

Kinzey, Bert, *P-51 Mustang, Part 1*, In Detail & Scale Volume 50, Squadron/Signal Publications, Carrollton, Texas, 1996.

Kinzey, Bert, *SB2C Helldiver*, In Detail & Scale Volume 52, Squadron/Signal Publications, Carrollton, Texas, 1997.

Kinzey, Bert, *TBF & TBM Avenger*, In Detail & Scale Volume 53, Squadron/Signal Publications, Carrollton, Texas, 1997.

Koehnen, Rick, *Boeing XF8B-1 Five-in-One Fighter, Naval Fighters Number 65*, Steve Ginter, Simi Valley, California, 2005.

Koehnen, Richard, *Chance Vought F6U Pirate, Naval Fighters Number 9*, Steve Ginter, Simi Valley, California, 1983.

Kowalski, Bob, *Curtiss XBTC-2 "Eggbeater," Naval Fighters Number 77*, Steve Ginter, Simi Valley, California, 2007.

Kowalski, Bob, *Curtiss XBT2C-1 Bomber / Torpedo Aircraft Prototype, Naval Fighters Number 62*, Steve Ginter, Simi Valley, California, 2003.

Kowalski, Robert J., *Grumman AF Guardian, Naval Fighters Number 20*, Steve Ginter, Simi Valley, California, 1991.

Kowalski, Bob, *Kaiser Fleetwings XBTK-1, Naval Fighters Number 48*, Steve Ginter, Simi Valley, California, 1999.

Kowalski, Bob and Ginter, Steve, *Douglas XSB2D-1 & BTD-1 Destroyer, Naval Fighters Number 30*, Steve Ginter, Simi Valley, California, 1995.

Lucabaugh, David and Martin, Bob, *Grumman XF5F-1 & XP-50 Skyrocket, Naval Fighters Number 31*, Steve Ginter, Simi Valley, California, 1995.

Maas, Jim, *F2A Buffalo in Action*, Aircraft No. 81, Squadron/Signal Publications, Carrollton, Texas, 1987.

Matthews, Birch, *Cobra! Bell Aircraft Corporation 1934-1946*, Schiffer Publishing Ltd., Atglen, Pennsylvania, 1996.

McCutcheon, Kimble D., *Tornado, Wright Aero's Last Liquid-Cooled Piston Engine*, Weak Force Press, Huntsville, Alabama, 2001.

McLaren, David, *North American P-51H Mustang, Air Forces Legends Number 209*, Steve Ginter, Simi Valley, California, 2000.

Moran, Gerard P., *Aeroplanes Vought 1917-1977*, Historical Aviation Album, Temple City, California, 1977.

Pace, Steve, *Bell P-59 Airacomet, Air Forces Legends Number 208*, Steve Ginter, Simi Valley, California, 2000.

Pace, Garry R. and Campbell, John M., *Northrop Flying Wings, A History of Jack Northrop's Visionary Aircraft*, Schiffer Publishing Ltd., Atglen, Pennsylvania, 1995.

Pape, Garry R., Campbell, John M. and Campbell, Donna, *Northrop P-61 Black Widow*, Schiffer Publishing Ltd., Atglen, Pennsylvania, 1995.

Pape, Garry R. and Harrison, Ronald C., *Queen of the Midnight Skies*, Schiffer Publishing Ltd., Atglen, Pennsylvania, 1992.

Pearcy, Arthur, *Lend-Lease Aircraft in World War II*, Motorbooks International, Osceola, Wisconsin, 1996.

Pęczkowski, Robert, *Lockheed P-38 L-J Lightning*, Stratus, Sandomierz, Poland, 2003.

Pelletier, A. J., *Beech Aircraft and Their Predecessors*, Naval Institute Press, Annapolis, Maryland, 1995.

Pelletier, Alain J., *Bell Aircraft Since 1935*, Putnam Aeronautical Books, London, England, 1992.

Price, Alfred, *Aircraft Versus Submarine*, Robert MacLehose & Co., Ltd., Glasgow, 1973.

Robbins, Guy, *The Aircraft Carrier Story 1908-1945*, Cassell & Co., London, 2001.

Rubensteun, Murray and Goldman, Richard M., *To Join with the Eagles: Curtiss-Wright Aircraft 1903-1965*, Doubleday & Co., Inc., Garden City, New York, 1974.

Scarborough, W. E., Captain, *F7F Tigercat in Action*, Aircraft No. 79, Squadron/Signal Publications, Carrollton, Texas, 1986.

Schlaifer, Robert, *Development of Aircraft Engines*, Harvard University, Andover, Massachusetts, 1950.

Scrivner, Charles L., *F8F Bearcat in Action*, Aircraft No. 99, Squadron/Signal Publications, Carrollton, Texas, 1990.

Scutts, Jerry, *Beaufighter in Action*, Aircraft No. 153, Squadron/Signal Publications, Carrollton, Texas, 1995.

Smith, Peter C., *Curtiss SB2C Helldiver*, The Crowood Press, Wiltshire, United Kingdom, 1998.

Smith, Peter C., *Dive Bomber!*, Naval Institute Press, Annapolis, Maryland, 1982.

Smith, Peter C., *Vengeance!* Airlife Publishing, Shrewsbury, England. 1986.

Stern, Robert, *SB2C Helldiver in Action*, Aircraft No. 54, Squadron/Signal Publications, Carrollton, Texas, 1982.

Stoff, Joshua, *The Thunder Factory: An Illustrated History of the Republic Aviation Corporation*, Motorbooks International, Osceola, Wisconsin, 1990.

Sullivan, Jim, *F4U Corsair in Action*, Aircraft No. 145, Squadron/Signal Publications, Carrollton, Texas, 1994.

Sullivan, Jim, *F6F Hellcat in Action*, Aircraft No. 36, Squadron/Signal Publications, Carrollton, Texas, 1979.

Swanborough, Gordon and Bowers, Peter M., *United States Military Aircraft Since 1909*, Putnam Aeronautical Books, London, England, 1989.

Thompson, Jonathan, *Vultee Aircraft 1932-1947*, Jonathan Thompson, Santa Ana, California, 1992.

Thompson, Kevin, *North American Aircraft 1934-1998, Volume 2*, Jonathan Thompson, Santa Ana, California, 1999.

Thompson, Warren E., *Northrop P-61 Black Widow*, WarbirdTech Volume 15, Specialty Press, North Branch, Minnesota, 1997.

Trimble, William F., *Wings for the Navy: A History of the Naval Aircraft Factory, 1917-1956*, Naval Institute Press, Annapolis, Maryland, 1990.

Wagner, Ray, *American Combat Planes of the 20th Century*, Jack Bacon & Co., Reno, Nevada, 2004.

Wegg, John, *General Dynamics Aircraft and their Pred-*

ecessors, Naval Institute Press, Annapolis, Maryland, 1990.

White, Graham, *Allied Aircraft Piston Engines of World War II*, Society of Automotive Engineers, Inc., Warrendale, Pennsylvania, 1995.

White, Graham, *R-4360, Pratt & Whitney's Major Miracle*, Specialty Press, North Branch, Minnesota, 2006.

Williams, Anthony G., and Gustin, Emmanuel, Dr., *Flying Guns, Development of Aircraft Guns, Ammunition and Installations 1933-45*, Airlife Publishing Ltd., Shrewsbury, England, 2003.

Zichek, Jared A., *The Boeing XF8B-1 Fighter: Last of the Line*, Schiffer Publishing Ltd., Atglen, Pennsylvania, 2007.

Monographs

AeroJet Engineering Corp., *Report from AeroJet, The Power of the Future*, AeroJet Engineering Corp., undated brochure.

Carter, Dustin W., *A Historical Brief on the Vultee XP-54 Airplane*, paper presented at the 2nd Annual Western Aerospace Historical Symposium, date unknown.

Matthews, Henry, *Chronology of MX-324, America's First Rocket Airplane, X-Planes Monograph-1*, HPM Publications, Beirut, Lebanon, 1995.

McFarland, Stephen L., *Conquering the Night, Army Air Forces Night Fighters at War*, U.S. Government Printing Office, Washington, D.C., 1998.

Young, James O., *Lighting the Flame: The Turbojet Revolution Comes to America*, Air Force Flight Test Center History Office, Edwards AFB, CA, 2002.

Young, James O., *Riding England's Coattails: The U.S. Army Air Forces and the Turbojet Revolution*, AFFTC History Office, Edwards AFB, CA, October 1995.

Periodicals

Allen, Francis J., "Northrop's Failed Fighter," *Air Enthusiast*, No. 32, December 1986-April 1987, pp. 63-72.

Allen, Francis, "Ascent Tail-First," *Air Enthusiast*, No. 51, August-October 1993, pp. 10-15.

Allen, Francis, "The Ultimate Escort?: McDonnell XF-85 Goblin," *Air Enthusiast*, No. 52, Winter 1993, pp. 17-23.

Allen, Francis, "Last of the Line: Boeing's XF8B-1 Multi-Purpose Fighter," *Air Enthusiast*, No. 55, August 1994, pp. 22-27.

Andrews, Hal, "End of the Line … The Last Curtiss Navy Fighter," *Air Enthusiast Quarterly*, No. 3, no date, pp. 98-108.

Balzer, Gerald H., "Request for data R40-C: The Origin of the XP-54, XP-55, and XP-56, Part 1," *AAHS Journal*, American Aviation Historical Society, Winter 1995, pp. 242-263, "XP-54/R40-C, Part 2," Spring 1996, pp. 28-53, "XP-55/R40-C, Part 3A," Summer 1996, pp. 90-113, "XP-55/R40-C, Part 3B," Fall 1996, pp. 162-177, "XP-56/R40-C, Part 4A," Winter 1996, pp. 242-265, "XP-56/R40-C, Part 4B" Spring 1997, pp. 34-51.

Beauchamp, Gerry, "Futuristic Hawks: A Story About the Curtiss X/YP-37Aircraft," *AAHS Journal*, American Aviation Historical Society, Vol. 21 No. 1 Spring 1977, pp. 12-25.

Beauchamp, Gerry, "Little Norway," *AAHS Journal*, American Aviation Historical Society, Vol. 17 No. 4 Winter 1972, pp. 273-276.

Beauchamp, Gerry, "XP-42, Perennial Test-Bed," *AAHS Journal*, American Aviation Historical Society, Vol. 19 No. 2 Summer 1974, pp. 82-92.

Bedford, Alan, "Early American Carrier Jets, Evolving Jet Operations with the U.S. Fleet, Part One," *Air Enthusiast*, No. 81, May/June 1999, pp. 13-19.

Berkowitz, Bruce D., "Monster Engines," *Air & Space*, December 1997/January 1998, pp. 80-87.

Berry, Peter, "Development of the "Straight-Through" Turbojet Engine," *AAHS Journal*, American Aviation Historical Society, Vol. 47 No. 3 Fall 2002, pp. 198-203.

Berry, Peter, "Kaiser XBTK-1," *Air Pictorial*, September 1982, p. 361.

Bodie, Warren M., "Thunderbolt," *Wings*, Special Edition No. 1, 1981, entire issue.

Bowers, Peter M., "Streamlining, Pt. II," *Airpower*, November 1991, pp. 10-25 and 34-43.

Bowers, Peter M., "Economy Fighter," *periodical unknown*, date unknown, pp. 42-47.

Boyne, Walt, "P-75 Eagle, GM's Flying Frankenstein," *Wings*, February 1973, pp. 9-16.

Boyne, Walt, "Brewster's Last Stand," *Wings* or *Airpower*, date unknown, pp. 10-16.

Boyne, Walt, "Sky Tiger," *Wings* or *Airpower*, date unknown, pp. 20-37, 62, and 64-66.

Boyne, Walt, "Vultee's Swoose Goose," *Airpower*, November 1972, pp. 8-15.

Boyne, Walt, "Ascender," *Airpower*, March 1973, pp. 6-16.

Breuhaus, Waldemar O., "The Variable Stability Airplane from a Historical Perspective," *AAHS Journal*, American Aviation Historical Society, Vol. 36 No. 1 Spring 1991, pp. 30-55.

Brulle, Robert V., "Don't Panic! It's Just a Compressibility Dive," *Air Power History*, Spring 1996, pp. 41-54.

Carter, Dusty, "The Vultee "P-38," *AAHS Journal*, American Aviation Historical Society, Vol. 31 No. 1 Spring 1988, pp. 18-22.

Casius, Gerard, "The St Louis Lightweight," *Air Enthusiast*, No. 16, 1981, pp. 33-44 and 65.

Christy, Joe, "Hawkman," *Wings*, February 1973, pp. 18-35.

Cleaver, Thomas McKelvey, "A Tiger's Tale – Erik Shilling," *Flight Journal*, December 2002, pp. 20-30.

Colchagoff, George D., Captain, "Final Report of the XP-77 Airplane," USAAF Technical Report 5359, Army Air Forces, Air Technical Services Command, Wright Field, Dayton, Ohio, reproduced in *AAHS Journal*, American Aviation Historical Society, Vol. 26 No. 4 Winter 1981, pp. 314-327.

Danforth, John, "The Ryan Legend," *Airpower*, March 1998, pp. 40-55.

Daniels, C. M., "Thunder-Maker: The Story of Alexander Kartveli," *Air Classics*, July 1971, pp. 18-32 and 50.

Daso, Dik Major, "Origins of Airpower, Hap Arnold's Command Years and Aviation Technology, 1936-1945," *Airpower Journal*, Fall 1997, pp. 94-113.

Dorr, Robert F., "The Bell XP-83 Fighter of 1945-46," *Aviation News*, 5-18 October 1984, p. 394.

Dorr, Robert F., "Beyond the Frontiers – McDonnell XF-85: The Built-in Fighter," *Wings of Fame*, Volume 7, 1997, pp. 26-35.

Dorr, Robert F., "Boeing XF8B, Boeing's Last Fighter," *Wings of Fame*, Volume 8, 1997, pp. 94-99.

Dorr, Robert F., "Grumman's XF5F-1 Skyrocket," *Aviation News*, 17-30 April 1987, p. 1279.

Furler, E. F., Jr., "Cobras for the Navy," *Air Classics*, date unknown, pp. 14-20.

Furler, E. F., "XP-41: Expanding the Envelope," *Air Classics Special*, Volume 3, 1993, pp 4-5.

Gann, Harry, "North American P-64," *AAHS Journal*, American Aviation Historical Society, Vol. 23 No. 4 Winter 1978, pp. 296-299.

Gann, Harry and Sloan, John, "North American P-64," *periodical unknown*, date unknown, pp. 6-7.

Gemeinhardt, Fritz, Lucabaugh, David and Martin, Bob, "The Brewster Blaster," *AAHS Journal*, American Aviation Historical Society, Vol. 32 No. 1 Spring 1987, pp. 58-73.

Gemeinhardt, F., Lucabaugh, D. and Martin, R., "The Bellicose Brewster, Part I," *Aeroplane Monthly*, November 1989, pp. 674-678, Part II," December 1989, pp. 714-717, Part III," January 1990, pp. 18-23.

Goodspeed, M. Hill, "Grumman TBF/TBM Avenger," *Wings of Fame*, Volume 13, 1998, pp. 32-91.

Gordon, Yefim, "P-39 in the USSR," *Wings of Fame*, Volume 10, 1998, pp. 144-151.

Green, William and Swanborough, Gordon, "The End of the Beginning … The Seversky P-35," *Air Enthusiast*, No. 10, 1979, pp. 8-21.

Gunston, Bill, "Prototype Pursuits," *Aeroplane Monthly*, July 1979, pp. 386-389, September 1979, pp. 466-467, October 1979, pp. 550-552, November 1979, pp. 580-583, December 1979, pp. 636-638, January 1980, pp. 51-52, February 1980, pp. 78-80, March 1980, pp. 134-135, April 1980, pp. 202-205.

Gunston, Bill with Dorr, Robert F., "North American P-51 Mustang," *Wings of Fame*, Volume 1, 1995, pp. 56-115.

Hall, C. L., "Final Report of Development, Procurement, Performance and Acceptance the XP-39E Airplanes," Air Corps Technical Report No. 5022, 21 September 1943, reproduced in *AAHS Journal*, American Aviation Historical Society, Vol. 27 No. 1 Spring 1988, pp. .55-63.

Hallion, Richard P., Dr., "Lockheed P-80 … The Story of a Star," *Air Enthusiast*, No. 11, 1979, pp. 54-70.

Heyman, J., "Talkback: Grumman History Revealed," *Air International*, June 1982, p. 313.

Historical Office, "Case History of XP-77 Airplane Project," Air Technical Service Command, Wright Field, Dayton, Ohio, reproduced in *AAHS Journal*, American Aviation Historical Society, Vol. 26 No. 4 Winter 1981, pp. 311-326.

Howeth, Larry, "Beech XA-38 Destroyer," *AAHS Journal*, American Aviation Historical Society, Vol. 5 No. 4 Winter 1960, p. 338.

Hucker, Robert, "Tucker's Forgotten Fighter, *International Air Review*, Spring 1992, pp. 4-16.

Kelsey, Harry F., "Reflections of a Bell Engineer," *AAHS Journal*, American Aviation Historical Society, Vol. 36 No. 4 Winter 1991, pp. 258-261.

Kempel, Robert W., "The World's Fastest Piston-Engine Airplanes," *AAHS Journal*, Summer 2002, pp. 141-150.

Klein, Bernhard, "Talkback: More on XTB2F-1," *Air International*, September 1982, p. 156.

Koehnen, Richard C., "Bell's No Name Fighter," *Airpower*, January 1982, pp. 18-25 and 44-46.

Kusenda, Mike, "XP-77," *AAHS Journal*, Winter 1982, Vol. 27 No. 4, p. 316.

Joffrion, Buddy, Colonel, "The Laminar Flow Wing and the P-51," *The Dispatch*, Spring 1993, pp. 7-8.

Lake, Jon, "P-47 Thunderbolt, Part 2," *International Air Power Review*, Volume 7, 2003, pp. 128-165.

Lowe, Thomas E. and Reinert, Earl, "The Last Lancer," *AAHS Journal*, American Aviation Historical Society, Vol. 23 No. 2 Summer 1978, pp. 112-119.

Lucabaugh, David and Martin, Bob, "The Scarce Skyrocket," *AAHS Journal*, American Aviation Historical Society, Vol. 34 No. 2 Summer 1989, pp. 96-107.

Maas, Jim, "Fall from Grace: The Brewster Aeronautical Corporation, 1932-42," *AAHS Journal*, American Aviation Historical Society, Vol. 30 No. 2 Summer 1985, pp. 118-135.

Martin, Bob, "Pretty Bird!: The Bell XFL-1 Airabonita," *AAHS Journal*, American Aviation Historical Society, Vol. 38 No. 3 Fall 1993, pp. 204-215.

Martin, R., "The Vitiated Vanguard," *AAHS Journal*, American Aviation Historical Society, Vol. 29 No. 2 Summer 1984, pp. 102-115.

Matt, Paul R., "Ryan FR-1 "Fireball," *Historical Aviation Album*, Vol. III, 1966, pp. 139-144.

Matthews, Birch, "Bell XP-77 Design Origin," *AAHS Journal*, American Aviation Historical Society, Vol. 28 No. 2 Summer 1983, pp. 119-120.

Matthews, Birch, "Airacobra Mystery," *AAHS Journal*, American Aviation Historical Society, Vol. 46 No. 4 Winter 2001, pp. 290-299.

McAuliffe, Jerry, "News & Comments: From Our Readers," *AAHS Journal*, American Aviation Historical Society, Vol. 47 No. 4 Winter 2002, p. 317.

McDowell, Ernest R., "Ryan's Fireball," *AAHS Journal*, Winter 1963, pp. 231-247.

Miska, Kurt H., "Development of the Grumman XTB3F and the AF "Guardian," *AAHS Journal*, American Aviation Historical Society, Vol. 18 No. 4 Winter 1973, pp. 218-225.

Miska, Kurt H., "The Plane That Never Was…: Grumman XTB2F-1," *Air Combat 1939-45*, Volume 4 Number 6, 1972, pp. 171-174.

No author stated, "Case History of the V-72, A-31 and A-35 Airplane Project," Air Technical Services Command, Historical Office, September 1944, reproduced in *AAHS Journal*, American Aviation Historical Society, Vol. 35 No. 4 Winter 1990, pp. 242-251.

No author stated, "Design Details of the Northrop P-61 (Part 1)," *Aero Digest*, 1 November 1945, page numbers uncertain, Part 2," 1 December 1945, page numbers uncertain.

No author stated, "XP-41: Granddaddy of the P-47 Thunderbolt," *Wings*, Volume 11 No. 5, October 1981, pp. 32-35.

No author stated, "XP-42: Search for Streamlining," *Air Classics Special*, Volume 3, 1993, pp. 6-9.

No author stated, "P-43: The Missing Link Fighter," *Air Classics Special*, Volume 3, 1993, pp. 16-21.

No author stated, "XP-49: Lightning Replacement," *Air Classics Special*, Volume 3, 1993, pp. 24-25.

No author stated, "XP-49, Built to Reach New Heights, Developed as 'Just in Case' Plane," *Lockheed Star*, 2 September 1954, p. unknown.

No author stated, "XP-50: A Twin for the Army," *Air Classics Special*, Volume 3, 1993, pp. 26-27.

No author stated, "XP-54: The Losing Winner," *Air Classics Special*, Volume 3, 1993, pp. 28-31.

No author stated, "XP-55: Play On Words," *Air Classics Special*, Volume 3, 1993, pp. 32-35.

No author stated, "XP-56: The Black Bullet," *Air Classics Special*, Volume 3, 1993, pp. 36-39.

No author stated, "XP-60: Attempt for Success," *Air Classics Special*, Volume 3, 1993, pp. 40-43.

No author stated, "XP-62: Hailed Heavyweight," *Air Classics Special*, Volume 3, 1993, pp. 44-45.
No author stated, "P-66: A Fighter for the World," *Air Classics Special*, Volume 3, 1993, pp. 46-53.
No author stated, "XP-67: The First Stealth?," *Air Classics Special*, Volume 3, 1993, pp. 54-59.
No author stated, "XP-70: Make-Shift Night Fighter," *Air Classics Special*, Volume 3, 1993, pp. 60-65.
No author stated, "XP-75: Spare Parts Fighter," *Air Classics Special*, Volume 3, 1993, pp. 66-73.
No author stated, "XP-77: Wooden Failure," *Air Classics Special*, Volume 3, 1993, pp. 76-79.
No author stated, "The Untossed Pancake: The Story of the Ill-Fated XF5U-1," *Air Enthusiast*, June 1973, pp. 287-293.
No author stated, "Fighter A to Z: Curtiss XP-42," *Air Enthusiast*, November 1976, p. 236.
No author stated, "Fighter A to Z: Curtiss XP-46," *Air Enthusiast*, November 1976, p. 236.
No author stated, "Fighter A to Z: Curtiss XP-60(D)," *Air Enthusiast*, November 1976, p. 237.
No author stated, "Fighter A to Z: Curtiss XP-60A," *Air Enthusiast*, November 1976, p. 237.
No author stated, "Plane Facts: Skyraider Ancestors," *Air International*, May 1978, pp. 240-241.
No author stated, "Fighter A to Z: North American (P-51H & M) Mustang," *Air International*, May 1989, p. 252.
No author stated, "Mr. Mac's First Phantom, The Story of the McDonnell FH-1," *Air International*, November 1987, pp. 231-235 and 258-260.
No author stated, "Republic XP-47J Thunderbolt," *Air International*, July 1991, p. 48.
No author stated, "Republic XP-72," *Air International*, July 1991, p. 49.
No author stated, "Tucker Lightweight Fighter," *Flying Review International*, October 1963, p. 62.
No author stated, "Twin-Pusher Curtiss," *Flying Review International*, May 1964, p. 61.
No author stated, "Naval Aircraft: Buccaneer," *Naval Aviation News*, December 1979, pp. 20-21.
No author stated, "Naval Aircraft: XBT2C-1," *Naval Aviation News*, September 1979, pp. 20-21.
No author stated, "Naval Aircraft: Fireball," *Naval Aviation News*, July 1980, pp. 20-21.
No author stated, "Naval Aircraft: XTB2D-1," *Naval Aviation News*, January 1982, pp. 20-21.
O'Leary, Michael, "XP-77: First of the Light Weight Fighters," *Air Classics*, March 1974, pp. 27-31.
O'Leary, Michael, "North American's First Fighter," *International Air Review*, Spring 1992, pp. 26-27, 30-32, and 62-63.
Ostrowski, David W., "Anacostia Flight Test Grumman XF5F-1 Skyrocket," *Skyways*, April 2002, pp. 2-22.
Pape, Garry R. and Harrison, Ronald C., "Dark Lady, Pt 1: The Design and Development of the Northrop P-61 Black Widow," unknown publication, date unknown, p. uncertain.
Pape, Garry R. and Thompson, Warren E., "Nocturnal Lightnings," *Air Enthusiast*, August 1978, pp. 80-87.
Pearson, Gregory, "Vought's Flying Disc," *Wings*, February 2002, pp. 50-55.
Pelletier, Alain J., "Consumptive Vengeance: Vultee A-35s in French Service," *Air Enthusiast*, No. 128, March/April 2007, pp. 75-79.
Pelletier, Alain J., "Not So Ideal: The McDonnell XP-67 'Bat'," *Air Enthusiast*, No. 96, November/December 2001, pp. 2-8.
Perkins, Kendall, "Design Development of the McDonnell FD-1 Phantom," *Aviation*, November 1946, pp. 40-48.
Peterson, Wayne, "The Hybrids, Part II," *Wings*, June 2005, pp. 12-19.
Phillips, Edward H., "Gunship," *Airpower*, November 1978, pp. 10-13, 16-19 and 58-60.
Rust, Kenn C. and Hess, William N., "The German Jets and the U.S. Army Air Force," *AAHS Journal*, American Aviation Historical Society, Vol. 8 No. 3 Fall 1963, pp. 155-184.
Schoeni, Arthur L., "Experimental Corsairs," *AAHS Journal*, American Aviation Historical Society, Vol. 13 No. 1 Spring 1968, pp. 67-68.
Schoeni, Art, "Pioneer Pirate," *Aeroplane Monthly*, December 1981, pp. 658-661.
Sheahan, Frank, "Curtiss P-60 – Successor to the P-40," *Armchair Aviator*, Vol. 2 No. 6, pp. 7-9.
Shores, Christopher, "Allison-Powered Mustangs," *Air Enthusiast Quarterly*, No. 2, no date, pp. 191-206.
Shores, Chris, "America's Spitfires," *Air Enthusiast*, No. 16, 1981, pp. 13-25.
Shores, Christopher and Smith, Frank F., "Diving Vengeance," *Air Enthusiast Quarterly*, No. 5, November 1977-February 1978, pp. 29-43.
Smith, Richard K., "An Escort Appended… The Story of the McDonnell XF-85 Goblin," *Flying Review International*, December 1967, pp. 1060-1062.
Spick, Mike, "Grumman's Night 'Cats," *Air Enthusiast*, No. 54, Summer 1994, pp. 60-65.
Stanley, Robert M., "Excerpts from Bell XP-39E Flight Test Report 23-943-039," 1 May 1942, reproduced in *AAHS Journal*, American Aviation Historical Society, Vol. 27 No. 1 Spring 1988, pp. 64-68.
Sunday, Terry L., "Convair's Flying Compromise," *Wings*, October 1987, pp. 37-47.
Thompson, Jonathan, "Air Force for Sale!," *Airpower*, May 1993, pp. 10-21 and 38-41.
Westell, Freeman, "Ed Heinemann & the Legend of the Skyraider!," *Airpower*, January 2002, pp. 8-21.
Whitney, Dan, "General Electric 'Type I Supercharger,' America's First Jet Engine: Part I – The British Connection," *AAHS Journal*, American Aviation Historical Society, Vol. 45 No. 1 Spring 2000, pp. 95-103.
Whitney, Dan, "General Electric 'Type I Supercharger,' America's First Jet Engine: Part II – General Electric Type I Superchargers," *AAHS Journal*, American Aviation Historical Society, Vol. 45 No. 2 Summer 2000, pp. 15-21.
Young, Edwards M., "Seizure of the North American NA-68 an NA-69," *AAHS Journal*, American Aviation Historical Society, Vol. 25 No. 3 Fall 1980, pp. 194-198.

Reports

Able, Charles R., Maj., *Final Report of the Procurement, Inspection, Testing and Acceptance of the Lockheed XP-49 Airplane*, Air Corps Technical Report No. 5271, 22 August 1945.
Able, Charles R., Maj., *Final Report of the Development, Procurement, Performance and Acceptance of the XP-55 Airplane*, Army Air Forces Technical Report No. 5306, 22 October 1945.
Aldridge, John F., Jr., Maj., *Final Report of the XP-67 Airplane*, Army Air Forces Technical Report No. 5412, 31 January 1946.
Aldridge, John F., Jr., Maj. and Herald, J. M., *Final Report on the Procurement, Inspection, Testing, and Acceptance of the General Motors Fisher Body Division XP-75 Airplane*, Army Air Forces Technical Report No. 5505, Air Materiel Command, 26 June 1946.
Colchagoff, George D., Capt., *Final Report of the XP-77 Airplane*, Army Air Forces Technical Report No. 5359, 15 November 1945.
Dillon, A. K., *Final Report of Development, Procurement, Performance, and Acceptance XP-61D Airplane*, Report No. 5693, United States Air Force, Headquarters, Air Materiel Command, 27 April 1948.
Eickstaedt, R. C., *Prototype Flight Tests on XP-58*, Report No. 4872, Lockheed Aircraft Corp., Burbank, California, 3 September 1944.
Hall, C. L., *A Review of the Curtiss XP-53 Interceptor Pursuit Airplane Project*, Memorandum Report No. EXP-M-50-697, Air Corps, Material Division, Experimental Engineering Section, 6 June 1942.
Hello, Bastian, 1Lt., *Final Report of Development, Procurement, Performance and Acceptance XP-80 Airplane*, Army Air Forces Technical Report No. 5235, 28 June 1945.
Mann, Roy E., Capt., *Final Report of the XP-86 Airplane*, Air Force Technical Report No. 6168, January 1952.
Morris, Frank G., 2Lt., and Leach, Everett W., Maj., *Flight Tests on the Curtiss XP-55, USAAF No, 42-78846*, Flight Section Memorandum Report Serial No. TSCEP5E-1807, 17 October 1944.
No author stated, *Army Aircraft Characteristics, Production and Experimental*, Report No. TSEST – A2, ATSC Wright Field, Ohio, United States Army, 1 April 1946.
No author stated, *Case History of Hughes D-2, D-5, F-11 Project*, History Section Intelligence, Air Materiel Command, Wright Field, August 1946.
No author stated, *Case History of L-1000 (XJ37-1) Jet Propulsion Engine*, Historical Division, Intelligence, T-2, Air Materiel Command, June 1946.
No author stated, *Case History of XP-54 Airplane*, Historical Study No. 41, History Office, Air Technical Service Command, Wright Field, November 1944.
No author stated, *Case History of XP-59, XP-59A, YP-59A, P-59A, P-59B, and XP-59B Airplanes*, Historical Office, Intelligence Department, Air Materiel Command, Wright Field, December 1947.
No author stated, *Case History of the XP-56 Airplane*, Historical Division, Intelligence, Air Materiel Command, Wright Field, January 1946.
No author stated, *Case History of the XP-62 Airplane*, History Office, Air Technical Service Command, Wright Field, August 1944.
No author stated, *Case History of the XP-71 Airplane*, History Office, Air Technical Service Command, Wright Field, October 1944.
No author stated, *Design Features of the Lockheed L-133*, Report No. 2571, Lockheed Aircraft Corp., 27 February 1942.
No author stated, *Final Report on the Procurement, Inspection, Testing, and Acceptance of the XP-54 Airplane* (Rough Draft), number or date unknown.
No author stated, *Manufacturer's Preliminary Brief Model Specification, Jet Propulsion Unit, Model L-133*, Report No. 2579, Lockheed Aircraft Corp., 27 February 1942.
No author stated, *Naval Aviation Confidential Bulletin*, No. 4-46, CONVAER-00-75-500, October 1946, Office of the Chief of Naval Operations and Bureau of Aeronautics, Navy Department, Washington, D.C., pp. 36-38.
Palmer, John, Jr., *Final Report on Proposed Development of XP-65 Airplane*, Memorandum Report No. EXP-M-50-702, Air Corps, Material Division, Experimental Engineering Section, 20 June 1942.
Rankin, Werner R., *Final Report of History, Estimated Performance, and Cancellation of Airplane Model XP-69*, Air Corps Technical Report No. 4975, 5 July 1943.
Smith, Paul B., *Final Report on XP-68 Airplane*, Material Command Engineering Division, 17 April 1943.
Swofford, Ralph P., Jr., *History of XP-52 Airplane Project*, Memorandum Report No. EXP-M-50-701, Air Corps, Material Division, Experimental Engineering Section, 19 June 1942.
Taylor, Joe Gray, *Development of Night Air Operations 1941-1952*, U.S. Air Force Historical Study No. 92, Historical Division, Air University, 1953.
Thornton, O. B., Capt., *Final Report of the Development, Procurement, and Acceptance of the Lockheed XP-56 Airplane*, Air Force Technical Report No. 5714, 30 July 1948.
von Kármán, Theodore, *Where We Stand*, USAAF, Washington, D.C., 1946.

Correspondence

Chrystie, Henry, formerly with Chance Vought Aircraft, Letter to John M. Elliot, Assistant Historian, Aviation History Branch, Department of the Navy, Washington, D.C., 25 July 1988.
Lester, William A., formerly with Bell Aircraft Corp., letter, subject XP-77, dated 20 May 1979.
Schwendler, William T., "Class VTB Airplane – Grumman Design No. 70 – Proposal for," Grumman Aircraft Engineering Corp., 8 September 1944, to Bureau of Aeronautics.
Israel, G., "Summary of Investigation of Jet Propelled Fighters, 19 January 1945, Inter-Office Memorandum, Grumman Aircraft Engineering Corp.
Wagner, Bill, "Ryan Announces XFR-4 Experimental Navy Fighter; Tests Flush Entry Air Ducting," Ryan Aeronautical Co., undated press release.

Other

Handbook of Operation and Flight Instructions for the Model YFM-1A Multi-Place Fighter Airplane, Technical Order No. 01-110HB-1, Materiel Division, Field Services Section, Wright Field, Dayton, Ohio, 20 December 1940.
No author stated, *NAVAER SD-353 Detailed Specification for Model XTB2F-1 Airplane Class VTB (Landplane, Monoplane, Three-Place)*, Navy Department, Bureau of Aeronautics, Washington, D.C., 20 September 1943.
No author stated, Notes on Design 56, found in TBF file, via Grumman History Center.
No author stated, Notes and drawings within the XTB2F-1 and Design 55 file at the Grumman History Center, Bethpage, New York.
No author stated, Various notes and report excerpts on Design 70 found in TB3F-1 file, via Grumman History Center.

Internet Sources

Cully, George and Parsch, Andreas, *Designations of U.S. Air Force Projects*, http://www.designation-systems.net/usmilav/projects.html

Index

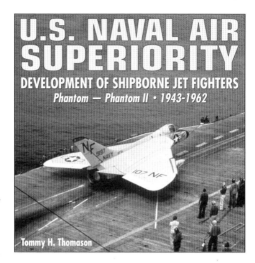

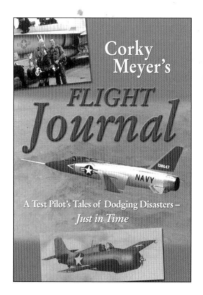

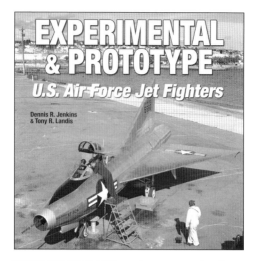

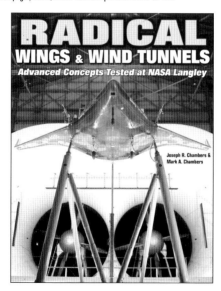